INTRODUCTION TO THE HISTORY OF CHRISTIANITY

Second Edition

TIM DOWLEY

LION

Published by Lion Books
an imprint of
Lion Hudson plc
Wilkinson House, Jordan Hill Road,
Oxford OX2 8DR, England
www.lionhudson.com/lion

ISBN 978 0 7459 5688 6

Original edition published as *A Lion Handbook: The History of Christianity*, 1977
This edition originally published by Augsberg Fortress, Box 1209, Minneapolis, MN 55440.
UK edition 2014

Acknowledgments
Scripture quotations marked NIV are from the Holy Bible, New International Version, copyright © 1973, 1978, 1984 International Bible Society. Used by permission of Zondervan and Hodder & Stoughton Limited. All rights reserved. The 'NIV' and 'New International Version' trademarks are registered in the United States Patent and Trademark Office by International Bible Society. Use of either trademark requires the permission of International Bible Society. UK trademark number 1448790.
Scripture quotations marked NRSV are from the New Revised Standard Version published by HarperCollins Publishers, copyright © 1989 by the Division of Christian Education of the National Council of the Churches of Christ in the USA, and are used by permission. All rights reserved.
Scripture quotations marked KJV are from the King James Version.

Cover image: Abraham with the angels (mosaic), Byzantine School, (6th century) / San Vitale, Ravenna, Italy / The Bridgeman Art Library; The Holy Family (Barcelona, Spain) ©iStockphoto / stan tiberiu loredan; Christ Pantocrator, 1607 (oil on panel), Bulgarian School, (17th century) / National Art Gallery, Sofia, Bulgaria / Giraudon / The Bridgeman Art Library
Cover design: Laurie Ingram

A catalogue record for this book is available from the British Library

Printed and bound in Singapore, May 2014, LH18

INTRODUCTION TO THE
HISTORY OF CHRISTIANITY

Editor

Dr Tim Dowley

Consulting Editors

John H. Y. Briggs

Director of the Centre for Baptist History and Heritage
and Senior Research Fellow in Church History,
Oxford University, formerly Pro Vice-Chancellor,
University of Birmingham, England

Dr Robert D. Linder

University Distinguished Professor of History,
Kansas State University, Manhattan, Kansas, USA

The late David F. Wright

Formerly Professor in Patristic and Reformed
Christianity, University of Edinburgh, Scotland

CONTENTS

CONTRIBUTORS

Dr John S. Andrews, formerly Sub-Librarian, University of Lancaster, England. *Hymns and Church Music; Hymns and Church Music after 1800.*

The late Canon James Atkinson, formerly Director of the Centre for Reformation Studies, University of Sheffield, England. *Reformation; Thomas Cranmer.*

Dr David W. Bebbington, Professor of History, University of Stirling, Scotland. *C. H. Spurgeon; William Carey; William Wilberforce.*

The late Dr Paul M. Bechtel, formerly Professor Emeritus of English, Wheaton College, Illinois, USA. *Blaise Pascal.*

Dr Janette Bohi, formerly Professor of History, University of Wisconsin, Whitewater, Wisconsin, USA. *A Crusade among Equals.*

John H. Y. Briggs, Director of the Centre for Baptist History and Heritage and Senior Research Fellow in Church History, Oxford University, formerly Pro Vice-Chancellor, University of Birmingham, England. *The First English Baptists; The First Industrial Nation; Present and Future.*

Dr Colin Brown, Senior Professor of Systematic Theology, Fuller Theological Seminary, Pasadena, California, USA. *Anselm; Reason and Unreason; A World Come of Age; Friedrich Schleiermacher.*

Revd Colin O. Buchanan, formerly Bishop of Woolwich, England. *The Sacraments in Medieval Europe; Organizing for Unity.*

Revd Dr Richard A. Burridge, Dean, Kings College, London. *Jesus*

Dr Robert G. Clouse, Senior Research Scholar in Liberal Arts and Professor Emeritus of History, Indiana State University, Terre Haute, Indiana, USA. *Columba; Patrick; Boethius; Flowering: the Western Church; Francis of Assisi; Thomas Aquinas; Savonarola; John of the Cross.*

The late Revd Dr Leonard W. Cowie, formerly Senior Lecturer in History, Whitelands College, London. *The First English Missions.*

Dr James A. DeJong, President and Professor of Historical Theology, Emeritus, Calvin Theological Seminary, Grand Rapids, Michigan, USA. *Expansion Worldwide.*

Dr Walter Delius, formerly Professor of Church History, Theological Faculty, Berlin, Germany. *Alcuin.*

Dr Bruce A. Demarest, formerly Professor of Theology and Spiritual Formation, Denver Seminary, Denver, Colorado, USA. *Jerome; Interpreting the Bible in the Middle Ages.*

Dr Wayne A. Detzler, Academic Dean and Professor of Biblical Studies and Missions, Southern Evangelical Seminary, North Carolina, USA. *Europe in Revolt; Pope Pius IX; The Bible Societies.*

Revd Dr John P. Donnelly, Professor Emeritus of History, Marquette University, Milwaukee, Wisconsin, USA. *Gasparo Contarini; The Jesuits; Pope John XXIII.*

Dr Tim Dowley, London. *John Wyclif, John Bunyan, Karl Barth.*

Dr James D. G. Dunn, Emeritus Lightfoot Professor of Divinity, University of Durham, England. *Pentecostalism and the Charismatic Movement.*

The late H. L. Ellison, Bible teacher and lecturer, England. *The Christian Church and the Jews.*

Dr Everett Ferguson, Distinguished Scholar in Residence, Abilene Christian University, Texas, USA. *Irenaeus; Origen; Tertullian; Athanasius; John Chrysostom.*

The late Dr Ronald C. Finucane, Distinguished Professor of History, Oakland University, Rochester, Michigan, USA. *Monasticism in the West; The Waldensians; An Age of Unrest.*

Dr Harlie Kay Gallatin, Senior Professor Emeritus of History, Southwest Baptist University, Bolivar, Missouri, USA. *The Eastern Church.*

Dr W. Ward Gasque, President of Pacific Association for Biblical Studies, Seattle, USA. *The Church Begins; Establishing Christianity*

Daniel Guy, MA, Marlborough, England: *Europe in Revolt*

The late Dr Colin Hemer, formerly Research Fellow, Tyndale House, Cambridge, England. *Archaeological and Earliest Christianity; Justin Martyr.*

The late Canon Michael M. Hennell, Manchester Cathedral, Manchester, England. *The Evangelicals; The Oxford Movement; John Henry Newman.*

Walter G. Hooper, Trustee and Literary Advisor to the Estate of C.S. Lewis. *C.S. Lewis.*

Dr Thomas Howard, Emeritus Professor of English, St John's Seminary, Brighton, Massachusetts, USA. *The Arts in the Christian West.*

Dr Larry W. Hurtado, Emeritus Professor of New Testament Language, Literature and Theology, University of Edinburgh, Scotland. *How the New Testament Came Down to Us.*

Dr F. W. Kantzenbach, formerly Professor of History of the Church and Christian Doctrine, University of Saarland, Germany. *Albert Schweitzer.*

Dr Alan Kreider, formerly Professor of Church History and Mission, Associated Mennonite Biblical Seminary, Elkhart, Indiana, USA. *Christians, War, and Peace; The Radical Reformation.*

A. N. S. Lane, Professor of Historical Theology, London Bible College, England. *A Flood of Bibles; William Tyndale and the English Bible.*

Dr Robert D. Linder, University Distinguished Professor of History, Kansas State University, Manhattan, USA. *Peter Abelard; The Catholic Reformation.*

The late Dr Andreas Lindt, formerly Professor of Modern Church History, University of Berne, Switzerland. *John Calvin.*

The late Dr H. Dermot McDonald, formerly Vice-Principal and Senior Lecturer, History of Doctrine and Philosophy of Religion, London School of Theology. *Marcion; Basil the Great; Nestorius; Cyril of Alexandria; William of Ockham.*

Dr Philip M. J. McNair, formerly Serena Professor of Italian, University of Birmingham, England. *Seeds of Renewal.*

Dr Caroline T. Marshall, formerly Professor of History, James Madison University, Harrisonburg, Virginia, USA. *Bernard of Clairvaux; Thomas Becket; Popular Religion; Jan Hus; Teresa of Avila.*

Dr Ralph P. Martin, formerly Distinguished Scholar in Residence at Fuller Theological Seminary, Pasadena, USA. *How the first Christians Worshipped.*

Dr James R. Moore, Professor of the History of Science, The Open University, Milton Keynes, England. *Christianity and the Rise of Modern Science; The Reasonableness of Christianity.*

Dr James I. Packer, Board of Governors' Professor of Theology, Regent College, Vancouver, Canada. *The Faith of the Protestants; Ignatius of Loyola.*

Dr C. René Padilla, President, Micah Network; Executive Director, Ediciones Kairos, Buenos Aires, Argentina. *An Age of Liberation, Hélder Câmara.*

Dr Pheme Perkins, Professor, Boston College, Boston, Massachusetts, USA. *The Thought-world of Early Christianity*

Dr Richard Pierard, formerly Scholar-in-Residence and Stephen Philips Professor of History, Gordon College, Wenham, Massachusetts, USA. *An Age of Ideology; Billy Graham.*

Arthur O. Roberts, Professor-at-large, George Fox University, Newberg, Oregon, USA. *George Fox and the Quakers.*

Revd Dr Wesley A. Roberts, Pastor, Peoples Baptist Church of Boston, Boston, Massachusetts, USA. *Martin Luther King, Jr.*

The late Dr Henderik 'Hans' R. Rookmaaker, first Professor of Art History, Free University, Amsterdam, The Netherlands. *Art and the Spirit.*

The late Dr Harry Rosenberg, formerly Professor of History, Colorado State University, Fort Collins, Colorado, USA. *The West in Crisis; Gregory the Great; Pope Innocent III.*

Dr Harold Rowdon, formerly Lecturer in Church History, London Bible College. *The Brethren; Hudson Taylor.*

Howard Sainsbury, formerly Senior Lecturer in Education, Edge Hill College of Higher Education, Ormskirk, England. *Jonathan Edwards.*

Dr Robert V. Schnucker, formerly Professor of History and Religion, Truman State University, Kirksville, Missouri, USA. *Theodore Beza; Martin Bucer.*

Dr Henry R. Sefton, Professor Emeritus of Church History, University of Aberdeen, Scotland. *Buildings and Belief; Post-Reformation Church Architecture.*

Dr Ian Sellers, formerly Honorary Lecturer in Church History, University of Manchester, England. *George Whitefield; Philipp Spener; The Unitarians.*

Revd Michael A. Smith, formerly Minister of Golcar Baptist Church, Huddersfield, England. *Worship and the Christian Year; Baptism; Eusebius; Peter; Paul; Ignatius of Antioch; Spreading the Good News; Clement of Rome; Ambrose of Milan; Leo the Great; Ascetics and Monks.*

Dr Keith L. Sprunger, Oswald H. Wedel Professor of History Emeritus at Bethel College, North Newton, Kansas, USA. *Puritans and Separatists.*

Dr Paul D. Steeves, Professor of History and Director of Russian Studies, Stetson University, DeLand, Florida, USA. *The Paulicians and the Bogomils; The Orthodox Church in Eastern Europe and Russia; The Russian Church: 1500–1900.*

The late Dr Robert Stupperich, Professor of Church History, University of Münster, Germany. *Martin Luther; Philip Melanchthon, Huldrych Zwingli*

Canon Dr Anthony C. Thiselton, Emeritus Professor of Christian Theology, University of Nottingham, England. *An Age of Anxiety.*

Revd Dr Derek Tidball, Visiting Scholar, Spurgeon's College, London. *D. L. Moody.*

Dr Richard A. Todd, Emeritus Associate Professor of History, Wichita State University, Wichita, Kansas, USA. *Constantine and the Christian Empire; The Fall of the Roman Empire; Clergy, Bishops, and Pope.*

Dr Andrew F. Walls, Professor of the History of Mission, Liverpool Hope University, Liverpool, England. *Outposts of Empire; David Livingstone; Samuel Ajayi Crowther; African Independent Churches.*

The late Revd Dr A. Skevington Wood, formerly Principal, Cliff College, Calver, England. *Awakening; John and Charles Wesley; Nikolaus von Zinzendorf.*

The late David E. Wright, formerly Professor in Patristic and Reformed Christianity, University of Edinburgh, Scotland. *Cyprian of Carthage; What the First Christians Believed; Councils and Creeds; The Church in North Africa; Augustine of Hippo; Pseudo-Dionysius the Areopagite; Cassiodorus.*

Dr Edwin Yamauchi, Professor Emeritus of History, Miami University, Oxford, Ohio, USA. *The religion of the Romans; The Manichaeans; The Gnostics.*

The late Dr John Howard Yoder, formerly Professor of Christian Ethics, University of Notre Dame, South Bend, Indiana, USA. *Christians, War, and Peace; The Radical Reformation.*

Dr Ruth Zerner, Associate Professor Emerita of History, Lehman College, City University of New York, USA. *Dietrich Bonhoeffer.*

LIST OF MAPS

LIST OF TIME CHARTS

LIST OF ILLUSTRATIONS/ PHOTOGRAPHS

PREFACE

Nearly two thousand years ago Jesus of Nazareth was put to death on a cross in an obscure corner of the Roman Empire. Today, worldwide faith in the risen Christ has grown as never before, not just in the so-called Christian West but in the new centres of Christianity in Africa, South-East Asia, and South America.

How has the belief of a handful of persecuted and frightened people in Jerusalem expanded so extensively? How did it outlive the mighty Roman Empire and outlast the more recent empires? How did the Christian churches, denominations, movements, doctrines, and beliefs we know today come into being? How has the faith passed from generation to generation, and from country to country? These are a few of the questions we attempt to answer in this book.

To write the full story of the rise of the Christian faith in one volume is an almost impossible task. In trying to tackle it, we have called upon the expertise of many contributors. We have involved writers from many countries throughout the world, and drawn on wide resources for photographs, illustrations, and maps. The aim has been to draw a rounded picture of the worldwide development of Christianity, focussing on key movements, outstanding Christian leaders, crucial turning-points, and revolutionary breakthroughs. This cannot claim to be a comprehensive history of the church; however, the compression necessary to a book of this length offers the prospect of exciting new perspectives across the centuries, a bird's-eye view of 2000 years of Christianity.

Is it objective history? Yes – if we mean that it is written by experts, well informed on their subjects, and abreast of modern views. Yes – if we mean that it claims to be accurate, scholarly, and balanced. But no history can be detached. It is written largely by scholars who are Christians, and who write with a sympathetic understanding that breathes life into their accounts. They are committed both to Christianity and to the unhindered pursuit of truth; they haven't disguised or avoided the darker, depressing, or disgraceful aspects of the varied story of Christianity.

The story is an exciting one, yet also complex; we have tried not to over-simplify difficult questions. Wherever possible, we have presented material visually and graphically, to give a 'feel' for the period concerned, to see the wood as well as the trees. We have principally in mind those who come new to the subject, excited by the discoveries, gripped by the unfolding story, and wanting an account which is not so superficial as to be unsatisfying but which wears its learning lightly. We have tried to let the facts speak for themselves.

PREFACE TO THE REVISED EDITION

This new revised edition adheres to the aims of the original book. However, we have redesigned and re-arranged material to make things clearer and easier to follow, and also taken the opportunity to update, and to bring the story down to the twenty-first century.

In summary, for this edition we have:

- Removed some introductory material on historiography to allow more space for the narrative history
- Completely revised, re-styled, checked, and re-edited the text throughout
- Added important new text – for example on Jesus, the Thought World of Early Christianity, and the Future
- Added dates for all significant named persons
- Added scripture references and texts
- Added a useful glossary of ecclesiastical and theological terms
- Created around 40 new full-colour maps
- Revised and re-designed all Timelines
- Created a single, comprehensive index
- Completely re-illustrated the book in full colour throughout
- Added section summaries, study questions, and suggested further reading for students
- Completely re-designed the entire book, with a larger format, more readable typeface, and clearer layout

It is the hope of editors and contributors alike that this book in its new form will open up the story of the Christian faith to a new generation of readers and students.

Tim Dowley
Dulwich, London 2013

THE CHRISTIAN CENTURIES

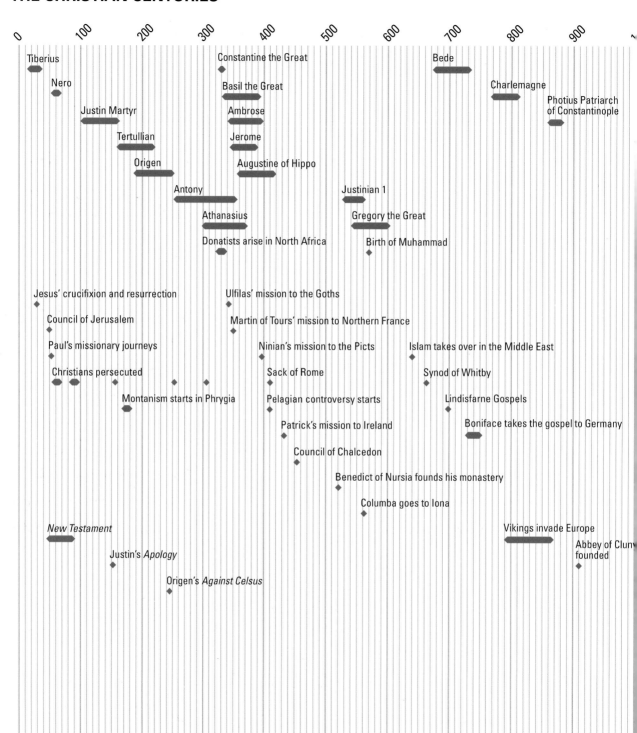

Timeline markings: 0, 100, 200, 300, 400, 500, 600, 700, 800, 900

Tiberius

Nero

Justin Martyr

Tertullian

Origen

Antony

Athanasius

Donatists arise in North Africa

Constantine the Great

Basil the Great

Ambrose

Jerome

Augustine of Hippo

Justinian 1

Gregory the Great

Birth of Muhammad

Bede

Charlemagne

Photius Patriarch of Constantinople

Jesus' crucifixion and resurrection

Council of Jerusalem

Paul's missionary journeys

Christians persecuted

Montanism starts in Phrygia

Ulfilas' mission to the Goths

Martin of Tours' mission to Northern France

Ninian's mission to the Picts

Sack of Rome

Pelagian controversy starts

Patrick's mission to Ireland

Council of Chalcedon

Benedict of Nursia founds his monastery

Columba goes to Iona

Islam takes over in the Middle East

Synod of Whitby

Lindisfarne Gospels

Boniface takes the gospel to Germany

New Testament

Justin's *Apology*

Origen's *Against Celsus*

Vikings invade Europe

Abbey of Cluny founded

1100   1200   1300   1400   1500   1600   1700   1800   1900   2000

Erasmus

Dürer

Martin Luther

Zwingli

Ignatius of Loyola

Francis Xavier

John Calvin

Teresa of Avila

J. S. Bach

Zinzendorf

John Wesley

George Whitefield

William Carey

Society for the
Propagation of
the Gospel founded

Moravians formed

Karl Barth

Bonhoeffer

Billy Graham

Pope John XXIII

Pope
John Paul II

World War I

Russian Revolution

World War II

...elm

William the Conqueror King of England

Pope Gregory VII

Peter Abelard

Bernard of Clairvaux

Francis of Assisi

Pope Innocent III

Thomas Aquinas

Dante

John Wyclif

Jan Hus

The Crusades

Rise of the universities

Cathedral building booms in the West

Fourth Lateran Council

Inquisition founded

Turks capture
Constantinople

Queen Elizabeth I of England

Galileo

Descartes

Rembrandt

Pascal

Newton

Anabaptists arise in Europe

Pilgrim Fathers reach New England

Inquisition revived

Council of Trent

First English Baptists

Thirty Years' War

Propaganda founded

Jesuit missions begin

James Watt's
steam engine

American Independence

French Revolution

David Livingstone

Kierkegaard

Pope Pius IX

Freud

Baptist Missionary Society founded

Church Missionary Society founded

British and Foreign Bible Society founded

Modern Pentecostalism begins

American Civil War

Salvation Army founded

Papal Infallibility promulgated

9/11

World Council of
Churches formed

Vatican II

Luther's *95 Theses*

Loyola's *Spiritual Exercises*

Calvin's *Institutes*

King James Version

The Pilgrim's Progress

Edinburgh World
Missionary Conference

The *Communist Manifesto*

Darwin's *Origin of Species*

Beginnings

AD 1–325

Summary

Christianity rapidly spread beyond its original geographical region of Roman-occupied Palestine into the entire Mediterranean area. Something of this process of expansion is described in the Acts of the Apostles in the New Testament. It is clear that a Christian presence was already established in Rome itself within fifteen years of the resurrection of Christ. The imperial trade routes made possible the rapid traffic of ideas, as much as merchandise.

Three centres of the Christian church rapidly emerged in the eastern Mediterranean region. The church became a significant presence in its own original heartlands, with Jerusalem emerging as a leading centre of thought and activity. Asia Minor (modern-day Turkey) was already an important area of Christian expansion, as can be seen from the destinations of some of the apostle Paul's letters, and the references to the 'seven churches of Asia' in the book of Revelation. The process of expansion in this region continued, with the great imperial city of Constantinople (modern-day Istanbul) becoming a particularly influential centre of mission and political consolidation.

Yet further growth took place to the south, with the important Egyptian city of Alexandria emerging as a stronghold of Christian faith. With this expansion, new debates opened up. While the New Testament deals with the issue of the relationship of Christianity and Judaism, the expansion of Christianity into Greek-speaking regions led to the exploration of the way in which Christianity related to Greek philosophy. Many Christian writers sought to demonstrate, for example, that Christianity brought to fulfilment the great themes of the philosophy of Plato.

Yet this early Christian expansion was far from unproblematic. The 'imperial cult', which regarded worship of the Roman emperor as a test of loyalty to the empire, was prominent in the eastern Mediterranean region. Many Christians found themselves penalized as a result of their insistence on worshipping only Christ. The expansion of Christianity regularly triggered persecutions. These were often local – for example, the Decian persecution of 249–51, which was particularly vicious in North Africa.

CHAPTER I

JESUS
His life, ministry, death, and its consequences

'Christianity' without 'Christ' is a meaningless word; and without Jesus Christ, there would be no Christianity about which we could write a history. 'Christ' is a Greek word, translating the Hebrew participle, 'Messiah', both of which simply mean 'someone who has been anointed'. The very first Christians applied this title to Jesus of Nazareth so quickly that, by the time of the letters of the apostle Paul a generation later, it functioned almost like a surname, Jesus Christ; thus it is hardly surprising that the early disciples were soon given the nickname, 'Christians', for those who belong to Christ (see Acts 11:27). It is a curious quirk of history that, while Jesus himself seems never to have had a proper education, was not formally trained or ordained, never held any rank or high office or earned much money, probably never walked further than a hundred miles from his home, during a brief period of wandering and preaching, and finally suffered a humiliating execution at a relatively young age, yet arguably his brief life, ministry, death, and its consequences have had a greater effect on human history than anyone else.

DID JESUS OF NAZARETH EXIST?
No serious historian really doubts that Jesus actually lived and died in the first-century Roman Empire, as evidenced by the major ancient historians. Tacitus (Annals 15.44.3) tells us that the early Christians, who were wrongly blamed by Nero for the fire in Rome in AD 64, took their name from Christ who was executed under Pontius Pilate in Judaea, while Suetonius says that debates about Christ led to such unrest that the Emperor Claudius expelled the Jews from Rome in AD 49 (Claudius, 25.4). Pliny writes to

THE ROMAN EMPIRE IN AD 14

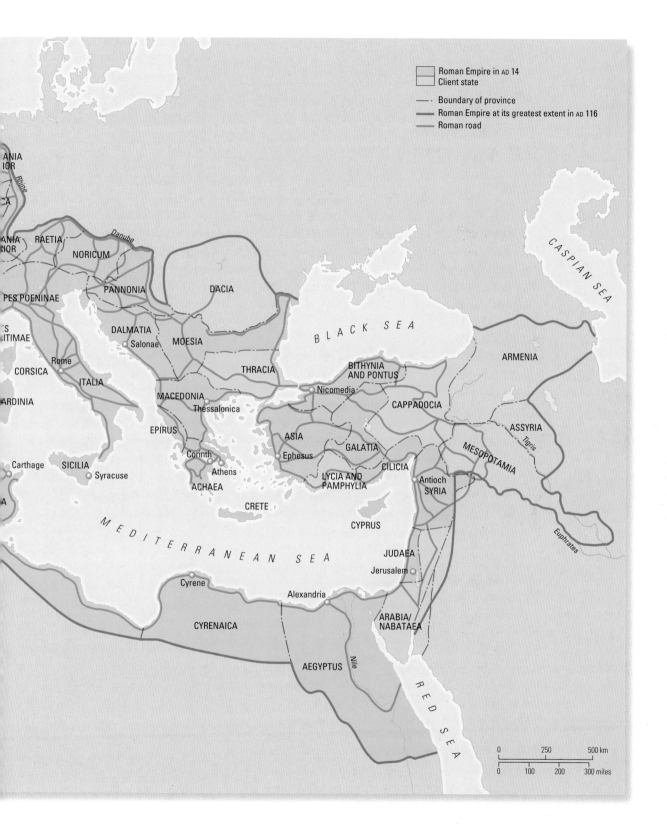

Roman Empire in AD 14
Client state
- - - Boundary of province
Roman Empire at its greatest extent in AD 116
Roman road

RAETIA
NORICUM
Danube
PANNONIA
DACIA
ANIA
IOR
ANIA
IOR
PES POENINAE
DALMATIA
Salonae
MOESIA
BLACK SEA
CASPIAN SEA
S
ITIMAE
Rome
CORSICA
ITALIA
THRACIA
BITHYNIA
AND PONTUS
ARMENIA
ARDINIA
MACEDONIA
Thessalonica
Nicomedia
CAPPADOCIA
ASSYRIA
EPIRUS
ASIA
Tigris
Carthage
SICILIA
Corinth
Ephesus
GALATIA
MESOPOTAMIA
Syracuse
Athens
CILICIA
A
ACHAEA
LYCIA AND
PAMPHYLIA
Antioch
SYRIA
CRETE
CYPRUS
Euphrates
M E D I T E R R A N E A N   S E A
JUDAEA
Jerusalem
Cyrene
Alexandria
ARABIA/
NABATAEA
CYRENAICA
AEGYPTUS
Nile
RED SEA

0   250   500 km
0   100   200   300 miles

the Emperor Trajan around AD 111 for advice about what to do with people in his province in Asia Minor who worship 'Christ as a god' (Letters, 10.96). In addition, later Rabbinic traditions say that 'Jesus of Nazareth' was executed 'because he practised sorcery and led Israel astray' (bSanhedrin 43.a). Such historical evidence from Romans and Jewish opponents alike is very significant and provides the core for research in what is often called the 'Quest for the Historical Jesus': the first phase of which started with German scholars such as Albert Schweitzer around the turn of the nineteenth and early twentieth century; the 'new Quest' began with Ernst Käsemann in 1953; while recent work by scholars such as E. P. Sanders and N. T. Wright is usually seen as the 'Third Quest', in which biblical and other sources are scrutinized to see what can be determined about the historical life and death of Jesus.

WHAT ARE THE MAIN SOURCES?

Beyond these historical mentions of Jesus in Roman and Jewish writers, the main sources about Jesus are the four Gospels 'according to' (rather than 'by') Matthew, Mark, Luke, and John found in the Bible. There are other texts also called 'gospels' not found in the canon of the Christian scriptures; these 'non-canonical' works are mostly less narrative or historical in form, being sayings, discourses, revelations of Jesus, and are probably written a couple of generations later than the canonical Gospels. These four have a similar structure, describing the life and ministry of Jesus from his baptism by John the Baptist, with an extended concentration on his final week in Jerusalem, his arrest, trial, and execution – and what happened afterwards. This means that their form and literary genre is very similar to ancient biographies of famous people, which concentrated on their public lives, exemplified

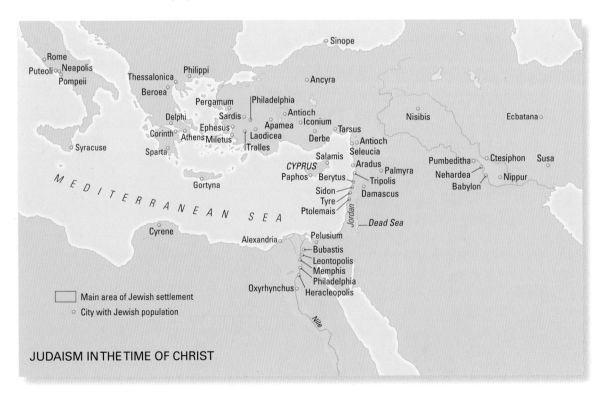

JUDAISM IN THE TIME OF CHRIST

THE THOUGHT-WORLD OF EARLY CHRISTIANITY

Twenty-first century students are familiar with terms such as cultural diversity and globalization. Christianity was born in a cultural setting that experienced its own forms of intellectual and religious diversity, brought into conversation with each other thanks to the global expansion of the Roman Empire. The Gospel of Luke and the Acts of the Apostles display the three distinctive threads in this tapestry: Jewish, Greek, and Roman. Jesus was born into a world of pious Jews, devoted to their traditions and to the Jerusalem Temple. At the same time, many first-century Jews imagined a day when God would raise up a new anointed one (messiah) to right the wrongs of injustice and liberate Israel from foreign rule. They found the religious vocabulary for these hopes in passages from the Hebrew prophets, especially Isaiah, Jeremiah, Ezekiel, and Daniel. So Luke's Gospel has the adult Jesus begin his public career by announcing that God's Spirit now rests on him. The time of fulfilment is at hand (Luke 4:14–21).

Though Jesus, himself, would have known those scriptures in Hebrew, and their translations into the Aramaic spoken in Palestine, Luke and the other New Testament authors employ the Greek translations used by diaspora Jews since the third century BC. Called 'the Septuagint' (LXX), these Greek versions sometimes create new meanings for Greek words to translate Hebrew concepts, or substitute a familiar Greek concept for the Hebrew. For example, the Greek word *diathēkē* ordinarily means a will or testament, but in the LXX it translates the Hebrew *berîth*, 'covenant'. Alexander the Great's Eastern conquests in the fourth century BC had spread Greek language, civic organization, and culture throughout the region. Attempts by his successors to create a thoroughly 'Greek city-state' and religious culture in Jerusalem resulted in persecution and rebellion in the mid-first century BC (1 Maccabees 1:1–15).

Important religious concepts emerge among Jews opposed to the world being created by Alexander's successors, illustrated in Daniel 7–12. The present world belongs to a predestined series of 'evil empires', hostile to God's righteous ones. A series of symbolic visions reveals the truth about history to the seer, including its eventual termination (7:15–18). Instead of the human series of flawed or pious leaders, cosmic powers, demonic or angelic, determine the apocalyptic story of empires, each more evil than its predecessor. God's righteous people felt themselves to be living in the last days, (Daniel 10:18–11:45). Finally, the angelic powers, represented by Michael, will end the situation. Divine judgment will be enacted punishing the wicked and rewarding the faithful (Daniel 12:1-12). The Lord's prayer asks God to protect believers from the

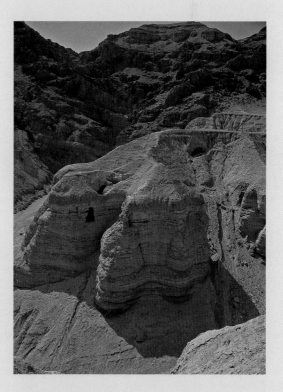

The limestone cliffs, above the Qumran archaelogical site, in which many of the Dead Sea Scrolls were discovered. Around three-quarters of the scrolls from the immediate area were found in 1952 in Cave 4Q, in the middle of the photograph.
TIM DOWLEY ASSOCIATES

perils of living in the evil days at the end of the world: 'do not lead us into [the time of] testing, and deliver us from the evil one' (Matthew 6:13).

EVIDENCE FROM THE DEAD SEA SCROLLS

Evidence for the importance of this apocalyptic view of the world was provided by discovery of a major collection of biblical manuscripts, liturgical books, community rule books, and other writings belonging to a sect of Jews claiming to be the righteous remnant, a community of the new covenant (Dead Sea Scrolls). A sharp dualism divided its members, 'children of light', from other Jews, 'sons of darkness'. The former were sustained in their strict adherence to the Mosaic Torah as interpreted by the sect by a Spirit of Holiness, or angel of light. The rest of humanity was deceived by the Prince of Darkness. As Christians would do later (Luke 24:25–27), the 'new covenanters' (Essenes) discovered predictions of their founder, the 'Teacher of Righteousness', of his opponent, the 'Wicked Priest', and of the eventual coming of priestly and royal messiah figures in words of the Hebrew prophets. These messianic agents are frequently depicted as heavenly figures. For example, a priestly figure claims, 'who shall be like (me) in my judgment […] for my position is with the gods' (4Q491) and an exalted royal figure 'will be called son of God, and they will call him son of the Most High' (4Q246).

With the advent of Roman power in the region, the final evil empire shifts from Alexander's successors, as in Daniel, to Rome. A work from the first century BC, the 'War Scroll,' provides elaborate descriptions of the final battles between the Sons of Light and the forces of evil, the 'Kittim', whose tactics reflect Roman military practice. The earthly struggle which engulfs the nations of the world mirrors a heavenly conflict that ends with the defeat of Evil. The New Testament concludes with a comparable apocalyptic overthrow of Rome, the nations under her sway, and the Satanic forces, but leaves 'the saints' out of the battle. It calls upon the righteous to endure suffering and reject any collusion or cultural accommodation with 'the beast' (Revelation 13:5–9).

PAX ROMANA

As Rome emerged from the civil wars that marked the end of the Republic into its own position as a global power, its divine right to rule nations was embodied in mythic tales and monuments. Virgil's *Aeneid* transformed the minor character who survived the Greek destruction of Troy into 'pious Aeneas', semi-divine founder of the Julio-Claudian line and of Roman military glory. Roman conquests made her the heir of Alexander's empire. Roman authors make extensive use of legends about Alexander, the Great. He can illustrate the moralist's cautionary tale against abandoning the simplicity of traditional Roman values for corruption by the wealth and luxury of the east. Or he can celebrate the overthrow of capricious, tyrannical regimes by a ruler who establishes a new order of peace based on justice.

Monuments such as temples, statues, and altars, represented imperial power as the source of justice and world peace. For example, Augustus' temple to *Mars Ultor* (the Avenger), meeting place for the senate when considering military affairs, included a monumental statue of the divinized Julius Caesar, as well as panels by Alexander the Great's court painter. Claudius even had its Alexander repainted as Augustus. An inscription from Ephesus (c. 49 BC) acclaims the living Julius Caesar, 'the god who has appeared visibly and universal saviour of human life'. Acclaiming Roman emperors as though their benefits to humanity entitled them to divine honours could spark conflict between Jews and Romans, as it did when Caligula

in their deeds and words, culminating in their death. It is important to recognize that even ancient history writing is not like what we call history today, and nor are the Gospels like video-diaries, simply recording what was done or said. Like other ancient 'lives', they seek to interpret eyewitness and other material to explain the importance of their subject –

ordered a monumental statue of himself erected in the Jerusalem temple (Philo, Leg. 203). Though Luke–Acts depicts Roman governors as more just than enraged local authorities who drag Christians before them, Luke cannot accept Augustus as the 'saviour' who brought peace to the world (Luke 2:1–14).

Alexander's conquests established Greek as the *lingua franca* of the region and the Greek style city-state as the dominant political organization. Alexandria in Egypt, with its great library, emerged as the centre of textual, literary, and scientific learning. Greek medicine, rhetoric, and philosophy also spread throughout the region providing a common cultural language for the educated elite. Even the isolationist 'new covenanters' employed common patterns of civic associations in their community rules and of Greco-Roman military manuals in the War Scroll.

GREEK PHILOSOPHY

Religious activities might assure the safety of one's household, the prosperity of a local community, or the continued peace of the empire, but it was philosophy which taught individuals to take rational control of their lives. Schools founded in fourth century BC Athens by Plato, Aristotle, Zeno (Stoics), and Epicurus pursued technical debates and developed further teaching. For larger audiences, the interest of the Greek philosophical schools lay in their therapies for disordered souls. What is the best way for human beings to attain happiness? How can passions such as anger, greed, and self-centredness be checked or overcome? What responsibilities do human beings have to the larger community?

Stoics understood human reason as part of a rational spirit which pervaded the entire universe and was responsible for its complex order. At the end of each cosmological cycle everything collapsed into the primordial fire from which it had devolved. Therefore bringing one's passions under control by self-control and self-examination could be described as living according to nature's law. Much unhappiness, the Stoic argued, flows from attachments to things not under our control. Hence Stoics were celebrated for a calculated indifference, and willingness to commit suicide, rather than suffer dishonour or public torture.

Epicureans countered that everything has emerged from the interactions of various types of atoms in an infinite universe. Death is nothing more than the atoms untangling. Gods have no interest in human affairs. They agree that many human passions are irrational sources of misery. But the solution is to live life as pleasantly as possible, without fear among like-minded friends. Unlike the Stoics, Epicureans advocated withdrawal from public affairs. Hence opponents accused Epicureans with atheism and hatred of humanity. The 'wicked' who think there is no afterlife in Wisdom 2:1–11 seem to be Epicureans. God's wisdom is vindicated when they are shown the immortal happiness of the righteous (*Wisdom* 3:1–4; 5:1–8).

Itinerant Christian missionaries might be confused with another philosophical type, the Cynic with rough cloak, leather bag, and staff. Cynics appealed to the figure of Socrates. They eschewed all social conventions, castigating audiences for their preoccupations with family, property, honour, and other things unnecessary to sustain life. Cynics also mocked other philosophers, who depended upon wealthy patrons for support. Paul's insistence on his own independence of external support would have sounded comparable (1 Corinthians 9:1–18). But as Paul insists, the Christian gospel of salvation through faith in a crucified messiah shatters the conceptual world of both Jew and Greek (1 Corinthians 1:18–25).

PHEME PERKINS

Jesus – after years of prayer and meditation through the inspiration of the Holy Spirit – to bring out the truth about Jesus' deeds and words, life and ministry, death, and resurrection. Most New Testament scholars think that Mark was written first, and his account is followed by Matthew and Luke, who also have access to collections of Jesus' teachings;

these three Gospels are often called the 'Synoptics', because they can be 'looked at' together, while John is probably composed independently of them, although he too includes some very early traditions.

WHERE DID JESUS COME FROM?

Ancient biographies usually begin with the person's public debut, with perhaps a brief story about their birth or childhood, and sometimes a note about the family history, genealogy, or ancestral city. Mark begins with the adult Jesus arriving to be baptized by John (Mark 1:2–11). Matthew takes it back to the story of Jesus' birth in Bethlehem, told from Joseph's viewpoint, with wise men coming to pay homage, and a genealogy that goes back to David and Abraham (Matthew 1–2). Luke begins with the birth of the fore-runner, John the Baptist, the journey of Mary and Joseph from Nazareth to Bethlehem, and Jesus' birth in an inn, narrated from perspective of Mary and the women, with humble poor shepherds coming to the manger; there is a brief story of the twelve-year-old Jesus in the Temple, and his baptism concludes with a more universal genealogy going right back to Adam (Luke 1–3). On the other hand, rather than human stories, John is clear that Jesus' origin is truly cosmic: 'in the beginning was the Word', who not only was 'with God', but who is also God, yet who took on human flesh and dwelt among us to reveal what God is like (John 1:1–18).

Sunset view across the Sea of Galilee – also known as Lake Tiberias, Gennesaret, and Kinneret – the setting of much of Jesus' ministry: see, for example, Matthew 4:18–22, 15:29; Mark 1:14–20, 7:31; Luke 5:1–11; John 6:1.
DREAMSTIME

WHERE DID IT ALL TAKE PLACE?

Like other ancient biographies, all four Gospels begin their main narrative with the subject's public debut, as Jesus is baptized by John the Baptist; he then undertakes an itinerant ministry of teaching, preaching, and healing. This was not at all uncommon in first-century Israel-Palestine, where such wandering prophets would gather groups of followers. So Jesus calls his first disciples, who were fishermen and workers in Galilee. Most of his ministry takes place in the towns and ports around this large inland lake. Mark devotes the first half of his Gospel to this period, which could all happen in the space of only a few months; after discussing his identity with his disciples, Jesus decides to go down to Jerusalem (Mark 8.27–38), where he is then arrested and dies. Following Mark, Matthew organizes his Gospel similarly, although he structures it around five major discourses of Jesus' sayings and teachings. Luke prefers to arrange it geographically, as the Galilean ministry leads into a long journey section from Galilee to Jerusalem (9:51–19:26), before Jesus' final week and Passion. Once again, John is different, as he describes various visits of Jesus up and down to Jerusalem over two to three years before his final Passover there. Again, like ancient lives, the bulk of the Gospels' narrative is taken up with their accounts of the subject's deeds and words, his teaching and his mighty acts, culminating in his final days and death.

WHAT DID JESUS DO?

Jesus' primary activity was to proclaim the 'kingdom of God' breaking into our world, which was accompanied by various healings and miracles. Once again, such preaching would be expected of such wandering prophet teachers and healers. Most of Jesus' miracles are healings, performed to help those crippled by sickness or disease, at their own request or that of their loved ones (for example, Jairus' daughter and the woman with the flow of blood, Mark 5:21–43); like some Old Testament prophets, Jesus sometimes even raised people from the dead (see for example Luke 7:11–17; John 11:1–44). Jesus' other miracles demonstrated his control over nature, such as the feeding of the 5,000 or the storm on the lake (Mark 6:30–52). Some people say we cannot be expected to believe this in our rational world; actually, such stories are very common in all forms of ancient literature, including their history books, as well as in other cultures. It really depends on our prior assumptions: if we rule such things out as impossible in advance, then they have no place in an historical account today. On the other hand, if we accept and believe in Jesus as the Son of God who was raised from the dead, then it should not be surprising that he could do extraordinary things. For the evangelists, the much more important question is what the purpose of these miracles was: often they remind us of, or even fulfil, Old Testament stories, and they point to who Jesus is, and what he is doing. Thus John calls miracles 'signs', as he links them to discourses and teachings which explain the significance of Jesus; see, for example, how his account of the feeding of the 5,000 leads into the debate about Jesus as the 'bread of life' (John 6:1–59).

WHAT DID JESUS SAY?

After his baptism and temptation in the wilderness, Jesus comes back into Galilee preaching that 'the kingdom of God is at hand' (Mark 1:15). The English word 'kingdom' sounds very masculine, concrete, and powerful, while both the Hebrew, *malkuth*, and Greek, *basileia*, are feminine abstract nouns, meaning 'rule' or 'sovereignty'. Jesus never defines the 'kingdom', preferring to tell short stories, or parables, about what it is 'like' – and they are very strange, full of seeds growing secretly, good and bad fish caught in the same net, wheat and weeds growing together until the harvest, managers rendering accounts to their superiors, lost coins, lost sheep, and lost children (see the collections of parables in Mark 4, Matthew 13, and Luke 15). It is all about what happens in the topsy-turvy world when we let God actually be God, rather than doing it our way. Interestingly, although Mark regularly calls Jesus 'rabbi', or describes him teaching (see Mark 1:21–22; 4:1–2; 4:38; 5:35, etc.), he records surprisingly little actual teaching. On the other hand, both Matthew and Luke include a lot of Jesus' teaching, which they probably derive from a shared source of his sayings, though scholars are divided about whether it was oral or written down. Matthew collects this teaching material together into five great sermons or 'discourses' (chapters 7–9, 10, 13, 18, 22–23), while Luke prefers to give it a narrative setting, often on the journey from Galilee to Jerusalem (9:51–19:26).

Jesus is regularly described, especially by those who do not consider themselves to be Christians, as one of the great moral teachers of the human race. However, his direct ethical teaching, often in pithy phrases with teasing word-play, is extraordinarily demanding, while appearing to be impractical or impossible to put into practice in the 'real world'. Money and possessions are to be given away (Mark 10:23–27; Matthew 6:19–33; Luke 12:22–34); marriage is enhanced, with no divorce permitted and celibacy commended (Mark 10:2–12; Matthew 19:12); non-violence is advocated to the point of 'turning the other cheek', praying for enemies, and putting away the sword (Matthew 5:38–44; 26:52; Luke 6:27–30). The Christian church has struggled to follow or obey this teaching in both personal and public affairs over two thousand years; not everyone can become a monk or nun with their vows of poverty, chastity, and obedience!

HOW DID HE DIE?

Like other ancient biographies, all four Gospels devote the largest amount of space – about a quarter to a third of their narrative – to the events of Jesus' final week in Jerusalem, leading to his death. The three Synoptic Gospels begin their accounts with Jesus' entry into Jerusalem and his protest about the commercialization in the Temple (although John places this at the very start of his ministry, John 2:13–22). Over the next few days, Jesus continues his ministry as a teacher and healer in and around the Temple courts, which produces challenges to the religious authorities, who respond in turn and question Jesus about his authority (Mark 11:27–33). On the Thursday evening, he gathers his disciples together for a 'last supper', in what seems to be a Passover meal in the Synoptics, in which he institutes the holy communion for his followers, although John describes Jesus washing the disciples' feet, rather than the eucharist (John 13:1–11). After this meal, he goes to a garden, called Gethsemane by Mark and Matthew, to pray; although it is on the way back to safety in Bethany, the delay to struggle in prayer to accept the will of God means he is still there when Judas arrives with soldiers to arrest him. Jesus is then subjected to hearings before the Sanhedrin, the assembly of the Jewish religious leaders, and before Pilate as the Roman authority. After being flogged, he is crucified: the most humiliating and painful execution in the ancient world.

Yet, the extraordinary thing is how each Gospel depicts the crucifixion as the climax of its story: Mark has shown how Jesus was misunderstood throughout his ministry, so now he feels abandoned even by God, while Matthew describes God's answer in the earthquake which ensues (Mark 15:34–39; Matthew 27:46–54). In Luke's Gospel, Jesus has been particularly concerned for women, and for bringing ordinary people into the kingdom in prayerful trust in his father, and now he dies as he lived, caring for women, his executioners, and the penitent thief (Luke 23:27–30, 34, 39–43, 46). Meanwhile, John brings to a climax his account of Jesus being divinely in control since 'in the beginning', showing how he is concerned for his mother even on the cross, where he fulfils scripture and finally accomplishes everything (John 19:25–26, 28, 30).

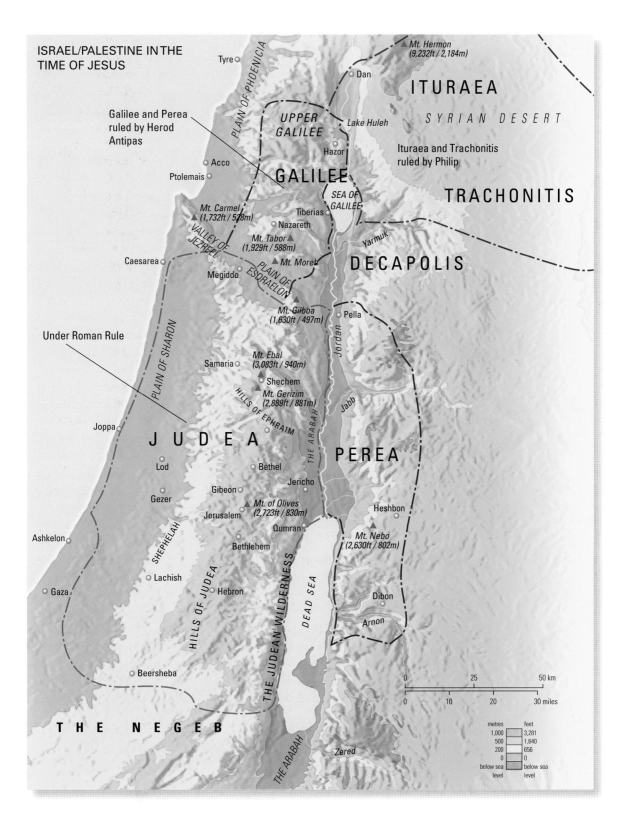

ISRAEL/PALESTINE IN THE
TIME OF JESUS

Tyre

PLAIN OF PHOENICIA

Mt. Hermon
(9,232ft / 2,184m)

Dan

ITURAEA

SYRIAN DESERT

Galilee and Perea
ruled by Herod
Antipas

UPPER
GALILEE

Lake Huleh

Hazor

Ituraea and Trachonitis
ruled by Philip

Acco

GALILEE

TRACHONITIS

Ptolemais

Mt. Carmel
(1,732ft / 528m)

SEA OF
GALILEE

Tiberias

Nazareth

VALLEY OF
JEZREEL

Mt. Tabor
(1,929ft / 588m)

Yarmuk

Caesarea

Megiddo

Mt. Moreh

PLAIN OF
ESDRAELON

DECAPOLIS

Mt. Gilboa
(1,630ft / 497m)

Pella

Under Roman Rule

PLAIN OF SHARON

Samaria

Mt. Ebal
(3,083ft / 940m)

Jordan

Shechem

Mt. Gerizim
(2,889ft / 881m)

Jabb

Joppa

HILLS OF EPHRAIM

THE ARABAH

JUDEA

PEREA

Lod

Bethel

Gezer

Jericho

Gibeon

Mt. of Olives
(2,723ft / 830m)

Heshbon

Jerusalem

Qumran

Ashkelon

Bethlehem

Mt. Nebo
(2,630m / 802m)

SHEPHELAH

Dibon

Lachish

Hebron

DEAD SEA

Gaza

HILLS OF JUDEA

THE JUDEAN WILDERNESS

Arnon

Beersheba

THE   NEGEB

THE ARABAH

Zered

0   25   50 km

0   10   20   30 miles

metres	feet
1,000	3,281
500	1,640
200	656
	0
below sea level	below sea level

Beside the family tomb of Herod the Great, Jerusalem, is a huge disc-like stone that would have sealed the entrance. The tomb of Joseph of Arimathea, in which Jesus was buried, had a similar stone blocking entry; see Matthew 28:57–60.
TIM DOWLEY ASSOCIATES

WHAT HAPPENED NEXT?

The Romans had long discovered that executing the ringleader was usually the best way to stop such enthusiastic religious renewal movements, and there are plenty of examples of their use of this tactic around the first century. The Christian movement is the only one which is different – in that the leader's humiliating death on a cross was not the end – and this demands an historical explanation. According to Luke's second volume, the book of Acts, the same disciples who betrayed and denied Jesus at his arrest and simply fled away, started to turn Jerusalem upside down a couple of days later with the extraordinary claim that God had raised him from the dead. The earliest witness is Paul's account of Jesus' appearances, which he had 'handed on' to the Corinthians in the early days; the list in I Corinthians 15 reads like a very early tradition that goes back before Paul himself to shortly after Jesus' death. The Gospels, which were written down some years after Paul, all contain descriptions of the empty tomb, with some accounts of Jesus' appearances to Mary, Peter, and others.

Modern historical enquiry can be uncomfortable about claims of people rising from the dead, and yet history has to provide some explanation of the change in the disciples, and why the Jesus movement did not die out like the others. If the authorities had the body of Jesus in safekeeping, it would have been easy to produce it to stop the early church in its tracks. However one assesses the historical arguments for the resurrection of Jesus Christ, it remains a fact that this is the constant thread throughout the rest of the New Testament, and in the experience of Christians for the next two thousand years, without which there would be no history of Christianity – and no need for this book!

RICHARD A. BURRIDGE

CHAPTER 2

THE CHURCH BEGINS
From Jerusalem to Rome

Jesus was executed by the Roman authorities in the city of Jerusalem around AD 30 on a trumped-up charge of sedition. Not a promising start for a new religion! But within three days the rumour was spreading around the city that he was alive, that he had been raised from the dead. Some of his closest followers claimed that they had actually seen him, and seven weeks later his resurrection was being boldly proclaimed in public in the city where he had been executed. The effects were startling; thousands of Jews and Jewish converts, who had returned from other parts of the Roman Empire to live in or visit Jerusalem, came to believe that Jesus was alive, and that his death on a cross was, in fact, part of God's plan to save humanity. During the following weeks and months many others joined them.

This marked the birth of the Christian church, as recorded in the book of Acts.

THE BIRTH OF THE CHURCH

During the days immediately following the resurrection, Jesus' followers claimed to have met him. After these encounters with the risen Jesus, no one could convince them that they were following mere pious hopes. They were not deluded: they had really *seen* their master and he was alive for ever!

They said Jesus explained to them things they had never understood before; for example, that it had been necessary for him to suffer and die before entering into his rightful glory. Now – in the light of his resurrection and the explanations he gave – the cross of Jesus took on an eternal dimension of significance for them, despite the wickedness of the people responsible for his death.

Overview of the 1:50 scale model of Jerusalem, based on research by the Jewish archaeologist Michael Avi-Yonah, now housed at the Israel Museum, Jerusalem. Top left, dominating the city, is Herod's Temple, with the four defensive towers of the Roman Antonia Fortress adjoining.
TIM DOWLEY ASSOCIATES

But belief in Jesus' resurrection did more than simply rebuild the faith of his disciples and cast new light on the meaning of his death. The apostles also said that he commissioned them to take into all parts of the world the good news of what God had done by sending him to rescue the human race. But they would not be alone in this task: Jesus promised them God's Holy Spirit to empower them (Matthew 28, Luke 24, and Acts 1).

PETER

Peter came from Bethsaida, on Lake Galilee, and his fisherman father John originally named him Simon. He was living in Capernaum, with his wife, brother, and mother-in-law, when first introduced to Jesus by his brother Andrew. He quickly became the leader of Jesus' twelve close followers, was often their spokesman, and was the first to declare publicly that Jesus was the Messiah, at Caesarea Philippi.

Jesus gave him the nickname 'Peter' (*Cephas* in Aramaic) meaning 'rock'. Rash and hot-blooded, Peter said that he was ready to die with Jesus, then three times denied knowing him on the night of Jesus' arrest. But Peter was one of the first to meet the risen Jesus, who specifically restored him to his position as leader.

After Jesus ascended, Peter took the initiative in the appointment of a successor to Judas among the Twelve, and was the chief preacher when the Holy Spirit came, on the Day of Pentecost. Peter and John took the lead in the early days of the church, disciplining Ananias and Sapphira after they deceived the believers, healing and preaching, and taking a special interest in the mission to Samaria.

PETER'S MISSION

Later, Peter had a vision which launched the mission to take the gospel to the Gentiles. Although he was wary of this new venture, and later wavered under the criticism of strict Jewish Christians at Antioch, Peter welcomed Paul's work among the Gentiles, and gave it his full support at the Council of Jerusalem, which welcomed Gentile converts without imposing on them all the rigours of the Jewish law. Peter was imprisoned by King Herod Agrippa I (r. AD 41–44),

but miraculously escaped the night before he was due to be executed.

Peter's later career is obscure. He may have worked in Asia Minor, perhaps visited Corinth, but ultimately settled in Rome, where he described himself as a 'fellow elder', which may mean that he was one of the church leaders, but not the sole leader. Two New Testament letters bear his name, and he was probably the main source for Mark's Gospel. Peter is believed to have been martyred at Rome during Nero's persecution of Christians, around AD 64.

Although he did not found the church at Rome, Peter's martyrdom in Rome gave it great prestige. Paul's association with the church added to this, and the Church of Rome later claimed to be the chief church in the West of the Empire, and the only one with assured apostolic roots. A considerable cult began to surround Peter and Paul from about AD 200. By the time of the Emperor Constantine, the site of Peter's martyrdom was held to be that now occupied by the Vatican basilica of St Peter's. In the time of Pope Leo I (c. 391/400–461), Peter was given greater prominence. The popes of Rome now claimed direct spiritual descent from Peter, the leader of the Twelve.

Several apocryphal works are attributed to Peter. A Gospel of Peter was banned from use at Rhossos (near Antioch) in AD 190 because of its heretical tendencies. The Apocalypse of Peter, which includes a graphic description of hell, and the Acts of Peter, which tells the famous '*Quo vadis?*' story of Peter returning to Rome to be crucified, also date from the later part of the second century.

MICHAEL A. SMITH

Some writers have suggested that a better name for the 'Acts of the Apostles' would be 'Acts of the Holy Spirit'. The book tells of the coming of the promised Holy Spirit, and how the earliest Christians witnessed to their Lord in various parts of the Roman Empire.

The account in Acts gives just part of the picture. It tells of only a few important churches and individuals – particularly Peter (the key figure in chapters 1–12) and Paul (who comes to the fore in chapters 13–28). But Acts gives a clear insight into the patterns of growth of early Christianity and – together with the New Testament letters – provides most of what is known about the spread of the gospel in the first century.

Above all, Acts stresses that the Holy Spirit's power enabled the disciples to witness effectively in their world. A tiny band of discouraged and disillusioned men and women was suddenly transformed into a bold company of enthusiastic evangelists. Their work began in Jerusalem, but quickly spread to other centres. Thirty years later, the new faith had reached most parts of the eastern section of the Roman Empire, and probably even beyond, as well as westwards to Rome itself.

Statue of Peter, holding the traditional keys of heaven and hell, outside the Cathedral of Syracuse, Sicily, Italy.
TIM DOWLEY ASSOCIATES

THE JERUSALEM CHRISTIANS

In spite of Jesus' commission to preach the good news in all the world, most of his followers in Jerusalem at first restricted themselves to evangelizing fellow Jews. This was not quite so limited as might appear, since thousands of Jews regularly flocked to Jerusalem for their most important religious festivals, and many actually settled permanently in Jerusalem – though doubtless maintaining links with their home countries. Paul's travelling companion, Barnabas, provides one example (see Acts 11). It was probably largely through the witness of these unknown Jewish converts from the earliest days that the Christian faith spread throughout the Empire and beyond in the first few decades, though Acts reveals little about this.

But among the Jerusalem Christians there were a few who were more forward-looking. They grasped the full meaning of Jesus' final command to his disciples and tried to reach beyond the orthodox Jews. One disciple, named Stephen, saw more clearly than others that the faith was for all people, and that a break with Judaism was inevitable. He belonged to a group of Jews called 'Hellenists', who spoke Greek and adopted a freer life-style than the more conservative Jews. Stephen came into conflict with some of the Jewish leaders as a result of his bold preaching. This led to his quick trial and summary execution, and a general outburst of persecution against the Jerusalem Christians, and particularly the Hellenists (Acts 6, 7).

PERSECUTION AND EXPANSION

Many Christians were forced to flee from Jerusalem because of this persecution, but they spread the good news about Jesus wherever they went – throughout the province of Judea and into Samaria. Philip, another Hellenist, led the way by evangelizing extensively among the despised Samaritans, who were half-caste and unorthodox Jews (Acts 8). This resulted in mass conversions.

Other Christians travelled to the coast of Palestine, to the island of Cyprus, and to Antioch in Syria, the third city of the Empire, preaching the message of Jesus with great success. It was in the metropolis of Antioch that the revolutionary step of evangelizing non-Jews was first taken by some of these nameless refugees from Jerusalem. This move was only reluctantly accepted by the Christians back in Jerusalem. It was in Antioch, too, that the followers of Jesus were first called 'Christians' (Acts 11:19–30).

During these early years, Peter evangelized among his fellow-Jews, but only within his own country. On one occasion he was rather reluctantly forced to preach the good news directly to Gentiles (Acts 10); but it took him at least ten years to decide that the gospel was for all people. It was left to a one-time opponent of Christianity to become the champion of Gentile evangelism and to pave the way for the integration of Jews and Gentiles into a common community.

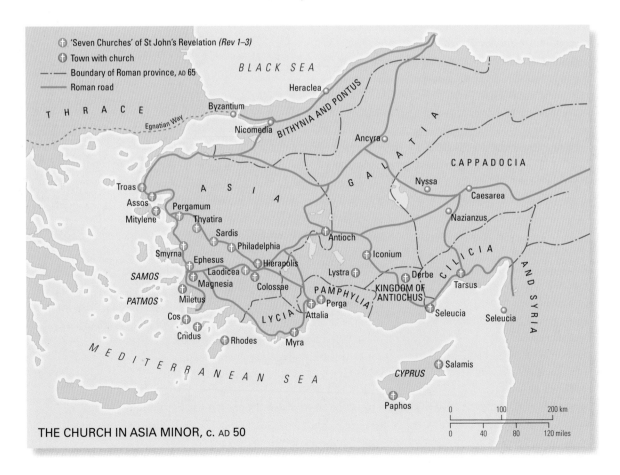

THE CHURCH IN ASIA MINOR, c. AD 50

PAUL: THE MODEL MISSIONARY

Saul of Tarsus is better known to us as Paul. Saul was his Jewish name; Paul his Roman name — or *cognomen*. He is mentioned in Acts as leading the persecution of Christians which followed the death of Stephen (Acts 7:54–8:3). For a time he violently opposed the Christian movement; but suddenly the chief persecutor became a leading witness to the risen Christ, as a result of his personal encounter with Jesus on the road to Damascus. After a period in Arabia (Nabatea), Paul returned home to Tarsus (near the south-east coast of modern Turkey), where he may have spent the next ten years or so, spreading the gospel (Acts 9:1–30).

When the Jerusalem believers sent a man called Barnabas to visit the Christians in Antioch, he fetched Paul from Tarsus to assist him. This marked the beginning of the well-documented part of Paul's life, which was to be so important for the expansion of Christianity. Paul quickly emerged as leader of the dynamic group of Christians in Antioch who now became the leaders in a concerted campaign to evangelize the Gentiles. Jerusalem was to remain important in the worldwide Christian community until the Roman army destroyed the city in AD 70 — and Paul reported back to the believers there after each of his missionary journeys abroad. But it was the church at Antioch which actually set the pattern for the future.

Paul was ideally equipped to be the greatest of all missionaries. He belonged to three worlds: Jewish, Greek, and Roman. His parents were strictly orthodox Jews who used the Hebrew language and observed Jewish customs at home. They were sufficiently concerned about a correct religious upbringing to send Paul to Jerusalem at an early age – possibly to live with an older, married sister (Acts 23:16-22). In Jerusalem Paul learned the traditions of his people and was ultimately taught by Gamaliel the Elder, one of the most famous rabbis of the day (Acts 22:2–5).

But Paul also inherited Greek culture, which had permeated the eastern Mediterranean following the conquests of Alexander the Great (335–323 BC). Paul later showed his mastery of Greek in his pastoral letters, which can be counted among the classics of Greek

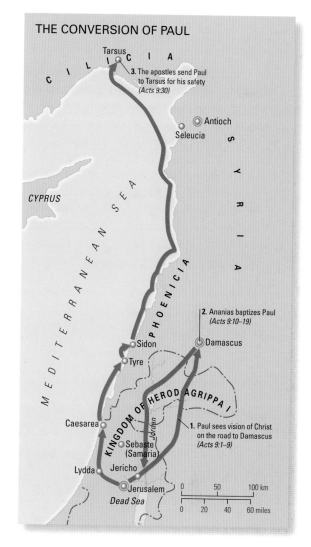

THE CONVERSION OF PAUL

Tarsus
CILICIA
3. The apostles send Paul to Tarsus for his safety (Acts 9:30)
Antioch
Seleucia
SYRIA
CYPRUS
MEDITERRANEAN SEA
PHOENICIA
2. Ananias baptizes Paul (Acts 9:10–19)
Sidon
Tyre
Damascus
KINGDOM OF HEROD AGRIPPA I
Caesarea
1. Paul sees vision of Christ on the road to Damascus (Acts 9:1–9)
Sebaste (Samaria)
Jordan
Lydda
Jericho
Jerusalem
Dead Sea

0   50   100 km
0 20 40 60 miles

Paul

A man small in size, with meeting eyebrows and a rather large nose, bald-headed, bow-legged, strongly built, full of grace; for at times he looked like a man, and at times he had the face of an angel.

SECOND-CENTURY DESCRIPTION OF PAUL

PAUL

Paul was born into a Jewish family in Tarsus, where his parents were Roman citizens. He was a strict Pharisee, and even as a young man was outstanding in his orthodox beliefs and in his hatred of followers of Christ. He was present at the stoning of Stephen, and was commissioned by the High Priest to arrest Christians in Damascus.

Paul was converted through a vision of the risen Christ on his way to Damascus. Temporarily blinded, he was befriended by a Christian called Ananias, and when cured began to preach Christ in Damascus. However, attempts were made against his life, and he escaped by being lowered down the city wall in a basket.

After a spell in Arabia, Paul may have returned to Damascus, but later went to Jerusalem, where he was befriended by Barnabas and introduced to Peter. Further Jewish threats against his life forced him to flee again, and he returned to Tarsus. There followed a period of roughly ten years about which little is known; but Paul must have been active in Christian work, for when the Gentile mission began to flourish at Antioch, Barnabas summoned him from Tarsus to join in the work.

PAUL'S MISSION

Paul visited Jerusalem again, taking famine-relief funds, and discussed the Gentile mission with Peter. Then Paul began the evangelistic work which made him the outstanding Christian missionary of the first century. He journeyed with Barnabas and John Mark to Cyprus and central Asia Minor (modern Turkey), founding a number of churches. On his return, he had a violent disagreement with Peter at Antioch about how far Gentiles had to accept Jewish customs when they became Christians. This question was settled soon after at the Council of Jerusalem (Acts 15).

Paul now set out again, this time with Silas (Silvanus), travelling through Asia Minor and crossing into Macedonia. Further successful missionary work followed, especially in Macedonia, Corinth, and Ephesus. After another visit to Jerusalem, Paul left with the youthful Timothy for further evangelism, finally returning to Jerusalem with money collected for the poor Christians there. On his arrival, Paul was seized by a Jewish mob and would have been lynched, but for the prompt intervention of the Roman garrison. He was kept in protective custody at Caesarea Maritima for two years by the Roman governor Felix, whose successor, Festus, suggested that Paul be tried at Jerusalem. But Paul refused to face such a biased court and appealed to the Roman Emperor for justice.

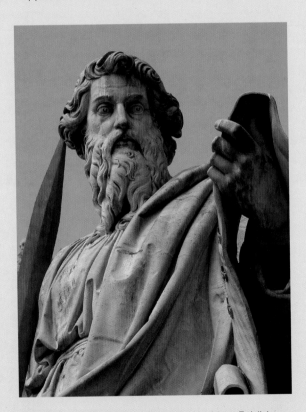

Nineteenth-century statue of the apostle Paul by Adamo Tadolini, outside St Peter's Basilica, Rome. The great missionary is shown brandishing a sword, possibly the 'sword of the spirit' (Ephesians 6:21).

Paul was taken to Rome, surviving a shipwreck at Malta on the way. After two years in Rome (at which point the account in Acts ends), Paul was probably released and spent further time in missionary work, before being martyred on a second visit to Rome during Nero's persecution of AD 64.

PAUL'S LETTERS

Paul's surviving letters are found in the New Testament. Galatians was probably written before the Council of Jerusalem; 1 and 2 Thessalonians date from Paul's first journey into Greece; and Romans and 1 and 2 Corinthians come from his last spell in Greece, before his arrest in Jerusalem. Philippians, Colossians, Ephesians, and Philemon were probably written from Rome during Paul's first imprisonment (though some scholars date them from an earlier imprisonment in Ephesus). 1 and 2 Timothy and Titus were probably written after Paul's first stay in Rome.

Paul's letters were highly valued during his lifetime, and were probably collected together soon after his death. In *1 Clement* (written about AD 95) they are already accepted on an equal basis with other Scripture. The letters were certainly in their present, collected form by the time of Marcion (about AD 140).

Paul's theology was not well understood in the period immediately after his death. This was partly because the heretic Marcion rejected the Old Testament and much that was Jewish in the New Testament, and made great use of Paul's writings to support his ideas. As long as Marcion's heresy was a threat, mainstream Christian teachers did not stress many of Paul's distinctive doctrines, such as law and grace. Augustine was the first to give full weight to Paul's theology.

MICHAEL A. SMITH

literature. In addition, Paul was a Roman citizen, which gave him special freedom of movement, protection in his travels, and access to the higher strata of society. Ultimately it meant that he probably died by the sword, a Roman prerogative, rather than on a cross.

PAUL'S ACHIEVEMENT

Paul's missionary achievements were immense. The years AD 35–45 remain obscure, but during the next ten or twelve years his activity was astounding. Between AD 47/48 (when he set sail with Barnabas on his first missionary journey) and AD 57 (when he returned to Jerusalem for the last time) he established flourishing churches in major cities in the Roman provinces of Galatia, Asia, Macedonia, and Achaia (Acts 13–23). When he wrote to the church in Rome, towards the end of this period, he spoke of his work in the eastern provinces as being essentially finished, and indicated that he was now thinking about visiting Spain (Romans 15:23-24).

How was it that Paul played such a decisive role in the early Christian mission? First, it was he who championed the mission to the Gentiles and won its acceptance by the rest of the church. Second, it was Paul who developed the theological defence of the Gentile mission that is clearly set out in Romans 1–11. He worked very hard to keep Jewish and Gentile

The reconstructed Stoa of Attalos, Athens, built by King Attalos II of Pergamon between 159 and 138 BC. The Stoic school of philosophers derive their name from the word 'stoa', where they met. The apostle Paul may have debated in the nearby Stoa Basilicos.
TIM DOWLEY ASSOCIATES

Christians united. With this purpose in view, he kept in constant touch with the mother church in Jerusalem, collected a considerable sum of money among Gentile converts for the needs of the Christians in Judea, and regularly underlined the importance of Christian unity in his letters.

Finally Paul's principle of being 'all things to all people' helped him move with relative ease between the synagogues, his base of operations, and Greco-Roman society, where ultimately the gospel received its greatest response. Paul's personal example as a self-supporting travelling missionary, and his concentration on important cities rather than rural areas, provided a pattern for others to follow.

THE CHURCH EXTENDS

Paul was not the only pioneer missionary among the early generation of Christians. In spite of the earlier hesitancy of Peter and the other apostles, they too probably travelled far and wide in the cause of Christ. Almost certainly Peter preached the gospel in Rome and the apostle John evangelized long and successfully in the province of Asia.

According to more disputed traditions, Mark helped found the church in the city of Alexandria, and Thaddeus (possibly also known as Lebbaeus or Jude, Acts 1:13) the church in Edessa (about 180 miles north-west of Syrian Antioch). Thomas is traditionally believed to have taken Christianity to India. Hundreds of unknown believers simply talked

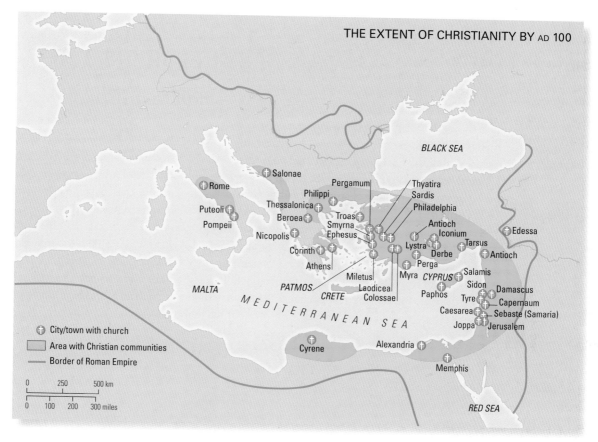

BLACK SEA

Salonae
Rome
Pergamum
Philippi
Thyatira
Sardis
Puteoli
Thessalonica
Philadelphia
Pompeii
Beroea
Troas
Antioch
Edessa
Nicopolis
Smyrna
Iconium
Tarsus
Ephesus
Lystra
Corinth
Derbe
Antioch
Athens
Perga
Miletus
Myra
CYPRUS
Salamis
Sidon
Damascus
MALTA
PATMOS
Laodicea
Paphos
Tyre
Capernaum
CRETE
Colossae
Caesarea
Sebaste (Samaria)
Joppa
Jerusalem

MEDITERRANEAN SEA

Cyrene
Alexandria

Memphis

RED SEA

City/town with church
Area with Christian communities
Border of Roman Empire

0   250   500 km
0 100 200 300 miles

about their new-found faith as they travelled to and fro throughout the Empire and beyond in the course of business or other responsibilities.

By the middle of the second century, little more than a hundred years after the death and resurrection of Jesus, flourishing churches existed in nearly all the provinces between Syria and Rome. Though their origins are shrouded in obscurity, there were probably also churches in the great cities of Alexandria and Carthage, as well as beyond the eastern fringes of the Empire and in Gaul (modern France).

A century later, a significant Christian minority existed in almost every province of the Empire and also in several countries to the east. After another fifty years, around AD 300, Christians formed a majority in parts of the provinces of Africa and Asia Minor. In addition, Osrhoene, with its capital of Edessa, adopted Christianity nationally, as did Armenia later. Finally, the Emperor himself began to support Christianity in AD 312.

WHY CHRISTIANITY EXPANDED

Several factors encouraged the rapid spread of Christianity in this short period. One was the existence of a unifying language and culture – at least in the cities – from Italy to India. In the East, Alexander the Great and his successors established Greek as the common language – often referred to as *koine*, the Greek word for 'common'. Paul and the other early Christians were able to use this language to spread their message.

Jews were scattered throughout the Empire and beyond, and provided Christian missionaries with an entry into the pagan world. Since the first Christians were Jews, they used the synagogues – both inside and outside Judea – as centres for evangelism. Although most of their fellow-Jews remained unconverted, many God-fearing Gentiles, who were attracted to Judaism but had not gone through the ritual of total integration into the Jewish community, became Christian converts. In fact, in spite of the growing divergence between the church and the synagogue, the Christian communities worshipped and operated essentially as Jewish synagogues for more than a generation.

With a few notable exceptions, three hundred years of peace and general prosperity prevailed throughout the Roman Empire from the time of Augustus. This period has become known as the *pax Romana* (Roman peace), and allowed great freedom of travel throughout the Mediterranean world. For example, Paul could travel along superbly engineered roads, and until the final years of his life also expect the protection of the Roman government.

The pagan world was experiencing a certain insecurity. Local political independence had disappeared, old loyalties and traditions were losing their hold, and sensitive people felt that their age was morally and religiously bankrupt. Many sought security in the intimate fellowship provided by the newly-popular Eastern religious cults, while others found escape in the excitement of the ever more brutal public games and entertainments. Such an atmosphere of dissatisfaction and unease prepared people to listen to the Christian gospel.

Early Christianity in no way depended solely upon professional leaders for its practice and growth. Each Christian was both 'priest' and 'missionary'. The churches have been described as the most inclusive and the strongest of all the various associations in the Roman world. The distinctions between Jew and Gentile, slave and freeman, male and female were in theory, and usually also in practice, abolished in the Christian community. All were active in sharing the message of Christ with others.

W. WARD GASQUE

BEGINNINGS

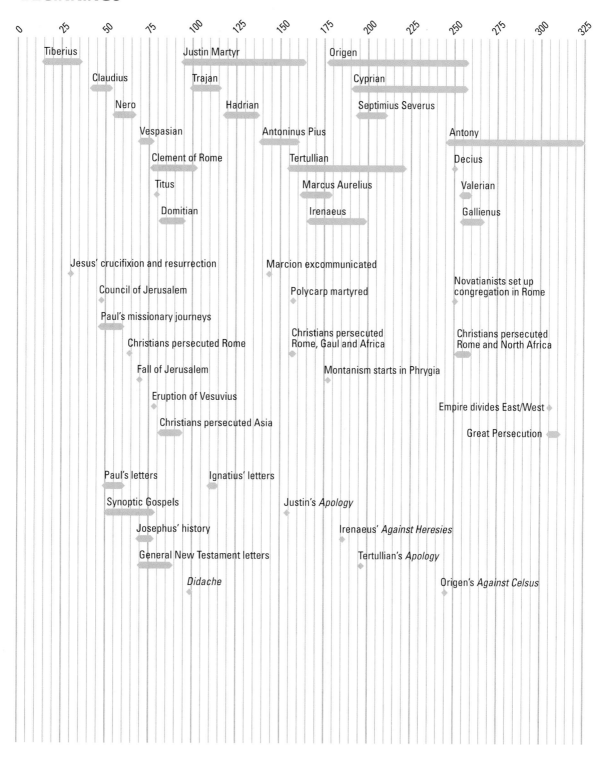

| 0 | 25 | 50 | 75 | 100 | 125 | 150 | 175 | 200 | 225 | 250 | 275 | 300 | 325 |

Tiberius

Justin Martyr

Origen

Claudius

Trajan

Cyprian

Nero

Hadrian

Septimius Severus

Vespasian

Antoninus Pius

Antony

Clement of Rome

Tertullian

Decius

Titus

Marcus Aurelius

Valerian

Domitian

Irenaeus

Gallienus

Jesus' crucifixion and resurrection

Marcion excommunicated

Novatianists set up congregation in Rome

Council of Jerusalem

Polycarp martyred

Paul's missionary journeys

Christians persecuted Rome, Gaul and Africa

Christians persecuted Rome and North Africa

Christians persecuted Rome

Fall of Jerusalem

Montanism starts in Phrygia

Eruption of Vesuvius

Empire divides East/West

Christians persecuted Asia

Great Persecution

Paul's letters

Ignatius' letters

Synoptic Gospels

Justin's *Apology*

Josephus' history

Irenaeus' *Against Heresies*

General New Testament letters

Tertullian's *Apology*

Didache

Origen's *Against Celsus*

CHAPTER 3

ESTABLISHING CHRISTIANITY
Challenges to the New Faith

The early followers of Jesus were marked out by their clear convictions about doctrine and ethics. They recognized only one message of salvation, only one God, and only one Saviour. Once a person became a follower of 'the Way', a new life-style was demanded of him or her. This exclusiveness of early Christian belief and behaviour attracted many people. But it was also a cause of offence; enemies accused Christians of aloofness and of hating the present world.

Strong forces were acting against the spread of Christianity. Paganism still maintained a strong grip on people, the world was as morally corrupt as it has ever been, and the young church soon attracted the unyielding opposition of the ruling authorities. Jesus, Paul, and Peter had all been executed by the state, and other leaders were similarly dealt with.

CAESAR VERSUS CHRIST

As long as the church was regarded as simply a Jewish sect, it was tolerated by the Roman authorities. For its first thirty years Christianity – like Judaism – enjoyed protection by Roman law. Partly for this reason, Paul emphasized the benefits of good government. But once Judaism and Christianity began to diverge, Christians lost the special privileges given to Jews.

Jews were specially exempted from taking part in the Roman cult of emperor-worship. Christians too sought this exemption, since they recognized only one God and served one Lord, Jesus Christ. But when the church became largely composed of Gentiles, it was no longer possible to shelter under the wing of Judaism. Christians refused to offer a pinch of incense on an altar to the divine Emperor – an act which most intelligent people considered to be merely symbolic – and this was interpreted as unpatriotic. As a result, the official Roman attitude towards Christianity became less and less favourable.

PERSECUTION

Adherents of the new religion were subjected to a series of persecutions. These began with brief, and apparently localized, persecution in Rome under Nero in July 64. According to Tacitus, a Roman historian writing 50 years later, Nero tried to shift the blame on to the Christians after a rumour arose that he had started a fire which destroyed much of the city of Rome. The scale and length of these persecutions seem to have become exaggerated. But Revelation, the final book of the Bible, gives evidence of the persecution of Christians in the province of Asia under the Emperor Domitian (AD 81–96).

Letters have survived between the Emperor Trajan (AD 98–117) and Pliny the Younger, Governor of Bithynia (AD 111–113), which make it clear that by their time profession of Christianity could be a capital offence. The policy which Pliny followed, and which was commended by the Emperor, did not involve seeking out Christians for special punishment. But if a person was discovered to be a Christian, he or she was given an opportunity to renounce the faith. Refusal to do so meant execution. This was probably normal policy at this period.

Seven letters of Ignatius, bishop of Antioch, written when on his way to Rome to be executed for being a Christian, survive from the beginning of the second century. In his letters he mentions others who 'preceded me from Syria to Rome for the glory of God'. One of his letters is addressed to Polycarp, bishop of Smyrna (Izmir in modern Turkey), who in turn became a martyr at the age of around eighty-six, about AD 156–160. Around the middle of the second century, Bishop Telesphorus of Rome was executed. During the reign of the Stoic Emperor Marcus Aurelius (161–180), who thoroughly disliked Christians, believers were executed in Rome itself, and in the provinces of Gaul and Africa.

The legal grounds for the persecution of Christians are often obscure. Popular rumour suggested that Christians were cannibals (based perhaps on a misunderstanding of the Lord's Supper), atheists (like the Jews, Christians had no images in their shrines), and incestuous (their 'love' for one another was well known). These accusations were easily answered by Christian writers, but little notice seems to have been taken of their arguments. Apparently, simply to bear the name 'Christian' was a crime, probably because rejection of the gods of the Romans was felt to threaten the peace and prosperity that the gods were believed to bring. Refusal to worship the Emperor could also be taken as a sign of treason.

NERO'S MASSACRE

Nero charged and tortured some people hated for their evil practices – the group popularly known as 'Christians'. The founder of this sect, Christ, had been put to death by the governor of Judea, Pontius Pilate, when Tiberius was Emperor. Their deadly superstition had been suppressed temporarily, but was beginning to spring up again – now not just in Judea but even in Rome itself, where all kinds of sordid and shameful activities are attracted and catch on.

First those who confessed to being Christians were arrested. Then, based on information obtained from them, hundreds were convicted, more for their anti-social beliefs than for fire-raising. In their deaths they were made a mockery. They were covered in the skins of wild animals, torn to death by dogs, crucified or set on fire – so that when darkness fell, they burned like torches in the night. Nero opened up his own gardens for this spectacle, and also gave a show in the arena, where he mixed with the crowd or stood dressed as a charioteer on a chariot. As a result people began to feel sorry for the victims, although they were guilty of being Christians and deserved death. They realized that they were being massacred, not for the public good, but to satisfy one man's mania.

TACITUS, ANNALS 15.44

Despite periods of persecution, the church continued to grow. Tertullian famously wrote: 'The blood of the martyrs is seed.' The later full-scale, systematic persecutions under the Emperors Decius (249–251) and Diocletian (284–305), the fiercest of all the early opponents of the Christian faith, helped to purge the church of some of its lukewarm members.

Very little is known about the details of church expansion during the second and third centuries. We have just glimpses of a lively church, steadily expanding in size and in its influence on society. The faith of a persecuted minority was quietly and gradually becoming a major force in the Empire.

THE RELIGIONS OF THE ROMANS

The Romans originally practised an agricultural religion, in which they worshipped a mysterious, impersonal force that pervaded nature. They placed strong emphasis upon correct ritual. For them religion was a contract, summarized in the Latin saying, 'I give that you may give.'

The Romans believed that they had to strive to preserve 'the peace of the gods' by such means as sacrifices, and by a special banquet where images of the gods were featured. Every Roman made offerings at each meal to the spirits of the farm, and the spirits of the larder.

THE ROMAN GODS

During the period of the Roman Republic (509–27 BC) the Romans adopted Greek myths and identified the Greek gods with their own native gods.

- Jupiter (the Greek god Zeus) was 'the best and the greatest', who made known his will by lightning and thunder. The Temple of Jupiter, built on the Capitoline Hill in Rome, was the most important of all, to which a victorious general or emperor made his way in the 'triumph', a ceremonial procession in which prisoners and plunder were paraded.
- Juno (Greek, Hera) was responsible for women and marriage. Her month of June – or more precisely the second half – was considered particularly favourable for marriages.
- Mars (Greek, Ares), the god of war, was second in importance only to Jupiter.
- Neptune (Greek, Poseidon) was the god not only of the sea, but also of rivers. His priests were known as 'bridge-builders' (in Latin, *pontifex*). The *pontifex maximus* (high priest) was an elected official, who supervised the religious calendar and sacrifices. This title has survived, and is today applied to the pope.
- Mercury (Greek, Hermes) was the god of both merchants and thieves – a suggestive combination.
- Venus (Greek, Aphrodite) was the goddess of love and beauty. In Corinth 1,000 sacred prostitutes plied their trade at her temple as part of her cult.

Many of the months of our year are named after terms in Roman religion. For example, January is named after the two-faced god Janus, whose gate was kept open during times of war and shut in times of peace. It was usually open.

READING THE SIGNS

The prediction of future events and the interpretation of past occurrences played a major role in Roman religion, politics, and warfare. The Romans regarded unusual occurrences as signs that the 'peace of the gods' had been broken. Signs or 'prodigies' included such freaks as a foal with five feet, hot stones falling from heaven, and shields sweating blood.

The Romans were especially concerned to discover the will of the gods from auguries, by observing the 'signs' given by birds. From the temple precinct they would observe the flight of birds, their numbers, and their calls. During military campaigns, the Romans also carefully observed the feeding of chickens. When some of his sacred chickens did not eat, one impatient naval commander threw the fowls into the sea with the comment, 'Let them drink since they will not eat!' But this impious act was said to have cost him the battle.

No military campaign or official act was supposed to be conducted without discovering the will of the gods by some act of divination. To disregard the signs was an act of ill omen, and to ignore the stars promised 'disaster'. In 44 BC Julius Caesar was forewarned of his assassination by dreams and other omens, which he ignored.

EDWIN YAMAUCHI

CHALLENGES FROM WITHIN

When we read Paul's first letter to the church at Corinth (I Corinthians), it becomes clear that many problems faced the church within its own membership. There was a tendency to divide into parties centred on the personalities of human leaders, and possibly also differences in emphasis over doctrines. A prominent member of the church was living in immorality, individual Christians were taking each other to the law-courts over minor disputes, there were misunderstandings about the meaning of Christian liberty, disorders during the weekly worship service, and even false teaching about the resurrection.

Paul's other letters also reveal controversies and power-struggles in the midst of encouragement and growth. Some people opposed the mission to the Gentiles, some questioned Paul's role in the church, and others tried to mix Christian and non-Christian religious beliefs. The first letter of John (I John) speaks of those who once belonged to the Christian community but had now departed, denying the true humanity of Jesus Christ.

RIVAL MOVEMENTS

Early in the second century, Gnostic ideas began to be strongly promoted within the churches. Church leaders recognized that such views would lead to the destruction of the Christian faith and had to be vigorously opposed.

Another challenge came from Marcion, a wealthy ship-owner, who came to Rome shortly before AD 140 and began to teach his own brand of anti-Jewish Christianity. Marcion organized his followers into a movement rivalling mainstream Christianity, establishing its own communities throughout the Empire, and presenting a real threat to the young faith.

A few decades later a movement arose in Phrygia, central Asia Minor, strongly emphasizing the imminent return of Christ and the end of the age. It became known as Montanism, and combined prophetic enthusiasm with strict asceticism, leading to a split in the church which lasted for more than a century. Later, theological controversies concerning the nature of Christ occupied much attention, disrupting Christian unity and weakening the church's witness.

The church brought together ideas and people from many backgrounds. It had to cope with people who had become Christians in disreputable seaports such as Corinth, notorious for its immorality. It had to resolve the pressures to revert to pagan practices or to Judaism, sort out its attitudes towards contemporary customs and cultures, and thrash out beliefs and opinions about issues on which there were no precedents to guide its thinking.

LEADING THINKERS

By the end of the second century, the new faith was on its way to becoming the most forceful and compelling movement within the Roman Empire. Many of the keenest minds of the day were emerging as followers of 'the Way'.

A series of writers defended the Christian faith against both popular accusations and more sophisticated attacks. Although most of the writings of these 'apologists' were dedicated to the emperors, their real audience was the educated public of the day. If such writers could answer the accusations of the enemies of Christianity and point out the inherent weakness of paganism, they hoped this would help to change public opinion concerning the good news and lead to conversions. Men such as Aristides the

MARCION

Marcion was born in Sinope, Pontus, on the Black Sea, the son of the bishop. He arrived in Rome about AD 140 and immediately fell under the spell of the Gnostic teacher Cerdo, who believed that the God of the Old Testament was different from the God and Father of the Lord Jesus Christ. The God of the Old Testament was unknowable; the latter had been revealed. The former was sheer justice; whereas the God of the New Testament is loving and gracious.

Marcion became the chief spokesman of this message and introduced his own distinctive ideas. Was Marcion a Gnostic? He was certainly gnostic in his belief that the physical body was inherently evil, and so arguing for asceticism and a docetic understanding of Christ. But he never supported the fanciful and mythological views of redemption held by other Gnostics. His garbled Christian views were firmly repudiated by the church in Rome, and Marcion was excommunicated in AD 144.

Justin Martyr asserted that Marcion was aided by the devil to blaspheme and to deny that God was the creator of the universe. Tertullian wrote *Against Marcion* about AD 207, regarding Marcion as a formidable foe of true Christian doctrine.

Marcion developed Cerdo's division between the God of the Old Testament and the New. He held that the Old Testament God was basically vengeful and the author of evil. God was solely concerned for the Jewish people, for whom he was prepared to destroy all others. In contrast, the New Testament God is a God of grace and love for all, who disclosed himself in Jesus Christ, his Son.

Marcion stated that Jesus Christ was not born of a woman; he suddenly appeared in the synagogue at Capernaum in AD 29 as a grown man. For Jesus was not like any other man, except in his appearance: he was a new being on the earth. Marcion's view of Christ was similar to that of the Docetists: although he stated that Christ's life and crucifixion were necessary for salvation, he also believed that Christ's human experiences and sufferings were merely apparent, not real. Since creation was not an act of the good God of the New Testament, the Christian must reject the world. The body must be denied and discarded, since the soul and spirit alone are redeemed. As a result, Marcion rejected the idea of the resurrection of the body.

MARCION'S SCRIPTURES

Believing that the God of the Old Testament favoured the Jews exclusively, Marcion rejected the entire Old Testament, and also those New Testament writings which he considered favoured Jewish readers – for example Matthew, Mark, Acts, and Hebrews. He removed from the rest of the New Testament what appeared to him to compromise his own views, including the Pastoral letters (1 and 2 Timothy and Titus). So he was left with only a mutilated version of Luke's Gospel (omitting the nativity stories) and ten letters of Paul, who he believed was the only apostle who did not corrupt the gospel of Jesus.

The Marcionites set up their own churches, modelled on orthodox congregations. They did not use wine at communion, because of the ascetic emphasis of their teaching. Some of the Marcionite ideas spilled over into the various Gnostic sects, and Marcionites were themselves affected by Gnostic views. Marcionite concepts spread throughout Italy and as far afield as Arabia, Armenia, and Egypt. In the East they exercised a considerable influence for many decades. A number of Marcionite villages are known to have existed near Damascus as late as the fourth century. In the West their influence declined, mainly as a result of their becoming linked with the Manichaeans.

H. DERMOT MCDONALD

Athenian, Justin Martyr, his disciple Tatian, Athenagoras (c. 133–190), Theophilus of Antioch (d. c. 185), the unknown author of the *Letter to Diognetus*, and Melito, bishop of Sardis, all directed their intellectual and spiritual gifts to this cause.

Towards the end of the second century Irenaeus, bishop of Lyons, Gaul, wrote five monumental books against the Gnostic heresies of his area, together with a book entitled *Proof* (or *Demonstration*) *of the Apostolic Preaching*. Several of his other books have been lost. His theology was grounded in the Bible and the church's doctrines and helped provide a steadying, positive influence in the church. Irenaeus wrote of the cosmic implications of the work of Christ and God's plan in history, and paved the way for the later Christian interpretations of history by writers such as Augustine.

TERTULLIAN

Tertullian, the 'father of Latin theology', was born in Carthage, in the province of Africa, around AD 150. He was converted to Christianity as a man of about forty, and soon began writing books to promote the Christian faith. The large number he wrote in Greek are now lost, but thirty-one in Latin survive.

Tertullian's *Apology* underlined the legal and moral absurdity of the persecution directed against Christians, while other books offered encouragement to those facing martyrdom. He attacked the heretics, explained the Lord's Prayer and the meaning of baptism, and helped develop the orthodox understanding of the Trinity,

TERTULLIAN

Tertullian (c. 160–c. 225) was the first major Christian author to write in Latin, and therefore the first to use many of the technical words common in later Christian theological debates. He lived most of, if not all, his life in Carthage, capital of the Roman province of Africa, receiving an education typical of the late second century.

Tertullian's surviving works date from between AD 196 and 212, and reflect three main concerns: Christianity's attitude to the Roman state and society; the defence of orthodox beliefs against heresy; and the moral behaviour of Christians. His own strict moral views led him to join the Montanists around AD 207.

Tertullian wrote in a witty and vigorous style, marked by startling turns of phrase. It was he who claimed that 'the blood of the martyrs is seed'. But his well-known questions, 'What has Athens to do with Jerusalem?' expressed a rejection of philosophy that was not true of his own work, where he demonstrated how pagan intellectual achievements could be made to serve Christianity.

Tertullian's masterpiece was his Apology, which argued effectively that Christianity should be tolerated. His longest work, the five books *Against Marcion*, defended the use of the Old Testament by the Christian church, and the oneness of God, both Creator and Saviour. In *Against Praxeas*, Tertullian developed the doctrine of the Trinity. Tertullian had two things against Praxeas: his opposition to the Montanist 'New Prophecy', and his view of God. Tertullian said that Praxeas 'did two works for the devil in Rome: he put to flight the Paraclete and crucified the Father'.

Tertullian also covered a number of other subjects. In *The Exclusion of Heretics* Tertullian used an argument from Roman law to claim the Scriptures as the exclusive property of the church, against Gnostic heretics. Tertullian's *On the Soul* is the first Christian writing on psychology. On Baptism is the earliest surviving work about baptism; in it Tertullian criticized the baptism of children. In other books, Tertullian argued for rigour in church discipline, remarriage, and fasting; and opposed flight to avoid persecution.

EVERETT FERGUSON

> If the River Tiber reaches the walls, if the River Nile does not rise to the fields, if the sky does not move or the earth does, if there is famine, if there is plague, the cry is at once: 'The Christians to the lion!' What, all of them to one lion?
>
> *TERTULLIAN, APOLOGY*

being the first to use the Latin word *trinitas* (trinity). Tertullian later joined the Montanist movement. His intellectual brilliance and literary versatility made him one of the most powerful writers of the time, almost as influential as Augustine in the development of theology in the West.

While Tertullian was at work in Carthage, Alexandria, to the east, was becoming another key intellectual centre for the Christian faith. Alexandria had been an important cultural capital since its foundation by Alexander the Great in the fourth century BC, and possessed one of the great libraries of the ancient world. It was probably in Alexandria that the Old Testament was first translated from Hebrew into Greek. The famous Jewish philosopher, Philo, lived in Alexandria at about the time of Jesus: he attempted to re-interpret Judaism in terms of Greek philosophy.

THE SCHOOL OF ALEXANDRIA

By about AD 185 a converted Stoic philosopher named Pantaenus was teaching Christians in Alexandria. He probably also travelled to India, and was a very able thinker. Pantaenus was succeeded as leader of the school for those preparing for Christian baptism ('catechumens') first by Clement, then by Origen. In spite of periods of intense persecution, the school at Alexandria gained great importance, strengthening the faith of Christians and attracting new converts to the faith. The crucial achievement of Clement and Origen was to communicate the gospel in terms which could be understood by people familiar with the highest forms of Greek culture. They established once for all the intellectual respectability of the new faith.

In addition to being a creative theologian, Origen also made an immense contribution to biblical scholarship. He was one of the few Christian scholars before the Reformation to learn Hebrew, so that he could read the Old Testament in its original language. He was later forced to leave Alexandria for Caesarea Maritima, where he continued writing and teaching.

During the third century the church extended its frontiers, both geographically and socially, at an unparalleled rate. It was beginning to assume the proportions of an empire within the Empire. The constant travel between different churches, the synods of bishops, the letters carried by messengers back and forth across the Empire, and the loyalty which Christians showed to their leaders and to one another impressed even the emperors. Yet such things could also easily be interpreted as a threat to the government.

VIOLENT PERSECUTION

In AD 250 the most violent persecution the church had yet faced was instigated by the Emperor Decius (249–251). Imperial edicts commanded all citizens of the Empire to sacrifice to the traditional Roman gods. Those who did so were given certificates (*libelli* in Latin) as evidence that they had obeyed the order. Those who refused to obey, and were unable (or unwilling) to obtain false *libelli* from sympathetic or corrupt officials, were

ORIGEN

Origen (c. 185–c. 254) was the greatest scholar and most prolific author of the early church. He was not only a profound thinker, but also deeply spiritual and a loyal churchman.

Origen was born into a Christian family in Alexandria, and became a teacher, first of new converts, and later of more advanced students. Origen, who led a very ascetic life, was forced to move to Caesarea, in Palestine, because of the antagonism of Bishop Demetrius of Alexandria. Origen travelled widely in response to invitations to mediate in church disputes, and to speak before prominent people. He died as the result of injuries inflicted during the persecution under the Emperor Decius.

Origen produced the *Hexapla*, the greatest piece of biblical scholarship in the early church. It put in parallel columns the Hebrew text of the Old Testament, a Greek transliteration, the Greek translations by Aquila, Symmachus, and Theodotion, and the *Septuagint*. The *Hexapla* was the basis for Origen's interpretations of the Old Testament. His church sermons and massive biblical commentaries illustrated his theory that three levels of meaning can be found in any biblical text: the literal sense, the moral application to the soul, and the allegorical or spiritual sense, referring to the mysteries of the Christian faith.

Origen's major theological work, *First Principles*, attempted to present systematically the fundamental Christian doctrines: God, Christ, the Holy Spirit, creation, the soul, free will, salvation, and the Scriptures. He tried first to set out clearly the faith expressed in the church, and then to clarify and draw out what was only implicit in the faith. *Exhortation to Martyrdom* and *Prayer* are examples of Origen's writing on the Christian life. *Against Celsus* was his sole major writing against pagan criticisms of Christianity.

Origen tried to express the Christian faith in terms of the prevailing Platonic philosophical ideas of his time. Some of his speculations, for example about the pre-existence of souls and universal salvation, were repudiated by the church, and helped bring about his later condemnation. But Greek Christian theology continued to be concerned with the problem which Origen tackled: the relationship between philosophy and the Christian tradition.

EVERETT FERGUSON

executed. Many Christians complied to save their lives. Others were able to obtain certificates without having actually sacrificed. But an unknown number of Christians were imprisoned or executed – among them the bishops of Rome, Antioch, and Jerusalem.

Fortunately for the church, this period of testing did not last very long. Within two years, Decius died in battle against Gothic invaders from the north. Although his successor, the Emperor Gallus (251–253), kept the anti-Christian measures alive, persecution was not so widespread as under Decius.

A few years later, persecution was renewed with fresh ferocity, towards the end of the reign of the Emperor Valerian (253–260). On this occasion, church leaders were singled out and ordered to worship the old gods, under the threat of exile or imprisonment. Christians were forbidden to hold church meetings, or visit Christian cemeteries, on pain of death. Finally, a particularly severe edict prescribed death for church leaders, and the confiscation of property, slavery, and even death for other Christians who would not desert the faith. Again, only a war against foreign invaders – this time the Persians – put an end to the Christians' ordeal.

DIOCLETIAN'S PERSECUTION

A few decades of relative peace and prosperity followed, only to be interrupted in 303 by the most severe persecution the church had yet faced, often known as the 'Great Persecution'. By this time Christianity had reached as far as the immediate family of the Emperor Diocletian (284–305). Many of his slaves and servants, as well as his wife and daughter, were believers, together with many others in high places – either Christian or favourably disposed to Christianity. Diocletian issued four edicts against Christianity, which were enforced with varying degrees of severity. His actions may have been intended to gain more enthusiastic support from the army, which tended to be strongly anti-Christian.

The decrees of 303 ordered the destruction of all church buildings, the confiscation of Christian books, the dismissal of Christians from the government and army, and the imprisonment of the clergy. A further edict, in 304, ordered all Christians to offer sacrifices to the pagan gods.

In Asia Minor, an entire town (probably Eumenia, Phrygia) and its inhabitants, who were predominantly Christian, was destroyed by soldiers. In Rome, church property was confiscated and many Christians were martyred. Christians in Palestine, Syria, and Egypt seem to have suffered particular violence.

LAPSED CHRISTIANS

Many Christians were willing to suffer as martyrs, rather than betray their Lord by acknowledging false gods. Some, however, renounced their faith under pressure of torture and imprisonment. Others persuaded pagan neighbours to sacrifice on their behalf, or obtained false certificates from sympathetic officials. At the opposite extreme, some Christians eagerly sought out martyrdom, even when it was not forced upon them, though this was strongly discouraged by Christian leaders.

Following each wave of persecution, the church was faced with the problem of what to do about those who repented after lapsing under the pressure of persecution. Baptism was generally held to cover only sins previously committed; serious post-baptismal lapses required special treatment. Some Christian leaders claimed that offences such as idolatry after baptism were unpardonable on earth; but others allowed one such occasion of forgiveness subsequent to baptism. The lapsed Christian who showed genuine penitence could be received back into church communion.

NOVATIAN

Callistus, bishop of Rome (217–22), was among the more moderate and appealed to Paul's letters and the parables of the lost sheep and the prodigal son (Luke 15) for proof that no sin is unforgivable if the sinner truly turns from his sins. His views enjoyed wide acceptance in the church, but were strongly opposed by Novatian (c. 200–258), a presbyter in the church of Rome during the persecution under Decius.

Cornelius, a more liberal man, was elected bishop of Rome; but a minority voted for Novatian, and demanded that those who had given up faith under oppression should not be welcomed back into fellowship. Novatian, a gifted theologian, and one of the earliest Latin authors among the Christians, is believed to have been martyred during the persecution of the Emperor Valerian.

Novatian split the church over this issue. Novatianists were theologically orthodox and spread quickly in the 250s. They set up a rival bishop at Carthage, gained the support of Marcian, Bishop of Arles, and also made headway in the East. They soon built up a network of small congregations, calling themselves 'Cathari' (pure ones), to distinguish themselves from all other churches, which they considered to be polluted as a result of their lenient attitude towards sinners. Those who joined the Novatianists had to be baptized afresh, as if they were joining the only true church. Novatianists later took their rigid stand further, refusing to have communion with people who had been married more than once, and rejecting the possibility of penance for any major sin after baptism.

Novatianists were treated as heretics until the time of Constantine, when an edict in 326 granted them toleration and the right to own church buildings and burial-places. A Novatianist bishop, Acesius, was present at the Council of Nicaea in 325. In the fourth century, Novatianists spread into Spain and Egypt.

Despite official toleration, Novatianists continued to be harassed by official churchmen. Nestorius attacked them at Constantinople in 428, but was restrained by the Emperor. In 429 Celestine, Bishop of Rome, deprived them of their buildings. The Novatianists were strong in Constantinople, but were probably reabsorbed into the mainstream churches with the passage of time. As early as the Council of Nicaea, Novatianist clergy were allowed to retain their rank if they returned to the 'catholic church'.

DONATUS

A similar division took place in North Africa, following the persecution under Diocletian. Here the arguments were clouded by personalities and questionable motives. A bishop of the church in Carthage was consecrated by a bishop who was believed to have surrendered the Scriptures to the police, and was therefore regarded as fatally tainted by stricter members of the church. A rival bishop was elected by the stricter group, and was in turn succeeded by Donatus, from whom the Donatist movement derives its name.

This controversy ultimately led to the principle that the reality of baptism and of ordination does not depend on the moral character of the person who performs it, but on Christ and the Spirit. It now became general practice to accept people back into the church following a temporary lapse from the faith, provided that they gave evidence of repentance. But the Donatists rejected this position – and even re-baptized orthodox Christians who joined their ranks.

MIRACLES AND MARTYRS

From the beginning, those Christians who gave their lives rather than betray their Lord were held in high honour by the church. The book of Acts gives considerable space to the martyrdom of Stephen (Acts 6, 7). The book of Revelation honours an otherwise unknown disciple named Antipas, acknowledged by Jesus as 'My witness, my faithful one, who was killed among you' (Revelation 2:13), and elsewhere promises a special reward for those who have sealed with their blood their witness for Christ.

During the later persecutions, the martyrdoms of Peter and Paul were given special significance. Ignatius thought of his own journey to Rome for execution as a conscious imitation of his Lord's last journey to Jerusalem and the cross. Martyrdom became regarded by many as the ultimate sign of Christian discipleship. As a boy in Alexandria, Origen had to be forcibly restrained by his mother from leaving home voluntarily to join the martyrs in their sufferings. Origen lived a strictly ascetic life; he may even have taken the instruction of Matthew 19:12 literally, and had himself castrated.

The martyrdom of Polycarp, whose execution was recorded so lovingly by a disciple, was celebrated annually by his church at Smyrna. This celebration became the pattern for the practice of venerating martyrs' remains and commemorating their death. Later the belief developed that prayers addressed to God through the martyrs were especially effective.

In the late third and early fourth centuries, the practice of the veneration of the martyrs grew rapidly. The events of the last, violent persecutions led to an exaggeration of the scale and extent of earlier persecutions. The number of martyrs and their sufferings were greatly magnified; the stories of their deaths were embroidered with all sorts of fantastic miraculous happenings and superstitions.

Some converts from paganism brought with them pre-Christian ideas, so that in the church the martyrs began to take on the role that the gods had earlier played in the old religions. Relics of the martyrs were superstitiously cherished, their graves became sites of pilgrimages and prayer, and they were believed to work miracles and guarantee special blessings to believers. Although not all church leaders approved of such things, the veneration of martyrs and other saints took an increasingly important place in popular religion.

NORTH AFRICAN CHRISTIANS

North African Christianity tended to be extremely rigorous, with martyrs seen as ideal Christians. Churchmen in North Africa tended towards a view of the church which regarded it as so pure as to forget that it consisted of a community of redeemed sinners, leading to repeated controversies and divisions.

Bishop Cyprian of Carthage (c. 248–258) provides an example of rigorous North African faith, although he advised moderation towards the back-sliders during the persecution under Decius, and in certain circles gained a reputation for compromise. Cyprian was under vows to remain single, and lived a life of poverty, though he was born into wealth. He rejected the reading of all literature other than the Bible and distinctively Christian books, despite being educated in some of the best schools of his day.

THE FIRST MONKS

In Syria and Egypt the earliest Christian monks appeared, in the late third century. Christian hermits or anchorites (from a Greek word meaning 'one who withdraws') forsook ordinary society for a life of prayer and solitude in the desert. One of the most famous of these early hermits was Antony of Egypt (c. 251–356), who gave away all his possessions at the age of twenty, in order to serve Christ free of distraction. In spite of his desire to be alone, he was constantly beset by curious visitors, and finally organized a cluster of hermit cells around him. Although physically withdrawn from the world, Antony strongly influenced Christians of his day and inspired many conversions to Christ.

CONSTANTINE BECOMES EMPEROR

At the height of the most severe of the persecutions directed against the Christians, the Emperor Diocletian voluntarily retired in 305 to live as a gentleman-farmer on his estate on the coast of Dalmatia (modern Croatia). He aimed to stabilize the government and avert civil war, by setting a precedent for orderly, peaceful succession to the office of Emperor. Earlier Diocletian had divided the Empire into two parts, the East and the West, each with its own capital and senior and junior emperors.

Diocletian succeeded in setting the administrative pattern for a divided Empire (and, later, a divided church) for many centuries to come. But he did not avert civil war. Upon the death of Constantius, the chief ruler of the Western Empire, his son Constantine took command of the army in Britain and Gaul, and demanded recognition as his successor. Galerius, the pre-eminent Emperor in the East, granted Constantine only junior status. Soon Maxentius, son of Constantius's predecessor in the West, murdered the senior Western Emperor and usurped his position.

Constantine returned to Italy and marched upon Rome. His rival, Maxentius, foolishly sallied forth to meet him, and was defeated at the crucial battle at the Milvian Bridge in 312. In this way Constantine, later called the Great, became the sole master of the West. After a further struggle with Licinius, successor to Galerius in the East, Constantine emerged as supreme victor in the entire Empire.

W. WARD GASQUE

CHAPTER 4

SPREADING THE GOOD NEWS
How and why Christianity expanded

Christians took two main approaches to spreading their faith. They used a variety of direct methods to communicate the good news, but they also explained the faith intelligently and countered the attacks of critics, an activity often known as 'apologetics'.

PUBLIC PREACHING

Public open-air preaching is often mentioned in the book of Acts. The Christian speaker would choose a place where a crowd gathered, attempt to catch their attention, and then proclaim the Christian message. This method must have become very hazardous after Nero's persecution, and it is rarely mentioned during the second and third centuries, though it was possibly practised in some places, because apocryphal stories about apostles dating from this time still mention it.

Preaching in the Jewish synagogues was a common tactic in the age of the apostles. Paul almost always started by preaching at the synagogue when he first arrived at a town. However, after the destruction of Jerusalem in AD 70, Jews took strong action against Christians in their midst, and certain anti-Christian additions were made to the synagogue prayers. Although there were Jewish Christians throughout the second century, the synagogues were now closed to Christian evangelism.

Preaching in the Christians' own places of worship offered another method of evangelism. The regular Sunday service gradually began to split into two parts. The first part was open to all, but the communion which followed was restricted to baptized believers. Although during the second century most church-attenders were people already sympathetic to Christianity, later the audience widened. During the long periods in the third century when Christians were not actively persecuted, many interested outsiders attended the first part of Sunday worship, and from them came a considerable number of candidates for baptism.

ARGUMENT AND INSTRUCTION

Philosophic argument in public can be traced at least as far back as the time of Socrates and the Sophists of the fifth century BC and Christians entered such debates very early. For a period, Paul argued daily with the philosophers in the market-place at Athens (Acts 17:16–34). This method continued, and often these public arguments were recorded. For example, Justin Martyr's famous dialogue with the rabbi Trypho at Ephesus, and the discussion recorded by Minucius Felix (*Octavius*), are both preserved in written form.

When public preaching became dangerous, semi-private instruction took over. This practice had already been utilized to supplement public preaching. At Ephesus, Paul hired the lecture-hall of Tyrannus for Christian teaching (Acts 19:9–10). In mid-second century Rome, Justin Martyr held classes for enquirers in a room over public baths; and in early third-century Alexandria, Pantaenus (d. c. 200), Clement of Alexandria, and Origen in succession headed a well-known 'school of instruction' for those wishing to become Christians. Later such teaching became formalized into a new converts' instruction-class for baptism (or 'catechetical school'), held each year during the period before Easter, which developed into Lent. Such instruction was also the method most frequently used by Christian splinter-groups for propagating their different doctrines.

PERSONAL WITNESS

Personal witness was by far the most common method of evangelism used by Christians, because it was the easiest to organize. Personal friendship formed the basis for bringing many people to Christ, but more casual encounters were used too. Justin Martyr became a Christian after talking with an old man at Ephesus, while Cyprian was converted through talking to a church elder. Later, family influence became a strong factor: Origen came from a Christian family and owed much to his parents for his Christian faith.

Some idea of the effectiveness of Christian witness is given by Celsus, a powerful opponent of the faith in the second century. Celsus mentions how Christians with little or no education seized every opportunity to witness to people, and even when confronted by educated pagans would not stop pushing their opinions.

Personal evangelism was often backed up by conspicuous acts of kindness. Another opponent of Christianity, Lucian of Samosata (125–180), told how a charlatan, Proteus

Those Christians

Christians are not differentiated from other people by country, language, or customs. They do not live in cities of their own, or speak some strange dialect, or have some peculiar lifestyle.

This teaching of theirs has not been contrived by the invention and speculation of inquisitive men; nor are they propagating mere human teaching as some people do. They live in both Greek and barbarian cities, wherever chance has put them. They follow local customs in clothing, food, and the other aspects of life. But at the same time, they display to us their wonderful, and certainly unusual, style of citizenship.

They live in their own countries, but as aliens. As citizens, they participate in everything with the rest; but endure everything as if they are aliens. Every foreign country is to them as their native country, and every homeland as a foreign country.

They marry and have children, just like every one else; but they do not kill unwanted babies. They offer a shared table, but not a shared bed. … They pass their days on earth, but are citizens of heaven. They obey the prescribed laws, but go beyond the laws in their own lives.

They love everyone, yet are persecuted by all. They are unknown and condemned; they are put to death and gain life. They are poor, and yet make many rich. They lack everything, and yet have plenty of all things. They are dishonoured, and yet gain glory through dishonour.

Their names are blackened, and yet they are cleared. They are mocked and bless in return. They are treated outrageously, and behave respectfully to others. When they do good, they are punished as evildoers; when punished, they rejoice as if being given new life. They are attacked by Jews as barbarians, and are persecuted by Greeks; yet those who hate them can give no reason for their hatred.

To put it simply: the soul is to the body as Christians are to the world. The soul is dispersed through all parts of the body – and Christians are scattered through all the cities of the world. The soul lives in the body, but is not of the body; Christians are in the world, but not of the world…

FROM AN ANONYMOUS *LETTER TO DIOGNETUS*, POSSIBLY DATING TO THE SECOND CENTURY

Perpetua on trial for her Christian faith

While we were under arrest, my father, out of his love for me, tried to persuade me to shake my resolve.

'Father,' I said. 'Do you see this vase here, for example, or this water pot or whatever?'

'Yes,' he said.

'Could it be called anything other than what it is?' I asked.

'No.'

'Well, in the same way, I can't be called anything except what I am – a Christian.'

My father was so angry at the word 'Christian' that he made as if he would tear my eyes out. But he left it at that and departed, defeated along with his devilish arguments.

During those few days I was baptized, and I was inspired by the Spirit not to ask for any other favour after the water, except physical perseverance.

A few days later we were lodged in the prison. I was terrified, as I had never been in such a dark hole. What a terrible time it was! With the overcrowding, the heat was stifling. There was also the extortion of the soldiers – and on top of everything else, I was tormented with worry about my baby.

I had to endure these trials for days. Then I obtained permission for my baby to be with me in prison. Immediately I regained my health, relieved of worry and anxiety about the child. Prison suddenly became a palace; I wanted to be there more than anywhere else.

Then one day, while we were having breakfast, we were suddenly rushed off to court. We arrived at the forum, and immediately the news flew around the neighbourhood and a huge crowd gathered. We entered the prisoners' dock. When they were questioned, the others all admitted their guilt. When my turn came, my father appeared with my son, dragged me from the bench, saying, 'Make the sacrifice – have pity on your baby!'

Hilarianus, the governor who succeeded the late proconsul Minucius Timinianus as judge, said, 'Have pity on your father's grey head; have pity on your infant son! Offer the sacrifice for the well-being of the emperors!'

'I will not,' I replied.

'Are you a Christian?' said Hilarianus.

'I am!' I confessed.

Then Hilarianus passed sentence on all of us: we were condemned to the beasts.

We returned to prison in high spirits.

EXTRACT FROM PERPETUA'S DIARY OF HER IMPRISONMENT

Peregrinus, was befriended by Christians. During outbreaks of plague at Alexandria, Christians tended the sick and buried the dead when almost everyone else had fled. In fact, the Christian life-style itself was a powerful influence in evangelism. In a society where kindness, honesty, and personal purity were rare, Christians who lived out these virtues were sure to attract comment – and often serious enquiry.

The personal witness of Christian martyrs also had some effect. Even hostile observers, such as the Emperor Marcus Aurelius, admitted that Christian bravery in the face of death was praiseworthy. As a result of the martyrdom of Perpetua and Felicitas at Carthage in 203, it was reported that the local prison governor was converted. The sufferings of Christian martyrs at Lyons and Vienne in Gaul in AD 177 encouraged several bystanders to declare themselves believers, even though it meant almost certain death for them, too.

LITERATURE

Throughout this period, Christians were writing to explain the faith and refute unfounded attacks. Luke and Acts may be the first examples; they were certainly written to instruct. By the second century, such writing was well under way, aiming to commend the faith to pagans and Jews, and to counter slanders made against Christians. Quadratus, Aristides, Justin Martyr, Athenagoras of Athens (c. 133–190), and Theophilus of Antioch all composed such works in the second century. From the third century come the great writings of Origen, refuting the extended attack on Christianity made by the pagan philosopher Celsus.

As Christians became more competent, their writings tended to specialize. Some authors concentrated on a particular audience (for example, the Jews), while others took a particular theme (for example, Lactantius's *The Deaths of the Persecutors*, which claimed that all emperors who persecuted Christians came to a bad end). Orthodox Christians also devoted much time to combating unorthodox groups and thinkers, an example being Tertullian's monumental work *Against Marcion*.

Translation of the Scriptures from Greek into other languages also aided evangelism. By AD 300 there were versions of the New Testament in Latin, Syriac, and Sahidic (a Coptic dialect), as well as collections of biblical texts.

Finally, some apocryphal fiction of this period may have had an evangelistic aim. It is possible that stories such as the *Acts of Paul and Thecla* (written in the second century) were produced to compete in the market of light, romantic fiction, and to commend Christian life-styles.

Ruins of ancient Laodicea, Turkey.
TIM DOWLEY ASSOCIATES

Christians were sometimes expatriates who could interest people from similar backgrounds. For example, the Christians of Vienne and Lyons, Gaul, came from Asia Minor. At this time Christianity was largely an urban movement; Paul tended to preach in big cities, and small Christian groups could more easily spring up in the anonymity of large towns. Deep penetration of the countryside only began in the third century, though the methods employed are unclear.

MEETINGS AND MIRACLES

Nearly every known Christian congregation started by meeting in someone's house, such as Philemon's house-church, possibly at Laodicea (Philemon v. 2). The home formed an important starting-point, though by the mid-third century congregations were beginning to have their own special buildings, because congregations had become too large to meet even in the courtyard of a large Roman house.

Although the apostles performed many miracles during their evangelistic work (see for example Acts 5:12–16, 14:8–10), miracles did not form a significant part of evangelism during the years that followed. Eusebius mentions only a very few miracles in his history of the church during this period – and in only one incident (the exorcizing of the Paneas spring) was any evangelistic use made of them. In fact, most Christian writers were surprisingly rationalistic, and tried to discredit contemporary pagan superstition, focussing on good living rather than supernatural 'signs'.

In the late third century came the first deliberate attempts by Christian missionaries to 'baptize' features of pagan religions, and so overcome them by absorbing them into Christianity. Churches took over from temples, martyrs replaced the old gods in popular devotion, and the festivals of the Christian year took the place of the high-days and holy days of paganism. Reports of the work of people such as Gregory the Wonderworker (or 'Gregory Thaumaturgus', c. 213–c. 270) in Pontus, northern Asia Minor, and Gregory the Illuminator (or 'Enlightener' c. 257–c. 331) in Armenia tend to exaggerate the success brought about by miracles. In Armenia, the conversion of the royal family was followed by a national acceptance of Christianity. Such methods of 'Christianization' became common in later centuries throughout Europe.

MICHAEL A. SMITH

CHAPTER 5

ARCHAEOLOGY AND EARLIEST CHRISTIANITY

What archaeologists can – and cannot – illuminate

Archaeology is properly the study of ancient times. In a narrow sense, it refers to the techniques of excavating ancient sites and interpreting the objects found there, but it may also be used in a wider sense to mean the study of many areas of ancient evidence that go beyond the province of the traditional historian using literary sources. There is no rigid boundary between history and archaeology in this sense. Where the early church is concerned, the archaeologist's interest may lie, for instance, in the study of papyri, of stone inscriptions (epigraphy), or of the development of church architecture.

The special value of archaeology is not usually to prove anything; rather, it helps build up a complete picture. Its data must be assessed and compared with literary sources. Archaeology cannot prove the Bible true. If a historical text is accurate in the kinds of detail which archaeology can confirm, there will be links between the two. Such details are valuable illustrations and may help to rule out mistaken theories, but they must not be given more weight as 'proof' than they deserve.

The book of Acts is a case in point. Many details of the names of people and officials, places and customs can be exactly illustrated from inscriptions. This does not prove the account to be historically true – but it rules out any view which holds that the writer was careless about such details. It also makes it more difficult to believe that the book was written long after the events.

Biblical archaeology has caught the popular imagination through spectacular discoveries, such as the Dead Sea Scrolls and the dramatic story of Masada. These great finds shed important light on the contemporary Jewish world, and this in turn helps us to understand the background to Christian beginnings. But these matters need cautious and rigorous assessment: instant sensations often turn out to have been ill-founded.

TRADITIONAL SITES

The Romans destroyed Jerusalem so thoroughly in AD 70 that today little remains visible of the city that Jesus knew. The many traditional sites are covered by churches, and the evidence for the original state of the localities has been destroyed or made inaccessible. We cannot visualize the tomb of Jesus by standing in the Church of the Holy Sepulchre – which is probably at or near its actual site. But we can illustrate what it was probably like from other tombs, such as the so-called 'Tombs of the Kings', where a disc-shaped rolling stone fits into a slot in the rock.

The first missions to the Gentiles, as presented in Acts, offer a fruitful field for archaeological study. Different kinds of detail interlock. For example, Paul met a Jewish couple in Corinth, after the Emperor Claudius had expelled the Jews from Rome (Acts 18:2).

A CHRISTIAN ANAGRAM?

A mysterious square made up of Latin words has been found scratched on walls in places as far apart as Cirencester, England; Pompeii, Italy; and Dura-Europos in Mesopotamia. The letters are so arranged that the words read backwards and forwards as well as up and down. Many people think it has a Christian significance, but its exact meaning remains a puzzle. The direct translation does not make much sense; various attempts have been made to find a hidden meaning.

R	O	T	A	S	the wheels
O	P	E	R	A	with care
T	E	N	E	T	holds
A	R	E	P	O	Arepo
S	A	T	O	R	the sower

It contains, jumbled-up, the words PATER NOSTER ('Our Father', the first two words of the Lord's prayer in Latin), together with A and O (the Greek letters 'alpha' and 'omega', used of God, for example in Revelation). So the square could be re-arranged like this:

```
              A
              P
              A
              T
              E
              R
    A   PATERNOSTER   O
              O
              S
              T
              E
              R
              O
```

This expulsion is mentioned in pagan literature and dated to AD 49 by a later writer. During Paul's long stay in Corinth, Gallio became governor (Acts 18:12). Gallio is known elsewhere from the writings of his famous brother Seneca, and his governorship can be dated to AD 51–2 by an inscription found in Delphi. This evidence helps build a consistent and fairly precise timeline for this part of Paul's life, and helps relate Acts and Paul's letters.

A test case is Paul's letter to the Galatians. The famous British investigator Sir William Ramsay (1851–1939) used the evidence of inscriptions to establish clearly the extent of Galatia, and then argued that Paul's letter was sent to southern cities such as Pisidian Antioch, in Phrygia, which Paul had visited on his first journey (Acts 13–14). This in turn suits a very early date for the letter. Thus the details of Paul's life contained in the letter may be straightforwardly related to those in Acts.

CITY LIFE

The city was a vital force in the ancient world, and it is crucial to see Christianity in its city setting. The faith first spread in those areas of the eastern Roman Empire where the cultures had become very mixed. Roman rule and institutions were imposed on Greek-speaking peoples, who were often deeply influenced by Eastern religions. There were also many Jews. It must have been very different from the picture given in surviving contemporary literature; Roman literature was only for the educated few, who despised such popular movements as Christianity.

The everyday life of a Roman city has been remarkably preserved at Pompeii and Herculaneum in Italy, which were both overwhelmed by the eruption of Mount Vesuvius in AD 79. Paul had found Christians at nearby Puteoli twenty years earlier, and there were probably Christians here, too, though the traces are tantalizingly uncertain. In Herculaneum a tiny room, perhaps belonging to a family slave, was found to have had a wooden cross nailed to the wall and later wrenched off. In Pompeii two examples of the *ROTAS-SATOR* word-square, which may have been of Christian origin, were found scratched on walls.

The book of Revelation was probably written around AD 95, at a time of conflict and persecution, and study of the cities of Asia to which the book was addressed reveals more about that period. The imagery used in the book was often much to the point. For instance, the people of Laodicea had constructed an aqueduct to supply their city, but the water was lukewarm and impure. The remains can still be seen, and thick deposits of calcium carbonate inside the pipes witness to the warmth of the water which once flowed through them. The words of Revelation 3:14–15 must have hit home powerfully in Laodicea; the writer said that this church was as useless and distasteful as that bad water.

THE WRITTEN WORD

The written word is the most important source of evidence about the earliest Christians. Books in the ancient world had usually been written on rolls made of papyrus or parchment, but this form of book was awkward to use, and the early Christians wanted to make their good news available as widely as possible. They may have been the first people to make wide use of the 'codex', the bound book with pages, such as we have today.

Tens of thousands of papyri have been preserved in the dry climate of Egypt. Those discovered include the oldest known fragment of the New Testament, a scrap of a papyrus codex of John's Gospel, copied about AD 130, known as the John Rylands Fragment P52, and now in Manchester, England.

These papyri are important in other ways. They include hundreds of letters, accounts, certificates, receipts, and other private documents, and offer a vivid picture of everyday life and society, and of the kind of Greek which was spoken and written by ordinary people. This is important because the New Testament was not written in very literary or religious language, and is often illustrated and clarified by these examples of more popular language.

GRAVES AND EPITAPHS

Epitaphs differ from most of the papyri in being phrased with a view to public display and posterity. The tombs of Christians are not at first easily recognized, for they use almost the same names and styles as their pagan neighbours. A famous and distinctive Christian epitaph is that of Abercius of Hierapolis, in Phrygia, dating from the late second century. Here poetic language about symbols, such as the shepherd and the fish, carried a hidden meaning for the Christian reader. Open confessions of faith are rare on tombstones, but there are some remarkable third-century examples from Phrygia which read 'Christian to Christian'. These appear to belong to the Montanists, who insisted that Christians publicly proclaim their faith in the face of persecution.

The most important evidence comes from the catacombs in Rome. These were huge complexes of underground burial-galleries, excavated by the Christians in the soft tufa-stone near roads outside the city. The total length of their corridors is said to be more than 500 miles (800 kilometres). Some 35 catacombs are known, the oldest of which, bearing the names of Lucina, Callistus, Domitilla, and Priscilla, date from later in the second century.

Fill me with the Fish, I pray thee, Lord Saviour.

May my mother sleep well, I pray thee, Light of the dead.

Aschandius, my father, dearly beloved of my heart, with my sweet mother and my brothers, remember thy Pectorius in the peace of the Fish.

PART OF A THIRD-CENTURY CHRISTIAN EPITAPH FROM AUTUN, GAUL

Third-century fresco of the Good Shepherd from the crypt of Lucina, in the Catacombs of San Callisto (St Callixtus), Rome.

Inscriptions and paintings from the catacombs help clarify the development of Christian art and symbolism, and thereby of Christian beliefs and devotion. The cross and the fish are common Christian emblems, although the history of their usage remains a puzzle. The fish probably came from an acrostic; the first letters of the Greek words *Iesous CHristos THeou Uios Soter* (Jesus Christ, God's Son, Saviour) make up the word *ICHTHUS* (Greek for fish). Here was a secret sign which also summed up the heart of Christian belief and served as a simple aid to help explain it.

However, there are huge gaps in the records. About many important subjects archaeology reveals little. Most of the information concerning the growth of the church comes from literature, and particularly from the Christian historian Eusebius. Christianity had become a powerful force when in the third century Rome tried to suppress it. There are traces in the inscriptions of the renewed strength of pagan cults. Yet material remains of the life and witness of the Christians are rarely found. Eusebius tells of an entire Christian town exterminated in the persecution of Diocletian: this may have been Eumenia in Phrygia, where there are many Christian epitaphs.

There is just the occasional glimpse of personal faithfulness to Christ. A crude third-century drawing in Rome depicts a boy with one hand raised in an attitude of worship before a crucified figure with an ass's head. Beneath are scribbled the mocking words, 'Alexamenos worships his god'.

THE FIRST CHURCH BUILDINGS

The earliest Christians had no special buildings, but often met in private houses, as mentioned in several places in the New Testament. Recent discoveries at Capernaum in Galilee have led some to believe that a very early house-church met there, in what may once have been the house of the apostle Peter. The earliest known church building is usually thought to be at Dura-Europos on the River Euphrates, where a house dating from AD 232–3 was adapted soon after its construction to make a larger hall suitable for about 100 people to assemble for worship. The walls feature painted scenes from both the Old Testament and the Gospels.

In Rome, about eighteen churches still bear the name of an early owner or patron, and their origins as house-churches go back before the time of Constantine. They are now almost wholly replaced by, or incorporated in, later buildings. After Constantine the picture changed completely; Christianity was officially recognized, and large, impressive churches were built in many places.

COLIN J. HEMER

CHAPTER 6

WHAT THE FIRST CHRISTIANS BELIEVED
The faith is defined

As the 'Jesus movement' grew and spread throughout the Mediterranean world, pressures from both inside and outside presented it with a series of important challenges. Internally, it had to spell out its foundation charter and terms of membership, and develop its structure and leadership. Externally, it had to work out its relations with Judaism, with other religions and philosophies, and with the Roman Empire itself.

As it came to terms with these challenges during the first three centuries, Christianity began to acquire a recognizable shape and sense of identity through various features: the New Testament Scriptures, the concepts of orthodoxy and heresy, the 'Rule of Faith' and the earliest creeds, the offices of bishop, presbyter, and deacon, the rise of Rome as a centre of reference and arbitration, patterns of argument against Jewish and pagan critics, schemes for the instruction of new converts ('catechumens') before baptism, elaborate orders of worship, and the basic outline of the Christian year.

Christianity attempted to take over from the cults and philosophies of the Roman world, and to satisfy both religious and intellectual needs. Its success was due partly to the rich variety of thought and life that developed within the one 'Jesus movement'.

JEWS AND CHRISTIANS SEPARATE

The first Christians were all Jews. They had come to believe the apostles' message that Jesus was the promised Saviour of God's people. 'Jesus the Messiah (Christ)' summed up all that the Jews were called upon to accept. In the earliest preaching to Jews, the resurrection of Jesus was emphasized more than his death, because it demonstrated that the person executed as a criminal was nevertheless God's Messiah.

Following guidelines laid down by Jesus himself, the apostles pointed to Old Testament passages which had been fulfilled in his career and in the beginnings of the church. 'This is what was prophesied' was a phrase frequently on their lips. They used Old Testament images to describe Jesus. He was the Passover lamb (John 1:29, 1 Corinthians 5:7); the second, or last, Adam (1 Corinthians 15:22, 45); the kinsman-redeemer (Galatians 4:4–7; Hebrews 2:11–18); and the stone rejected by the builders, but chosen by God to be the 'cornerstone' in the construction of his church (1 Peter 2:4–8).

This central concern of the earliest Christian preaching and teaching is especially emphasized in Matthew's Gospel and, from a different angle, in the letter to the Hebrews. But all early Christian theology was Jewish, since the language and concepts it used were quarried chiefly from the Old Testament.

Some Jewish Christians were so conservative that they demanded, in effect, that Gentiles had to become Jews in order to be true Christians. They insisted on circumcision and other Jewish legal requirements, and frowned on social contact with 'unclean' Gentiles (Acts 11:2). These 'Judaizers' appealed to the Jerusalem church, where James 'the Just', the brother of Jesus, led a community of thousands of 'staunch upholders of the Law' (Acts 15:1, 21:17–25). But Paul refused to tolerate any demands imposed on Gentile converts which threatened the good news of 'grace alone through faith alone' (Galatians 2:11–21).

In Jerusalem the harmony maintained between James and the Jewish authorities failed to survive Paul's martyrdom in AD 62 and the Jewish war with Rome (the First Jewish Revolt) which began four years later. Jewish–Christian relations continued to deteriorate later in the first century. Judaism entrenched itself within the tight limits set by the rabbinic Pharisees, excluding non-conformist Jews like the followers of Jesus.

THE EBIONITES

Conservative Jewish-Christianity disappeared into obscurity. Its strength filtered off into side-channels, such as the heretical Ebionite groups, who placed special value on voluntary poverty. It may also have merged with currents from other brands of Judaism, which similarly lost out after the disastrous revolt against Rome. The Qumran community, whose library – known as the 'Dead Sea Scrolls' – was discovered in 1947, helped

THE GNOSTICS

The Gnostics were followers of a variety of religious movements in the early Christian centuries which held that people could be saved through a secret knowledge (gnōsis in Greek). The clearest evidence for these movements, collectively known as Gnosticism, comes in Christian writings of the second century which viewed the various Gnostic groups as heretical perversions of Christianity. Gnosticism may also have been more independent of Christianity. Some scholars find Gnostic traces wherever there is an emphasis on 'knowledge' for salvation, as for example in the Dead Sea Scrolls. Others emphasize the stress in Gnosticism on an opposition between the spiritual world and the evil, material world.

GNOSTIC TEACHINGS

In Gnostic beliefs there is a sharp dualism: they set a transcendent God over against an ignorant creator (often a caricature of the God of the Old Testament). Some Gnostics taught that the creation of the world resulted from the fall of Sophia, 'wisdom', whilst all Gnostics viewed the material creation as evil. Sparks of divinity, however, have been encapsulated in the bodies of certain 'spiritual' individuals destined for salvation, but are ignorant of their heavenly origins. God sends down to them a redeemer, who brings them salvation in the form of secret knowledge (gnōsis) of themselves, their origin, and their destiny. Thus awakened, the 'spirituals' escape from the prison of their bodies at death, and pass safely through the planetary regions controlled by hostile demons, to be reunited with God.

Since they believed that salvation depended solely upon the knowledge of one's 'spiritual' nature, some Gnostics indulged in very licentious behaviour, claiming they were 'pearls' who could not be stained by any external mud. In the second century AD Carpocrates of Alexandria, for example, urged his followers to sin. The Cainites perversely honoured Cain and other villains of the Old Testament, while the Ophites venerated the serpent for bringing 'knowledge' to Adam and Eve.

Most Gnostics, by contrast, had a radically ascetic attitude towards sex and marriage. Humans were originally unisex. The creation of woman was the source of evil; the procreation of children simply multiplied the souls in bondage to the powers of darkness.

Gnosticism enjoyed great success in the ancient world, especially on the fringes of Christianity. It offered explanations of the evil and confusion of the world and the human race, and a way of escape which led back to humanity's spiritual home.

Until the nineteenth century, our knowledge of the Gnostics rested entirely on the writings of such Christians as Irenaeus, Hippolytus, Origen, Tertullian, and Epiphanius. Some of these preserved extracts from original Gnostic documents, but for the most part their accounts are in the form of counter-arguments. Scholars were not sure how accurate these accounts were; however twentieth-century discoveries, such as the Nag Hammadi texts, have confirmed some of them.

NEW EVIDENCE

In the nineteenth century two original Gnostic manuscripts were published: the Askew Codex (also known as Codex Askewianus, now in the British Library), containing the *Pistis Sophia*, and the Bruce Codex (Codex Brucianus, now in the Bodleian Library, Oxford) containing the *Books of Jeu*. All of these are relatively late Gnostic documents. A third manuscript, the Berlin Codex (Akhmim Codex, or Papyrus Berolinensis), though acquired in the nineteenth century, was not fully published until 1955. It contains a *Gospel of Mary* (of Magdala), a *Wisdom* (*Sophia*) *of Jesus*, *Acts of Peter*, and an *Apocryphon of John* (a work mentioned by Irenaeus in AD 180). These three manuscripts are in Coptic, a late version of the Egyptian language.

In 1946 a priceless cache of twelve Coptic codices and fragments was discovered near Nag Hammadi, in Upper Egypt, by a peasant searching for fertilizer. This collection, which was deposited about AD 400, contains about fifty works – texts which have already thrown much new light on Gnostic beliefs and practices.

Among those which have been published are:
The Gospel of Truth, which some have ascribed to the famous Gnostic leader Valentinus, and which deals with ignorance as the cause of humanity's lost state.
The Treatise on the Resurrection (sometimes called *The Letter to Rheginos*), also possibly by Valentinus, claims that Christians should consider themselves already spiritually resurrected.
The Gospel of Thomas, an important collection of 114 *logia*, or sayings attributed to Jesus. (This is distinct from another apocryphal *Gospel of Thomas* which describes the miracles supposed to have been done by the child Jesus.)
The Gospel of Philip, by Valentinus, which discusses several sacraments, including baptism, anointing with oil, and the 'wedding chamber'.
The Apocryphon of John, which gives a detailed account of the origins of the universe, similar to that of the Sethians and Ophites, Gnostic groups mentioned by early Christian writers.
The Revelation (Apocalypse) of Adam, in which Adam reveals to Seth how Noah was saved from the flood and Seth's seed is saved from destruction by fire. Although some allusions – for example to a virgin birth and physical suffering – may be explained as references to Christ, Christianity is not explicitly mentioned in the text. Some have therefore argued that this document represents pre-Christian Gnosticism.

GNOSTIC SURVIVORS

The small Mandaean communities living today in Iraq, Iran, Syria, and Jordan are the sole surviving remnants of ancient Gnosticism. Three major texts from the Mandaeans were translated early in the twentieth century:
The Ginza, a detailed account of the beginnings of the universe.
The Drasa, containing some late traditions about John the Baptist.
The Qolasta, a collection of prayers and liturgies.

The manuscripts of these texts date from the sixteenth to the nineteenth centuries; there are also earlier magic bowl texts (AD 600), and some magical lead amulets which may possibly date from as early as the third century AD. Though a number of scholars have assumed a pre-Christian date for the origin of the Mandaeans, the firm evidence suggests a date no earlier than the second century AD. Hence it is anachronistic to interpret the New Testament on the basis of Mandaean texts.

GNOSTIC LEADERS

Although the New Testament itself (Acts 8) does not describe Simon Magus as a Gnostic (he is called a *magos*, 'magician'), early Christian writers unanimously regarded Simon as the fount of all heresies. Unlike the later Gnostics, Simon appears to have claimed to be divine, and taught that salvation involved knowledge of himself rather than any knowledge of one's self.

Simon was followed by a fellow Samaritan, Menander, who taught at Antioch in Syria towards the end of the first century. He told his followers that those who believed in him would not die. Needless to say, his own death demonstrated that he was a false prophet. Also teaching in Antioch, at the beginning of the second century, was Saturninus, who believed that Christ was the redeemer. But like other Gnostics he maintained that Christ was not a material being and only *appeared* to be a human (the Docetic view).

Cerinthus taught in Asia Minor. (Irenaeus tells the story that the apostle John fled from a bath-house in Ephesus when he learned that Cerinthus was there!) He taught that Jesus was merely a man upon whom 'the Christ' descended as a dove. As Christ could not suffer,

to produce strongly ascetic forms of Christianity east of the River Jordan and to the north in Syria. Fringe Judaism of one kind or another also fertilized the emerging Gnostic sects which loomed so large in the second century.

The martyr Stephen's boldness in declaring the old covenant obsolete (Acts 7:1–53) reflects the ideas of more liberal, Greek-speaking Jewish Christians scattered throughout the Empire. They had been won to the new faith from the Jewish communities of the Dispersion (or 'Diaspora') found throughout the Mediterranean world. They preached the new faith in Alexandria, where the thoroughly Hellenized Judaism of Philo (20 BC–AD 50) also contributed to distinctive Alexandrian varieties of Christianity.

A GENTILE CHURCH?

Towards the middle of the second century Justin Martyr was asked by a Jewish teacher whether Jewish converts to Christianity would be saved if they continued to keep the law of Moses. Justin replied that they would, provided they did not insist on other Christians doing likewise; but he also warned that not all Christians shared his tolerant attitude. The incident reveals that the church was by this time a predominantly Gentile body.

According to Christian writers in the second and third centuries, relations between Christians and Jews apparently became increasingly hostile. These writers tried to support believers who were faltering under the force of the Jewish objection, 'How can Jesus be the Messiah if so few Jews have accepted him?' They responded by portraying Israel as an unbelieving and apostate people from first to last, helping to create a tradition of anti-Semitism.

But Jews and Christians were often on friendlier terms as neighbours in the local community than official hostility and irregular persecution would indicate. Church he departed from Jesus before the crucifixion. (This tradition is also found in the Qur'an: 'They slew him not nor crucified, but it appeared so unto them.')

Marcion of Pontus was an important, though not typical, Gnostic. He insisted upon faith in Christ, but rejected the humanity of Jesus and the resurrection of the body. Other Gnostic teachers included Basilides and his son Isidore, and Carpocrates and his son Epiphanes – all of whom taught at Alexandria, in Egypt. The most famous Gnostic teacher was Valentinus, who taught at Alexandria and came to Rome in AD 140. He had a number of able followers, among them Theodotus in the East, and Ptolemy and Heracleon in the West. Heracleon's commentary on the Gospel of John is the earliest known commentary on a New Testament book.

EDWIN M. YAMAUCHI

leaders repeatedly denounced Christians who joined in Jewish practices, sometimes following the 'rediscovery' of Old Testament commands. Such denunciations would have been unnecessary were not Christians in practice frequently ignoring them. Jewish festivals could be enjoyable occasions, as Christmas is for post-Christian pagans in the West today.

The second-century churches of the Roman province of Asia held the Christian *Pascha* to celebrate the passion, resurrection, and exaltation of Christ on the same day as the Jewish Passover. (This was probably the general custom of the earliest Christians.) Some of their opponents believed that Sunday was the only appropriate day to end the fast that preceded *Pascha*, and accused them of Judaizing, labelling them '*Quartodecimans*' – 'fourteenthers'. (Passover fell on the fourteenth day of the Jewish month *Nisan*.) In time, the Sunday *Pascha* became standard practice, and formed the basis of Easter today.

CHRISTIAN USE OF THE OLD TESTAMENT

Jews keenly resented the Christians' claim that the Old Testament belonged to them exclusively since they alone understood it aright. Christians followed the example of Jesus and the apostles, and accepted the Old Testament as inspired and authoritative Scripture. They normally used the Greek Septuagint version of the Old Testament (often abbreviated LXX). Latin translations of the Septuagint first became available in the West late in the second century.

At some periods sections of the early church also used a number of other Jewish writings. Most of these, such as the Wisdom of Solomon, were first written in Greek and were included in the Septuagint. They are now known as the Apocrypha. There is much argument about how far they were given a status equal to the books of the Hebrew Bible. In the West, largely through Augustine's influence (but against Jerome's arguments), they later became widely accepted as part of the 'canon' of Scripture, whereas Eastern churches usually recognized only the Hebrew books. Melito of Sardis (d. c. AD 180) travelled to Palestine in about AD 170 to investigate the contents of the Hebrew Scriptures, and compiled the earliest known Christian canon of the Old Testament.

Early Christians went to exaggerated lengths to make the Old Testament into a Christian book speaking everywhere about Christ and his church. Their interpretations of Scripture often kept to the historical pattern of promise and fulfilment, shadow and substance, which the New Testament writers largely used, but they soon became much freer and looser.

Most of the Gnostics rejected the entire Old Testament, at least in any straightforward meaning. They blamed the 'inferior' God of the Old Testament for creating the evil material world. Marcion himself posed sharper problems by listing the contradictions between Old and New. He claimed that the Old Testament God who ordered battles and slaughter, and was driven by anger rather than love, was incompatible with the merciful Father of Jesus Christ.

Other critics pointed the finger at the polygamy and other misbehaviour of the Jewish patriarchs, the psalms which lusted for the destruction of enemies, and the crude descriptions of God's 'back parts' and the like. The Old Testament also seemed to concentrate on earthly prosperity as the reward of piety; this was embarrassing in an age of martyrs and widespread asceticism.

Christianity inherited many of the objections that Greek and Roman intellectuals levelled against the Jewish Bible, and therefore could take over traditional Jewish arguments to refute them. But Marcion's charge that the Old Testament was sub-Christian was not so easily answered. Tertullian's defiant response was to 'mingle the law and the prophets with the Gospels and apostolic writings'. As a result, his own Christianity has been called 'baptized Judaism'; and his follower Cyprian 'mingled' Christian ministers with Old Testament priests, and Christian ordinances with Old Testament sacrifices.

Most churchmen found peace on this front only by allegorizing or spiritualizing the Old Testament. They followed the example set by Philo and some of the Gnostics, as well as Platonic interpreters of Homer and Hesiod, the revered poets of Greece. The *Letter of Barnabas*, possibly from Alexandria, claimed that the law of Moses had never been meant to be taken literally; even the number of Abraham's 318 servants pointed to the cross of Jesus!

Origen was the most influential allegorizer of Scripture. He developed a sophisticated theory of the different levels of Scripture:

> The Scriptures were composed through the Spirit of God, and have both a meaning which is obvious, and another which is hidden from most readers. For the contents of Scripture are the outward forms of certain mysteries, and the reflection of divine things ... The whole law is spiritual, but the inspired meaning is not recognized by all — only by those who are gifted with the grace of the Holy Spirit in the word of wisdom and knowledge.

The use of allegorical interpretations infuriated pagan objectors, whose criticisms depended on taking the Old Testament at face value. It also enabled Origen to discover secret teaching concealed beneath the surface of the Scriptures, like a Christian Platonist or true Gnostic. After Origen, Christians found it easier to live with their conviction that the Bible was inspired and therefore both consistent and significant in every detail, when spiritually understood.

CHRISTIANS RECOGNIZE THE NEW TESTAMENT

The earliest Christian congregations quickly appreciated the value of letters written by apostles such as Paul. Some of them were obviously intended for public reading, perhaps in place of, or alongside, a sermon on the Old Testament, and for circulating among the churches. Christians also treasured what they learned about the life and teaching of Jesus. The first Gospels were not produced until the 60s, but their contents were partly available in written form before this time.

It is uncertain how long reliable, spoken traditions about Jesus lived on. Papias, a Phrygian bishop early in the second century, confidently believed that he had discovered fresh information from the 'living and abiding voice' of the elders or followers of the apostles. The little that remains of his writings suggests he was mistaken!

The example of the Old Testament 'canon' encouraged the gradual collection of a list of Christian writings which would constitute the standard, or rule, of the churches. (The Greek word *kanōn* meant 'measuring rod'.) These were the books read publicly in the congregations and regarded as having special authority.

Paul's letters were brought together the earliest, probably around the end of the first century. The Synoptic Gospels (Matthew, Mark, and Luke) were formed into a group by the middle of the second century. John's Gospel, which appealed particularly to the Gnostics, and later the Montanists, was treated with some reserve and took longer to be generally accepted.

Marcion is generally believed to have published the first formal canon-list about AD 140. It consisted of the expurgated Gospel of Luke and ten of Paul's letters (but not the Pastoral letters). This restricted collection, together with the Gnostics' use of their own gospels and apocalypses bearing apostolic names, challenged the church. It was also feared that the Montanists would claim the status of scripture for the utterances of their New Prophecy. Possibly the earliest appearance of the words 'New Covenant (Testament) of the Gospel' to mean a body of writings is found in an anti-Montanist writer late in the second century.

The late second century also saw the production of several 'acts' of apostles whose missionary labours are not recorded in Luke's Acts. In addition there appeared the first of a number of gospels written to satisfy curiosity about, for example, the childhood of Jesus and the life of Pilate. These mainly imaginative books served as the novels and romances of popular Christianity. Most of them popularized the ideas of fringe Christian groups, particularly Docetism, and the rejection of sex and marriage.

THE MONTANISTS

Around AD 172, an enthusiastic young Christian named Montanus began to attract attention as a prophet in Phrygia, a region of western Asia Minor. Two prophetesses, Prisca (sometimes called Priscilla) and Maximilla, soon joined him, claiming to be mouthpieces of the Paraclete, the Greek title used in John's Gospel for the Holy Spirit. At times God spoke through them in the first person, as with the Old Testament prophets. They were the 'New Prophecy', whose main message was the nearness of the end and the return of Christ, for which Christians needed to be fully prepared.

Montanists called all Christians to a demanding asceticism. Marital relations were to be abandoned in favour of chastity, fasts multiplied, and food eaten dry. The Montanists' holy, Spirit-led communities at Pepuza and Tymion in Phrygia were named 'Jerusalem'. Maximilla predicted: 'After me there will be no prophecy, but the End.' Through their oracles, the Montanists urged Christians to relish persecution: 'Do not hope to die in bed . . . but as martyrs.' Montanists were 'gloriously martyred' in Gaul and Africa.

The most distinguished Montanist was Tertullian of Carthage in his later life. He too believed that the prophecies given by the Paraclete perfected the church's discipline — by refusing forgiveness for serious sins after baptism, and banning remarriage and flight from persecution.

The Montanists soon ran into trouble. In Asia they were excommunicated by the first synods of bishops we know of in the history of the church. Why they were condemned is uncertain: they were fanatics, but not heretics. (One bishop of Rome apparently recognized their gifts as of the Spirit, but later changed his mind.) Their visions, speaking in tongues, and intense religious excitement attracted suspicion. The claims made for their prophecies seemed to question the emerging canon of New Testament Scriptures. Maximilla's predictions were not fulfilled. The Montanists scolded the 'unspiritual' church for rejecting their Paraclete. In short, allegiance to the New Prophecy created discord at a time when the bishops were working towards a united, stable church which conformed with the tradition of the apostles.

Montanist groups survived into the fifth century in Africa, and longer still in Phrygia, and the church lost something by excluding them. Despite their excesses, the Montanists stood for the conviction that the Spirit was as active in the contemporary church as at the beginning; greater manifestations, not lesser, were promised for 'the last days'. Their similarity to today's Pentecostal and charismatic movements has often been exaggerated.

DEFINING THE CANON

By the late second century, Christian writers felt it vital to spell out which books were accepted by the church. Irenaeus had no doubt that there could be only four Gospels, neither more nor less. A document known as the Muratorian Canon (discovered in eighteenth-century Milan by Ludovico Muratori) lists the four Gospels, thirteen letters of Paul, Acts, two letters of John, Jude, and the Revelation of John, together with the Wisdom of Solomon, and, with reservations, the Revelation of Peter. Hebrews is, surprisingly, missing; it had been much used by Clement of Rome a century earlier. This list has traditionally been dated around AD 170, but several scholars place it much later.

By the early third century, a consensus had been reached throughout the church concerning the main contents of the canon, and only a handful of books continued to be debated. Hebrews was not accepted in the West, possibly because doubts about who wrote it were stiffened by the Montanist use of chapter 6. Revelation was unpopular in the East because it was used to support millenarian ideas.

Eusebius summed up the situation at the outset of the fourth century. The only books still disputed at that stage were James, 2 Peter, 2 and 3 John, and Jude. These were 'spoken against' by some but 'recognized by most churchmen'. Eusebius was clearly bewildered by the Revelation of John. He placed it with the undisputed books, but knew that its authorship was uncertain and its contents unwelcome to some. Dionysius of Alexandria (d. AD 265) had earlier worked out, with remarkable skill, that Revelation was not by the author of the Fourth Gospel: but he did not for that reason deny its authority.

The Eastern Church finally arrived at a consensus by 367, in which year Athanasius' Easter Letter from Alexandria listed solely the twenty-seven books of the New Testament. It also allowed new converts to read the *Didache* and *The Shepherd of Hermas*. Other orthodox books which had until then been accepted for a time in some churches were I Clement and

EUSEBIUS: 'FATHER OF CHURCH HISTORY'

Eusebius (c. 263–c. 339) was the first to attempt to write a history of the church on a grand scale. Born in Palestine, he was on the run during the Great Persecution of the church (303–305), seeing many martyrdoms in Egypt, and was himself imprisoned for his faith. In 313/14 Eusebius was made bishop of Caesarea, Palestine, and later became a close friend of the Emperor Constantine, for whom he composed many flattering speeches. His political ideas helped create the Christian Empire of Byzantium, and he became a typical court-bishop of the period. During the Arian dispute, Eusebius' own theology came under suspicion. He supported the banishment of Athanasius at the Council of Tyre (335). A voluminous writer, Eusebius' works include works to justify Christianity directed against pagans, biblical and theological works and letters, and above all his *Church History*. He was a keen follower of Origen.

Eusebius's *Church History* was completed initially in either 303 or 311, but several supplements were added by him to bring the story up to 324 and the final triumph of his admired friend, the Emperor Constantine. Eusebius dealt mainly with the succession of Christian bishops and teachers from apostolic times, heresies, the sufferings of the Jews, and the persecution and martyrdom of Christians. He also recounted traditions about the New Testament writers, and details about the canon of Scripture. Eusebius wrote in a heavy, verbose, and difficult style; however, his book is invaluable since it preserves extracts from otherwise lost works. Much of his history is told by means of long quotations from previous writers. As a writer, Eusebius was neither utterly credulous nor very critical; he does not stuff his work with improbable miracles, but accepts most of his sources at face value.

Although he was not the first church historian – Hegesippus (c. 110–c. 180) and Julius Africanus (c. 160–c. 240) wrote before him, though only fragments of their works survive – Eusebius was the first to attempt a history on a comprehensive scale. He set the pattern for future church historians, and was used extensively by later Christian writers, such as Jerome (c. 347–420) and Bede (672/73–735).

MICHAEL A. SMITH

the Letter of Barnabas. For centuries the Syriac Church used Tatian's Diatessaron (c. AD 160–175), a harmony of the Gospels, instead of the four separate ones. Later, it also rejected Revelation and demoted the general letters. They were all restored by the mid-sixth century.

In the West, complete canon lists were approved by the African Councils of Hippo (393) and Carthage (397). In time the Western Church followed the East in accepting Hebrews within the canon, its contents proving so attractive that they overcame doubts about its writer. Christians at Alexandria claimed at an early stage it was by Paul, a view that was eventually accepted everywhere.

Although church leaders in a literal sense created the canon, they were only recognizing the books that had already stamped their own authority on the churches. The criteria for accepting a book as canonical were sometimes complex. Above all, it had to be written – or sponsored – by an apostle, and also be recognizably orthodox in content, and publicly used by a prominent church or majority of churches. Known forgeries, such as the *Acts of Paul*, were rejected; as were other books which contained heretical teaching.

Some books suffered because of the unacceptable use other Christians made of them. The Montanists' love of Revelation was made the excuse for discrediting the book for a time.

CLEMENT OF ROME

Little is known of the life of Clement, one of the early bishops or presbyters of Rome, whose name was linked to a general letter usually known as *1 Clement*, and who died about AD 100. *1 Clement* is an open letter from the Church at Rome to the Church at Corinth, probably written at the end of the first century, shortly after the persecution by the Emperor Domitian. It is likely the earliest surviving Christian writing apart from the New Testament, and was written to counter the disruption and disturbance in the Church at Corinth, where some of the older leaders had been deposed by a younger clique.

The letter sheds interesting light on church life soon after the age of the apostles. There is no trace of a single ruling bishop; instead the leaders of the church are called either bishops and deacons or elders (presbyters). The martyrdoms of Peter and Paul are referred to, but only in very vague terms. The letter appeals to a simple form of apostolic succession.

1 Clement puts great stress on good order within the church, and on Christian faith being accompanied by good works, claiming that Abraham was saved 'by faith and hospitality'. The book quotes extensively from the Old Testament, Jewish books outside the canon, and writings of the apostles. It became widely known and popular because it was believed that its author knew Peter and Paul, and because it contained earnest exhortations to Christian humility and love. It was known to Hermas of Rome and Dionysius of Corinth in the later second century, and was occasionally even read in church.

2 Clement, another early work, was claimed to be written by Clement of Rome, but is an anonymous sermon, perhaps dating from AD 150. Several additional writings dating to the fourth century were falsely claimed to be by Clement.

MICHAEL A. SMITH

Some people were embarrassed about the differences between the Gospel of John and the other Gospels, and also at the variations and massive overlap between the Synoptic Gospels.

But the eventual shape of the New Testament shows that the early church wanted to submit fully to the teachings of the apostles. It had been created by their preaching and now grounded itself upon their writings.

THE ROOTS OF THE FAITH

The ancient world had a great respect for tradition and precedent, especially in religion; but Christianity seemed to be quite new, which presented a serious stumbling-block. Christian writers tried to overcome this problem by demonstrating that their faith had centuries-old roots in Israel and in the wisdom of the Greek philosophers. Justin Martyr wrote: 'Christ is the *Logos* in whom every race of men shared. Those who lived in accordance with *Logos* – true reason – are Christians, even though they were regarded as atheists; for example, Socrates and Heraclitus among the Greeks.'

Tertullian and most early Christian writers believed that truth was older than error. Heresy came later than orthodoxy, like some corrupting parasite. Origen wrote: 'All heretics are at first believers; then later they deviate from the rule of faith.' The early Christian writers believed that the orthodox faith was transmitted full-grown to the churches by the apostles. A delightful legend described how the Twelve composed the Apostles' Creed jointly, each contributing a clause.

JUSTIN MARTYR: CHRISTIAN APOLOGIST

Justin (c. 100–c. 165) was a convert from paganism who became the most notable of the second century 'apologists' (writers defending the Christian faith). Details of his life come chiefly from his own writings.

Justin was born at Flavia Neapolis (now Nablus) in Palestine. As a young man, he searched energetically for truth in a variety of philosophical schools. One day, while meditating alone by the seashore – perhaps at Ephesus – he met an old man who exposed the weakness of his confident thinking. This stranger then pointed him to the Jewish prophets who bore witness to Christ. Justin had already been impressed by the remarkable moral constancy of Christians in the face of death. These themes were later to recur in his writings. Justin responded wholeheartedly by becoming a Christian and taking his new faith into the philosophical schools. He believed he now possessed in Christ a more perfect philosophy, revealed fully by the God who had been known only in part through the wisdom of the ancient world. He taught in Ephesus and Rome, where Tatian was one of his pupils.

JUSTIN'S WRITINGS

Justin's writings are vigorous and earnest, but discursive – urgent appeals to reason, thrashed out under the threat of persecution. His *First Apology* was addressed to the Emperor Antoninus Pius (AD 138–161), and aimed to clear away prejudice and misunderstandings about Christianity. He claimed that popular charges that Christians were atheists and immoral were unfounded, arguing that Christian beliefs and practices actually reflect a higher reason and morality. His *Second Apology* is brief and passionate, protesting against injustice, provoked by the summary execution of people innocent of any crime, except confessing the name of Christ.

The longest of Justin's three surviving works is the *Dialogue with Trypho*, which apparently recounts an actual encounter at Ephesus years earlier. Trypho was a cultured Jew who objected that Christians broke the Jewish law and worshipped a human being. The debate was conducted with respect and courtesy on both sides, despite deep disagreement. Justin argued from the Scriptures they shared: the Scriptures spoke of Christ, in whom the law is set aside. Justin's words are valuable examples of the way that early Christians interpreted the Bible.

Justin was martyred in Rome about AD 165. He had presented his faith as both scriptural and reasonable in the face of objections by both Jews and pagans.

COLIN J. HEMER

But the preaching and teaching of the apostles was not the same as the orthodoxy about which the theologians wrote; historical development had been at work in the interim. Nevertheless, from a very early stage sharp lines were drawn between true and false versions of the Christian message. Rival gospels were condemned outright. In Galatians, Paul curses those who add Jewish legal requirements to the gospel. 1 John established that Christians must believe that Christ came 'in the flesh'. 1 Corinthians stipulated that belief in the historical resurrection of Jesus is another indispensable basis of salvation.

ORTHODOXY, HETERODOXY, AND HERESY

False accounts of Christ and his achievement were in circulation from the very beginning. Many scholars believe that in some regions views later condemned as heresy predominated at first. It appears that in Alexandria Christian teaching was quickly combined with Jewish

God made this universe by his word, reason, and power. Your philosophers also agree that the maker of the universe seems to be *Logos* – that is, word and reason … (for example, Zeno and Cleanthes) … We also claim that the word, reason, and virtue, by which we have said that God made all things, have spirit as their substance … This Word, we have learned, was produced from God, and was generated by being produced, and therefore is called the Son of God, and God, from unity of substance with God. For God too is spirit.

When a ray is projected from the sun, it is a portion of the whole sun; but the sun will be in the ray because it is a ray of the sun; the substance is not separated but extended. So from spirit comes spirit, and God from God, as light is kindled from light … This ray of God … glided down into a virgin, in her womb was fashioned as flesh, was born as man mixed with God. The flesh was built up by the spirit, was nourished, grew up, spoke, taught, worked, and was Christ.

TERTULLIAN, *APOLOGY XXI*

and Greek beliefs. Then prominent Christian Gnostic groups arose there, before orthodox Christianity became dominant towards the end of the second century. It was not until this period too that orthodox teaching prevailed in Syriac-speaking Christianity. Here however the extreme asceticism, known as 'encratism', deriving from unorthodox Jewish Christianity, continued to dominate.

The churches were hardly ever free from disputes over vital aspects of the faith. In the early centuries, Christian leaders did not distinguish clearly between heretical movements and schisms which split the mainstream church. It was difficult to believe that separatists could be really orthodox; while heretics who denied the faith of the church logically belonged outside the church. But paradoxically, heretics contributed to the way in which Christianity developed. The pioneering challenge of heresy did much to shape Christian orthodoxy – a rounded, systematic exposition of the implications of basic Christian convictions.

The core of earliest Christianity centred on the Scriptures, the Lord's Supper, and fellowship (*koinōnia*) in the Spirit, as well as faith in Christ and the Father. Out of this core, provoked by the challenge of heretics, patterns of orthodoxy were developed. They were not identical in every region, but they were sufficiently similar for each region's church to be in communion with the others. Prior to the Council of Nicaea (325), no universal touchstone of orthodox faith existed – except perhaps in the New Testament.

The differences between the orthodoxy in, for instance, Alexandria and Carthage, arose out of the different ways of thinking of their theologians. Each reflected his own culture. Tertullian used the language and thought-forms of law, rhetoric, and Stoicism – and Montanism; Clement and Origen used the concepts of Platonism and Pythagoreanism – and Christian Gnosticism. Origen, and even Tertullian, may at times have been so heavily influenced by these thought-forms as to cross the narrow frontier that separates orthodoxy from heresy.

INCARNATION?

Christians inherited from the Jews the belief that the world was created by God. But the Creator also entered fully into human life in the incarnation. The Word who 'became flesh' was the same Word through whom 'all things came to be' (John 1:1–3, 14).

The philosophers rejected these Christian fundamentals. They held that a transcendent god could not be directly involved in the physical world; nor change, as the doctrines of creation and incarnation implied. Gnostics denied them too, since they believed that spirit alone belonged to God; the material world was corrupt and corrupting. Many Gnostics held that Christ only *appeared* to be human, like a phantom.

Others who took this view of Christ were known as 'Docetist', from the Greek verb 'to seem' or 'appear'; their views were attacked in 1 and 2 John. Jews too objected to the idea of divine incarnation, and some Jewish Christians described Christ's coming as a 'theophany', a temporary visitation by God, more angelic than human.

For all these reasons, second-century Christian writers stressed that God's world was good; that the body as well as the soul was destined for salvation; and, consistent with both these doctrines, that Jesus was a man of flesh and blood. Ignatius wrote: 'Jesus Christ was of the race of David, the child of Mary, who was truly born and ate and drank, was truly persecuted under Pontius Pilate, was truly crucified and died.'

The most important anti-Gnostic author was Irenaeus of Lyons. He taught that, if the body could not be saved, 'the Lord did not redeem us with his blood, nor is the cup of the eucharist the communion of his blood, nor is the bread which we break the communion of his body'. Theology, worship, and salvation were all connected. Ignatius believed that martyrdom was meaningless if Christ had not truly shed his blood.

THEOLOGY OF THE *LOGOS*

Christian writers developed a theology of the *Logos* in order to justify their belief in divine creation and incarnation. *Logos*, translated 'Word' in John 1, also meant 'reason, purpose, wisdom'. This term was used in Stoicism, Middle Platonism, and the writings of Philo to mean a cosmic principle of order and harmony, or the pattern or power by which God impinged upon the world.

Justin Martyr and others developed these two meanings, and taught that the *Logos* was eternally with God, as his mind or wisdom. But in creation, revelation, and finally incarnation, the *Logos* went forth, acting upon and within the world. God the Father was therefore not directly in contact with the physical world, nor subject to change; for the *Logos* never ceased to be his eternal wisdom. Some Christian writers were strongly influenced by philosophical ideas of divine unchangeability, quite different from the consistent steadfastness of the living God of the Bible.

IGNATIUS OF ANTIOCH

Ignatius was bishop of the Church at Antioch early in the second century. What little is known of him comes almost entirely from seven letters written during his journey to Rome to be executed, about AD 98–117. His seven letters (others attributed to him were added in the fourth century) were addressed to the churches at Ephesus, Magnesia, Tralles, Rome, Philadelphia, and Smyrna, and to Polycarp, bishop of Smyrna. He argued strongly that there should be one 'bishop' in charge of each congregation, in order to prevent splits in the church and to ensure that correct beliefs were preserved.

He strongly condemned Docetist ideas current in churches in Asia Minor, where it was held that Jesus only *seemed* to be a man, and was in fact a pure spirit-being, uncontaminated by this material world. Ignatius put high value on the eucharist (communion) as a means of ensuring unity, and of stressing the reality of Jesus' becoming man.

Ignatius believed that he possessed the Holy Spirit's gift of 'prophecy', though he considered himself inferior to the apostles. He was rather neurotic, given to strong ideas and forceful language. Ignatius was so keen to become a martyr that he begged the Christians in Rome not to prevent his expected execution.

MICHAEL A. SMITH

The *Logos* who issued from God was certainly seen as divine. But the *Logos* easily appeared to be some impersonal power of God. It was often argued that the *Logos* was generated as Son (so that God became Father of the Son) only prior to creation (Tertullian), or even the incarnation (Hippolytus).

Some of the difficulties arose from language. If God was Father, this seemed to imply that he once existed without his Son. Origen established that such language referred to an eternal relationship between the Father and the Son. His doctrine that the Son was eternally being generated was an important step forward.

The theologians of Alexandria did not assert divine creation and incarnation as unambiguously as, say, Irenaeus. Origen lived in an age of persecution and was a Christian Platonist; therefore he instinctively looked through and beyond the visible, historical world to the transcendent and spiritual. For him, the material world was only a passing phase, where spirits who had fallen in an earlier existence were purified as punishment.

WAS CHRIST REALLY GOD?

The Christians took over the Jews' uncompromising belief that: 'The Lord our God is one God' (Deuteronomy 6:4). But they also soon came to the belief that 'Jesus is Lord' (Romans 10:9). They applied to Christ Old Testament passages referring to *Yahweh*, the Lord; they worshipped Christ as God.

IRENAEUS

Irenaeus (c. 115–c. 202) was born in Asia Minor and studied under Polycarp, Bishop of Smyrna. He then went to Gaul, where he became Bishop of Lyons (Lugdunum), Gaul, in AD 177. His books aimed to counteract the Gnostic ideas common in this region. Two major writings by Irenaeus survive: *Against Heresies* ('Five Books Exposing and Overthrowing the so-called 'Knowledge''') and *Proof of the Apostolic Preaching*, an instructional book demonstrating that the basic Christian faith fulfils the Old Testament.

Irenaeus stressed the fundamental Christian doctrines that were being challenged by Gnosticism: that the world was created by one God; that Jesus Christ, son of the Creator, died to save humanity; and that there will be a resurrection of the body. He appealed to the historical roots of the Christian faith, and argued that Scripture contained a succession of covenants through which 'one and the same God' progressively revealed his will to men and women, as they were ready to receive it. Irenaeus

developed the idea that Christ – fully man as well as fully God – retraced the steps of Adam, with a different result. Because Christ passed through every age of life, all humanity shares in his sanctifying work.

The Gnostics claimed to possess secret traditions passed down from the apostles. To counter this, Irenaeus developed an argument involving another form of apostolic succession. He claimed that the churches preserved public, standard beliefs handed down from apostolic times by the teachers in the churches.

Irenaeus developed Christian theology in several ways: for example, the 'canon (or rule) of truth' preserved in the church as the key to interpreting Scripture; the view that the eucharist contains 'an earthly and divine reality'; and the place of the virgin Mary (the 'new Eve') in theology. At the same time he tried to base his teachings and arguments on Scripture.

EVERETT FERGUSON

In worship and other activities, the Christians did not necessarily feel any tension between these two basic beliefs. But both Jews and pagans such as Celsus accused Christians of having two gods. Some Christians were also making unacceptable statements about Christ. The issue of the Trinity (a later term) became an unavoidable problem. It was particularly difficult to resolve because of the influence of the Greek concept of unity, as perfect oneness, excluding any internal distinctions.

Docetists and Jewish Christians, such as the Ebionites, saw no problem. The Docetists regarded Christ as merely a temporary appearance of God disguised as a human. The Ebionites saw Jesus as an ordinary person indwelt by God's power at his baptism. Neither believed that Jesus Christ was truly God.

Some writers tried to safeguard both monotheism and the deity of Christ with the *Logos* theology – which tended to be rather academic. It failed to give an adequate picture of the personal divinity of the *Logos*, especially prior to creation. Writers such as Irenaeus and Tertullian developed this into an 'economic' doctrine of the Trinity – so called because it spoke of the relations between Father, Son, and Spirit chiefly in terms of the divine 'economy', or plan for the world, rather than in terms of the internal life of God in eternity. It emphasized the successive activities of Father, Son, and Spirit as God dealt with creation, and stressed that the one God was responsible for both creation and redemption, thus countering Gnostic views.

THE MONARCHIANS

In the late second and early third centuries a backward-looking theology known as Monarchianism emerged in Asia Minor and flourished in the West. It was anxious to emphasize the divine unity, or 'monarchy'. (The Monarchians are also known as 'Sabellians' after one of their leaders, Sabellius.) They claimed that God existed in different 'modes' (so were sometimes also called 'Modalists'), but only in one mode at any one time. God's different names – Father, Son, and Spirit – described the different roles he played at different times. The Monarchians were also called 'Patripassians' by their opponents, because they taught in effect that the Father (Latin, *pater*) suffered (Latin, *passus*) as the Son. They felt they could not believe that God was one, and that Christ was fully God, without rejecting the belief that God was always three.

The Monarchians were assailed on all sides – in Rome by Hippolytus and Novatian, in Africa by Tertullian, and in Alexandria by Origen. In writing a book to refute Praxeas – possibly a nickname for a Roman bishop – Tertullian gave the Latin West a theological vocabulary that has hardly yet been bettered. He drew upon Stoicism and Roman law for his language, and taught that God was one being (Latin, *substantia*) but three concrete individuals (Latin, *personae*). The Son and the Spirit did not issue from the Father by a division of his being, but as extensions from his being, like rays from the sun. Tertullian's theology was backed up by the Roman theologians, and ensured that the Western Church was scarcely disturbed by the problems raised by Arius in the fourth century.

Origen's teaching dominated the East in the third and fourth centuries. Against the Monarchians, he insisted that Father, Son, and Spirit were three eternally distinct persons (Greek *hypostaseis* – roughly the same as *personae*). The Son owed his being eternally to the Father (the eternal generation of the Son), and was inferior to him. As genuine Son of the

Father he was truly divine, but subordinate; the Spirit was even lower. Origen's ideas were deeply coloured by Middle Platonism, which graded existence into different levels. His teaching pointed in various directions, and for this reason could be appealed to later by most parties in the Arian controversy.

Before the Council of Nicaea (AD 325) all theologians viewed the Son as in one way or another subordinate to the Father. Around AD 250, a dispute between Dionysius, Bishop of Rome, and Dionysius, Bishop of Alexandria, illustrated the different approaches of the churches in the West and East. The West was stronger on the unity of God and weaker on the permanent distinctness of the three; in the East, the position was reversed.

CHRISTIANS SUMMARIZE THEIR BELIEFS

The early Christians often summarized what they believed. These summaries varied according to the contexts in which they were used, the writers or churches which produced them, and the errors or attacks which they had to resist.

In addition to statements made at baptism (for example, Acts 8:37), and solemn commands (for example, Acts 3:6 and 2 Timothy 4:1), scholars have discovered summaries of the teaching of the apostles (for example, I Corinthians 15:3, 4), as well as statements of belief in hymn form:

> *(Christ) appeared in human form,*
> *Was shown to be right by the Spirit,*
> *And was seen by angels.*
> *He was preached among the nations,*
> *Was believed in the world,*
> *And was taken up to heaven.*
> *(I Timothy 3:16)*

Some formulas mention Christ alone, for example: 'Jesus is the Christ' (for a Jewish setting) or, more widely: 'Jesus is Lord' (I Corinthians 12:3). Persecutors often demanded that Christians should curse Christ and say: 'Caesar is Lord.' Other formulas include God the Father too (I Corinthians 8:6; I Timothy 2:5), while forms naming Father, Son, and Spirit appear in baptism (Matthew 28:19), worship (2 Corinthians 13:14), and summaries of doctrine (Ephesians 4:4–6).

Later writers recorded more elaborate declarations of faith. Ignatius' declaration against Docetism was quoted earlier (p. 79).

Some hostile or inquisitive outsiders called for statements of what Christians believed. Here is the account of Aristides, one of the earliest writers to defend Christianity:

> *As for the Christians, they trace their origins to the Lord Jesus Christ. He is confessed to be the Son of the most high God, who came down from heaven by the Holy Spirit and was born of a virgin and took flesh, and in a daughter of man there lived the Son of God ... This Jesus ... was pierced by the Jews, and he died, and was buried; and they say that after three days he rose and ascended into heaven ... They believe God to be the Creator and Maker of all things, in whom are all things, and from whom are all things.*

Similar summaries were made by Justin Martyr.

One important outline of basic Christian beliefs in the late second and early third centuries was the 'Rule of Faith'. Origen described it as: 'the teaching of the church preserved unaltered and handed down in unbroken succession from the apostles'. In reality it indicated what particular writers or churches taught, especially against heretics, but also to new converts, as the central message of the Bible. The Rule was also known by several other names: 'the faith', 'the tradition', 'the preaching', and the 'Rule of Truth'. It claimed to represent an apostolic tradition of teaching, and was even appealed to in the dispute over the Christian *Pascha*.

Irenaeus is the first writer to record a clearly identifiable Rule. Its main content was as follows:

> ... this faith: in one God, the Father Almighty, who made the heaven and the earth and the seas and all things that are in them; and in one Christ Jesus, the Son of God, who was made flesh for our salvation; and in the Holy Spirit, who made known through the prophets the plan of salvation, and the coming, and the birth from a virgin, and the passion, and the resurrection from the dead, and the bodily ascension into heaven of the beloved Christ Jesus, our Lord, and his future appearing from heaven in the glory of the Father to sum up all things and to raise up anew all flesh of the whole human race ...

This is clearly anti-Gnostic: it emphasizes the 'bodily ascension' and alludes to Irenaeus's distinctive idea of the 'summing up' in Christ of all God's dealings with humanity.

Other versions of the Rule reflect not only the battle with Gnostics and other heretics, but also the writers' personal concerns. The Montanist Tertullian described lengthily 'the Holy Spirit, the Paraclete, the sanctifier of the faith of those who believe in the Father, the Son, and the Holy Spirit'. The speculative Origen not only includes paragraphs on the soul, free will, devils, and angels, but also claims that the apostles left much else 'to be investigated by those who were fit for the higher gifts of the Spirit'.

BAPTISMAL CREEDS

But the Rule of Faith was not a creed with fixed wording. Fixed creeds of this kind developed chiefly in the context of baptism, and originally consisted of question-and-answer. Although at first people were often baptized in the name of Christ alone, it soon became standard to be baptized in the name of the Trinity. By Justin's time at Rome, those being baptized answered questions about their belief in 'God, the Father and Lord of the universe', 'Jesus Christ, who was crucified under Pontius Pilate', and 'the Holy Spirit, who through the prophets foretold all things about Jesus'.

Hippolytus's account of baptism at Rome at the outset of the third century is very important:

> When the person being baptized goes down into the water, he who baptizes him, putting his hand on him, shall say: 'Do you believe in God, the Father Almighty?' And the person being baptized shall say: 'I believe.' Then holding his hand on his head, he shall baptize him once. And then he shall say: 'Do you believe in Christ Jesus, the Son of God, who was born by the Holy Spirit of

the Virgin Mary, and was crucified under Pontius Pilate, and was dead and buried, and rose again the third day, alive from the dead, and ascended into heaven, and sat at the right hand of the Father, and will come to judge the living and the dead?' And when he says: 'I believe,' he is baptized again. And again he shall say: 'Do you believe in the Holy Spirit, in the holy church, and the resurrection of the body?' The person being baptized shall say: 'I believe,' and then he is baptized a third time.

BAPTISM

Baptism was usually by immersion, either in a river or in the bath-house of a large house. The person was normally immersed three times, in response to three questions about belief in the three persons of the Trinity. From the early second century, baptism by pouring of water was allowed in cases of emergency or sickness. From the third century, the baptismal service also included the laying-on-of-hands by the chief minister of the church (the bishop), with a prayer that the candidate would receive the Holy Spirit.

Baptism seems normally to have taken place on Sundays. At first, baptism was probably administered only to adults. The first definite mention of child baptism comes early in the third century, and infant baptism was beginning to be widespread by the mid-third century. Both adult *and* infant baptism were practised until the sixth century, after which, usually, only infant baptism was practised.

As early as the end of the second century, some people had come to believe that baptism had a magical effect. Tertullian mentions prayer to 'sanctify' the water, and from then on it was widely believed that baptism automatically washed away sins. From this period, too, there arose the practice of exorcizing the candidate before baptism, often accompanied with ceremonial anointing with oil.

MICHAEL A. SMITH

By this time other items of belief had been attached to the third question, which sometimes mentions 'the forgiveness of sins'. In addition, the question about Christ had been considerably expanded, probably influenced by the Rule of Faith, to uncover and exclude Gnostics and heretics. Although it is in question-and-answer form, Hippolytus's 'Old Roman' creed is the earliest close parallel to the Apostles' Creed – which has no direct link with the apostles, and of which the earliest exact text dates from about AD 400.

Creeds in statement form (I believe …) developed from the mid-third century by adaptation of the questions-and-answers. Such creeds were originally used in the closing stages of the instruction of converts prior to baptism. The earliest clear example is the creed of the Church of Caesarea in Palestine.

The Creed of Nicaea inaugurated a new era. The old creeds were creeds for converts, the new creed was for bishops; the old creeds had been local, the new one was to be universally binding. It took over from the old Rule of Faith as a test of orthodoxy.

INSTRUCTION BEFORE BAPTISM

At the birth of the church, converts were baptized with little or no delay (see for example Acts 8:36, 16:33). But soon a course of instruction prior to baptism became customary, especially for non-Jewish converts. Justin explained that before baptism: 'All those who are convinced and believe the things which are taught by us and said to be true, and promise to live accordingly, are instructed to pray and to call on God with fasting.'

Hippolytus of Rome again provides valuable evidence. A convert's occupation and personal relations were scrutinized, and then followed pre-

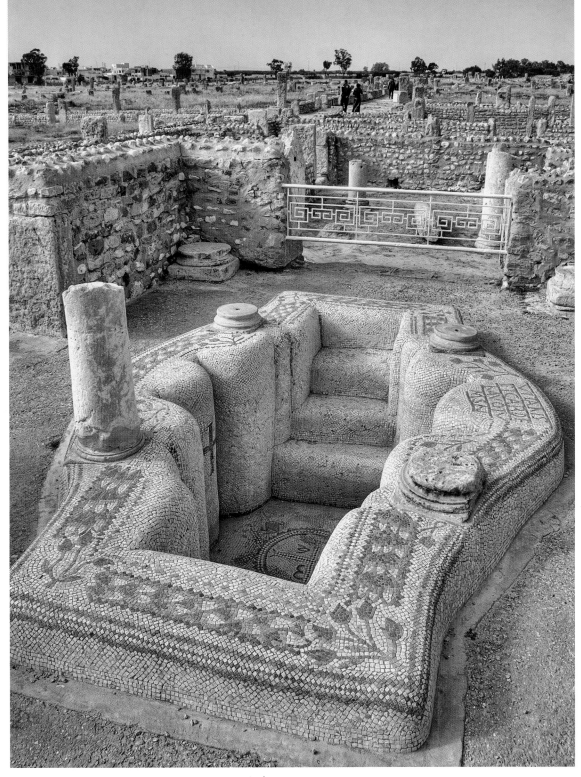

Baptistery of the Basilica of St Vitalis, Sufetula, modern Sbeïtla, Tunisia.
© MARCIN CIESIELSKI/SYLWIA CISEK/DREAMSTIME.COM

baptismal instruction, which took three years (even longer in Syria!). Good progress, or the imminence of persecution, could shorten the period. A convert who was martyred before baptism was regarded as experiencing a better 'baptism in blood'. More intensive preparations, including fasting, exorcism, and blessing, immediately preceded baptism. The converts were often taught by laymen, such as Justin in Rome and Origen in Alexandria, in independent Christian 'schools', which were also open to enquiring pagans.

By the fourth century, the clergy had taken over the instruction of converts ('catechumens'), and the bishop had become personally responsible for the concentrated teaching and discipline immediately before baptism. (Here lay the origins of Lent; from the second century baptisms normally took place at Easter.)

By now this period of preparation included the ceremonial 'handing over' of the creed, which the candidates would affirm in the baptismal questions-and-answers. After the bishop had explained it and the candidates had memorized it, they would 'give it back' in a later ceremony. The same was often done with the Lord's Prayer. These formulas were not presented in written form; they were treasured secrets to be concealed from the uninitiated, in the same way as what happened at the Lord's Supper. From this era survive several notable series of addresses delivered before, and immediately after, baptism.

Careful preparation for baptism was seen as essential, because baptism was commonly thought of as dealing with a person's past corruption, but not his or her future faults. This explains the practice of delaying baptism, the development of a system of penitence to cover sins after baptism, and even Tertullian's insistence on purity before baptism, with the result that baptism became almost a prize.

The systematic teaching of new converts along these lines flourished particularly in the great era of Christian expansion in the third and fourth centuries. As infant baptism became increasingly common, the practice faded. Little is known about the instruction of children within the early Christian community.

WHO LED THE CHURCH?

The first leaders of the church were the apostles, assisted in Jerusalem by 'the elders' (Acts 11:30, 14:23), and the practical help of the Seven (Acts 6:1–6). Other gifted and Spirit-filled individuals were prominent in the early decades: missionary preachers, evangelists (including some of the Seven), teachers, and prophets (see, for example, Acts 8:26, 11:27, 28, 12:25, 13:1). They were not normally officially appointed, but undertook a widely-recognized travelling ministry.

By the early second century, the Spirit-gifted leadership had largely disappeared. The *Didache* shows that, in one region, some prophetic teachers were settling down, others had become self-seeking, and 'bishops and deacons' were gaining new prominence. Nevertheless, the prophetic tradition continued with people such as Ignatius of Antioch, Hermas of Rome, Melito of Sardis, and the Montanists; and freelance teachers or philosophers still existed – such as Justin, Clement of Alexandria, Origen, and even Tertullian.

At an early stage local leaders emerged. Congregational life was directed by a team or group, commonly known as 'presbyters' – that is, elders or fathers in the faith (possibly based on Jewish or Old Testament models) – or 'bishops' (that is, guardians or overseers, probably derived from Hellenistic patterns, although there were interesting parallels in the ascetic community at Qumran). Other titles were also used: pastor or shepherd, teacher, deacon or servant, ruler, and president. The status and function of the different posts were still flexible; in earliest Christianity there was no counterpart to 'the minister' of today. Until at least the third century, churches met in small, house-based gatherings.

By the time of Ignatius (d. about 98–17) churches in Asia Minor were ruled by the 'three-fold ministry', consisting of a single bishop (Ignatius links his authority to that of the single God), a body of presbyters (patterned on the band of apostles), and several deacons (who 'served' as Christ did). This structure became universal before the third century, though the churches of Rome and Greece had no single bishop in Ignatius' day, nor did Alexandria until about AD 180.

The number of bishoprics varied considerably from region to region. Numerous small communities in Asia Minor and Africa acquired their own bishops; elsewhere, for example in Gaul, the bishop of a large town would supervise congregations in the surrounding area. About AD 250 the church at Rome still had only one bishop, together with forty-six presbyters, seven deacons, and seven sub-deacons, as well as forty-two 'acolytes' or attendants, and fifty-two exorcists, readers, and door-keepers.

The bishop gradually emerged as undisputed leader of the Christian community, which was brought about by a number of factors. Congregations often needed one from the group of presbyters or bishops to take the initiative, or represent them – for example, by presiding at the Lord's Supper, contacting other churches, teaching, or guarding church property and offerings. Also, one-person leadership was suggested by the roles played by the founding apostle or missionary, especially if he had settled in one place for an extended period; and by the single agents of the apostles, such as Timothy in Ephesus and Titus in Crete; and by James, who was apostle-cum-bishop-cum-high-priest of the Jerusalem Church. Some of their functions had to be continued in the churches.

HEIRS TO THE APOSTLES?

Clement of Rome urged the Christians at Corinth to preserve the arrangements made by the apostles for controlling the congregation's affairs. But this was simply the kind of provision any pioneer missionary organizes for the leadership of a new church.

The Gnostics soon began to appeal to a succession of teachers traced back to the apostles (normally Philip, Thomas, and Matthias) to whom, they claimed, Jesus entrusted secret wisdom before he ascended. Their views were countered by stressing the continuity of the open teaching (for instance, the Rule of Faith) and of teachers (bishops or presbyters) from the time when the apostles founded the churches.

This argument was first outlined by Hegesippus (c. 110–c. 180), who travelled from Palestine to Rome in the mid-second century, associated with numerous bishops, and heard (so he says) the same teaching from all. 'In every succession and city, what the law and the prophets and the Lord preached is faithfully followed.' He drew up succession-lists of bishops, at least for Corinth and Rome. He may also have taken note of the Jerusalem Church's attempt to maintain a hereditary leadership from among the 'relatives of the Lord', similar to the succession of Jewish high priests.

Irenaeus, Tertullian, and others in the West followed in the anti-Gnostic path mapped out by Hegesippus. They held that the succession of bishops stemming from the apostles guaranteed the unbroken handing-on of the apostles' doctrine. Irenaeus still felt close to living tradition; only the generations of Polycarp and John separated him from Jesus. But in fact the apostles had not appointed bishops in every church, and succession-lists of bishops were seriously unreliable.

Later the threat from the Gnostics receded, and lapse of time eroded the appeal to tradition. But apostolic succession was given a new lease of life, chiefly by Cyprian. Now the bishop became the basis and criterion of the church's life; being in the church was made dependent upon communion with the bishop. The apostles were now seen as the first bishops, and bishops were called apostles. Succession assumed a more mechanical character.

Cyprian's theory prevailed in the medieval West; but the East was never sold on the idea. For Cyprian, the 'one and undivided episcopate' was embodied in the provincial or pan-African councils he frequently called and presided over. In Africa and elsewhere, the provinces of the Roman Empire supplied the basis for the regions of the church. The provincial capital normally became the ecclesiastical centre, and its bishop enjoyed special status as metropolitan bishop.

CYPRIAN OF CARTHAGE

Cyprian became a Christian about AD 246, when he was already a rich and cultured man of Carthage, the chief city of Roman Africa, and probably destined for high government office. He now dedicated himself to celibacy, poverty, and the Bible with such distinction that within two years he was made Bishop of Carthage.

When the persecution of the Emperor Decius began in AD 250, Cyprian left the city. Many church leaders scorned flight from persecution, and Cyprian lost face. From his hiding-place he had difficulty restraining the 'confessors', Christians whose sufferings earned them great spiritual prestige. They were urging lenient treatment for 'lapsed' Christians who denied the faith under pressure. After Cyprian returned in AD 251, a council of bishops fixed stricter terms for readmitting them to the church, whereupon the dissidents split off. To oppose their action, Cyprian wrote his most important work, *The Unity of the Catholic Church*.

From AD 255 Cyprian defiantly opposed Stephen, Bishop of Rome, over the question whether Christian baptism could be received outside the catholic (mainstream) church. Cyprian believed that the Spirit's gifts of life and salvation were restricted to the Catholic Church. Unlike Stephen, he demanded that people baptized in separatist groups who entered the church should be rebaptized. The dispute faded after Stephen's death and Cyprian's exile and courageous martyrdom in AD 258.

Cyprian was above all a churchman; a clear-headed administrator but a simple theologian, whose writings deal with practical church matters. By calling regular councils of bishops, he put into practice his conviction that the church depended for its unity on their harmony and equality.

Cyprian believed that all bishops were in theory equal – just as the apostles had been. He regarded ministers as priests, and the Lord's Supper as the sacrifice of the cross, and tried to integrate the Spirit-dominated puritanism of Tertullian with the church of the bishops. Cyprian's pastoral zeal was best shown when he helped people during a terrible plague in AD 252–4.

DAVID F. WRIGHT

ROME TAKES THE LEAD

When Irenaeus presented his succession-list for the Church of Rome, he described it as: 'the very great, very ancient, and universally known church, founded and organized at Rome by the two most glorious apostles, Peter and Paul.' Because Christians from all parts were found there, it was a microcosm of the whole Christian world.

Irenaeus' statement hints at some of the reasons why Rome acquired a leading position among the churches. All roads led to Rome, the capital of the Empire, not least the roads that Christians travelled. A remarkable number of prominent Christians made their way to Rome: Ignatius, Polycarp, Marcion, Valentinus, Tatian, Justin, Hegesippus, Irenaeus, Tertullian, Praxeas and other Monarchians, and Origen – as well as Peter and Paul in the sixties.

Rome was the only Western Church to receive a letter from an apostle (and what a letter!). Luke's long, miraculous account of Paul's journey to Rome reflects the importance attached to his reaching the capital (Acts 27, 28). Nothing boosted the prestige of Christian Rome so much as the fact that the two chief apostles were martyred there under Nero. By the mid-second century, memorial shrines to Paul and Peter had been erected in Rome, on the Appian Way and the Vatican Hill respectively. Remains of the latter were uncovered in excavations during the 1950s and 1960s.

The Fall of Jerusalem in AD 70 enhanced the standing of the Roman Church in the long term. It now became almost impossible to evangelize the Jewish settlements in Parthia to the east, and Christianity's centre of gravity shifted west – where Rome was well suited to play a central role. However, the letter to the Church at Corinth known as *1 Clement* (c. AD 95–97) did not imply any Roman claim to superior authority.

Second-century Christianity in Rome appears very varied. It included independent schools like Justin's, and immigrant groups such as the Asians, who followed their traditional observance of the *Pascha*. Not until the 190s did a strong bishop emerge – Victor (r. AD 189-199), an African and the first Latin speaker. He threatened to excommunicate the Asian churches over the *Quartodeciman* dispute. Meanwhile the new succession-lists and the shrines of Peter and Paul bolstered a growing self-confidence, and the Roman bishop's attitude towards Montanism was widely noted.

In his dispute with Cyprian, Stephen (r. 254–257) was the first Bishop of Rome to claim a special authority derived from Peter by appealing to Matthew 16:18–19: 'And I tell you that you are Peter, and on this rock I will build my church, and the gates of Hades will not overcome it. I will give you the keys of the kingdom of heaven; whatever you bind on earth will be bound in heaven, and whatever you loose on earth will be loosed in heaven' (NIV). Paul's position alongside Peter in the earliest Roman church now began to be lost sight of. Cyprian regarded every bishop's seat as 'the see of Peter', although he admitted that the Roman Church had a special importance because it had been founded so early.

The Roman Church soon possessed considerable wealth, including the first of its underground burial-chambers (catacombs) outside the city, and several large houses whose upper floors were adapted for use as churches (*tituli*). Constantine's family enriched it by giving the Lateran Palace, and by erecting basilicas, including two as memorials to Peter and Paul. In the 270s, when the Emperor Aurelian was petitioned to settle a dispute about church property in Antioch, he allocated it 'to those with whom the bishops of the doctrine in Italy and Rome should communicate in writing', thus indicating their special authority.

During the fourth century, the Church of Rome and its bishop considerably enlarged their claims to first place in honour and jurisdiction. They benefited from reaction against excessive interference by the Emperor in Eastern Church affairs, and because Rome was consistently orthodox throughout the upheavals over doctrine in the East.

CHRISTIANS AND THE ROMAN STATE

Different attitudes towards the Roman Empire are evident in the earliest Christian writings, and a variety of views persisted into the second and third centuries. Following Romans 13 and Acts, apologists writing in defence of their faith stressed that the Christians were law-abiding citizens, who paid their taxes and prayed for the emperors. They did not serve in the armies, but engaged in a more effective spiritual warfare, and by prayer contributed to Rome's victory in just wars.

These writers attempted to demonstrate that those who did not worship the Roman gods could nevertheless be good Romans. They argued that the special connection between Roman religion and the Roman state should be broken, and that emperors should allow the practice of other religions, such as Christianity.

Some Christian writers falsely claimed that only corrupt emperors had persecuted the church. Some suggested that the church and Empire might have a common destiny; they began together (Jesus was born in the reign of the first Emperor, Augustus) and prospered together. They claimed that the peace won by the Emperor – the *Pax Romana* – was God-given to facilitate the spread of Christianity, 'the philosophy which goes with the Empire' (Melito).

Tertullian was less optimistic, and followed the apocalyptic tradition of the Revelation of John. He believed that the whole fabric of social and public life was fouled by idolatry, and that it was unthinkable that a Christian should enter the imperial service, let alone be an emperor. North African Christians generally displayed a more scornful and defiant attitude to Roman power. In AD 180 one of the six martyrs from Scillium declared, 'I do not recognize the empire of this world.'

During the first half of the third century, it became fashionable to combine the worship of different gods in one religion. Some of the emperors showed a particular interest in Christianity. The Emperor Alexander Severus (r. 222–235) reputedly included a representation of Jesus among the statues in his chapel. His mother had contact with Hippolytus and Origen, who also corresponded with the Emperor Philip the Arabian (r. 244–249) and his wife.

But Christianity first became the religion of kings and princes outside the Roman Empire. Royal families adopted the faith in Edessa, one of the chief centres of Syriac-speaking Christianity, in the early third century, and in Armenia and Georgia a century later.

DAVID F. WRIGHT

THE MANICHAEANS

Mani (AD 216–76), a Persian born in Mesopotamia, established a religion which claimed to be the final, universal revelation. This was a dualistic religion which maintained the sharp opposition between the principles of light and of darkness, like other Gnostic movements. Mani's followers, the Manichaeans, were zealous missionaries who carried their gospel to Africa, Europe, and even China. The Manichaeans posed a threat to the church in the fourth century, and numbered Augustine among their adherents prior to his conversion. The Manichaeans probably bequeathed some of their beliefs to heretical groups that flourished in Asia Minor and Europe in the Middle Ages.

MANI

Mani was brought up among a sect of Jewish Christians, but left them when he received 'revelations', calling himself 'the apostle of Jesus Christ'. Mani converted members of his family and commenced his far-flung ministry of more than thirty years. An early source describes Mani's appearance, with a book in one hand and a staff in the other (he may have been lame), and wearing flamboyant clothing – a blue cloak and red and green trousers. Mani preached in Mesopotamia and throughout Persia, and even reached India, allegedly delivering many from demons and diseases. Mani died in prison in AD 276, after which he was decapitated, and his corpse buried by his followers at Gundishapur, in south-west Persia.

Mani, a gifted painter, composed the *Ardahang*, a picture book, to propagate his faith among the illiterate. He also wrote seven works. Mani taught that there were two independent eternal principles: light and darkness, God and matter. In the first epoch, light and darkness were separate; in the second epoch they were intermingled; and in the final epoch they were to be separated once more. Jesus and other religious leaders came in order to release souls of light from the prison of their bodies.

The Manichaeans were sharply divided between an elite circle known as the 'elect' and the mass of lay people known as 'hearers'. The hearers lived the lives of ordinary citizens. They offered daily gifts of fruit, cucumbers, and melons – which were believed to possess a great deal of light – to the elect, who were ascetics and vegetarians. At death, the souls of the hearers were reborn as other people. Only the elect, who were distinguished by white robes, were eligible for offices and for the most sacred rites.

MANICHAEISM IN THE WEST

Manichaeism spread at an early date to Syria and Palestine, an army veteran bringing the new religion from Mesopotamia in AD 274. Their arrival in North Africa elicited Diocletian's harsh edict of AD 297, which condemned the Manichaeans as hostile Persian agents who were to be executed. After the spread of Manichaeism in many areas in the fourth century, the forceful refutations of Augustine of Hippo, his disciple Evodius, and other church leaders stemmed the tide. By the sixth century Manichaeism was in decline in the West.

The Paulician movement, which spread in Armenia from the seventh to the twelfth century, though it repudiated Manichaeism, resembled it in its dualist views. The Paulicians came to Bulgaria in the tenth century and helped to develop the Bogomils, who flourished in the Balkans in the eleventh and twelfth centuries. The latter movement in turn stimulated the Manichaean-like heresy of the Cathars, or Albigensians, who were widespread in southern France and northern Italy in the twelfth and thirteenth centuries. A crusade was proclaimed against them by Pope Innocent III in 1208, and by the fourteenth century, the last heirs of Manichaeism had finally been suppressed by the Inquisition.

EDWIN YAMAUCHI

CHAPTER 7

HOW THE FIRST CHRISTIANS WORSHIPPED

Since the first Christians came to faith in Jesus as Messiah and Lord out of a Jewish background, it is not surprising that Jewish influences are seen in the patterns of early Christian worship. The two great centres of Jewish worship, the Jerusalem Temple and the network of local synagogues throughout Palestine and the ancient world wherever Jews had scattered, handed on a recognizable legacy to the Christian church. The synagogue played the more dominant role in both Judaism and early Christianity. Its pattern of Scripture readings and sermon within a framework of praise and congregational prayers was taken over by the Jewish Christians. Luke 4:16–21 gives a valuable description of Jewish worship:

> ...on the Sabbath day he went into the synagogue, as was his custom. And he stood up to read. The scroll of the prophet Isaiah was handed to him. Unrolling it, he found the place where it is written: 'The Spirit of the Lord is on me...' [Isaiah 61:1, 2] Then he rolled up the scroll, gave it back to the attendant and sat down. The eyes of everyone in the synagogue were fastened on him, and he began by saying to them, 'Today this scripture is fulfilled in your hearing.'

Later, the apostles used the synagogue as a springboard for their evangelism and teaching. Scripture reading is referred to occasionally in the New Testament, and the sermons reported in the book of Acts give models of early Christian preaching, sometimes in synagogues.

PAUL ON WORSHIP

In 1 Corinthians, which gives probably the earliest description of worship in the Christian church, Paul constantly draws on the Old Testament. This letter, written about AD 55, pictures the church as the new Israel, living a pattern of the Christian life that is based on the new exodus. Paul uses ideas drawn from the Jewish Passover, which celebrated God's saving favour and strength in calling Israel to be his people, and rescuing them from tyranny in Egypt.

According to Paul, the church succeeded the old Jewish community, and combined both Jews and Greeks within God's one family of converted men and women. This fellowship of believers in Jesus stood at the dawn of a new age in God's dealings with the old Israel. They were the first generation of a new people in world history, marked out by their joyful awareness of living in a new relationship to God, and sharing in a new age of grace and power. All this was made possible through the gift of the Holy Spirit, which followed the resurrection and ascension of Jesus. This one fact of experience stamps New Testament worship as unique, however much the church owed to its Jewish inheritance.

That inheritance was, of course, considerable. Paul used the framework of the Passover meal to interpret the Lord's Supper. But other elements were also intertwined, such as the fellowship meal, called the *agape*, or 'love feast', which had its counterpart in Jewish table-customs. At public prayer, the response of *amen* (a Hebrew word meaning a confirming of what was being expressed in prayer) was the natural way to show agreement.

The setting of worship was 'the first day of the week'. This referred to the day of Christ's resurrection, as in the Gospels, and is distinct from the Jewish Sabbath. The Christian Sunday was not made a 'day of rest' until Constantine decreed it in AD 321. Paul also speaks about baptism, a rite of initiation with roots in Jewish washings for ceremonial purpose, and especially in the service of *tevilah*, the ritual 'bath' necessary for all converts to Judaism from paganism.

Several of these practices were being misused at Corinth, and Paul objected to their abuse and misunderstanding. Baptism should be in the name of Jesus, not in the name of Christian leaders, as if they were in charge of some cult. 'In the name of Jesus' meant that the new converts passed under his authority, and confessed him as Lord.

TWO SPECIAL MEALS

The love feast, or *agape* meal, had become an occasion for selfishness and drunkenness; Paul pointed to the breakdown of fellowship – which it was the purpose of both the *agape* and the Lord's Supper to promote. Paul believed the Lord's Supper served both to unite Christians with the Lord in his death and risen life, and to join believers in a bond of union as 'one body' in Christ. The excesses at Corinth destroyed both aims. By their greed and drunkenness, they were turning the meal into an orgy; by their superstitious attitude to the bread and wine, they were undermining Paul's teaching on the need for a personal receiving of Christ by faith and in love (I Corinthians 11).

> For I received from the Lord [the teaching] I also handed on to you, that the Lord Jesus on the night when he was betrayed took a loaf of bread, and when he had given thanks, broke it and said, 'This is my body that is for you. Do this in remembrance of me.' In the same way he took the cup also, after supper, saying, 'This cup is the new covenant in my blood. Do this, as often as you drink it, in remembrance of me.'
>
> 1 CORINTHIANS 11:23–25, NRSV

In addition, the enthusiasm of the Corinthian Christians led them to misuse 'ecstatic tongues' and other gifts of the Spirit. Paul tried to curb this, by insisting that worship must promote the healthy growth of the entire community of Christians. Personal whims and the private enjoyment of the gifts of the Spirit were to be brought firmly under control (I Corinthians 12).

Not all the features of early Christian worship at Corinth are clear. It is not known what 'baptism for the dead' implied (I Corinthians 15:29). Paul did not attach great importance to it, but used it simply to illustrate another matter. He also mentioned the 'holy kiss' (I Corinthians 16:20) without explanation.

SINGING AND PRAYERS

'Singing' with the mind and with the spirit indicates a musical side to the meeting, but references to musical instruments do not make it clear whether they were used in worship (I Corinthians 14:15). Exactly what these hymns were, and whether snatches of them have survived, is unclear. Passages such as Philippians 2:6–11, Colossians 1:15–20, and I Timothy 3:16 contain what may be early hymns, offered, as later among Christians in Bithynia about AD 112, to Christ as to God. Ephesians 5:14 is the most likely example of a hymn from the churches instructed by Paul. The setting of that three-line invocation is clearly a service of baptism:

> *Sleeper, awake!*
> *Rise from the dead,*
> *and Christ will shine on you.* (NRSV)

Prayers, whether very short like *Maranatha*, meaning 'Our Lord, come' (I Corinthians 16:22), or longer, played an important part in worship at Corinth. Problems arose concerning women who attempted to pray with uncovered heads. Paul resisted this practice, though he freely granted the right of women believers to act as prophets and leaders of prayer in the assembled church (I Corinthians 11:2–16).

Both prophesying and praying are gifts of the Spirit. The freedom that the Corinthians were exercising to the full was to be held in check. Paul crisply summed up: 'Let all things be done decently and in order' (I Corinthians 14:40).

Evidence about Christian worship from writers who lived between the time of Paul and the middle of the second century is scarce and difficult to piece together. Worship gradually became more formal and stereotyped in the period following Paul's death. Bishops and deacons possibly helped in this trend. New converts (catechumens) were given instruction in preparation for baptism. Worship forms connected with this have been seen in such writings as I Peter and I John.

Short snatches of an elementary creed are found in such verses as Romans 10:9 ('Jesus is Lord'); later examples are lengthened and developed, as in I Timothy 3:16 and I Peter 3:18–22:

> *For Christ died for our sins once for all, the righteous for the unrighteous, to bring you to God. He was put to death in the body but made alive by the Spirit, through whom also he went and preached to the spirits in prison who disobeyed long ago when God waited patiently in the days of Noah while the ark was being built. In it only a few people, eight in all, were saved through water, and this water symbolizes baptism that now saves you also — not the removal of dirt from the body but the pledge of a good conscience towards God. It saves you by the resurrection of Jesus Christ, who has gone into heaven and is at God's right hand — with angels, authorities, and powers in submission to him.*

STATEMENTS OF FAITH

The rise of false teaching, against which the letters of John were written, required Christians to state their faith in Jesus Christ as true man and true God. This was to counteract the Docetists, who denied Christ's humanity, and the Ebionites, who threw doubt on Jesus' unique status as Son of God.

At first, when a person was baptized he or she affirmed a creed which was concerned mainly with statements about Christ's person, as in the addition to the text at Acts 8:37: 'I believe that Jesus Christ is the Son of God'. Examples of more formal creeds, stating belief in the three persons of the Godhead, which goes back to the baptismal commission recorded in Matthew 28:19 ('… make disciples of all nations, baptizing them in the name of the Father and of the Son and of the Holy Spirit…'), occur in descriptions of baptismal services reported by Irenaeus and Hippolytus of Rome. The Apostles' Creed derives from the late second-century baptismal creed used in Rome.

The puzzling document known as the *Didache* probably originated in the Syrian churches in the late first or early second century. It consists of a moral tract concerning the 'Two Ways' – of life and of death – followed by sections about early procedures for baptism, the *agape*, and the Lord's Supper. It is clear that the *agape* and Lord's Supper included set prayers and were celebrated during a public gathering on the Lord's day, when Christians assembled 'to break bread and give thanks'. This was preceded by the confession of sins and offering of gifts.

Clement of Rome also provides evidence that Sunday worship was becoming formalized. Clement included a great prayer of intercession, drawn from the church's liturgy (a word used for the form of service, normally the Lord's Supper), in his letter *1 Clement* (late first/early second century). He also insisted that worthy celebration of the Lord's Supper is possible only when conducted by church leaders, called bishops or presbyters.

Ignatius also emphasized that the eucharist is the focal point of the church's unity, and so must be celebrated only under the authorized church leader, the bishop or his delegate. Ignatius' letters shed much light on early Christian worship, and include an early hymn to Christ and an explanation of the meaning of the Lord's day.

The correspondence between the Emperor Trajan and Pliny, the governor of Bithynia (AD 111–113), reveals that Christians used to meet for public worship on a 'fixed day' (Sunday) before sunrise. They would join in a hymn sung responsively, offered

Instructions for worship and leadership

On Sunday, the Lord's own day, come together, break bread, and carry out the eucharist, first confessing your sins so that your offering may be pure. Let no one who has a quarrel with his friend join the meeting until they have been reconciled, so that your offering is not polluted. For this is the offering spoken of by the Lord: 'Everywhere and at all times offer me a pure sacrifice. For my kingdom is great, says the Lord, and my name is wonderful among the nations.'

Appoint for yourselves therefore bishops and deacons worthy of the Lord; men who are meek and not money-lovers, true and approved, for they also perform for you the ministry of prophets and teachers. So do not despise them; they are the honourable men among you, together with the prophets and teachers.

DIDACHE 14:1–15:1

An outsider's view of Christian worship

They were in the habit of meeting on a certain fixed day before it was light, when they sang an anthem to Christ as God, and bound themselves by a solemn oath (*sacramentum*) not to commit any wicked deed, but to abstain from all fraud, theft, and adultery, never to break their word, or deny a trust when called upon to honour it; after which it was their custom to separate, and then meet again to partake of food, but food of an ordinary and innocent kind.

PLINY, *LETTERS* X.96; AD 112

A service in second-century Rome

At the end of the prayers, we greet one another with a kiss. Then the president of the brethren is brought bread and a cup of wine mixed with water; and he takes them, and offers up praise and glory to the Father of the universe, through the name of the Son and of the Holy Ghost, and gives thanks at considerable length for our being counted worthy to receive these things at his hands. When he has concluded the prayers and thanksgivings, all the people present express their joyful assent by saying Amen. ('Amen' means 'so be it' in Hebrew) … Then those whom we call deacons give to each of those present the bread and wine mixed with water over which the thanksgiving was pronounced, and carry away a portion to those who are absent.

We call this food 'eucharist', which no one is allowed to share unless he or she believes the things which we teach are true, and has been washed with the washing that is for remission of sins and into a second birth, and is living as Christ has commanded. For we do not receive them as ordinary bread and ordinary drink; but as Jesus Christ our Saviour, having been made flesh by the word of God, had both flesh and blood for our salvation; similarly we have been taught that the food which is blessed by the word of prayer transmitted from him, and by which our blood and flesh are changed and nourished, is the flesh and blood of that Jesus who was made flesh. For the apostles, in the memoirs called Gospels composed by them, have delivered to us what was enjoined upon them; that Jesus took bread, and when he had given thanks, said, 'This do in remembrance of me, this is my body'; and that, in a similar way, having taken the cup and given thanks, he said, 'This is my blood'; and gave it to them alone.

JUSTIN, *APOLOGY* 1:65–66; AD 150

to Christ 'as God', and vowed to renounce all practices inconsistent with their Christian faith. They shared 'holy meals', and it seems that by now the *agape* had been separated from the Lord's Supper. In fact, continuing abuse of the love feast led to its gradual disappearance in its original form, while the solemn meal of 'holy communion' was given more and more significance as a sacrament. Ignatius described it as 'a medicine of immortality, the antidote that we should not die, but live for ever in Jesus Christ'.

LATER PATTERNS OF WORSHIP

The Christians gradually standardized their worship and gave increasing prominence to the Lord's Supper as the focal point of the liturgy. From the time of Justin Martyr to Athanasius, three major descriptions offer new evidence.

Justin's *First Apology*, written about AD 150, contains what has been called 'the oldest systematic description of Sunday worship', based on practices in the Church in Rome at that time. In Justin's day, Christian worship was becoming distinctively ecclesiastical, by shedding its Jewish elements, though the framework was still modelled on that of the synagogue. The domestic atmosphere of the Passover meal was giving way to formality, and a new vocabulary was introduced to give a more other-worldly, even transcendental, character to worship.

For Justin, the act of communion was a 'memorial of the passion' of Christ. The elements of bread and wine over which thanks had been given nourished the lives of Christians by assimilation – a thought derived from Jesus' teaching in John 6:25–58. This idea played a growing role in explanations of the eucharist as a sacramental sharing in the divine life. Justin and Irenaeus possibly allude to a special prayer, later known as the *epiclesis*, which 'called upon' the divine Word to come upon the bread and wine. It is not surprising that, especially among Gnostics, magical ideas about the nature of the consecrated elements began to emerge. Irenaeus also wrote of the 'altar in heaven' to which prayer and offerings were directed.

Justin's evidence is important for other reasons. He described the framework of Scripture readings as including 'the memoirs of the apostles' (that is, the Gospels of the New Testament), the exposition delivered by the presiding leader, prayers for all people, offered standing, and the kiss of peace. This 'service of the word' (as it was later called) led into the eucharist itself, when bread and wine were presented to the leader, who offered a thanksgiving prayer extempore, to which the congregation assented with 'Amen'. The deacons handed the bread and wine to all present, and arranged to have them distributed to those believers who were absent. A collection was taken, looked after by the leader and then distributed to those in need.

Evidently, what has come to be regarded as a service of worship was already more or less fixed in Justin's time. It soon became clear, as Origen implies, that the first part of the service was open to converts under instruction, and probably enquirers too, but the second part restricted to baptized communicants. This distinction became standard, with a clear dividing-line between the two parts – particularly in the Syrian *Apostolic Constitutions* and later in Chrysostom's writings.

The *Apostolic Tradition* of Hippolytus, usually dated about AD 215, contains a full account of the ordaining and ordering of ministers, and also includes much interesting information about baptism. However, its chief value lies in its teaching about the eucharist. The Holy Spirit was invoked on 'the offering of the church', but this was more a prayer for the Christians in their act of offering than for the elements themselves. The bishop who laid his hand on the offering was to do so 'with all the presbyters' sharing with him: the act clearly involved both the bishop and the presbyters.

The Sacramentary of Serapion (who was an Egyptian bishop at the time of Athanasius) was written primarily for bishops, but gives interesting general descriptions of worship and particularly prayer. The Word (Logos) is asked to come upon the offerings to make them 'the body of the Word', 'the blood of the Truth'. The bread on the church's altar is believed to *become* 'the likeness of the holy body' of the Lord.

RALPH P. MARTIN

HOW THE NEW TESTAMENT CAME DOWN TO US

An overwhelming number of handwritten texts are available for studying the New Testament in the original Greek. A recent count lists more than 120 papyri (manuscripts made of papyrus, and generally the earliest), around 300 uncial manuscripts (written in Greek capital letters, generally on leather), and more than 2,900 minuscule manuscripts (written in cursive Greek script, and usually later in date than uncials). In addition, there are more than 2,450 lectionary manuscripts – church reading books which contain the parts of the Gospels and letters to be read on fixed days of the church year. But most of these manuscripts date from the eighth century or later, and few have been studied in detail.

The earliest complete New Testament manuscript still available is the *Codex Sinaiticus*, which dates from the fourth century, and is now in the British Library, London. 'Codex' is the name for an early form of book, made by sewing leaves of writing material together. *Codex Vaticanus*, from which a few leaves are missing at the end of the New Testament, dates from the same period and has been housed in the Vatican Library, Rome, since at least the fifteenth century.

Less complete New Testament manuscripts date back as early as the late second or early third century, and one fragment of the Gospel of John (the Rylands Library Papyrus P52, now at the John Rylands University Library, Manchester) dates from approximately AD 130. The Chester Beatty Papyri contain parts of the Gospels, Acts, Paul's letters, Hebrews, and Revelation, and date from the first half of the third century. Bodmer Papyrus II (P66), dating from about AD 200, has significant fragments of John's Gospel; other papyri in this collection, from about AD 175–225, contain parts of Luke and John, as well as the letters of Peter and Jude.

Codex Alexandrinus, from about the fifth century, another important early manuscript containing most of the New Testament, is also now in the British Library. *Codex Bezae*, from the fifth century, contains most of the Gospels and Acts, in Greek and Latin on facing pages, and is now in Cambridge, England; *Codex Washingtonianus*, dating from the fourth or fifth century, includes nearly all of the four Gospels, and is now in Washington DC.

St Catherine's Monastery, in the Sinai Peninsula, one of the oldest monasteries in the world. The German archaeologist Constantin von Tischendorf retrieved part of the *Codex Sinaiticus* manuscript of the New Testament here in the mid-nineteenth century.
TIM DOWLEY ASSOCIATES

Scholars examine these Greek manuscripts in the following ways:

- By attempting to date and place a manuscript by its style of writing and other clues.
- By looking for any divergences from other manuscripts in its text.
- By discovering relationships between manuscripts, they work out how far they agree with each other. More exact methods for measuring the amount of agreement between manuscripts have been developed.

Manuscripts with significant amounts of agreement are grouped into 'text-types'. So far, four possible main text-types have been found:

1. The Alexandrian, Neutral, or Egyptian text-type, which underlies most modern New Testament translations
2. The Western text-type, found particularly in Old Latin translations from the Greek
3. The Byzantine, Syrian, Ecclesiastical, Traditional, Constantinopolitan, Majority, or Antiochian text-type, the standard text in the Greek Orthodox Church, and underlying most Protestant translations of the Reformation era.
4. The Caesarean text-type suggested by some scholars to be found in certain Greek manuscripts of the Gospel

GETTING BACK TO THE ORIGINAL TEXT

The main aim of all this detailed work is to establish a Greek text which is as close as possible to the wording of the New Testament documents as they first came from the hands of the authors. For those Christians for whom the Bible's teaching is the starting-point, exact theological thinking depends upon an accurate Greek New Testament. In addition, scholars are trying to discover how the history of the church may have affected the copying of the New Testament text.

The overwhelming mass of variations in the many manuscripts studied consist of accidental spelling differences or omissions. But some variations are clearly deliberate, most of them seemingly attempts to 'im-prove' the style, to remove ambiguity, or sometimes to harmonize parallel accounts in different books.

A few of the variations appear to be caused by a copyist's concern about doctrine. For example, in Mark 3:21, the original text seems to suggest that Jesus' friends or relatives were worried about his sanity ('…people were saying 'He has gone out of his mind'' NRSV). This appears to have embarrassed some scribes; in some early manuscripts they have changed the wording so it is the crowd – not his family – who try to seize Jesus, and the worry is about the excitement of the crowd rather than Jesus' sanity. Because of its rather non-literary Greek, Mark's Gospel appears to have suffered most often from these kinds of deliberate alterations during copying.

COPYING THE NEW TESTAMENT

Clearly the New Testament writings were considered important in the early church, since many copies were made – for private reading as well as church use. However, though the writings were considered important, this did not always guarantee scrupulous, exact copying of them. While no manuscript is free of either accidental or deliberate variations, some manuscripts seem to reflect a more careful tradition of copying, while others reveal a much freer attitude towards the actual words of the New Testament.

Several translations of the New Testament were made at an early date, the most important of which are the Syriac, Latin, and Coptic. There was an intense interest in making the New Testament available to different language-groups in the Roman world. These translated versions can often show how the New Testament was interpreted during the second and third centuries and later, when they were first produced. But these translations were not always prepared by people with a good command of Greek, and are often very imperfect.

Quotations from the New Testament in the works of some of the early Christian writers can also help in studying the New Testament text. But these early writers were often very free in their use of the New Testament, and quoted from memory, or merely para-

Can the New Testament text be trusted?

Perhaps we can appreciate how wealthy the New Testament is in manuscript attestation if we compare the textual material for other ancient historical works. For Caesar's *Gallic War* (composed between 58 and 50 BC) there are several extant manuscripts, but only nine or ten are good, and the oldest is some 900 years later than Caesar's day. Of the 142 books of the *Roman History* of Livy (59 BC–AD 17) only thirty-five survive; these are known to us from not more than twenty manuscripts of any consequence, only one of which, and that containing fragments of Books iii–vi, is as old as the fourth century. Of the fourteen books of the *Histories* of Tacitus (about AD 100) only four and a half survive; of the sixteen books of his *Annals*, ten survive in full and two in part. The text of these extant portions of his two great historical works depends entirely on two manuscripts, one of the ninth century and one of the eleventh. The extant manuscripts of his minor works (*Dialogus de Oratoribus*, *Agricola*, *Germania*) all descend from a codex of the tenth century. The *History* of Thucydides (about 460–400 BC) is known to us from eight manuscripts, the earliest belonging to around AD 900, and a few papyrus scraps, belonging to about the beginning of the Christian era. The same is true of the *History* of Herodotus (about 488–428 BC). Yet no classical scholar would listen to an argument that the authenticity of Herodotus or Thucydides is in doubt because the earliest manuscripts of their works which are of any use to us are over 1,300 years later than the originals.

But how different is the situation of the New Testament in this respect! In addition to the two excellent manuscripts of the fourth century ... which are the earliest of some thousands known to us, considerable fragments remain of papyrus copies of books of the New Testament dated from 100 or 200 years earlier still. The Chester Beatty Biblical Papyri, the existence of which was made public in 1931, consist of portions of eleven papyrus codices, three of which contained most of the New Testament writings. One of these, containing the four Gospels with Acts, belongs to the first half of the third century; another, containing Paul's letters to churches and the Epistle to the Hebrews, was copied at the beginning of the third century; the third, containing Revelation, belongs to the second half of the same century.

Earlier still is a fragment of a papyrus codex containing John 28:31–33, 37ff., now in the John Rylands University Library, Manchester dated on palaeographical grounds around AD 130.

F.F. BRUCE, *THE NEW TESTAMENT DOCUMENTS*

phrased the passage, which makes it difficult to decide what type of New Testament text they used. The early Christians revered and used the New Testament greatly, but did not treat the exact wording with care.

From the time they were first produced, the New Testament writings were always closely linked with the church and its worship, evangelism, beliefs, and institutions. The information available concerning the New Testament in the early period shows how New Testament Scripture and the church interacted and affected each other at that time. The church was concerned to make Scripture widely available; some of the variations in early New Testament manuscripts reveal a concern over misunderstanding of Scripture, or perhaps misuse by heretics.

LARRY W. HURTADO

The Early Church Recognizes the New Testament

All dates approximate

AD 100

Different parts of our New Testament were written by this time, but not yet collected and defined as 'Scripture'. Early Christian writers such as Polycarp and Ignatius quote from the Gospels and Paul's letters, as well as from other Christian writings and oral sources. Paul's letters were collected late in the first century. Matthew, Mark, and Luke were brought together by AD 150.

AD 200

New Testament used in the Church at Rome (the 'Muratorian Canon')

Four Gospels; Acts; Paul's letters; Romans; 1 & 2 Corinthians; Galatians; Ephesians; Philippians; Colossians; 1 & 2 Thessalonians; 1 & 2 Timothy; Titus; Philemon; James; 1 & 2 John; Jude; Revelation of John; Revelation of Peter; Wisdom of Solomon

To be used in private, but not public, worship

The Shepherd of Hermas

AD 250

New Testament used by Origen

Four Gospels; Acts; Paul's letters:; Romans; 1 & 2 Corinthians; Galatians; Ephesians; Philippians; Colossians; 1 & 2 Thessalonians; 1 & 2 Timothy; Titus; Philemon; 1 Peter; 1 John; Revelation of John

Disputed

Hebrews; James; 2 Peter; 2 & 3 John; Jude; The Shepherd of Hermas; Letter of Barnabas; Teaching of Twelve Apostles; Gospel of the Hebrews

AD 300

New Testament used by Eusebius

Four Gospels; Acts; Paul's letters:; Romans; 1 & 2 Corinthians; Galatians; Ephesians; Philippians; Colossians; 1 & 2 Thessalonians; 1 & 2 Timothy; Titus; Philemon; 1 Peter; 1 John; Revelation of John (*authorship in doubt*)

Disputed but well known

James; 2 Peter; 2 & 3 John; Jude

To be excluded

The Shepherd of Hermas; Letter of Barnabas; Gospel of the Hebrews; Revelation of Peter; Acts of Peter; Didache

AD 400

New Testament fixed for the West by the Council of Carthage

Four Gospels; Acts; Paul's letters; Romans; 1 & 2 Corinthians; Galatians; Ephesians; Philippians; Colossians; 1 & 2 Thessalonians; 1 & 2 Timothy; Titus; Philemon; Hebrews; James; 1 & 2 Peter; 1, 2 & 3 John; Jude; Revelation

FURTHER READING

JESUS

Richard A. Burridge, *Four Gospels, One Jesus? A Symbolic Reading*, 2nd ed., London/Grand Rapids 2004.

Richard A. Burridge, *What are the Gospels? A Comparison with Graeco-Roman Biography*, 2nd ed., Grand Rapids, 2005.

Richard A. Burridge, *Imitating Jesus: An Inclusive Approach to New Testament Ethics*, Grand Rapids, 2007.

Graham N. Stanton, *The Gospels and Jesus*, 2nd ed., Oxford, 2002.

E. P. Sanders, *The Historical Figure of Jesus*, London, 1993.

N. T. Wright, *Jesus and the Victory of God*, London, 1996.

THE EARLY CHURCH

Ivor J. Davidson, *The Birth of the Church: From Jesus to Constantine AD 30–312*, Oxford, 2004.

W. H. C. Frend, *The Rise of Christianity*, London, 1984

J. Stevenson ed., rev. W. H. C. Frend, *A New Eusebius, Documents Illustrating the History of the Church to AD 337*, London, 1987.

Frances Young, *The Making of the Creeds*, London, 1991.

STUDY QUESTIONS

1.   Why was the destruction of Jerusalem in AD 70 significant for Christianity?

2.   What factors influenced the recognition of the New Testament canon?

3.   What was the *Pax Romana* and did it impact the growth of Christianity?

4.   Why and how did Judaism and Christianity divide?

5.   When and why did the Roman state oppress Christians?

6.   How does archaeology inform our knowledge of the early church?

7.   Who were the Gnostics and how did they threaten the early church?

8.   Describe the main elements of Christian worship in the first three centuries.

9.   To which regions had the Christian faith spread by AD 300?

10.   What was the impact of Hellenistic philosophy on Christian theology?

2 Acceptance and Conquest

AD 325–600

Summary

Christianity was given official recognition as a 'legitimate religion' by the Roman state in 313, when Constantine, a recent convert, was joint emperor. From that point onwards, Christianity became not merely a recognized faith, but the official religion of the Roman Empire.

This period of Christian history was marked by a number of controversies over the identity of Jesus Christ and the Christian doctrine of God. A series of councils was convened to resolve these differences, and to ensure the unity of the Christian church throughout the Empire. The most important of these was the Council of Chalcedon (451), which set out the definitive Christian interpretation of the biblical witness to the identity of Jesus Christ as 'true God and true man'.

The fall of the Roman Empire – traditionally dated to 476 – led to widespread insecurity within the Western Church. In the East, the church continued to flourish, as the Eastern Empire, based at Constantinople, was largely unaffected by the attacks from northern European invaders which eventually terminated Roman power in the West. The removal of Rome as a stabilizing influence, however, gave a new role to the church in the West, and particularly to its monasteries. The founding of the first Benedictine monastery at Monte Cassino around 525 is widely seen as a landmark in this process. The increasingly important role of the pope as a political force also began to emerge during this period.

CHAPTER 8

CONSTANTINE AND THE CHRISTIAN EMPIRE
Christianity recognized

Momentous changes occurred in both the church and the political structure of the West during the fourth, fifth, and sixth centuries. The Western Roman Empire disappeared under the repeated assaults of the German barbarian tribes on its northern frontier. Christianity, a persecuted minority faith at Constantine's conversion in AD 312, had become the religion of the Empire by the end of the fourth century. The Bishop of Rome, whose leadership in the church had been largely a primacy of honour, now claimed supreme and universal authority in Christian lands and began to make good this claim in the West, at least over the church. By the time of Pope Gregory I ('Gregory the Great', r. 590–604) the collapse of the Western Empire left the Roman bishop the real ruler of much of central Italy.

THE CONVERSION OF CONSTANTINE

Throughout the fourth century, relations between the church, the emperor, and pagan religion were changing continually. Constantine's defeat of Maxentius at the Battle of the Milvian Bridge in the autumn of 312, and his interpretation of that victory as the response of the Christian God to his prayer for help, propelled church and state into a new age for which neither was prepared. Out of this new relationship between Christian church and Christian emperor stemmed the turbulent history of church/state relations in the later Roman Empire and throughout the Middle Ages.

Constantine's account of his conversion, told by the emperor himself to the church historian Eusebius of Caesarea towards the end of his life, is well known. Constantine, alarmed by reports of

A giant sculpted white marble head of Constantine the Great (c. 280–337), Rome, Italy, from a colossal statue that once stood in the Roman Forum.
© RON CHAPPLE/DREAMSTIME.COM

Maxentius' mastery of magical arts, prayed to the 'Supreme God' for help. The response was a sign, a cross in the noonday sky 'above the sun', and with it the words, 'Conquer by this.' That night Christ appeared to Constantine in a dream and commanded him to use the sign – apparently Chi-Rho, the initial letters of the name of Christ – 'as a safeguard in all engagements with his enemies'. According to the historian Lactantius, Constantine put this sign on the shields of his solders, and then marched on Rome, confronted Maxentius – who was miraculously induced to fight outside the city fortifications – and conquered.

This story has been doubted. But Constantine's attitude towards the Christian church after he became emperor, and his new laws, demonstrate that his allegiance to Christianity was genuine, though his understanding of the Christian faith was at first no doubt imperfect. Indeed, Constantine did retain the pagan high priest's title of *Pontifex Maximus*; for a decade his coins continued to feature some of the pagan gods, notably his own favourite deity, the Unconquered Sun; and he delayed Christian baptism until the end of his life. However, delayed baptism was the custom of the age, a device for avoiding mortal sin; and retaining the pagan symbols was a necessary compromise with his pagan subjects, still very much in the majority.

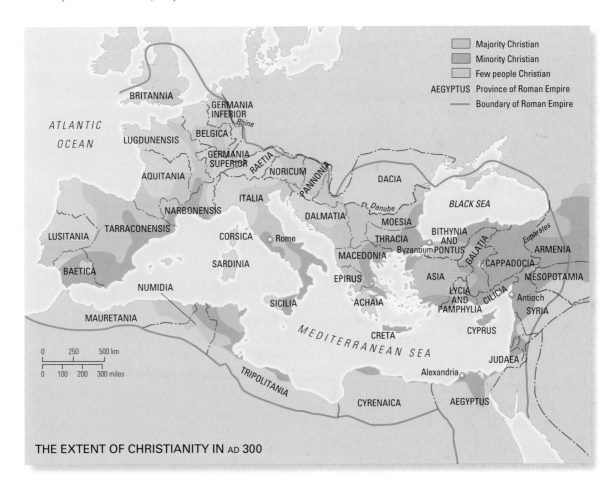

THE EXTENT OF CHRISTIANITY IN AD 300

Constantine treated Christianity as the favoured, though not yet the official, religion of the Empire. He granted immunities to the clergy and lavished gifts on the church; in his letters and edicts he spoke as if the Christian God were his own.

It is important to understand Constantine's previous religion, the worship of the Unconquered Sun. If the story of the cross in the sky is true, he may have interpreted the sign as his own special deity commending the worship of the Christian God. Perhaps Constantine continued to identify the sun with the Christian God in some way – a belief made easier by the tendency of Christian writers and artists to use sun imagery in portraying Christ. For them, Christ is the source of light and salvation; a mosaic from a third-century tomb found under St Peter's, Rome, even shows him as the sun god in his chariot. When in 321 Constantine made the first day of the week a holiday, he called it 'the venerable day of the Sun' (Sunday).

Another result of Constantine's conversion was renewed interest in the Holy Land by people in the West. Since the failure of the Second Jewish Revolt of Bar Kokhba (132–35), Jerusalem had been a pagan city; Constantine and his mother Helena now made it into a Christian city. The traditional place of Jesus' burial was found beneath the Emperor Hadrian's Temple of Venus, and Helena discovered what was believed to be the 'True Cross' on which Jesus had been crucified. Here – with the Church of the Holy Sepulchre – and elsewhere, Constantine and Helena built churches, and pilgrims came in increasing numbers to the holy places.

CHRISTIANITY AND PAGAN CUSTOMS

The Christian church began to take over many pagan ideas and images. From sun-worship, for example, came the celebration of Christ's birth on 25 December, the birthday of the Sun. *Saturnalia*, the Roman winter festival of 17–21 December, provided the merriment, gift-giving, and candles typical of later Christmas holidays. Sun-worship hung on in Roman Christianity, and Pope Leo I, in the mid-fifth century, rebuked worshippers who turned round to bow to the sun before entering St Peter's Basilica in Rome. Some pagan customs which were later Christianized, for example the use of candles, incense, and garlands, were initially avoided by the church because they symbolized paganism.

THE VIRGIN MARY

The veneration of the Virgin Mary was probably stimulated by parallels in pagan religion. Some scholars believe the worship of Artemis (Diana) was transferred to Mary. Ephesus, a city which belonged to Artemis until the end of the pagan era, was also associated with Mary from an early date.

Many people connected Mary with Isis, the Egyptian goddess, whose worship had spread throughout the Empire in the Christian era. In her travels, Isis became identified with many other goddesses, including Artemis, and was the 'universal mother' of later pagan religion. The devotees of Isis, herself called 'the Great Virgin', 'Mother of the God', and 'Queen of Heaven', naturally tended to look to Mary for comfort when paganism was outlawed and their temples were destroyed at the end of the fourth century. Some surviving images of Isis holding the child Horus are in a pose remarkably similar to that of some early Christian madonnas. However, the original aim of such titles for Mary as 'bearer of God' (Greek, *Theotokos*) was to honour the divine Son.

SAINTS AND MARTYRS

The cult of saints and martyrs grew rapidly in the fourth century, another example of the blending of the old paganism with Christianity. Chapels and even churches began to be built over the tombs of martyrs, a practice which influenced church architecture. Competition for saintly corpses soon degenerated into a superstitious search for relics, and in parts of the East it sometimes became a fight for the bodies of saintly hermits, still alive but expected to expire shortly. Although the cult arose among the people, it was approved and encouraged by the great Christian leaders of the age – Jerome, Ambrose, and Augustine. Ambrose, for instance, discovered the bodies of several forgotten saints.

The Christian historian Theodoret of Cyrrhus, Syria (c. 393–c. 457) boasted that in many places saints and martyrs took the place of pagan gods, and their shrines the place of pagan temples. Saints were claimed variously to cure barrenness, protect travellers, detect perjury, foretell the future, and heal the sick. Particularly popular was the shrine near Alexandria of St Cyrus and St John, physicians who in their earthly practice charged no fees. To the shrine of St Felix of Nola, who was believed to detect perjury, Augustine sent two clergymen who had accused each other, to discover which was lying.

The church never went as far as to teach that saints were to be worshipped, but it was suggested that they were in a special position to hear petitions and present them directly to God. The saint's position in heaven was compared to that of the great man at court, who might be expected to get results for a lowly petitioner, by presenting his request directly to the emperor.

Augustine and others protested against abuses of the traffic in relics. In 401, an African church council insisted that, before a chapel was consecrated, the saint or martyr celebrated must be proved genuine. We have only one surviving suggestion by an orthodox Christian that attachment to shrines or relics marked a return to pagan superstition. Vigilantius, an obscure priest from Aquitaine, wrote:

> *We almost see the rites of the pagans introduced into the churches under the pretext of religion; ranks of candles are lit in full daylight; and everywhere people kiss and adore some bit of dust in a little pot, wrapped in a precious fabric.*

Vigilantius' protest survived only because some outraged priests sent a copy to Jerome, who refuted it in a typically scathing reply.

CONSTANTINE AND THE CHURCH

'What has the Emperor to do with the church?' retorted Bishop Donatus famously, when presented with an unfavourable decree from the Emperor Constans (r. 337–350). Most of the conflict between church and state during the fourth century relates to this question. From the very beginning of Constantine's reign, most Christians agreed with the Emperor that he had a great deal to do with the church.

THE DONATIST DIVISION

Although they later complained about the Emperor's interference, it was the Donatists who first asked Constantine to intervene, less than six months after his victory over Maxentius. The Donatists were a strict party in North Africa, who refused to recognize Caecilian as bishop of Carthage because, they alleged, he had been ordained by a *traditor*, one who had 'handed over' or 'betrayed' Scriptures to the authorities in the recent persecution.

Constantine did not hesitate to accept jurisdiction, although he referred the matter to a council of bishops. When the Donatists refused to accept the authority of this and a subsequent council, the Emperor lost patience and threatened to go to Africa to set things right himself:

> *I am going to make plain to them what kind of worship is to be offered to God ... What higher duty have I as emperor than to destroy error and repress rash indiscretions, and so cause all to offer to Almighty God true religion, honest concord, and due worship?*

Though the visit to Africa did not materialize, Constantine ordered the Donatist churches to be confiscated and their leaders banished. The Donatists resisted tenaciously – over the years producing a host of martyrs – and Constantine soon realized that his policy of repression was futile and revoked it. Despite intermittent attempts to root them out, the Donatists survived for three centuries; they only disappeared with the obliteration of Christianity in North Africa after the Muslim conquest.

The Roman Emperor, as head of the state religion, had always been responsible for maintaining good relations between the people and their gods, and Constantine naturally saw himself in a similar role as Christian Emperor. He believed strife in the church, such as the Donatist and Arian controversies, was likely to bring down the wrath of the Christian God on him and the people entrusted to his care.

The willingness of the church to accept, indeed to ask for, the intervention of the Emperor in matters so clearly outside his expert knowledge is surprising. The explanation is in part the self-interested desire of one faction or another to gain advantage in the various desperate struggles of the fourth century. Another problem for the church was that the only precedent for the role of a Christian emperor was that of the Old Testament kings of Israel, who had a great deal to do with maintaining peace and purity of religion in their kingdoms. In the Byzantine East, once the doctrine that the Emperor was above the church had been established, it was never effectively challenged.

THE ARIAN CONTROVERSY

Constantine's handling of the Arian controversy was more astute, and at first more successful, than his approach to the Donatist split. The council of Nicaea, where the controversy should have ended, was his great triumph.

When Constantine became master of the East in 324, he found a dispute already raging between Alexander, Bishop of Alexandria, and his presbyter, Arius, who was attempting to solve the difficult problem of the relation of the Son to God the Father. He suggested that the Son, though Creator, was himself created, and therefore could not be truly divine like the Father. Alexander and his bishops judged this heretical and excommunicated Arius, who found support elsewhere in the East.

Constantine hoped to settle the matter 'out of court', and sent a letter to the contending parties describing the dispute as 'very trifling and indeed unworthy to be the cause of such a conflict'. When he saw that this dispute was not to be settled so easily, Constantine called a council of the whole church, the first 'ecumenical' (general) council, at Nicaea in 325.

The Emperor himself presided over the critical session, and it was he who proposed the reconciling word, *homoousios* (Greek for 'of one essence'), to describe Christ's relationship to the Father (though it was probably one of his ecclesiastical advisers, Ossius of Cordova – also known as Osius or Hosius – who suggested it to him). Nicaea was a triumph both for orthodoxy, since Arius could not accept the word, and apparently for Constantine's goal of church unity, since only two bishops finally stood with Arius.

The orthodox statement of doctrine produced at Nicaea, with some later modifications, became one of the great creeds of Western Christianity. But Constantine's achievement of unity proved a hollow victory. Conflict flared up again when the anti-Arian party, led by Athanasius – who succeeded Alexander as bishop of Alexandria – refused to receive back repentant Arians into the church. Constantine's continued attempts to attain unity were frustrated, as he saw it, by the obstinate refusal of first one faction and then the other to make any compromise.

Constantine died in 337, tolerant towards Arian sympathizers, and with Athanasius defiant in exile – thus failing to achieve his goal of unity in the church. Against this must be balanced his successes. He had begun to Christianize the Empire. He founded Constantinople (in 330) and so shifted the focus of the Empire eastward, contributing both to the decline of the West and to the independence of the Western Church. The effect of Nicaea and its creed far outlived his own failure to solve the Arian controversy. Finally, Constantine established, permanently in the East, and for a time in the West, his own answer to the question: 'What has the Emperor to do with the church?'

CHURCH, STATE, AND PAGANISM

The division of the Empire between Constantine's three sons, after his death in 337, soon resulted in a civil war with theological overtones. From this struggle Constantius, who was inclined towards Arianism, emerged victorious in 353. Constantius' efforts to unite the church under an anti-Nicene banner are seen in the series of councils held in various parts of the Empire between 354 and 360. Through these, he finally succeeded in forcing an anti-Nicene creed on reluctant bishops, and secured the condemnation of Athanasius, leader of the Nicene party. The climax of imperial intervention came at Milan in 355, if Athanasius' account is accepted. Certain bishops were summoned before Constantius at his palace and ordered to condemn Athanasius. When they dared to appeal to the canons of the church, the Emperor replied, 'Whatever I will, shall be regarded as a canon … Either obey or go into exile.'

In spite of all this, neither Athanasius nor the other Nicene bishops at first questioned the Emperor's authority to intervene in church disputes. They simply held that he was wrong, deceived by his advisers. By 358, however, Athanasius' views had changed:

> *When did a judgment of the church receive its validity from the Emperor? … There have been many councils held until the present, and many judgments passed by the church; but the church*

*leaders never sought the consent of the Emperor for them, nor did the Emperor busy himself
with the affairs of the church ...*

This was not quite true – but well might Athanasius forget the events of Constantine's reign when confronted with the audacity of Constantius.

Even old Ossius of Cordova, who had helped shape Constantine's policy towards the church, now quoted Jesus against imperial interference:

*Do not intrude yourself into church matters, nor give commands to us concerning them ...
God has put into your hands the kingdom; to us he has entrusted the affairs of his church ...
It is written, 'Render therefore unto Caesar the things that are Caesar's; and unto God the
things that are God's' [Matthew 22:21, KJV].*

PAGANISM SUPPRESSED

The sons of Constantine were bolder than their father in the attack on paganism. Constantine had to proceed slowly, since most of his subjects were still pagan – particularly the army and the nobility, from whom he drew his officials. His 'Edict' of Milan (313) proclaimed toleration for both pagan and Christian subjects. He did close a few temples particularly offensive to Christians for such things as ritual prostitution, and stripped many others of their treasures to deck his new capital city, Constantinople. He also banned private sacrifices and divining, and probably prohibited public sacrifice too, near the end of his reign.

Constantine's sons proceeded more vigorously. A law of 341 apparently suppressed pagan cults, while a stronger decree by Constantius, in 356, closed the temples and prohibited sacrifice on pain of death. Some temples were actually shut down, but the law seems not to have been rigidly enforced, for pagan priesthoods and rituals continued in Rome, and probably elsewhere. In 357, Constantius, on a visit to Rome, removed from the Senate House the Altar of Victory, on which senators had offered incense since the age of the Emperor Augustus (27 BC–AD 14).

Athanasius came to regard Constantius as worse than the biblical villains Saul, Ahab, or Pilate, and as a herald of the Antichrist, but such a view is too harsh. Constantius was, after all, acting in the same spirit as Constantine, to bring about unity in the Empire. Furthermore, he thought the church was on his side, since he had the support of a large part of the Eastern church, and Christianity was stronger in the East. But Constantius' reign does show that truth and liberty can suffer when unity is the ultimate goal.

JULIAN THE 'APOSTATE' (R. 361–63)

Some of the Nicene leaders thought better of Constantius when confronted with Julian, who became emperor in 361. Julian was a nephew of Constantine, and barely escaped the general massacre that followed his death in 337. As emperor, he could at last reveal that he had for some years been a secret pagan. His conversion was due to many factors, including the massacre of his family, and a lonely childhood filled with fears – imagined and real – of enemies at the Christian court of Constantius. In his education, Julian had felt closest to Plato and other great writers of ancient Greece, whom he studied under sympathetic tutors. He was also influenced by the skill of the Neoplatonic magician and medium, Maximus.

Julian, sometimes also known as 'the Philosopher', now attempted to convert the Empire to a religion that he called 'Hellenism', which was more than a mere revival of the old, uncoordinated paganism. Julian made a unique attempt to combine many old elements in an organized, pagan 'church', in which the principal deity was Plato's 'Supreme Being', whose chief visible representative was the life-giving Sun, identified with Helios and Mithras in the mythologies of the day. Syncretism prevailed, making it possible to regard all the old and new gods, with their cults and rituals, as originating from the Sun. Thus the world of Greek culture, mythology, and ritual could be retained without sacrificing the lofty monotheism of the Sun.

Julian paid tribute to the Christian church, by attempting to incorporate in his 'Hellenism' some of the more successful features of Christianity. He tried to set up a hierarchy like that of the church, with metropolitans of provinces set over the local priesthoods and answerable to the Emperor as *Pontifex Maximus*. Julian was concerned that the 'Hellenists' should not be outdone in holiness and charity by the 'Galileans' – as he called the Christians – and that the lives of his priests should be worthy of their high calling. A letter to Arsacius, High Priest of Galatia, is in this spirit:

> *Why do we not notice that it is their kindness to strangers, their care for the graves of the dead, and the pretended holiness of their lives that have done most to increase atheism [i.e. Christianity]? I believe that we ought really and truly to practise every one of these virtues. And it is not enough for you alone to practise them, but so must all the priests in Galatia, without exception ... In the second place admonish them that no priest may enter a theatre, or drink in a tavern, or control any craft or trade that is base and not respectable ...*

Although Julian restored pagan worship all over the Empire, and the special privileges enjoyed by Christian clergy were removed, there was no open persecution of Christians. In fact, toleration was decreed for all religions, though pagans were particularly favoured in the civil service, and imperial justice was not always even-handed when settling the violent disputes that arose in some cities over the religious changes.

But Julian raised the strongest protest when he prohibited Christians from teaching literature in the schools. He knew that upper-class Christians would continue to send their children to the ordinary schools, which prepared them for public life, even if their teachers were pagan, thus exposing the young to pagan propaganda. A curious solution to the dilemma was found by two Christian professors, who attempted to make the Scriptures a suitable vehicle for the preferred classical education, by translating the Old Testament into epic and tragedy, and the New Testament into Platonic dialogue. However Julian died in 363 before this stratagem could be tested.

'Be of good courage; it is but a cloud which will quickly pass away', Athanasius told his weeping congregation on hearing that Julian had ordered him into exile. Athanasius was right, for the zeal had gone out of paganism – at least Julian's kind of paganism. Its failure was apparent even before Julian's death.

CHRISTIAN EMPERORS

Jovian, the emperor who followed Julian in 363, was a Christian, and proclaimed toleration,

AMBROSE OF MILAN

In 374, following the death of the Arian Bishop of Milan, Ambrose was elected bishop by popular acclaim, although at that time he was not even baptized. Ambrose (339–97) came from a noble Roman family, received a classical education, and became a provincial governor in northern Italy, residing at Milan.

He read widely, especially the Greek theologians, and following his election as bishop became famous both as a preacher and as a church administrator and politician. Ambrose was the leading spokesman against the petition of the pagan Symmachus in 384 to have the Altar of Victory restored to the Senate House in Rome; it was his influence that ensured the altar was not reinstated.

Ambrose took a strong stand against Arianism, and completed its overthrow in the West. He clashed with the Empress-mother Justina, mother of Valentinian II, and in 385 organized a sit-in when she tried to take over one of the churches of Milan for Arian worship, making her give up the idea.

Later, Ambrose became a close adviser of the Emperor Theodosius, when he had his court in Milan. He used his position to prevent the Emperor from punishing rioting monks who had burned down a synagogue at Callinicum, but also forced the Emperor to make a public confession after he had sanctioned a massacre of civilians at Thessalonica. Ambrose was the first church leader successfully to use his office to coerce civil rulers.

Ambrose did much to encourage early monasticism in the West; and had considerable influence on Augustine, baptizing him in Milan in 387. He introduced community hymn-singing in the church, during the sit-in against Justina, and at least four Latin hymns are correctly credited to him. Ambrose's writings mainly concern matters of Christian practice.

MICHAEL A. SMITH

as did Valentinian I (364–75), who shortly succeeded him. Ammianus, a pagan historian, praised Valentinian because: 'he kept a middle course between the different sects of religion; and never troubled anyone, nor issued any orders in favour of one kind of worship or another ...' Valentinian extended toleration to Arians and most other heretics, though he himself was of the Nicene faith.

Valens (364–78), the younger brother of Valentinian, chosen by him to rule the East, was less tolerant. He did not attack paganism, but felt obliged to proceed against the Nicene party, and exiled some of its bishops. Valens, however, was killed at the Battle of Adrianople in 378, and subsequent emperors – in the East as in the West – were orthodox.

A dispute over the election of the Bishop of Rome in the reign of Valentinian scandalized the pagan Ammianus. The resulting bloody battle between the followers of Damasus (r. 366–84) and Ursinus (also known as Ursicinus) left 137 dead in the Basilica of Sicininus, which, Ammianus noted, 'is a Christian church'. The historian concluded that the Roman bishopric had become a prize worth fighting for, and described the luxury of the Roman clergy, 'enriched by offerings from women, riding in carriages, dressing splendidly, and feasting luxuriously, so that their entertainments surpass even royal banquets'. Not all lived luxuriously however: many lived frugal, even austere lives, as did bishops Ambrose and Augustine, and recommended the same simple life to their congregations.

Gratian (375–83) succeeded his father, Valentinian, in the West, and became ruler of the East too upon the death of Valens. Wisely recognizing that he could not govern the whole Empire alone, he chose an experienced soldier, Theodosius, to rule the East. Gratian was a talented, pious, and cultured young man who received a classical, but Christian, education from the poet Ausonius. He was also an accomplished sportsman, and could have 'excelled in every sphere if he had put his mind to the art of government, for which he was unsuited by temperament and training'. Gratian's inability to win the loyalty of the armies led to his death during the rebellion of a Spanish officer, Magnus Maximus (383).

THE END OF PAGAN RELIGIONS

The reigns of Gratian and of Theodosius I (379–95) finally decided the fate of paganism. Both Gratian and Theodosius strongly supported the orthodox faith, while the imperial policy of outlawing heresy and pagan religion during these years was in part the work of the great bishop Ambrose, elected to the see of Milan, Italy, in 374.

When Auxentius, the Arian Bishop of Milan, died in 373, the new governor, Ambrose, was afraid the Catholic/Arian controversy would break into violence. When the people of Milan poured into the cathedral to elect their bishop, Ambrose spoke a few words to calm the crowd. Suddenly a voice was heard (a child's voice, it is said), 'Ambrose, bishop!' The congregation took up the cry, and Ambrose found himself elected bishop, much to his surprise and against his will, for he was unbaptized and had received no church training. He tried to flee and hide, but eventually was persuaded that this election was the will of God.

Ambrose became bishop at the age of thirty-four and held the position for twenty-three years. He was particularly influential because Milan, rather than Rome, was at this time the Emperor's residence in the West. The Western Emperors Gratian and Valentinian II (375–92), came under his direct influence, as did Theodosius when in the West during some of the most critical years of his reign.

Gratian at first tolerated other religions as well as orthodox Christianity, but soon changed his mind under Ambrose's influence, and began to suppress pagans and heretics. He once again removed the Altar of Victory from the Senate House in Rome

Statue of Ambrose (c. 330–97), Archbishop of Milan, by Arturo Dazzi, in San Carlo al Corso, Rome, Italy.
© FABRIZIO TROIANI/DREAMSTIME.COM

(Julian had restored it), confiscated the revenues of the Vestal Virgins and other Roman priesthoods, and refused the title of *Pontifex Maximus* (High Priest), which previous Christian emperors had taken.

In 381 and 385, Theodosius prohibited sacrifices for divination, which seems to have stopped all sacrifice. Petitions to destroy individual temples, or convert them into Christian churches, were received and many were destroyed. Theodosius ordered all the temples in Alexandria to be demolished, following pagan-Christian unrest. It is reported that when the first blow at the great bronze statue of the god Serapis in the famous Serapeum produced only a swarm of rats, and divine retribution failed to follow the destruction of the temple, many pagans became Christian believers.

Finally, in 391, Theodosius prohibited all sacrifices and closed all temples, and the following year banned private pagan worship too. Paganism had one last chance in the West, during the brief reign of the usurper Eugenius (392–94), whose chief supporters were zealous pagans who restored the ancient worship in Rome. However Theodosius' final triumph in 394 put an end to that.

Nevertheless, the laws against paganism were not rigidly enforced, and pagan worship continued openly in some places for several generations – and secretly for a great deal longer. In much of the Empire, the countryside remained pagan for several centuries. Pagan *belief* was not prohibited, and pagans still managed for some time to attain high positions in the Empire.

Early in his reign, Theodosius began to act against heretics. In 380 he ordered all his subjects to subscribe to the faith brought by Peter to Rome and now held by Pope Damasus and by Peter, Bishop of Alexandria. The following year he summoned the Council of Constantinople, which drew up a definition of faith on the Nicene model. But Arianism had by now lost its vitality, except among the Gothic tribes – still mostly outside the Empire – and Theodosius met little opposition.

PRISCILLIAN EXECUTED

In Gratian's reign began the strange and sad case of Priscillian, in which the usurper, Magnus Maximus (383–88), became the first Christian emperor to inflict the death penalty on a heretic. These events foreshadow the later medieval practice of handing over heretics condemned by the church for execution by the state.

Priscillian was the Spanish leader of a strict Christian ascetic movement, first accused by prominent Spanish church leaders of heretical beliefs and immoral practices, but escaping outright condemnation. Later the case was referred to Maximus, who was biased against Priscillian and his followers. Finally, Priscillian and six of his associates were condemned and executed at Trier in 385, despite the personal appeal of the saintly Bishop Martin of Tours, who also objected to the case being tried before secular rulers. Although Priscillian and his followers were ultimately condemned for the civil crime of sorcery, no one doubted that their real offence was Priscillian's unusual beliefs and religious practices. He was perhaps more an eccentric than a heretic, although he was involved in magic and the occult.

To the credit of the church, the executions brought a strong reaction. Martin reappeared at Trier to denounce the Emperor Maximus; and Ambrose and Pope Siricius refused to have fellowship with Priscillian's accusers. Finally, in 388, the anti-Priscillian bishops were deposed and their party destroyed. Though a few fanatical church leaders were willing to execute people for heresy and use the state as the church's executioner, most drew back from that severe view.

WHAT HAS THE EMPEROR TO DO WITH THE CHURCH?

Two encounters between Ambrose and the Emperor Theodosius show a dramatic increase in the power of the church since the time of Constantius. The first occurred in 388, after rioting in the town of Callinicum on the River Euphrates. The Christians had been led on by the bishop to rob and burn a Jewish synagogue. Theodosius ordered the stolen property to be restored, and the synagogue rebuilt, at the bishop's own expense; just compensation, it appears. But Ambrose sent Theodosius a letter insisting that to make a Christian bishop rebuild a place of worship for the Jews, the 'enemies of Christ', amounted to apostasy. 'The maintenance of civil law is secondary to religious interests,' wrote Ambrose. When Theodosius ignored Ambrose's letter, the bishop felt obliged to preach on the subject in the presence of the Emperor, who, partly because he was weak in the West, finally had to give in and withdraw his order.

The second encounter, in the summer of 390, shows Ambrose in a better light. The people of Thessalonica had murdered the military commander of the city because he had refused to release a favourite charioteer. Theodosius avenged his death by a massacre of the inhabitants, despite Ambrose's protest. The Emperor repented, but too late; 7,000 or more citizens, both guilty and innocent, had been slaughtered in the theatre. Ambrose sent a secret letter, excommunicating the Emperor until he did public penance; Theodosius was again obliged to give way, and asked forgiveness for his sin publicly in the church.

Ambrose's answer to the question, 'What has the Emperor to do with the church?' was that the Emperor was within the church, not above it. However, this did not mark the end of imperial interference in the church's affairs. The Emperor in Constantinople kept control of the Eastern church, and occasionally interfered in the West, particularly during the sixth century, after Justinian reconquered Italy.

By the late fifth century, the Bishop of Rome, Gelasius I (r. 492–96), had developed the view that the Emperor was directly subject to the head of the church, the Bishop of Rome (or pope), and should rule the Empire for the good of God's people. This exalted idea could not be applied in the late Empire because of the church's political weakness, but was picked up in the Middle Ages. Ambrose demonstrated how it might work in practice.

RICHARD A. TODD

> Nothing can be found in this world more exalted than priests or more sublime than bishops.
>
> AMBROSE

ACCEPTANCE AND CONQUEST

300 325 350 375 400 425 450 475 500 525 550 575 600

Athanasius

Theodosius I

Leo I

Constantine the Great

Valentinian II

Zeno

Basil the Great

Honorius

Theodoric the Ostrogoth, King of Italy

Constantius II

John Chrysostom, Bishop of Constantinople

Jerome

Anastasius I

Augustine of Hippo

Gelasius I, Bishop of Rome

Julian the Apostate

Justinian I

Valentinian I

Theodosius II

Gregory the Great, Bishop of Rome

Valens

Leo the Great, Bishop of Rome

Damasus, Bishop of Rome

Ambrose, Bishop of Milan

Gratian

Donatists arise in North Africa

Patrick's mission to Ireland

Council of Nicaea

Huns under Attila invade Italy

Ulfilas' mission to the Goths

Council of Chalcedon

Martin of Tours' mission to Northern France

Vandals under Gaiseric capture Rome

Odoacer the German deposes the last
Western Emperor, Romulus Augustulus

Council of Constantinople

Division of Roman Empire into
East and West becomes permanent

Conversion of Clovis, King of the Franks

Vandals invade Gaul and Spain

Benedict of Nursia
founds his monastary

Rome sacked by Alaric and the Visigoths

Pelagian controversy starts

Columba goes to Iona

Council of Ephesus: Nestorius deposed

Lombards invade Italy

Vandals form a kingdom in Africa

Birth of Muhammad

CHAPTER 9

COUNCILS AND CREEDS
Defining and defending the faith

From the outset, Christians were people who believed certain things. The beliefs they expressed in worship and witness, especially about Jesus Christ, were fundamental to the very existence of the church. The fourth, fifth, and sixth centuries were marked by prolonged controversies, chiefly in the Eastern Church, about how Christ, the Son of God, was himself God (the doctrine of the Trinity), and how he was both man and God (the doctrine of the person of Christ, or Christology).

   Numerous councils of bishops were held, four of which – Nicaea (325), Constantinople (381), Ephesus (431), and Chalcedon (451) – came to be accepted as general, or ecumenical (universal), councils, binding upon the whole church. (Some areas of Eastern Christianity rejected the decisions made at Ephesus or Chalcedon.) Two later general councils – at Constantinople in 553 and 680–81 – dealt with similar questions, but have influenced Western Christianity much less. Many creeds and statements of doctrine were produced, including the famous Nicene Creed and the Chalcedonian Definition, which became touchstones of orthodoxy throughout most of

The Nicene Creed

We believe in one God,
the Father, the almighty,
maker of heaven and earth,
of all that is,
seen and unseen.

We believe in one Lord Jesus Christ,
the only Son of God,
eternally begotten of the Father,
God from God, Light from Light,
true God from true God,
begotten, not made,
of one Being with the Father,
Through him all things were made.
For us men and for our salvation
he came down from heaven;
by the power of the Holy Spirit
he became incarnate of the Virgin Mary, and was
made man.
For our sake he was crucified under Pontius Pilate;
he suffered death and was buried.

On the third day he rose again
in accordance with the Scriptures;
he ascended into heaven
and is seated at the right hand of the Father.
He will come again in glory
to judge the living and the dead,
and his kingdom will have no end.

We believe in the Holy Spirit,
the Lord, the giver of life,
who proceeds from the Father and the Son.
With the Father and the Son he is worshipped and
glorified.
He has spoken through the prophets.

We believe in one holy catholic and apostolic church.
We acknowledge one baptism for the forgiveness
of sins.
We look for the resurrection of the dead,
and the life of the world to come.

Amen

the Christian world. This was an era of unparalleled importance in the formation of Christian theology.

At the same time it was an age of interference, and even domination, by the emperors, of colourful and abrasive personalities, and of bitter antagonism between leading bishoprics. Technical terms without biblical origins were made key-words in authoritative statements of belief; their use contributed to the Latin-speaking West and the Greek-speaking East misunderstanding and misrepresenting one another. Even between different segments of the Greek Church misunderstandings arose; these disputes contributed to major divisions in the Christian world.

In theory the first appeal was to Scripture, but the Bible was often used in curious or questionable ways. People frequently appealed to Scripture to confirm their theology, rather than to decide it. Above all, the disputes were shot through with the feeling that, unless God and Christ were truly what Christian devotion and worship claimed, salvation itself was endangered. Passions ran high because the fundamentals of the Christian religion were felt to be at stake.

IS THE SON REALLY GOD?

Arius was a senior presbyter in charge of Baucalis, one of the twelve 'parishes' of Alexandria. He was a persuasive preacher, with a following of clergy and ascetics, and even circulated his teaching in popular verse and songs.

Around 318 Arius clashed with Bishop Alexander. Arius claimed that the Father alone was really God; the Son was essentially different from his Father. The Son did not possess by nature or right any of the divine qualities of immortality, sovereignty, perfect wisdom, goodness, and purity. He did not exist before he was begotten by the Father, who produced him as a creature. Yet as the creator of the rest of creation, the Son existed 'apart from time before all things'. Nevertheless, he did not share in the being of God the Father, and did not know him perfectly.

As if to salvage something from the wreckage, Arius allowed that the Son was called 'God' by grace and favour, and was sinless and unchangeable in practice, if not by nature. Moreover, the Son received enough wisdom and light from the Father to enable him to reveal the Father to mankind. Nevertheless, by dividing off the Son from God the Father, Arius undermined Christ's standing as God's revelation, and the redeemer of mankind.

We are not certain of Arius' precise teaching and motives. It may be that he wanted chiefly to explain the incarnation without difficulties. He undoubtedly believed that the *Logos*, or Son, took the place of the human soul in the earthly Christ. The *Logos* was united only with a human body, not with a full human nature. It was much easier to understand how the *Logos* could be united with human flesh when he was lowered to the status of a perfect creature or honorary god.

Arius' ideas parallel and contrast with Origen's teaching; they owe much to secular Greek concepts of God. He had a sharply logical mind and appealed to biblical texts which apparently backed up his arguments – for example, John 17:3 ('the only true God'), I Timothy 6:16 ('alone possesses immortality'), Colossians 1:15 ('first-born of all creation') and Proverbs 8:22 (in the Septuagint, 'the Lord created me at the beginning of his work').

A council at Alexandria of Egyptian and Libyan bishops soon excommunicated Arius and a dozen other clergy, including two bishops, but the affair was not so easily settled.

Arius sought the backing of former fellow-pupils of Lucian of Antioch, an influential teacher martyred a few years earlier, including Eusebius, Bishop of Nicomedia, the imperial headquarters on the Asian side of the Bosphorus. Eusebius skilfully used his closeness to the court to benefit 'the Eusebians', as sympathizers of Arius came to be known, and later moved across the Bosphorus to the see of Constantinople, the new capital.

THE COUNCIL OF NICAEA

Eusebius of Caesarea, the church historian, also rallied support for the Arians in his region, but soon found himself in deep water as a consequence. Constantine, now Emperor of East as well as West, was dismayed to discover in 324 that his new territories were split over a 'theological trifle'. His religious adviser, the Spanish Bishop Ossius, was sent to Alexandria, but failed to reconcile the parties, so Constantine summoned a general assembly of bishops to meet at Ancyra (modern Ankara) the following year. Hoping to avoid a divisive result, the Emperor subsequently changed the venue to Nicaea, near Nicomedia, where the Council met in the imperial palace under imperial auspices. Constantine presided at the opening session, surrounded by survivors of the Great Persecution, and he, or Ossius, may also have taken the chair when the Arian question arose.

All this underlined the change in relations between church and state. However, Constantine's ambitions for a fully church-wide attendance were disappointed. Of some 220 bishops present, only a handful, including Ossius, were from the West, with Bishop Sylvester of Rome represented by two presbyters. The Council's 'universal' status depended largely on its subsequent universal acceptance.

THE CREED OF NICAEA

Much more is known about the outcome of the council than of its proceedings. Arius was quickly condemned by his own words. Three bishops previously banned or suspended, including Eusebius of Caesarea, were cleared.

To exclude Arian error, the council produced its own creed, which we call the Creed of Nicaea to distinguish it from the Nicene Creed:

> *We believe in one God, the Father, Almighty, maker of all things visible and invisible;*
>
> *And in one Lord Jesus Christ, the Son of God, begotten of the Father, only-begotten, that is, from the substance (*ousia*) of the Father; God from God, Light from Light, Very God from Very God, begotten not made, of one substance (*homoousios, consubstantial*) with the Father, through whom all things were made, both in heaven and on earth; who for us men and for our salvation came down and was incarnate, was made man, suffered, and rose again on the third day, ascended into heaven, and is coming to judge the living and the dead;*
>
> *And in the Holy Spirit.*
>
> *And those who say: 'There was a time when he was not', and: 'Before he was begotten he was not', and: 'He came into being from nothing', or those who pretend that the Son of God is 'Of another substance (*hypostasis*), or essence (*ousia*)' [than the Father] or 'created' or 'alterable' or 'mutable', the catholic and apostolic church places under a curse.*

Based on a traditional Syrian or Palestinian creed, the Creed of Nicaea became entirely distinctive because of its technical language and solemn curses (anathemas). (Apparently Arius could agree to any statement using solely biblical language.) Constantine supported the introduction of the word 'consubstantial' – probably suggested by a Western bishop. 'Consubstantial' (*homoousios*) had been introduced to Christian theology by Gnostics, who believed that the heavenly powers shared in the divine fullness. Origen probably applied it similarly to the Son, as a true offspring of the Father, but later bishops had been unhappy about its implications. For many at Nicaea, it probably implied that the Son was no less divine than the Father; that the two were equally divine, as an earthly father and son are equally human. For the Westerners and a few Easterners – Alexander and Athanasius, his personal assistant, Eustathius of Antioch, and Marcellus of Ancyra – it meant that Father and Son were one in a single Godhead.

Both these senses ruled out Arian misconceptions. But some bishops hesitated at the Council, and many more reacted in alarm afterwards, fearing that the Greek word *homoousios* split the Godhead into two, as if it were a material substance. The word was used, for example, to describe two coins made from the same metal; its use in the Creed of Nicaea must have resulted largely from intimidation, or overawing persuasion, by Constantine.

Only two bishops actually refused to subscribe to the Creed, and Constantine rejoiced in the God-given concord, which later events showed to be so deceptive. Eusebius of Caesarea signed only by making tortuous evasions; Eusebius of Nicomedia also signed, but was later exiled for entertaining the Arians *en route* for Illyria, on the Danube frontier, where Constantine had banished them. Genuine Arians were very few in number.

THE CHURCH'S ORGANIZATION

The Council of Nicaea also issued twenty 'canons' regulating various aspects of the church's life, which – because of the prestige surrounding the Council – formed the core of later collections of canon law. These dealt with the admission of members of splinter groups, restrictions on the functions of deacons and on business activities by the clergy, the giving of the eucharist to those about to die out of communion, probation before ordination after baptism, and a ban on clergy transferring from one city to another.

Other canons strengthened the organization of the church into provinces, and recognized that the bishops of Rome, Alexandria, Antioch, Caesarea, and Jerusalem had superior authority. While Rome alone is mentioned in the West, the four in the East were soon joined by Constantinople. The pretensions of this 'upstart', as well as the rivalry between ancient Antioch and Alexandria, rapidly aggravated the continuing conflicts over doctrine.

The Council of Nicaea set many precedents. The Emperor called it, influenced its decision-making, and used his civil power to give its decrees virtually the status of imperial law. The Council introduced a new kind of orthodoxy, which for the first time gave non-biblical terms critical importance. The Creed's own form of expression was influenced by the heresy it outlawed. Only in the long term did the whole church recognize that Nicaea had decisively developed its understanding of the divinity of Christ.

THE REACTION TO NICAEA

Nicaea was followed by more than half a century of discord and disorder in the Eastern Church, which at times spilled over into the West. The 'faith of Nicaea', as the Creed was commonly called, was for most of this period out of favour with most churchmen. Numerous other statements of belief were drawn up, some quite near to it, others a great distance from it, but none containing the word *homoousios*. The Eastern emperors between Constantine and Theodosius I were at best unsympathetic to Nicaea, at worst openly friendly towards Arianism.

Throughout this half-century the basic dispute about doctrine was intertwined with other complications – local factions, rivalries between the leading bishoprics, the personal failings or follies of Christian leaders, the emperors' intervention, and confusion arising from differences in language – especially as rifts opened up between the Latin and Greek churches.

ATHANASIUS

Athanasius (c. 293/8–373) is one of the giants of Christian history, because of his part in defining the doctrine of the Trinity in the Arian struggles. As a deacon of the Church at Alexandria, Athanasius accompanied his bishop, Alexander, to the Council of Nicaea in 325; and he succeeded Alexander as bishop in 328. Changing political fortunes, due to the involvement of the Emperor in the affairs of the church, resulted in Athanasius being exiled five times (335–37, to Trier in Gaul; 339–46, to Rome; 356–61, when he lived among the monks in the Egyptian desert; 362–63 and 365–66, in concealment in Egypt). Athanasius' flock stayed loyal to him, and each time he was welcomed back from exile.

On the Incarnation (335–37, but dated by some as early as 318) sets out Athanasius' basic theological viewpoint: Christ 'was made human that we might be made divine'. This concern with salvation motivated Athanasius as he argued against Arius and his followers. The Arians said that Christ was a created being, made by God before time; Athanasius argued that if Christ was less than God then he could not be our saviour. Only God could restore the human race to communion with himself. For this reason, Athanasius defended Nicaea's definition of Christ as of the same substance with God, and Nicaea's rejection of Arianism.

Most of Athanasius' writings aim at opposing Arianism, dealing with it historically, doctrinally, or from Scripture. Athanasius stood like a rock in defence of the creed adopted at Nicaea: his personality, preaching, and writings did more than anything else to achieve victory for the Nicene position. His zeal made him uncompromising – even harsh – in dealing with opponents, and slow to recognize good in those he disagreed with. The counterpart of his harshness towards opponents was blindness – or excessive indulgence – to the faults of friends and supporters. Athanasius was not a speculative theologian; what mattered for him was not so much the terms used in the Creed of Nicaea as its message. He used Scripture as inadequately as his contemporaries.

Athanasius' *Life of Antony* did much to promote monasticism by praising the life of the desert ascetics. Athanasius found echoes of his own experiences and emotions in the psalms (*Letter to Marcellinus*), and helped to introduce the personal devotional use of the psalms which Christians have adopted ever since. His *Easter Letter 39* (367) is the earliest witness to the 27-book New Testament canon.

EVERETT FERGUSON

Athanasius, backed by the solid ranks of Egyptian churchmen and monks, remained the one unyielding champion of Nicaea in the East. Five times exiled from Alexandria, he lived long enough to welcome the 'new Nicene' theology of the 360s and the Cappadocian Fathers.

The Western Church had able theologians such as Hilary of Poitiers ('Hammer of the Arians', c. 300–c. 368) and Ambrose of Milan, but they contributed little to solving the troubles of the East. The Western Church consistently supported Nicaea and Alexandria (whose isolation in the fourth century arose partly because it had expelled Origen in the third); this did their cause little good, and much harm, in the East.

While Constantine remained alive, no one openly dared to attack his beloved Council. Instead the reaction against Nicaea had to proceed indirectly, seizing the opportunities offered by the Emperor's restless quest for harmony. The Eusebians, and even Arius, were brought back into favour, while the leading enthusiasts for Nicaea were sent packing.

A CHRISTIAN EMPEROR

After he had been cleared at Nicaea, Eusebius of Caesarea went on to develop a theology of the Christian empire and emperor. He claimed that both empire and church were images of the kingdom of heaven; through

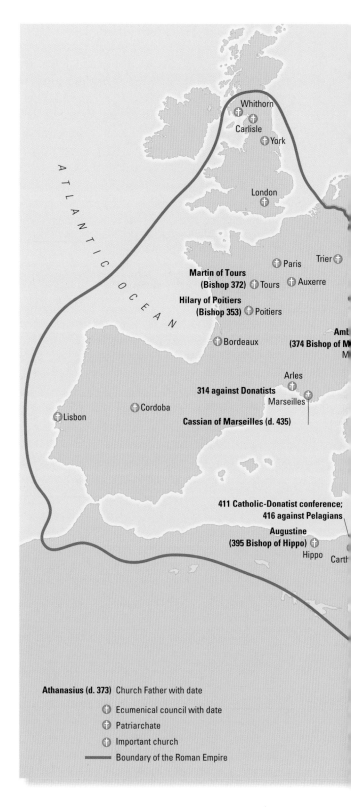

Athanasius (d. 373) Church Father with date

✝ Ecumenical council with date

✝ Patriarchate

✝ Important church

— Boundary of the Roman Empire

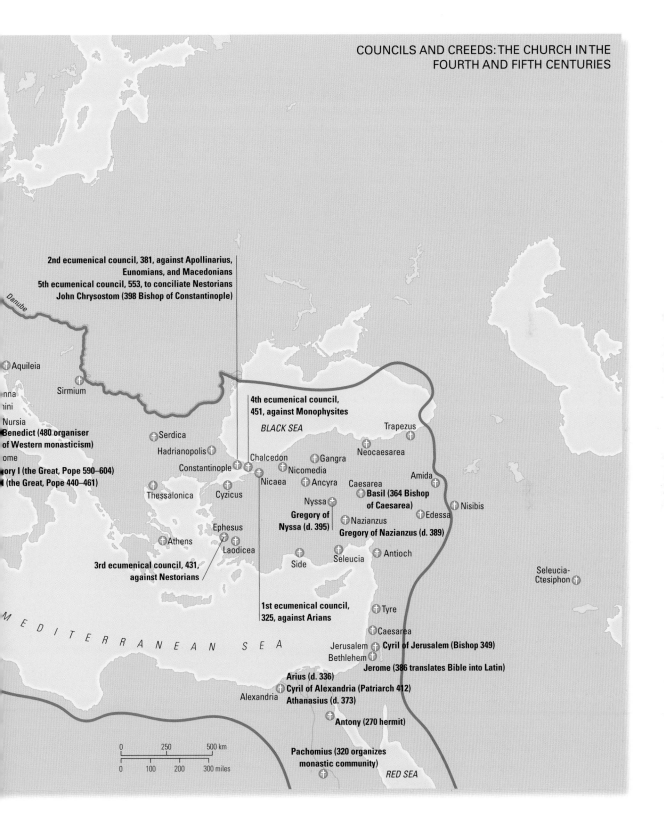

Danube

✠ Aquileia

✠ Sirmium

2nd ecumenical council, 381, against Apollinarius,
Eunomians, and Macedonians
5th ecumenical council, 553, to conciliate Nestorians
John Chrysostom (398 Bishop of Constantinople)

nna
hini

Nursia
**Benedict (480 organiser
of Western monasticism)**
ome
**ory I (the Great, Pope 590–604)
(the Great, Pope 440–461)**

✠ Serdica
Hadrianopolis ✠

✠ Thessalonica

Cyzicus ✠

4th ecumenical council,
451, against Monophysites

BLACK SEA

Trapezus ✠

Chalcedon ✠ Gangra
Constantinople ✠✠ ✠ Nicomedia
Nicaea ✠ Ancyra ✠
Neocaesarea ✠

Amida ✠

Caesarea
**Basil (364 Bishop
of Caesarea)**

Nyssa ✠
**Gregory of
Nyssa (d. 395)**
✠ Nazianzus
Gregory of Nazianzus (d. 389)

✠ Edessa
✠ Nisibis

✠ Athens

Ephesus ✠
✠ Laodicea

**3rd ecumenical council, 431,
against Nestorians**

Side ✠

Seleucia ✠

✠ Antioch

Seleucia-
Ctesiphon ✠

**1st ecumenical council,
325, against Arians**

✠ Tyre

✠ Caesarea

Jerusalem ✠ **Cyril of Jerusalem (Bishop 349)**
Bethlehem ✠
Jerome (386 translates Bible into Latin)

Arius (d. 336)
✠ **Cyril of Alexandria (Patriarch 412)**
Alexandria **Athanasius (d. 373)**

✠ **Antony (270 hermit)**

**Pachomius (320 organizes
monastic community)**
✠

M E D I T E R R A N E A N   S E A

RED SEA

| 0 | 250 | 500 km |
| 0 | 100 | 200 | 300 miles |

both God was saving humanity. The empire replaced anarchy with monarchy, which represents on earth the God who alone rules in heaven; the church replaced polytheism with the worship of the one God. In the Christian emperor, the two images began to merge. Constantine is seen as the earthly image of the *Logos*, who had fully revealed the heavenly monarchy and kingdom, and he was specially inspired to rule by the *Logos*.

Eusebius drew his ideas from Hellenistic writers on divine kingship – although the Old Testament offered similar patterns – and his thinking was adopted by Eastern Christians. Since Alexander the Great, the East had been used to regarding rulers as divine. Inevitably the emperors became supreme in church as well as state.

ARIANS RESTORED

Eusebius of Nicomedia was recalled from exile after a couple of years, and threw himself into organizing opposition to Nicaea. Arius was likewise recalled after confusing Constantine with a statement of faith that dodged all the crucial issues, but he no longer had any influence.

Among the supporters of Nicaea, Eustathius of Antioch was the first to be dislodged. The reasons given ranged from insulting Constantine's mother Helena to exaggerated criticism of Origen. Marcellus of Ancyra was condemned directly for heresy. He was another critic of Origen's ideas, and presented a single God who expanded into three in creation and redemption and then contracted to one again. This seemed like a form of Sabellianism, which Origen had taught Eastern churchmen to resist with unparalleled intensity. Marcellus' appeal to I Corinthians 15:24–28 (the Son at the end hands the kingdom over to the Father, and is made subordinate to him, so that God is all in all) led eventually to the inclusion in the Nicene Creed of the words 'whose kingdom shall have no end'.

Athanasius annoyed Constantine by refusing to rejoice when the Arians were reconciled. The Eusebians plotted to depose him in 335 at Tyre, where the bishops assembled before celebrating the thirtieth anniversary of Constantine's reign with the dedication of his Church of the Holy Sepulchre in Jerusalem. Athanasius was charged with conduct unbecoming a bishop, including violent treatment of dissident clergy, charges with some substance. When Athanasius fled to Constantine himself, his enemies accused him of threatening to cut off vital grain supplies for Constantinople, by calling a dock strike in Alexandria. Constantine banished him to Trier in Gaul – banishment had become customary for those the church condemned.

When Constantine died, baptized by Eusebius of Nicomedia, and praised by Eusebius of Caesarea, the Creed of Nicaea remained officially in force. Until the end, Constantine had worked for peace in the church. His son Constantius, Emperor of the East until 361, and of the West too after Constans' death in 350, pursued the same policy. The only difference was that his quest for unity did without the settlement of Nicaea.

CONFUSION UNDER CONSTANTIUS

A breathing-space after Constantine's death saw the return of the exiles: Athanasius, Marcellus, and Paul, bishop of the strategic see of Constantinople, who was expelled as often as Athanasius. But the slide towards total rupture between East and West soon resumed.

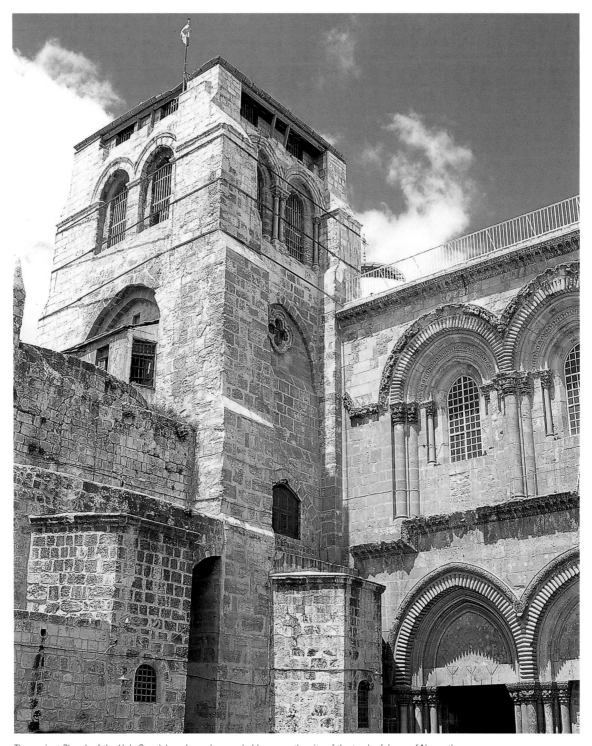

The ancient Church of the Holy Sepulchre, Jerusalem, probably covers the site of the tomb of Jesus of Nazareth.
TIM DOWLEY ASSOCIATES

Although efforts to heal the divisions had some success, when Constantius died Arianism was practically dominant in the East, while the Emperor's theology of compromise ruled the West. Yet there were hints of a brighter future for the 'faith of Nicaea'.

Constantius was not long in power before Athanasius and Marcellus were banished again. Eusebius had now moved from Nicomedia to Constantinople. The two exiles went to Rome, where in 340 a council under Bishop Julius undid their excommunication and declared Marcellus orthodox. The Eastern Church saw these acts as arrogant and simple-minded, feeling Rome had been hoodwinked by Marcellus, who managed to avoid being pressed on the weak points of his beliefs. Moreover, Rome did not actually have the power to overrule councils of Eastern bishops.

At a council at Antioch in 341, the Greek bishops were free to express their own views. They repudiated both Arius and Marcellus (their chief target), and refused to reconsider the case of Athanasius. They drew up creeds, not intending to supplant Nicaea's, but implying that it was inadequate. The second creed of Antioch was repeatedly referred to in the years following as a true mirror of Eastern theology. It was inadequate in teaching that Father, Son, and Spirit are 'three as persons' but one only 'in agreement', or harmony of will. It clearly excluded Arianism, but went out of its way to condemn Marcellus and his supposedly Sabellian ideas.

Constans persuaded Constantius to call a general council at Sardica (modern Sofia, Bulgaria) in 342/3, but this council split into opposing camps, which bombarded each other with anathemas. A theological statement from the Western side innocently exposed the problems of mutual understanding. By refusing to describe Father, Son, and Spirit as 'three *hypostaseis*' (which it understood as implying 'three Gods'), and by arguing for a single *hypostasis* of Father and Son, it confirmed Eastern fears that the West sincerely backed Marcellus' Sabellian viewpoint. Adding offence to the Eastern Church, the Western council gave the Bishop of Rome the right to hear appeals from bishops condemned in their own provinces.

VIRTUAL SCHISM

For the first time East and West were in a state of virtual schism, from which they never fully recovered. The situation improved for a time as Constans pressed, and Constantius was distracted by the Persians. The West and Athanasius quietly abandoned Marcellus, and Athanasius was even allowed to return to Alexandria, where in 346 he embarked upon his 'golden decade'.

But after taking over control of the Western Empire in 350, Constantius allowed the Arians to advance to fresh triumphs. He pursued his goal of harmony in the church, at the expense of Nicene theology and theologians. At councils he forced the Western bishops to condemn Athanasius, and banished those who resisted to the end, such as Ossius and Hilary. Constantius could then confidently exile Athanasius again in 356, though his replacement was inducted to his office only by force against massive popular opposition.

ARIANISM MODERATED

The provinces of Illyria had become a stronghold of Arianism as a result of Arius' banishment to this region. (It was from here that the Visigoths adopted Arian

Christianity, launching it on its second career as the new religion of the migrant peoples who overwhelmed the Western Empire.) A local anti-Nicene bishop, Valens of Mursa, influenced Constantius strongly during the 350s. A creed published at nearby Sirmium in 357, which Hilary labelled 'the Blasphemy of Sirmium', banned the use of philosophical words such as *ousia*, and implied clearly Arian beliefs. It was welcomed by the Anomoians, extreme Arians who claimed that the Son was unlike (*anomoios*) the Father.

These excesses provoked a reaction, spearheaded by Marcellus' successor, Basil of Ancyra, whose supporters – sometimes misleadingly called 'semi-Arians' – taught that the Son was like the Father in all respects, including his essential being (*ousia*). They described the Son as 'of like substance to' (*homoiousios*) the Father, rather than 'of one substance with' (*homoousios*), thus unmistakably distinguishing between Father and Son. Hilary and Athanasius viewed this movement as the most promising development since Nicaea itself.

Constantius' reign ended with a moderated Arianism dominant. In the West all dissent had ceased, except for Hilary, in exile. Constantius extorted from joint councils at Rimini in Italy, and Seleucia (on the coast of Asia Minor), a universal creed which feebly confessed the Son to be like (*homoios*) the Father. Jerome wrote, 'The whole world groaned in astonishment at finding itself Arian.' This shock was similar to the dismay which had followed Nicaea in the Eastern Empire. Churchmen would not acquiesce in an imperial settlement which had not won their own agreement. But Basil's constructive contribution was still to bear fruit, focusing attention in a new way on the central theological issue.

SURPRISING AGREEMENT

Emperor Julian the 'Apostate' permitted all those exiled by Constantius to return. But instead of the destructive inter-church warfare which he expected, there came major advances in mutual understanding. Athanasius, now somewhat mellowed, called a 'statesmanlike little council' in Alexandria in 362, where the bishops agreed that the Creed of Nicaea should be confessed by all without any additions, and discovered that, in spite of differences in technical terms, they were in agreement. 'Three *hypostaseis*' did not mean three Gods, or three beings with different natures, or as separate from each other as three men. Nor did the phrase 'one *hypostasis*' involve its users in Sabellianism; it spoke of the oneness of the Godhead as a single essence.

Other problems that concerned this council were the God–man union in the incarnate Christ, and the teaching of Egyptian supporters of Nicaea that the Holy Spirit was a superior angel, not of one substance with the Father and the Son. Athanasius had written against them, and the council backed him up. Although Scripture was less explicit on this matter, and Nicaea itself had said little, the acceptance that the Son was fully God cleared the way for the same acceptance concerning the Spirit. For Athanasius, only a divine Spirit could make us 'partakers of the divine nature'. This issue arose more threateningly outside Egypt.

DIVISIONS IN ANTIOCH

Elsewhere in the East, many people rallied to the faith of Nicaea, or to the second creed of Antioch of 341. But divisions continued among the Antioch Christians and threatened further progress. Ever since Bishop Eustathius had been deposed in 330, the Nicene

Christians had met in a separate congregation, now led by Paulinus. The official bishops of Antioch were Arians of one variety or another until Bishop Meletius, who was deposed when he showed his colours.

Meletius' supporters formed a second anti-Arian congregation in Antioch, with wide backing in the East. Athanasius, followed by Rome and the West, continued in communion with the old Nicenes under Paulinus. Church order and theology could not have been more tightly interwoven. Antioch was an important church; by refusing to recognize Meletius and the new Nicenes, Alexandria and Rome offended Eastern churchmen.

Valens, the Eastern Emperor (364–78), reminded the world that the 'Homoian' creed of Constantius was still official orthodoxy. During the 'second Arian persecution' by Valens, old and new Nicenes suffered alike, although Athanasius' fifth exile did not last long. The Emperor devastated congregational life, and heretical groups proliferated; the confusion was 'like a sea-fight in the fog'. Apollinarius' teaching (see below) was popular, and around Constantinople the Pneumatomachians, 'fighters against the Spirit', denied that the Spirit was fully God in the same sense as the Son. (They were later improperly called 'Macedonians', after a former bishop of Constantinople.) They claimed that the Bible says nothing to deny that the Spirit is a lower being.

THE CAPPADOCIANS' THEOLOGY

Athanasius' greatest contribution was in routing mainstream Arianism; he had less success in re-establishing the faith of Nicaea. However, as his attitude softened with the years, he happily accepted the new approaches of Basil of Ancyra, Meletius of Antioch, and Basil the Great, Bishop of Caesarea in Cappadocia (eastern Asia Minor), r. 370–79.

Basil the Great was an extremely able administrator, who set about repairing 'the tattered old coat of the church' by letters, and by influencing the appointment of bishops in the provinces of Asia. But in relations with the West, he had little success. Basil sent four delegations to Pope Damasus, which produced no tangible aid. The two sides disagreed strongly about the division in Antioch: Western churches still suspected the theology of the so-called 'new Nicenes' such as Meletius and Basil himself. Damasus' insensitive and ill-informed detachment further endangered the recovery of harmony between East and West.

Basil worked closely with his brother Gregory of Nyssa (c. 335–c. 395) and their friend Gregory of Nazianzus (c. 329–90). These three Cappadocians finally convinced the East that it was quite possible to accept both Nicaea (*homoousios*) and the distinct persons (*hypostaseis*) of Father, Son, and Spirit simultaneously. It was not enough to show that the Son was equal with the Father, for this might suggest there were two Gods; Father and Son must also be recognized as one God. The Cappadocians established *ousia* as the Greek equivalent to the Latin *substantia*. Meanwhile, further linguistic confusion reared its head. The closest Greek parallel to the Latin 'three *personae*' was 'three *prosōpa*', but the latter term, meaning 'face, mask, or role', was popular with the Sabellians, and the Cappadocians insisted on the stronger 'three *hypostaseis*' (beings).

The Cappadocians' doctrine of the Trinity is complex, and at points controversial. They were accused of suggesting that there are three Gods, and also of the opposite error, Sabellianism. They used analogies that they knew were inexact – but one in particular, of

BASIL THE GREAT

Basil displayed immense gifts in public speaking, church statesmanship, and theological insight, and was outstanding in social concern and the monastic way of life. The trio of Basil, his brother Gregory of Nyssa, and friend Gregory of Nazianzus, are often known as the 'Cappadocian Fathers'.

Basil was born into a distinguished and wealthy Christian family in Caesarea in Cappadocia about 330. Despite a first-class education, he turned aside from a career in rhetoric, was baptized, and lived as an ascetic on his family estate in Pontus (357). From the outset he was completely dedicated, especially to biblical study. With Gregory of Nazianzus, he compiled an anthology of Origen's works; his sure theological touch helped strengthen Origen's place within orthodoxy.

In 364 Basil was ordained presbyter, and in 370 he succeeded Eusebius as Bishop of Caesarea. His new monastery was at the heart of a complex of hospitals and hostels he founded, largely from his own pocket, out of concern for the sick and needy. He took a firm stand against the state-supported Arian party, and wrote several works to oppose their errors. He backed Meletius (Bishop of Antioch, 360–81), which damaged his attempts to win practical help from Damasus, Bishop of Rome, and cooled his relationship with Athanasius. Basil refused to accept the Roman bishop as supreme judge of the universal church, although he recognized his authority in the area of doctrine.

Basil's writings on the monastic life had enormous influence in Eastern Christianity: no one before had laid so much stress on community and love in the monastic life. In *On the Holy Spirit* Basil opposed the Pneumatomachians ('fighters against the Spirit'), who denied that the Holy Spirit was truly divine. He also wrote homilies on a number of the psalms, a long commentary on Isaiah chapters 1–6, and many sermons and letters.

By giving precise meanings to the terms used in talking about the Trinity, Basil paved the way for the work of the Council of Constantinople (381). Suspected in turn of the opposite errors of Sabellianism and tritheism, Basil could be convicted of neither. He died in Caesarea on the first day of 379.

H. DERMOT MCDONALD

the single humanity shared by father, mother, and child, easily misled. Basil argued that the Trinitarian baptismal formula and doxology (whether 'Glory be to the Father together with the Son, with the Holy Spirit' or 'Glory be to the Father through the Son in the Holy Spirit') demanded that Father, Son, and Spirit are equal, but distinct. According to the Cappadocians, the three operated inseparably, none ever acting independently of the others. 'Every divine action begins from the Father, proceeds through the Son, and is completed in the Holy Spirit.' They 'coinhere', inter-penetrate each other; 'everything that the Father is is seen in the Son, and everything that the Son is belongs to the Father'.

On the basis of John 15:26 ('When the Advocate comes, whom I will send to you from the Father, the Spirit of truth who comes from the Father, he will testify on my behalf.' NRSV)

> ## All Constantinople talks theology
>
> If you ask anyone in Constantinople for change, he will start discussing with you whether the Son is begotten or unbegotten. If you ask about the quality of bread, you will get the answer: 'The Father is greater, the Son is less.' If you suggest taking a bath you will be told: 'There was nothing before the Son was created.'
>
> GREGORY OF NYSSA

they taught that the Spirit 'proceeds' from the Father through the Son, as the counterpart of the Son's generation. Basil remained diffident about calling the Holy Spirit 'God'.

THE END OF ARIANISM

The Cappadocians' theology made little formal headway until Theodosius (347–95), a Westerner and keen supporter of Nicaea, became Eastern Emperor in 379. It was he who conclusively established Christianity as the official religion of the Empire: a famous decree of 380 required all peoples to adhere to 'the religion that is followed by Pope Damasus and Peter, Bishop of Alexandria'.

In 381 Theodosius summoned the Council of Constantinople, to reaffirm the faith of Nicaea. No doctrinal statement put out by this council has survived, but at the Council of Chalcedon in 451 the Nicene Creed – regarded as the Creed of Nicaea appropriately modified after later controversy – was attributed to the Council of Constantinople. The Nicene Creed was probably independently produced by the council, republishing the teaching of Nicaea rather than repeating its wording.

THE COUNCIL OF CONSTANTINOPLE

The Council of Constantinople marked the end of Arianism within the Empire. Unlike the other three early ecumenical councils, it was not followed by decades of doctrinal strife. Theodosius had proved the man for the moment, but in matters of church order, peace was more elusive.

The council confirmed Gregory of Nazianzus' appointment as Bishop of Constantinople, rejecting the rival claimant backed by Alexandria. When Meletius died, Gregory succeeded him as president of the council, but in this exposed seat he was buffeted from all sides, and he retired sadly into private life. In his place, the council chose as Bishop of Constantinople and its own president a prominent layman, who belonged to no party, and was unbaptized. Anti-Western feelings were strong, and the schism at Antioch went on.

Alexandria's interference in Constantinople and Antioch was clearly in mind when the council drew up its canons. The second of these adopted the dioceses (groupings of provinces) in the Eastern Empire as regions for church purposes, and forbade intervention in the affairs of another diocese. The third canon read: 'The Bishop of Constantinople shall have the primacy of honour after the Bishop of Rome because Constantinople is new Rome.' The elevation of this upstart see greatly offended the ancient church of Alexandria, for centuries the leading city in the Greek world, and provoked bitter conflict between the two. Rome, too, was dismayed because the canon assumed that political importance determined status in the church. Rome based her supremacy on religious grounds, claiming to be founded by Peter, the apostle. The new ruling would leave Rome's future position uncertain instead of unassailably supreme, on the basis of history and tradition. The Roman Church repudiated it – delaying until the sixth century Western recognition of the Council of Constantinople (which was attended only by Eastern bishops) as ecumenical. The canon itself was accepted at the Lateran Council in 1215.

The new settlement of orthodoxy concerning the Trinity was enforced by imperial edict in both East and West, where Ambrose spurred the emperors into clearing up the last pockets of Arianism. But in government and discipline, East and West went separate ways, still divided over Antioch. Doctrinal order had been restored, but in the process the seeds of irreparable disruption had been sown between East and West, and in Alexandria's isolation in the East.

THEOLOGY OF THE TRINITY

The Cappadocians' theology of the Trinity remained fundamental to all subsequent Greek and Byzantine statements, such as John of Damascus' eighth-century *The Orthodox Faith*. John developed their doctrine of the mutual indwelling of the three persons of the Trinity.

Latin expositions reached their peak in Augustine's writings, especially his principal work on *The Trinity*, an intensive and profound discussion, from the traditional Western starting-point that God is one single substance. His distinctive contribution was elaborate analogies: of the lover, the loved, and the love which binds them, as a picture of relationships within the Trinity; and of the inner man reflecting the image of God in a trinity of mind or memory, knowledge or understanding, and will or love. Marius Victorinus, a converted Neo-platonist, had speculated along somewhat similar lines in refuting Arianism, shortly before Augustine wrote.

Augustine, like Ambrose and Jerome, taught that the Spirit proceeded not from the Father alone, but also from the Son. (The Greek theologians for the most part thought of the Spirit proceeding from the Father through the Son.) This so-called 'double procession' of the Spirit was incorporated into the 'Athanasian' Creed, which in reality was written in Latin, probably in southern Gaul in the late fifth century. This creed, Augustinian in inspiration, is directed against the 'modalism' (similar to Sabellianism) which Priscillianism had revived in Gaul and Spain in the fourth and following centuries, and against the Arianism of the Goths and Vandals, which made the Son and the Spirit into second- and third-rank divinities.

The 'double procession' of the Spirit found its way into the Nicene Creed by the addition of the word *Filioque* (Latin, 'and the Son'), the first evidence of which comes from the Third Council of Toledo, Spain (589). The Roman Church refused for centuries to accept this addition, which later became a major bone of contention between the Latin and Greek Churches.

WAS THE LORD OF GLORY CRUCIFIED?

The relationship between the divine and human natures in the incarnate Christ was inevitably interwoven with the questions about the Trinity in the Arian controversy. However, it remained a minor theme until the divinity of the Son had been firmly established. So long as the Son was viewed as inferior to the Father in his deity, its union with humanity in Christ was not an urgent problem.

The issue was discussed at Athanasius' little council or synod at Alexandria in 362, probably in connection with the teaching of Apollinarius (or Apollinaris, c. 310–90), Bishop of Laodicea in Syria. What was decided is not clear, except that it was agreed that the incarnation was not 'the Word indwelling a holy man, as he did the prophets', but 'the Word himself becoming man for us from Mary after the flesh'. Athanasius' account of the agreement reflects the approach to the subject favoured in Alexandria; Apollinarius' bold exposition of this approach was universally condemned.

Origen regarded Christ's rational soul as the ideal meeting-point with the *Logos*, because they shared a perfect natural affinity. (Platonists viewed the soul as the essential person and, like Stoics, held that the *Logos* directing the universe and the *logos* in human individuals were homogeneous.) It was a short step to conceive of the *Logos* not merely swallowing up the soul, but replacing it.

The Word, therefore, was the sole agent in the life of Christ. This framework of understanding was followed by both Arius and Athanasius, although they differed totally in their estimates of the Word. Whether or not Athanasius disbelieved in, or changed his mind about, the existence of a human soul in Christ (the debate still rages), he certainly attached no theological significance to it. For him, Christ is always the divine Word active in human flesh. It was the Word-as-incarnate who was tired, or ignorant, or suffered; from start to finish, the incarnation was a divine work of salvation. The Alexandrians' use of allegory in understanding Scripture enabled them to be less bothered by the human experiences of Jesus in the gospel story.

As a consequence, this doctrine of Christ grasped strongly the unity of his person, and was at times inclined to mix divine and human. The incarnate union brought about a real interchange of attributes between the two: the Lord of glory actually suffered crucifixion.

APOLLINARIUS

Apollinarius was a staunch theologian in the Nicene tradition. Reacting against teaching from Antioch, he denied that Christ possessed a human soul: the soul was intrinsically corrupt, and could not be responsible for motivating a Saviour of sinful people. He asserted that the virgin birth marked the divide between the human race and Christ, and that humanity was the sphere – not the instrument – of salvation. Christ was 'one nature composed of impassible divinity and passible flesh', 'one enfleshed nature of the divine Word'. In the union, Christ's flesh took on a divine character. In the eucharist, a communicant could be confident of receiving Christ's life-giving flesh.

Apollinarius' teaching first attracted notice in the 350s, but was not prominent until the 370s, when the supreme heresy-hunter, Epiphanius, Bishop of Salamis, Cyprus, denounced it. It was condemned in East and West, and conclusively at the Council of Constantinople in 381. If God in Christ did not lay hold of our full humanity, then it is not saved. 'What is not assumed [by the Word] is not healed' (Gregory of Nazianzus). Apollinarius made the incarnation seem like a mere appearance of God, and Christ's humanity monstrous or mutilated.

After the condemnation of Apollinarius, Alexandrian theologians no longer denied that Christ had a human soul. Yet little significance was attached to human agency or experience in the incarnation. Apollinarius' writings continued to circulate, often masquerading under orthodox names such as Athanasius.

TWO NATURES?

The Antioch school of theologians normally interpreted Scripture in a straightforward historical manner. Serious consideration was given to the human figure of the Gospels, whose example and achievement were regarded as possessing saving virtue. In Christ the human will, which in other people turns freely to sin, proved obedient and victorious.

Antiochene theologians consequently stressed the complete humanity of Christ, regarding human nature as a unity of body and soul, following Aristotle. This union did not in any way affect the completeness and normality of the human nature. Antiochenes feared that if the human soul were excluded, the Word would be demoted in Arian fashion in order to accommodate the evidence of the Gospels. It might be possible to ascribe Christ's physical experiences, such as growth, hunger, and pain, to flesh alone; but not his mental and emotional life of sorrow, ignorance, and exasperation.

After the Word became flesh, the two natures remained distinct. In Antiochene teaching, they could easily seem like two beings, God and the man Jesus, Son of God and son of Mary, joined, associated, even juxtaposed, rather than personally united. This seemed to open up the possibility of separating 'the man who was assumed' from 'the Word who assumed'. As a vessel indwelt by the Word, he was not unlike prophets and apostles, except that he enjoyed perfect fullness of grace and power.

This dualistic approach allotted what Christ did or underwent either to his divine, or to his human, nature. Undeniably the New Testament spoke of the Son of God suffering, or the human Jesus working miracles, but this was seen as merely a literary convention, acceptable to the ordinary believer, but not to the theologian.

These characteristic emphases were developed by Eustathius, by Diodore, Bishop of Tarsus (r. 378 – c. 390), and supremely by Theodore, Bishop of Mopsuestia (east of Tarsus) (r. 392–428), in direct opposition to Apollinarius. Diodore and Theodore had been presbyters at Antioch.

NESTORIUS DEPOSED

Nestorius was a famous preacher at Antioch, before being appointed Bishop of Constantinople by Theodosius II in 428. It is difficult to prove that Nestorius' teaching went beyond that of his master, Theodore. Like the latter, he doubted whether it was right to describe Mary as *theotokos*, 'God-bearer', the title used by Apollinarius, but also well established in Christian devotion, especially in monastic circles.

Nestorius (c. 386–c. 451) was undoubtedly rather outspoken in expounding his Christology. The incarnate Christ he weakly described as 'one *prosōpon*', the single historical figure of the Gospels. In his own words, 'I hold the natures apart, but unite the worship.' Nestorius was condemned more for ecclesiastical than doctrinal reasons: as the Emperor's nominee in the hot seat of Constantinople, he was soon widely hated for his assaults on Jews and heretics. He also rapidly incurred the implacable hostility of Cyril, the Patriarch of Alexandria (r. 412–44), a distinguished expositor and theologian, but an unscrupulous and violent controversialist. Cyril, sufficiently alarmed by Nestorius' teaching and 'new Nicene' background, was outraged when Nestorius listened to the complaints of some Alexandrian clergy deposed by Cyril. Western disapproval of Nestorius was ensured when he gave refuge to some Pelagian exiles who had been excommunicated in the West, though his action probably had nothing to do with the fact that some Pelagian emphases were similar to Antiochene theology. There was also confusion over language: *physis* was used by Alexandrians of the single 'person' of Christ, but by Antiochenes of his two 'natures'.

Cyril opened his attack on Nestorius late in 428. His forceful arguments for Alexandrian Christology were bedevilled by his own unwitting use of works by

NESTORIUS

Condemned for heresy at Ephesus, Nestorius was a native of Germanicia, in Euphratesian Syria. Born around 381, he was taught the theology of Antioch by Theodore of Mopsuestia, whose views he echoed. He was instituted Bishop of Constantinople in 428, and immediately began an offensive against Arian heretics and the Novatians. His support of his chaplain Anastasius made him declare his own views, which brought about his condemnation for heresy at the Council of Ephesus (431).

Nestorius, in his defence of Anastasius, and his repeated rejection of the word *theotokos* (the popular designation of Mary as 'bearer of God'), made it appear that he held Christ to be consti-tuted of two persons. He did not deny the deity of Christ; but in emphasizing the reality and integrity of his humanity, he pictured the relation between the two natures in terms of a moral 'conjunction', or merging of wills, rather than as an *essential* 'union'. Although he never divided Christ into 'two sons', Son of God, and son of Mary, he refused to attribute to the divine nature the human acts and sufferings of the man Jesus. He objected that to as-sert that Mary was mother of God was tantamount to declaring that the divine nature could be born of a woman, or that God could be three days old. Nestorius distinguished the two natures in Christ with admirable realism, but was unable to reduce the two to the unique, and clearly undifferentiated, one Jesus Christ of the Gospels. The twelve anath-emas hurled against him by his chief opponent, Cyril of Alexandria, were countered by twelve from Nestorius. After exile in 431, he wrote his apology, which survived in Syriac, under the pseudonym *The Bazaar of Heracleides*, in which Nestorius attempts to justify his position and answer Cyril's criticisms. Nestorius died in Upper Egypt around 451.

H. DERMOT MCDONALD

Apollinarius. He stirred up accusations that Nestorius was an adoptionist, and slandered him to Rome, where Pope Celestine was upset about his having received the Pelagians. Celestine commissioned Cyril to carry out a Roman synod's judgment against Nestorius, and Cyril demanded that Nestorius should agree to twelve 'anathemas' which condemned the Antiochene doctrine in the harshest terms.

At the Council of Ephesus in 431, called by Theodosius II – who had until then supported Nestorius – Cyril got Nestorius deposed before the late arrival of his Syrian supporters. They in turn, led by John of Antioch, condemned Cyril and Bishop Memnon of Ephesus. Finally the Roman legates arrived and approved the action of Cyril, whose synod reassembled to excommunicate the Syrian bishops and distribute favours to his allies. Cyril was able to count on the backing of metropolitan bishops such as Ephesus, who resented Constantinople's superior authority, and Jerusalem, who wanted independence from Antioch. Cyril's campaign also rallied ordinary Christians, who only too easily pictured Christ as God in human guise, and worshipped his incorruptible flesh in the eucharist.

After further machinations, Theodosius II eventually acquiesced in the decisions of Cyril's first assembly at Ephesus, which became the third Ecumenical Council. Nestorius was sent off to Antioch, and died around 450 in exile in Egypt. Few of his supporters accepted his excommunication.

Under pressure from the Emperor, Cyril and the Syrians began to understand each other, and in 433 they signed a Formula of Union drawn up by Theodoret, Bishop of Cyrrhus (north of Antioch). Largely Antiochene, it included the description *theotokos* (bearer of God), and showed that some mutual understanding had existed at Ephesus in 431, when most of it was drafted. Both sides agreed to drop demands – the Syrians for Nestorius' reinstatement, Cyril for recognition of his twelve anathemas. Extremists on both wings were dissatisfied, but the compromise held while Cyril and John of Antioch were alive.

THE 'MONOPHYSITE' COUNCIL OF EPHESUS

In the early 440s a new generation took over. John died in 441/2; Leo I became Bishop of Rome in 440; the ruthless Dioscorus succeeded Cyril in 444; Flavian was made Patriarch of Constantinople in 446. Of the earlier protagonists, only Theodoret survived.

Dispute soon raged around Eutyches, an aged monastic superior in Constantinople, who provocatively attacked the doctrine of 'two natures after the union'. In almost 'single-nature' (Monophysite) terms, he suggested that Christ's humanity was absorbed by his divinity, like a drop of wine in the sea. Although attacked by Theodoret, and condemned under Flavian in 448, Eutyches had influence at court and was supported by the unprincipled Dioscorus.

Amid counter-charges, intrigues, and disorder, Theodosius II summoned another council for Ephesus in 449. Leo sent a statement of doctrine for the bishops to approve: this was the first major Western contribution — unoriginal, but a useful mediating statement. It rejected Eutyches and supported 'two natures after the union', yet incorporated some Alexandrian positions. (Tertullian had long ago provided the structure and language — two *substantiae* in one *persona* — of a Latin Christology, which to a remarkable extent anticipated the outcome of these Eastern disputes.)

Dioscorus dominated this second Council of Ephesus. Leo's *Tome* (his statement of doctrine) was refused a hearing, Flavian was deposed, and Eutyches rehabilitated. The Formula of Union and its two-nature doctrine was banned, and its supporters, including Theodoret, excommunicated. Leo labelled the synod a 'den of robbers'; it amounted to a shameless attack on Constantinople by Dioscorus.

CYRIL OF ALEXANDRIA

Although he was an important figure who became a brilliant representative of the Alexandrian theology, the early life of Cyril is obscure. He was accepted into the ranks of the clergy by his nephew, Theophilus, Patriarch of Alexandria, and in 403 accompanied Theophilus to Constantinople. Despite opposition, Cyril was elected in 412 to succeed Theophilus as Patriarch of Alexandria. His main concern was to combat Nestorianism. Acting on behalf of Celestine of Rome, Cyril convened the Council of Alexandria in 430, which demanded that Nestorius recant. Cyril's twelve anathemas against Nestorius were countered with twelve from Nestorius. Cyril headed the Council of Ephesus (431), which deposed Nestorius.

Cyril's theological talent was devoted to preserving Christ's person as a living unity, against Nestorian dualism. While acknowledging the completeness of Christ's human nature, he held that the human nature which the Word assumed was not really 'personal'. In his resulting definition, however, the two natures were virtually resolved into one, and by using the phrase 'one nature' he was blamed for reviving Apollinarianism, and giving rise to Eutychianism, with its resulting Monophysitism.

Against Nestorius, as well as heretics, Jews, and pagans, Cyril showed himself a ruthless antagonist. The conflict with Nestorius was in part a clash between the rival sees of Alexandria and Constantinople. Cyril died in 444.

H. DERMOT MCDONALD

LEO THE GREAT

Leo (c. 391–461) was born in Tuscany, Italy, and rose through the bureaucracy of the church to become Bishop of Rome in 440. He advanced the primacy of the Roman Church in the West, and was the first Bishop of Rome to make extensive use of the text 'You are Peter...' (Matthew 16:19) as speaking of the pope himself. He also received legal backing for the status of the Bishop of Rome from the Emperor Valentinian III, although by this time edicts from the Western Emperor were mostly unenforceable. Leo was one of the church's earliest great administrators, his style strongly influenced by Roman law. He was also a notable preacher.

Leo took a leading part in the controversies of the fifth century about the nature of Christ, fighting energetically against ideas that stressed the deity of Christ at the expense of his humanity. The *Tome* of Leo – his statement about the person of Christ – was disregarded at the 'robber synod' of Ephesus (449), but two years later, at the Council of Chalcedon (451), it was one of the main sources used to draw up the Chalcedonian Definition on the person of Christ. In line with mainstream beliefs, Leo stated that Christ has both a fully human nature and a fully divine nature, and yet was not a split personality.

Leo increased his personal prestige, as well as that of his office as Roman bishop, when he persuaded Attila the Hun to turn back from Rome (452), and later managed to minimize the damage done to the city when it was captured by the Vandal leader Gaiseric (455). The Roman bishop was beginning to act as a civil ruler.

MICHAEL A. SMITH

THE COUNCIL OF CHALCEDON

No redress was possible until Theodosius II died the next year, in a fall from his horse. His sister, Pulcheria, succeeded him, reigning jointly with her new husband, Marcian. Pulcheria had been sympathetic to the cause of Leo and Flavian, and the great Council of Chalcedon (across the Bosphorus from Constantinople) was summoned for late 451.

More than 400 Greek bishops attended, with legates (representatives) from Rome, and Pulcheria's own commissioners controlled the proceedings. The acts of the 'robber synod' (Second Council of Ephesus) were undone, and Dioscorus deposed. Theodoret at last disowned Nestorius. The Council put out a composite Definition, which consisted of the Creeds of 325 and 381, two letters of Cyril refuting Nestorius, Leo's *Tome*, and, despite some reluctance, a new confession, compiled largely from Cyril, Leo, and the Formula of 433:

> *We all with one voice confess our Lord Jesus Christ one and the same Son, at once complete in Godhead and complete in manhood, truly God and truly man, consisting of a reasonable soul and body; of one substance with the Father as regards his Godhead, of one substance with us as regards his manhood, like us in all things, apart from sin; begotten of the Father before the ages as regards his Godhead, the same in the last days, for us and for our salvation, born from the Virgin Mary, the God-bearer (theotokos), as regards his manhood; one and the same Christ, Son, Lord, Only-begotten, to be acknowledged in two natures, without confusion, without change, without division, or without separation; the distinction of natures being in no way abolished because of the union, but rather the characteristic property of each nature being preserved, and coming together to form one*

person (prosōpon), and one entity (hypostasis) not as if Christ were parted or divided into two persons ...

This distinguished statement undoubtedly reflects the fact that the Antiochene standpoint had the stronger influence.

Rome was disturbed by some of this council's canons, which included important regulations concerning monks and monasteries. Canons 9 and 17 allowed appeals from Eastern provinces to be addressed to Constantinople, instead of to the chief bishop (exarch) of the diocese. Canon 28 reaffirmed the third canon of 381, explicitly stating that the earlier council gave Rome the primacy because she was the imperial city. The Roman legates appealed in vain to Nicaea's canons, before Constantinople even existed! Leo even delayed recognizing the Council of Chalcedon's doctrinal settlement for a couple of years.

THE ACACIAN SCHISM

Chalcedon's decrees became imperial law, which was now normal practice. They offended Eastern Churches who cherished Cyril's one-nature portrayal of the incarnate Christ; these dissidents were henceforth known as 'Monophysites'. For the most part they could no more be called heretics than Cyril himself.

Anti-Chalcedonianism soon dominated Egypt, where the Coptic language served to express dissent, especially among the monks, and where the Greek-speaking Chalcedonian minority was dubbed 'the Emperor's men'. In Syria, where the Syriac language played a similar role, the Monophysites had to struggle for ascendancy; but here too their leadership far excelled that of the Chalcedonians.

The division threatened the imperial throne itself during the Emperor Zeno's reign. He subsequently issued the *Henoticon* – a peace formula which condemned Nestorius and Eutyches, sanctioned Cyril's anathemas in addition to the Creeds of 325 and 381, and put a curse on any contrary doctrine 'whether taught at Chalcedon or elsewhere'. From 484 to 518, under the Emperors Zeno and Anastasius, the *Henoticon* was official orthodoxy. The pope's excommunication of Zeno and Acacius, the Patriarch of Constantinople, created the 'Acacian schism' between the Greek and Latin churches, the longest formal breach thus far.

THE GROWTH OF NESTORIANISM

The Empire's adoption of this compromise Monophysitism encouraged the Persian Church to accept Nestorianism, in order to widen its divorce from the imperial church, and so appear less obnoxious to Persia's rulers. After Nestorius' condemnation in 431, Nestorian strength had concentrated at Edessa, east of the River Euphrates. The Monophysite reaction after Chalcedon prompted the Nestorians to migrate across the frontier into Persia, and make Nisibis their centre. In 486 the Persian Church became officially Nestorian. The works of Diodore and Theodore were preserved in Persian as well as Syriac.

After the *Henoticon* was abandoned, efforts to meet the Monophysites half-way continued, especially under the Emperor Justinian I (Justinian the Great, 527–65), who set his sights on the political and religious reunification of East and West. In 543/4 he condemned three propositions, or 'chapters', which listed Theodore of Mopsuestia and his works, and specified writings of Theodoret and Ibas (Bishop of Edessa, 435–57) – all three alleged

MAXIMIANVS

Sixth-century mosaic of the Emperor Justinian I, surrounded by his retinue, including Bishop Maximian; from the Basilica of San Vitale, Ravenna, Italy.
SONIA HALLIDAY PHOTOGRAPHS

Nestorians left uncondemned by Chalcedon. Pope Vigilius (r. 537–55) hesitated under extended pressure, but finally consented to the anathematizing of these propositions at the fifth Ecumenical Council at Constantinople in 553. The West was divided over the affair. The same council condemned Origen as a heretic, and approved the development of Chalcedon's doctrine worked out by Leontius of Byzantium.

MONOPHYSITE CHURCHES FORM

The emperors persecuted, as well as wooed, the Monophysites, which stimulated the formation of separate ecclesiastical organizations. Severus, Patriarch of Antioch (512–38), gave Monophysite theology its definitive Cyril-derived shape, while Jacob Baradeus, Bishop of Edessa from 543 until his death in 578, vigorously created Monophysite bishoprics throughout the East in the mid-sixth century. As a result, the Syrian Jacobites, and the Copts of Egypt and Ethiopia – which was always closely dependent on Alexandria – formed themselves into autonomous Monophysite churches. Armenia, too, became Monophysite in the same period, largely in order to gain her independence of the Empire and of Constantinople. Georgia took up Chalcedonianism partly to gain imperial aid in resisting Armenian control.

In the seventh century, Persian and, later, Arab invasions made reconciliation with the Monophysites even more imperative; but two further attempts at achieving harmony of doctrine came to nothing. The beliefs that Christ possessed a single principle of activity or 'energy' (Monergism) and a single will (Monotheletism) were both condemned at the sixth General Council at Constantinople in 680–81. This Council decreed that in Christ 'there are two natural wills and modes of operation without division, change, separation, or confusion ... His human will follows, without any resistance or reluctance but in subjection, his divine and omnipotent will.'

Once again the failure to resolve doctrinal conflict was a major factor in the creation of ecclesiastical divisions, which in the eastern Mediterranean area weakened the Empire's defences against the Muslim invaders. Issues of faith and order had proved to be disastrously interwoven. The creeds and confessions of the ecumenical councils were bought at considerable cost to peace.

DAVID F. WRIGHT

CHAPTER 10

BUILDINGS AND BELIEF
Early church structures

The first Christians gathered in existing buildings, usually the homes of individual believers. The earliest known church of which traces remain is at Dura-Europos, Syria, where a normal courtyard house was adapted for the purpose. Two rooms were put together for the celebration of the Lord's Supper, another room – decorated with frescoes – served as the place for baptisms, and yet another may have been used for the instruction of applicants for church membership.

Wealthy Christians in Rome likewise adapted parts of their houses for worship. The catacombs, or underground burial chambers, were not used for regular meetings, as is sometimes supposed, but for the annual celebration of the deaths of the martyrs. This began the link with the remains of the faithful departed which has been a feature of much Christian worship and which has influenced the design and arrangement of churches. Most obviously, it has meant the use of the church as a burial-place, and its setting within a cemetery or churchyard.

BASILICA CHURCHES

Constantine's pronouncement of freedom of worship for all in the 'Edict' of Milan (313) soon brought a great change in the circumstances of the church, which is reflected in the buildings for Christian worship. Gone was the need for secrecy and the need to adapt existing buildings. Shortly afterwards recognized as the official religion of the Roman Empire, Christianity found an appropriate pattern for its impressive new buildings in the Roman basilica, built to accommodate crowds attending a law court, market, or other kind of assembly. The Emperor himself built a new church in Rome that symbolized the dawn of a new era: this Church of St John Lateran was a basilica, and in all the main centres of the Empire this style of church seems rapidly to have replaced the house-church.

The main architectural features of the basilica were a rectangular hall, divided into three sections by two (sometimes four) rows of columns parallel with the longer sides, and an 'apse', or semi-circular niche, opening off one of the shorter sides. The roof covering the wider central space was higher than the roofs over the side sections. The outer walls, including that of the apse, were blank, with the only daylight coming through the doorways or windows pierced in the walls of the central space, above the columns. These are the ancestors of the 'clear-storey' (or clerestory) nave and side-aisles long associated with churches. Here was a direct ancestor of the familiar nave and side aisles of a church.

The appearance of this new, and fully-developed, plan for church buildings has led to the suggestion that Constantine imposed it on the church, and commanded that it be followed everywhere. It seems more likely that the plan was gradually adopted by the builders of churches simply because it was the most suitable available, and that these developments began before the time of Constantine.

The basilica plan was followed because it provided what the church needed in its altered circumstances – most obviously, space for the much larger congregations which now gathered for worship. The house-church had usually provided enough room for the persecuted Christians; now that Christianity was respectable and officially recognized, the numbers of worshippers increased rapidly.

Pagan temples were not designed to house a worshipping assembly, although occasionally they were taken over and adapted by the Christians for their own worship in smaller, or less wealthy, communities. Such adaptation has been described as 'turning the temple inside out'. The space between the outer pillars was filled in with walls, the original inner walls of the temple were pierced, and an apse was added. In other words, the temple was made as similar to a basilica as possible.

CLERGY AND LAITY SEPARATE

Worship in the house-church had been of an intimate kind, in which all present had taken an active part. But by the beginning of the fourth century, the distinction between clergy and lay people was becoming more pronounced. About this time, the liturgy changed from being 'a corporate action of the whole church' into 'a service said by the clergy to which the laity listened'. This may have influenced the choice of the basilica plan for the new churches.

Certainly the basilica pattern made it easier for the distinction between clergy and lay people to harden. The apse was reserved for the clergy, where a throne was set up in the centre for the bishop, with benches for the presbyters ranged on either side. This stately chair reflected the bishop's position as a trusted, imperial servant as much as a pastor of the flock. The table for the Lord's Supper became a permanent altar at the front of the apse, and under it were often placed the remains of a saint or martyr. The central space, or 'nave', was occupied by the choir, who sang the service, and by the lower ranks of clergy. The ordinary worshippers tended to be confined to the side aisles – men on one side, and women on the other. Those under instruction (the catechumens) or under discipline (the penitents) were restricted to the porch, at the rear of the nave.

The basilica had no direct lighting, as the windows were immediately under the roof of the nave in the 'clear-storey'. This was not regarded as a disadvantage, for it enhanced the light of the candles and lamps near the altar, and heightened the sense of mystery. Churches were normally orientated towards the west, so that the rays of the rising sun fell on the face of the clergyman celebrating the eucharist as he stood behind the altar, facing the congregation.

SITING THE CHURCHES

St John Lateran in Rome was built on a site without any special associations, but the Churches of St Peter and of St Paul were built by Constantine on the traditional sites of the apostles' martyrdom or burial. In the Holy Land, churches were built on sites associated with particular events in the life of Christ. This affected the plan of the church, for attention had to be drawn to the sacred spot which was the reason for the church being built there. Thus in the Church of the Nativity in Bethlehem, the traditional birthplace is covered by an octagonal building which is linked to a rectangular basilica. In St Peter's, Rome, the place of martyrdom was marked by a structure at the front of the apse, and given further prominence by the addition of transepts (cross-aisles) on either side of the basilica..

BAPTISTERIES AND *MARTYRIA*

Besides the basilica, two other types of Christian building developed. These were the baptistery, where baptisms took place, and the *martyrion*, a chapel built over the tomb or relics of a martyr or saint. In the East, it was thought important to keep the altar distinct from the relics of the saint, which were often housed in a separate building. Both of these types of building were constructed with a central focal point, and a dome was a frequent feature. When these buildings were designed for congregational use, the altar was not placed in the centre over the tomb, but in an apse added to the original plan.

The tradition of the buildings built for martyrs (*martyria*) was strong enough for their centralized plan to influence church architecture. In the Holy Land, Syria, and Mesopotamia, centralized churches became the rule; and since such churches required a dome, architects developed their skills until they succeeded in constructing a cupola over a square. In this way, the basilica and centralized styles of construction could be combined, making possible the architectural miracle of St Sophia, Constantinople, the supreme example of the domed basilica. St Sophia (Hagia Sophia) was built by the command of the Emperor Justinian, and completed in 537. Its great central dome was damaged by an earthquake twenty-one years later, but was repaired by 563, since when it has remained.

Buildings of a similar style do occur in the West, but there the basilica-plan was the basis of most church architecture. In time, the rounded Romanesque arches were replaced by pointed Gothic ones, and the ground-plan was often elaborated into the form of a cross. With the development of trade and the expansion of towns, churches became more and more magnificent, an expression of civic pride.

THE ALTAR

Despite their apparent differences, Eastern and Western Churches have one important development in common: both separate the altar from the ordinary worshipper. This is partly the result, partly the cause, of an emphasis on the 'mystery' of the liturgy in the East and of the mass (eucharist) in the West. In the East the separation is made by means of the *iconostasis*, a massive solid screen adorned with icons, or pictorial representations of the saints. When the doors on this screen are closed, the altar is invisible to the ordinary worshippers, who are in this way sharply distinguished from the priests, who pass inside the *iconostasis*.

In the West the means of separation is different, but the effect is similar. Churches in the West are divided into a chancel (or room for the clergy) and a nave (or room for the laity). The two are usually divided by an open-work screen with a large crucifix on top, known as a rood-screen, or, less commonly, by a solid screen known as a *pulpitum*. The chancel contains the high altar and seats for the clergy – often intricately-carved stalls – while the nave contains the pulpit for the preaching of sermons and often a second altar. For worship the people would either stand or bring their own seats. The baptismal font is usually at the back of the nave, near the entrance to the church. These arrangements prevailed throughout the Middle Ages, but were complicated by the erection of numerous side altars in the aisles of the nave, and the addition of chapels, each with its own altar. These often contained relics, and were primarily for the saying of masses for the souls of the founders and their friends.

HENRY SEFTON

CHAPTER 11

WORSHIP AND THE CHRISTIAN YEAR
The making of the Christian Calendar

When Christianity became a tolerated religion, in the time of Constantine, worship and festivals had not yet been rigidly formalized. The main festivals of the Christian year were Easter (the *Pascha*) and Pentecost. Easter was still at this time only a one-day festival, celebrating together the death, resurrection, and exaltation of Christ, on the Sunday following 14 Nisan in the Jewish calendar. It ushered in a period of rejoicing over the resurrection of Christ, which lasted for the seven weeks, until Pentecost. (The whole period was often known as Pentecost.) The weeks immediately before Easter Sunday were used for preparing candidates for baptism. In addition, a number of days were probably kept as the anniversaries of local martyrdoms.

Christian worship in this period was almost entirely in Greek, although in a few places local languages such as Syriac, Coptic, or Latin were probably beginning to be used. In general, services in this period were extempore, the local bishop being free to pray or preach as the Spirit led, within certain fairly broad guidelines. There were a few fixed formulas in use, including the dialogue beginning 'Lift up your hearts' (*Sursum corda*), the hymn beginning 'Holy, holy, holy' (*Sanctus*) based on Isaiah 6, and the 'Words of Institution', commemorating the Last Supper, at the communion service. The doxologies at the end of prayers, the creed, and the form of words at baptism were also of a set pattern, although the words of the creed could vary slightly from one church to another.

SUNDAY A HOLIDAY

The toleration of Christianity under Constantine produced a few immediate changes. Constantine ordered that Sunday was to become a public holiday – similar to other Roman holidays – which made possible wider developments in worship, and larger congregations in the churches. Sunday services became bigger occasions, and worship imported some practices from court ceremonial, such as the use of incense, the carrying of candles as a mark of honour, and curtaining around the altar used at the eucharist. But Constantine's act of toleration also started trends

> ## The Apostles' Creed
>
> I believe in God the Father almighty;
>
> and in Christ Jesus, his only Son, our Lord,
>
> who was born of the Holy Spirit and the Virgin Mary,
>
> who was crucified under Pontius Pilate and was buried,
>
> on the third day rose from the dead,
> ascended into heaven,
> sits on the right hand of the Father
> whence he will come to judge the living and the dead;
>
> and in the Holy Spirit,
>
> the holy church,
>
> the remission of sins,
>
> the resurrection of the flesh
>
> (the life everlasting).
>
> THE OLD ROMAN CREED

Egeria's Pilgrimage to the Holy Places

Next we came, in the name of Christ our God, to Edessa [in northern Mesopotamia]. When we arrived there, we immediately went to the church and memorial chapel of the holy Thomas. And when we had offered up our prayers there in the customary way, and had done all the usual things at the holy places, we read something there about the saintly Thomas. Now the church there is very large, very beautiful, and built in a new style; it is a worthy home of God.

And since there were many things I wished to see, I had to stay there for three days. I saw in the city several commemorative chapels, and also holy monks, some of whom live near the chapels, and others in hermitages further from the city, in more isolated places. The bishop of the city – a truly pious man, a monk, and confessor – received me warmly and said: 'Since I see, my daughter, that from a spirit of religion you have gone to such great efforts to journey here from distant places, we shall, if you desire it, show you all the places here which Christians like to see.' Then I thanked God first of all and afterwards him, and eagerly urged him to carry out his promise. He brought me first to the palace of King Agbar …

TRAVELS OF EGERIA 19

which only became really noticeable later: the gradual growth of formality, ceremonial, and superstition. Churches still had to draw people in: during the fourth century this was often done by great pulpit-orators, who were cheered (or occasionally booed) by intensely-involved congregations.

Greater leisure meant that Christian festivals tended to multiply. Constantine's mother Helena went on a pilgrimage to the Holy Land (326–27), which made a great impression, and such visits to Bible lands now became quite common. A short pamphlet appeared in 333 describing a pilgrimage route from Bordeaux to Jerusalem. Considerable effort was devoted to finding various biblical sites, erecting churches on them (for example, the Church of the Holy Sepulchre), and celebrating there the events linked to them. The Church at Jerusalem took the lead in this, and was rapidly followed by others. In this way, the idea of the Christian year as a re-enactment of the life of Jesus became increasingly central.

EASTER

It was probably early in the fourth century that Easter expanded into a week-long festival, and the marking of Christ's death was made distinct from the Easter Sunday resurrection festivities. Good Friday, Maundy Thursday, and Palm Sunday were now all separately celebrated. Easter had often been spent by baptismal candidates fasting on a vigil, a practice now generally adopted by the church. At the same time, the week after Easter became the special period when newly-baptized Christians received teaching about baptism and the eucharist.

The period before Easter for preparing candidates for baptism became formalized into the forty days of Lent. Several sets of baptismal instruction addresses have survived, usually consisting of an extended explanation of the creed that the candidates had to memorize. At the beginning of Lent, people who wanted to be baptized gave in their names at church, and their moral fitness for baptism was examined. Lent as a period of austerity and fasting only developed in the Middle Ages.

CHRISTMAS

The first mention of Christmas as a festival of the church on 25 December refers to AD 336, and comes in the *Philocalian Catalogue* (354), a civil and religious calendar compiled in Rome. But in the East, 6 January, known as Epiphany, was favoured as the anniversary of Christ's birth and baptism. The Western date was introduced to the East by John Chrysostom, near the end of the fourth century, and subsequently the birth of Christ was celebrated by both East and West on 25 December. Meanwhile Epiphany had come from the East to the West, where it commemorated the revealing of Jesus to the Gentiles – originally to the Wise Men.

ADVENT

As Christmas began to rival Easter in importance, it also acquired a preparatory period similar to Lent that was called Advent. Because Advent came at the point where the liturgical year ended, it was viewed both as preparation for the celebration of Jesus' birth, and as a period of looking forward to his second coming.

SAINTS' DAYS

During the period of persecution under the Roman Empire, martyrs were regarded with the highest esteem. The date of a martyr's death – the saint's day – was often celebrated annually by his or her local congregation. Such celebrations tended to be local festivals only, although in the case of some apostles, such as Peter, Paul, and John, these anniversaries – often referred to as 'birthdays' – were widely celebrated. However, even by the fourth century an average church observed only about six such days per year. When, after the persecution of Diocletian, martyrdom became almost unknown for Christians, other notable Christians, such as hermits, ascetics, or great missionaries, became venerated. Possibly the first of these was Martin of Tours (316-397). A special service of communion was held to celebrate the martyr's anniversary, sometimes at his or her tomb.

Although there was no great increase in the number of festivals of martyrs in the fourth century, martyrs did receive greater attention. Private ceremonies were held in the cemeteries, although these were often condemned because of disreputable behaviour. Also, many of the martyrs' tombs were decorated: for example, Bishop Damasus' many fine inscriptions in the catacombs in Rome. New discoveries of supposed relics of martyrs were celebrated with great joy, as at the finding of the relics of saints Gervasius and Protasius at Milan, in 386. A few churches were formally dedicated at this time, such as the great new church at Antioch in 341. The Roman festival of the throne of Peter (*Cathedra Petri*), first mentioned in the *Philocalian Catalogue*, is probably the earliest celebration of the patron saint of a particular church.

Those imprisoned for the faith had been permitted the privilege of forgiving penitent sinners. From this arose the belief that a martyr might still be able to obtain blessings for his or her local church. Some churches were built around the tomb of a martyr, and on the anniversary of the martyrdom it became customary to call on the martyr's prayers. In time, a similar practice extended to include the saints and the Virgin Mary, and was often connected with the idea that the communion was an offering on behalf of the living and the dead.

WRITTEN LITURGIES

With Christian worship evolving into public ceremonial, there came a move towards fixed, written forms of service, though during the fourth century this change was fairly slow.

The catecheses given at Jerusalem by Bishop Cyril (348–86) and Bishop John (386–417) include fixed wording, but also opportunity for extempore prayer. Ambrose of Milan quotes several long passages from the great eucharistic prayer in his work on the sacraments written 390–91.

At the same time, languages other than Greek were being used in worship. Egeria, a Gallic pilgrim to Jerusalem in the late fourth or early fifth century, mentions services there being conducted in Greek, Latin, and Syriac, and preaching to baptismal candidates in all three languages. In Egypt, both Coptic and Greek were used for worship. Although there was a gradual move towards fixed forms in worship, language and regional differences ensured considerable variations from one church to another, and such differences could even involve additional ceremonies. The Church at Milan, for example, practised ceremonial foot-washing at baptism (based on John 13:1–19), though this was unknown in Rome. Prominent churches such as Rome used their power to try to enforce some kind of uniformity, but local variations continued for a long time.

During the fifth and sixth centuries the trends begun in the fourth century continued; however, East and West now diverged more sharply. In the East, the ritual tended to become uniform, leaving no room for variation. This was perhaps due to the greater political stability there, which allowed uniformity to be more easily enforced. But fixed forms of worship were also the rule in churches disowned by the state-church, such as the Nestorians and the Monophysite Coptic Church. Only in the Syrian Jacobite Church did the practice of composing eucharistic prayers, attempted by almost every great churchman, live on; yet even here the liturgy of James was pre-eminent. At least eight local rites are known from the sixth century, but these gradually gave way to the liturgies of Chrysostom and Basil.

THE CHRISTIAN CALENDAR

In the West, the liturgy varied according to the calendar. Probably by the mid-fifth century, the Roman rite included a fixed eucharistic prayer, to which Leo the Great is traditionally credited with making a minor alteration. A wide selection of prayers was available in a sixth-century compilation from Verona, Italy, known as the *Leonine Sacramentary*; however, the central prayer is fixed in form.

A similar arrangement was to be found in other rites in the West; for example, the Mozarabic in Spain, the Gallican rites of France, the Celtic rites, and some early rites in northern Italy. It was possible to vary all but their basic form (for instance, in the mass only the opening preface, the *Sanctus*, and the Words of Institution could not be varied), but written forms were provided for different festivals. No two mass-books were identical, but all provided fixed written prayers – although in an emergency an eloquent bishop, such as Sidonius Apollinaris, might still extemporize a whole service. The Roman rite gradually spread throughout the West, and was already beginning to displace various local rites when it was made official by Charlemagne in the late eighth century.

By the year 600, many other festivals had been added to the Christian calendar, several going back to the fourth century, and what was to become the classic pattern of the Christian year had been established in all but a few details. The Christmas period acquired a number of saints' days: St Stephen (26 December), St John (27 December), Holy

Innocents' Day (28 December), to commemorate the infants massacred at Bethlehem, and the Circumcision of Jesus (1 January). The entire week after Easter was especially observed, and the Ascension of Jesus was celebrated in addition to Pentecost. In the week before Easter, Maundy Thursday was celebrated as the day when the eucharist was instituted. Saints' days became more common, and included not only apostles, but also the Virgin Mary, and various local saints, such as Martin of Tours, Germanus of Auxerre, and Cyprian of Carthage. Celtic churches now began to celebrate All Saints' Day (1 November), and to make long prayers to the saints.

LITURGICAL BOOKS

In the West, by the mid-fourth century Latin had replaced Greek as the language of worship. Greek and Latin prayers were both used in Rome until about 350. Latin remained alive after the fall of the Western Empire, because most of the barbarian languages had not yet been reduced to written form.

As the Christian year evolved, service books were compiled for use by the clergy in the West. These included 'sacramentaries', containing all the forms of services needed in a church during the year; 'lectionaries', with the set Bible readings for the various days of the year; and 'homiliaries', books of sermons for the use of clergy who were not well enough educated to write their own.

New ceremonies were gradually added to church services from the fifth century onwards, while some older ceremonies fell out of use. Believer's baptism declined, and the baptism of infants became the norm. Because infant mortality rates were high, baptism usually took place early in life, becoming a private ceremony, often not even performed in a church building. At the same time, the examples of Jerusalem and the growing monastic communities encouraged daily services of prayers and Bible readings. Ordination, at one time a ritual merely tacked on to the eucharist, had grown into an important, distinct ceremony. Laying-on-of-hands was accompanied by the giving of articles to symbolize the job – a Gospel-book for the deacon, a chalice for the priest.

MICHAEL A. SMITH

CHAPTER 12

CLERGY, BISHOPS, AND POPE
The church builds an organisation

The growth of the church in the third century so increased the responsibilities of the bishop, at least in the cities and larger towns, that it was no longer possible for him to know all his flock. Theoretically, a bishop could have been appointed for each small congregation, but the idea of dividing the church by having more than one bishop in a city seems never to have been considered in the West. Instead, the number of presbyters (priests) assisting the bishop was increased, and more minor clergy were appointed.

By the mid-third century in Rome, exorcists had joined readers on the bishop's liturgical staff, and sub-deacons and acolytes had become his personal and secretarial assistants. The bishop closely controlled this developing organization.

In the fourth century, these clerical offices became a formal hierarchy, similar to the succession of posts held by the ambitious Roman aristocrat. The aspiring church leader began as a reader – often in childhood – proceeding to acolyte (assistant), and sub-deacon, up to the age of thirty. Then followed five years as deacon, and ten as priest, so that the minimum age for a bishop was set at forty-five. Although this was the norm in the Western Church, exceptions were made, as the career of Ambrose illustrates: he passed from baptism to Bishop of Milan in a single week!

All the churches of a city were under the direct pastoral care of its bishop. In Rome, for example, the bishop himself took all baptisms, and each Sunday the elements consecrated for the eucharist were carried from the bishop to the various churches of the city by acolytes. Although several priests were attached to each church, there was no parish priest, at least until the end of the fifth century.

FINANCING THE CHURCHES

The bishop also controlled the finances of all the churches and clergy of the city. By the third century, churches had begun to acquire property; but it was the extraordinary growth of church wealth in the fourth century that changed the pattern of church support. After Constantine, endowments, supplemented by government subsidies, provided the major income, though voluntary offerings always remained an important part of church revenue. Earlier on, the bishop alone allocated these revenues, which resulted in abuses. By the end of the fifth century, the Church at Rome had devised a system by which all income from rents and offerings was divided into four parts – for the bishop, the clergy, the poor, and for the repair and lighting of the churches. Elsewhere the distribution varied.

Under this system, the bishop received an income much greater than that of priests and deacons – though he had to spend a considerable amount on hospitality. Another contrast was between rich and poor churches. The wealth of the Roman bishop was enough to make the great pagan senator Praetextatus say, 'Make me Bishop of Rome – and I will become a Christian tomorrow!' On the other hand, the regular income of some country clergy was so small that they had to rely primarily on the generosity of the Christians of their congregation.

COUNTRY CHURCHES

The Christian church was primarily a church of the cities for the first centuries of its existence. However, by the beginning of the fourth century it had begun to move into the countryside in the West (earlier in the East), usually as a result of preaching tours by bishops, who set up churches in the larger villages to care for their new converts. At first these churches were under the care of clergy sent out from the city. Only in the sixth century, and primarily in Gaul, did each country church come to have its own clergy. Priests in these country parishes were still consecrated and controlled by the city bishop, but could administer the sacraments. The church was beginning to take on the form of local parish ministry familiar in the Middle Ages and modern times.

At the same time, another kind of country church developed: the church building given by a landowner to benefit those on his private estate. The landowner would normally provide an endowment for the upkeep of the church, and have the right to appoint its clergy. Such clergy, though subject to the bishop, were not under his control to the same extent.

AUTHORITY

Church organization grew in two ways: by the development of the authority of church councils, and by the increase in the authority of certain bishops over other bishops. Councils developed out of irregular meetings of bishops of neighbouring communities to discuss common problems, meetings which became more frequent during the third century, when some local and provincial councils began to meet annually.

Constantine called larger councils to settle matters that could not be resolved by local or provincial synods. Arles, in 314, was a General Council of the Western Church, and Nicaea, in 325, the first General Council of the whole church. The decrees of these and subsequent councils became the canon law of the church.

THE BISHOP OF ROME PRE-EMINENT

Meanwhile, the growth in the authority of the Bishop of Rome was of vital significance. In theory, all bishops were equal, but from earliest times some were more prominent than others, because of the importance of their cities. The most important were Alexandria, Antioch, Rome, and Carthage. The Council of Nicaea recognized the first three of these as pre-eminent in their own regions. Constantinople was added in 381, when the church council meeting in that city declared it second only to Rome.

The bishop of Rome objected to this, because it implied that the position of church and bishop depended on the status of their city in the Empire. The pre-eminence of Rome did not depend on any such historical accident, nor on the decrees of any synod, declared a Council of Rome, probably in 382, under Pope Damasus' leadership. On the contrary, Rome's status was due to the pope's position as successor to Peter, the founder of the Roman Church, on whom Christ had promised he would build his church. This exalted view, though not for some time accepted even in the West, was the foundation for the eventual supremacy of the Bishop of Rome in the church of the Middle Ages.

CONSTANTINE AND THE BISHOP OF ROME

Constantine's reign as the first Christian Emperor was immensely significant for the Bishop of Rome. The Roman Church suddenly found itself not only free of persecution, but also gifted with churches and estates. Constantine ordered a basilica to be begun over the shrine of Peter on the Vatican Hill, and another over the shrine of Paul on the Ostian Way; in addition, the Lateran Palace of the Empress Fausta was given to the Bishop of Rome as his official residence. But Constantine was certainly not the emperor of later legend, prostrate before Pope Sylvester, stripped of his imperial regalia, begging forgiveness for his sins – or handing over to the pope the rule of Rome, Italy, and the West, as the forged Donation of Constantine has it (see p. 197).

DAMASUS' PAPAL THEORY

Until Damasus (r. 366–84) the popes of this period were at best undistinguished men, who were unable – and sometimes unwilling – to stop the Emperor from dominating the church. The dramatic change at the end of the fourth century, when the church came to dominate the Emperor, was due to Ambrose, the great Bishop of Milan. But it was Ambrose's contemporary, Damasus, who made the theory about Peter an essential part of papal doctrine: he was the first pope consistently to refer to the Church of Rome as the 'apostolic see', and to address bishops of other churches as 'sons' rather than 'brothers'.

Damasus' successor, Siricius (r. 384–99) was the first to use the 'decretal', a letter of instruction modelled on the Emperor's decree sent to provincial governors. In using this type of letter, the pope was claiming the same kind of binding authority for himself in the church as the Emperor had in secular affairs. The successors of Siricius – Innocent I (r. 401–17), Zosinus (r. 417–18), and Boniface I (r. 418–22) – continued and built on the claim to Peter's authority, although theory often ran ahead of practice. Innocent claimed universal authority for the Bishop of Rome, declaring that nothing done in the provinces could be regarded as finished until it had come to his knowledge, and that the pope's decisions affected 'all the churches of the world'.

The ineffective Zosimus made just as exalted claims, but his success was meagre, for he managed to fall foul of the Emperor, the fiercely independent North African Church, and some strong-minded bishops in Gaul. Zosimus reversed Innocent's condemnation of Pelagius, but was forced to change his decision by pressure from the Emperor and the North African Church.

LEO I AND GELASIUS I

Popes Leo I (440–61) and Gelasius I (492–96) were undoubtedly the most significant of the fifth century. The climax of barbarian attacks on the Empire made the imperial court at Ravenna desperate for the support of any authority that might help to hold together the Empire. This is the background to the decree of the Emperor Valentinian III in 445, instructing Aëtius, the Roman commander in Gaul, to compel the attendance at the papal court of any bishop who refused to come voluntarily. An emperor's edict had turned into law the pope's claim to authority over other bishops.

The accounts of Leo's intercession with Attila the Hun, and Gaiseric the Vandal king, suggest that the pope could now perform imperial services, at a time when the civil government was disintegrating. Leo also had a moment of triumph in the East when his skilful *Tome* (on the divine and human natures of Christ) was read before the fourth General Council of Chalcedon (451), and was received with the cry, 'St Peter has spoken through Leo!' But the Council of Chalcedon rejected the Petrine basis for the pope's supremacy, declaring that a city's ecclesiastical status was determined by its civil status, and that the church of 'New Rome' (Constantinople) had a legal position similar to the church of Old Rome. The Roman delegates refused to sign — and departed in protest.

Leo set out more clearly than any before him the concept that the papacy was Peter's own office, not only as founder, but also as the present ruler of the church, through his servant, the pope. Leo claimed it did not matter how unworthy any particular pope might be, as long as he was the successor of Peter, and was acting according to canon law.

Gelasius I completed the papal theory of the Middle Ages. He insisted that the Emperor must guard the church, but also submit himself to the guidance of the pope, who was himself guided by God and St Peter. It followed that clergy should not be judged in secular courts, and that the pope himself could not be judged by any man. As Gelasius put it, 'Nobody at any time, and for whatever human pretext, may haughtily set himself above the office of the pope, who by Christ's order was set above all and everyone, and whom the universal church has always recognized as its head.'

For more than half a century after Gelasius, the real position of the pope was very much less than these exalted claims. Popes were used, and sometimes abused, first by the Gothic kings in Italy, and then, after Justinian reconquered the West, by the Eastern emperors. There were scenes of humiliation, as when Pope John I, on the orders of Theodoric the Ostrogothic King of Italy, travelled to Constantinople in 525 to plead with the Emperor on behalf of Arian Christians. When he returned in failure, he was thrown into prison, where he died. The papacy remained subservient to Constantinople long after the death of Justinian and the failure of Roman rule in Italy. Until 741, papal elections had to be confirmed by Constantinople, or by the imperial exarch of Ravenna.

GREGORY I AND THE LOMBARDS

The Lombard invasions ended Roman imperial domination of Italy, and gave the pope a new independence, though they threatened to overwhelm the city of Rome in a barbarian flood. Fortunately for Rome, and the Roman Church, Gregory the Great (540–604), pope during the critical last decade of the sixth century, was equal to the challenge. Gregory was a Roman of noble birth who was made prefect of the city about 573, but soon after gave up his wealth and estates to become a monk. A few years later, he was recalled to Rome by the pope for administrative work, and then to serve as ambassador to Constantinople.

When Gregory became pope, in 590, Rome's situation was desperate. The Romans faced the Lombard threat, with no hope of help from the imperial exarch at Ravenna, while famine and plague were also ravaging the land. Without hesitation, Pope Gregory I took command, provisioned the city, provided for its defence, sent orders to generals in the field, negotiated with the Lombards, and finally concluded peace without the Emperor's authorization. No pope before Gregory had dared do half as much.

In the midst of all this, Gregory was administering the estates of the church, caring for the spiritual needs of his flock, strengthening the churches in Gaul and Spain, defending the rights of the Church of Rome against the claims of Constantinople, and sending missionaries to England. Gregory's period as pope, by its extension of the pope's authority, marks the transition from the ancient world of imperial Rome to medieval Christendom, united by the Roman Catholic Church.

INTO THE MIDDLE AGES

The Roman Church played a central role in the transition to the medieval world, since it was primarily the church – the principal surviving institution from the ancient world – that transmitted Roman culture to the Middle Ages. In many ways, the Roman Church had taken on the shape of the Roman world in which it had grown to maturity. The most obvious example of this is the way in which the church's organization followed the pattern of the imperial administration. Each city was entitled to a bishop, and each province to an archbishop. Within the bishop's diocese, the hierarchy of officers was virtually the same as that of the Roman civil administration. Church canon law was modelled on Roman law. At first it contained only decrees of church councils, but eventually it also included papal decretals, which paralleled imperial edicts.

The Latin language also contributed a unity to the Christian world. Though little ancient literature joined the mainstream of medieval culture, Christian literature and learning were patterned on Latin models. Christian architecture too was naturally Roman in origin, the obvious example being the development of the basilica-church, and later the medieval cathedral, from the Roman meeting-hall known as the basilica (see pp. 140–1).

RICHARD A. TODD

CHAPTER 13

THE CHURCH IN NORTH AFRICA
The making of a distinctive tradition

The Great Persecution initiated by Diocletian affected Africa, directly and indirectly, more severely than anywhere else in the West. For example, during the persecution all forty-seven Christians from Abitina were martyred at Carthage. The African Church had massively expanded during the third century. Moreover, response to the imperial decrees, and esteem for confessors and martyrs, caused conflict, resulting in the division between the Donatists and the Catholics.

THE DONATISTS

The Donatists were a protest movement, standing for a holy church, purity of discipline and unflinching defiance of godless rulers. They were named after Donatus, their bishop in Carthage from 313 to about 355. They elected their own first bishop of Carthage in 312 after rejecting Caecilian, the catholic bishop, because one man who consecrated him, Felix of Apthungi, had allegedly been guilty of *traditio*, the 'handing over' or 'betrayal' of the Scriptures during the Great Persecution. African Christianity, like Judaism, was a religion of the holy book, and the surrender of precious biblical manuscripts to persecutors was naturally viewed by many as apostasy.

The dissidents were motivated by a number of other grievances. The bishops of Numidia (some whom were themselves guilty of *traditio* and similar compromises) felt slighted. Caecilian's hasty consecration had precluded their own archbishop from taking his traditional place in consecrating the bishop of Carthage. The ambitions of disappointed clerics, the greed of frustrated presbyters and the pique of a formidable lady rebuked by Caecilian for her superstitious devotion to a martyr's relic all played their part. Caecilian had been rather cool towards the confessors awaiting martyrdom, and his predecessor Mensurius had almost gone alone with the authorities.

WHAT DONATISTS BELIEVED

The Donatists believed that they constituted the true church, and that the Catholics were apostate. When Constantine restricted his grants and immunities to Caecilian's party, the Donatists demanded adjudication of their cause. Repeated enquiries cleared Felix and Caecilian, and an impatient Constantine attempted, with catholic backing, to coerce the Donatists (317–21). The Donatists flourished despite – and because of – persecution by emperors. A protracted assembly in the latter years of Constantine gathered 270 Donatist bishops. Constantine had to acquiesce when they took over a basilica he had built in the Numidian city of Cirta (renamed Constantine), and granted the Catholics another building.

Persecution and martyrdom, the fate of all the righteous, confirmed them in their convictions. Further oppression under the Emperor Constans in 347–48 left them depleted until Julian's tolerant reign in the 360s, and provoked Donatus' famous question 'What has the Emperor to do with the church?' The Circumcellions' violence provided one answer. They were wandering 'warriors of Christ' on the fringe of the Donatists, righting wrongs and intimidating Donatist waverers and catholic clergy. They were devoted to martyrdom.

THE DECLINE OF THE DONATISTS

After Julian's reign, the Donatists dominated the fourth-century church in North Africa. Social protest was expressed in religious dissent. In Donatus and Parmenian they had gifted leaders, and could even afford to expel the ablest African theologian of the years between Tertullian and Augustine – Tyconius, who lost an internal Donatist debate about the nature of the church.

After Parmenian (who succeeded Donatus) Donatism declined. In the 370s and 390s some Donatists supported local revolts against Roman rule and suffered when they were put down. Above all, in Aurelius of Carthage and in Augustine the Catholics at last had leaders who were a match for the Donatists. Augustine issued exhaustive historical and theological counter-arguments and a justification of coercion, while Aurelius' organizing ability produced effective action. Yet it took legal sanctions to check Donatism – especially the Edict of Unity (405) and the proscription which followed the convention in Carthage in 411.

Donatism was inspired by the traditions of African Christianity, as represented by Tertullian and Cyprian. It inevitably gathered up currents of popular social and economic discontent without being itself a nationalist or revolutionary movement. Under Vandal rule (429–533) the Catholics and Donatists suffered together – which probably encouraged mutual acceptance.

Subsequently Donatism flourished again, apparently diverging less and less from the catholic body. It survived until North African Christianity was submerged by the invading Moors in the seventh century. Its repression in Augustine's time may have permanently weakened the African church's ability to withstand such a challenge.

In the early fourth century lived two African orators and apologists who were noted writers. Arnobius the Elder from Numidia was the teacher of Lactantius, who died around 320. Lactantius served as a tutor in Diocletian's court at Nicomedia, and again later, after becoming a Christian, in Constantine's. His elegant Latin earned him the title 'The Christian Cicero'. His book *The Deaths of the Persecutors* luridly demonstrates that persecutors come to bad ends, and three other apologetic works, including *The Divine Institutes*, commend Christianity to educated readers. His theology was defective, being often rationalistic and moralistic in tone.

What is man?

Can any praise be worthy of the Lord's majesty? How magnificent is his strength! How inscrutable his wisdom! Man is one of your creatures, Lord, and his instinct is to praise you. He bears about him the mark of death, the sign of his own sin, to remind him that you thwart the proud. But still, since he is part of your creation, he wishes to praise you. The thought of you stirs him so deeply that he cannot be content unless he praises you, because you made us for yourself and our hearts find no peace until they rest in you.

FROM AUGUSTINE'S *CONFESSIONS*

MANICHEISM

Manicheism was also successful in Africa, despite being banned in around 302. It gathered up remnants of the Gnostic tradition, and its austerity and radicalism also appealed to minds as distinguished as Augustine's, who recruited other converts.

Augustine's appointment as presbyter and bishop of Hippo marked the beginning of a catholic resurgence, and hastened the downfall of the Donatists, who at their peak around 394 assembled 310 bishops. The Donatist Circumcellions, who had easily been confused with the aggressively orthodox roving monks of the East, had discredited asceticism. Augustine stimulated the monastic movement within the catholic church. From his cathedral chapter-cum-seminary emerged several bishops for African churches.

Above all, Augustine raised the self-confidence and intellectual level of African Catholicism. (He had himself encountered enlightened catholic Christianity only outside Africa.) Under Aurelius, bishop of Carthage 391/2 to about 430, councils of bishops again became influential in the church's life. The Councils of Hippo (393) and Carthage (397) published the first complete canons of the New Testament in the West. Councils were important in uniting the bishops on issues such as Donatism.

The Donatists resisted reasoned argument, and managed to avoid the public debates in which Augustine routed leading Manicheans. But they felt the force of anti-heretical legislation in the late fourth and early fifth centuries. After the imperial enquiry under the commissioner Marcellinus at Carthage in 411, when 286 catholic bishops confronted 284 Donatists, they suffered harsh repression, especially in the better-policed cities nearer the coast. Donatist strength came to be concentrated in Numidia. In the process of defeating Donatism, African churchmen found themselves on the side of the Empire with untypical enthusiasm.

The African church had known close, but rarely subservient, relations with the church of Rome at least since Tertullian's time. The Donatists found it expedient to maintain a Roman congregation for a period. In their anti-Donatist campaign the African bishops sought Roman support, and the Pelagian controversy meant that they uncharacteristically became more dependent on Roman bishops.

Africa had taken the initiative in condemning Celestius in 411 – the same year as the catholic–Donatist confrontation at Carthage. Issues of baptism and the doctrine of the church were involved in both cases. After acquittals in Palestine, Pelagius too was first condemned at councils of Carthage and Milevis, in 416. When Pope Zosimus lifted his predecessor's ban on the pair, another Council of Carthage in 418 weightily repeated earlier African verdicts. Zosimus bowed to the Africans, and the Pelagians' fate in the West was finally decided.

Not all African church leaders shared Augustine's keen opposition to Pelagian teachings. In the late 420s monks at Hadrumetum, in Byzacena (Tunisia), and Carthage suggested modifications to his anti-Pelagian doctrines that amounted to what was misleadingly called 'semi-Pelagianism'.

The case of Apiarius is an example of the African bishops asserting their traditional independence of Rome. Apiarius, a Numidian presbyter, had appealed to Zosimus against deposition by his bishop. Zosimus attempted to reinstate him – but this led to a decree by the Council of Carthage in 418 banning such appeals to authorities outside Africa. The Roman bishop rested his authority on the canons of Sardica which his collection of canons

AUGUSTINE OF HIPPO

Augustine, whose influence was to dominate the medieval church in the West, was born to African parents of Romanized Berber origins in Tagaste in Numidia (modern Algeria) in 354. From childhood he was a catechumen, learning the Christian faith from his earnest mother Monnica, but his baptism was delayed until 387 by a lengthy religious and philosophical pilgrimage, described in his *Confessions*.

He excelled in the literary education of his time, except in Greek, and lectured in rhetoric at Carthage. In 373 a work by Cicero converted him to love the divine wisdom; but he was repelled by the Bible's apparent barbarity. He became a follower of Manicheism, a Gnostic religion with a dualistic mythology which encouraged asceticism and intense devotion to Christ. He persisted with Manicheism for nine years, although he soon began to distrust its claims to demonstrate the truth by rational means.

Disillusioned, he went to Rome, where for a time he shared the 'Academics" despair of reaching any certainty. He was even tempted to taste the pleasures of Epicureanism. But in 384 he was appointed imperial rhetorician at Milan and exposed to the influence of Bishop Ambrose and the ideas of Neoplatonism. Together they undermined the obstacles which had alienated him from the orthodox faith.

From Ambrose he discovered that Christianity could be eloquent and intelligent and learnt that the difficult stories of the Old Testament could be treated as allegories. The Neoplatonists revealed the spiritual perfection of God and sought insight and vision through inward contemplation. Augustine came to believe that the cause of evil, which preoccupied him all his days, lay in the absence of good, rather than being a power in itself as the Manichees believed.

He was now challenged to abandon 'the flesh and the world'. He had lived with a common-law wife for over ten years, and seemed destined for high office (which would gratify Monnica). The challenge to 'conversion from the world' came through repeated stories of heroic renunciations such as Antony's and Victorinus'. The chain finally snapped as he read Romans 13:13–14 in a garden in Milan.

Weathered statue of Augustine of Hippo by Jan Bedrich Kohl, from the Charles Bridge, Prague, Czech Republic.
© ALESSANDRO0770/DREAMSTIME.COM

ORTHODOX CHAMPION

Prior to baptism Augustine retired to Cassiciacum, where a few companions spent their disciplined leisure as Christian philosophers. On returning to Africa in 388 after Monnica's death, he formed a monastic community for study and contemplation at Tagaste. However, in 391 he was press-ganged into the priesthood at Hippo on the coast (modern Annata), and by 396 he was the catholic bishop. For the rest of his life he was preacher and pastor, minister of the sacraments, judge and intercessor, trustee and organizer of charity, as well as a tireless defender of catholic orthodoxy and a voluminous writer. Hippo's half-pagan Catholics and stubborn Donatists rapidly turned him from the confident humanism of a Christian Neoplatonist to a more biblical and pessimistic view of human nature, society and history. The *Confessions* were an early fruit of this new outlook. *The City of God* a more mature one.

Augustine developed his influential principle, 'Believe in order to understand', as he opposed the rationalism of the Manicheans. He used the principle himself in numerous writings, above all in *The Trinity*. Against the Donatists he insisted that the church was a mixed field of wheat and tares, believers and unbelievers, growing together until the harvest. He undercut Donatist rebaptism by claiming that Christ is the chief minister of the sacraments, so that they remained true sacraments even if administered by un-worthy people. Yet the sacraments brought no benefit

Augustine describes his conversion

I probed the hidden depths of my soul and wrung its pitiful secrets from it, and when I gathered them all before the eyes of my heart, a great storm broke within me, bringing with it a great deluge of tears . . . For I felt that I was still enslaved by my sins, and in my misery I kept crying, 'How long shall I go on saying 'Tomorrow, tomorrow'? Why not now? Why not make an end of my ugly sins at this moment?'

I was asking myself these questions, weeping all the while with the most bitter sorrow in my heart, when all at once I heard the sing-song voice of a child in a nearby house. Whether it was the voice of a boy or a girl I cannot say, but again and again it repeated the chorus, 'Take it and read, take it and read.' At this I looked up, thinking hard whether there was any kind of game in which children used to chant words like these, but I could not remember ever hearing them before. I stemmed my flood of tears and stood up, telling myself that this could only be God's command to open my book of Scripture and read the first passage on which my eyes should fall. For I had heard the story of Antony, and I remembered how he had happened to go into a church while the Gospel was being read and had taken it as an instruction addressed to himself when he heard the words, 'Go home and sell all that belongs to you. Give it to the poor, and so the treasure you have shall be in heaven; then come back and follow me.' By this message from God he had at once been converted.

So I hurried back to the place where Alypius was sitting, for when I stood up to move away I had put down the book containing Paul's Letters. I seized it and opened it, and in silence I read the first passage on which my eyes fell: 'No orgies or drunkenness, no immorality or indecency, no fighting or jealousy. Take up the weapons of the Lord Jesus Christ; and stop giving attention to your sinful nature, to satisfy its desires.' I had no wish to read more and no need to do so. For in an instant, as I came to the end of the sentence, it was as though the light of faith flooded into my heart and all the darkness of doubt was dispelled.

AUGUSTINE'S *CONFESSIONS* VIII.12

as long as those receiving them remained outside the fold of the Spirit's unity and love. Augustine also justified the coercion of dissident Christians as being an act of loving correction.

Pelagian refugees from sacked Rome occupied Augustine's attention from 411. He attacked them only after Celestius questioned the grounds for infant baptism (which Augustine helped to make normal practice). The eventual condemnation of the Pelagians in the West came largely as the result of African pressure spearheaded by Augustine. They provoked him to develop further his doctrines of the fall and original sin, as both corruption and guilt; the necessity of grace to free the will in turning to God; and the predestination and perseverance of the 'fixed number of the elect'.

The Arian Vandal invaders were besieging Hippo when Augustine died in 430. Living amid the shocks and disruptions of the disintegrating Roman Empire, Augustine taught Christians to endure the world, where evil reigns invincibly, and to seek the peace of the heavenly city. He stood at the close of the creative era of Latin Christianity and was to dominate the minds of medieval and Reformation church leaders.

DAVID F. WRIGHT

attributed to Nicaea. Africa knew better. When the situation was repeated a few years later, the Africans insisted on African independence, while recognizing that Rome had a primacy of honour. Recently discovered letters of Augustine reveal similar attitudes over the case of Anthony of Fussala. Augustine nearly resigned.

VANDALS INVADE

The Vandals crossed to Africa from Spain in 429, captured Carthage in 439, and ruled until 533. As a result, Catholics and Donatists alike were persecuted for a long period. The Vandals, who were Arian Christians, sought church unity in time-honoured Roman fashion, and imposed rebaptism, exiled bishops and prevented their replacement, and dissolved monasteries. There were peaceful interludes, especially under Gunthamund (484–96), when Dracontius, Africa's only Christian poet of distinction, flourished at Carthage, and under Hilderic (523–30), during whose reign an all-African council met in the capital (525).

Arianism became an inevitable concern of catholic writers. They included Quodvultdeus, Bishop of Carthage, whose exile in 456/7 was followed by a vacancy in the see for a quarter of a century. Another exile, Victor, Bishop of Vita, compiled an invaluable history of the Arian persecution in about 485. Vigilius, bishop of Thapsus, fled to Constantinople around 484, where he wrote extensively against the Eastern heresies, especially Monophysitism. Fulgentius was a monk and founder of monasteries before becoming bishop of Ruspe. He spent fifteen years in exile in Sardinia with numerous other bishops, and as a keen Augustinian wrote against both Arians and Pelagians. Exiled African clergy and monks contributed helpfully to church life in Spain, Italy and Gaul.

After Justinian's general Belisarius reconquered Africa in 533, catholic Christianity recovered much of its vigour. It was now directed more against the Eastern emperors' compromises with the Monophysites than against the Donatists, who were buoyant, especially in Numidia. Mutual toleration between Catholics and Donatists under Arian persecution seems to have resulted in practice in each 'denomination' recognizing the other. Pope Gregory I repeatedly rebuked the African bishops for their slackness in opposing the Donatists.

In the seventh century African church leaders, reinforced by the great Eastern Theologian Maximus the Confessor, again resisted the imperial theology of Monotheletism (646). But time was running out for African Christianity. The Muslim Saracens began their invasion in 642/3, took Carthage in 698, and completed the conquest by 709. The decline of the church is not easy to trace. By 1100 only a handful of bishoprics survived, but a Christian community of some sort lived on in Tunis until the sixteenth century. Only literary remains and impressive archaeological monuments today bear witness to the life and independence of early African Christianity.

DAVID F. WRIGHT

CHAPTER 14

THE FALL OF THE ROMAN EMPIRE

How and why it came to an end

Since the time of Augustine, many have tried to explain the fall of the Roman Empire, by which is meant the end of the Roman Empire in the West. The Eastern Empire, based on Constantinople – 'East Rome' – survived for another 1000 years. Although the underlying reasons for the fall of the Western Empire are still disputed, the immediate cause was the Germanic invasions of the fifth century.

THE VISIGOTHS BECOME ARIAN CHRISTIANS

Germanic tribes had threatened the Roman frontier for several centuries. But the tribes who finally destroyed the Western Empire were new to the Romans: Goths, Vandals, Burgundians, Lombards, and others. Most important of these were the Goths, who began to attack the Empire around the middle of the third century. The Visigoths, the western branch of the Goths, occupied the Roman province of Dacia (roughly modern Romania and Moldova) and forced the Emperor Aurelian to abandon it in 271.

   The Visigoths were introduced to Christianity during their occupation of Dacia, by Roman prisoners captured during raids into the Empire. About the end of Constantine's reign, Ulfilas (c. 310–83), a descendant of one of these Christian Roman prisoners, was consecrated head of the Christian community there by an Arian bishop. Therefore the Visigoths became Arian Christians, and eventually spread their particular kind of Christianity to most of the other German tribes on the border of the Empire. Ulfilas' most important achievement was the translation of the Bible into the Gothic language, for which task he had to invent a Gothic alphabet.

   After its recovery from the chaos of the third century, the Empire enjoyed almost a century of relative security. The first hint of ultimate disaster was the Battle of Adrianople, in 378. The Visigoths had secured refuge from the Huns within the Empire, but when mistreated by the Romans, they rebelled and destroyed the Emperor Valens and his army at Adrianople. Theodosius, chosen to settle the East by the Western Emperor Gratian, managed to subdue the Visigoths; but they were allowed to remain within the Empire as Roman allies, under their own rulers, and with a regular subsidy.

ALARIC SACKS ROME

In 395, the Empire was divided between Arcadius and Honorius, the two young sons of Theodosius. Alaric, the new King of the Visigoths, began to exploit the differences that now developed between East and West. Encouraged, apparently, by Constantinople, he invaded Italy in 401. On the night of 24 August 410, Alaric stormed the walls of Rome in a surprise attack, and pillaged the city for three days. The event had little permanent effect on the Empire, since Alaric soon abandoned the city; but the psychological blow was enormous. For the first time in 800 years, Rome had been captured by a foreign

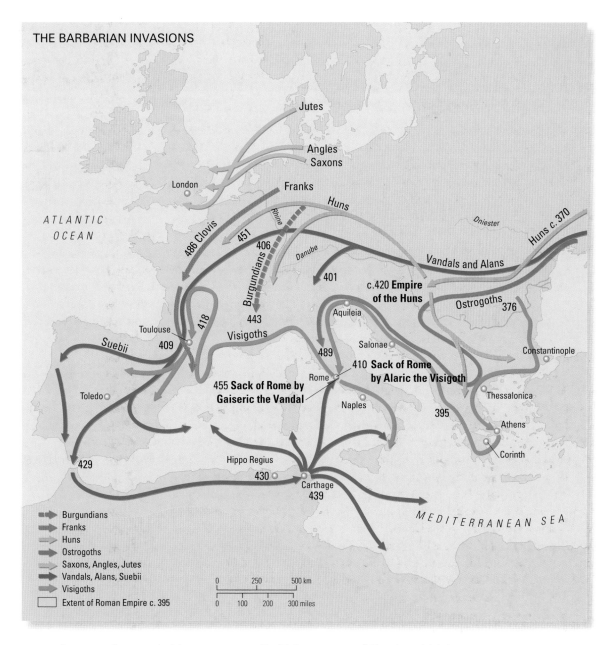

enemy. Jerome – far away in his monastery at Bethlehem – wept: 'The city which has taken the whole world is itself taken!'

DIVINE PUNISHMENT?

Some pagans claimed that the catastrophe was due to the recent rejection by the Romans of their ancestral gods. Augustine of Hippo, the great North African bishop and theologian, countered this accusation in his book *The City of God*. Augustine wrote that, within the Roman Empire, two 'cities' were intertwined: the City of God, the community

JEROME

Jerome (c. 345–420), the leading biblical scholar of his time in the Western Church, was born in a small town in north-east Italy. He studied the classical disciplines and was baptized at Rome, and then journeyed through Gaul, where he was converted to ascetic Christianity, joining an ascetic community near his home at Aquileia. Later at Antioch in 374, Jerome had a vision criticizing his preoccupation with secular learning, and accusing him of being a 'follower of Cicero and not of Christ'. This led the learned scholar to withdraw to an ascetic life in the Syrian desert, south-east of Antioch, where he mastered Hebrew and transcribed biblical manuscripts.

After ordination at Antioch, Jerome travelled to Constantinople, where he studied with the Eastern theologian Gregory of Nazianzus in 380. He then acted as secretary to Pope Damasus in Rome in 382, where he also became involved in experiments in monastic living by aristocrats. While in Rome, Jerome was commissioned by the pope to make an improved Latin translation of the Bible. Following the death of Pope Damasus, Jerome visited Antioch, Egypt, and the Holy Land, but in 386 finally settled to monastic life in Bethlehem, where he spent the rest of his days in seclusion, completing his translation of the Scriptures into Latin and writing commentaries on the books of the Bible.

THE VULGATE

Jerome achieved distinction in his studies of the text of the Bible and his biblical exegesis, based on his unsurpassed skills with languages. Pope Damasus wanted a Latin version of the Scriptures to replace the confusion of corrupted 'Old Latin' manuscripts then in circulation. Jerome went back to the Greek version of the Old Testament (the Septuagint) and the Greek New Testament to prepare fresh Latin translations of the Psalms, other Old Testament books, and the Gospels. Later, convinced of the need to base his Old Testament translation on the Hebrew original, rather than on the Greek of the Septuagint, Jerome reworked his Latin translation of the Old Testament to conform more closely to the Hebrew Bible. After twenty-three years, Jerome completed his revision of the Latin Scriptures (382–405). Known as the 'Vulgate Bible', it was eventually accepted as the authorized Latin version of the Western Church, and, although the text became corrupted during the Middle Ages, its supremacy was reaffirmed by the Council of Trent (1546).

Jerome, who was a biblical scholar rather than a theologian, wrote commentaries on most of the Bible. As a result of his use of Hebrew and Greek, his profound knowledge of early church writings, and his familiarity with Bible lands gained by much travel, Jerome's comments on Scripture are of considerable significance. He sought to steer a course between an allegorical and a woodenly literal interpretation of Scripture. Although he avoided the unrestrained use of allegory of many contemporaries, he commended a threefold interpretation (finding historical,

of true Christians living according to God's law, and the City of Man, pagan society following its own desires and seeking material gain. Such a community could only come to a disastrous end. But to Christians, citizens of the City of God, the sack of Rome was not a catastrophe, despite their suffering. The loss of goods can deprive Christians of nothing, since their hearts are set on heavenly things; suffering and deprivation are part of their Christian instruction. The City of God alone is eternal, yet the two cities will coexist inseparably until the end of the world.

Augustine did appreciate the achievement of Rome, though it stood under judgment: Rome provided the just government needed for an ordered society, and for the control symbolic, and spiritual senses) which resulted in numerous arbitrary and mystical explanations.

Jerome's commentaries on Scripture were prepared at great speed. His exposition of Galatians was written at the rate of 1,000 lines per day, while his Matthew commentary was completed within a fortnight. His exposition of Scripture leans heavily on Jewish tradition, and also involves extensive quotations of numerous authorities of the early church. Quite often Jerome's comments are indistinguishable from those of other interpreters. Nevertheless, Jerome ranks with Origen and Augustine as an early biblical interpreter of the first order. He also translated into Latin several works by Greek theologians, and with merciless passion engaged in one controversy after another.

One of the most cultured and learned of the Fathers, Jerome's reputation as a keen biblical scholar endures. 'The great hermit of Bethlehem had less genius than Augustine, less purity and loftiness of character than Ambrose, less sovereign good sense and steadfastness than Chrysostom, less keenness of insight and consistency of courage than Theodore of Mopsuestia; but in learning and versatile talent he was superior to them all' (Farrar).

BRUCE A. DEMAREST

Jerome's Latin Bible

I am not so stupid as to think that any of the Lord's words either need correcting, or are not divinely inspired; but the Latin manuscripts of the Scriptures are proved faulty by the variations which are found in all of them. My aim has been to restore them to the form of the Greek original, from which my critics do not deny that they have been translated.

JEROME, *LETTERS* XXVII

of evil. God gave Rome this authority, and the Christian must obey such government, unless commanded to do evil.

THE END OF THE EMPIRE IN THE WEST

The sack of Rome was not a serious blow to the Empire as a whole, since the Visigoths returned to Gaul after Alaric's death, and Rome had ceased to be the administrative centre of the West. The Emperor and his court were safe behind the marshes at the Italian coastal city of Ravenna.

Gaul, however, was in desperate straits, attacked by a new group of barbarian tribes — Vandals, Alans, Suevi, Franks, and Burgundians. Meanwhile Britain was occupied by Anglo-Saxons from northern Europe. The legendary Arthur, though certainly not the royal hero of the Round Table, may have been the last successful military leader of Christian Britain against the pagan invaders (490–510).

Attila the Hun is possibly the most famous of barbarian kings, although the Huns made a less permanent impact than the Visigoths, Vandals, and some other barbarians. In 452 Attila invaded Italy, but was persuaded to withdraw — according to tradition, by a Roman delegation led by Pope Leo I. Attila died the following year, his army dissolved, and the Huns were absorbed into the surrounding population.

Meanwhile another Germanic people – the Vandals led by Gaiseric – had crossed from Spain into North Africa in 429, and by 435 controlled much of the coast. They next mastered the sea, and in 455 dared to attack Rome itself, which was unprepared and leaderless. It is reported that Leo again saved Rome, by pleading with Gaiseric for restraint in his fourteen-day sack of the city.

The final act of the drama is quickly told. The next two decades were filled with wars against the Vandals and complex intrigues, whereby puppet emperors were set up and deposed at will by barbarian generals. Eventually, the barbarian Roman army in Italy revolted – the army of true Romans had by this time completely disappeared – and elected as their king Odoacer, one of the barbarian officers of the imperial guard. In 476, Odoacer deposed the last Roman Emperor in the West, little Romulus Augustulus, and sent his imperial regalia to the Eastern Emperor Zeno, affirming his allegiance to the government at Constantinople, and seeking to be recognized as ruler of the West.

THE CHURCH AND THE POOR

Salvian, a presbyter of Marseilles, reveals something of life in Roman Gaul in the mid-fifth century. His book, *The Government of God* (*De gubernatione Dei*), tries to answer a question similar to that addressed by Augustine: why God would bring suffering on a Christian people. He shows that the terrible experience of Christian Gaul does reflect God's just rule; it is his righteous judgment on a wicked people, particularly on wealthy aristocrats and greedy public officials who mercilessly oppress the poor. This sympathy for the common man sets off Salvian from most writers of the ancient world. Landowners, governors, municipal officials, and tax collectors, says Salvian have all conspired to rob the poor, who can least afford to pay. No wonder the poor prefer life among the barbarians or in the monasteries.

Salvian's picture is certainly overdrawn, for there were many prosperous peasants, merciful landlords, and honest officials in the mid-fifth century. Nevertheless, the peasant's life was usually hard, and sometimes desperate; peasants were at the bottom of the pile when the crunch came, as in times of famine. Taxes were collected from the poor, even when they were starving, while rich landowners were often able to arrange remission of their taxes.

Sometimes the church was part of the oppressive system, for example when its lands were managed by harsh, or corrupt, administrators. Such cases occurred on the estates of the Roman Church in Sicily in the time of Pope Gregory the Great, but were quickly rectified when they came to Gregory's attention.

But the church was generally on the side of the poor and oppressed. Ambrose protested about the expulsion of non-residents from the city of Rome in time of famine, and eventually money was raised to buy grain for distribution. The same thing happened at Edessa, at the urging of Ephrem the Syrian (Ephraem Syrus, c. 306–73). In this case not only was bread distributed, but an open-air hospital of 300 beds was set up. Sometimes church officials shared in the relief effort; the bishop was usually a conscientious shepherd of his flock. It was the church's care for its own poor, and for outsiders, that so impressed the pagan Emperor, Julian the Apostate.

CHRISTIANS AND MORALITY

The success of the church in dealing with other social evils of the day is more debatable. It succeeded in ending gladiatorial combats, but chariot-races, wild beast hunts, and an extremely immoral theatre continued, despite Christian condemnations and, in some cases, imperial prohibition. The rigid sexual standards of the church were not observed by the majority of Christians, apart from the large numbers who fled to monasteries or desert hermitages, or the few who, like the women friends of Jerome and Ambrose, could afford to live privately as virgins in their own homes.

For many it was thought difficult to live a Christian life in the secular world. The Christian magistrate, for example, might have to order torture or execution. Thus Christians were often advised, for the sake of their souls, to leave public office, an attitude that probably contributed to the decline of public morality in the late Empire, as posts were often filled with people of lower ideals.

It is surprising that the harsh treatment of the lower classes in the late Empire did not produce more uprisings, like that of the Bagaudae in Gaul; most of the peasants seemed not to care *who* ruled them. The Circumcellions of North Africa, a militant fringe of the Donatists, are a special case, since they were inspired by both religious and social grievances. The Circumcellions were peasants who lived around the shrines of their martyrs, where they stored their food. They raided the country villas of catholic landlords, combining economic and religious protest.

WHY ROME FELL

Ever since the eighteenth-century English historian Edward Gibbon concluded that his account of the fall of the Roman Empire traced 'the triumph of Barbarism and Religion', there has been a special interest in trying to explain *why* it fell. The immediate cause is, of course, the barbarian attacks on the Western Empire in the fifth century, which resulted in the replacement of Roman government by Germanic kingdoms in the Western provinces. But it is surprising that the barbarian attacks, which had harassed the Empire since before the Christian era, should suddenly prove fatal in the fifth century.

Numerous unsatisfactory explanations have been offered: change in climate, soil exhaustion, and race mixture, for example. One popular idea is that the Empire fell because of a decline in morality. Immorality there certainly was in plenty in the Roman Empire – but throughout its history. The late Empire was probably no more immoral than any other period, except possibly in the area of public administration, where corruption and brutality seem to have increased. The church, while it preached against such abuses, contributed to the decline by discouraging good Christians from holding public office, as noted above.

A much more important cause for the end of the Western Empire was a failure of human and material resources. The West had always been poorer than the East, and conditions had become worse in the two or three hundred years before the disastrous fifth century. The problem was that too many non-productive members of the society had to be fed by too few productive labourers. The army had doubled in size since the third century, and the bureaucracy had expanded considerably, while the number of producers had shrunk. In addition, the great senatorial landowners, who possessed a vastly disproportionate share of the wealth of the Empire, frustrated imperial attempts to make them pay a fair share of taxes, or to conscript their agricultural labourers into the army. But whatever the causes that made the West weaker than the East, the most important reason for the fall of the Roman Empire in the West was the unprecedented severity of barbarian attacks in the fifth century.

WAS CHRISTIANITY TO BLAME?

Gibbon himself complained that 'a large part of public and private wealth was consecrated to the specious demands of charity and devotion; and the soldiers' pay was lavished on the useless multitudes of both sexes, who could only plead the merits of abstinence and chastity.' Though Gibbon's anti-religious bias is evident, the numerous monks and clergy were certainly among those non-producers who had to be fed from the diminishing resources of the Empire.

Furthermore, the church, in focusing attention on the heavenly 'City of God', encouraged neglect of the earthly 'City of Man' – the Empire. The church attracted the most creative minds, and the most capable leaders, of the day. Athanasius, Ambrose, Augustine, and Gregory the Great are only the most famous of hundreds of capable bishops who might have staffed the imperial civil service, which was so desperately in need of leadership. Ambrose, Gregory, and Sidonius Apollinaris were all magistrates before they responded to the call of God.

Christians in the West tended, if not to welcome the barbarians, at least to accept them as God's judgment, and to reach an understanding with them. For example, Pope Gregory the Great despaired about the decaying city of Rome, and negotiated with the invading Lombards (without imperial authorization). But while submitting to barbarian political rule, the church converted the barbarians to orthodox Christianity.

Christians thus shared responsibility for the fall of the Western Empire. But by the fifth century was the Empire worth saving? It had proved itself unable to deal not only with the barbarian problem, but with political, social, and economic problems too. We may well regret the passing of 'the glory that was Greece and the grandeur that was Rome'; but the fall of the Western Empire was offset in the long run by the conversion of the barbarians of Western Europe to Christianity.

ITALY UNDER THEODORIC AND JUSTINIAN

Odoacer, the Gothic chief who deposed the last Roman Emperor in the West, was himself overthrown in 493 by Theodoric, chief of a group of Ostrogoths, who had served previously in the Eastern Empire. Theodoric now ruled a Gothic kingdom in Italy, taking over all the old Roman administration, including the Senate. His government of both Romans and barbarians worked surprisingly well, at least until near the end of his reign, when harmony was destroyed in intrigues that accompanied the death of the statesman Boethius.

The Ostrogoths were Arian Christians, but tolerant, like the Visigoths and Burgundians. Although Theodoric made sure that the popes did as he wanted, he tried to maintain friendly relations with his Catholic (mainstream Christian) subjects. In North Africa, the church suffered more from the barbarians. Augustine's death in 430, during the siege of the Vandals, marked the end of the brilliant period in its history. The Vandals were intolerant Arians, who sent nearly 5,000 Catholics to the southern desert, and shipped Catholic bishops to the island of Corsica to cut timber for their fleet.

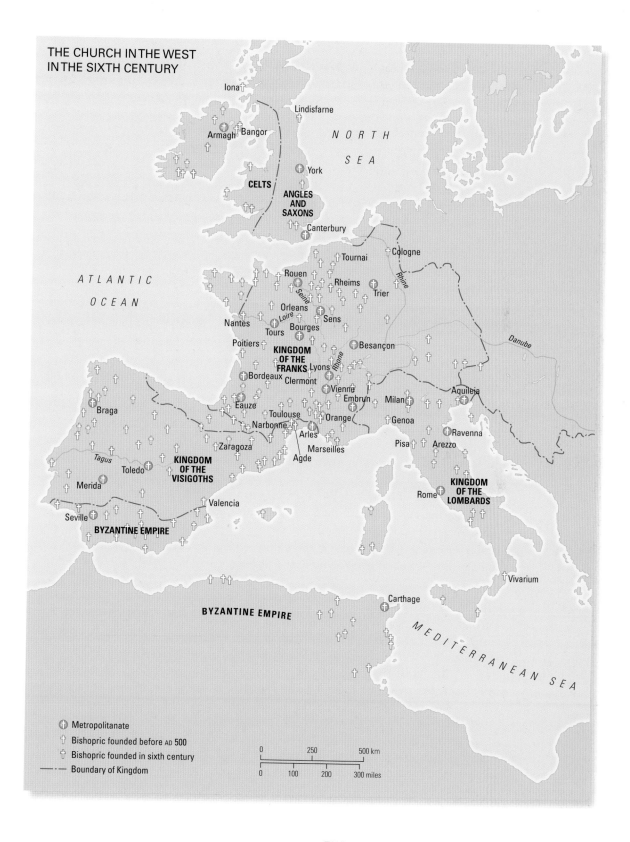

THE CHURCH IN THE WEST
IN THE SIXTH CENTURY

NORTH SEA

Iona

Lindisfarne

Armagh Bangor

York

CELTS

ANGLES
AND
SAXONS

Canterbury

ATLANTIC
OCEAN

Tournai

Cologne

Rouen

Rheims

Trier

Rhine

Orleans

Sens

Nantes

Loire

Bourges

Tours

Poitiers

Besançon

Seine

KINGDOM
OF THE
FRANKS

Lyons

Rhône

Danube

Bordeaux

Clermont

Vienne

Embrun

Milan

Aquileia

Braga

Eauze

Toulouse

Orange

Genoa

Ravenna

Narbonne

Arles

Pisa

Arezzo

Zaragoza

Agde

Marseilles

Tagus

KINGDOM
OF THE
VISIGOTHS

Toledo

Merida

KINGDOM
OF THE
LOMBARDS

Rome

Valencia

Seville

BYZANTINE EMPIRE

Vivarium

BYZANTINE EMPIRE

Carthage

MEDITERRANEAN SEA

⊕ Metropolitanate

✝ Bishopric founded before AD 500

✝ Bishopric founded in sixth century

—·— Boundary of Kingdom

0		250		500 km

0	100	200	300 miles

BOETHIUS: THE CONSOLATION OF PHILOSOPHY

Boethius is ranked among the founders of the Middle Ages because of his great influence on medieval education and thought. A statesman and philosopher, Anicius Manlius Torquatus Severinus Boethius (c. 480–524) was educated in Athens and Alexandria, and served the Arian king of the Ostrogoths in Italy, Theodoric the Great. Living in the twilight of the Roman Empire, he was the last Western scholar before the twelfth century to be thoroughly familiar with the Greek texts of Aristotle's philosophical works. He planned to translate the works of both Plato and Aristotle into Latin, but was able to complete only Aristotle's works on logic, together with some commentaries on them.

He also wrote five *Tractates (Opuscula Sacra)* in defence of orthodox theology. One of these books, which systematically applied Aristotle's logic to Christian theology, earned him the title of the 'first scholastic' – one who was attempting to harmonize faith and reason.

Towards the close of his life Boethius was accused of treason against Theodoric, and was imprisoned and executed. While in prison he wrote his best-known work *The Consolation of Philosophy*, a dialogue between Boethius and 'Philosophy', who leads him from despair over his situation to 'that true contentment which reason united with virtue can give'.

ROBERT G. CLOUSE

After the death of Theodoric in 526, the generals of the Eastern Emperor, Justinian (527–65), temporarily reconquered Italy. But the imperial army was unable to defend Italy against the Lombard invasions after Justinian's death, and Italy was once more dominated by barbarians. Although the imperial army managed to hold Ravenna and some other parts of Italy, Rome itself was now governed by her bishop.

CLOVIS AND THE CHURCH IN GAUL

In Gaul, Clovis, pagan king of the Franks, married a Catholic Christian princess and was converted to orthodox Christianity in 496. This proved extremely significant for Christianity in the West. Legend makes Clovis a second Constantine, praying in battle to the Christian God, and receiving baptism after his victory. Gregory of Tours reported that Clovis' reign was attended by miraculous signs of divine approval; the pious bishop had to see the hand of God in a victory which meant the triumph of Catholic Christianity in Gaul. But though Clovis' conversion brought the Gallo-Roman Church to his side, it changed neither his character nor his reign, which continued to prosper on treachery, brutality, and murder.

RICHARD A. TODD

CHAPTER 15

ASCETICS AND MONKS
The rise of Christian monasticism

Ascetic Christianity may be defined as a more rigorous practice of the faith than normal for the average Christian. It can involve a variety of practices: abstaining from certain things normally considered good (for example, marriage) and adding further requirements or routines (for example, extra set periods of prayer). Asceticism encourages the idea of a double standard, with a spiritual elite set above the general level of Christians. There can also be, in monasticism, the additional step of withdrawing from society and seeking solitude.

ASCETICISM AND THE BIBLE

Parts of the New Testament have been held to encourage asceticism; but there it is advocated for practical reasons, with no suggestion that it is especially praiseworthy. Jesus said that 'there are some who are eunuchs for the sake of the kingdom of God', but this was specifically 'for those who can receive it'. Similarly, Paul's preference for the single life was based on his feeling that Christ's return might come very soon and that marriage ties might impede evangelism.

On the other hand, the New Testament strongly condemns some types of asceticism. Jesus rejected the Pharisees' scruples over clean and unclean food, and Paul attacked the teaching that it was wrong to marry or to eat certain foods.

The Jews had traditions of asceticism, both individual and communal, reaching back into the Old Testament. The Nazirite vow involved temporary abstinence from wine and other restrictions. Later in Israelite history, prophets gathered into special groups for teaching and prayer, under the leadership of notable holy men such as Elisha. Regular puritanical groups, such as the Rechabites, came into being later; they kept apart from normal Israelite life and aimed at a purer and more faithful devotion to God.

In New Testament times there were both individual and communal ascetics in Palestine. Josephus, the Jewish historian, mentions that he received some of his teaching from a hermit called Banus. John the Baptist, living a solitary ascetic life in the Judean desert, also represents this tradition. On the communal side, the best-known are the Essenes, of whom the group at Qumran who produced the Dead Sea Scrolls were the most prominent. But some Essenes lived ascetic lives in their community, as did some of the Pharisees.

None of the earliest Christians appears to have lived as a hermit or in an ascetic community. Individuals, however, were noted for their rigour of life and devotion to God. James, the Lord's brother, for example, was admired by many non-Christian Jews for his constant fasting and prayer. Also, in the early period, any consistent Christian life was likely to be viewed as extremely ascetic by a morally lax society. Some noble Roman ladies, who may have been Christians, are reported by pagan sources to have lived in mourning and seclusion for years, presumably because they had no time for the pagan social life surrounding them.

While Christianity was under threat of persecution, congregations tended to be small, and to keep very high moral standards (even if there were some lapses, which were severely punished). Martyrdom was valued as the supreme example of devotion to God. Although some churches may have had church membership requirements that were ascetic (for instance, some Syriac-speaking churches appear to have accepted as baptized members only those who were celibate), there was no sign of an organized 'spiritual elite' inside the church apart from groups of widows and virgins. On the fringes of mainstream Christianity, for example among Jewish-Christian groups, Marcionites, and Montanists, asceticism was very popular, often in the form of 'encratism' (Greek for 'self-control'). Encratites rejected marriage, wine, and meat. Clement of Alexandria and Origen laid the foundations for an orthodox theology of asceticism.

THE FIRST MONKS

The late third and early fourth centuries saw the beginnings of monastic asceticism in Christianity. General toleration of Christianity even before Constantine produced an influx of new members into the churches, and growth in numbers was accompanied by a lowering of standards. At the same time martyrdom became less and less frequent, and the martyrs and confessors were replaced as the spiritual elite by the first monks. The monks aimed to live the Christian life to the full, and felt that continued residence in the 'world' hindered this. They tried to achieve a pure Christianity and a deep communion with God which they considered unattainable in the existing churches.

There is considerable debate as to where monasticism began. The first monks were individuals who retreated to the desert in Egypt or Syria. Sometimes these retreats were only temporary, and may have been prompted by the need to flee persecution; often they became permanent. Although he may not have been the earliest, Antony (about 256–356), a Coptic peasant from Egypt, was the first famous hermit. His example was followed by others, and soon there were many hermits, living either singly or in loosely-associated groups on the edge of the desert.

The main routine of the hermit was prayer and meditation, supplemented by reading of the Bible. Fasting was also important, and they attempted many other rigorous feats such as standing for hours while praying. Some of the prayers were rather mechanical, involving the repetition of short set formulas.

The prolonged loneliness and the shortage of food and sleep fostered hallucinations as well as growth in spiritual awareness of God. Conflicts with demons were frequent. Many of the visions, trances, and strange experiences of the desert hermits have obvious psychological explanations (for example, the appearance of the devil as a seductive woman could be the result of repressed sexual feelings). Those who retreated to the desert inevitably abandoned family life, and celibacy was the rule, although some married couples retreated together into the desert, but lived without sexual intercourse. Most hermits remained fairly stationary, but there were some wanderers, especially in the regions of Syria, including more extreme groups such as the unruly Messalians who wandered about, sleeping rough and keeping up a continual chanting.

Antony would eat only once a day after sunset, and sometimes he did not taste food for two or frequently for four days. His food was bread and salt; he drank only water.

ATHANASIUS

Some hermits went to unnatural extremes, such as living at the top of pillars, or walling themselves up in caves. Early hermits were largely lay people. Occasionally they might meet to receive the eucharist, or a priest who was a hermit would minister to a group throughout an area. But the eucharist had little place in the routines of the early hermits.

PACHOMIUS STARTS A COMMUNITY

Communal monasticism was begun about 320 by Pachomius. He was a converted soldier, and after discharge he spent some time as a hermit before setting up his first ascetic community at Tabennisi, by the River Nile in Egypt. The rule for his community survives in a Latin translation made by Jerome.

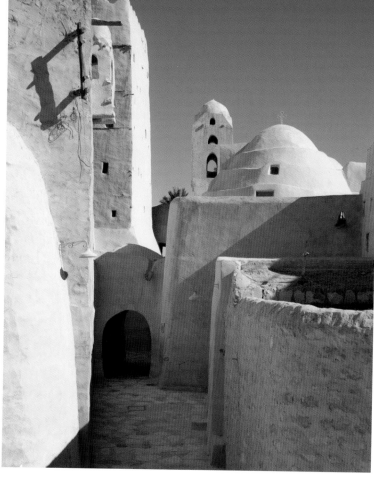

The Coptic Christian monastery of St Antony, in the Eastern Desert, Egypt, one of the oldest monasteries in the world, founded by followers of Antony (c. 251–356), the pioneer monk.
© ALEXEY BYKOV/ DREAMSTIME.COM

Pachomius set his face against extremism. He insisted on regular meals and worship, and aimed to make his communities self-supporting through such industries as the weaving of palm-mats or growing fruit and vegetables for sale. Entrants to his community had to hand over their personal wealth to a common fund, and were only admitted as full members after a period of probation. To prove their initial earnestness they were required to stand outside the monastery door for several days. Part of the qualification for full membership was to memorize parts of the Bible; and if the candidates were illiterate they were taught how to read and write. Although Pachomius' first communities were for men, before his death he supervised the establishment of the earliest communities for women as well. Pachomius created the basic framework which was followed by all later monastic communities.

Monasticism appeared first out of Eastern Christianity. It was first brought to the notice of the Western Churches by Athanasius. While he was in exile in the West between 340 and 346, he was accompanied by two Egyptian monks. Athanasius spent parts of his later exiles hiding among the hermits of the Egyptian desert, and subsequently wrote the life of Antony. This biography provides almost all our knowledge about Antony, and largely helped to spread the ideals of the ascetic movement. It was soon translated into Latin, and among those influenced by it was Augustine of Hippo. In the West monasticism had the backing of church leaders such as Ambrose from the very beginning.

BISHOPS AND MONKS

After Pachomius, Basil the Great (330–79) made the most important contribution to Eastern monasticism. After being educated at Constantinople and Athens, in 356 Basil returned to his home in Cappadocia, determined to renounce the world and live as a hermit. He visited many of the ascetics before setting up his own community with the help of Gregory of Nazianzus. His monastic planning comes from this period, but was influenced by the fact that he was ordained in 364 and became bishop of Caesarea (in Cappadocia) in 370. Basil was both a bishop and an ascetic.

Basil integrated the monastic communities more closely with the church, believing the bishop should have ultimate authority over a monastery. At the same time, monasteries started to become more outward-looking. Basil's monastery provided medical treatment for the sick and relief for the poor, and also did some work in education. He disapproved

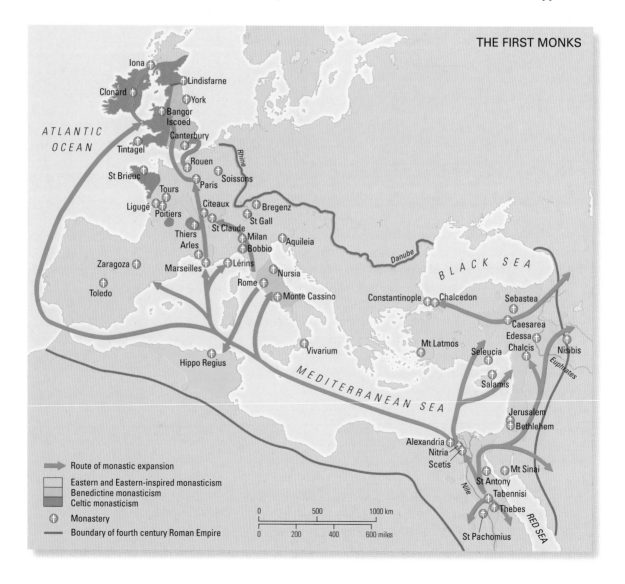

THE FIRST MONKS

Route of monastic expansion

Eastern and Eastern-inspired monasticism
Benedictine monasticism
Celtic monasticism

Monastery
Boundary of fourth century Roman Empire

strongly of individualistic piety which ran to extremes, and laid down set times of prayer, eight times daily.

Basil's ascetic theory was summed up in two monastic 'rules'. While these owe something to an older friend of his, Eustathius of Sebaste (c 300–80), and have also been modified later, they remain basically the work of Basil. The rule of Basil is still observed in Eastern monasteries today. Basil saw the monastic life as the climax of Christian achievement, with its aim of freeing the soul from the entanglements of the body through discipline. Basil stressed the need for self-examination, but believed that people could in fact fulfil the commandments of God.

MONASTICISM IN THE WEST

In the West, monasticism was stimulated by Martin of Tours, who died in 397. Martin took up the hermit's life after military service and lived in a solitary cell near Ligugé, in France. His sanctity resulted in many others coming to join him, and a form of community was set up. Rather against his will, he was persuaded to become bishop of Tours in 372, and for some time lived as a hermit in a cell next to the church. The continued distraction of his curious visitors compelled Martin to retreat to Marmoutier, where he set up a monastery as a springboard for evangelizing much of the still-pagan rural France. His monastery was also a nursery for bishops, as a result of its rigour and sanctity. Most of our knowledge of Martin of Tours comes from an extremely popular biography of him written by Sulpicius Severus which helped spread Martin's example throughout the West. Many early churches were dedicated to him, and he is probably the first non-martyr to be venerated as a saint. Martin of Tours set the pattern for the 'holy man' for the succeeding centuries.

Augustine of Hippo introduced a new aspect to monasticism; the arrangement whereby a group of celibate clergy lived together and served a local church. Jerome and Rufinus had belonged to a similar group in north-east Italy. After his conversion and return to North Africa in 388, Augustine gathered a group of his friends to live together in an ascetic community, devoting themselves mainly to study. They continued after Augustine was made bishop of Hippo in 395. Here were the roots of the later cathedral 'chapters' and the medieval practice of the bishop of a town surrounding himself with a 'family', comprising his subordinate clergy and often young men under training for ordination. The monastic rules circulating under his name in the Middle Ages originated in part with Augustine, but had been worked over extensively by later writers.

MILITANT MONKS

In Egypt, and to a lesser extent in Syria, monastic communities took part in political warfare. Organized and armed crowds of monks took sides in theological disputes and overawed church councils by their presence. Foremost in this activity was Schnoudi, the fierce abbot of the White Monastery in Egypt, who supported Cyril of Alexandria violently and effectively when he got Nestorius condemned for heresy at the council of Ephesus in 431. With the connivance of cynical bishops, such as Theophilus of Alexandria, monks were also responsible for destroying pagan temples, and for harassing and even murdering pagans and heretics. In this they were no better than the pagan mobs of earlier periods who had often persecuted Christians savagely at Alexandria and elsewhere.

CASSIODORUS

This long-lived Roman aristocrat, who died around 583, forged lasting links between classical and early Christian civilization and the medieval world of monks and barbarians. Cassiodorus attained high office as a minister of Theodoric and other Ostrogothic rulers. In drafting official documents, collected and known as his *Variae*, he drew upon traditional Latin rhetoric to serve a barbarian court, and influenced later practice. He encouraged Theodoric's regard for the cultural legacy of Rome. *The History of the Goths*, his most original work, is now lost.

Cassiodorus wanted to create a Christian academy at Rome, but was frustrated by the Gothic wars – although a library was collected about 535 under Pope Agapetus. Cassiodorus fulfilled his ideals in the monastery he established on his estate at Vivarium ('fish-pond', from the landscaped gardens) near the southern Italian coast, where he settled after 540.

His *Introduction to Theological and Secular Studies* advocated a marriage of biblical study and the liberal arts. His enthusiasm for secular learning, which was not shared by Benedict or Gregory the Great, strongly influenced later Benedictine practice. Vivarium's library and scriptorium (room set apart for writing) preserved and passed on manuscripts of the early Christian writers and the classics alike. Cassiodorus supervised the translation from Greek into Latin of works by such Christian writers as Clement of Alexandria, Didymus the Blind, and the church historians, as well as Josephus. He also made earlier Latin theology more readily available, especially Augustine's commentary on the Psalms and Pelagius on Paul's letters.

Cassiodorus' ideal was *civilitas*, 'humane values and order'. For the privileged it meant monastic culture, civilized study in a refined setting, welding together Roman and Christian, just as earlier he had reconciled the Gothic and the Roman.

DAVID F. WRIGHT

In the West in the fifth century, monasticism flourished in southern Gaul. Honoratus founded a monastery on the island of Lérins, which became the training ground for many monk-bishops. John Cassian began work at Marseilles at the same period. He had trained as a monk in Bethlehem and Egypt. After a period in Constantinople, he came west and in 415 founded a monastery and a convent at Marseilles.

MONKS AND LEARNING

Cassian is the West's great writer on monasticism, and his detailed instructions for monasteries served to promote the monastic movement widely. He went into great detail, covering not only subjects such as clothing and the form of monastery services, but also examining the temptations against which a monk had to fight. He was a keen observer and painstaking administrator. Cassian reacted against what he felt to be an over-emphasis on human weakness in the theology of Augustine. He held that people are able to make some response to God in their own strength, even though they cannot totally fulfil God's commands. Cassian's viewpoint, probably brought from the East, was especially common in the monastic communities of southern France, and is often called semi-Pelagianism. In addition to Cassian, its most notable teacher was Vincent of Lérins. Semi-Pelagianism became quite popular in southern France until it was condemned by the Synod of Orange in 529.

The next great name in Western monasticism is Cassiodorus (490–583), who came from a distinguished Roman senatorial family and held high office under Theodoric

The Greek monastery of Mar Saba, or Sabas the Sanctified, is among the oldest inhabited monasteries in the world. Situated near Bethlehem, in the West Bank, the monastery was begun in 483 by Sabas, but today houses only a handful of monks. John of Damascus (676–749) lived here as a monastic priest.

TIM DOWLEY ASSOCIATES

PATRICK: MISSIONARY TO THE IRISH

Patrick (c 389–461), the great missionary to the Irish, was probably born in Roman Britain. He was the son of a deacon and magistrate named Calpurnius. The details of his life are disputed and have been overlaid with many pious legends. The small amount of definite information about him is found in his two writings: *The Confession* and *A Letter to the Soldiers of Coroticus*, a chief in north Britain.

At the age of sixteen, while at his father's farm, Patrick was seized by raiders and sold as a slave in Ireland. After six years of service as a shepherd, he escaped and eventually reached home again. He also spent some time in Gaul. During his captivity, his Christian faith had been decisively deepened and he became convinced he should return and evangelize Ireland. Once in a dream he heard the voice of the Irish calling, 'We beseech you to come and walk among us once more.'

Patrick returned to Ireland as a bishop in 432 and spent the next thirty years ministering there. He had a great influence on several chieftains and special ties in the areas of Tara, Croagh Patrick, and Armagh. Although he was not well educated, he encouraged learning and, possibly through contact with strict monasteries in Gaul, he began to emphasize the ascetic life and monasticism. In the later Irish Church the basic unit became the monastery led by the abbot, rather than the bishop's diocese. Patrick also communicated the priority of mission to Celtic Christianity, which produced great numbers of monks who evangelized Western Europe during the sixth and seventh centuries.

ROBERT G. CLOUSE

the Great, the Ostrogothic king of Italy. In 540 he retired to the monastery he had founded at Vivarium, in Calabria (southern Italy). He placed great emphasis on the copying of manuscripts and the study of ancient writings, and some scholars believe Benedict of Nursia derived his stress on study from Cassiodorus. The emphasis on monastic learning ensured that Greco-Roman culture survived into the Middle Ages.

CELTIC MONASTICISM

Monasticism seems to have begun among the Celts in the late fifth or early sixth century, but its origins are obscure. Although its establishment was later attributed to Patrick, there is no certain evidence from his writings that he founded monasteries or that he was a monk himself. Patrick himself seems to have encouraged the private type of asceticism favoured before 325. However, in the late fifth century, monasticism seems to have taken root in Ireland in a form which owed much to the Egyptian pattern. Martin of Tours' monastic ideals may have reached Ireland *via* Ninian's monastery at Whithorn in Scotland.

The extreme rigour of Irish hermits, and the arrangement of cells within an outer boundary wall, both reflect Egyptian influences. Irish monks also acquired a great enthusiasm for scholarship, which may have been encouraged by continental scholars who fled to Ireland from the barbarian invasions of the fifth century. Contemporary Ireland was a tribal society without large towns, and the monasteries exerted a great influence on church life. Unlike Western monasticism in mainland Europe, Irish monks put little value on staying in one place, and from the sixth century onwards the wandering Celtic monk became a common figure on the European continent. Such wandering monks founded some of the most famous of the early continental monasteries – including Luxeuil in Burgundy, St Gall in Switzerland, and Bobbio in Italy; they also promoted the evangelization of much of central Europe.

COLUMBA: CELTIC MISSIONARY

Columba (521–97), who became a famous abbot and missionary, was born of noble parents in Donegal, Ireland, the land of the 'Scots'. He was educated at the schools of Finbar at Moville and Finnian at Clonard, and after ordination preached widely and helped to establish churches and monasteries, such as those at Derry and Durrow.

In 563 Columba left Ireland, determined to 'go on pilgrimage for Christ'. There is some disagreement over why he left his homeland. He had been involved in a dispute over the possession of a manuscript he had copied out, and he fell into disfavour for his part in causing the civil war which followed between his clan and the High King Diarmid. His departure may have been partly a self-imposed penance.

With twelve companions Columba sailed to the island of Iona, on the west coast of Scotland, where he established a monastery which served as a base for evangelism among his fellow Scots and among the Picts. A courageous man, almost warlike at times, Columba preached to people who were under the influence of Druid opponents of Christianity. His faithfulness was rewarded when rulers such as Brude, king of the Picts, were converted. Many churches were founded, and much of the religious, political, and social life of Scotland Christianized. The extent of Columba's influence beyond the west of Scotland is uncertain.

Columba combined deep visionary piety and a forceful involvement in the affairs of kings and chiefs with a concern for scholarship and a love of nature, and is a figure typical of the Celtic Church. His achievements illustrate the importance of the Celtic Church in reviving Christianity in Western Europe after the fall of the Roman Empire. An important early *Life of Columba* was written about 688–92 by Adamnan, the ninth abbot of Iona.

ROBERT G. CLOUSE

THE RULE OF BENEDICT

Benedict of Nursia provided the definitive rule for monasteries in the West; from the late sixth century his system gradually superseded other Western monastic rules. Very little is known of the life of Benedict apart from the details given in a biography attributed to Gregory the Great. Only in the time of Charlemagne, and through the efforts of Witiza, who called himself Benedict of Aniane (c. 747—821), was the Benedictine rule widely published and imposed on monasteries. Benedict was born at Nursia, in Umbria (north-central Italy), and studied at Rome before withdrawing to live as a hermit. He founded several small monasteries, but had little success until he moved to the monastery at Monte Cassino. He wrote his rule during his early years as a monk, and died at Monte Cassino about 547. When the monastery there was destroyed by the Lombards, some of the monks fled to Rome where they brought his rule to the notice of Gregory the Great.

The Rule of Benedict is based on two activities: prayer and work. The individual monk had to show high moral character, and Benedict insisted a monk should remain in the same monastery where he had taken his vows. The abbot was the spiritual head of the monastery and exercised all the normal discipline. The monasteries' stable, well-ordered communities, with their emphasis on worship, greatly helped to keep up spiritual standards during these centuries. Perhaps thanks to the influence of Cassiodorus, the Benedictine monasteries also became centres of learning.

Life in Benedict's monastery

In every aspect all shall follow the *Rule* as their guide: and let no one depart from it without good reason. Let no one in the monastery follow his own inclinations, or brazenly argue with his abbot . . . The abbot, for his part, should do everything in the fear of the Lord and in obedience to the *Rule*, knowing that he will have to account to God for all his decisions.

If a brother is insubordinate, or disobedient, proud or a grumbler, or in any way acting contrary to the holy *Rule* and despising the orders of his seniors, let him, according to the Lord's commandment, be privately warned twice by his seniors. If he does not improve, let him be publicly rebuked before them all. But if even then he does not correct himself, he should be excommunicated, if he understands how severe this penalty is. If, however, he is beyond conviction, he should be physically punished.

The brothers shall take turns to wait on each other so that no one is excused from kitchen work, unless prevented by sickness or taken up with some vital business . . . An hour before each meal the week's servers are to receive a cup of drink and a piece of bread over and above their ration, so they can wait on their brothers without grumbling or undue fatigue.

At the brothers' meal times there should always be a reading . . . There shall be complete silence at table, and no whispering or any voice except the reader's should be heard. The brethren should pass

The Celtic high cross of St Martin, sculpted from a single stone, stands outside the west door of Iona Abbey, on the island of Iona, Scotland. Its west face depicts scenes from the Bible; the east face is decorated with bosses and serpents. The abbey was founded by Columba and his Irish missionaries in 563.

TIM DOWLEY ASSOCIATES

The Rule of Benedict observed in monasteries today is still largely that of the founder, although copies of the rule have been enlarged and altered to fit later developments. Some historians believe Benedict's rule owes a great deal to another monastic rule of similar date, known as the *Regula Magistri*, the 'Rule of the Master', and that Benedict's genius lay in making the harsher requirements of this older rule more human.

CELIBATE CLERGY
The idea that the clergy should remain unmarried developed only slowly. From the New Testament, it is reasonable to suppose that most of the apostles were married. Certainly

to each other in turn whatever food is needed so that no one needs to ask for anything. If anything should be wanted, ask for it by sign-language rather than by speech.

Above all, care must be taken of the sick . . . Baths should be available to the sick as often as necessary: to the healthy, and especially the young, less often. The eating of meat shall also be allowed to the sick and the delicate to aid recovery. But when they have got better, they shall all abstain from flesh, as is normal.

In winter, that is from 1 November until Easter, as far as possible they must get up at the eighth hour of the night, so that they rest for a little over half the night, and rise when they have had a good sleep. But the time that remains after 'vigils' shall be spent in study . . .

As the prophet says, 'Seven times in the day do I praise thee.' We will complete this sacred number seven if, at lauds, at the first, third, sixth, ninth hours, at vesper time and at compline we carry out the duties of our service.

Idleness is the enemy of the soul. Therefore, at fixed times, the brothers should be busy with manual work; and at other times in holy reading. We believe these ought to be arranged in this way: from Easter until 1 October, on coming out of *Prime* they shall do the work needing attention until the fourth hour. From the fourth hour until about the sixth, they should concentrate on reading. After the meal on the sixth hour, they shall rest on their beds in complete silence; anyone who wishes may read to himself as long as he does not disturb anyone else. *None* shall be said a little early, about the middle of the eighth hour; after that they shall work at their tasks until evening.

A mattress, woollen blanket, woollen under-blanket, and a pillow shall be enough bedding. Beds are to be searched frequently by the abbot for private belongings. And, if anyone is found to possess anything he did not receive from the abbot, he shall be very severely disciplined. To abolish private property, everything necessary shall be given by the abbot: a hood, tunic, shoes, long socks, belt, knife, pen, needle, handkerchief, tablets, so that they can have no excuses about needing things.

A monastery should, if possible, be built so that everything needed – water, mill, garden, bakery – is available, so that the monks do not need to wander about outside. For this is not at all good for their souls.

We intend to found a school to train men in the service of the Lord, but where we shall not make the rules too strict and heavy . . . If we seem to be severe, do not get frightened and run away. The entrance to the path of salvation must be narrow, but as you progress along the life of the faith, the heart expands and speeds with love's sweetness along the pathway of God's commandments.

SELECTIONS FROM BENEDICT'S *RULE*

this is true of Peter (his mother-in-law is mentioned) and the brothers of Jesus; and it was regarded as normal that an apostle could take his wife with him on church work. At the same time, Paul recognized the practical advantages of remaining unmarried. Also, with sexual excesses all around them, it is likely that some Christians reacted against sex from a fairly early period. However, this was not formally set out or made a matter of special praise. In fact, special vows by younger women to abstain from marriage were discouraged by Paul.

During the period which followed, abstinence from marriage was left a matter of personal choice, although in most Gnostic sects marriage was actively discouraged on the grounds that it entangled the spiritual soul with the evil physical world. Some Jewish and

Christian traditions blamed sexual differences on the fall, and believed salvation included a return to 'unisex' life. In the mainstream churches, leaders such as Melito of Sardis became known for their austere personal lives, with abstinence from marriage part of this. In many churches, too, Christian women may have had difficulty in finding suitable husbands. Tertullian spells out the problem of a Christian woman with a pagan husband in a tract dedicated to his own wife! For such reasons some women remained unmarried, which could give them more time for prayer and devotion. In the same way, men who were free from family ties had more time to devote to church affairs, and were often obvious choices as leaders.

By the third century, celibacy was beginning to be valued as a mark of holiness. Even so, extremes were frowned upon, and Origen earned considerable disapproval because he made himself a eunuch, believing this was commended in the Gospels. As martyrdom declined, asceticism began to become the measure of spirituality; the leaders regarded as more spiritual in the churches tended to be those who practised an ascetic way of life. However, the clergy were not generally obliged to be celibate and some important church leaders, such as Hilary of Poitiers (c. 300– c. 368), were married. In the fourth century also some men in public life were ordained later on in life, after they had married. In some cases they continued to live with their wives, but abstained from sexual intercourse.

In the fourth century, moves were made to restrict marriage after ordination. The Council of Ancyra, about 315, declared that deacons had to choose between marriage and celibacy before ordination, and could not marry afterwards; the Council of Neocaesarea, about 320, ruled that presbyters who married after ordination were to be deposed. However, it is uncertain how far these rules were enforced. As the fourth century proceeded, the pressure for Christians to be celibate became very great. Jerome was the most enthusiastic supporter of celibacy, and was criticized because many of his pronouncements seemed to denigrate marriage. Some Western theologians believed original guilt entered into the soul of the infant through the act of conception and thus cast doubt on sexual intercourse. In spite of protests that celibacy was Manichean (the Manichees held that all aspects of the physical world were evil), supporters of celibacy persuaded the churches that celibacy and holiness were closely connected.

Celibacy of the clergy introduced two great abuses. Many so-called celibate clergy in fact lived with women who were not their wives (called *subintroductae*), a practice repeatedly condemned by church councils and writers. Jerome was particularly biting about such disgraceful behaviour. Also, enthusiastic men were tempted to desert their wives in order to follow the celibate life. A Roman law of 420 expressly forbade this.

In the fifth century and after, two codes of practice evolved. In the Eastern Churches, presbyters and deacons were allowed to marry before ordination, but bishops were always chosen from among the celibate clergy (very often they were monks). This practice was accepted as the norm by Justinian and remains in force in Eastern Christianity today. In the West there was strong pressure for complete clerical celibacy. Leo the Great wanted to forbid marriage even for subdeacons, but it is uncertain whether this was ever enforced during his time. Certainly, during the fifth and sixth centuries married men such as Sidonius Apollinaris (c. 430–489) became bishops. However, during these centuries the monasteries came to be regarded as the main centres of spirituality, which meant that increasingly the best bishops tended to be celibate. Celibacy of the clergy continued to be praised as an ideal, although it was not enforced legally and effectively until the time of Hildebrand (Pope Gregory VI, r. 1073–85).

DAILY PRAYER

Ascetic communities influenced the liturgy considerably, especially in the matter of daily services. Early in the second century the *Didache* had encouraged Christians to pray three times a day. Another early practice was for Christians to rise and pray at midnight – common by the time of Tertullian. Morning and evening prayer in church became customary during the fourth century, especially at centres of pilgrimage such as Jerusalem. Egeria (sometimes known as Aetheria or Silvia), a lady pilgrim to the Holy Land in the late fourth century, mentions four daily services attended by clergy and monks in Jerusalem. The seven-times-daily order of prayer evolved in the monasteries soon after, and was claimed to be sanctioned by the text from Psalm 119, 'Seven times a day will I praise thee.'

The routine was made up from the three hours of prayer (9 a.m., 12 noon, 3 p.m.), the morning and evening prayers, and two additional services. The complete cycle was:

Lauds (the old morning prayer)
Prime (to fill the gap between Lauds in the small hours and Terce)
Terce (at 9 a.m.)
Sext (12 noon)
None (3 p.m.)
Vespers (old evening prayer)
Compline (prayer just before bedtime).

These services varied in content, but included prayers and intercessions, reciting of psalms, the reading of the Bible, and a certain amount of singing, mainly by a solo singer, with the congregation repeating a refrain at intervals. On occasions there was also antiphonal singing, where the congregation divided into two choirs and sang alternate halves of the verses of a psalm; but this only happened where the training of singers could be relied on. On the anniversaries of martyrs or saints, the Bible reading might be replaced by a reading from the account of the martyrdom or from the 'Life' of the particular saint.

MICHAEL A. SMITH

FURTHER READING

A. H. M. Jones, *Constantine and the Conversion of Europe*, London, 1948.

Ivor J. Davidson, *A Public Faith: From Constantine to the Medieval World AD 312–600*, Oxford, 2005.

Frances Young, *From Nicaea to Chalcedon*, London, 1983.

J. Stevenson ed., rev. W. H. C. Frend, *Creeds, Councils and Controversies: Documents Illustrating the History of the Church AD 337–461*, London, 1989

Philip Jenkins, *The Lost History of Christianity: The Thousand-year Golden Age of the Church in the Middle East, Africa and Asia*, New York, 2008.

Peter Brown, *Augustine of Hippo: A Biography*, London, 1969.

STUDY QUESTIONS

1. Why did Constantine recognize Christianity?

2. What attracted Christians to the monastic life in this period?

3. Why did Christians argue so much about the doctrine of the Trinity?

4. What were the main immediate effects of the official recognition of Christianity?

5. Why is Augustine of Hippo regarded as such an important figure?

6. Why did the Roman Empire decline and fall?

7. What differences appeared during this period between the church in the West and the church in the East?

8. Patrick or Jerome: which do you think is of greater importance in the history of the church – and why?

9. How did the church in North Africa differ from the church in Western Europe?

10. Describe life in a Christian monastery of this period.

3 A Christian Society

AD 600–1500

Summary

The major disruptions within the Roman Empire in the fifth century led to a growing rift between the Western and Eastern Churches. Increasing tension over political as much as theological issues led to the Great Schism of 1054. By this point, the influence of the Eastern Church had extended as far north as Moscow.

In Western Europe, Christianity underwent a major renaissance during the period 1000–1500. This era – the Middle Ages – saw the renewal of church life at every level. The political and social influence of the church was consolidated, and the personal authority of the pope to intervene in political disputes of the region reached new levels. The form of theological thinking known as 'scholasticism' developed, with thirteenth-century writers such as Thomas Aquinas and Duns Scotus achieving great theological sophistication.

Scholasticism was increasingly questioned. The European Renaissance, which began to become a major cultural force in Western Europe in the fourteenth century, pointed to the importance rather of returning to the roots of Christendom. The humanist movement – linked with the Renaissance – believed it essential to study Scripture in its original languages, creating pressure for new Bible translations.

The rise of Islam in the seventh century had a significant negative impact on Christianity in North Africa and the Middle East. It seemed poised to extend yet further in 1453, when Islamic armies captured Constantinople, 'the gate to Europe'. By the early sixteenth century, Islam was poised to enter Austria, though military defeats in fact limited its influence to the Balkans.

By this stage, however, Western Europe was convulsed by new controversies, as the movement we know as the Reformation gained momentum.

CHAPTER 16

THE WEST IN CRISIS

Pope Gregory I, Gregory the Great (r. 590–604) stands at a crossroads in the development of the Christian church. The division between its Eastern (Greek and Orthodox) and its Western (Latin and Catholic) halves had been in existence from at least the fourth century; any semblance of political unity between East and West under the eastern Roman Empire was mere pretence.

From 400 to 600 the emperors in the West increasingly relied on bishops to assist in secular matters. The fall in population and the penetration of the German peoples into the interior of the Roman Empire helped create a need for new leaders, and it was the Christian bishop who increasingly filled this role. By the year 600 the effective legislation and leadership of Western Europe was provided by the Christian clergy, particularly the bishops meeting in local councils.

Intense competition had arisen earlier among the bishops of the great imperial cities – Antioch, Alexandria, Rome, and Constantinople. Long before 600 Rome and Constantinople had emerged as the two chief rivals for pre-eminence. Constantinople was, of course, the junior of the two, but since it was associated with the imperial capital, the Church of Constantinople inevitably rose in prestige and influence.

THE POPE AND THE INVADERS

As pope, Gregory the Great reflected the new status of the papacy. He criticized the Patriarch of Constantinople for using the term 'Ecumenical Patriarch', asserting that such a title belonged only to the bishop of Rome. When his Eastern counterpart refused to agree, Gregory dropped the disputed title rather than share it, and called himself instead 'servant of the servants of God'.

Gregory sought to develop ties with the pagan and Arian Christian Germanic kingdoms. When the Germanic tribal groups pushed into the Roman Empire in the late fourth century, they came as Arian Christians. Although the Germanic kings tried to integrate their tribes with the local orthodox Catholic populations, the religious difference was too great an obstacle. Catholic antagonism towards the heretical rulers resulted in constant tension between the ruling elite and the rest of the population.

The bishops of Rome had come to enjoy great power in Rome and in Italy as a result of the decline and eventual disappearance of effective imperial authority in the West and throughout their extensive landholdings. While the legal basis for the Papal States ('the Patrimony of St Peter') was probably not established until the eighth century, its origins clearly go back to the fourth century. The title 'Republic of St Peter' appears in papal documents as early as the late seventh century.

The last of the Germanic tribes to enter the Roman Empire, the Arian Lombards, arrived in Italy in 568. The ineffectiveness of the imperial governor at Ravenna in combating them brought home to the papacy the need to find another protector. Conversion of the invaders to Catholic Christianity was one possible solution – which

GREGORY THE GREAT

Of all the bishops of Rome between Constantine the Great and the Reformation, none was more influential than Gregory I, 'the Great' (540–604). Indeed, the medieval papacy clearly makes its appearance with the career of this remarkably able churchman. Gregory, who came from a distinguished Roman aristocratic family with a long tradition of imperial service and, later, service to the church, also began his career in public administration.

But Gregory turned away from public life and became a monk. He was the first pope who had been a monk and he introduced monasticism to the papacy. Gregory stressed ascetic ideals – ideals associated with the rule of Benedict which became the prevailing style of monasticism by the ninth century.

Gregory marked his period as pope by his claim to 'universal' jurisdiction over Christendom, notably in a controversy with the Patriarch of Constantinople over the latter's right to use the title of 'Ecumenical Patriarch', and in Gregory's efforts to cultivate the rulers of Germanic kingdoms in Western Europe. One matter of outstanding importance was Gregory's decision to send a team of monks to the kingdom of Kent in Britain. The Christianization of the Anglo-Saxons and the victory of Roman Christianity over the Celtic Church were the long-term result of Gregory's missionary policy.

Gregory's prolific writing resulted in the production of a basic textbook for training the medieval clergy and increased popularity for allegorical interpretations of the Bible and interest in saints' lives – the truly popular Christian literature of the Middle Ages. He gave to early medieval Catholicism its distinctive character, stressing the cult of saints and relics, demonology, and ascetic virtues. Finally, Gregory confirmed the authority and hierarchy of the papacy and the church; he proclaimed the 'Christian Commonwealth' in which the pope and the clergy were to be responsible for ordering society.

HARRY ROSENBERG

Gregory did in fact try. He supported the Lombard Queen Theodelinda, who was a Catholic Christian. Eventually the Lombards were weaned away from Arian to Catholic Christianity, though this did not solve the political problems of the papacy. But Gregory pointed the way to the future solution, namely looking west and not east for protection.

Gregory wrote a series of important letters to Germanic rulers elsewhere in the West. By this time, the Arian Visigoths in Spain had accepted Catholic Christianity, and Gregory's letters to Reccared I (559–601), the first catholic Visigoth king of Spain, demonstrate the pope's desire to make his influence felt there.

CLOVIS IS CONVERTED

The Frankish kings in Gaul were the only Germanic tribes to enter the Roman Empire as pagans and not as Arian Christians. About 500, Clovis – the first great ruler among the Franks – decided to accept Catholic baptism, following his marriage to Clotild, a catholic Burgundian princess. According to a Frankish history, Clovis agreed to accept Christ if the Christian God gave him victory over another tribe with whom he was at war. Clovis won his battle against the Alemanni; then, with 3,000 of his warriors, he was baptized. This event points up the general pattern of early medieval conversions: the change to Christianity was essentially a matter of royal policy. The ruler's conversion decided the religion of his subjects. Catholic queens and princesses did much to bring about the conversion of their husbands – and their kingdoms.

Clovis' conversion laid the foundations for an important alliance between the papacy and the Franks. Although the Franks showed great devotion to Peter and the Roman Church from a very early stage, this did not mean the pope immediately had great influence on royal policy. The harsh, even barbaric, conditions of Gaul under the Merovingian dynasty of Frankish rulers proved very detrimental to the church during the sixth and seventh centuries.

Pope Gregory, determined to revive the Church in the West, attempted to launch reform in Gaul. He was thwarted by the Merovingian rulers, who indulged in such practices as appointing laymen as bishops and selling church appointments, simply assuming the church was freely at their own disposal. Gregory's efforts pointed the way to the reform of the eighth century.

ANGELS – NOT ANGLES!

Gregory's relations with the Merovingian kings did have one positive result: the mission to England and the conversion of the Angles, Saxons, and Jutes. This enterprise best demonstrates Gregory's vision to convert the 'barbarians' and make them members of a 'Christian commonwealth' led by the pope. Gregory's vision became reality in medieval Europe.

The mission to England is described in a simple, perhaps apocryphal, story by a pious papal biographer. Gregory, while still a monk in Rome, one day saw some attractive young children in the slave market. On inquiring who they were, Gregory learned they were *Angli* from England, and that they were pagans. He replied that these young boys were not 'Angles' but 'Angels'!

It is certain that Gregory had such contacts, for in 595 he ordered his representative in Arles, in southern France, to purchase Anglo-Saxon slaves to be brought to Rome for training as clerics. Gregory also had good information about the political and religious situation in England. In 596 he assembled a team of forty monks under Augustine, the prior of the pope's own monastery in Rome. With Frankish priests as interpreters, the team arrived in England just before Easter 597. Gregory's intelligence indicated that the Jutish kingdom of Kent should be the target of the mission, as its king, Ethelbert, was married to a Catholic Frankish princess, Bertha. Ethelbert accepted Catholicism, and, since he was nominal overlord of the neighbouring Anglo-Saxon kingdoms of Essex and East Anglia, Catholic Christianity came to three of the twelve Anglo-Saxon kingdoms.

By late 597, the pope appointed Augustine archbishop of the Church in England. King Ethelbert gave the new archbishop his own palace in Canterbury, which became the first episcopal centre in England. Pope Gregory instructed the rather unimaginative Augustine how to convert the pagans – they were to be weaned slowly away from their current religion.

Evangelistic efforts among the Angles and Saxons proceeded gradually, and were directly affected by intense political and religious competition among the kings. Archbishop Augustine was also concerned about the Celtic Church – its attitude towards the Anglo-Saxon mission, and its practices, which differed from those of Rome. Bede, the historian, wrote that Augustine's attempts to unite the Celtic Church and Rome failed on three basic issues: namely his requirements that the Celtic Church adopt the Roman

A ninth-century manuscript of Pope Gregory I, 'the Great', dictating, inspired by the Holy Spirit (represented by the dove); from the Bibliothèque Nationale de France, Paris.

SONIA HALLIDAY PHOTOGRAPHS

method of arriving at the date of Easter, adopt the Roman tradition of baptism, and join his mission to convert the Anglo-Saxons.

CELTIC CHRISTIANS OBJECT

Relations between Augustine and the Celtic churchmen turned sour. The Celtic bishops took offence when the archbishop refused to stand to greet them and they refused to accept him as their archbishop.

The Celtic Church already had a long history when Augustine arrived. British bishops were present at the Council of Arles, convened by Constantine in 314. In the late fourth and early fifth centuries Christianity thrived in Britain. But in the face of the invasions of Britain by the Angles, Saxons, and Jutes, from the mid-fifth century on, much of the Celtic-Roman British population, as well as the Celtic Church, retreated to the south-west. British conservatism, caused by the long period of isolation from continental Christianity, together with hatred of the foreign invaders, were the major barriers to unity between Augustine and the British Church.

The British Church finally fused with Roman Christianity during the course of the following century. This occurred when the mission among the Anglo-Saxons succeeded, with both Celtic-British and Roman Christians participating. By the third quarter of the seventh century a generation of church leaders emerged who combined the order and authority of Rome with the emotional and imaginative vigour of Celtic Christianity. Aidan of Lindisfarne (d. 651), the first Celtic churchman to take an active part in the mission to the Anglo-Saxons, with a number of other Anglo-Saxon churchmen, such as Wilfrid of York (634–709), took the lead in overcoming paganism and racism. Again with royal support, this time that of Oswy, King of Northumbria, this mission achieved success. The Synod of Whitby, in 664, confirmed the Romanization of British Christianity.

Five years later two church leaders were sent to England by the pope to complete the reordering of the Church in England. Theodore of Tarsus (602–90), a Greek who served the pope as Archbishop of Canterbury, and Hadrian, from North Africa, stand out as the real founders of the Catholic Church in England. They built on the foundations laid by Pope Gregory and Archbishop Augustine, and drew on the spiritual and intellectual vigour of Celtic Christianity.

The new leaders carried out effective administrative and educational work. Theodore wisely followed a policy of reconciliation with Celtic Christianity. He and Hadrian brought Mediterranean Christian culture to Canterbury, contributing a permanent framework to the Anglo-Saxon Church. By establishing a 'national' body which transcended local boundaries and local patriotism, Theodore's reorganization of the church helped develop secular government as well as bringing order out of chaos. The church conveyed the concepts of unity and centralization to the secular leaders.

Archbishop Theodore, who had previously studied in Athens, also contributed to the development of Anglo-Saxon culture. Assisted by Hadrian and Benedict Biscop (c. 628–90), an Anglo-Saxon deeply interested in Christian learning, the archbishop founded at Canterbury a school where the cultures of British and Mediterranean Christianity fused, resulting in a remarkable intellectual flowering in the arts and humanities. The Venerable Bede (c. 673–735) is an outstanding example of the literary achievement of this rebirth of biblical and historical studies. The superb artistic skills of the Celts in illustrating manuscripts are seen in remarkable Bibles such as the *Lindisfarne Gospels* (now in the British Library) and *The Book of Kells* (in Trinity College Library, Dublin). The culture and learning of the Anglo-Saxon Church, as well as its fervour for the gospel, contributed directly to the revival of religious and intellectual life in Europe during the century after Theodore.

THE RISE OF ISLAM

Meanwhile another development with far-reaching consequences for the history of Christianity and the medieval and modern world was taking place. At the very time when Gregory the Great was turning away from the eastern Mediterranean and seeking to extend papal influence throughout the West, there began in Arabia the career of a remarkable religious leader, Muhammad of Mecca (c. 570–632), whose teachings had an almost immediate impact. The movement of Islam was born and spread outside Arabia with dramatic speed after the prophet's death.

The course of history in both the Orthodox East and the Catholic West was drastically affected. The rise of Islam directly influenced the political and economic development of both halves of Christendom, and Islam became medieval Christianity's greatest opponent. By the tenth century the Islamic community, stretching from Baghdad to Cordova, had become the most prosperous of the early Middle Ages.

Although cradled in Arabia, with Arab cults and social habits somewhat defining its outlook and influencing its ritual, the new religion was in many ways an offshoot of Judaism and Christianity, though it was also influenced by Zoroastrianism, the religion of Persia. Islamic culture shared the same background as early Christian thought – the Jewish and Hellenistic cultures which prevailed in western Asia. Thus, medieval Islamic civilization shared a common basis with medieval Christian civilization, which made contacts between the two easier.

THE PROPHET'S CALL

Following his religious call in 610, Muhammad proclaimed the message of Islam (Arabic for 'submission to the will of God'). His teachings included: the impending judgment of the world, with reward and punishment for each individual's actions, and the teachings of *Allah*, the creator and judge. The message of Muhammad imposed five main obligations upon Muslim believers: the confession of faith ('There is no god but *Allah*, and Muhammad is his prophet'), prayer five times a day, charitable gifts, fasting in the holy month of *Ramadan*, and the pilgrimage to Mecca.

The basic source of the divine revelation was the *Qur'an* (which was collected and committed to writing by Uthman ibn Affan, c. 579–656), the third caliph and second leader after Muhammad). In addition there was the *Hadith*, which recorded the traditions of the habits and sayings of the prophet. Finally the *Ijma*, consisting of the 'accord of the faithful', formed the body of law followed by devout Muslims. Taken together these three religious sources constitute the *Sunna* or 'The Path'. A subsequent division within Islam between the Sunnites and the Shiites left the *Sunna* in dispute. This schism, caused by the problem of choosing a successor to Muhammad, still persists.

When Muhammad's proclamation was ill-received in Mecca, he made the fateful decision to leave for Medina in June 622. This emigration to Medina, the city of the prophet, is known as the *Hegira*. It marked the beginning of a new era, a change in fortune for Muhammad, and the beginning of the Islamic calendar. With Medina as his base of operations, Muhammad developed the rudiments of what became the major characteristics of Islam worldwide. Idol-worshippers had to accept Islam or the sword, but monotheists — Jews and Christians — enjoyed a special status; they were tolerated on condition they paid a special tax. Eight years after leaving Mecca, Muhammad returned there in triumph and purified the city by removing the various idols in the ancient Arab shrine, the *Kaaba*. By the time of his death two years later, the whole of Arabia was committed to Islam.

A NEW WORLD-RELIGION

The Islamic community was now led by the caliphs, literally 'successors'. Although other factors contributed to the expansion of Islam outside Arabia, the chief force was the extraordinary religious enthusiasm generated by Muhammad and his immediate converts, the 'Companions'. Within a century of the prophet's death, Islam had reached the Atlantic Ocean (Morocco) and the River Indus (Pakistan). Within this vast area, there was created a

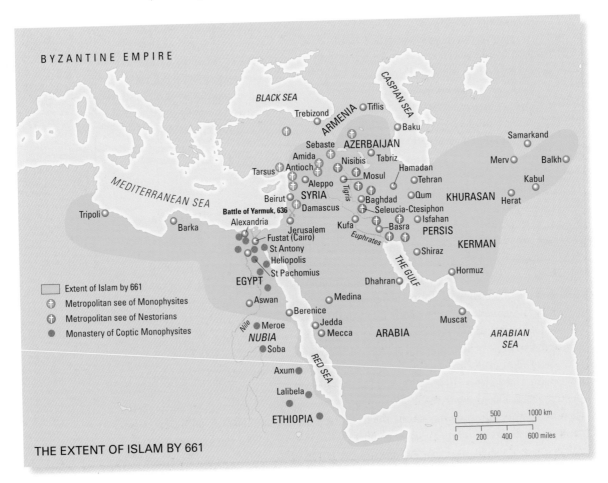

THE EXTENT OF ISLAM BY 661

theocratic empire led by the caliphs, who combined religious and political functions. Arab military commanders became the civil governors of the occupied areas, as representatives of the caliphs.

This new world empire soon divided into a series of caliphates, based primarily upon Mecca, Baghdad, Damascus, and Cairo, together with a number of separate states. But the Islamic states had a coherent and homogeneous civilization, thanks to their basic Arab core. This was due, in the first instance, to the fact that no translation of the *Qur'an* was allowed, and thus the Arabic language dominated not only the religion of Islam, but also the closely allied areas of law, language, and education. Islam influenced a vast array of ethnic groups, cultures, and religions. Contrary to the generally accepted view in the West, forced conversions were the exception.

By the beginning of the eighth century, Islam reached its northernmost limits of growth. Following a series of sieges of the great imperial stronghold of Constantinople, a Muslim-Byzantine frontier was established. In the West, the Muslims rapidly occupied Visigothic Spain. Raiding parties probed into Frankish Gaul, but were defeated by the Carolingian leader, Charles Martel, at the Battle of Poitiers (or Tours) in 732. Although the Muslims were prevented from penetrating into the heart of Europe, they did succeed in gaining control over the Western Mediterranean.

In Spain, the mutual exchange of ideas among Arabs, Berbers, Jews, and Christians produced a unique culture in the Middle Ages. But Catholic Europe was concerned above all about its religious differences with the Muslim community, a concern expressed in unrelieved hostility. Islam, and its prophet, Muhammad, were identified with the beast in the book of Revelation, or with the Antichrist. Medieval Christian authors portrayed Muhammad as an imposter and Islam as a religion of violence and idolatry. Meanwhile, the Muslim community believed their civilization was superior to all others, since the revelation to Muhammad was the final one, supplanting all previous ones, such as the Old and New Testaments.

ENGLAND AND IRELAND EVANGELIZE EUROPE

After Gregory the Great, European Catholicism went through a difficult period. The papacy suffered at the hands of both the Lombards in Italy and the Byzantine rulers. In Frankish Gaul the Merovingian kings became increasingly ineffective, and the moral, spiritual, and intellectual quality of the clergy steadily declined. Effective church government was weakened as a result of constant interference by secular rulers. In his writings, Gregory, bishop of Tours (c. 538–94), reveals a sordid picture of society, also revealing that women were particularly important in sustaining sincere religious endeavour, especially by supporting monasteries.

The revival of religious life in Gaul and, indeed, throughout Latin Christendom, came about in the eighth century, led by the Anglo-Saxon missionaries, who came in great numbers, by a revitalized papacy, and by a new royal house in Frankish Gaul.

Missionaries from the Irish-Celtic Church had engaged in missions to Europe from the late sixth century. Outstanding among them was Columban (Columbanus, 540–615), who was active in Gaul and Italy. Gallus, a member of his group, founded the monastery of St Gallen, Switzerland, at an important junction along the road linking Italy and Germany, and it remained a vital centre of monastic life and culture throughout the early Middle Ages. Celtic missionaries also found their way into Bavaria and central Germany.

Although vigorous and venturesome, these missionaries paid little attention to consolidating their work; constant movement characterized Celtic Christianity. For this reason much of their work had to be done over again by the late seventh century. The Anglo-Saxons, themselves objects of a mission from Europe at the beginning of the century, were in turn impelled to carry the gospel back into Europe. Unlike their Celtic predecessors, however, these new missionaries brought with them Roman church organization and sense of order. In addition, they had close ties with the papacy. Outstanding among these hardy and courageous missionaries was Wynfrith of Crediton (680–754), better known as Boniface.

Boniface had consultations in Rome and received papal consecration as 'Bishop of the German Church'. He then evangelized among the Hessians of Bavaria and Thuringia, established the famous monastery of Fulda, and finally became Archbishop of Mainz. He is justly known as the 'Apostle to the Germans', bringing Germany into Christian Europe, under papal leadership.

A NEW ROYAL HOUSE

In addition, Boniface played a critical role in the revival of the Church in Gaul. Earlier Anglo-Saxon missionaries to Germany had received the support of Charles Martel, a member of the Carolingian family, the rising power in Frankish politics. He backed their missions because of his desire to expand his rule eastwards into Bavaria. The church and the papacy were grateful for his support, and for Charles' victory over the Muslims when they crossed the Pyrenees to invade Gaul. But Charles Martel incurred the wrath of the church because he took away church lands. Initially, the church had agreed to the use of its lands and incomes to help fight off the Muslim invaders, but Charles did not return the lands. In addition, he refused a papal request for an attack on the Lombards in Italy, because the Lombards had been his allies against the Muslims.

A new era began with the accession of Martel's heirs, Carloman and Pepin, who had been raised in the monastery of St Denis, near Paris. These two Frankish rulers were helped by Boniface to carry out a major reform of the Frankish Church. These reforms of the clergy and church organization brought about a renewal of religious and intellectual life, and made possible the educational revival associated with the greatest of the Carolingian rulers, Charlemagne.

After his brother entered a monastery, Pepin was in a position to complete the Carolingian quest for legitimate authority. Negotiations between Pepin and Pope Zachary in 751 resulted in Boniface, the Pope's legate, anointing the new King Pepin at Soissons. Another milestone in church–state relations was passed when Pope Stephen II (r. 752–57) appealed to Pepin for aid against the Lombards. The pope placed Rome under the protection of Pepin and recognized him and his sons as 'protectors of the Romans'.

LOOSENING TIES WITH THE EAST

This sequence of events, together with the coronation of Charlemagne as emperor, gave the pope the opportunity he wanted to loosen ties with the Eastern Empire and

Constantinople. Religious developments in the East provided the papacy with an opportunity finally to break free. The 'Iconoclastic controversy' engulfed the East after Emperor Leo III banned the use of icons (images of Christ, the Virgin Mary, or a saint) in 726. The supporters of icons ultimately prevailed after a century and a quarter of bitter, disruptive dispute. Meanwhile Pope Gregory II not only rejected the edict banning the use of icons, but went on bluntly to flaunt his disrespect for the Emperor's authority in the West. Gregory's bombastic letter included much bluffing, but also a dramatic statement that clearly reveals the differences between the state Church of the Orthodox East, where the secular ruler always played a leading role in church affairs, and the papal church of the West, where the papacy was attempting to eliminate secular influence. Gregory wrote: 'Listen! Dogmas are not the business of emperors but of pontiffs.'

The presence of what was regarded as a heretical dynasty in the East gave the pope the excuse he needed to separate from the East and to find a new, devoted, and orthodox protector in the West. The alliance between the papacy and the Carolingians represents the culmination of the papal quest, and opened a new and momentous chapter in the history of medieval Christianity.

In response to Pope Stephen's appeal for help, Pepin recovered territories in north-east and central Italy from the Lombards and gave them to the pope, an action known as the 'Donation of Pepin', thus confirming the legal foundation of the Papal States. At about the same time, the pope's claim to sovereign rule in Italy and independence from the Eastern Roman Empire was reinforced by the appearance of one of the great forgeries of the Middle Ages, the Donation of Constantine. This document alleged that Constantine had bequeathed Rome and the Western part of the Empire to the bishop of Rome when he relocated the capital of the empire in the East, and was not exposed as a forgery until the fifteenth century.

Mosaic of the Virgin Mary between the emperors Justinian I and Constantine I, over the south portal of Hagia Sophia, Istanbul, built as the Orthodox patriarchal basilica in 360.
SONIA HALLIDAY PHOTOGRAPHS

Charlemagne: God's deputy

Always remember, my king, that you are the deputy of God, your king. You are set to guard and rule all his members, and you must render an account for them on the day of judgment. The bishop is on a secondary plane.

Our Lord Jesus Christ has set you up as the ruler of the Christian people, in power more excellent than the pope or the Emperor of Constantinople, in wisdom more distinguished, in the dignity of your rule more sublime. On you alone depends the whole safety of the churches of Christ.

EPISTOLAE KAROLINI AEVI, II, 503; 288

ALCUIN

Alcuin (d. 804), an Anglo-Saxon scholar, became head tutor at the court of Charlemagne at Aachen, and in 796 Abbot of Tours. Previously he had for a time been master of the cathedral school in York.

He profoundly influenced the intellectual, cultural, and religious direction of the Carolingian Empire, as revealed by his more than 300 surviving letters. Alcuin's importance is best shown in the manuscripts of the school at Tours, in his educational writings, revision of the text of the Bible, biblical commentaries, and in the completion of the Gregorian Sacramentary version of the Roman liturgy. He standardized spelling and the style of writing, reformed missionary practice, and contributed to the drawing up of collections of church regulations.

Alcuin was also the leading theologian in the struggle against Adoptionists in Spain, who believed that the man Christ was God's 'adopted son'. Alcuin upheld orthodox belief and the authority of the church, the eminence of the Holy Roman see, and Charlemagne's sacred position as Emperor.

WALTER DELIUS

The Emperor Charlemagne kneels before the altar: from a thirteenth-century window at Chartres Cathedral, France.

CHARLEMAGNE CROWNED EMPEROR

The concluding act in the papal attempt to free itself from Constantinople came on Christmas Day 800, when Pope Leo III revived the Empire in the West by crowning Charlemagne as emperor. However, Charlemagne did not relish the thought of owing his crown to the pope, and in the last fourteen years of his reign he made the papacy subordinate in his empire. He continued the largely educational reform of the church begun by his father Pepin and Boniface. His chief educational adviser was the Anglo-Saxon Alcuin of York; it was an age that needed to go to school and in Alcuin it found a masterful teacher.

From the palace school at the royal court, a generation of Alcuin's students went out to head monastic and cathedral schools throughout the empire that Charlemagne created. Even though this empire barely outlived its founder, the revival of education and religion associated with Alcuin and Charlemagne brightened European culture throughout the bleak and chaotic period that followed. This 'Carolingian Renaissance' turned to classical antiquity and to early Christianity for its models, with the emphasis on Latin literature; efforts at Greek were tentative and quite artificial. The Irishman Johannes Scotus Eri(u)gena (c. 815–c. 877) was the only

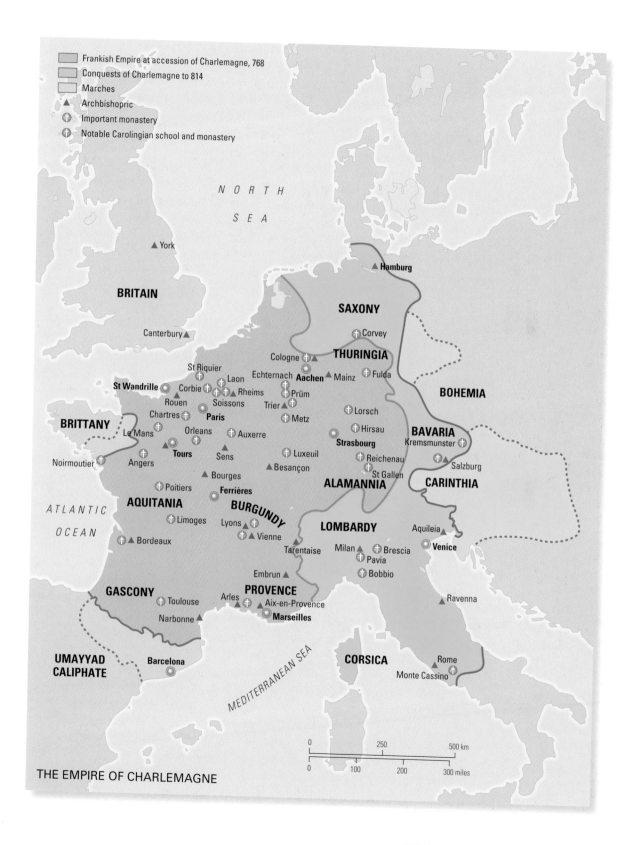

Legend:
- Frankish Empire at accession of Charlemagne, 768
- Conquests of Charlemagne to 814
- Marches
- ▲ Archbishopric
- ✚ Important monastery
- ✚ Notable Carolingian school and monastery

NORTH SEA

▲ York

BRITAIN

Canterbury ▲

▲ Hamburg

SAXONY

THURINGIA

✚ Corvey

Cologne ✚ ▲

Echternach ✚ Aachen ▲ Mainz

Fulda ✚

St Riquier ✚
Laon ✚
Corbie ✚ ✚ Rheims ✚
Rouen ✚ Soissons ✚
Chartres ✚ Paris
Le Mans ✚
Orleans ✚
St Wandrille ⊙

Prüm ✚
Trier ▲
Metz ✚

Lorsch ✚

BOHEMIA

BRITTANY

Auxerre ✚

Hirsau ✚

Strasbourg

BAVARIA
Kremsmunster ✚

Tours ⊙
Angers ✚
Sens ▲

Luxeuil ✚

Reichenau ✚
St Gallen ✚

Salzburg ✚

Noirmoutier ✚

Bourges ▲
Poitiers ✚
Ferrières ⊙

Besançon ▲

ALAMANNIA

CARINTHIA

ATLANTIC OCEAN

AQUITANIA

Limoges ✚

BURGUNDY

LOMBARDY

Aquileia ▲

Lyons ▲ ✚
Vienne ✚ ▲

Milan ▲
Pavia ✚

Brescia ✚
Venice ⊙

Bordeaux ⊙▲

Tarentaise

Bobbio ✚

GASCONY

Embrun ▲

PROVENCE

Ravenna ▲

Toulouse ✚
Narbonne ▲

Arles ▲▲
Aix-en-Provence ▲
Marseilles

UMAYYAD CALIPHATE

Barcelona

CORSICA

Rome ▲

MEDITERRANEAN SEA

Monte Cassino ✚

THE EMPIRE OF CHARLEMAGNE

Scale: 0   250   500 km
0   100   200   300 miles

accomplished Greek scholar in the Carolingian world. The activity in the copying rooms of Carolingian monasteries was of major importance for Western culture, as the works of both pagan and Christian classical authors were copied. Many original texts have not survived: these manuscripts give us our only access to the original writings.

EAST–WEST DIFFERENCES

The intellectual vigour of the Carolingian Renaissance and the political dynamism of the revived Empire stimulated new theological activity. There was some discussion and writing about the continuing iconoclastic problem in the Orthodox East. Political antagonism between the Eastern and the Carolingian emperors also led to an attack by theologians in the West on the practices and beliefs of the Orthodox Church. These controversial works on the 'Errors of the Greeks' proliferated during the ninth century as a result of the 'Photian Schism', when the Patriarch of Constantinople was deposed by the Eastern Emperor. The deposed patriarch appealed to Pope Nicholas I (858–67), as did his replacement, Photius. But when Nicholas ordered the restoration of Ignatius as Patriarch, relations between Constantinople and Rome worsened.

By this time the icon supporters had triumphed at Constantinople. Latin theologians also criticized the Eastern Church for its different method for deciding the date of Easter, the difference in clergymen's tonsure-style, and over the celibacy of the clergy. (The Eastern Church allowed clergy to marry, but required monks to be celibate.)

The major theological controversy involved the *filioque* question. Did the Holy Spirit descend 'from the Father *through* the Son' or 'from the Father *and* the Son'? From the time of Photius, Orthodox theologians bitterly attacked the Western Church on this issue, declaring that the Western position of 'and the Son' (*filioque*) was a late addition to the Nicene Creed (as indeed it was), this issue further alienating the Eastern and Western Churches. The Greek-speaking East and the Latin West were also divided in language: 'East and West could not understand each other because they could not understand each other!'

NEW QUESTIONS OF BELIEF

Carolingian theologians often anticipated later medieval theological issues. The Adoptionist heresy, alleging that Christ in his humanity was only the 'adopted' Son of God, arose in Spain in the late eighth century and appeared again later in the Carolingian Empire. Alcuin combated it vigorously in his work, *Against Felix*. Several Carolingian monks disputed the question of the perpetual virginity of Mary, a view widely accepted from the fifth century. Carolingian concern to protect the holiness and sinlessness of Mary points toward the later medieval emphasis on the Virgin Mary.

A significant discussion arose over the question of predestination. A Carolingian monk named Gottschalk, who studied Augustine's theology carefully, appears to have been the first to teach 'double predestination', the belief that some people are predestined to salvation, while others are justly predestined to eternal judgment. He was tried and condemned for his views by two synods and finally imprisoned by the Archbishop of Rheims, dying twenty years later still holding to his views.

The other major theological issue of the Carolingian era concerned the Lord's Supper. The influential Abbot of Corbie, Paschasius Radbertus (785–865), wrote a treatise *On the Body and Blood of the Lord*. This was the first clear statement of a doctrine of the 'real presence' of Christ's body and blood in the eucharist, suggesting what was later called transubstantiation. Ordinary Christians readily accepted the idea that the actual body and blood of Christ were present in the sacrament of the mass.

REFORMING THE CLERGY

The reform synods of King Pepin and Boniface focussed attention on the behaviour of non-monastic clergy, insisting that priests should lead lives beyond reproach. The repetition of this requirement at synod after synod during the sixth, seventh, and eighth centuries clearly witnessed to the need for reform among the clergy. Among the violations criticized were the rejection of celibacy, over-eating and drunkenness, unnecessary and unwise relationships with women, hunting (and keeping hunting animals – dogs and hawks), carrying arms, and frequenting taverns.

Chrodegang, bishop of Metz (d. 766), did most to reform the clergy, by preparing a rule for his cathedral clergy, a rule which eventually spread throughout the Carolingian Empire. The spirit of reform was strongly supported by Pepin and Charlemagne themselves.

Monastic developments at this time were particularly significant, with the emphasis on standardization and centralization. Between 813 and 817 a revised Benedictine rule was adopted for the whole of the Carolingian Empire. Another Benedict, a monk from Aniane in Burgundy, was responsible for an exceedingly strict regime based on the Benedictine rule, a model that was soon copied in all the monasteries of Burgundy. Charlemagne's successor, Louis the Pious (778–840), appointed Benedict the overseer of all monasteries in the realm, and a few years later his revised Benedictine rule was made obligatory for all monasteries, though with little long-term effect.

When Louis the Pious succeeded Charlemagne, the pope was able to reassert his independence, following the long period of domination by Charlemagne. The new trend towards an imperial theocracy during Charlemagne's era would have yielded a 'state church', as in the Eastern Orthodox Empire. But the papacy stressed the superiority of the spiritual power over the secular, reinforced by the forged Donation of Constantine, with its emphasis on papal pre-eminence in the governing of the western half of the Roman Empire. The pope's crowning of Charlemagne was a further demonstration of the pope's claim to decide who should wear the imperial crown.

After Charlemagne, the Carolingian Empire was torn by civil wars. The political chaos, as well as the prevailing system of church control, threatened the independence of the bishops. Laymen controlled churches by means of the 'proprietary' system, providing the land and erecting the church building. Increasingly the lay patrons felt free to choose the clergymen to serve in these churches. Associated with this system there arose the abuse of simony, the sale of church posts, often with little or no regard to the clerical qualifications of the purchaser. These arrangements persisted throughout succeeding centuries, the age of classic feudalism, and as a result the church was seriously compromised.

The Carolingian era did see a major effort to deal with this problem. In the diocese of Rheims between 845 and 853, clergymen produced another remarkable forgery, the *Pseudo-Isidorian Decretals* or *False Decretals*. This fabrication, done with great inventiveness, was designed to provide 'law' to protect the rights of the bishops. To strengthen the argument, the authors invoked the principle of the supremacy of the pope. Their intent was not to aid the papacy, but in fact it was the papacy which ultimately benefited most from the *False Decretals*. This compendium of church law, which incorporated the Donation of Constantine, became a vital part of medieval canon law, and buttressed the papal claims to supremacy in the church and over secular authority. The first pope to make use of this collection was Nicholas I (r. 858–67), the most important pope in the period between Gregory the Great and Gregory VII. Nicholas saw clearly the danger of a church dominated by civil rulers, and was determined to avert this possibility by stressing that the church's government was centred on Rome.

DESPAIR AND DARKNESS

From the late ninth century until the mid-eleventh century, internal and external problems steadily weakened Western Christendom. The Carolingian Empire fragmented and no major military power existed in the West. The continued attacks of the Muslims in the south, a new wave of attackers from central Asia – the Magyars (Hungarians) – and the almost overwhelming movement of Norsemen from Scandinavia, brought yet more fragmentation and chaos. A contemporary chronicler lamented, 'Once we had a king, now we have kinglets!' The end of the world seemed at hand – and was seriously expected by many as the year 1000 approached.

For the papacy this was an era of despair; the pope no longer had Carolingian 'protectors' to come to his assistance. The papacy was increasingly involved in the power struggle among the nobility for the rule of Italy, with popes becoming captive partisans of one political faction or another, resulting in spiritual and moral decline. Pope Stephen VI, for example, took revenge by having his predecessor's body disinterred and brought before a synod, where it was propped up in a chair for a trial. Following conviction, the body was thrown into the River Tiber. Within a year Stephen was overthrown, and subsequently strangled in prison.

There was an almost total collapse of civil order and culture in Europe during the tenth century. Everywhere church property was either devastated and ransacked by foreign invaders, or fell into the hands of catholic nobility. Noblemen treated bishoprics and monasteries as their private property to dispose of as they wished. The clergy became indifferent to duty, and their ignorance and immorality increased.

For the papacy the tenth century was indeed a dark age. Without imperial protection, the popes became the helpless plaything of the Roman nobility, who strove to gain control by appointing relatives or political favourites. The fascinating chronicle by Liutprand, the German bishop of Cremona, presents a picture of sexual debauchery at the papal court, but must be read with caution since the author was very anti-Roman.

Although there were incompetent and immoral popes during the tenth and the first half of the eleventh century, the papal institution continued to operate and to be respected throughout the West. The papal administration still functioned, even though at a reduced level. The nerve centre of papal government, the chancery, continued to issue letters to all parts of Europe, dealing with a variety of issues. Bishoprics and abbeys were founded by laymen after they had obtained the approval of the papal court. Pilgrimages to Rome hardly slackened during this age, as Christians visited the most important shrines in the

West – the tombs of Peter and Paul – as well as a host of other relics that were venerated in the papal city.

OTTO RESCUES THE PAPACY

At the lowest ebb of the tenth-century papacy, during the reign of Pope John XII (955–64), a major change in Italian politics directly affected the position of the popes. A strong, independent German monarchy emerged. The Saxon dynasty began with the election of Henry I (876–936) and was vigorously continued in his son, Otto I (r. 936–73). Otto the Great developed a very close relationship with the church in Germany. Bishops and abbots were given the rights and dignity of princes of the realm and the church was given generous grants of land. By means of his alliance with the church, Otto sought to offset the power of the rebellious hereditary nobles of his kingdom.

The 'spiritual aristocracy' created by the Saxon kings was not hereditary. The loyalty of these men could therefore be counted on much more readily, and in fact the German bishops contributed money and arms to help the German kings expand into Italy, eastern Germany, and Poland.

Otto the Great provided the desperately needed assistance to raise the papacy out of the mire of Roman and Italian politics. His entrance into papal and Italian affairs was indeed a fateful decision. Otto marched south into Italy to help Adelaide of Burgundy, to marry her, and to declare himself king of the Lombards. A decade later, he was again in Italy, this time invited by Pope John XII. In February 962, the papacy revived the empire in the West when John XII crowned Otto and Adelaide in St Peter's, Rome. The price paid by the papacy for the support of the secular state was interference in the internal affairs of the church.

The events of 962–63 initiated another decisive phase in church–state relations. Until 1250 each German ruler was to follow up his election as king by making the journey to Rome to be crowned Emperor. German involvement in papal affairs meant emperors deciding who should be pope, or recognizing 'anti-popes'. In 963 Otto returned to Rome and made the Romans promise not to elect a pope thereafter without his or his son's consent. Then he convened a synod, which tried Pope John, found him guilty of a list of sordid crimes, and finally deposed him. In his place they chose a layman, who received all his ecclesiastical orders in one day to become Pope Leo VIII.

HARRY ROSENBERG

A CHRISTIAN SOCIETY

550 600 650 700 750 800 850 900 950 1000

Bede

Boniface takes the gospel to Germany

Emperor Charlemagne

Photius Patriarch of Constantinople

Emperor Otto the Great

Abbey of Cluny founded

Synod of Whitby

Lindisfarne Gospels

Iconoclastic Controversy

Muhammad flees from Mecca

Muslims conquer the Middle East

Arabs conquer Spain and Portugal

Vikings invade Europe

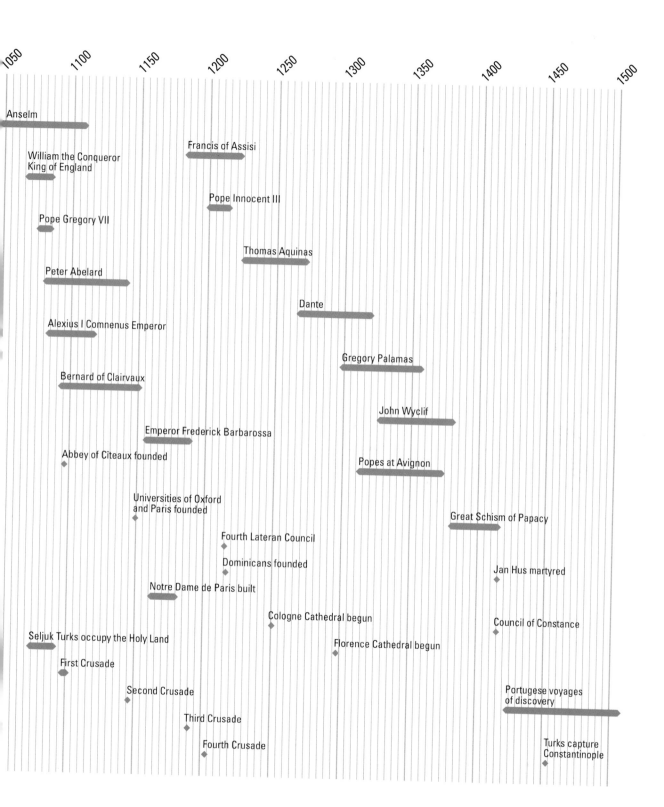

1050　1100　1150　1200　1250　1300　1350　1400　1450　1500

Anselm

Francis of Assisi

William the Conqueror
King of England

Pope Innocent III

Pope Gregory VII

Thomas Aquinas

Peter Abelard

Dante

Alexius I Comnenus Emperor

Gregory Palamas

Bernard of Clairvaux

John Wyclif

Emperor Frederick Barbarossa

Abbey of Cîteaux founded

Popes at Avignon

Universities of Oxford
and Paris founded

Great Schism of Papacy

Fourth Lateran Council

Dominicans founded

Jan Hus martyred

Notre Dame de Paris built

Cologne Cathedral begun

Council of Constance

Seljuk Turks occupy the Holy Land

Florence Cathedral begun

First Crusade

Second Crusade

Portugese voyages
of discovery

Third Crusade

Fourth Crusade

Turks capture
Constantinople

CHAPTER 17

THE EASTERN CHURCH

Many of the characteristics that today distinguish Eastern Christianity developed very early in Christian history. As soon as the fifth century, the legacy of unresolved differences separating East and West began gradually to mount up. By the end of the twelfth century, the Eastern and Western parts of the church had come to the point of thinking of each other as separated bodies. Unfortunately, but predictably, each area held the other responsible for having abandoned the true Christian tradition.

CREATING A TRADITION

The Christian message was, of course, first proclaimed in the context of the predominantly Jewish culture of Palestine. But long before AD 100, through contacts with the dispersed Jews who were part of the 'hellenized' population influenced by Greek culture, Christianity made its way to regions far from Jerusalem. Christianity next moved to various hellenized Gentile cultures – in Egypt, Syria, Asia Minor, Greece, and Hellenistic outposts in the cities of the West. By the mid-second century AD, Christianity had begun to spread from the hellenized people of Egypt and Syria into the Coptic and Syriac sub-cultures. Similar developments in other regions of the Roman Empire brought Christianity into contact with a still wider range of cultures by the end of the second century.

The word 'catholic', meaning general or universal, as opposed to particular or local, began to be used regularly during the second century to refer to Christianity's common body of beliefs and practices. Although a large part of this Catholic Christian tradition was shared by all Christians, no matter what their language or culture, many differences of interpretation, emphasis, and practice emerged from the diverse cultural circumstances. Indeed, during the following centuries further differences developed, which caused new tensions and problems within the Christian community.

'NEW ROME'

By 324 Constantine the Great had made himself master of the Roman world, ushering in an epoch of general peace and prosperity. He established a new capital on the Bosphorus. A symbol of the new era, the city was originally designed as a Christian counterpart of Rome, and was called 'New Rome'. However, during its long and illustrious history, as the centre of a thriving civilization and seat of economic and political power, it has more often been known as Constantinople – the city of Constantine. It was to become – and to remain for many centuries – the greatest city in the Christian world, the cultural and political hub of the Byzantine or East Roman state. This was the focus around which the Eastern Church took form.

By bringing about reconciliation between the Roman Empire and the Christian church, Constantine greatly influenced Christianity as a whole, and the traditions of the Eastern Church in particular. His achievement was of pivotal importance for the cultural and political future of Western civilization.

Constantine found Christianity divided and torn over differences in doctrine and practice, and was superstitiously anxious that God would hold him personally responsible for these divisions and quarrels among the Christians. If Christianity lacked cohesion and unity, how could it be a proper religion for the Emperor? Constantine, and many later emperors, made every effort to lessen the divisions and increase agreement about the faith.

Constantine adopted a procedure already developed by the Christians to settle differences of opinion at a local or regional level: he called the leaders of the entire church to assemble in his presence in order to define and agree upon the correct tradition. This procedure itself became a part of the Christian tradition. From the first ecumenical council at Nicaea (325), to the seventh, also held at Nicaea (787), it was always the Emperor who called the council and presided over it – either personally or by deputy. Eastern Christians today still place great emphasis on these seven ecumenical councils, sometimes referring to themselves as 'The Church of the Seven Councils'.

The Emperor believed it was just as important to achieve and maintain a uniform tradition as it was to decide what the correct tradition was. Uniformity in the whole church could be most easily secured by controlling its leaders. Whatever the Christian leaders agreed upon in an ecumenical council was immediately pronounced as law by the Emperor. Church leaders who dissented from the beliefs and practices judged by the council to be orthodox were labelled 'heretics' or 'schismatics', and deposed from office. The government then frequently deported the deposed leader to some distant corner of the Empire, where his influence could have little effect.

But this procedure was of little help in dealing effectively with the widespread and deep-seated doctrinal controversies which the church endured from the fourth to the seventh centuries – Arianism and Monophysitism in particular. Even the most energetic emperors, such as Justinian I and Heraclius, were unable to avoid or to moderate such controversies. Statesmanlike emperors such as Zeno or Constans II, who demanded that all debate on controversial issues should cease, only stirred up the wrath of both parties against themselves.

A PATTERN OF GOVERNMENT

One reason why the emperors did not achieve unity and uniformity lay in the pattern of organization used from very early times, a polity still carefully maintained by the Orthodox Church today. Every bishop is bound to uphold Scripture and the apostolic tradition. But the actual government of the local church rests in the local synod or council, consisting of the bishop together with the local clergy (priests and deacons) and influential laymen, who may be monks or scholars.

Each bishop was elected by the local synod and congregation, although he was often nominated by a neighbouring bishop. After his election, neighbouring bishops (at least two) gathered to ordain their new colleague. Once consecrated, he normally served for life, and could be deposed only if charges against him were accepted by a synod of his fellow bishops in the same province. All bishops were in theory equal, but those in the larger cities easily came to exercise more influence than the bishops from smaller places in the province. As a result, the synod of bishops in the province recognized the bishop of the capital city, the 'metropolitan bishop', as their presiding officer. Normally the metropolitan bishop had the right to approve all candidates for episcopal ordination before they were consecrated, and the right to carry out any disciplinary actions voted by the provincial synod.

By Constantine's day, the bishops of the cities of Rome, Alexandria, and Antioch were recognized as 'chief metropolitans', reflecting the fact that they were customarily called upon to approve the candidates for metropolitan bishop in adjoining provinces, and to preside at any synod which involved those metropolitans and their bishops. Eventually the chief metropolitans became known as 'patriarchs'. The bishops of Constantinople and Jerusalem were later also recognized, making a total of five patriarchs, each representing a section of the total church called a patriarchate. Representatives of all five patriarchs had to be present in order for a council to be recognized as truly ecumenical, and any change in Christian teaching or practice required the approval of such an ecumenical council.

In theory, each patriarch's authority as a bishop was equal, as was his importance in relation to the clergy of his patriarchate. Each patriarch was also seen as equally responsible to the Emperor and to the decrees of the ecumenical councils. However, the patriarch bishop of Rome was regarded as first among equals at the first ecumenical council, because of the status of the ancient capital. At the next ecumenical council (381) it was agreed that the Patriarch of Constantinople was to rank second, because Constantinople was the 'New Rome'. The Patriarch of Constantinople, sometimes known as the 'Ecumenical Patriarch', became the spokesman for Eastern Christianity. Though the Emperor's immediate presence was a powerful influence with which other patriarchs did not have to deal, the Patriarch of Constantinople never became simply an imperial agent in charge of religious affairs, nor did his authority exceed that of the other patriarchs.

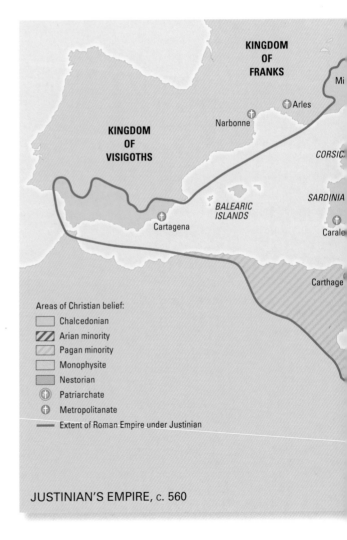

Areas of Christian belief:

- ☐ Chalcedonian
- ▨ Arian minority
- ▨ Pagan minority
- ☐ Monophysite
- ☐ Nestorian
- ✚ Patriarchate
- ✚ Metropolitanate
- —— Extent of Roman Empire under Justinian

JUSTINIAN'S EMPIRE, c. 560

GOD'S CHOSEN DEPUTY

The emperor, 'the living image of Christ', stood at the head of the church. The notion that his office was sacred, a mixture of priest and king, was not originally a Christian idea. Pagan emperors of Rome had carried the title of chief priest ('*pontifex*'), and performed official religious duties as part of their office. Leading Christians saw Constantine as God's chosen deputy, whose imperial power was an earthly reflection of God's heavenly sovereignty. The emperor, as head of the church, presided over certain local synods at Constantinople, and over all general councils. He had the right to approve all candidates for the post of patriarch. Hence, in the Eastern Church, the ecclesiastical role of the imperial head of state became traditional, so that after Roman emperors ceased to exist in the fifteenth century, the church conferred its attention on Russian emperors as a substitute. This helps to explain the strong national identity of modern orthodox churches.

During the pagan centuries the emperor had set out official religious policy. This principle remained basically unchanged. Certain forms of religious behaviour were limited or prohibited, and selected cults were favoured and patronized. Constantine began by granting Christian priests and bishops the same sort of privileges as the pagan priesthoods had enjoyed. He also prohibited the most immoral of pagan rites. It was Theodosius I

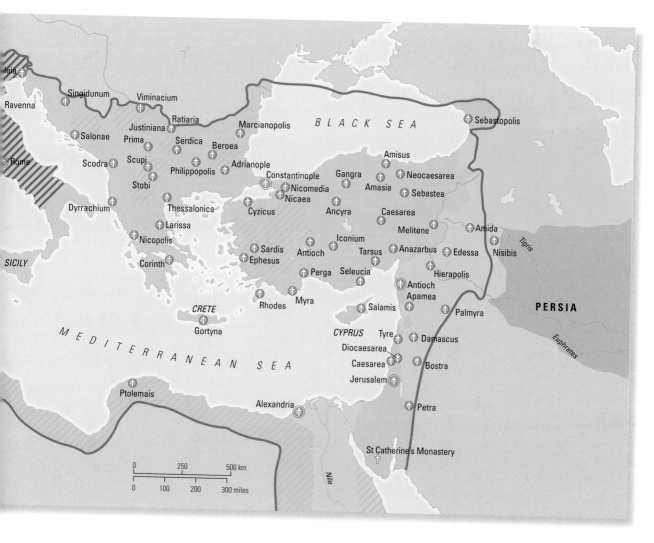

(379–95) who took the final step of totally outlawing paganism and establishing orthodox Christianity as the only official religion of the Roman Empire.

In imitation of the gifts of earlier emperors to pagan cults, Constantine granted funds for new furnishings and new church buildings to many Christian congregations. Later emperors did the same. But the most famous of all was Justinian I (527–63), whose extensive construction programme of church buildings across the Empire included the huge and impressive Church of Hagia Sophia. It was the largest and most elaborate of about twenty new churches he erected in or near Constantinople, and it still stands in modern Istanbul as a museum.

COMBATING DECLINE

In time the church began to regard correct belief as much more important than correct behaviour, even for the clergy. Correct behaviour for the clergy was gradually narrowed down to a ritualistic life-style, involving only the traditional duties of the priest and such superficial things as distinctive dress and special haircut.

JOHN CHRYSOSTOM: MASTER PREACHER

John, who became known as the greatest of Christian preachers, was born about 350 at Antioch. He was brought up by his devoted mother Anthusa, who at twenty was left a widow with an infant son. John's teacher, the pagan orator Libanius, paid Anthusa the tribute, 'God, what women these Christians have!'

John was baptized at the age of eighteen, and became a reader in the church. His devotion to ascetic practices, including two years living alone in a mountain cave, ruined his health. Returning to the city, he was ordained a deacon in 381 and presbyter in 386. From the latter date he was appointed to preach in the principal church in Antioch, where he built up his reputation as a preacher.

In 397 John was chosen bishop of Constantinople against his will, and consecrated to that position in 398. Unsuited for the intrigues and pressures of Constantinople, his efforts to raise the moral climate of the capital met strong opposition. His enemies joined forces: the Empress Eudoxia, stung by his attacks on sin in high places; local clergy who found John too strict; and Theophilus, patriarch of Alexandria, jealous of a churchman from Antioch in the capital. They had John deposed at the 'synod of the Oak' in 403, a decision that the Emperor accepted and exiled him. The people of Constantinople rioted in support of their bishop; frightened by this response, the Emperor recalled John the following day.

John's brave, if tactless, preaching angered Eudoxia again, and his enemies tried to banish him once more. The Emperor ordered him to cease his official church duties, which he refused to do. While gathering catechumens for baptism, John was driven out of the church by soldiers, and blood stained the baptismal waters. This exile (404) ended in his death in 407. His remains were brought back to Constantinople in 438 and buried in the Church of the Apostles.

John Chrysostom has been honoured for his courage and piety. From the sixth century he has been known as the 'Golden mouth' ('Chrysostom'), for he was a master of preaching. His insights into the meaning of the Greek Bible, and skill in applying it practically to his hearers, are the enduring contribution of his hundreds of surviving sermons.

EVERETT FERGUSON

Preaching was given great importance, especially in the fourth and fifth centuries. Through long, eloquent, but heavily theological sermons, Gregory of Nazianzus in Asia Minor and John Chrysostom ('golden mouth') at Antioch and Constantinople, with a host of less celebrated preachers, instructed throngs of converts in Christian belief and behaviour. Christian ideas were so popularized that they often became items of everyday conversation. Yet there was no immediate transformation of society.

The rich liturgical tradition which forms part of the Eastern Orthodox Church's uniqueness developed at Constantinople from the fourth century. The elaborate liturgy of Basil, Bishop of Caesarea in Cappadocia (370–79), was brought to the capital shortly after it had been written and is still used for ten special services during the Orthodox Church year. During the rest of the year Orthodox worshippers use the shorter liturgy, introduced at Constantinople by John Chrysostom, patriarch 398–404. Some additions were made to Chrysostom's liturgy in the ninth century, on the basis of the liturgy then in use at Jerusalem. Also, most of the hymns that have survived with this liturgical tradition originated in Constantinople. Those written there in the sixth century by the Syrian, Romanus the Melodist, are particularly important.

PSEUDO-DIONYSIUS THE AREOPAGITE

The name of Dionysius, Paul's convert in Athens, was borrowed by the unidentified early sixth-century Syrian who wrote *The Divine Names*, *Mystical Theology*, *The Celestial Hierarchy*, *The Ecclesiastical Hierarchy*, and some letters. Although Monophysite Christians were the first to refer to them, they were soon accepted as authentic by Chalcedonians such as Leontius of Byzantium. Maximus the Confessor's paraphrases finally established their authority in the East, while in the West Gregory the Great and the Lateran Council of 649 accepted them as first-century writings.

Pseudo-Dionysius' writings depend closely on the Neoplatonists Plotinus and Proclus (d. 485). He views the universe as a hierarchy, with the heavenly pattern reflected in the church. The 'triads' of angel choirs which mediate between God and humanity correspond to the 'triads' of sacraments, of orders of clergy, and of classes of 'inferior Christians'. Moreover, three stages of spiritual life – purification, illumination, and union – lead to the goal of becoming like God himself. The ascent through these stages consists of advances in 'unknowing' – by shedding sensible and rational perceptions; illumination is by a 'ray of divine darkness'. This 'mysticism of darkness' has secular Greek roots, identifying spirit with pure intelligence, rather than using biblical concepts.

This synthesis of Christian and Neoplatonist concepts enormously influenced Byzantine theologies of mysticism and liturgy, and Western mystics, scholastics, and Renaissance Platonist thinkers. Dionysius' works were translated into Latin by Eriugena about 850. Lorenzo Valla first questioned their authenticity in the fifteenth century; as was widely doubted in the Reformation era, although not disproved until the end of the nineteenth century.

DAVID F. WRIGHT

EASTERN MONASTICISM

Monasticism from its earliest stages made many important contributions to Eastern Christianity. It began in the eastern regions of the Empire in the fourth century and spread rapidly. Many pious people, both laypersons and clergy, were troubled by the apparent failure of the church to escape worldly entanglements, and turned to asceticism and monasticism. Basil, the Bishop of Caesarea in Cappadocia, provided a set of rules for those in his area who had chosen monastic life. This 'Basilian Rule' has remained the basic constitution for all monasteries connected with the Orthodox Churches. In the Eastern Church the great majority of monks were laymen. After the middle of the sixth century, it became customary to select and ordain monks to fill the highest posts in the church. Eastern monks were better known for their piety and contemplative prayer than for their scholarship. After the tenth century a group of monasteries on Mount Athos, near Thessalonica, today known as 'Holy Mountain', became increasingly important.

In the fourteenth century a movement of radical mysticism, based on the tradition of contemplative prayer, began. Gregory Palamas (1296–1359) was the leader and theologian of this new movement, which the Orthodox Church accepted.

BYZANTIUM BESIEGED

Since the Christian and political institutions of Byzantine society were closely related, secular events often directly influenced the development of Christianity. In the two hundred years following Justinian I's death (565), the Empire fell on evil times and was nearly obliterated. In the early seventh century Sassanid Persia in the east and the Avar kingdom of central Europe co-operated in a war effort. This culminated in a joint attack on Constantinople (626) that came very close to success. Emperor Heraclius (610–41), with the aid of wealth generously offered by the church, led the imperial forces to victory over both Avars and Persians. However he was unable to check the advance of the Arabs into the imperial territories of Syria, Palestine, and Egypt during his last years. Inspired by their new religion, Islam, the Arabs pushed on relentlessly to conquer all North Africa and a great part of Asia Minor. Twice their forces advanced to the bulwarks of Constantinople, but without success. The emperors also had to contend with the expanding power of the Lombards in Italy, the various Slavic peoples in Greece, and the Bulgarians in the valley of the River Danube.

The Empire survived with only a fraction of its former territory, but Constantinople remained the cultural, political, and economic focus of its existence. Large numbers of Orthodox Christians left the regions that had been devastated by the Persians and then the Arabs. These refugees included many monks and clergy who settled in the central and western parts of the Empire, especially around Constantinople, in southern Italy, and near Rome.

By 800, four of the five patriarchates of the church were in new hands. Alexandria, Antioch, and Jerusalem were under Muslim rule, and their patriarchs, unable to maintain their positions or exercise their powers, frequently chose to live in exile at Constantinople. The pope, the new contemporary title for the patriarchal bishop of Rome, felt abandoned by Constantinople in the face of the Lombard menace and after 750 forged a political alliance with the Frankish kings. In 800 he crowned the Frankish king, Charlemagne, as 'Emperor of the Romans'. Thus, for all practical purposes, a separate Roman Empire was created in the West.

The increasing political, economic, and cultural fragmentation of the Empire after 800 challenged the unity of Christianity as never before. Paying lip-service to the ideal of unity, each isolated region of the church became more and more independent of, and divergent from, the others. Eastern Christianity was now concentrated more than ever at

Constantinople, and its own tradition was still developing. At the sixth ecumenical council held in Constantinople in 681, the long struggle with Monophysitism was laid to rest and the doctrine for which orthodox leaders had contended since the middle of the fifth century was affirmed. Monophysitism arose out of dissatisfaction with the doctrinal definitions of the Council of Chalcedon (451), and its greatest popular support had been in the very regions of the East that were now conquered by the Arabs. In those areas, the Monophysites continued to enjoy freedom to create independent churches, some of which have endured to the present.

WHAT IS 'HOLY'?

Soon yet another religious controversy began to rage across the Byzantine world. On the surface it was a disagreement over the use of icons, that is, images. But at a deeper level it was a disagreement over which things were sufficiently sacred or holy to deserve worship. Christian clergy are set apart by ordination; hence, they are holy. Church buildings are set apart by dedication; they are holy. The martyrs and heroes of the faith are set apart by their

Virgin Mary (Theotokos) and child mosaic from the apse, Hagia Sophia, Istanbul, Turkey.

deeds, and they are normally called 'saints' (which means 'holy ones'). Do they not deserve the same reverence as the clergy? And as the martyrs became holy by their self-sacrifice, so monks sacrificed the normal routines of everyday life. Do they, too, deserve worship?

The holiness of the saints was supported by the miracles reported as taking place in connection with the saint's tomb, relics, or even icon. By the beginning of the seventh century many of the cities of the Empire had one or more local saints whose icons were revered as having special powers of intercession and protection. Examples include Saint Demetrius of Thessalonica, the miraculous Christ-icon of Edessa, and the miracle-working icon of Mary, the Virgin *Hodegetria*, of Constantinople.

From the sixth century, both the church and the imperial government encouraged the recognition given both to monastic holy men and Christian icons, failing to realize that the uncontrolled multiplying of icons and holy men would encourage people to confine their Christian devotion to unique local shrines and figures. Most ordinary Christians failed to distinguish between the holy object or holy person and the spiritual reality it stood for and thus fell into idolatry.

Such idolatry had its precedents. In pagan Rome the icon of the emperor was revered as if the emperor himself were present, and special agents of the emperor were also given royal treatment. Even after the emperors became Christian, the imperial image on coins, in court-houses, and in the most prominent places in the major cities continued to be an object of devotion. Constantine and his successors had the habit of erecting huge statues of themselves at Constantinople. Justinian first broke with this tradition and erected instead a huge statue of Christ over the main gate, the Chalke Gate or 'Bronze Gate', of the imperial palace at Constantinople. During the following century icons of Christ or Mary came to replace the imperial icon in many settings. Eventually, in the reign of Justinian II (685–95, 705–11), the icon of Christ began to appear on the reverse side of the coinage.

LEO THE ICONOCLAST

Emperor Leo III (717–41) launched an attack on the use of icons, perhaps motivated by a sense of the nation's guilt. Christianity taught that God punished the children of Israel because of their idolatry; possibly the humiliating defeats and losses of the previous century, as well as the calamitous earthquake early in Leo's reign, were intended to bring 'God's new chosen people' to their senses. Christian antagonism to the use of icons developed during the seventh century in the eastern regions adjacent to the Arab frontier where Leo grew up. Before becoming emperor, Leo served as governor-general of western Asia Minor, where several bishops were beginning to speak out against icons.

After successfully repulsing the Muslim armies in their second major attack on Constantinople (717–718), in 726 Leo openly declared his opposition to icons for the first time and ordered the icon of Christ over the Chalke Gate to be replaced with a cross. In spite of angry rioting which spread to many cities, Leo called in 730 for the removal and destruction of all religious icons in public places and churches.

Under Leo III and his son Constantine V (741–75), those supporting icons were vigorously persecuted. The pope at Rome dared officially to condemn iconoclasm, that is, the destruction of icons. The Emperor retaliated by removing Sicily, southern Italy, and the entire western part of the Balkans and Greece from the patriarchate of Rome and claiming these areas for the patriarchate of Constantinople. This, as much as anything else, forced the bishop of Rome to seek the support and protection of the Franks.

A synod of bishops met at Hieria in 1753 and described all use of icons as idolatry. All remaining icons were destroyed, and supporters of icons in the area around Constantinople were excommunicated, mutilated, and sent into exile. Constantine V deliberately destroyed the reputation and influence of monks in general and the popular, highly venerated ascetics in particular. An estimated 50,000 of these holy men fled from the region immediately around Constantinople to escape persecution and humiliation. The Emperor also attempted to limit the practice of saint-worship by destroying relics and condemning prayers made to saints.

The iconoclasts wanted to replace the religious icons with the traditional Christian symbols of the cross, the Book (Bible), and the elements of the Lord's Supper. These objects alone were to be considered holy. Beyond this, only ordained clergy and dedicated buildings possessed a kind of holiness. Constantine V argued that, when consecrated, the elements of the Lord's Supper were the true icon of Christ, apparently believing that the consecrated bread and wine were identical in *substance* with the flesh and blood of the divine and human Christ. A proper icon must consist of the same *substance* as what it stands for.

A DEFENCE OF ICONS

The icon supporters consisted largely of monks and other ascetics, together with their uneducated and superstitious followers from the general population. Although not all monks were in favour of icon usage, some monasteries were in the lucrative business of making and selling them. Reasoned defence of their position came from a distant source. John Mansour (c. 655–749), in a monastery in Arab-controlled Palestine, formulated the ideas that were eventually used to justify religious icons. Mansour, better known as John of Damascus (his birthplace) or Damascene, was the greatest theologian of the eighth century, and is recognized today by the Orthodox Churches as the last of the great teachers of the early church, the so-called 'Fathers'.

John explained that an image was never of the same substance as its original, but merely imitated it. An icon's only significance is as a copy and reminder of the original. To deny, as the iconoclasts did, that any true icon could depict Christ, was, in effect, to deny the possibility of the incarnation. Although it was wrong to worship an icon, the presence of an icon of Christ could instruct and assist the believer in the worship of the true Christ. Icons should be honoured and venerated in much the same way as the Bible or the cross. It also came to be accepted that icons of Mary, the apostles, the saints, and even the angels could be used; but the pictures themselves were no more than reminders to help the faithful give proper respect and reverence.

Constantine V's son and successor, Leo IV (775–80), was not an energetic iconoclast, and his widow Irene, regent for their son Constantine VI (780–97), overturned the dynasty's iconoclastic policy. Under her instigation the seventh ecumenical council assembled at Nicaea in 787 and condemned the whole iconoclastic movement, affirming the position taken by John of Damascus.

But this was not the end of iconoclasm. An influential block of support developed in the professional military class, partly as a reaction to the series of military disasters,

THE PAULICIANS AND THE BOGOMILS

The Paulicians were a Christian group who appeared in the eastern parts of the Byzantine Empire after 650. Their founder, Constantine, rejected the formalism of the Orthodox state church which dominated the religious life of the Empire, basing his teaching on the written word of God alone, but held that only the Gospels and letters of Paul were divinely inspired. An evil deity, he declared, had inspired the rest of the New Testament and the Old Testament. The Paulicians claimed this evil deity was the creator and god of this world; the true God of heaven, they said, was opposed to all material things. In order to save people's spirits from the evil of the physical world, the true God sent an angel who appeared to be a man, Jesus. From this dualistic view came the Paulicians' ideas about the Scriptures and church.

Since the Old Testament both declared that God created the world and provided the basis for the theocratic principles of the Byzantine union of church and state, they believed that it must have been produced by the evil spirit. Since the Orthodox Church involved so much that was physical and material – such as the sacraments, priesthood, images, liturgy, and secular influence – it, too, must come from the same evil spirit.

The origin of the Paulicians' ideas is unclear. They are similar to some of the earlier ideas of Marcion, and especially the Manichaeans, but not identical with either. Constantine changed his name to Silvanus (Silas), the name of one of the associates of Paul. After Silvanus was stoned to death, the next leader took the name of Titus and was subsequently burned alive. Other leaders adopted the names of Timothy and Tychicus. This attempt to associate themselves with the apostle Paul probably led to their name of 'Paulicians'.

During the 'Iconoclastic Controversy' of the eighth century, the persecution of the Paulicians eased. But in the ninth century, the Empress Theodora ordered the massacre of tens of thousands of Paulicians, who were most numerous in the area of Armenia. In response, the Paulicians organized armies which proved skilful in battle. Therefore, the emperors moved many Paulicians from their Armenian homeland to the

diplomatic humiliations, and economic problems the state experienced in the quarter century after Nicaea. Finally, Emperor Leo V, the Armenian (813–20), decided that iconoclasm should again become the official policy of his government. A synod of church leaders in 815 reaffirmed the position taken by the anti-icon synod of 754 – except that they no longer regarded the icons as idols. Key leaders of the opposition, such as the deposed Patriarch Nicephorus and Theodore the abbot of the Studios monastery in Constantinople, were imprisoned. A few other unbending church leaders were deposed, and several monks gained notoriety by openly and violently confessing pro-icon views.

THE END OF THE CONTROVERSY

With Leo V's death, active persecution of the pro-icon party waned for seventeen years, before bursting out again in 837 under the leadership of John Grammaticus, patriarch of Constantinople. Under John's influence Emperor Theophilus (829–42) decreed exile or capital punishment for all who openly supported the use of icons.

Theodora, widow of Theophilus and regent for their son Michael III (842–67), determined that her son must abandon the iconoclastic policy to retain the widest support for his rule. A synod early in 843 condemned all iconoclasts (except Theophilus), deposed patriarch John Grammaticus, and confirmed the decrees of the

Balkans (present-day Bulgaria) to help defend the Empire against threats from Slavs and Bulgars. However, the Paulicians had a greater impact on the Bulgars in the religious than the military field, preaching their beliefs to these recent converts to Christianity. Some Bulgars adopted Paulician ideas into a new religious system that acquired the name 'Bogomilism'.

THE BOGOMILS

The organizer of the new movement, it appears, was a priest named Bogomil, whose name means 'beloved of God'. Around the middle of the tenth century, Bogomil began to teach that the first-born son of God was Satanael. Because of his pride, this deity was expelled from heaven, so he made a new heaven and earth, in which he placed Adam and Eve. Satanael and Eve became the parents of Cain, who was the source of all evil among humans. But God sent the Logos, his second son, to save humanity from the control of Satanael. Although Satanael killed the incarnate Logos, Jesus, his spiritual body was resurrected and returned to the right hand of God. Satanael was in this way defeated.

In contrast to the Paulicians, the Bogomils adopted a rigidly ascetic life-style. They despised marriage, although they permitted it in the case of less-than-perfect believers, and condemned the eating of meat and drinking of wine. They rejected baptism and communion as Satanic rites, since both used material things.

Bogomilism flourished in Bulgaria while it was an independent country in the tenth, and again in the thirteenth centuries, and Bogomil ideas probably spread to western Europe, where they influenced the Cathars and Albigensians. When the Turks destroyed the Bulgarian Empire in 1393, the Bogomil sect disappeared, although Paulicians continued to exist in Armenia into the nineteenth century.

PAUL D. STEEVES

seventh council. Thereafter the relationship of the Orthodox Church and the Byzantine government became more one of harmony and cooperation. Each year Orthodox Churches still celebrate the first Sunday in Lent as the 'Feast of Orthodoxy', to commemorate the end of the iconoclastic controversy.

In today's Orthodox Church buildings, paintings and mosaics frequently fill spaces on ceilings and walls. A screen or low partition called the *iconostasis* stretches across the front of the church, between the congregation and the altar area, for the purpose of displaying all the special icons pertaining to the liturgy, the holy days, and seasons.

In the period from the sixth to the eleventh centuries the widening cultural divide between the Eastern and Western regions did not prevent the faithful from continuing to think of the church as a single, universal body. Episodes of intense disagreement were relatively infrequent, and a harmony more apparent than real, based perhaps on frail human assumptions and the enormous difficulty of maintaining regular communication, masked the fact that a growing number of controversial issues stood unresolved. The Western Church's inclusion, and the Eastern Church's alleged exclusion, of a phrase in the Nicene Creed was the basis of charge and counter-charge on more than one occasion. The controversial insertion, the Latin word *filioque* meaning 'and the Son', remains today one of the significant points of disagreement between Eastern and Western Churches.

ATLANTIC OCEAN

Trondheim

Uppsala

NORMANS

Don

Kiev

Prague
Vistula
Krakow
Danube
Halicz

ROME

CONSTANTINOPLE

BLACK SEA

Ravenna
Belgrade

Rome
Naples
Salerno
SICILY

Constantinople Chalcedon
Nicaea
Thessalonica

Antioch

MEDITERRANEAN SEA

MUSLIM

0   500   1000 km
0   200   400   600 miles

THE FINAL RIFT: THE 1054 SCHISM

In 1054, an angry rift between the agents of the Roman pope, Leo IX (1049–1054), and the patriarch of Constantinople, Michael Cerularius (1043–58), proved to be the final one. Repeated initiatives to heal the schism and reunite the Roman Catholic and Eastern Orthodox parts of the church have so far failed.

HARLIE KAY GALLATIN

CHAPTER 18

FLOWERING: THE WESTERN CHURCH
Reform and resurgence

In the West, a great struggle developed in this period between lay people and clergy over the control of the church. During the ninth and tenth centuries, when the Carolingian Empire was declining, feudal nobles had gone far beyond their historic rights in selecting candidates for church posts and controlling church affairs. This was one symptom of a general crisis through which Europe passed due to the invasion of the Magyars, Saracens, and Vikings, which destroyed both morale and property. Examples of the sorry state of the church included untrained clergy, simony (purchase of church posts), general sexual laxity, and lay investiture (control of the appointment and allegiance of abbots, bishops, and popes).

Sometimes it is darkest before the dawn, and in the case of the medieval church this proved to be the case. Growing out of the reform movement of the monastery at Cluny, a great renewal came to eleventh-century Christianity which helped the church gain control over medieval Europe. The Cluniac order, founded in 910 in France, reinvigorated monasticism. A new method of organization developed to promote the reform movement; each new monastery founded was tied to the mother house. They were exempt from any local control, and responsible only to the pope. Eventually the Cluniac order came to include 300 priories, which produced a host of prominent church leaders, and inspired many institutions and individuals who were not members of the order.

REFORM

One of these men, Hildebrand (Pope Gregory VII), has given his name to the papal reform of the eleventh century, called the 'Hildebrandine' or 'Gregorian' reform, although several individuals in the court of Pope Leo IX (1048–54) were responsible for reforming the church. Eventually they were to engage in a bitter struggle with the

The Romanesque abbey church of Cluny, Burgundy, France still stands.
© BEATRICE PREVE/DREAMSTIME.COM

Holy Roman emperors, though at first this was not apparent. In fact it was the Emperor Henry III (1039–56) who aided the reformers to gain control of the papacy.

In addition to Hildebrand, prominent leaders of this movement included Humbert of Moyenmoutier, Peter Damian, Frederick of Lorraine, and Otho of Lagery (Pope Urban II, r. 1088–99), all of whom desired the freedom of the church – that the church should be subject only to the commands of God as revealed through canon law and the Scriptures. The church, which meant in effect the whole of society, viewed as Christian people, was to be governed by the hierarchy of clergy. The pope was superior to secular rulers, and everyone was to obey him.

Although this programme seemed revolutionary in its day, the reformers claimed they were restoring the ancient and true law of the church that had been neglected and perverted by their time. As they examined canon law, they learned that the initiative for choosing a pope should lie with the clergy and the people rather than with a king or emperor. The canons also stated that buying and selling of church offices (simony) was wrong, and so must stop. In a similar manner, church law taught that clerics should not be married, so that celibacy should be enforced for clergy.

LAY INVESTITURE

The main controversy between the reformers and the emperors came to be lay investiture – the choice of important clergymen. In 1059 the reform position was laid out in a decree of Pope Nicholas II (r. 1059–61), which included the statement that the election of future popes was to be by the vote of the College of Cardinals. In addition, the papal legate's job was made more important, and through his office the power of Rome could be felt throughout western Europe. Under Pope Gregory VII the conflict with the secular forces came to open warfare. In 1075, he drew up a considered statement of clerical power, the *Dictatus Papae*. Simony, clerical marriage, lay investiture were all forbidden and papal power was declared absolute. All secular forces owed him submission, and he could depose emperors and kings.

The struggle which followed between the Emperor Henry IV and Pope Gregory VII was marked by a dramatic incident at Canossa. Because of rebellion in his Empire and his own excommunication, Henry went to Italy in 1077 and stood in the snow for three days in front of the fortress at Canossa where Gregory was staying, thus prevailing on the pope to forgive him. Although regarded as a humiliation for Henry, it actually enabled him to continue his fight against the reformers. The popes allied themselves variously with German rivals to the Emperor, the Normans of south Italy, and the cities of north Italy and gradually wore down imperial power.

KING VERSUS POPE

Eventually the papacy came to stand for the reform programme in the minds of Christians. Each of the major areas of Western Europe – England, France, and the Holy Roman Empire – accepted the pope as supreme in the church. When Duke William of Normandy decided to conquer England, the reformers had an opportunity to control the church there more effectively. The pope sanctioned this invasion; William was not a disappointment and Lanfranc, one of the reformers, was made Archbishop of Canterbury.

Although he retained the right to lay investiture, William the Conqueror never questioned the spiritual superiority of the pope, and the need for obedience. The king worked to separate church courts from secular courts, but ordered that the pope could exercise authority in England only with royal approval. The reformers thus made significant gains under William I.

William II, who became king on the death of the Conqueror in 1093, appointed Anselm as Archbishop of Canterbury. A dedicated reformer, the new archbishop struggled with the king and it was not until the reign of King Henry I (1110–35) that an agreement was reached. Bishops were to be elected by the cathedral chapter in the king's presence and, after election, the bishop was to do homage for his temporal possessions to the king and then be invested with his spiritual dignity by the archbishop.

Other lands of Western Europe reached a similar settlement on this question. In France, King Philip I (r. 1060–1108) approved a settlement by which the king would invest the bishop with the temporal powers of the office and the church would give the spiritual authority. In the Empire, the agreement reached between Emperor Henry V and

William the Conqueror

King William ... was a man of great wisdom and power ... Though stern beyond measure to those who opposed his will, he was kind to those good men who loved God. On the very spot where God granted him the conquest of England he caused a great abbey to be built; and settled monks in it and richly endowed it. During his reign was built the great cathedral at Canterbury, and many others throughout England.

ANGLO SAXON CHRONICLE, 1086

THOMAS BECKET

Thomas Becket, Archbishop of Canterbury 1162–70, struggled with King Henry II (1154–89) over the conflicting claims of church and stage in England. Becket had been nominated by Henry, who hoped to make good the crown's superior rights over those of the church. From being the king's dutiful minister, Becket became the uncompromising champion of the church.

The issues involved were the independence of the church courts, which claimed exclusive authority over anyone in holy orders, the right of appeals to Rome, and the alienation of church lands. Henry II attempted to establish his jurisdiction over clergy guilty of criminal offences and to forbid appeals to Rome in the *Constitutions of Clarendon*, 1164. The resulting conflict drove Becket into exile in France.

A truce was arranged in 1170, and Becket returned to Canterbury for Christmas. Immediately upon his return, he excommunicated several English bishops who had supported the king, who in turn violently criticized Becket. Four knights, impelled by the king's anger, appeared at Canterbury on 29 December, and murdered the archbishop before his own high altar.

Christian society throughout Europe was shocked, and at once a cult developed around the martyred Becket. In 1173 he was canonized by Pope Alexander III, and Canterbury became one of the three great Western shrines for pilgrims. The king did public penance. Becket's courage and defiance in the face of armed knights, and his commitment to 'the liberty of the church', which he felt he had been called upon to defend in the face of a weak pope and a rapacious king, were remarkable.

CAROLINE T. MARSHALL

King Henry II and
Thomas Becket
depicted in a
thirteenth-century
stained-glass
window in the
Trinity Chapel,
Canterbury
Cathedral.

SONIA HALLIDAY
PHOTOGRAPHS

the church was called the Concordat of Worms (1122). The emperor agreed to cease
the traditional investiture with the ring and staff (which symbolized the conferring of
ecclesiastical power) and in exchange the pope recognized the Emperor's right to confer the
regalia (temporal rights) by investiture with the sceptre.

THE POPE AND THE EMPEROR

The struggle between the Empire and the papacy was not finally settled by the agreement
reached in the twelfth century. This was only a compromise, which left each side feeling
an opportunity would come to gain the upper hand. By the second half of the century
the German electors had chosen a new emperor, Frederick I of Hohenstaufen (*Barbarossa*,

r. 1152–90), who turned out to be a man of great ability, aiming to establish peace in Germany and lead an army into Italy to make imperial control effective there.

After several warlike campaigns Frederick I realized that force would not resolve the situation, and he resorted to diplomacy. Once the north Italian towns had acknowledged his control, he agreed to allow them to govern themselves. He also made peace with the southern Italians and his heir married the aunt of the king of Sicily. When Frederick died, his son, Emperor Henry VI, became ruler of Germany, northern Italy, Sicily, and southern Italy. If the Hohenstaufen emperors could control these lands effectively, the pope would be caught in a pincer. As events unfolded, this proved impossible, because Henry died in 1197 while in his early thirties, leaving his possessions to a three-year-old son, Frederick (1194–1250). Anarchy resulted in both Germany and Italy.

The imperial weakness worked to the advantage of the papacy, since a very competent pope acceded – Innocent III (r. 1198–1216). The son of a noble Roman family, he was trained in both theology and law. Innocent was determined to build a strong papal state in Italy, so that secular rulers could not so easily use material means to force the papacy to do their bidding. Frederick became Innocent's ward, and was established as Emperor Frederick II with the pope's help.

However, after Innocent's death, Frederick turned out to be a disappointment to the pope's cause. He attempted to control both northern and southern Italy, resulting in a life-

POPE INNOCENT III

The medieval papacy attained the peak of its authority and influence under Innocent, who was pope 1198–1216. He had a unique ability to apply abstract concepts to concrete situations. His aristocratic background, together with his outstanding personal abilities, sharpened by a precise training in canon and civil law as well as theology, fitted him to become a cardinal. In papal service he demonstrated unusual skill in dealing with the enormous variety of religious and secular problems which arose.

Innocent's diplomatic skills enabled him to wield papal authority to a remarkable degree throughout Christendom, although not always with the success he desired. He successfully upheld papal political power in Italy when it was threatened by the union of the kingdom of Sicily with the German Empire, but was unable to rescue King John from his rebellious English barons.

Because he believed the pope had unique authority as the 'Vicar of Christ', and as the successor of Peter, Innocent claimed the right to set aside any human actions, since these were contaminated by sin and therefore came within his competence. Consequently he decreed an election for the German kingship null and void because, while one candidate had the majority of the votes, Innocent's candidate had the 'saner' votes.

The Fourth Lateran Council, called by Innocent in 1215, was the fitting climax to his career. This general council symbolized the mastery of the papacy over every feature of Latin Christendom (and seemingly over Greek Christendom, since the Fourth Crusade had led to a short-lived Latin Empire of Constantinople between 1204 and 1261). Innocent's council confirmed the shameful isolation of Jews from society at large, requiring among other things that they wear a special badge, and increasingly confining Jews to living in ghettos.

HARRY ROSENBERG

and-death struggle with the pope, who tried to crush his power. Frederick's own character complicated this struggle, for he combined a Western outlook with the style of an oriental sultan. Himself a linguist, physician, hunter and poet, he organized southern Italy into a kingdom that set an example for later Renaissance states. Although a persecutor of heretics, Frederick shared many of the ideas of his Muslim subjects, including a fatalist outlook and a belief in astrology. Insatiably curious, he kept a zoo of exotic animals as well as a harem.

While on a crusade, Frederick II (r. 1220–50) made a treaty with the Muslims, and visited the Church of the Holy Sepulchre and the Islamic Shrine of Omar in Jerusalem with equal zeal. Though successful in Italy, he gained for his heirs the hatred of the papacy, causing the extinction of his line.

THE PEAK OF PAPAL POWER

Innocent III also led the papacy to victory over the kings of France and England. In 1205 King John argued with the pope over the appointment of the Archbishop of Canterbury, and Innocent arranged the election of Stephen Langton to the post. John refused to accept him, so England was placed under an interdict in 1208, with the result that the church refused to marry, baptize, or bury people. John retaliated by seizing church lands and forcing most of the bishops out of England. In 1209 Innocent excommunicated the English king and in 1212 declared the throne of England vacant, inviting the French to invade the country. This proved effective, and John agreed to accept Langton and return church property. He resigned the crown of England, receiving it back as a feudal retainer of the pope. Although the indignity inflicted on the king was not realized at first by the English, taxes exacted by the pope in the thirteenth century resulted in a bitter hatred of the papacy in England.

Innocent was just as successful against the king of France, with whom he quarrelled over a moral issue. With the permission of a synod of French bishops, King Philip Augustus left his wife for another woman, on the grounds that the queen was a distant relative. She appealed to Rome, and Innocent ordered Philip to take her back. France was placed under an interdict and after a long struggle the queen was restored.

The leadership of the clergy and pope over society was affirmed under Innocent's direction at the Fourth Lateran Council of 1215. The power of the church was demonstrated by the wide range of participants in this convocation, including archbishops, bishops, abbots, priors, the heads of the religious orders, and representatives of the secular rulers.

The Council demanded that each archbishop hold a council every year to make certain that

The Moon and the Sun

The Creator of the universe set up two great luminaries in the firmament of heaven; the greater light to rule the day, the lesser light to rule the night. In the same way for the firmament of the universal church, which is spoken of as heaven, he appointed two great dignities; the greater to bear rule over souls (these being, as it were, days), the lesser to bear rule over bodies (these being, as it were, nights). These dignities are the pontifical authority and the royal power. Furthermore, the moon derives her light from the sun, and is in truth inferior to the sun in both size and quality, in position as well as effect. In the same way the royal power derives its dignity from the pontifical authority: and the more closely it cleaves to the sphere of that authority, the less is the light with which it is adorned; the further it is removed, the more it increases in splendour.

INNOCENT III ON THE EMPEROR AND THE PAPACY IN *SICUT UNIVERSITATIS CONDITOR* 1198 bishops were doing their duty. Provincial meetings of monks were to be held annually to see that each community adhered to its rule. Ignorance and heresy were to be crushed by the setting up of an efficient educational system. The bishops were to inspect the churches of the diocese to make certain that they supported schools where the children of the rich could be taught for a fee and where the sons of the poor could receive a free education. Lay people were commanded to respect church property, obey church courts, and observe the Christian rules of marriage. The clergy were warned to abstain from sexual disorder, fighting, and drunkenness, and procedures were established for the trial of erring clerics.

Although the church reached the height of its power in the early thirteenth century the seeds of its subsequent decline had already been sown. To defeat the emperors, the church strengthened other European royal houses. It was one of these, the Capetians in France, who would defeat the papacy and bring about its removal from Rome to Avignon in the fourteenth century.

NEW MONASTIC ORDERS

The spirit of revival or renewal in the church expressed itself not only in organizational change by the papacy, but also in the formation of new monastic orders. The success of the reformed papacy and the growth of culture led to a crisis in Benedictine monasticism in the later eleventh century. The monastic tradition of handing on order and culture was superseded by the rise in the power of popes, bishops, and kings. Education now became centred in the bishops' schools rather than in the monasteries. Non-monastic clergy and stable civil government guaranteed an order in society that made obsolete the monasteries' previous function as oases of culture. New monastic movements emphasized the spirit of prophecy rather than the spirit of power.

The most influential of the new groups was the Cistercians, founded in 1097 at Cîteaux, as an offshoot from a Benedictine house at Molesme. Stephen Harding (d. 1134), third abbot of the new group, drew up a rule for the order which emphasized manual labour instead of scholarship, and private rather than corporate prayer. They were to construct their own community houses in the most desolate places, while accepting no titles, gifts, or lay patrons. Hiring no servants and believing that 'to work is to pray' (Latin, *laborare est orare*), they took upon themselves the tasks of farming, cooking, weaving, carpentry, and the many other duties of life. Their churches were plain, with no ornaments or treasures, they owned no personal possessions, and they were allowed seven hours of sleep in the winter and six in the summer. Gathering for communal prayer periodically, the brothers spent the rest of the day in manual work, meditation, reading, and divine service. Cistercians ate sparingly of vegetables, fish, and cheese – this only once a day in summer, and twice a day in winter. Even in the coldest regions, a fire was allowed only on Christmas Day.

This strict rule met with phenomenal success, and by the end of the twelfth century there were hundreds of Cistercian monastic houses. The ethos of this movement appealed to medieval people, and the group was doubly fortunate in having a remarkable leader in the person of Bernard of Clairvaux (1090–1153), who arrived at Cîteaux in 1112. Later, at Clairvaux, he founded the first of more than sixty-five new monasteries, and as an abbot was able to wield a Europe-wide influence. He was so persuasive in persuading men to enter the monastery that it is said that mothers hid their sons, and wives their

BERNARD OF CLAIRVAUX

Bernard (1090–1153), the Abbot of Clairvaux, was the most influential Christian of his age. He bridged two worlds: the ages of feudal values and of the rise of towns and universities. He was the first of the great medieval mystics, and a leader of a new spirit of ascetic simplicity and personal devotion.

Born near Dijon to a noble family, Bernard took on the ideals of feudalism and chivalry characteristic of his class. However, he was also moulded by the Gregorian and Cluniac reforms, and was educated in the studies of the *trivium* (rhetoric, grammar, and logic). At the age of twenty-one he entered the monastery of Cîteaux, the centre of the Cistercian order, in the wild valley of the River Saône, France. In 1115 he led a dozen Cistercians to found the new house of Clairvaux, in the Champagne region.

Bernard wished to turn his back on the world and its comforts, and lead a life of prayer and self-denial. He emphasized God's love and believed that Christians come to know God by loving him. Bernard preached that physical love, which was natural to man, could be transformed by prayer and discipline into a redeeming spiritual love, the passion for Christ.

Aggressively self-righteous, he did not hesitate to criticize and correct the powerful leaders of his age, and in 1130 intervened in a controversy over the selection of a new pope. Bernard unhesitatingly backed the claimant he considered morally more worthy, and scolded the rest of Europe into doing likewise. He made peace between King Louis VII and his feudal subjects, wrote a rule for the order of Knights Templar, condemned the scholastic rationalism of Peter Abelard, and preached the Second Crusade. Privately Bernard practised the most rigorous self-denial until, worn out by strenuous asceticism, he died.

CAROLINE T. MARSHALL

husbands, when he came fishing for men. Bernard described the Christian life as an experience of progress in love, and it is easy to understand how an age that was moved by the adventures of knights searching for the Holy Grail would respond to his teachings.

Despite Bernard's success, by the end of the twelfth century the Cistercians had already become lax and ineffective. They had rapidly grown wealthy and had become as famous for their agricultural skills as for their spiritual life.

PREACHING MONKS

The decline of the Cistercian order coincided with the passing of the importance of cloistered monasteries. During the twelfth and thirteenth centuries Europe became more settled and the security of the monastery was less necessary. Towns and cities were developing and offered a new challenge to the church as traditional expressions of faith failed to cope with worldliness and the growth of population.

Many clergymen recognized the need to bring a new form of spirituality to the people and found a method that would enable them to work in the world while at the same time living under a spiritual rule. A group of clergy would live together under a strict rule but go out to work among the ordinary population. Among the orders that operated in this fashion were the Premonstratensians, who had a rule resembling the Cistercians', and the Augustinians or Austin monks, who used the Rule of Augustine. Both orders followed as much of the monastic life as was possible, while carrying out their duties of preaching and teaching in the world.

At the beginning of the thirteenth century new groups of preaching monks, the friars, arose. Extremely ascetic, and working in towns and cities, they gained the respect of society. The friars preached in the parishes and town squares, taught in the schools,

FRANCIS OF ASSISI

Francis of Assisi (1182–1226), a popular youth who led a carefree life, was destined for a career as a knight, until converted through illness, a pilgrimage to Rome, a vision and the words of Jesus in Matthew 10:7–10. He was the son of a wealthy Italian cloth merchant, and his father was angry because Francis interpreted the gospel to mean that goods should be freely given to the poor. Leaving home in a ragged cloak, he wandered the countryside with a few followers, begging from the rich, giving to the poor, and preaching. His charm, humility, and kind manner attracted many followers.

In 1210 Francis obtained approval from Pope Innocent III for his simple rule devoted to apostolic poverty and began to call his associates the Friars Minor ('Lesser Brothers'). The new group, which followed its founder in preaching and caring for the poor and sick, met yearly at Portiuncula, near Assisi. A society for women, the Poor Clares, or Order of St Clare, began in 1212 when Clare, an heiress of Assisi, was converted and commissioned.

To encourage missionary activities, Francis tried to go to Syria (1212) and to Morocco (1213–14) but was thwarted by misfortune. In 1219 he travelled to the Middle East, where he tried unsuccessfully to convert the Sultan of Egypt.

While Francis was away, problems arose among the members of his order in Italy; upon his return he was forced to deal with them. Cardinal Ugolino was asked to be the protector of the order, and the appointment of a politically-minded brother, Elias of Cortona, as vicar-general led to a change in the character of the movement. In 1223, Pope Honorius III confirmed a new rule, which allowed for an elaborate organization. Holding to his original ideals, Francis laid down his leadership and retired to a chapel at La Verna, Tuscany, where he allegedly received the stigmata (bodily representations of the wounds of Christ). In spite of illness, pain, and blindness he composed his 'Canticle to the Sun', his *Admonitions*, and his *Testament* before submitting gladly to 'Brother Death' in 1226.

Francis did not turn to nature as a refuge from the world, as many monks did, but rather saw in created things objects of love that pointed to their Creator. For this reason he enjoyed the solitary life, and it is reported that even birds and animals enjoyed his sermons. However, his major concern was the growing cities, where he spent most of his time preaching the gospel while living in utter poverty among ordinary people.

ROBERT G. CLOUSE

and eventually dominated many of the universities. One group, the Franciscans, developed from the teachings of Francis of Assisi (1182–1226), who gave up his wealth, renounced his inheritance, and settled outside his native town to live a life of prayer and poverty. Gathering a band of followers, he wandered the hills of Umbria, worked at part-time jobs, and served others by preaching and nursing the sick. Francis taught that complete poverty relieved the brothers from cares and made them joyful before God. Approved by the pope in 1209, the brothers were known as the Minor Friars (*fratres minores*), wore dark grey (and so were called the Grey Friars) and went barefoot. As the organization grew it became difficult to continue a life of poverty and in time the order was permitted to own property. However, some wanted to continue to live according to the strict teachings of Francis, insisting upon a life of poverty and a renunciation

Fresco of Francis of Assisi, displaying the stigmata – marks resembling Christ's wounds – by Simone Martini (1285–1344), in the lower church at the Basilica of St Francis of Assisi, Italy.

SONIA HALLIDAY PHOTOGRAPHS

The Rule of Francis

1. This is the rule and way of life of the Brothers Minor: to observe the holy gospel of our Lord Jesus Christ, living in obedience, without personal belongings and in chastity …

2. If any wish to take up this way of life and join our brothers, they shall send them to the provincial ministers; to them alone, and to no others, permission is given to receive brothers. And the ministry shall carefully examine them in the Catholic faith and the sacraments of the church. And if they believe all these, and will confess them faithfully and observe them steadfastly to the end; and if they have no wives, or if they have them and the wives have already entered a convent … the ministers shall tell them, in the words of the gospel, to go and sell all they have and give it carefully to the poor. But if they are not able to do this, their good intention is enough … After that they shall be given the garments of the probationers: two gowns without hoods and a belt, and stockings and a cape

of endowments. They became known as the spiritual Franciscans (or *Fraticelli*). Because they refused to obey the pope's order to alter their rule, this group was persecuted, and became associated with other suppressed movements. Those brothers who accepted the changes to the order were known as 'Conventuals'.

WATCHDOGS OF THE LORD

The second great order of medieval friars, the Dominicans, was founded by Dominic de Guzman (1170–1221), a studious cleric from Castile who was sent to Provence to preach reaching the belt ... And, when the probationary year is over, they shall be received into obedience, promising always to observe this way of life and the rule ... And those who have now promised obedience shall have one gown with a hood and another, if they wish it, without a hood. And those who really need them may wear shoes. And all the brothers shall wear humble garments, and may repair them with sackcloth and other remnants, with God's blessing ...

3. The clerical brothers shall perform the divine service according to the order of the holy Roman Church ... And they shall fast from the feast of All Saints to the Nativity of the Lord; but as to the holy season of Lent ... those who fast during this time shall be blessed of the Lord, and those who do not wish to fast shall not be bound to do so. At other times the brothers shall not be bound to fast except on Friday; but when there is a compelling reason the brothers shall not be bound to observe a physical fast. But I advise, warn and exhort my brothers in the Lord Jesus Christ that, when they go into the world, they shall not quarrel, nor contend with words, nor judge each other. But let them be gentle, peaceable, modest, merciful, and humble, as is fitting. They ought not to ride, except when infirmity or necessity clearly compels them to do so ...

4. I strictly command all the brothers never to receive coins or money either directly or through an intermediary. The ministers and guardians alone shall make provision, through spiritual friends, for the needs of the infirm and for other brothers who need clothing.

6. The brothers shall possess nothing, neither a house, nor a place, nor anything. But, as pilgrims and strangers in this world, serving God in poverty and humility, they shall continually seek alms, and not be ashamed, for the Lord made himself poor in this world for us ...

11. I strictly charge all the brethren not to hold conversation with women so as to arouse suspicion, nor to take counsel with them ...

12. Whoever of the brothers by divine inspiration may wish to go among the Saracens and other infidels shall seek permission from their provincial ministers. But the ministers shall give permission to go to none but those whom they see to be fit for the mission.

Furthermore I charge the ministers on their obedience that they demand from the lord pope one of the cardinals of the holy Roman Church, who shall be the governor, corrector and protector of the fraternity, so that, always submissive and lying at the feet of that same holy church, steadfast in the Catholic faith, we may observe poverty and humility, and the holy gospel of our Lord Jesus Christ, as we have firmly promised.

The original Rule of Francis consisted of a few instructions from the Gospels. When the order expanded, a new rule was produced, but this was felt too strict and was never used. The final version of the rule, quoted above, was approved by Pope Honorius III in 1223, three years before Francis' death.

against the Albigensians. Realizing the need for an educated clergy able to communicate with the people through sermons, he founded the new order, recognized in 1220, which emphasized the friar's calling to teach and preach. Hence the Dominicans' official title was the Order of Preachers and, wearing a white habit and black cloak (scapular), and so known as the Black Friars, they spread throughout Europe as 'the watchdogs of the Lord' (a pun on the Latin name *Dominicanus = domini canis*) to hunt down heresy and ignorance.

The academic emphasis of the Dominicans contrasted with Franciscan anti-intellectualism. The friar preachers established colleges and seminaries not only for their own members but also for other clergy who might wish to attend, and produced leading medieval theologians such as Albert the Great and Thomas Aquinas. However, the two orders gradually became more alike, as the Franciscans found it necessary to train young friars, and thus also set up educational foundations.

The friars accomplished social, pastoral, educational, and missionary work. As Francis and the early brothers had done, they continued to serve lepers and other sick people, a practice which encouraged the study of medicine. They showed courage and loving care while working with the sick during the frequent medieval plagues. Friars were also effective preachers, although they frequently met difficulties with the local clergy. More thoroughly trained than the parish ministers, encouraged by their wider contact with brothers of their order, and burning with the zeal of first love, the friars made a notable impression on their audiences. Their sermons were marked by humour, and effectively used rhyme and stories from everyday life.

The friars were also busy in education, establishing a school at each house for young men entering their orders. Houses were also founded at the newly-formed universities of Paris, Oxford, Cambridge, and Bologna. The Franciscans could boast of such famous scholars as Bonaventura (1221–74), Alexander of Hales (1170–1245), William of Ockham, and Roger Bacon (c. 1214–92).

The missionary activity of the friars added a challenging facet to their work. Francis himself preached the gospel abroad, and sent friars to Spain, Hungary, and the East. The orders encouraged the study of Eastern languages so that missionaries could communicate with the Muslims. During the thirteenth century they preached and founded houses in North Africa, the Middle East, and Eastern Europe.

EAST AND WEST DIVIDE

The preaching of friars in the East might have resulted in a more peaceful penetration of the area by Latin Christianity, had it not been for a breakdown of relations between Byzantium and the West. At the beginning of the eleventh century the Greek Church was not obviously separated from the Western Church, but the position was to change during the next two centuries. After the Crusaders' conquests in the Middle East there came to be two rival claimants for each of the major Eastern Sees – one Latin and the other Greek.

The Eastern Orthodox Church had been drifting apart from the Roman Catholic Church for centuries. Distinctive features of the two churches can be listed – such as a different ritual, the use of a different type of communion bread, a different version of the Nicene Creed, and different attitudes towards the use of statues (icons) in the church – but none of these problems marked a decisive break between the two communions. For centuries contact between western Europe and the East had been limited. However, with the Crusades, commerce and communication between the two were reawakened. Paradoxically, the final break came at the time of this new closeness – because of the new attitude of the reformed papacy and the behaviour of the Crusaders.

The eleventh-century popes, as described, wanted effectively to control Christianity, but the Patriarch of Constantinople was not willing to accept the pope's mandates and legates. When Humbert of Moyenmoutier arrived in Constantinople in 1054 as a representative of the pope, the patriarch refused to submit to him. Humbert thereupon published a

THE SPREAD OF FRANCISCAN
MONASTERIES BY 1300

document excommunicating the patriarch. As the pope's control of the Western Church tightened, the split with the East widened. Eastern theory emphasized control of the church by a council of the five important leaders of the Christian world (the patriarchs), while the papal reformers believed the church should be ruled by the pope alone.

A NEW ENEMY

The Crusades also contributed greatly to the schism between East and West. These were religious wars fought by western Europeans to recover the Holy Land from the Muslims. The remarkable growth of Islam threatened to engulf Byzantium (Constantinople). Threatened on all sides by enemies, the Eastern emperors of the tenth century fought a series of wars, defeating in turn the Muslims, the Bulgars, and the Armenians. A new foe appeared, however, in the form of the fierce Seljuk Turks, who defeated the forces of Byzantium at the Battle of Manzikert (1071) and invaded Asia Minor, depriving the Eastern Empire of more than half its territory.

After repeated appeals to the West for aid, it was a message from the Eastern Emperor Alexius Comnenus to pope Urban II in 1095 that finally attracted the attention of Latin ears. The pope responded with a sermon to a convocation at Clermont, southern France, where church dignitaries as well as the common people heard Urban explain:

> From the confines of Jerusalem and from the city of Constantinople a horrible tale has gone forth … an accursed race, a race utterly alienated from God … has invaded the lands of those Christians and depopulated them by the sword, plundering and fire.

The pope proceeded to list Turkish atrocities, including the desecration of churches, the rape of Christian women, and the torture and murder of men. He also appealed to French honour:

> Recall the greatness of Charlemagne. O most valiant soldiers, descendants of invincible ancestors, be not degenerate. Let all hatred between you depart, all quarrels end, all wars cease. Start upon the road to the Holy Sepulchre, to tear that land from the wicked race and subject it to yourselves.

At the conclusion of his address a shout rose from the crowd, 'Deus Vult! Deus Vult!' (God wills it). Pleased with this response, Urban made Deus Vult the battle-cry of the Crusades, and suggested each warrior wear the sign of the cross on his clothing. The Crusade joined together two themes which were developing strongly in eleventh-century Europe: the holy war, or military expedition blessed by the church, and the pilgrimage to a holy place.

In the months that followed, the pope's representatives travelled throughout Europe, enlisting recruits to go to the Holy Land to fight the Turks. The pope issued incentives to go on crusade, such as immunity from taxes and debt payment, protection of crusaders' property and families, and especially the indulgence, which guaranteed the Crusader's entry into heaven and reduced or abolished his time in purgatory. The papacy also organized financial support and sought to provide transport, usually by sea.

The leaders of this first Crusade represent a medieval Europe's *Who's Who* and included Robert of Normandy, Raymond of Toulouse, Bohemond of Taranto, Robert of Flanders, Godfrey of Bouillon, Baldwin of Boulogne, and Stephen of Blois. The imagination of many who romanticize medieval Europe has conjured a picture of the Crusaders as great, armour-clad warriors who rode out on huge steeds. In reality, the average knight stood about five feet three inches (1.6 metres) tall, and wore a hauberk and a leather coat protected by chain mail.

THE CRUSADERS FAIL

When they arrived in Constantinople the Crusaders misbehaved and the Emperor Alexius became frightened. He had imagined Urban would help him recruit mercenaries for his own armies; now a horde of 50,000 Western Christians had descended on his city. He provisioned them well, surrounded them with guards, extracted an oath of allegiance from their commanders, and got them safely across the Bosphorus into Asia Minor.

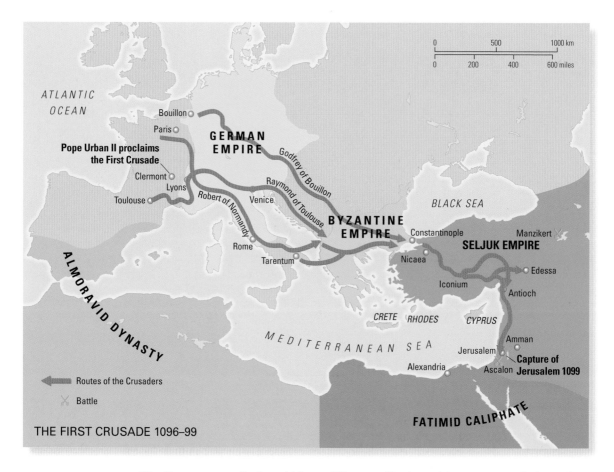

THE FIRST CRUSADE 1096–99

The Emperor now displeased his new Western allies by making treaties with the Turks while they were fighting. This seeming treachery on the part of the Eastern Empire enabled the Crusaders to defend the carving out of their own states in the Middle East. They had invaded at a fortunate time, because Islam was divided between the caliphates of Baghdad, Cairo, and Cordova into rival factions and sects. Driving south through Syria and Palestine, the Crusaders captured Jerusalem in 1099.

The conquests of the Crusaders extended along a strip of eastern Mediterranean coastline and were divided into the 'Latin Kingdom' of Jerusalem, the County of Edessa, the Principality of Antioch, and the County of Tripoli. For almost 200 years they represented a toehold of Western Christianity in the East; but these territories were also where the clash between Greek Orthodox and Catholic had resulted in total alienation. For example, Antioch in Syria, captured by the Crusaders, had a Greek bishop (John of Antioch) who was in communion with the Patriarch of Constantinople. When Alexius wanted the city restored to the Eastern Empire and the Crusaders refused, the bishop's position became untenable; he left the city and moved to Constantinople. The Westerners chose another church leader, a Latin, but John refused to resign, leaving two claimants to the Patriarchate of Antioch. A similar situation arose when Jerusalem was conquered, and also in Constantinople, when it fell to the Fourth Crusade.

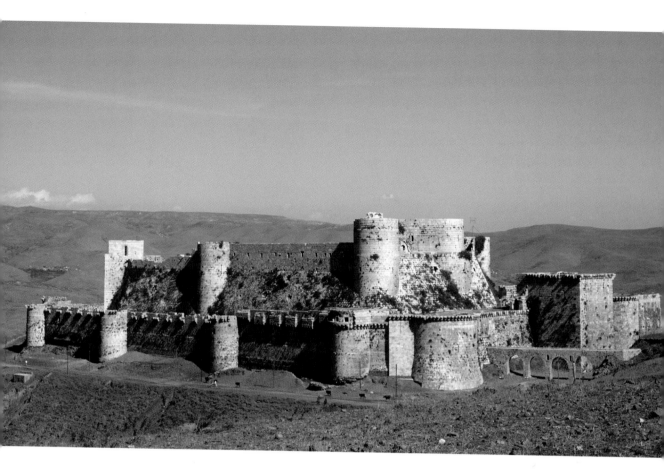

The first Crusade was far more successful than later expeditions, even though the twelfth and thirteenth centuries saw a great development in the theology and organization of crusades. The Europeans' hold on the Middle East was always fragile. The Italian maritime cities such as Venice, Genoa, and Pisa provided a lifeline – not only helping streams of pilgrims get to the Holy Land, but also sending supplies and recruits to fight the Muslims. Two new religious orders were formed for the purpose of defending the Holy Land: the Knights Templar and the Knights Hospitaller. The young men who formed these orders served as soldier-monks but, despite their efforts, the County of Edessa fell to the Muslims.

FURTHER CRUSADES

A Second Crusade (1147) was encouraged by the preaching of Bernard of Clairvaux, and led by King Louis VII of France and Conrad III, the Holy Roman Emperor. This expedition was marked by a series of disasters, culminating in Damascus, where the Crusaders were ambushed and prevented from taking the city. After two years their forces melted away: the crusade preached by the man with the greatest name for sanctity in Europe and led by royalty had failed. The Christian hold on the Holy Land depended on Muslim disunity, but after 1150 the Muslim leaders Nureddin

The Crusader castle of Krak des Chevaliers was built by the Knights Hospitaller in Syria between 1140 and 1170, and at its peak housed around 2,000 soldiers. It was captured by the Muslim Mamelukes in 1271.
SONIA HALLIDAY PHOTOGRAPHS

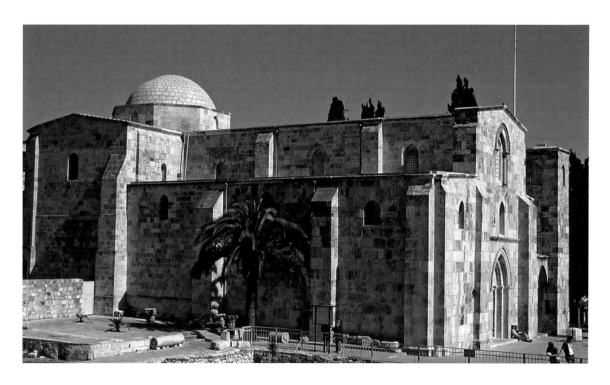

The Church of St Anne, Jerusalem, built by the Crusaders over the site of a grotto believed to be the birthplace of Anne, mother of the Virgin Mary. Completed in 1138, after Saladin retook the Holy Land, he converted the building into an Islamic seminary. Today it is administered by the Roman Catholic White Fathers.
TIM DOWLEY ASSOCIATES

(1118–74) and Saladin (1137/8–93) united the Near East and Egypt under one dynasty. In 1187 Saladin defeated the crusaders at Hattin, captured Jerusalem, and overran the Crusaders' lands.

Defeat astounded and angered medieval Christians and, as they tried to understand the situation, the treachery of the Greeks began to appear to them the main reason. As a result, Bernard started to suggest that a campaign be mounted against Constantinople. He achieved his wish in 1204, when the Doge of Venice persuaded an expedition of knights (the Fourth Crusade) to besiege and conquer the great Eastern city. The rape of Constantinople made an indelible impression on the Orthodox, and whatever ties still existed between them and Rome were severed. A Latin Empire set up in Byzantium lasted from 1204 till 1261, with the lands of the Empire divided into feudal holdings and presented to the Crusaders. A Latin patriarch was appointed, but the Western Church made little impression on the Greek population.

The Crusades may be seen as part of the expansion of Christian Europe after centuries of being on the defensive against Islam and paganism, and Crusading enthusiasm remained strong until at least 1250. The number of Crusades is normally given as seven or eight, but this gives the misleading impression of a few expeditions with long gaps in between. It is better to see the Crusades as a continuous movement, featuring many smaller expeditions in addition to the larger ones; after about 1150 there was a regular stream of soldiers, pilgrims, and merchants from Europe to Syria.

Some Crusades were pathetic, like the Children's Crusade, others militarily effective, such as the one Frederick II embarked upon when he was excommunicated. But with the fall of the Crusader states in 1291 the movement lost its impetus.

The Crusades failed in their aims. The Crusaders were a small minority in the East, and those who had settled there for two or three generations tended to adopt Eastern customs, to the disgust of new arrivals from Europe. As well as alienating Eastern Christians, two centuries of contact with the East caused cultural changes which in turn had a lasting effect on life in the West.

As time went on the Crusading movement was increasingly diverted from the Holy Land, and in the thirteenth century the popes launched crusades not only against European heretics such as the Cathars and Albigensians, but also against Catholic rulers such as Frederick II. In the thirteenth century, too, there arose criticism of the crusading principle; people such as Raymond Lull argued for peaceful missions to convert the Muslims, rather than armed expeditions to subdue them. Nevertheless the Crusades, attracting people from all the countries of Europe, were a striking example of both the unity and the religious zeal of medieval Europe.

Most arguments that were used to suppress heresy and encourage crusades were also applied to Jews. Religious regulations forced Jews into cities and limited their employment to banking and money lending, activities believed to be unfit for Christians. Consequently, to religious reasons for persecution were added socio-economic motives. The same ideas that sent thousands of Western Europeans on crusades led them to loot and burn Jewish ghettos: thus the pogrom was invented, and Jews were given the choice of baptism or death. Wild stories were widely circulated, such as that Jews kidnapped Christian children for ritual sacrifice, practised cannibalism and magic, poisoned wells, and profaned the sacrament of Holy Communion.

THE CATHARS AND ALBIGENSIANS

The church and the papacy were naturally alarmed by the rapid growth of the Cathars, a heretical sect. In 1208 Pope Innocent III launched a crusade against them in southern France. The crusade was successful, destroying Cathar political power by 1250, and ruining the civilization of the area in the process. After the crusade, the Inquisition was established in 1231–33, to root out heresy by relentless persecution. However, the preaching of the newly-established friars was also effective in winning people from Catharism, and in Italy this was probably the chief cause of its disappearance in the late fourteenth century. The Cathars should in no sense be regarded as medieval Protestants, as writers have sometimes mistakenly suggested.

The Cathars (Greek *Katharoi*, 'Puritans') flourished in western Europe in the twelfth and thirteenth centuries and, like the earlier Manicheans, believed in two gods, a good god who created the invisible spiritual world, and an evil god who created the visible material world. Matter, including the human body, was evil and was ruled by the evil god, whom the Cathars identified with the God of the Old Testament. He had, they claimed, imprisoned the human soul in its earthly body, and death merely caused the soul to migrate to another body, human or animal. Salvation could be attained only by breaking free from this miserable cycle, and Christ, the Son of the good God, had been sent by him to reveal to the human race the way of this salvation. Christ was a life-giving Spirit, whose earthly body was only an appearance.

The Cathars accepted the New Testament and various Christian teachings, but of course rejected the incarnation and the sacraments, since they completely separated spirit

The fortress-like Cathedral of Saint Cecilia, Albi, France, built following the brutal crusade to put down the Cathars of this region.
© PAKMOR/DREAMSTIME.COM

and matter. The one Cathar sacrament, which they believed enabled the soul to escape from the evil material world, was the *consolamentum*, or spiritual baptism, administered by the laying-on-of-hands. This they held was the baptism instituted by Christ, which gave to recipients the Holy Spirit, removed their original sin, and enabled them on death to enter the pure world of spirit and be united with the good God. The *consolamentum* had been handed down from the apostles by a succession of 'good men', but the church had perverted Christ's teachings and ordinances, and was enslaved by the evil god of matter.

The Cathars were divided into two classes, the Perfect, who had received the *consolamentum*, and the Believers, who had not. The former lived in strict poverty as ascetics, involving chastity, frequent fasts, vegetarianism, and the renunciation of marriage and oaths. They received unquestioning obedience and great veneration from the Believers, as the Perfect alone could pray directly to God. Most Believers delayed receiving the *consolamentum* until they were in danger of death, as the rigour necessary among the Perfect was too much for them.

After 1100, and especially after 1140, Catharism spread through western Europe, gaining its greatest strength in northern Italy and southern France, where it developed an advanced organization. The French Cathars were called 'Albigensians', being most numerous in the district of Albi. The holiness and simplicity of the Perfect undoubtedly contrasted with the riches of the Catholic Church and the corruptions of many of its clergy, and large numbers must have found that Catharism answered their spiritual needs in a way that Catholicism did not. By 1200 it seemed possible that southern France might become entirely Cathar, as the Cathars were protected by the sophisticated and anti-clerical merchants and nobles, notably the Count of Toulouse. It was this threat that provoked Innocent's crusade.

HERESY AND DISSIDENCE

The exercise of choice (Latin, *haeresis*) in religious doctrine has posed a problem in Christianity since the days of the apostles; by the fifth century Augustine could list no fewer than 88 different heresies. Yet throughout the early Middle Ages, heretics were mainly individual intellectuals or idiosyncratic rabble-rousers, and the response of the church was localized and sporadic. From the twelfth century, however, the problem of heresy became

THE WALDENSIANS

A wealthy merchant of Lyons, who came to be known as Peter Waldo or Valdes (c. 1140– c. 1218), experienced conversion in about 1175. He gave away his worldly goods and decided to follow the example of Christ by leading a simple life of poverty and preaching. He had translations made from the Latin New Testament into the vernacular, which formed the basis of his evangelism.

Similarly dedicated men and women rallied to him, and this ideal of illiterate lay folk living in simple poverty was given the approval of Pope Alexander III at the Third Lateran Council (1179). The pope added a condition, however, that they must obtain the permission and supervision of local church authorities before engaging in preaching. The Waldensians spread the message of the Bible and exalted the virtues of poverty, and by so doing were a living condemnation of the wealth and laxity of the established church.

When the Archbishop of Lyons prohibited their scriptural preaching around 1181, the Waldensians responded by preaching even more zealously. The 1181 condemnation was echoed in an excommunication of 1184 at Verona, this time by Pope Lucius III, who also directed that the Waldensians and other similar groups should be eliminated by episcopal inquisition and secular punishment. In not much more than a decade, what had begun as an enthusiastic popular movement had been branded as heresy, though before long Waldo himself faded from the picture.

The Waldensians fled from Lyons rather than submit, and started to organize as a church with bishops, priests, and deacons, eventually claiming to be the 'true' church. They spread throughout two regions of Europe notorious for unorthodox beliefs – Lombardy and Provence – also regions of Cathar strength. Their growth was something the reigning pope, Innocent III, would not allow.

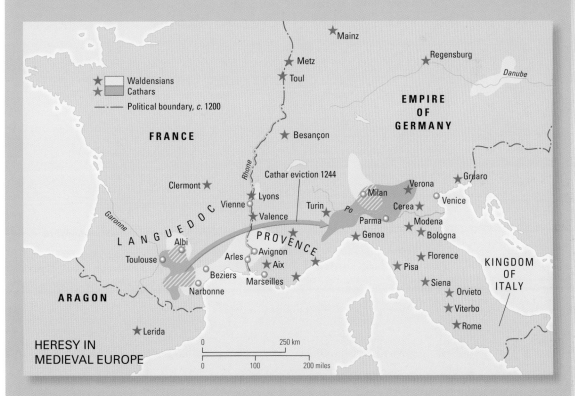

HERESY IN
MEDIEVAL EUROPE

Although some Waldensians re-converted to the established church following a debate in 1207, and Innocent received them back and gave them his special protection, this success was not to be repeated. In 1214 he described the Waldensians as heretics and schismatics, and in 1215, at the great Fourth Lateran Council, Innocent III repeated the general denunciation of heretics, including Waldensians.

Such outbursts by the pope only tended to convince the Waldensians themselves that the Catholic church was the 'Whore of Babylon', and need not be acknowledged. The Waldensians had expanded so far geographically and doctrinally that in 1218 they called a general council at Bergamo, Italy, where certain doctrinal differences between the Waldensians of Lombardy and France were discussed. By the end of the thirteenth century, although hounded by the newly-strengthened Inquisition, the Waldensians had infiltrated practically the whole of Europe except for Britain, and had become one of the most common and widespread persecuted movements.

WALDENSIAN BELIEFS

The doctrines which distinguished the Waldensians, and which the church considered heretical, were many and varied, and some altered during the later Middle Ages. The greatest objection to the Waldensians – who began within the church – was that they ended by rejecting that church altogether. The unauthorized preaching of the Bible and rejection of the intermediary role of the clergy were the two issues which gained the Waldensians the description of heretics.

One of the sources of their doctrines is a treatise written about 1320 by Bernard Gui, inquisitor in southern France at a time when the Waldensians were still among the strongest dissident movements. Writing as a critical outsider, Gui emphasized that the Waldensians rejected ecclesiastical authority, especially by their conviction that they were not subject to the pope or his decrees of excommunication. They rejected or re-interpreted all the Catholic sacraments except confession, absolution, and the eucharist. In theory, all Waldensian men or women could administer these sacraments, and the eucharist was usually held only once a year. There seems also to have been some kind of Waldensian baptism.

All Catholic feast days, festivals, and prayers were rejected as human creations, not based upon the New Testament, excepting Sundays, the feast-day of Mary, and the Lord's Prayer. Gui accused them of setting themselves up as an alternative church in which the 'priest' was simply the good individual, rather than someone in clerical orders, which seemed to him more serious than the other Waldensian hallmark, and of missionary preaching in the local language. Gui also noted the refusal of Waldensians to take oaths, except under special circumstances, since they said the Bible prohibited this. The Waldensians also denied purgatory, for which they could find no basis in the New Testament, leading them also to reject the Catholic belief in the value of prayers for the dead. For the Waldensians, if the dead were in hell they were beyond hope and, if in heaven, they had no need of prayer. Similar reasoning led them to reject prayers to images of the saints.

As to organization, Gui found the Waldensians to be divided into superiors and ordinary believers, a far more marked, and the reaction of the church correspondingly more rigorous. During the thirteenth century a strong papacy directed this response.

During the twelfth century, whole areas of Europe began to show tendencies either to purify (for example, the Waldensians), or to provide alternatives to (for example, the Cathars), the established church. Both these movements were persecuted by lay rulers as well as diocesan authorities; by the end of the twelfth century, the papacy had entered the battle against such disruptive groups. Pope Alexander III in 1162–63 suggested that lay and clerical informers who brought reports of heretics should be supplemented by officials who went out to discover evidence of heresy. He called upon lay rulers to distinction similar to that among the Cathars. The superiors were expected to lead more austere lives, depend on the alms of their followers, and evangelize as wandering preachers in the tradition of the apostles.

The points noted by Inquisitor Gui in the fourteenth century were repeatedly brought out by other later inquisitors well into the fifteenth century, with certain features apparently becoming more radical. For example, by 1398 the Waldensians were accused of rejecting all the physical trappings traditionally associated with the church: buildings, cemeteries, altars, holy water, liturgies, pilgrimages, and indulgences. The trend towards radicalism also appears in their rejection of all 'saints' not named in the New Testament.

WHERE WALDENSIANS PROSPERED

Although the Waldensians spread throughout Europe, they were strongest in central and eastern Europe. Waldensian beliefs themselves were sometimes influenced by contact with other dissident movements. In southern France, for example, the inquisitors often discovered that Cathar rejection of the created world was combined with the traditional Waldensian rejection of the established church. French Waldensians continued to be harassed to the end of the Middle Ages, culminating in a crusade against them in 1488 in the Dauphiné. In Italy they likewise continued to hold out against the Inquisition, taking refuge especially in Piedmont, where they were also attacked in 1488.

In their main region – central and eastern Europe – their work was later to influence the course of the Reformation. The inquisitors were active and

> They go about in twos, barefoot, in woollen garments, owning nothing, holding all things in common like the apostles.
>
> THE WALDENSIANS APPEAR IN ROME IN 1179

– at least when papal-imperial politics allowed it – successful in seeking out Waldensians throughout these areas in the later Middle Ages. Peter Zwicker and Martin of Prague, for example, were the leading persecutors in Bohemia, Moravia, Brandenburg, Pomerania, and Austria in the decades round about 1400. Other regions of central and eastern Europe, including northern Germany, Poland and Hungary, were similarly scoured by inquisitors in the later fourteenth century.

During the fifteenth century, despite repeated campaigns against them, there was considerable coming and going of Waldensians in central Europe, and some interchange of ideas between the Bohemian Hussites, English Wyclifites who were also to be found in this area, and the Waldensians. Though there were sporadic attempts to unite Hussites and Waldensians, these failed because of fundamental differences in doctrine. Nevertheless, such activity provided the charged atmosphere in which the great religious changes of the sixteenth century would occur, when many Waldensian beliefs entered the mainstream of the Protestant movement.

RONALD FINUCANE

combat heresy, and in the Third Lateran Council of 1179 announced a crusade against the Cathars of France. These efforts were not particularly effective.

Alexander's successor, Lucius III, decreed in 1184 that bishops should take action against heretics such as the Cathars, Patari, Humiliati, Waldensians, and Arnoldists. A particular characteristic of this decree, establishing the bishops' inquisition, which was echoed in a contemporary imperial edict, was that a suspect, once convicted of being a heretic, was to be handed over to the secular arm for punishment. The death penalty was not yet official, although medieval heretics had been burned at the stake – often by mobs of lay people – at least from the early eleventh century.

Innocent III further defined and extended the attitude of the papacy towards heresy. For example, Innocent was the first pope to talk about heresy in terms of 'treason' (1199). By his time the Cathars had spread widely in France and Italy, and he found it difficult to rouse local bishops to stamp out their dualistic doctrines. He sent Cistercians into the Midi region of France, with little success. He then sent others, more devoted to preaching and exemplary living, including Dominic Guzman, whose followers – the Dominicans – were to become the foremost order of the Inquisition.

Innocent's successor, Pope Honorius III (1216–27), allowed the Albigensian Crusade to intensify, assisted by the French King Louis VIII, who in 1226 issued an ordinance under which bishops would judge, and French law punish, heretics. Emperor Frederick II had issued a similar decree in 1220, and in 1224 he ordered the burning of heretics. When in 1231 another great pope, Gregory IX (1227–41), in *Excommunicamus*, issued further decrees against heretics, and repeated this law of 1224. Execution by the secular authorities had finally and officially become papal policy. Under Gregory the Inquisition as a church institution was practically completed, and the new orders of friars, especially Dominicans, had become its favoured papal agents. The finishing touches were supplied by Pope Innocent IV (1243–54) who, in the bull *Ad extirpanda* (1252), incorporated all earlier papal statements about the organization of the Inquisition, as well as condoning the use of torture.

WHAT WAS THE INQUISITION?

The Inquisition was a special court with a peculiar power to judge intentions as well as actions. It was made up of several officials, who assisted inquisitors in various ways: delegates – examiners who handled preliminary investigations and formalities; the *socius* – a personal adviser and companion to the inquisitor; familiars – guards, prison visitors, and secret agents; and notaries, who carefully collected evidence and filed it efficiently for present and future instances of suspected heresy. Usually a few dozen councillors were present, but since the inquisitor was not bound to follow their advice, their role was often merely formal. The bishop, too, would be represented, even though there was not always co-operation between bishops and inquisitors.

As to classifying suspected heretics, the widest and most vague description would be applied in the first instance, and eventually specialized phrases came to be used. Distinctions were made between heretics who had additional beliefs and those who denied orthodox beliefs, and between perfected and imperfect heretics; or again, since mere suspicion was sufficient cause to be summoned, individuals were classified as lightly suspect, vehemently suspect, or violently suspect. The web was carefully woven, and it was often simpler to confess than to try to defend oneself.

The inquisitor or his vicar would arrive suddenly, deliver a sermon to the townspeople calling for reports of anyone suspected of heresy, and for all who felt heresy within themselves to come forth and confess, within a period of grace. This was the 'general inquisition'. When the period of grace expired, the 'special inquisition' began, with a summons to suspected heretics who were detained until trial.

At this trial the inquisitor had complete control as judge, prosecutor, and jury. The proceedings were not public, evidence from two witnesses was sufficient, and it was usually possible to learn only the general nature of the charges. The names of witnesses, who might be of most questionable character, were equally difficult to discover. The suspect was not allowed a defence lawyer or, rather, lawyers quickly discovered that defence of a suspected heretic might result in their own summons to the holy tribunal. Certain pleas might be accepted as an alternative to admitting the charges; for example, ignorance, or that the charge was brought by malice – but since the suspect did not know the names of his accusers, he could at best merely provide the court with a list of individuals whom he suspected of such hatred towards him. Trials might continue for years, during which the suspect could languish in prison. Torture was a most effective means to secure repentance. Though it could not be repeated, torture could be continued, and though torture of children and old people had to be relatively light, only pregnant women were exempt – until after delivery.

'Penance' following confession might be light, such as the hearing of a number of masses, or, more commonly, pilgrimage to specific local or distant shrines, where scourging might be prescribed. Confessed heretics were sometimes forced to wear symbols denoting their fallen state, such as crosses of special design and colour. Penitents might instead (or in addition) be fined or have their property confiscated. In some countries, heirs who were not heretics might subsequently recover these lands. A sentence to the inquisitorial prison was among the heaviest of penances, and degrees of detention were specified as open or strict. Besides loss of liberty, heretics suffered civil 'death', and were disqualified from holding office or making legal contracts. In many cases sentences could be cut for a price. But the papacy found this and many of the other penances too harsh or extortionate, and at times particular inquisitors were directed to cool their ardour.

For a final group of heretics, the 'unreconciled' – classified as insubordinate, impenitent, or relapsed – a much more terrible fate was in store. The first two categories could still save themselves from the flames, to suffer less severe punishment. But for the last, especially after the middle of the thirteenth century, the only possibility was death at the stake. This the Inquisition entrusted to the secular authorities, which pronounced and carried out the sentence, since the church could not shed blood.

WHERE DID THE INQUISITION SUCCEED?

The success of the Inquisition varied from one region to another, depending upon political relations with the papacy and the amount of co-operation given by local church dignitaries. Its influence was affected by events such as the Avignon 'Captivity' of the papacy and the papal Schism. In Spain the Inquisition had come under secular control as early as 1230, but it was not until 1480 that the Catholic monarchs Ferdinand and Isabella made the Spanish Inquisition a royal instrument with its centre at Madrid. This near-independence in Spain produced a unique institution, which remained very influential until the nineteenth century.

In Germany, papal and imperial feuds meant that the course of the Inquisition never ran smoothly. Conrad of Marburg (1195–1233) is perhaps the best-known of thirteenth-century inquisitors; his reign of terror resulted in his murder. In the middle of the fourteenth century further attempts to enforce inquisitorial procedure in Germany met with little success, and by the end of the fifteenth century the papacy allowed Germany church dignitaries to oversee the Inquisition.

France was the scene of extensive activity by the Inquisition. Though the Cathars were of little importance after the mid-fourteenth century, constant demands were made upon the Inquisition. For example, after the condemnation of the Franciscan Spirituals in 1317, the Inquisition in Languedoc directed its energies against them and in 1318 four Spirituals were executed at Marseilles. The Beguines, too, came under attack, and some were executed about 1320; but the Waldensians proved more elusive.

Northern France, too, saw some inquisitorial activity. The Inquisitor Robert le Bougre, 'Hammer of the Heretics', active during the 1230s, was himself imprisoned by the pope for an excess of zeal, after rampaging through northern France in search of heretics. In the fourteenth century the north European Brethren of the Free Spirit suffered some executions, but after the mid-fourteenth century the French *Parlement* and the University of Paris tended to manipulate the Inquisition for political ends. During the fifteenth century, pressure from the Inquisition declined generally except for sporadic condemnations of those with Hussite views.

Italy, too, had much business for the Inquisition, particularly against the Cathars, who were strong in the north. After the assassination of the Inquisitor Peter of Verona (1206–52) in 1252, the Dominican inquisitors in Lombardy were increased from four to eight. There was much local resistance to this papal institution in those states which had a tradition of political independence. Venice especially resented the intrusion of the Inquisition, and heresy remained a matter for the civil government of that powerful city-state. In the Papal States themselves, inquisitors found that any enemy of the pope was automatically suspected of heresy, but, on the other hand, in the Alps the Waldensians managed to survive through the fourteenth and fifteenth centuries despite harassment.

In two countries, England and Bohemia, the Inquisition made little impact. Heresy became a problem in England with Wyclif's doctrinal and the Lollards' political-social movements of the fourteenth and early fifteenth centuries. But the fact that Parliament passed a statute in 1401 for the burning of heretics indicates how little reference there was to the Inquisition, since according to church law, such a statute was superfluous. Although inquisitors entered Bohemia in 1318, little headway was made during the fourteenth and fifteenth centuries in the independent atmosphere before the Hussites. In both England and Bohemia the political situation clearly restricted the effectiveness of the Inquisition.

Inquisitors were not all agitated zealots like Conrad of Marburg; many were well-educated and devoted to what they considered their duty. But some have earned the reputation of being sadists or thieves, depending on whether you are appalled by torture or disgusted by the unjust seizure of heretics' property. It is well to remember that 'the same widespread and fervent breath of reform that made people long to go on pilgrimages, to enter ascetic monasteries, and to become mystics also impelled them to attack and murder heretics and Jews and to undertake holy wars against the Moslems.'[1]

---

[1]   Jeffrey Burton Russell, *A History of Medieval Christianity, Prophecy and Order* NY, Thomas Y. Crowell Co. 1968

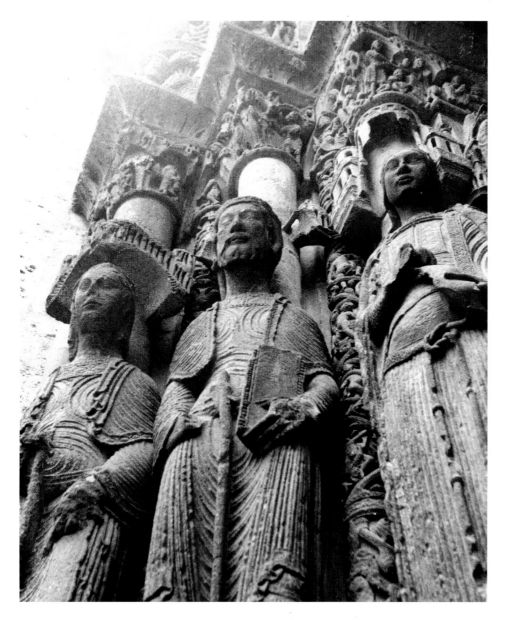

Weathered stone statues on the West façade of the Cathedral of Notre Dame, Chartres, mainly built between 1194 and 1250, and one of the finest examples of the French High Gothic architectural style.
TIM DOWLEY ASSOCIATES

THE GROWTH OF LEARNING

The stability and optimism reflected in the papal reform movement also resulted in the growth of learning and of the universities. Education during the age of Charlemagne and the tenth and eleventh centuries was carried on mainly by the monasteries and cathedral schools, the former being more prominent until the eleventh century.

A learned monk was appointed to teach novices (new monks) and when he was a famous scholar, adult monks from other houses would come to study under him. Other young men from well-to-do families would also be sent to study under the monastic tutor, and many of these would join the clergy or take up secular work.

THE SACRAMENTS IN MEDIEVAL EUROPE

During the second five hundred years of the Christian era in the West, the doctrines of baptism and communion developed considerably – both in a slightly 'magical' direction. Baptism was greatly affected by Augustine's controversy with Pelagius and his followers, as the doctrine of original sin, which Augustine set out, made it vital for the church to believe in the necessity of baptism for salvation. People took this to imply that unbaptized infants who died went to hell, or at least to 'limbo', on the borders of hell. The high rate of infant mortality at this period led to baptism being carried out within minutes of birth, often by midwives. (A carry-over survives to this day, when newborn infants are in danger of death.)

During this same period Western Europe came to be regarded as 'Christendom' – a Christian society. As a result virtually all baptisms were of infants, with this new and enormous pressure to baptize quickly. The older tradition of Easter baptisms ceased, and it also became impossible for the bishop to lay on hands (or anoint) at baptism. Indeed, in the larger dioceses of France and Britain, this practice was often neglected entirely, so that many people were never 'confirmed' at all. Aquinas even argued that confirmation was not necessary for ordination.

By 1000, more and more people believed that, at communion, the sign is itself that which it signifies (the 'realist' position). A controversy concerning the use of unleavened bread (*azymes*) in the eighth century standardized the use of wafers at communion in the Western Church. Ratramnus in the ninth century was one of the last writers to describe the elements at the eucharist as 'symbols', but his book was condemned in 1050. He opposed Paschasius, who took the 'realist' doctrine a long step further towards transubstantiation. The last opponent of this trend was Berengar of Tours in the eleventh century, whose denials of 'realism' provoked further definitions (for example, by Lanfranc who opposed him). Transubstantiation was finally adopted as orthodox at the Fourth Lateran Council in 1215, teaching that the underlying, permanent reality of the bread and wine are changed at consecration into Christ's body and blood.

THE SACRAMENTS SYSTEMATIZED

Meanwhile the sacraments were increasingly organized as a system. Hugh of St Victor in the early twelfth century still listed thirty sacraments, following Augustine's pattern. But his contemporary, Peter Lombard, in *The* Sentences, produced a tightly

By the twelfth century, the cathedral schools had surpassed the monastic establishments, and the chief cathedral dignitary after the bishop and dean was the chancellor, who taught the seven liberal arts and theology to the advanced students. Other teachers would instruct the younger scholars in Latin grammar. Students in these schools were generally destined for service as clerics. A licence to teach, given by the chancellor, was the predecessor of a university degree.

During the eleventh century the leading cathedral schools in northern Europe were at Laon, Paris, Chartres, and Cologne. Debates were carried on that reawakened intellectual life in Europe and helped expand the vocabulary and depth of Christian thought. Their thinking was carried on against the background of what had gone before – the classical philosophy of ancient Greece, the Bible, and the teaching of the early Christian writers. One of the significant controversies involved Berengar (c. 999–1088), a pupil of Fulbert of Chartres, who became the teacher in the cathedral school of Tours.

organized scheme of seven sacraments (which he divided off from the lesser 'sacramentals'). Lombard's views were pronounced orthodox by the Fourth Lateran Council, and his system finally entrenched by Aquinas, who expounded it in his *Summa Theologiae*.

Lombard's seven sacraments are baptism, confirmation, eucharist, penance, extreme unction, ordination, and matrimony. Their distinctive mark is that they are outward signs of inward grace, and were instituted by Christ. Lombard and Aquinas taught that the sacraments confer grace simply by being performed (*ex opere operato*). People receiving them can, through unbelief, create a barrier to grace – though this is of course impossible for an unconscious infant or a dying person.

The new system left many problems unsolved. The question as to where and how Christ had instituted these seven sacraments was left to the Reformers to discuss. Meanwhile the nature of the outward sign of the sacraments came under discussion. The Council of Florence (1438–45) defined the outward sign at ordination as the handing on of the paten and chalice to candidates for priest's orders.

During this period, too, came the idea that a 'seal' was made indelibly on the soul by the sacraments of baptism, confirmation, and ordination; this was held to make them unrepeatable. This was a logical conclusion from Augustine's claim that Donatist baptism was valid, and thus did not need repeating when Donatists were reconciled to the Catholic Church.

The doctrine of the eucharist was developed after the Fourth Lateran Council. Aquinas discussed it in terms of Aristotelian categories, and the doctrine of transubstantiation itself gave rise to new emphases: the building up to a climax of adoration in the rite; an increase in devotions outside the liturgy; the new feast of Corpus Christi ('the body of Christ'); and the barring of lay people from receiving the wine (lest the spilling of transubstantiated wine should occur and cause scandal). Theories were developed that, through the offering of Christ himself under the forms of bread and wine in the sacrifice of the mass, atonement was made for both the living and the dead, which in turn led to the later medieval proliferation of masses for the dead.

COLIN BUCHANAN

Discussion revolved around the meaning of the words of consecration in the mass, 'This is my body, this is my blood.' Berengar held that a real and true change takes place in these elements, but that the change is spiritual, and that the bread and wine remain of the same substance. Lanfranc and other theologians debated with him, believing that the underlying substance of the bread and wine was changed to Christ's blood and body, while the 'accidents' (touch, taste, sight, and smell) of the bread and wine remained the same. During a long and bitter controversy (1045–80) the term 'transubstantiation' emerged and took on Lanfranc's definition. Berengar was condemned and forced to disown his views.

ATONEMENT

Another controversy concerned Christ's work on the cross. How was it that the death of Christ could work a reconciliation between God and man? Before the eleventh century the dominant teaching on this subject was as old as Origen, who believed that through sin mankind had made itself subject to the devil, and that the mark of this subjection was

ANSELM

Anselm (1033–1109), one of the great archbishops of Canterbury, is today remembered chiefly as a philosopher and a theologian. Anselm was part of the Norman conquest of England. Taking monastic vows in 1060, he succeeded Lanfranc as prior of Bec, in Normandy, in 1063. Thirty years later he succeeded Lanfranc as Archbishop of Canterbury. His time as archbishop was marked by conflict with King William II (Rufus, r. 1087–1100) and his successor Henry I (1100–35), and he was exiled more than once. As archbishop, he was known as a reformer, encouraging regular church synods, enforcing clerical celibacy, and suppressing the slave trade.

Anselm was one of the early scholastic theologians. He taught that faith must lead to the right use of reason: 'I believe, in order that I may understand.' It was Anselm who first put forward the 'ontological argument' for the existence of God, an attempt to prove God's existence by reason alone, starting with the idea of the most perfect being ... God is 'that than which no greater can be conceived'. But if 'that than which no greater can be conceived' is greatest in every respect except for existence, then clearly it would be inferior to the greatest being which did actually exist.

Anselm himself expressed the argument in several different forms. Even today it is the subject of intense debate among the philosophers. But most thinkers agree that it contains something of a conjuring trick, for it treats existence as if it were a quality which a thing may or may not have. The thing is either there or not there. And the only way of knowing is to ask for some tangible evidence.

Anselm's greatest work of theology was his *Cur Deus Homo (Why God Became Man)*. Anselm replied that sin runs up a debt with God which humans can never themselves repay, but Christ's death was of such worth that it 'satisfied' God's offended majesty and earned a reward. Hence the Father gives humanity salvation on account of the merits of Christ. Anselm's work showed deep insight into humanity's need of atonement, but expressed it in terms of the thinking of his day. The New Testament speaks of Christ dying for humanity; Anselm tried to explain it by means of medieval ideas of merit and rewards.

COLIN BROWN

I do not seek to understand that I may believe, but I believe that I may understand: for this I also believe, that unless I believe I will not understand.

ANSELM OF CANTERBURY

death. God in his grace wished to free men, but he was unable to because the devil's claim was just. To neutralize Satan's claim, a ransom had to be paid in the form of a valuable person over whom Satan had no right – a sinless person. Thus the devil was tricked when Christ was crucified, because the Son of God was sinless; now God can with justice save whomsoever he pleases.

This theory was challenged by Anselm of Canterbury in *Cur Deus Homo* (*Why God became Man*). He argued that when a person sins, he or she breaks the order of the universe and is alienated from God. Because he is just, God must be given satisfaction for sin before he can forgive the sinner. Christ was sinless, sent by the mercy of God; thus he was able to offer to God the satisfaction owed by the human race. This explanation was widely accepted in Europe, and changed the entire understanding of the incarnation and atonement.

PETER ABELARD

A dynamic, popular teacher, Peter Abelard's life was one of constant personal turmoil and confrontation with authority. Born in Brittany in 1079, Abelard studied as a young man with some of the most respected theologians of his day. However, he soon became convinced he knew more than his teachers, arrogantly challenging and quarrelling with them on a variety of subjects. He finally withdrew to set up his own lectures, to which enthusiastic students flocked.

A brilliant lecturer and slashing debater, Abelard's reputation grew until he became known as Paris's brightest intellectual star. However, his celebrated love affair with the beautiful and talented Héloise almost shattered his academic career and cut short his intellectual influence. In 1115, at the age of thirty-six, Abelard agreed to tutor the teenage niece of Fulbert, a canon of Notre Dame Cathedral in Paris. A relationship developed, which resulted in a son called Astrolabe. When the scandal broke, Héloise retired to a local convent and Fulbert hired some thugs to castrate Abelard.

Following this humiliation, Abelard became a Benedictine monk, but soon resumed teaching and once again became involved in controversy. In 1121, the Council of Soissons condemned his views on the Trinity without a hearing. For the next twenty years Peter Abelard lived a harassed existence, constantly on the move, and followed by large numbers of students. Finally, around 1136, he returned to Paris, where he enjoyed renewed popularity and wrote several important works. In 1141, several statements selected from his writings were condemned at the Council of Sens. Abelard decided to appeal to the pope, but died near Cluny on his way to Rome in 1142.

Abelard was the major Christian thinker of his period. Particularly after becoming a monk, he struggled with many of the problems that were to emerge as major theological issues in the next centuries. Abelard's book *Sic et Non (Yes and No)* (1122) set the stage for discussing the relationship between faith and reason in Christian theology. Also, by pointing out that established authorities often conflicted, Abelard called attention to the fact that they needed to be systematized, clarified, and reconciled. He believed genuine Christianity was both reasonable and consistent, and his desire to reconcile faith and reason in the context of Christian theology set the stage for the work of Thomas Aquinas in the thirteenth century. One of the pioneers of scholasticism, Abelard also wrote poems, hymns, and an autobiography.

ROBERT D. LINDER

PETER ABELARD

Possibly the leading figure of the schools of Europe in the period just before the founding of the universities was Peter Abelard, who studied in Paris with two teachers of logic: Roscelin, the leading Nominalist, and William of Champeaux, a Realist philosopher. Later Abelard left Paris temporarily for Laon, where he studied theology with Anselm. It was probably Abelard's methods more than his conclusions that upset many important medieval church leaders. He stated: 'The first key to wisdom is this constant and frequent questioning ... For by doubting we are led to question, by questioning we arrive at the truth.' Using this approach, Abelard wrote *Sic et Non* (*Yes and No*) in which he demonstrated that tradition and authority alone were not sufficient to answer such questions as: 'Is God omnipotent?', 'Do we sin without willing it?' and, 'Is faith based upon reason?' He quoted authorities on both sides and left the contradictions unresolved.

A pupil of Abelard, Peter Lombard (1100–60), used reason to answer many of the same questions in his book, *The Sentences*, a popular theological textbook of the Middle Ages. This scholastic technique of setting up contradictory statements about a problem, and then resolving them by reason, was also used by Thomas Aquinas.

The scholastic method was also popularized in the twelfth century by Gratian in his systematizing of canon law in the *Decretum*. In this great work, he would state a law and, if it was not contradicted, it was allowed to stand. But if there were opposing statements, he tried to reconcile them through logic.

This law code, as applied by church courts, was to guide the Christian on earth. Certain cases involving personal offences were to be tried in church courts, and any crime committed by a clergyman was to be punished by canon law courts. There was a large area of overlap between secular and church courts, which led to tension between monarchs and the church during the Middle Ages.

THE UNIVERSITIES ARISE

The cathedral schools culminated in the foundation of the first universities. The term *universitas* was used to describe a guild or corporation of teachers or scholars who might band together in self-defence against the town in which they were located, or to discipline lazy or profligate students (or professors). A city with a well-known cathedral might become the centre for a great number of schools. At first scholars would rent rooms and students would pay to come and listen to their lectures. Guilds of professors organized the universities of northern Europe, while in Italy it was the students who formed the guilds. The first universities obtained a charter from the pope; those established later applied to the secular ruler.

The gradual development of universities makes it difficult to date them, but a list of the first universities would include Bologna, Paris, Salerno, Oxford, Cambridge, Montpellier, Padua, Salamanca, and Toulouse. The universities taught the seven liberal arts – a late Roman system of knowledge thought necessary to make an educated person. Although these included grammar, logic, and rhetoric (together the 'three ways', *trivium*) as well as arithmetic, geometry, astronomy, and music (the 'four ways', *quadrivium*), the teaching of logic or philosophy tended to dominate the undergraduate curriculum. Graduate faculties taught medicine, law, and theology.

THE CURRICULUM

Medieval universities were relatively small by modern standards, the largest having between 3,000 and 4,000 students. At Paris, the most famous, a boy could begin his studies at the age of twelve, but the privilege of lecturing in theology was not granted until a man (there were, of course, no female students) was thirty-five. The only entrance requirement was a knowledge of Latin; the first four years' studies consisted of the liberal arts. The next two years' work consisted of study, a teaching assistantship, thesis defence and culminated in the MA degree. This enabled a student to go on to study law, medicine, or theology. At Paris, if he decided to earn the DD (Doctor of Divinity) degree in theology, he would

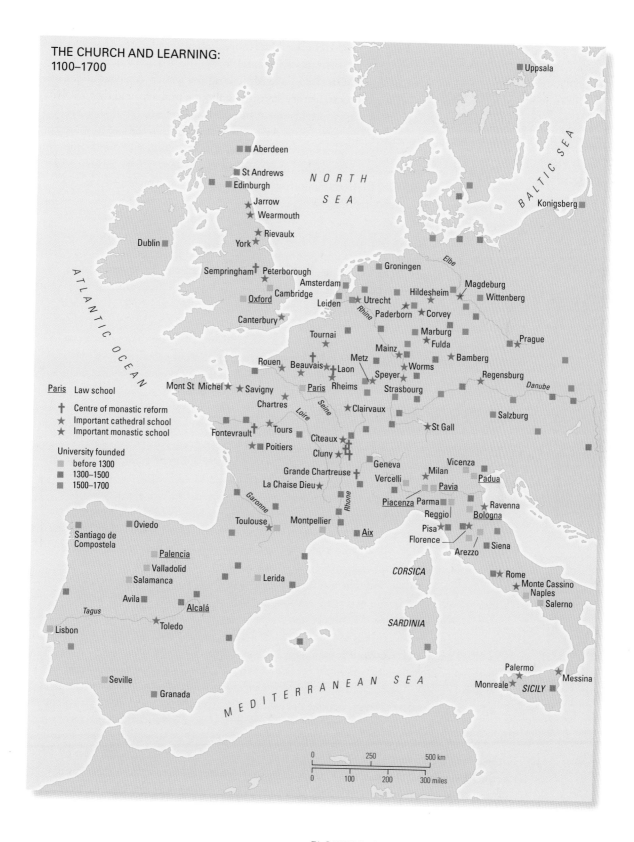

THE CHURCH AND LEARNING:
1100–1700

NORTH SEA

BALTIC SEA

ATLANTIC OCEAN

Uppsala

Aberdeen

St Andrews
Edinburgh

Konigsberg

Jarrow
Wearmouth

Rievaulx

Dublin

York

Sempringham   Peterborough

Groningen

Elbe

Magdeburg

Amsterdam   Hildesheim   Wittenberg

Oxford   Cambridge

Leiden   Utrecht

Paderborn   Corvey

Rhine

Canterbury

Tournai

Marburg

Prague

Mainz   Fulda

Bamberg

Rouen   Beauvais   Laon

Metz

Worms

Regensburg

Mont St Michel   Savigny

Paris   Rheims   Speyer

Strasbourg

Danube

Chartres

Seine

Clairvaux

Salzburg

Loire

Fontevrault   Tours

Cîteaux

St Gall

Poitiers

Cluny

Geneva   Vicenza

Grande Chartreuse

Milan

La Chaise Dieu

Vercelli   Pavia   Padua

Rhone

Piacenza   Parma

Ravenna

Reggio   Bologna

Oviedo

Toulouse   Montpellier

Pisa

Santiago de
Compostela

Florence   Siena

Garonne

Arezzo

Palencia

Lerida

Aix

CORSICA

Rome

Valladolid

Monte Cassino
Naples

Salamanca

Salerno

Avila   Alcalá

Tagus

SARDINIA

Lisbon   Toledo

Seville

Palermo

Granada

Monreale   *SICILY*   Messina

MEDITERRANEAN SEA

Paris   Law school

✝   Centre of monastic reform

⭐   Important cathedral school

★   Important monastic school

University founded
before 1300
1300–1500
1500–1700

0   250   500 km

0   100   200   300 miles

spend six years studying the Bible and Peter Lombard's systematic theology (*The Sentences*). Finally, three years' study of the writings of the early church theologians and the Bible led to the STD (Doctor of Sacred Theology), which qualified the scholar to teach theology in the same way as the MA entitled him to teach the arts.

Students paid their fees to each professor as they left his class; in return they received the reading of a text and the teacher's comments upon the book. This method was necessary because hand-copied books were rare and expensive; it could take over a year to copy the Bible. Most students could own only one or two books, and the lecturer had to dictate their textbooks to them. Later, comments of the outstanding lecturers were incorporated into the dictated materials. Since parchment was expensive, the student often had to remember the lesson. Students at first settled in rented rooms but, beginning in the thirteenth century, colleges were founded, where they could live cheaply, with some regulation by the older students and professors.

At Paris the most famous college was the Sorbonne, founded in 1256. England modelled its universities, Oxford and Cambridge, on Paris. The colleges at these two universities resembled the groups of canons of a cathedral, where clerics lived together under a rule. The religious origins of the colleges at Oxford and Cambridge are evident in the way that their chapels are arranged in a similar manner to a monastic chapel, with facing choir stalls. Although the professors and students at medieval universities were supposed to be clerics, their conduct suggests their minds were often on other matters.

ARISTOTLE REDISCOVERED

Scholastics tried by means of reason to reconcile the Christian revelation with Aristotle's philosophy, which was transmitted to western Europe through the Muslims and Jews of Spain and southern Italy. One of the earlier controversies resulting from the rediscovery of Aristotle concerned the problem of universals. In the early Middle Ages Platonic idealism prevailed: the view that in God's mind there are 'ideas', perfect forms or essences, such as chair, man, honour, and tree, and that the individual things which people actually perceive correspond to these 'ideas'. Defenders of the Platonic position were called 'realists' because they believed in the reality of these 'ideas' or 'universals'; they were challenged by 'nominalists', who maintained that 'universals' were only useful 'names' for talking about the world.

Abelard suggested a middle position between these two, stating that universals are ideas formed in the mind by abstracting characteristics which really do apply to the objects sensed. This view enabled Western minds to appreciate the more advanced work of Aristotle (*On the Soul*, *Physics*, and *Metaphysics*), which became available by 1200. The shock of these new ideas is difficult to exaggerate, and is comparable with the impact of Darwin's theories in the nineteenth century. Aristotle presented a complete explanation of reality, without any reference to a personal God. He challenged Christian and Muslim theology, and strained Jewish faith too. All these beliefs were confronted by a system which taught that matter and form were eternal, that there was no individual immortality apart from the body, and that no cosmic progress was possible – rather, history was an endless cycle of existence, striving to be like the 'Unmoved Mover', but never reaching its goal.

Muslims had to come to terms with Aristotle earlier than the West. Since the work of Islamic scholars such as Averroes (Ibn-Rusd, 1126–98) accompanied Aristotle to

Western Europe, it is important to notice the intellectual turmoil caused by his thought in Islam. Among Muslim scholars one of those who tried to come to terms with Aristotle was Al-Ghazali (1058–1111). Although at first he tried to reconcile faith and reason, he later interpreted philosophical concerns as antagonistic to religious belief and wrote a book entitled *The Incoherence of the Philosophers*, condemning Aristotle's theory of knowledge. Averroes replied proposing a 'double-truth' outlook – that philosophy is one category of truth, and theology deals in quite another kind of reality. Some Christian scholars, among them Siger of Brabant (c. 1240–84), followed Averroes, while others felt that Aristotle should be banned.

ALBERT, AQUINAS, AND ARISTOTLE

Most Christian schoolmen, or 'scholastics', tried to come to terms with the new knowledge. Two of the most famous of these were Albert the Great and his pupil Thomas Aquinas (1225–1274). Impressed by Aristotle's philosophy, yet a profound Christian, Thomas harmonized, at least to his own satisfaction, faith and reason. Accepting Aristotle as a guide in reason, and Scripture as the rule of faith, Aquinas believed there was a meaningful relationship between the two. Revelation, he felt, supplements but never contradicts reason.

A sample of Aquinas' application of this method to the problem suggested by Aristotelian logic is his discussion concerning the providence of God. Aristotle had stated that God (or the 'Unmoved Mover') neither knows nor cares about the world; yet the Bible states frequently that God is intimately concerned with his creation. Thomas explained this was not a real contradiction because God, as the Maker of the world, is its ultimate cause, and knows of the effects of this creation. Since he knows everything in himself, he knows of the whole creation. Also, because he created time, his knowledge of his work is eternal.

Proceeding in this fashion, Thomas explained in as logical a way as possible the doctrines of immortality, creation, and judgment. He made a clear distinction between the way knowledge is gained in the present world, and what an individual learns after death. In this world, knowledge is gained through experience, either directly or indirectly; but in heaven an individual will learn through mystic knowledge. He stated that the apostles and prophets were privileged individuals, who could experience God in a mystic fashion before their death, but that this knowledge was limited to them. By distinguishing in this way between sense experience and heavenly knowledge, Thomas differentiated clearly between science and the Christian hope.

Not all medieval scholastics followed the method of Aquinas. Bonaventura (1221–74), governor-general of the Franciscans and professor of theology at Paris, taught that rational knowledge of God is impossible, because God is different from a human being in quality as well as quantity. Thus, knowledge of God can only be equivocal, hazy, and by analogy. God is experienced by an individual when he or she withdraws from the world and seeks reflections or shadows of God in material things.

Another group of Franciscans, led by Roger Bacon (c. 1214–92) and Robert Grosseteste (c. 1168–1253), resisted Aquinas' method and laid the groundwork for modern science in their experimental studies of the behaviour of light, prisms, rainbows, and mirrors. These scholars emphasized observation, experiment, and the use of measurement for understanding the world. Bacon came to recognize the practical

THOMAS AQUINAS

Thomas Aquinas (1225–74), the greatest scholastic theologian of the Middle Ages, was born into a wealthy noble family in Aquino, Italy. Thomas was a fat, slow, pious boy who at the age of five was sent to the abbey of Monte Cassino. At the age of fourteen he went to study at the University of Naples. Impressed by his Dominican teacher, he decided to enter that order. His family was angered by his decision, and tried to dissuade him by tempting him with a prostitute, kidnapping him, and offering to buy him the post of Archbishop of Naples. All of these attempts were unsuccessful and he went to study at Paris.

Although nicknamed the 'Dumb Ox' because of his bulk, seriousness, and slowness, Thomas demonstrated his brilliance in public disputation. He studied under Albert the Great in Paris and Cologne, returning to Paris in 1252, and spent the rest of his life teaching there and in Italy.

A prolific writer, Thomas's works fill eighteen large volumes. They include commentaries on most of the books of the Bible and on Peter Lombard's *The Sentences*, discussions of thirteen works of Aristotle, and a variety of disputations and sermons. His two most important works are the *Summa Theologiae* and the *Summa Contra Gentiles*. Together they represent an encyclopedic summary of Christian thought, the first based on revelation, and the second designed to support Christian belief with human reason. Both works use Aristotelian logic in unfolding the connections and implications of revealed truth.

Thomas was challenged by secular Aristotelian thought, which came to Western Europe through the Muslims in Spain. Although an enthusiastic student of the new knowledge, he insisted on separating what was acceptable to Christianity from what was not. Following Aristotle, Thomas emphasized that all human knowledge originates in the senses. Aquinas stressed that philosophy is based on data accessible to all; theology only on revelation and logical deduction from revelation. His famous 'Five Ways' were attempts to prove God's existence by reasoning based on what can be known from the world. But this 'natural theology' teaches very little about God, and nothing that is not also clear in Scripture. He developed one of the most internally-consistent systems of thought ever devised, but it did not receive universal acceptance even in his own day. Some of his statements were condemned by the University of Paris in 1277, and a group of scholars, including Duns Scotus and William of Ockham, criticized him for not recognizing that reason and revelation often contradict one another.

Years later, however, Thomas's work gained a prominence in Roman Catholic thought which it has retained. At the Council of Trent (1543–63) the Roman Catholic reformers used the works of Aquinas in drafting their decrees; and in 1879 the pope declared Thomism (Aquinas's theology) eternally valid.

ROBERT G. CLOUSE

possibilities of his studies, dreaming of a world in which the pope would have an army equipped with new types of weapon that could destroy with one blow the Islamic armies and bring peace to the world.

CHURCH-BUILDING BOOM

The most important area of artistic achievement during the Middle Ages was the churches — and the sculpture and painting associated with them. Two building styles predominated during this period, the Romanesque and the Gothic.

The Romanesque style, named after the Romans, appeared in a great burst of church construction during the eleventh century, which produced an estimated 1,587 new buildings in France alone. These massive churches were richly decorated. The wooden roof (a fire hazard) was replaced by a thick half-cylinder of stone called a barrel vault, whose weight forced the builders to construct uniform, heavy walls. Because of the need to support the roof, windows had to be few and small, and the structures tended to be dark inside. In an attempt to brighten the interior, churches were hung with tapestries or painted in bright colours, with gilding or jewels used on statues, chalices, and reliquaries. Free-standing stone sculpture, which had not been used in the West since the fifth century, was re-introduced to lighten the heavy effect of Romanesque construction. The desire to develop a free and less monotonous appearance led architects to use cross-vaulting down the nave, which transferred the weight of the roof to a series of posts or pilasters. The Romanesque style emphasized horizontal lines, and tended to give the worshipper a feeling of repose and solidity.

THE SHIFT TO GOTHIC

The shift in style from Romanesque to Gothic is not essentially a matter of dates, as the forms overlap. Romanesque reached its peak in 1150 and continued into the thirteenth century; while Gothic originated in 1137 and reached its climax about 1250. Gothic first appeared in the construction of the Church of St Denis in Paris (1137–44), under the direction of Suger, adviser to kings Louis VI and Louis VII of France. Wishing to build a fitting tribute both to the Franks and to Dionysius (Denis), the supposed founder of the monastery, Suger created a building of great beauty and originality.

Characterized by delicacy, detail, and light, the Gothic style places the support needed for the structure outside the walls, in the form of flying-buttresses. The pointed arch, another innovation of Gothic construction, made it possible to build a very tall structure which emphasized vertical lines, and caused people who entered to share a feeling of striving upwards towards heaven. The builders of Gothic churches, like the medieval theologians who set up their arguments in a straight-forward manner, aimed for a structural explicitness; that is, they wanted all to see how their buildings were constructed.

In the following century, rivalry arose to see which city could build the highest cathedral structure. Notre Dame de Paris soared to 114ft/34.8m; Chartres to 123ft/37.5m; and Amiens to 138ft/42.1m. Beauvais tried to reach 157ft/47.9m, but the vault collapsed and the city ran out of money trying to rebuild it. These churches were light in two ways; because of the design, the stone-work seemed to lose its massive weightiness, and the stained-glass windows constituted a vast wall of colour, dispelling darkness. Not only the windows were works of art; the pillars, doors, and every possible part of the cathedral were sculpted.

The bishop acted as the patron or sponsor of a new cathedral, but practical oversight of the building was the task of the chapter. They had to arrange for adequate supplies of stone and timber and engage the services of a 'master', who acted as both architect and clerk of works. The master was generally a stone-mason with a practical knowledge of his craft, who had also learnt some geometry and how to draw up plans. He supervised not only the masons but also the work of the master-carpenter, the master-smith and the other skilled workers. Capable masters were much in demand and therefore in a position to bargain.

The west façade of Notre Dame de Paris Cathedral, France, a fine example of French gothic architecture, where building commenced in 1163 and was completed in 1345. Severely damaged during the French Revolution, the church was subsequently extensively renovated.

TIM DOWLEY ASSOCIATES

THE MEDIEVAL CATHEDRAL

Medieval artistic achievement reached its height in the Gothic cathedral, which combined the medieval version of a place of worship, theatre, art gallery, school, and library. The original purpose of a cathedral was to provide a church in which the bishop and his household of priests could celebrate the mass and sing the daily services. Gradually the bishop became taken up with the administration of his diocese – and often he was also employed on the king's business. He visited his cathedral only on special occasions. The household of priests became the 'chapter' of the cathedral, and took over its administration and services.

The cathedral itself was developed in size and magnificence far beyond what was needed for its original purpose. The bishop's church became a screened enclosure within a very much larger structure, which came to be a house of many rooms. There was the room known as the chancel or choir, containing the high altar, the bishop's *cathedra*, and stalls for the clergy, who sang the daily services. The other main room, known as the nave, provided for the religious needs of the people: a nave altar for mass, a font for baptisms, and a pulpit for sermons. But there were many smaller rooms, in which side-altars were set up and at which masses were said for the dead. These were endowed either by wealthy individuals or by guilds of merchants and craftsmen.

Since it was the house of people as well as the house of God, and because medieval art emphasized the unity of all knowledge, the cathedral was intended to be a mirror of the world. The carvings were naturalistic and detailed representations of beasts, Bible stories, and allegories of vices and virtues. The structure of society was represented in carvings of the hierarchies of both church and state, and portrayed ministers, knights, craftsmen, peasants, and tradesmen in various activities. In the windows of Chartres cathedral, no less than forty-three trades of the city are represented, while at Wells there is a vivid carving of a person with toothache!

Theology was reflected in the structure of the building; the upward striving towards God; the cross-shape; and the altar situated in the east, facing Jerusalem. Every detail of the creed – from the Trinity to creation, and from the passion of Christ to the Last Judgment – appeared in sculpture and stained glass. The harmony represented by such a structure signified the ideals of medieval art and thought.

Suger of St Denis kept an account of the work on his cathedral and when it was finished he described his reaction to it:

> I seemed to find myself, as it were, in some strange part of the universe which was neither wholly of the baseness of the earth, nor wholly of the serenity of heaven, but by the grace of God I seemed lifted in a mystic manner from this lower towards that upper sphere.

But the cathedral was not used solely for religious purposes; as the largest building in the town it was a natural meeting-place for social activity and even trade. At Chartres the transepts of the cathedral served as a kind of labour exchange, and the crypt beneath the church was always open for the shelter of pilgrims and the sick. The sounds of services often mingled with the greetings of friends and the haggling of traders. A market would be established in the area of the cathedral, plays were staged on its steps, strangers slept there, and townsfolk would meet in the side-aisles.

MIRROR OF CHRISTIAN SOCIETY

Medieval artistic expression was essentially different from modern art. Today there is no generally accepted coherent system of goals and values, and the language of art is largely personal. Medieval art expressed a coherent system of values and a view of the universe based on an understanding of Christianity. Its purpose was to point to the spiritual reality that underlay the material world, and medieval artists used symbolism and allegory to present their ideas.

Pictures, statues, architecture, poetry, hymns, legends, and the theatre were all used to teach those who could not read. The artists created a highly-developed system of symbols, whereby most things had a spiritual as well as a literal meaning. For example, fire represented martyrdom and/or religious fervour; a lily stood for chastity; an owl, the bird of darkness, often represented Satan; and a lamb stood for Christ, the sacrifice for sin.

EXPANSION SOUTH AND NORTH

The Crusades were only one of the ways in which Europeans responded to the non-Christian peoples who surrounded them. During the twelfth and thirteenth centuries the Muslims lost much of their territory in the Iberian peninsula, most of the pagan peoples in the remainder of Europe were Christianized, and Christian missionaries went on preaching tours which took them as far as East Asia.

In Spain, at the beginning of the eleventh century, Christian rule was confined to a narrow strip of states in the north, while the rest of the area was held by the Muslims.

With the collapse of the Caliphate of Cordova (1034), Islamic power there came to an end. The tide of the Christian reconquest ebbed and flowed, but by the middle of the thirteenth century Muslims controlled only the small state of Granada in the far south. In the reconquered territories, Muslims were treated in a similar way to Christians under Islamic control. They were free to practise their own religion and culture, but suffered from civil disabilities, including the payment of special tithes and taxes. Under these circumstances, Islam declined and many of its adherents migrated to Africa, while others became Christians. The Franciscans and Dominicans were especially successful in winning Muslims to the church.

SCANDINAVIA

Even before the flowering of medieval Christianity, attempts had been made to reach the Scandinavians for Christ. In Denmark, Norway, and Sweden conversion occurred as a community affair, following the royal lead, and resulted in greater control over the nobles by the kings. The impetus for missionary work in northern Europe came chiefly from England; the Viking conquests brought closer contact with the English, and the Scandinavians feared German political power. King Cnut (Canute) of Denmark (r. 1018–35), King Olaf I Tryggvason of Norway (r. 995–1000), and Olaf Skötkonung (r. 995–1021) of Sweden were responsible for introducing Christianity into their respective lands.

Although these peoples were officially Christianized by their rulers' actions, the church took several generations to instruct them in the faith and develop an organization. Monks and secular priests from abroad, the skalds (bards), and respected lay converts all helped spread the gospel. Diocesan boundaries usually paralleled political divisions, and by the close of the twelfth century each country had its own archbishop.

Christianity revolutionized the Scandinavians' way of life. Many resisted the new faith because marriage customs had to change, horsemeat (a Viking delicacy) could no longer be eaten, and church duties such as fasting, penance, and tithing were considered too burdensome. Despite pagan-inspired civil wars fought in opposition to both the monarchy and clergy, old customs gradually disappeared. The Viking fleets ceased to terrorize Europe, and more humane attitudes became characteristic of the descendants of the Norsemen.

INTO EASTERN EUROPE

Another area that challenged Christian missionary enthusiasm was eastern Europe. The Russians were converted through their contact with Constantinople and the Orthodox Church. The Poles, Hungarians, and Bohemians were won to Latin Christianity. As in Scandinavia, it was the action of rulers that gave the gospel its opportunity. Wenceslaus of Bohemia (Czech, Václav, r. 921–35), Bolesław I Chrobry of Poland (r. 992–1025), and Stephen I of Hungary (r. 1001–38), encouraged by the German Church, based their rule on Christianity. As a result, a band of states depending on Germany for their culture arose along her eastern frontier.

Many of the native people were oppressed farmers, who resented Christianity and the immigrant Germans who settled in the cities. These rural folk only gradually adopted Christianity, following decades of instruction, recruiting, and training of clergy, the development of dioceses and parishes, and the administration of the sacraments. By the early fourteenth century not only the Bohemians, Poles, and Hungarians but also the Wends (Slavs east of the River Elbe), Pomeranians, Lithuanians, Prussians, and Baltic peoples had adopted the Christian faith. The German-inspired push to the east might even have included the Russians, if the Teutonic knights, one of the agents of the conversion process, had not been defeated at the Battle of the Ice (or Battle of Lake Peipus, 1242) by the forces of the Republic of Novgorod.

MISSIONS TO THE EAST

By this time Russia had been invaded by the Mongols and was cut off from the West and the creative ferment of early modern Europe. However the vast Mongol Empire, which extended from China to the Caucasus and from the frozen north to the Himalayas, provided the opportunity for many Franciscan friars to spread Christianity. Two Franciscans, John of Planocarpini and William of Rubriquis, travelled to the court of the Mongol Khan in China in about 1250. Others followed them to the east, preaching in Persia and India, as well as China.

Their journeys met with such success that early in the fourteenth century a chain of Christian missions extended from Constantinople to Beijing, and it seemed at one time as if even the Mongol rulers might accept the Christian faith. This promising beginning did not lead to permanent results, however, since the western Mongols became Muslims and prevented the missionaries from travelling through their territories. Travel was made even more dangerous when the Mongol Empire broke up into many quarrelling states, while Western Europe itself lost its enthusiasm for mission during the fourteenth century as a result of wars, plague, and renewed arguments between secular and church power.

ROBERT G. CLOUSE

POPULAR RELIGION

In the Middle Ages, popular religion concentrated on the less abstract expressions of faith. Particularly popular were veneration of the saints, especially the Virgin Mary, emphasis on relics and their shrines, pilgrimages, and heroic efforts to recapture the Holy Land.

The ordinary Christian retained much of his or her pagan heritage, translated into Christian terms. The old spirit-shrines and pagan festivals became the new holy relics and holy days. Sophisticated theologians understood the absolute difference between the saints and the Trinity, but it is doubtful whether most lay people did. In the effort to achieve mass conversions during the Christianizing of Europe the church made ready use of festivals of pagan religion. It was easy to transfer the powerful character of pagan gods to Christian saints. Often pagan temples became Christian churches.

THE VIRGIN MARY

The growth of popular devotion in the twelfth century greatly advanced the role of the Virgin Mary. She became the 'universal mother', the great intercessor with her divine Son, almost his rival. The universal authority of the Virgin was heightened by the belief that she was taken up body and soul into heaven at the end of her earthly life. This belief made it impossible to confine her cult in time and space in the same way as that of other saints. The introduction from the East of the rosary, with its prayers to the Virgin, gave additional support to her cult in the West.

During the central Middle Ages emphasis was given to the humanity of Christ. The waves of devotion and emotion which swept Europe from the twelfth century onwards were fed by an increased interest in the life and death of the human Jesus. In this drama his mother became the central figure; the story of mother and son had great human appeal. Mary's appeal was as the beloved mother and protectress of all men. No sin was too dreadful, no transgression too vile, to escape her compassionate pleading with her son on behalf of the sinner.

Peasants, knights, and kings begged her help, and she became a romantic obsession. With the rise of the tradition of chivalry, the Virgin Mary became the focus of a romantic cult that it is difficult for the modern mind to appreciate. The great Gothic cathedrals cannot be fully understood until it is recalled that they were built partly as trophies for a beautiful woman, forever young, forever kind.

RELICS

With the growth of popular devotion, the traffic in holy relics swelled. The desire to own a memento of a revered and powerful religious figure was universal. Every new church building needed a relic for its altar, and the official church kept a vast stock of them. Merchants carried splinters of the true cross to protect them from thieves. Knights concealed saints' teeth, bones, or hair in their sword-hilts, while peasants bought drops of the Saviour's bloody sweat and the Virgin's milk at local fairs. Cities cherished – and stole from one another – the bodies of famous saints. Martin Luther's patron, Frederick the Wise of Saxony, possessed a huge and valuable collection of relics. The Reformation saw the destruction of millions of such relics.

PILGRIMAGE

Closely related to the adoration of relics and the cult of the saints was the passion for pilgrimage. The impulse to travel was fed partly by a belief that a visit to a great shrine could bring physical and spiritual healing. But there was also a new and restless desire to explore the mystical holy places and to experience the sights and smells of foreign places.

Pilgrimages to the Holy Land were hard and dangerous, and consequently restricted to the very devout and those obliged to do particularly serious penances. The most popular Western shrines

PILGRIM ROUTES OF MEDIEVAL EUROPE

Pilgrim centre
Main route of pilgrimage

0   500   1000 km
0   200   400   600 miles

St Andrews
Cologne Hamburg Lübeck
Canterbury Corvey
Chartres
Trier Fulda Prague
Mont St Michel Paris
Tours Augsburg
Vézelay
Santiago de Compostela Einsiedeln
Clermont Venice
Ostabat Arles Turin Padua
Zaragoza Marseilles Lucca
Barcelona Rome Mt Gargano Constantinople Chalcedon
Bari Thessalonica
Ephesus
Patmos
Jerusalem
Mt Sinai

ATLANTIC OCEAN

SICILY
CYPRUS
CRETE
MEDITERRANEAN SEA

When in April the sweet showers fall
And pierce the drought of March to the root,
and all ...
Then people long to go on pilgrimages
And palmers long to see the stranger strands
Of far-off saints, hallowed in sundry lands,
And specially, from every shire's end
In England, down to Canterbury they wend
To seek the holy blissful martyr, quick
To give his help to them when they were sick....

CHAUCER, *THE CANTERBURY TALES*

included Rome, Canterbury (Thomas Becket), and St James (Santiago) of Compostela in north-west Spain. Most pilgrimage routes were carefully arranged, with hostels spaced along the way, and a pilgrimage could be a light-hearted affair (witness Chaucer's *Canterbury Tales*). Like modern tourists, pilgrims tended to travel in groups, gossiping, singing, and stopping at minor shrines along the way. The pilgrimage gave the faithful a combination of religious duty and holiday relaxation.

CAROLINE T. MARSHALL

CHAPTER 19

MONASTICISM IN THE WEST

In the centuries after 600, the monastic rule established by Benedict was gradually accepted throughout western Europe. In the earlier centuries, however, it always existed alongside other types of monastic life. The most important of these was Celtic monasticism, which, from its centres in Ireland, sent out missions to Britain and Europe. Irish monasticism was distinguished by an ascetic rigour, a high level of cultural attainment and, in organization, by the very subordinate position of the bishop. The great Irish missionary figures were Columba in Scotland and Columbanus (540–615), whose missionary work took place in the Rhineland and the Alps. Columbanus founded the abbeys of Luxeuil in Gaul (c. 590) and Bobbio in north Italy (612), both cultural centres of great importance, and was responsible for the introduction of much Celtic influence into continental monasticism.

ENGLISH MISSIONS TO EUROPE

However, it was monasticism based on the Benedictine rule that was to become the normal and, indeed, official form. In 600 this rule was simply one of many. The monasteries of Gaul, for example, were influenced by Eastern, Celtic, and Italian models. By the reign of Charlemagne (768–814), however, the Benedictine rule was universal within his domains. The rule had been taken to England by Wilfrid (634–709) and ultimately replaced the earlier influence of Celtic monasticism.

From England missionary monks such as Boniface (Wynfrith) evangelized the pagan Germans, using the Benedictine monastery as the base for his work. The abbey of Fulda, founded under Boniface's influence in 744, became a great cultural and religious centre in the following centuries. Later missionary work among the Slavs and Scandinavians made use of the monastery as a centre in a similar way.

MONASTIC MANUSCRIPTS

The form of Benedictine monasticism widespread in Europe by the eighth century showed many differences from its early days. Increasingly monks were drawn from the nobility. It was common practice for nobles to 'devote' their sons and daughters to a monastery while still children. As a result of such changes, the monks' share of manual work had been gradually reduced and replaced by liturgical and cultural activities. This concentration on scholarly and artistic work made the great monasteries of the eighth to the tenth centuries – such as Reichenau, St Gallen and Corbie – the cultural and educational centres of Europe. They possessed large libraries and their monks copied the manuscripts which were to transmit ancient literature and learning to later centuries. In fact, the great majority of ancient Latin prose and poetry comes down to us only via early medieval monastic manuscripts. The monks' creative achievements were in the development of script and the illumination of manuscripts. In Ireland and Britain these beautiful works are best represented by the *Book of Kells* and the *Lindisfarne Gospels* respectively.

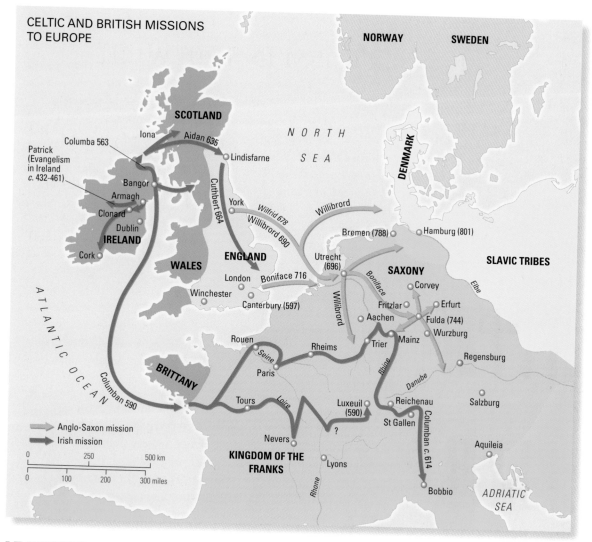

CELTIC AND BRITISH MISSIONS
TO EUROPE

NORWAY   SWEDEN

SCOTLAND

Columba 563   Iona   Aidan 635   N O R T H

Patrick   S E A   DENMARK
(Evangelism
in Ireland   Lindisfarne
c. 432-461)
          Bangor   Cuthbert 664
        Armagh   York   Wilfrid 678   Willibrord
      Clonard   Willibrord 690   Bremen (788)   Hamburg (801)
        Dublin
      IRELAND   Utrecht   SLAVIC TRIBES
                                                             (696)   SAXONY
  Cork   WALES   ENGLAND   Corvey   Elbe
                           London   Boniface 716   Boniface   Fritzlar   Erfurt
              Winchester   Aachen   Fulda (744)
                          Canterbury (597)   Willibrord   Mainz   Wurzburg
                                                                              Trier   Regensburg
A T L A N T I C   Rouen   Rheims   Rhine
                  Seine   Danube
          BRITTANY   Paris   Reichenau   Salzburg
O C E A N   Luxeuil   St Gallen
        Columban 590   Tours   Loire   (590)   Columban c. 614
                                                  ?   Aquileia
                          Nevers   Bobbio
  ──▷ Anglo-Saxon mission   ADRIATIC
  ──▶ Irish mission   KINGDOM OF THE   Lyons   SEA
                                         FRANKS
  0   250   500 km   Rhone
  0   100   200   300 miles

LINKS WITH SOCIETY

Between the sixth and eighth centuries, too, the monasteries became far more closely
linked with the society within which they existed. Their abbots and monks were related
to local noble families; lands were granted to them by kings and magnates; they achieved
both economic and political importance. Instead of a group of individuals fleeing from
the world to live a life of perfection, the monastic community was becoming a religious
corporation which served a definite function in society. Its duty consisted of maintaining
a continual sequence of praise and prayer. In a sense, the monks prayed on behalf of the
rest of humankind. In the never-ending battle with the forces of evil, the monks undertook
penance and intercession for others, and thereby increased their chances of salvation. They
were seen as spiritual counterparts of the feudal knights.

This close connection with society aroused some criticism. Much of the history of
monasticism from the ninth century onwards revolves around repeated attempts at reform, with

varying goals. Already in 817 Benedict of Aniane had attempted to reform the monasteries in the direction of greater severity, more manual labour, and less study, greater central control, and a curtailment of the outside activities of monks. This attempt was stillborn and, in the next century and a half, the monasteries fared badly. Renewed barbarian attacks from Vikings, Saracens, and Magyars destroyed many of the great abbeys and dispersed the monks and their cultural treasures. By 950 the destruction or decay of many monasteries, and the confusion caused by their relative independence, led to a determined attempt at reform.

CLUNY RESTORES DIGNITY

The tenth-century reform is closely associated with the abbey of Cluny in central France, founded about 909. Cluny's long-ruling abbots (Odo, 927–42; Odilo, 994–1049; Hugh the Great, 1049–1109), spiritual and political figures of European importance, led the movement. The 'Cluniac' reform had both a religious and an organizational aspect. The religious task of the monks was seen as, above all, the performance of the daily cycle of worship. In Cluny this was carried to its extreme: almost the whole of the monks' day was taken up with church services. The Cluniac churches were highly decorated and adorned to create a service as magnificent and solemn as possible. The widespread admiration that Cluny inspired shows this aim was generally respected, in both church and lay society.

The institutional reforms made by Cluny led to the creation, by the eleventh century, of a complex and strongly centralized organization. Earlier monasteries had been quite independent, linked only by shared emphases, such as the form of their observance, or by

Pope Urban II (r. 1088–99) consecrates the new church of the Abbey of Cluny, France.

SONIA HALLIDAY PHOTOGRAPHS

A CHRISTIAN SOCIETY

A contented monk

Our food is scanty, our garments rough; our drink is from the stream and our sleep often upon our book. Under our tired limbs there is but a hard mat; when sleep is sweetest we must rise at a bell's bidding … Self-will has no scope; there is no moment for idleness or dissipation … Everywhere peace, everywhere serenity, and a marvellous freedom from the tumult of the world. Such unity and concord is there among the brethren, that each thing seems to belong to all, and all to each … To put all in brief, no perfection expressed in the words of the gospel or of the apostles, or in the writings of the Fathers, or in the sayings of the monks of old, is lacking to our order and our way of life.

AILRED, *SPECULUM CARITATIS*, 1.17

historical association, such as that between a founding abbey and its 'daughter' houses. The abbots of Cluny, especially Odilo, created a large chain of dependent houses. Instead of an abbot, these houses had a prior appointed by the abbot of Cluny. The obedience of a monk to his abbot, a central feature of Benedict's rule, was extended to all the monks of the dependent houses, who were regarded as 'monks of Cluny' too.

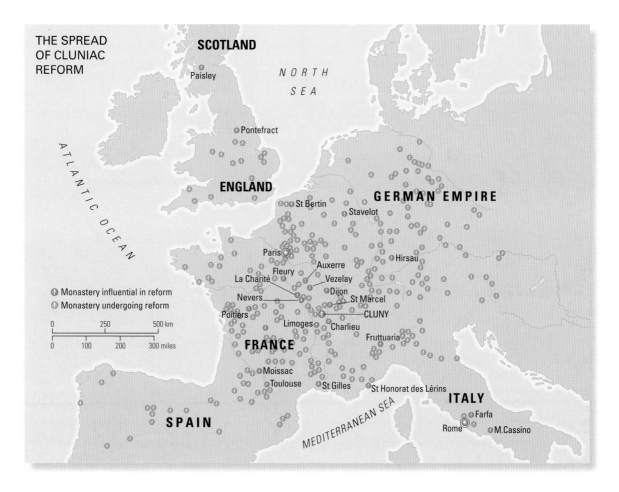

THE SPREAD OF CLUNIAC REFORM

⊕ Monastery influential in reform
⊕ Monastery undergoing reform

One of the advantages of being a Cluniac monk was that Cluniac monasteries were independent both of the local bishop and the local lay nobility, since Cluny had been founded in direct dependence on the pope. This became important during the eleventh century, as the popes sought to free the church from the control of secular powers. The Cluniacs tended to support this movement.

Cluny's influence was also through example. The tenth-century monastic reform movement in England, led by Archbishop Dunstan (909–88) and assisted by King Edgar (959–75), was indirectly influenced by Cluny via the monastery of Fleury. More than fifty monasteries were established or re-established in England after the ravages of the Viking invasions. These rich and cultured foundations formed the nucleus of future English monasticism. Cluniac houses were directly introduced into England after the Norman Conquest of 1066.

MONASTIC RENEWAL

Other movements of monastic renewal were taking place in the tenth century. In Lorraine and western Germany, the influence of the abbey of Gorze was similar to that of Cluny, although the Gorze reformers were less rigorous about excluding lay authority. In Italy the hermit form of monasticism was renewed, whereby monks lived together inside an enclosure, and might meet for common meals and services, but otherwise lived solitary lives. This was an attempt to return to the type of organization of the first monastics in the deserts of Egypt. The eleventh century foundation of Camaldoli by Romuald, and of Vallombrosa by John Gualbert both aimed at solitariness and severity.

The activities of the monastic reformers of the tenth century and their alliance with the new expansionist papacy of the eleventh century made these the classic centuries of Benedictine monasticism. But already a new wave of reform was imminent. The wealth of the Cluniac monasteries, their easy relations with the world at large and their emphasis on the church service led some reformers to seek a more austere and primitive path.

A discontented monk

Everything here and in my nature are opposed to each other. I cannot endure the daily tasks. The sight of it all revolts me. I am tormented and crushed down by the length of the vigils, I often succumb to the manual labour. The food cleaves to my mouth, more bitter than wormwood. The rough clothing cuts through my skin and flesh down to my very bones. More than this, my will is always hankering after other things, it longs for the delights of the world, and sighs unceasingly for its loves and affections and pleasures.

WALTER DANIEL'S *LIFE OF AILRED*

Some, for example, Bruno of Cologne, who founded La Grande Chartreuse in southern France in 1084, turned to the hermit type of monastery. The Carthusian order, which arose from this, remained one of the most rigorous throughout the Middle Ages. Their proud claim was that they were never reformed because their original ideals were never lost. The alleged laxity of some of the great Cluniac houses led to the foundation of several strict Benedictine orders around 1100: those of Grandmont, Fontevrault (a distinctive 'double order' of monks and nuns), and Savigny.

THE CISTERCIANS

But the most important and successful of the orders seeking to revive the primitive Benedictine life was that of the Cistercians or 'White Monks'. Their mother house was Cîteaux in Burgundy, founded in 1098 by Robert of Molesme, with Stephen Harding and other reforming monks. While Englishman Stephen Harding (d. 1134) was abbot, Cistercian houses spread throughout western Europe. They aimed at a complete break with the Cluniac past. Their churches and services were to be simple and unadorned, and their abbeys were founded in remote and desolate regions, again recalling the ideal

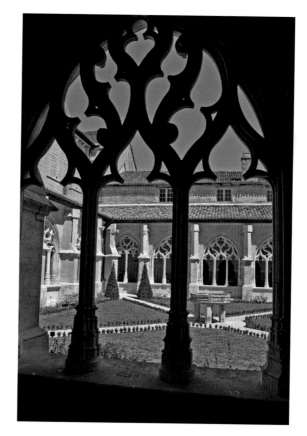

The cloister – which became a synonym for the monastic life – formed a barrier between the enclosed world of the monks and the outside world of the others who served in a monastic cathedral or church. Cadouin Abbey, in the Dordogne, France, which boasts a fine gothic cloister, was founded in 1115, and taken over by the Cistercian order shortly afterwards. It became a pilgrimage centre due to its possession of a cloth alleged to be part of Christ's shroud.
TIM DOWLEY ASSOCIATES

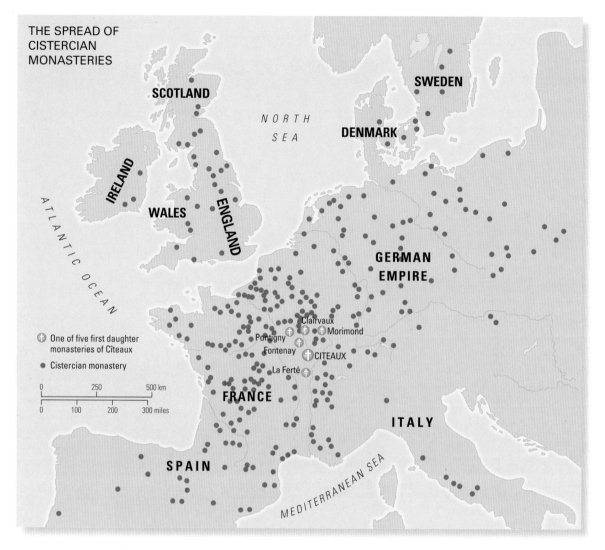

THE SPREAD OF
CISTERCIAN
MONASTERIES

SCOTLAND

SWEDEN

NORTH
SEA

DENMARK

IRELAND

WALES   ENGLAND

ATLANTIC OCEAN

GERMAN
EMPIRE

Clairvaux
Morimond
Pontigny
Fontenay   CÎTEAUX
La Ferté

✠ One of five first daughter
   monasteries of Cîteaux

● Cistercian monastery

FRANCE

ITALY

SPAIN

MEDITERRANEAN SEA

0   250   500 km

0   100   200   300 miles

of the earlier Christian monastics, who fled to the 'wilderness'. Silence and austerity were stressed, and a renewed emphasis was placed on manual work. The constitution of the order was set out in the *Carta Caritatis* of 1119. Each house had to be visited annually by the abbot of its mother house, while every year a general assembly (chapter) of all the abbots was to be held at Cîteaux, to lay down ordinances for the whole order. The severity and organization of the Cistercians proved remarkably successful, and by 1300 more than 600 monasteries and nunneries were in existence.

The Cistercians soon came under attack, however, on unexpected grounds. As their houses had to be founded in remote wastes, because of their flight from the world, they were gradually forced to develop techniques of survival in such regions. They learned how to turn these wastes into productive agricultural land, and in due course their economic activities, especially sheep-farming, made them a wealthy order. The monks withdrew from manual work, leaving this to the 'lay brothers', normally illiterate folk who joined the order but were not offered full membership, and lived in separate buildings on monastic lands. As a result of the wealth derived from their wide estates and the labour of the lay brothers (known as the *conversi*), the Cistercians were soon accused of the sin of greed. Spoiled by worldly success, their initial aim of austerity was ironically reversed.

YET MORE ORDERS

Before this stage was reached, however, the Cistercian ideal was generally admired, and had been imitated by other strict orders. The Premonstratensians, founded by Norbert of Xanten (c. 1080–1134) in northern France around 1120, and the Gilbertines, founded by Gilbert of Sempringham (c. 1083–1190) in Lincolnshire were deeply influenced by the Cistercian ideal. The Gilbertines, a double order of monks and nuns, was the only new order established by an English person within England in the monastic movement of the later medieval period. These two orders took

Page from the fifteenth-century Latin 'Book of Hours for Parisians' showing the various monastic orders; from the Bibliothèque Nationale de France, Paris.
SONIA HALLIDAY PHOTOGRAPHS

as their rule not that of Benedict, but the more flexible Augustinian rule which, although based on advice given by Augustine, only came into practical use in the eleventh century. They were canons – clergy living in community – rather than monks. The adaptability of their rule meant that the Augustinian canons included not only more cloistered orders, such as the Premonstratensian and Gilbertine, but also many houses where canons took up teaching or hospital work in the towns. The founding of a house of Augustinian canons was generally less expensive than a Benedictine abbey, and so benefactors found a new outlet in endowing such houses rather than Benedictine abbeys – by this time largely declining in public favour.

The military orders were also influenced by monastic ideals. These orders consisted of monk-knights, who originally intended to fight in the Holy Land, and were a logical extension of monastic involvement in the Crusades. The chief crusading orders adopted forms of the Cistercian regulations. The Knights Templar (founded about 1118, and suppressed in the early fourteenth century), the Hospitallers (late eleventh century), and the Teutonic Knights (late twelfth century) came to wield great political and economic power for several centuries.

MONASTICISM IN DECLINE

By 1200, however, monasticism had passed the peak of its appeal and influence. The initiative was now taken by the new begging orders of friars, especially the Dominicans and Franciscans, and by the universities. Although new monasteries were founded, the total number of monks began to decline, and standards of monastic life fell as strictness was relaxed. Ingenious means were sometimes found to keep to the letter of monastic constitutions, while deviating greatly from the spirit of those early rules. Community life was gradually modified, and divisions appeared within abbeys between the abbot, the monastic officials, and the monks. Increasingly, abbots and priors came to live and eat apart from the monks. Religious houses became more and more involved in the running of their estates and in legal squabbles. Many monks spent much of their time in supervising estates, collecting revenues, and battling for property rights. In Europe the 'commendatory' system brought in lay people to take over the income and administration of monasteries. Everywhere the system of allowing 'corrodies' – virtually supporting lay people out of monastic income in exchange for a lay grant – took the monk farther and farther from the life of prayer and into the world.

Nevertheless, attempts at reform continued throughout the later centuries of the Middle Ages. Some were initiated by popes, such as Innocent III in 1215, or Benedict XII in 1336. Others took the familiar form of a return to strict observance of the Benedictine rule. The Sylvestrines (1231), Celestinians (later thirteenth century), and Olivetans (1319) adopted this approach. The general attempt at church reform in the fifteenth century, associated with the great Councils, also saw further attempts at monastic reform. In the German lands the monasteries of Kastl, Melk, and Bursfeld were centres of reform, while St Justina in Padua provided an example for Italy and Spain. Other new movements include the Brethren of the Common Life, the Brigittines, a Swedish order of the fourteenth century, and the Minims, a fifteenth-century order which combined aspects of monasticism with the Franciscan rule.

The overall picture of late medieval monasticism, however, is one in which the monks have become an established and integrated part of society, but are no longer respected and attractive as their predecessors had been before 1200. It is significant that many monastic-type movements in the last two medieval centuries were based rather upon lay participation, and were in effect a result of lay devotion. Growing criticism of monastic abuses, and even of the very principle of monasticism itself, foreshadowed the great attack the institution was to experience in the Protestant Reformation.

RONALD FINUCANE

INTERPRETING THE BIBLE IN THE MIDDLE AGES

The fall of the Roman Empire led to widespread illiteracy and ignorance. For centuries, in the absence of public education, all learning and study of the Scriptures was restricted to the monasteries. Medieval theologians held that Scripture could be interpreted only by the learned few, under the direction of the church.

The medieval church believed it should uphold the traditions and dogmas of the early Christian writers, so, in general, biblical scholars were content to collect and synthesize the traditional explanations of theologians as far back as Origen. One scholar of the period wrote: 'It is better not to be taken up with supposedly new ideas, but to be filled from the fountain of the ancients.' As a result medieval scholars produced massive volumes of dogma and morality which claim to explain Scripture, but which in reality have little connection with the biblical text.

Following the methods of many early Greek and Latin Christian writers, medieval interpreters for nearly a thousand years used a fourfold scheme of biblical interpretations: 'The literal teaches the events, allegory what you are to believe, the moral sense what you are to do, the anagogical (spiritual) where you are to aim.' The literal, historical sense of the biblical text was smothered by a swarm of mystical interpretations. Thus, for example, the word 'water' in Scripture was often interpreted in the following fourfold way: literally, water, the physical element; allegorically, baptism, the nations, or grace; morally, sorrow, wisdom, heresy, or prosperity; spiritually, eternal happiness. An unbridled imagination was a prime requisite for interpreting Scripture!

OBSCURE

Never has biblical interpretation been made so obscure as during the early Middle Ages. Few interpreters paid attention to the historical and literal sense of the biblical text; still fewer had more than an elementary knowledge of Hebrew and Greek. For about four hundred years priests and monks tediously compiled early Christian writings, characterized by rigid dogmatic sentences, moral platitudes, mystical play on numbers, and false word-meanings.

Bede, the Anglo-Saxon historian and theologian, devoted his entire life to the study of Scripture in a monastery. Following Philo and Origen, he tried to extract the spiritual kernel of truth from the Bible, using an allegorical interpretation. Bede's comments on Scripture are little more than a patchwork fashioned from Ambrose, Jerome, Augustine, and Gregory. Alcuin and Walafrid Strabo (808–49) similarly produced highly allegorical commentaries on Scripture, compiled largely from excerpts from earlier writers. Johannes Scotus Eriugena (c. 815–c. 877) summed up the medieval attitude towards the Word of God: 'The sense of God's work is infinitely varied, and like a peacock's feather glows with many colours.'

SCHOLASTIC INTERPRETATION

Scholastic theologians continued to bypass the biblical languages of Greek and Hebrew and perpetuated the multi-sense interpretation of the Bible, while striving to reinforce the traditions of the church. Peter Lombard, a pupil of Abelard, and later bishop of Paris, produced a theological textbook of scholasticism entitled *The Sentences* (1158). This well-organized one-volume system of medieval dogma was primarily a collection of the opinions of previous writers – for example, Hilary, Ambrose, and Augustine. Lombard's numerous commentaries on Scripture were similarly an unimaginative collection of the moral and spiritual opinions of earlier writers.

MYSTICAL INTERPRETATION

Reacting to the sterile formalism and traditionalism of the scholastics, there arose mystical interpreters and theologians, who stressed the devotional study of the Bible aided by the free use of allegory. They replaced dialectical reasoning with ecstasy and intuition as the accepted yardstick for interpreting.

Bernard of Clairvaux, regarded as the father of medieval mysticism, wrote 86 sermons on the Song of Solomon, which are characterized not by the logical subtleties of scholasticism, but by highly esoteric mystical explanations.

Hugh of St Victor (c. 1096–1141), head of a theological academy at the monastery of St Victor, Paris (the principal centre of medieval mysticism), while allowing certain mystical meanings, emphasized the literal sense of Scripture. But Hugh adhered to the dogmatism of his time by affirming that the scholar first decides what he ought to believe and then goes to Scripture to confirm his judgment. The Franciscan mystic Bonaventura (1221–74) was influenced by the scholasticism of his day. The book of seven seals in Revelation allows the sevenfold sense of Scripture: the historical, anagogical, allegorical, tropological, symbolical, synechdochical, and hyperbolical. Only a learned monk could fathom the depths of wisdom contained in such a book!

Thomas Aquinas, the master of scholastic theology, has a much less distinguished reputation as an interpreter of Scripture. His *catena* (a stringing together of observations from the ancient authorities) on the Gospels quotes no less than twenty-two Greek and twenty Latin writers. Furthermore, Thomas allegorizes even the most simple texts. For example, he interprets Genesis 1:3, 'Let there be light', thus: historically, it refers to the act of creation; allegorically, 'let Christ be love'; morally, 'may we be mentally illuminated by Christ'; anagogically, 'may we be led to glory by Christ'.

THE SIMPLE SENSE

Meanwhile the plain sense of the Bible was being revived by certain Jewish commentators. Writing on the Pentateuch, Rashi (Rabbi Shlomo Yitzhaki, from Troyes, Frances, 1040–1105) concentrates on 'the simple sense of the Bible'. His Old Testament commentaries devote unusual attention to philology, grammar, and sentence construction. The Spanish scholar, Abraham ibn Ezra (1089–1167), wrote commentaries on most of the Old Testament, and strengthened the Jewish shift towards a modern historical and grammatical interpretation. He identified five traditional methods of biblical interpretation, but preferred the plain approach, which explains the meaning intended by the biblical writer.

Nicholas of Lyra (c. 1270–1349), a Franciscan at the University of Paris, was primarily responsible for bringing the approach of Rashi and his followers to Christian scholarship. Lyra wrote about 85 volumes covering the whole of the Bible. A master of Old Testament Hebrew, he prepared the first Bible commentary to be printed. It was published in Rome in 1471–2 and was widely consulted. While repeating the common medieval definition of the fourfold sense of Scripture, Lyra claimed that the plain sense of the text had priority: 'I intend to insist upon the literal sense and sometimes to insert brief mystical expositions, though rarely.' Lyra's contribution towards a responsible method of interpretation, and the dissolution of the iron grip of church tradition, led to the proverb, 'Had Lyra not played his lyre, Luther would not have danced.' The Reformer did in reality lean heavily upon the biblical interpretation of the French scholar.

The early English reformer Wyclif claimed that 'the whole error in the knowledge of Scripture, and the source of its debasement and falsification by incompetent persons, was the ignorance of grammar and logic'. For such reasons the Bible lay buried and obscured for centuries. With the Renaissance revival of the study of the languages and literature of Greece and Rome, scholasticism finally toppled.

BRUCE A. DEMAREST

CHAPTER 20

THE ORTHODOX CHURCH
in Eastern Europe and Russia

About the year 860, Rastislav, Prince of Moravia, requested the Byzantine Emperor Michael III to send missionaries to instruct his people in the ways of Christ. The Moravians, ancestors of the modern Czechs, belonged to the Slavic race, which had come from Asia and spread throughout the eastern plains of Europe. In response, Patriarch Photius provided two Greek brothers who were to be among the most influential of Christian missionaries.

MISSION TO MORAVIA

The two brothers, Cyril and Methodius, had grown up near Slavs who had settled in Macedonia and therefore they knew the Slavic language. Before embarking upon their mission, the evangelists began to prepare an alphabet for the hitherto unwritten language, so that the converts could have the Scriptures and liturgy in their native tongue. This script, known as Glagolitic, was the forerunner of the form of writing now used in southeastern Europe and Russia, which is called Cyrillic, after the younger brother. By this means, Orthodox Christianity, and with it the culture of Byzantium, spread among the Slavic tribes.

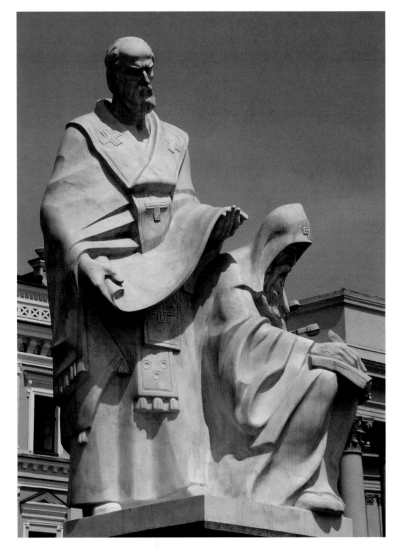

Statue in Kiev, Ukraine, of the Byzantine Greek brothers Cyril and Methodius, who became pioneering Christian missionaries among the Slavic peoples in the ninth century.

© TUPUNGATO/DREAMSTIME.COM

THE SLAVIC BIBLE

In 862, Prince Rastislav (or Rostislav) of Great Moravia requested the Emperor Michael III and the Patriarch Photius to send missionaries from Constantinople to translate the Bible into the Slavic language. Two brothers from Thessalonica, Cyril (born Constantine, 827–69) – who had theological training and knew both Arabic and Latin – and Methodius (815–85), were chosen for this mission. The brothers devised the 'Glagolitic' alphabet for the Slavic language – not previously reduced to written form – and also created a new vocabulary to convey concepts specific to the Christian faith. They then translated into 'Old Church Slavonic' the New Testament, the Psalms, and parts of the Old Testament, together with some of the church's liturgy. Although Rome generally objected to worship in any language other than Latin, the brothers were granted permission to use Slavic in the Moravian church's liturgy.

After the death of Methodius, his followers were exiled from Moravia and found refuge in Bulgaria, which had accepted Christianity in 865. Until this time, worship there was conducted only in Greek, but the Slavic translation of Cyril and Methodius was now accepted, and under czar Simeon I ('the Great', r. 893–927), Slavic literacy and liturgy blossomed. Use of the Glagolitic alphabet soon declined in favour of the new and simpler 'Cyrillic' alphabet, modelled on the uncials of the Greek alphabet. By the end of the tenth century, Bibles and liturgical books were being exported from Bulgaria as far as Kiev in the east and Serbia in the west.

This Byzantine culture determined the main lines of development for these peoples, especially the Russians, for centuries. Thus Cyril and Methodius rightly earned the title of 'The Apostles of the Slavs'.

The Moravian mission of Cyril and Methodius met with success in its first three years, but any long-term results were lost when the invading Magyars destroyed the state of Moravia. The church of this area eventually developed along Western Catholic lines. The brothers' work did not disappear, however, because their followers carried their message and Slavonic books southward to the Bulgarians, who became fervently attached to Byzantine Orthodoxy.

BULGARIAN ORTHODOXY

The Bulgarian czar Boris, who accepted Christianity for his people, prevailed upon the Emperor and Patriarch of Constantinople to recognize, in 870, the Bulgarians' right to have an independent church organization, under the Ecumenical Patriarch. The Bulgarians also won approval for their liturgy to be conducted in the Slavonic language. In this way a distinctive form of Orthodoxy was established in Eastern Europe, with state churches employing local languages. In 927, the chief bishop of the Bulgarian Church was raised to the rank of patriarch.

From Bulgaria, the Old Church Slavonic liturgical language and Byzantine Christianity were transplanted to Serbia, the third Slavic nation to be Christianized in the second half of the ninth century. The Serbian Church remained in the shadow of the Bulgarians until the time of the most celebrated Serbian Christian, Sava (1174–1236), who in 1219 was consecrated Archbishop of Serbia. The Serbian archbishopric was promoted to a

ORTHODOX MISSIONS 860–1050

patriarchate in 1346, at the height of the Serbian Empire under King Stefan Dushan. Bulgarian influence also drew the Church of Romania into the Orthodox fold.

VLADIMIR'S CHOICE

The most illustrious fruit of the brothers' Slavonic influence appeared when the pagan prince of Kiev, Vladimir, officially adopted Orthodoxy as the religion of his state. The magnificent legend of the conversion of the Russians narrates how Vladimir, around 988, decided that the interests of his realm required that he take up one of the major religions. According to the *Russian Chronicle*, Vladimir sent envoys to investigate Islam, Judaism, Latin, and Byzantine Christianity. The first three failed to suit, but he was won over by the report of those who returned from Constantinople, declaring that when they attended the mass in the great Church of St Sophia they could not tell whether they were on earth or in heaven. Vladimir ordered the mass baptism of the Russians according to the Orthodox form, and Orthodoxy became the state religion of Russia.

Although the details of the legend probably do not record actual history, they do reflect one of the most significant features of Russian Christianity. The forms of worship have always been more important than other aspects, such as theology or ethics. The primary

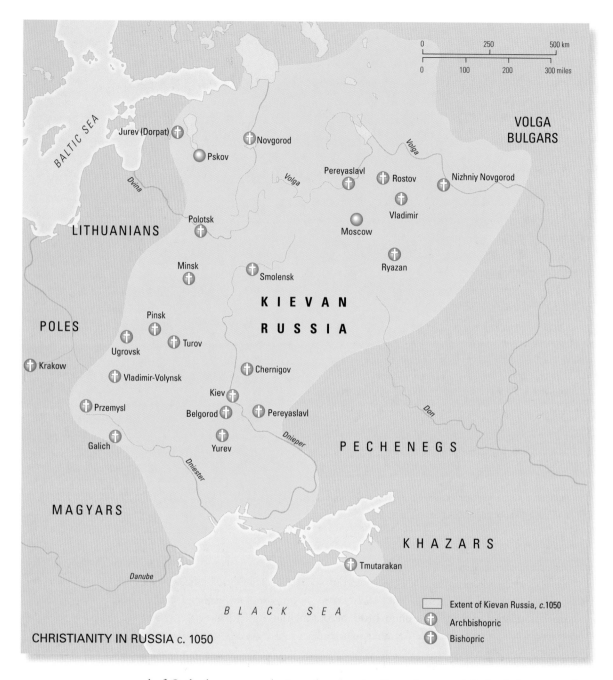

CHRISTIANITY IN RUSSIA c. 1050

Map labels:
Baltic Sea
Jurev (Dorpat)
Pskov
Novgorod
Volga
VOLGA BULGARS
Pereyaslavl
Rostov
Nizhniy Novgorod
Vladimir
Dvina
Volga
LITHUANIANS
Polotsk
Moscow
Minsk
Smolensk
KIEVAN RUSSIA
Ryazan
Pinsk
POLES
Turov
Ugrovsk
Krakow
Chernigov
Vladimir-Volynsk
Kiev
Don
Przemysl
Belgorod
Pereyaslavl
Galich
Yurev
Dnieper
PECHENEGS
Dniester
MAGYARS
Danube
KHAZARS
Tmutarakan
BLACK SEA

Extent of Kievan Russia, c.1050
Archbishopric
Bishopric

appeal of Orthodoxy was aesthetic, rather than intellectual or moral. Indeed, the name of the religion in Slavonic, *Pravoslavie*, means 'true worship', reflecting the pre-eminence of the liturgy to the Russian mind.

After Vladimir's conversion, the Slavonic books of Cyril and Methodius were brought to Kiev, so that the Russians received a benefit which Christians of the Latin-using Western Church did not enjoy. Their religious liturgy and writings existed in a language that was intelligible to all of them. Thus the church both civilized the Russian tribes and stimulated the growth of their native culture.

Vladimir's son and successor, Yaroslav I, the Wise, (r. 1019–54), cemented the bonds between the Russian Church and Byzantine Orthodoxy by accepting for his realm a bishop appointed by the Ecumenical Patriarch. In this way he acknowledged Constantinople as the overseer of the Russian Church. Yaroslav provided the bishop, consecrated as the Metropolitan of Kiev, with a cathedral which he dedicated as St Sophia's, in imitation of the mother church in Constantinople. For most of the next four hundred years, the head of the Russian Church was a Greek appointed by the Patriarch of Constantinople.

Yaroslav's death coincided with the year traditionally regarded as marking the final rupture between the Latin and Greek Churches (1054). The newly-converted Russians quickly learned to despise the Catholics as 'heretics'. Their hatred of the Latin Christians was greatly reinforced when German knights tried to take advantage of the chaos caused by the invasion of Russia by Genghis Khan's Mongol hordes in the thirteenth century and launched a Catholic crusade against the northern Russians. The Western invaders were repulsed by the heroic leadership of Alexander Nevsky in 1242. He was later recognized as a saint for his achievements.

Nevsky established an important precedent for the Russians by submitting voluntarily to the rule of the Khan. For over two hundred years the Russians lived under the 'Mongol Yoke'. During this period, the Russian Church continued to be led by the Metropolitan of Kiev and Vladimir, who was usually appointed and consecrated by Constantinople, but approved by the Khan. This situation goes a long way towards explaining why Russia never experienced a Renaissance and Reformation as Western Europe did.

THE RUSSIAN TRADITION

The period under the Mongol yoke included the life of one of the greatest of Russian Christians, Sergius of Radonezh (c. 1314–92). In search of solitude, Sergius withdrew around 1350 into the forest about twenty-five miles north of Moscow where he soon became the elder of the monastic community of the Holy Trinity, which is now the headquarters of the Russian Orthodox Church (*Zagorsk*). From the monastic tradition begun by Sergius, Russian spirituality began to penetrate in an unprecedented manner to the lower levels of Russian society.

Sergius' monastery inspired the emergence of the Russian artistic genius expressed in the creation of magnificent icons. The greatest icon painters, Andrei Rublev and Daniel Chornei, flourished in the years around 1400, decorating the churches in Sergius' Holy Trinity monastery, and in Moscow and the surrounding principalities. In their works distinctively Russian art forms appeared.

Sergius influenced Russian society in a third important way, by kindling the spirit of Russian national resistance to Mongol overlordship. In 1380 he inspired Dmitry, Prince of Moscow, to lead a Russian allied army against the Khan's forces. Dmitry's troops won a significant battle on Kulikovo Field. Although the Mongol yoke was not immediately cast off, the Prince of Moscow had demonstrated that the Mongols were not invincible, and the hope of final liberation smouldered in the Russian breast. It was amidst these events that Moscow rose to the leading position among Russian cities, its prestige heightened by Dmitry's achievements, Sergius' reputation, and the transfer of the Russian Metropolitan to the city.

THIRD ROME

By the second half of the fifteenth century, conditions were right for Moscow to emerge as the world's leading Orthodox city. Late in the fourteenth century, the Ottoman Turks occupied Bulgaria and Serbia, placing these Orthodox states under Islamic authority. In 1453, they captured Constantinople itself, killing the Byzantine Emperor and making the Ecumenical Patriarch a virtual prisoner of the Muslim conquerors. Shortly after, Ivan III of Moscow married Sophia Palaiologina, niece of the last emperor, and subsequently repudiated Mongol domination. Ivan adopted the Byzantine double-headed eagle as the symbol of his power.

Russian Church theorists saw profound theological significance in these events. Moscow, they declared, had become 'The Third Rome'. They claimed that the Church of Rome fell because of its heresy and was succeeded by Constantinople, the Second Rome. But this city, too, was punished by God by means of the infidel Turks. The monk Philotheus wrote to Ivan's son:

> The Church of Moscow, the new 'third Rome', shines throughout the entire world more brightly than the sun ... Two Romes have fallen, but the third stands and a fourth can never be.

The now thoroughly national Russian Church thus claimed to be chief protector of Eastern Christianity.

PAUL D. STEEVES

CHAPTER 21

AN AGE OF UNREST
The Western Church in the Late Middle Ages

Many important changes affected European society in the later Middle Ages. During the fourteenth and fifteenth centuries, new economic and political conditions altered the outlines of medieval society. There was a decline in the importance of landed wealth; agriculture became less profitable for many reasons. The fourteenth-century decline in population was made far worse by the Black Death of 1348–49 and by later epidemics. Towards the end of the Middle Ages, growth in commerce tended to draw more workers into towns and ports, where a new set of economic principles guided human relationships. The older, traditional medieval social patterns were beginning to dissolve.

Politically, this was an age of growing community self-consciousness. It is too early to speak of 'nations'; but increasingly people were getting used to considering themselves 'English' or 'French' whenever their thoughts went beyond their own town or region. Monarchs were growing efficient in the business of governing, which in itself helped their subjects to see themselves as belonging to a wider political 'state'.

In every century of the Middle Ages, from about 400 to about 1500, the church was a dominant element in society. Just as there were changes in later medieval society, so too there were many important changes in the church in the years between 1300 and 1500, changes which tended to bring disunity and unrest, pointing to the Reformation. Such changes involved the papacy itself, monasticism, lay people's faith and heresy, and missions.

The thirteenth century closed with the election and unheard-of abdication of Pope Celestine V in 1294. His resignation posed problems for his successors, since it could always be argued that no pope had the right to give up his office. This threw the first pope of the fourteenth century, Boniface VIII (1294–1303), under a cloud of uncertainty and foreboding.

BONIFACE VERSUS FRANCE

Boniface was quite different from Celestine, who was a feeble ascetic. Boniface, a canon-lawyer with wide experience, set to work immediately, reforming papal finances and bringing peace to the Papal States and Rome, a programme which brought him into conflict with the crowned heads of Europe. For example, his bull *Clericis laicos* (1296) limited the power of kings to tax their clergy. In retaliation France prohibited the export of bullion, and in England King Edward I threatened to remove royal protection from the clergy. At the very beginning of the period, papal and royal policies came into conflict. These unseemly squabbles recurred again and again until the end of the Middle Ages.

Boniface later modified his views, though the French found his leniency too grudging, putting pressure on him by supporting an Italian family, the Colonna, who were his greatest rivals. This escalated until Boniface agreed to disregard *Clericis laicos* and give in to other French demands, including the canonization of King Louis IX, in 1297.

The pope won a victory of sorts by announcing a plenary indulgence (ensuring immediate entry into heaven after death) for pilgrims to Rome in the Jubilee Year of 1300, which enhanced his prestige at least for the moment. By 1301 he was again in difficulties with the French. A bishop had been arrested in France and charged with treason. The pope demanded his release, which was refused. Boniface reactivated *Clericis laicos*, and issued another bull – *Ausculta fili* – emphasizing the pope's superiority over secular rulers. In reply, Philip IV stirred up French public opinion against the pope. Boniface answered with yet another bull, *Unam sanctam*, in 1302, summing up extreme papal claims. Finally, the French took direct action. Nogaret, the king's agent, went to Italy to bring back the pope: the issues were to be heard in France, and the pope's fate decided. Meanwhile Boniface excommunicated the French king. Finally, in September 1303, Nogaret, with help from the Colonna family, attacked the pope at Anagni. With the aid of the townsfolk Boniface escaped to Rome. He died at the Vatican a month later.

The problems arising between Boniface and the French have tended to overshadow all other aspects of this pope's reign. Though he was arrogant and guilty of nepotism, he had less unfortunate traits. He added to canon law in the *Liber Sextus*, arranged more efficient papal administration, helped establish a university in Rome, and laid the foundations for an effective archives department. He even took an interest in the current battle between the friars and non-monastic clergy. In the end, however, his pontificate was ominous for the future, a future very much involved in secular politics.

When Boniface died, the French were still determined to exert pressure on the papacy to bring it into line. The new French monarchical state was prospering under the astute control of Philip the Fair (Philip IV, r. 1285–1314). Much pressure was exerted on the College of Cardinals to elect a docile pope. In 1303 Benedict XI was elected, but his rather weak policy of conciliation had no time to develop before he died in 1304. By the time of the next election, the cardinals were split into a pro- and an anti-French faction.

THE POPE MOVES TO AVIGNON

Eventually, by 1305, the Archbishop of Bordeaux was elected pope, as a result of French pressure. He took the name of Clement VI (1305–14), but never went to Rome – partly because of his own unwillingness to leave his native country, partly because of pressure from the French king. Clement created French cardinals to balance the earlier predominantly Italian element in the College of Cardinals and fixed on Avignon in southern France as his residence, though he continued to travel widely throughout Philip the Fair's kingdom.

Hence, Clement V became the first Avignon pope, the first to live under what was known as the 'Avignon Captivity'. There were protests against this from all sides, among the loudest that of Petrarch (d. 1374), one of the greatest figures of the Italian Renaissance. For most of the fourteenth century no pope lived in Rome. This divorce between the head of the Western Christian world and Rome itself caused great scandal and unrest.

Clement approved the French plan to destroy the Order of the Knights of the Temple, or 'Templars', the military crusading order which came to an end while he was pope. Various charges – such as sacrilege, sodomy, and idolatry – were hurled at the Templars, especially in France, and torture was used to obtain 'confessions'. Those working to destroy them were aiming partly to disendow this wealthy and influential order which by the fourteenth century had become practically a European banking corporation. England and other kingdoms, as well as France, went along with papal directives, though to a lesser degree. The property of the order passed to the Hospitallers, or occasionally to other organizations, though in France the greatest beneficiary was the king. The destruction of the Templars included the execution of the Templar Grand Master, Jacques de Molay, and others, in 1314 and was yet another incident gradually bringing the papacy into disrepute.

THE POPES FAVOUR FRANCE

For the moment, however, the papacy at Avignon received a vigorous infusion of new blood in Pope John XXII (1316–34). He was one of the most efficient – and ruthless – of fourteenth-century popes. He was a decidedly French pope, but also independent to an unusual degree. John was well versed in papal and secular politics, and took a great interest in the affairs of Europe from his papal headquarters at Avignon. Among his many schemes was a reform in papal administration. His other interests included a controversy with the Franciscan Spirituals, aspects of speculative theology, compiling sermons, and tireless devotion to reading and making summaries of what he had read.

John was among the greatest of papal financiers, much interested in discovering better ways to increase papal income. At the same time he wished to make his power felt throughout the Christian West. In a sense he was president of a giant corporation with varied financial and political interests, seeing the papacy in administrative far more than spiritual terms.

Pope Benedict XII (1334–42) – who followed him – was a theologian, a Cistercian, and another Frenchman. He was greatly interested in the ever-increasing problems of heresy. Benedict began the construction of the papal palace archives at Avignon, and saw to it that the papal archives still in Rome were sent to him in France. He worked in co-operation with the French king, doing what he could for France during the Hundred Years' War, which began while he was pope. The pope wished to make his influence felt among the religious orders of the church – but they were not particularly enthusiastic. He also saw to it that recognition of the pope's supreme power percolated more effectively through all other levels of church government.

His successor, Pope Clement VI (1342–52), also supported France against the English during the Hundred Years' War. He had been a French cardinal, once Archbishop of Rouen, and was experienced in affairs at the papal court. He now used his expertise to the utmost to provide revenue for the French. While he was pope, in 1348, the city of Avignon was officially purchased by the papacy. Clement was a forerunner of the great Renaissance popes, lavish in expenditure on pomp and ceremony, and open in his support of members of his own family. His personal life left much to be desired from the moral standpoint. Observers, though impressed by his magnificent court, were well aware of the vast amounts of money spent on such display.

This waste of money was discontinued by the next Avignon pope, Innocent VI (1352–62), who paid more attention to the reformation of abuses within the church, and to regaining papal control in Italy. Ever since the popes had departed – and indeed before this – local Italian families and princes had created difficulties. With the pope far away in

Avignon, these inter-family quarrels and battles for control of parts of Italy grew worse, and among the areas to suffer were the Papal States. In addition to the pope's wish to resume power over these areas, there was by now growing pressure on the popes to return to Rome. It seems Innocent VI seriously attempted to do what he could to bring this about.

By now, too, the situation around Avignon was dangerous. Roving bands of mercenaries, a by-product of the Hundred Years' War, brought trouble to the very gates of the pope's residence. Great walls were built around Avignon in 1357, and still impress today. As part of his programme to protect the Papal States and Rome, the pope sent Cardinal Albornoz to Italy. This very capable papal agent remained there for thirteen years (1353–66), during which time he succeeded, at least temporarily, in regaining control. Albornoz succeeded in carrying out many of the pope's plans in preparation for a return to Rome, before he could move from Avignon, the pope died. The move back to the Holy City would be left to his successor, Urban V (1362–70).

RETURN TO ROME

Pope Urban V was a canon-lawyer who led a simple life and wanted to see reform in the church. He reduced expenditure on non-essentials. He wished for peace in Italy and hoped to be able to dismiss his mercenaries. He also planned to call a Crusade, and to achieve union with the Greek Church. In 1367 Urban at last returned to Rome, where he successfully imposed his authority on the various factions. Much of the ancient city was restored. In spite of this encouraging beginning, the pope failed to achieve many of his political aims. In 1368 he fell back into the tradition of the Avignon popes by appointing several French cardinals. Finally, in 1370, he gave up and returned to Avignon, where he died in the same year.

Urban's successor, Gregory XI (1370–78), realized it was necessary to return to Rome. After gaining the upper hand against Italian city-state factions, he left Avignon in 1376, perhaps influenced by the mystic Catherine of Siena, who urged a return to Rome. He was in Italy by late 1376, and entered Rome itself early in 1377. Peace moves were made towards Florence and Milan, but before anything could come of these, Gregory died. But the papacy had at last returned to the Eternal City.

In one sense the Avignon papacy marked an advance in papal affairs. It was during the fourteenth century that the papal court became more bureaucratic, and a more centralized, effective – but more complicated – papacy developed. A more expensive papacy, too. The papacy of the fourteenth century, a kind of international corporation, employed about 500 people in the papal palace alone. On average, about 100 honorary papal chaplains were created each year of the Avignon papacy. The French continued to dominate papal government. About 82 per cent of all cardinals created in the Avignon period were French, 13 per cent Italian, and 5 per cent other nationalities.

THE PAPAL MACHINE

Papal government became more efficient, especially in financial matters. The *Camera Apostolica*, or financial and political office, was one of the most highly bureaucratic. Other offices, such as the Apostolic Chancery and Rota, also had numerous officials assigned to them. The archives increased with this growth of 'red tape'. For the popes from John

XXII to Gregory XI, more than a quarter of a million 'business' documents remain in the archives, many still unexamined. New sources of income were developed to support this gigantic machine, such as special taxes ('annates') from the clergy. The average annual income under John XXII, a pope much concerned with financial matters, was about a quarter of a million gold florins. For Pope Gregory XI, it amounted to half a million. John's average running costs, however, were about the same as his income. Even so, he was able to leave a surplus of one million florins at his death.

The financial activities of the papacy were attacked more often than anything else by those wanting reform. But in the fourteenth century the growing costs of the papal courts, and of Italian wars, aroused more and more clamour for reform. The spiritual role of the papacy seemed forgotten in the rush to collect income in exchange for some privilege or favour. This increased papal interference was sometimes objected to by other European powers. In 1351, for example, England made it illegal for the pope to give foreign clergy positions in the English Church. In 1353, England limited appeals from her clergy to the papal court.

Even with the best organization in the world, however, the papacy could not mend its own inner divisions. These were evident following the death of Pope Gregory XI in 1387. Now the papacy was back in Rome. Angry crowds gathered demanding a Roman – or at least an Italian – pope. Eventually the cardinals went along with them by electing Urban VI (1378–89), who soon proved to be too much of a dictator for the cardinals. Using the disorderly behaviour at his election as an excuse, some of the cardinals gathered and elected another pope, Clement VII. The cardinals had become very independent-minded.

THE PAPACY SPLITS

After armed battles for control of Rome between the forces of the rival popes, Clement VII retired to Avignon in 1381. This marked the beginning of the Great Schism, a split at the very top of the government of the church which had political as well as religious repercussions. Some countries, such as Italy, the Empire, the eastern and Scandinavian areas, Hungary, and England, supported Urban VI of Rome. France and its territories, Spain, and Scotland supported Clement VII in Avignon. In the earlier medieval period two and even three popes had occasionally co-existed, but this Schism was far more serious. Unlike earlier schisms, the problem originated within the papal court itself, among the cardinals.

This division affected all levels of the clergy, although changes of allegiance from one pope to the other were not unheard of. Non-monastic clergy, cathedral, and college chapters, and even religious orders sometimes found their allegiance split. Urban's extreme stubbornness made an easy solution impossible: he even had some of his unbending cardinals tortured to death. Even after Urban's death in 1389, the problem continued, with parallel elections continuing into the next century.

By now, the embarrassment of the situation was clear even to the king of France. He attempted to heal the Schism, even at the cost of abandoning the Avignon pope. Various solutions were suggested, of which the three most important were for one pope to give way to the other, for one to conquer the other, or for both to compromise.

The farcical situation continued in Rome when Innocent VII became pope from 1404 to 1406 and was succeeded by Gregory XII (1406–15), in spite of general protests from

The magnificent Baptistery of St John, Pisa, the largest in Italy, built between 1152 and 1363, adjacent to the cathedral and the celebrated leaning tower.

TIM DOWLEY ASSOCIATES

church leaders and theologians. Meanwhile the rival colleges of cardinals – one at Rome, the other at Avignon – began to compromise and discuss ways of ending the Schism. Finally, since neither pope would agree to give way, some of their cardinals called a council to meet in Pisa in 1409 where, it was hoped, the Schism would be ended.

The popes refused to attend, so the cardinals deposed both of them and elected in their place Alexander V (1409–10). Neither the Avignon nor the Roman pope recognized this new choice, so the result of the council was three popes, where there had been two. More significantly, the Council of Pisa raised an important principle by its actions: a council may be superior in power to a pope, in effect calling papal supremacy into question.

COUNCIL OF CONSTANCE

The issues were not settled at Pisa. At the greatest council of the period, the Council of Constance (1414–18), it was hoped that they would be. Another pope now reigned – John XXIII, who in 1410 had succeeded Alexander V. The Council attracted wide interest, and by 1415 scholars, church dignitaries, and various secular officials had arrived. Even the Greek Orthodox sent representatives. Over the next three years some forty-five main sessions were held, with scores of lesser committee meetings. Eventually, after a trial in 1415, John XXIII was forced to give up his claim to the papacy. In the same year Gregory XII resigned, leaving but one pope, the Spanish Benedict XIII. He too was tried and deposed in 1417, though he went on living in Spain under the delusion that he was the only true pope, until his death in 1422.

No council had accomplished so much in healing breaches within the church since the very early general councils. The way was clear to elect one pope who would once more represent all Western Christians. This was done in 1417; the new pope was Martin V. The problem was raised, however, as to whether the council which had created him was superior to the pope who claimed supremacy. For the moment the claim of the council lapsed.

Other problems considered at Constance included the administration of the eucharist. The Hussites, especially after the execution of Jan Hus at the Council in 1415, held that all Christians should receive both bread and wine, which the Council prohibited. John Wyclif was condemned for heresy by the Council in 1415, and his body disinterred from holy ground in 1427.

JAN HUS

Jan Hus (c. 1369–1415) achieved fame as a martyr to the cause of church reform and of Czech nationalism. Jan was ordained a priest in 1401, and spent much of his career teaching at the Charles University in Prague, and as preacher in the Bethlehem Chapel, close to the university.

In his writing and public preaching, Hus emphasized personal piety and purity of life. He was heavily indebted to the works of Wyclif. Stressing the role of Scripture as an authority in the church he consequently lifted preaching to an important status in church services. In the process he became a national hero. In his chief work, *On the Church*, he defined the church as the body of Christ, with Christ as its only head. Although he defended the traditional authority of the clergy, he taught that only God can forgive sin.

Hus believed that neither popes nor cardinals could establish doctrine that was contrary to Scripture, nor should any Christian obey an order from them that was plainly wrong. He condemned the corruptness of the clergy and criticized his people for worshipping images, belief in false miracles, and undertaking 'superstitious pilgrimages'. He criticized the church for withholding the cup of wine from the people during communion, and condemned the sale of indulgences.

Hus was at the centre of lengthy struggles in Prague, and his case was referred to Rome. In 1415 Hus attended the Council of Constance in order to defend his beliefs. Although travelling under the Emperor's safe-conduct, he was tried and con-

Engraving of Jan Hus (1369–1415) priest, philosopher, and reformer from Charles University, Prague.
© GEORGIOS KOLLIDAS/DREAMSTIME.COM

demned to be burnt at the stake, with no real opportunity to explain his views. However, his heroic death aroused the national feelings of the Czech people, who established the Hussite Church in Bohemia, until the Hapsburgs conquered in 1620 and restored the Roman Catholic Church. The Hussite reform was closely associated with the resistance of the Czechs to German domination.

CAROLINE T. MARSHALL

Besides a few other issues, mainly political, the Council initiated reforms, and decreed in 1417 and 1418 that further councils should be held. In addition, changes were to be made in the College of Cardinals, in the bureaucracy of the papacy, and in abuses of tithes and indulgences. The real issue, however, was papal power.

Martin V showed himself to be a pope of the 'old school', after his return to Rome in 1420, which he finally subdued in 1424. He started a renovation scheme in Rome, reorganized the Papal States, and made good use of his extensive blood-ties with the Colonna family. But he was interested only in administrative reform; he let religious reform take second place.

Martin V died in 1431, having brought peace to the Papal States. He was succeeded by Eugene IV (1431–39), whose tactlessness provoked discontent among the cardinals, who wished to regain control of papal government. As a result of a decree issued by Martin V before his death, a council met at Basle in 1431. The new pope was not interested in attending and ordered the Council to dissolve. This was disregarded by the assembled members. Most of the College of Cardinals favoured the Council, as a continuation of the spirit of Constance. One of the major issues at Basle was the question of union with the Greek Church, officially separated from Rome since the eleventh century. From 1433 envoys were exchanged between the Council and Constantinople, but the pope too sent his own representatives to the East and the question of union was lost in the competition between pope and council for 'credit' in achieving the reunion.

The pope had the Council transferred to Ferrara. At Basle, reforms were difficult to carry through in the face of papal hostility. In Ferrara from 1438 the reassembled Council again dealt with the union of East and West. But little interest was shown by the Western powers, and the Council was again moved – to Florence – in 1439. Ever since 1438, when the pope transferred the Council, a Basle contingent continued to sit. In effect, there were two rival councils, one at Basle, and another, first at Ferrara, and then at Florence. Schism seemed about to return. The Basle Council deposed Eugene IV and elected Felix V (1439–49); once again there were two popes. Eugene IV's death in 1447 was followed by the election of Nicholas V (1447–55). The crisis ended only when, in 1449, largely because of political pressures, Felix V resigned.

The Basle Council broke up and dispersed. Its end marks the end of conciliarism, the reform movement within a framework of church councils. Reform would have to come from some other source. Meanwhile the papacy withdrew into itself, becoming an Italian power with Italian interests. The age of the Renaissance popes now began.

HUMANIST POPE

Pope Nicholas V set the tone for his successors: he was concerned with the architectural adornment of Rome, and with promoting humanism, especially the study of Greek. This aspect of scholarship was prominent following the sack of Constantinople in 1453 and the flight of Byzantine refugees to the West. The Vatican Library was reorganized and many manuscripts added. The ideal, but not the reality, of a crusade also attracted his attention.

The next pope, Alfonso Borgia (Calixtus III), who died in 1458, actually engineered schemes leading to a Crusade, and spent a great deal of money towards it. The results were hardly worth the effort. His successor, Pius II (1438–64), was one of the more interesting Renaissance figures in his own right. One of the greatest of humanist church leaders, he was widely travelled and fully experienced in affairs of the Empire, papal court, and councils. He too worked conscientiously for a Crusade against the Turks, but again this came to nothing. Pius left many writings, including an extensive collection of memoirs, from which the lifestyle of a Renaissance pope can be reconstructed. His successor, Paul II (1464–71), was not on friendly terms with the humanists, but more interested in lavish processions, pompous display, and his own reputation, rather than that of the office and dignity of the pope.

With Sixtus IV (1471–84) the papacy is sometimes said to have reached a new low. Although he was the general of the Franciscans, Sixtus, when elected, acted in a most un-Franciscan manner. Guilty of the most flagrant nepotism, of the thirty-four cardinals he elevated, six were his own nephews. He was involved in political intrigues, interfering in the affairs of Florence, and even being implicated in the assassination of two de Medicis in 1478. As to the Crusade, Sixtus at first expressed interest in the venture, but was unable to draw together enough material support. This was true even after the Turks landed on Italian soul, in Apulia.

THE INFAMOUS BORGIAS

The need for greater amounts of money, in the form of 'gifts', led to further bureaucratization of the papal court. Sixtus exploited the sale of offices and peddling of indulgences, requiring more money partly for his patronage of humanistic studies, art, and architecture. He was a man of complex motives and interests; this was the pope who built the Sistine Chapel in Rome. He also established a hospital for deserted children, cancelled the decrees of the Council of Constance, reorganized the Vatican Library, and condemned

Relief of Catherine of Siena, Rome, Italy.
©ZATLETIC/ DREAMSTIME.COM

SAVONAROLA

Girolamo Savonarola (1452–98) was an Italian preacher of reform who was executed for his activities. Born in Ferrara, Italy, he studied humanism and medicine, but renounced these pursuits to become a Dominican in 1474. He served in several north Italian cities and by 1491 was Prior of San Marco and a popular preacher in Florence. His sermons warned of a great judgment coming on the city, after which a golden age would arrive, when Florence would unite all Italy in a just commonwealth. These predictions seemed to be fulfilled when Charles VIII, King of France, invaded Italy and the Medici rulers of Florence fled.

Under the new government, Savonarola rose to a position of power through his preaching. He initiated tax reforms, aided the poor, reformed the courts, and changed the city from a lax, corrupt, pleasure-loving place into a virtual monastery. Having reformed Florence, he next denounced Pope Alexander VI and the corrupt papal court. The quarrel which followed resulted in his excommunication and the threat of an interdict against Florence. This frightened the people and led to his execution.

Savonarola became a hero to many of the early Protestants, even though he retained a Catholic theology. They saw in his opposition to the papacy a useful example for them to follow. His success came at the height of the Italian Renaissance and demonstrates a deeply religious attitude among the people of that era which is often overlooked.

ROBERT G. CLOUSE

the excesses of the Spanish Inquisition. Such was the anxiety aroused by this High Renaissance pope that there was even talk of another general council to bring him under control – but this came to nothing.

Pope Alexander VI (1492–1503) was one of the most controversial of all the popes. He was Rodrigo Borgia, a wily politician, rich, well-connected, and careless of morals. Born in Spain about 1430, Rodrigo studied at Bologna, moving on to become a cardinal and then vice-chancellor in the papal court of his uncle, Calixtus III. The many children of Rodrigo, born before his election as pope (for example, Isabella, Jeronima, John, Peter, Geoffrey, Caesar, and perhaps the best-remembered, Lucretia – born in 1480), were all well provided for from church revenues, both before and after their father became pope.

Alexander was a careful and efficient manager of the Papal States. Wising to avoid foreign intrigues and entanglements in Italy, he was not above using even Turkish help, for example against the French. In the midst of these political skirmishes, the preacher Savonarola was executed at Florence because of his opposition to Borgia, and his friendship with the French, whom he saw as the hope of Italy. The pope was called upon to act as mediator between Spain and Portugal, dividing the 'new world' between them. His reign, which closed the fifteenth century, witnessed the discoveries which opened up a new chapter in world history, and in the history of the church.

The character of the papacy was changing during the later Middle Ages, as was the attitude of many Christians towards it. The Avignon episode, and especially the Schism, brought about popular estrangement from the popes. Eventually the idea of 'national churches' would emerge, opposed to a universal papal church. The papacy grew in wealth and complexity, and the prestige of the office was lowered by its political involvement and increased bureaucracy. In addition, the important church councils challenged papal superiority. The tastes and morals of some fifteenth-century popes left much to be desired. In the midst of all these cross-currents, certain problems continued to intrude. One of these was the split between the Western Church and the Byzantine or Orthodox Church, centred on Constantinople.

THE WEST LOOKS EAST

A special relationship had grown up in Constantinople between the Eastern Emperor and the Patriarch. Secular influence over the spiritual power was far more acceptable in the East than in the West. This meant, among other things, that political considerations more directly affected the attitudes of the Eastern Church. This relationship, or 'Caesaro-papism', as it was called in the West, was not acceptable to the Western papacy. There were also complex theological differences between the two churches.

In addition, the entire cultural background in which each church followed Christian traditions was different. The Latin-speaking Western Church had its own customs and history, and the Greek-speaking Eastern Church similarly had a tradition of which it was proud. The rift between the two was not helped by the Fourth Crusade, when the Western Crusaders, transported by Venice and at the mercy of her sea-power, were diverted to Constantinople itself, which they captured in 1204. For much of the thirteenth century the power of the Greek Emperor was replaced by the so-called Latin Kingdom of Constantinople, under Western leadership. By 1261 the Greeks had retaken their capital city and ousted the uncouth Westerners. The thirteenth century, then, was hardly a promising era in which to improve relationships between the Churches of East and West.

Clement V, the first Avignonese pope, renewed the call to Crusaders to recapture Constantinople, but with little response. The French King Charles IV (1322–28) expressed some interest in the scheme, but nothing lasting came of this. Meanwhile a new development in the East was eventually to alter papal as well as Byzantine policy: the rise of the Ottoman Turks. By the middle of the fourteenth century these 'savage hordes' seemed to pose a real threat not only to the East but to the West too. United in fear, East and West began to grow closer together, for mutual protection.

As early as 1339, faced by the Ottoman Turks, the Greeks expressed an interest in a union with the West. Under Emperor John VI (1347–54), several missions were sent to Avignon to test the attitude of the papacy. Eventually it was accepted that an ecumenical council would be the best way to go about considering the union of Greek Orthodox and Roman Catholic Christianity. Unfortunately the outbreak of the Western Schism after 1378, and subsequent rivalry between popes and councils, ruined these prospects. Competing popes and councils appealed to the Eastern Emperor for recognition. These were political moves, and in the process the real issues were brushed aside. The East's response varied. On the one hand the Byzantines had no wish to get disagreeably involved in Western religious politics; on the other hand the Ottomans were menacing them.

Finally, Emperor Manuel II Palaiologos (1391–1425) journeyed to the West to try to resolve the issues. His reception was mixed – even lukewarm – and promises of armed assistance were not encouraging. His efforts were, in the event, unnecessary since immediate disaster was averted in the East. The Ottoman threat was quelled by the rise of a new intervening force, Tamburlaine, in 1402. For the moment, the Ottoman scourge seemed tamed. It was still discussed in the West, but with little real concern. For example, though the Turkish threat was raised at the Council of Constance in 1415, it was quickly pushed aside as a secondary issue.

The papacy was once again battling for independence, at the councils of Basle and Ferrara-Florence. This led each side, council and pope, to appeal to the Eastern Emperor for political support, and each side worked towards union with the Greeks. Whichever side achieved this could thereby claim the greater glory and prestige. In 1439 the papacy scored the victory, and a decree of union was agreed upon, though this news was not well received back in Constantinople itself, where there was much popular resistance to a religious union with the West, whatever the political advantages might be. It was not until 1452 that the decree of union was officially published in Constantinople. But this was too little, too late. The very next year, 1453, Constantinople, the ancient capital of Byzantium and stronghold of Orthodox Christianity, was captured by the Muslim Turks. The conflict between Roman and Greek Christianity was thus resolved.

POOR FRANCISCANS?

The dispute with the Greek Orthodox Church was only one among many problems of the later medieval papacy. Other conflicts were internal. One concerned the Franciscan Order, founded in the early thirteenth century with papal approval. The father of the order, Francis of Assisi, died in 1226. As early as 1245 difficulties which also involved the papacy had arisen within his organization of friars.

The question was, should the Franciscans be allowed to own property, or should they keep to the original ideal of poverty, as Francis had directed? Franciscans who favoured poverty discovered a justification in the writings of the mystic Joachim of Fiore (c. 1135– 1202). The other camp found a champion in Pope Innocent IV (1243–54), who declared that Franciscan property belonged to the church, and then allowed it to be re-allocated to the order – a mere technical avoidance of the rule of poverty.

The split within the Franciscans widened. Another papal decree of 1279, along much the same lines, also failed to unite the order. By the end of the thirteenth century the Franciscans had divided into a group of 'Spirituals', who supported the ideal of poverty, and one of 'Conventuals', who tried to find a compromise solution. They wished in theory to maintain the spirit of their order, but in practice avoid the burdens of poverty. Although an agreement of sorts was reached under the early Avignon popes, for example at the Council of Vienne (1311–12), the Spirituals began to move to a radical position, ultimately wishing to cut all links with the order. In 1317 John XXII ordered them to rejoin the other Franciscans. Some Spirituals who continued to refuse fell under the judgment of the Inquisition, and four 'Fraticelli' were executed in 1318.

This controversy involved basic problems for the papacy. In general, the Franciscans accepted that poverty was an ideal practised by Christ and the apostles. From this arose the idea that the church hierarchy should remain aloof from entanglements in the world. If extended to the papacy, this put in question the position of the pope as ruler of the princes of Christendom, and the massive wealth of the church as a whole came under scrutiny.

JOHN WYCLIF

John Wyclif (c. 1320–84) was a prominent English reformer of the later Middle Ages. He came from the north of England, became a leading philosopher at Oxford University and was invited to serve at court by John of Gaunt, who was acting as ruler at this time. Wyclif offended the church by backing the right of the government to seize the property of corrupt clergymen. His views were condemned by the pope in 1377, but Wyclif's influential friends protected him.

Wyclif pushed his anti-clerical views further, and began to attack some of the central doctrines of the medieval church. He opposed the doctrine of transubstantiation, claiming rather that Christ was spiritually present in the eucharist. Wyclif held that the church consisted of God's chosen people, who did not need a priest to mediate with God for them.

The reformer was gradually deserted by his friends in high places, and the church authorities forced him and his followers out of Oxford. In 1382 Wyclif, a sick man, went to live at Lutterworth, in the Midlands, where he died in 1384. He wrote many books, including a *Summa Theologica* and initiated a new translation of the Latin *Vulgate* Bible into English: *The Wyclif Bible*.

A group of followers arose around Wyclif at Oxford. He attracted support by his energetic preaching and lecturing. His followers spread to Leicestershire, and became known as 'Lollards', which may mean 'mutterer' or 'mumbler'. By 1395 the Lollards had developed into an organized group, with their own ministers and popular support.

John Wyclif, c. 1320–84), English scholar, translator, and reformer, sometimes known as 'Morning Star of the Reformation'.
TIM DOWLEY ASSOCIATES

The Lollards stood for many of the ideas set out by Wyclif, believing particularly that the main task of a priest was to preach, and that the Bible should be available to all in their own language. From the beginning of the fifteenth century, the Lollards were suppressed, particularly when their protest became linked with political unrest. But Lollardy continued to thrive in some parts of England, and prepared the way for the coming of Lutheranism in the next century.

TIM DOWLEY

Eventually Pope John XXII condemned the Franciscan doctrine of poverty in 1323 and some Franciscan leaders were excommunicated. This problem continued to trouble fifteenth-century popes, by which time the Spirituals were known as 'Observants'. In effect they had become a separate order from the Conventuals, though in theory still under a single rule. In 1517 this division was formally recognized. The Observants then constituted the larger party, the Conventuals the minor. It cannot be said that the conflict among the Franciscans, which began in the thirteenth century, was successfully resolved by the medieval papacy.

CRITICS OF THE PAPACY

This period witnessed a decline in prestige of the papacy. Simultaneously, there was a rise in various dissident religious movements. Some Spirituals were burnt by the Inquisition, declaring clearly their discontent with the church. During the fourteenth century, one particularly bizarre movement was the Flagellants, with their practice of whipping themselves. Other lesser groups also fell outside the lines of orthodoxy, for example the Brothers of the Free Spirit. The Black Death of the mid-fourteenth century brought hysteria as well as havoc and death to most of Europe.

The two most troublesome movements were those initiated by Hus and by Wyclif, whose followers came to be called Lollards. By the end of the Middle Ages they had come to attack the very foundations of the medieval hierarchy, including the papacy itself.

The attack came not only in the sophisticated Latin writings of professional theologians. Much of the vernacular literature of the later medieval centuries reveals discontent with the condition of the church and papacy. Examples occur in anti-clerical asides of the writer Boccaccio (1313–75), and the condemnation of church wealth by the English writer William Langland (c. 1332–c. 1386). Certainly Geoffrey Chaucer shows no love for the materialism of the church in fourteenth-century England.

Everywhere more and more people began to question the basic tenets of the church. Society was changing, and the church was not changing with it. The critics attacked the hierarchy and its wealth, and the doctrine and dogma of the sacramental system. In the universities, the Aristotelian philosophical basis for Christian theology – scholasticism – developed by Aquinas in the thirteenth century was being questioned by such men as William of Ockham (sometimes 'Occam', c. 1288–c. 1348) and Duns Scotus (c. 1265–1308) in England, and the Frenchmen Jean Buridan (c. 1300–after 1358) and Nicole Oresme (c. 1320–1382).

The later Middle Ages show an obvious change in yet another sphere of Christian activity. During the eleventh and twelfth centuries the founding of monasteries was one of the more praiseworthy acts of piety among wealthy lords and ladies. But in the later medieval period this enthusiasm for foundation, reform and growth had died out. New houses of monks and nuns were seldom built and endowments were less easy to obtain. Monasteries had fallen on evil times. For example, some were forced to sell room and board to private individuals and families, meaning in effect that some monasteries became a form of retirement home for those who could afford the fees. This was not the case everywhere. Some larger houses managed to carry on, so extensive were their lands. The smaller ones had the worst time of it, as changes in the agrarian economy and inflation lowered the value of their landed properties. Even before the end of the Middle Ages, smaller monasteries occasionally had to be closed down.

But people still wished to give towards establishing havens for holy men. Now, however, they would more often endow smaller places run by Augustinian canons, rather than Benedictine monks. The canons required a smaller endowment of land, worked in smaller groups, and seemed to contribute to the new town-dwelling society in which they settled. Canons worked in and with society; monks turned their backs

> We ask God then of his supreme goodness to reform our church, as being entirely out of joint, to the perfectness of its first beginning.
>
> THE LOLLARD CONCLUSIONS, 1394

on it – or so it appeared. Society was no longer tolerant of the exclusiveness of monks.

Another way pious lay people tried to reassure themselves of their chances of salvation was by establishing private chantries. During the fourteenth and fifteenth centuries more and more of these chantries were endowed. The idea was simple enough: a wealthy individual or family, even a guild, provided a sum of money for a priest to sing a mass periodically and, in 'perpetual chantries', for ever, for the soul of the benefactor. Sometimes special chantry-altars were built – private chapels licensed by the local church authority. This was an easy way for poor priests to make a bit of money, and was one of the things the more conscientious reformers disliked.

RELIGION BECOMES MORE PERSONAL

Private chantries represent a break with the institutional, official, and distant mediation on the part of the church. They satisfied the need for direct contact with one's own priest, who said one's own mass for one's own soul. Religion had become more personal, more individual. Church art and the liturgy also suggested this. The suffering Christ replaced God, the stern judge. The pitiful

WILLIAM OF OCKHAM

William of Ockham was a thinker of first-rate importance. He was born around 1288, probably in the village of Ockham in Surrey, England, and died in Munich around 1348. After entering the Franciscan order, he began theological study at Oxford around 1309, and completed the requirements for the status of Master with his lectures on Peter Lombard's *Book of Sentences* (c. 1318–20).

Apparently denounced as heretic to Pope John XXII by the university's former chancellor, William was summoned to Avignon in 1324. While there, he was embroiled in a controversy about apostolic poverty which made him more critical of the papacy. He called for a college of popes to rule the church, and claimed Christ was the church's only head – teachings which looked forward to the conciliar movement. Ockham entirely rejected papal authority in secular matters. In 1328 he fled to the service of the Emperor, Louis of Bavaria, supporting him in his struggles with the papacy.

In philosophy, William elaborated a new form of Nominalist theory. He rejected the prevailing view that 'universals' really exist, arguing that they are simply artificial products of the human mind, necessary for communicating by means of language. Only individual or 'particular' things have real existence. William's Nominalism became known as 'the modern way' (*via moderna*) over against 'the old way' (*via antiqua*) of Aquinas. Since knowledge was based on experience of individual things, natural science took a new significance.

In his many writings, William discussed with masterly logical skill the great themes of philosophy and theology. By the principle known as 'Ockham's razor' he insisted that 'What can be done with fewer [assumptions] is done in vain with more'; the mind should not multiply things without necessity. William made an elaborate criticism of philosophical proofs for the existence of God, although he himself had a strong, positive theology. He stressed that God was known by faith alone, not by reason or illumination, and that God's will was absolutely supreme. In these and other respects William of Ockham paved the way for Reformation theology.

H. DERMOT MCDONALD

Virgin Mary was made more human. The cult of the Virgin became particularly popular in later medieval Christianity, with shrine after shrine dedicated to her throughout Europe. The use of the rosary, the 'Hail, Mary', and feasts of the Virgin became increasingly common.

In art, the pierced and bleeding heart of Christ began to take its place more often among the other motifs. 'Miracles of the eucharist' became more frequent after the thirteenth century. Christ was worshipped in a way that replaced older saint-veneration: the 'monstrance' in which the elements were put on display was merely a newer-style saint's reliquary.

The standard of saintliness seems to have been changing. Joan of Arc was an ignorant peasant, unlike most of the saints revered earlier in the Middle Ages. Obviously, in her case, political considerations were important. The older approaches to popular religion still survived; for example, the credulous belief in relics and in astounding miracles. Behind all this was a profound swing away from an institutional, towards a personal, religion.

MYSTICS FLOURISH

This change is even more clearly documented in another area: the last two medieval centuries were noted for mysticism, perhaps the most personal form of expressed relationship between an individual and God to be found in medieval Christianity. Mysticism continued to flourish.

This tradition was strong in the Dominican order. Meister Eckhart (c. 1260–c. 1327) and Henry Suso (c. 1300–66), for example, stimulated the mystical outpourings of Johannes Nider (1380–1438). In his entertaining book *Formicarius*, though, Nider proved himself to be as aware of the real world as of the mystical. Nicholas of Cusa (1401–64) was another well-known mystic; his empirical studies in science and languages produced a unique mystical vocabulary. Using Neoplatonic ideas to approach the Unknowable God, Cusa created similes based upon optics and mathematics. Germany was the foremost land of mysticism.

Other regions also produced fine examples. Catherine of Siena (1347–80) was a well-known mystic from Italy. In England, an anonymous author contributed *The Cloud of Unknowing* to mystical literature, while Richard Rolle (1290–1349), Walter Hilton (d. 1396) and the late fourteenth-century anchoress Julian of Norwich (c. 1342–c. 1416) also wrote significant English mystical works.

Our Lord shewed me a little thing, the quantity of an hazelnut, in the palm of my hand; and it was as round as a ball. I looked thereupon with the eye of my understanding, and thought, 'What may this be?' And it was answered generally thus: 'It is all that is made.' I marvelled how it might last, for methought it might suddenly have fallen to naught for littleness. And I was answered in my understanding: 'It lasteth and ever shall last for that God loveth it. And so All-thing hath Being by the love of God.'

In this Little Thing I saw three properties. The first is that God made it, the second that God loveth it, the third that God keepeth it.

JULIAN OF NORWICH, *REVELATIONS OF DIVINE LOVE*, V, LATE FOURTEENTH CENTURY

MISSIONS TO MONGOLS AND MUSLIMS

Christianity was expanding to hitherto non-Christian parts of the world. The periods of greatest missionary activity in the Middle and Far East were the thirteenth and fourteenth centuries, and the Franciscans and Dominicans particularly concerned in these ventures. Francis himself went to Egypt in a fruitless effort to convert the Muslims. Further missions to North Africa followed, occasionally ending in martyrdom. Two sees, Fez and Morocco, were established, at least temporarily.

In addition, missionaries were also sent to central Asia. One of the motives behind this was to convert the Mongols and bring them into alliance with the Christians against the Muslims. An incidental effect of the movement was a new interest in oriental languages, which began to be studied in the West. Among the most important Franciscan and Dominican missionaries were Raymond Lull, Lawrence of Portugal, John of Plano Carpini, and William of Ruysbroeck.

Eventually the Franciscans established six mission fields or 'vicariates', three for the Mongols, one for North Africa, and two for Russia and south-east Europe. Pope John XXII also sent Dominicans to govern other Eastern sees, for example, in southern India and Samarkand. Ultimately the attempt to convert the Mongols to Christianity failed and Muslim missionaries succeeded before the Christians. The Mongol Khan Uzbek (d. 1340) was converted to Islam, and his 'Golden Horde' followed his example.

In the Far East, the thirteenth-century Venetian merchant family of the Polos was among the earliest messengers of the pope. The Franciscans followed up these preliminary steps. From 1289 John of Montecorvino (1247–1328) worked in China, founding a see at Peking after he was created archbishop in 1307. Six suffragan or junior bishops were established in the area under his control.

Ultimately these missionary activities in the Middle and Far East, among the Mongols and the Chinese, declined and died out after the middle of the fourteenth century. This was probably partly because of the Black Death, which came into western Europe at this time, disrupting both church and secular life. The failure was also due to the growth of Islamic influence among the Mongol people, and the confusion following Tamburlaine's rise to power. In China itself, a change to the new Ming dynasty in 1368 brought anti-Christian powers to the fore. These spelled the virtual end of eastward expansion for Christianity – and of Christian missionary activities – for some centuries.

During the fifteenth century in Portugal, at the other extremity of Europe, a strong royal house came to power with an interest in overseas exploration. Under Prince Henry 'The Navigator' (1394–1460), Portuguese ships nosed south along the west coast of Africa in search of commerce and converts. At the end of the Middle Ages, Catholic Christianity had retreated in the Orient; now a new field of mission was about to open up. It was to be the Portuguese and the Spaniards who would take their religion and their missionaries to the newly found lands of the west, to South and Central America, to Mexico.

RONALD FINUCANE

Missionaries will convert the world by preaching, but also through the shedding of tears and blood and with great labour, and through a bitter death.

RAYMOND LULL

FURTHER READING

Richard Fletcher, *The Cross and the Crescent: Christianity and Islam from Muhammad to the Reformation*, London, 2003.

Peter Brown, *The Rise of Western Christendom: Triumph and Diversity AD 200–1000*, Oxford, 1997.

G. R. Evans, *The Church in the Early Middle Ages*, London 2007.

Christopher Tyerman, *God's War: A New History of the Crusades*, London 2006.

Kallistos Ware, *The Orthodox Church*, London, 1963.

Tibor Szamuely, *The Russian Tradition*, London, 1974.

STUDY QUESTIONS

1. What were the main threats to the church in the West between AD 600 and 1000?

2. How did the rise of Islam impact the church before AD 1000?

3. In what ways was Pope Gregory I 'Great'?

4. Why did the Great Schism occur?

5. How did the church begin in Russia and Eastern Europe? Was it distinctive?

6. Why was monasticism so popular for much of this period? Why did it decline?

7. What issues divided the church and state in the West?

8. Are the Crusades defensible?

9. Who criticized the Roman Catholic Church? Why?

10. What was the legacy of the medieval church?

Reform and Renewal

1500–1650

Summary

The sixteenth century gave rise to a major upheaval within Western Christianity, usually referred to as the 'Reformation'. Alarmed at what they perceived to be a growing disparity between apostolic and medieval visions of Christianity, men such as Martin Luther and Huldrych Zwingli pressed for reform. Luther believed that the teachings of the church had been distorted during the Middle Ages and needed to be brought back into line with Scripture. For Luther, the question of how we enter into a right relationship with God – the doctrine of justification – needed radical revision in the light of the Bible.

Although the need for reform was widely conceded within the church, in the end both Luther and Zwingli found themselves creating reforming communities outside the mainline church. By the time of John Calvin and his reformation of the city of Geneva, Protestantism had emerged as a distinct type of Christianity, posing a major threat to the Catholic Church.

In the late 1540s, the Catholic Church itself began a major process of reformation and renewal, often known as the 'Catholic Reformation', and formerly the 'Counter-Reformation'. The religious orders were reformed, and many of the beliefs and practices that reformers such as Luther found objectionable were eliminated. Nevertheless, significant differences remained between Protestantism and Catholicism.

The discovery of the Americas led to a new interest in spreading the gospel abroad. The Society of Jesus, the Jesuits, founded by Ignatius Loyola in 1540, took the lead within the Catholic Church and sent missionaries to the Americas, India, China, and Japan. Christianity also expanded by other means, one of the most important being large-scale emigration from Europe to North America, beginning in the late sixteenth century.

CHAPTER 22

SEEDS OF RENEWAL
The origins of the Reformation

The great religious revolution called the Reformation broke out in 1517, but it is necessary to go back at least 100 years to understand what caused it. Although the seeds of renewal had been sown in prepared soil, the roots of abuse were old and deep. Martin Luther reckoned things began to go badly wrong with the Christian church in the eighth century. Today most Catholics and Protestants would say that several generations before Luther's protest against indulgences it was evident there was something radically wrong with the Roman Catholic church.

HOW CORRUPT WAS THE CHURCH?

It is difficult to form an objective picture of the corruption of the clergy in the century before the Reformation. By most accounts, negligence, ignorance, absenteeism, and sexual immorality were widespread among the clergy, and taken for granted by lay people. But not every lurid contemporary description should be taken at its face value: some high-minded Catholics of the time may have painted a blacker portrait of their church than was warranted by the facts. Nor was later mud-slinging always as accurate as it claimed. But corruption is one thing, official sanction of corruption is quite another; the heart of the rotten condition of the Catholic Church lay in papal protection and promotion of abuses.

The political writer Machiavelli said that the nearer one got to Rome the more corruption one found; and, in 1510 – seven years before his public protest – Luther was shocked by what he saw when he visited the holy city. But just as today vice hits the headlines while virtue goes unsung, so in the pre-Reformation church the scandals tend to be remembered and the piety forgotten. No doubt there was much hidden devotion in all ranks of society in the fifteenth century, and pockets of piety even in Rome. There were undoubtedly parish priests, like Chaucer's 'poor parson of a town', who lived useful lives of dedicated godliness: but they did not make history.

EUROPE UNDER THREAT

The period of the Reformation was rich in conflicting personalities, institutions, and events, and it featured factors other than church practice and abuse. The lives of ordinary people in the Catholic West were threatened by two major menaces from outside the Christian church: the plague and the Turk. Both suddenly appeared on the scene around the middle of the fourteenth century, and both were regarded by popular preachers as the scourge of God to punish the failings of Catholicism.

Bubonic plague first struck Europe in 1347, in an epidemic known as the Black Death, which in three years killed about one third of the inhabitants of the Catholic West. After that, it remained endemic for centuries, causing many deaths from time to time (in London, for example, in 1665). People lived in the shadow of this pestilence, and during the fifteenth century Europe could be described as a death-orientated society.

The Muslim Ottoman Turks became a political threat when they captured Gallipoli in 1354 and began their advance into Europe. Throughout the fifteenth century they continued their career of conquest to the north and west. The reign of their Sultan Mehmed II (1451–81), who died two years before Luther was born, saw spectacular territorial gains. Constantinople fell to him in 1453, Negroponte in 1470, and in 1480 his forces even made a landing at Otranto, on the heel of Italy.

All through Luther's lifetime and beyond, the Turks were as real a menace as the plague – indeed more real to coast-dwellers south of Rome, for Turkish raiding-parties would pounce in the night from the sea and carry off pretty girls for the Sultan's harem. The writer Tasso's sister was nearly abducted from Sorrento. In Machiavelli's comedy *Mandragola*, written within months of Luther's protest, a woman asks her confessor: 'Do you think the Turk will come into Italy this year?' It was a worry never far from the minds of those living near the Mediterranean.

NEW LANDS, NEW NATIONS

Europe (this title is itself a fifteenth-century concept) was meanwhile finding new outlets for expansion overseas by exploration, for this was the age of navigation and geological discoveries. Martin Luther was five years old when Bartholomew Diaz founded the Cape of Good Hope, nine years old when Columbus discovered America, and fifteen when Vasco da Gama opened up the sea-route to India. In fact, the voyages and exploits of Cabot, Cortés, Magellan, and Pizarro all fell within the lifetime of Luther; practically every year some new horizon was disclosed.

Great political developments at home matched great geological discoveries abroad. This was the age of emerging national consciousness in Europe. The three most powerful Western monarchies were all growing in confidence, with greater royal authority in provincial life. In England the new monarchy dates from 1485, in France from 1491, and in Spain from 1492.

But it was in the field of church politics that the conflict of the Reformation was joined, and the most powerful and pretentious contestant was the pope. When the fifteenth century began, there were two rival popes in the West, each seeking to undo the work of the other, and from 1409 there were three. This unhappy state in the leadership of the Western Church reflected a blight which affected the quality of Christian life at almost every level.

For all its ideals, piety, and art, Catholicism differed from the church of the New Testament in doctrine, morals, and administration. Most men and women of conscience realized this, and called with increasing urgency for 'reform in head and members'. Some – such as Jan Hus the Bohemian disciple of John Wyclif – would not wait for Rome to reform herself, but separated from the unity of the Roman Catholic church for the honour of Christ and his gospel.

THE RENAISSANCE

The words 'Renaissance' and 'humanist' have been used in referring to some of the fifteenth-century popes. *Renaissance* is a term which nineteenth-century historians began to apply to the broad cultural change which came over Western Europe in the fifteenth and sixteenth centuries. It means re-birth, and is used to describe the reviving of the values of classical Greek and Roman civilization in the arts, politics, and habits of mind, which originated in Italy and spread over most of Western Europe. Meanwhile, many of the attitudes and institutions which are thought of as 'medieval' persisted throughout this period even in centres of the new culture.

The Renaissance began with the revival of classical learning by scholars who have come to be called 'humanists'. A humanist was originally someone who taught Latin grammar, but the word later came to mean a student of Latin and Greek who not only read classical writings but moulded his life on what he read. Thus humanists stand in contrast to the scholastics, and humanism in contrast to scholasticism. But although Renaissance humanists read non-Christian authors, such as Cicero and Plato, they were not necessarily opposed to Christianity; in fact most of the early humanists professed faith in Christ. Only later, in the heyday of the classical revival, did many Renaissance thinkers reject or ignore Christianity to admire pagan virtues and practise pagan vices. For example, anyone reading *The Prince* by Niccolò Machiavelli (1469–1527) – written four years before Luther's protest – might be tempted to suppose that Christianity had never existed.

BACK TO THE CLASSICS

The home of humanism was Italy, and the first known humanist was Lovato Lovati (1241–1309), a judge in Padua who introduced a new way of treating the Latin classics by attempting to imitate their spirit as well as their letter. Besides composing Latin verse and cultivating literary friendships, he discovered manuscripts of forgotten classics in the library of the Benedictine abbey of Pomposa, thus launching a search for the hidden treasures of antiquity which became one of the hallmarks of humanism.

The Italian with whom humanism came of age was Francesco Petrarca, or Petrarch (1304–74), whose writings have had an enormous effect on European literature. Petrarch was a sensitive writer and a Christian by conviction (his favourite reading was Augustine), who reacted against the Aristotelian form in which Christianity was presented by the medieval scholastics. He was not a speculative thinker, and hated the logic-chopping of the schools, the sterility of medieval rhetoric, and the 'barbarism' of scholastic Latin.

The importance of Petrarch in the history of the church is that he polarized Christian opinion between the old scholasticism and the new humanism, between authoritarian tradition and the cult of original texts. In the next two centuries, both the Protestant and Catholic Reformations occurred in the context of this polarization. Petrarch has been called 'the first modern man', and it is true that some of his activities and attitudes (such as climbing a mountain to enjoy the view from the top) are more typical of our own day than of his. But in fact he shared with his contemporaries many medieval prejudices and limitations. His Christian humanism agonized between Augustine and Cicero, yet the inheritance he left for his successors was the ideal of a world of classical values recaptured and displayed within the context of a restored Christianity.

Apart from his friend and admirer, Giovanni Boccaccio (1313–75), a fellow-humanist who wrote voluminously in Latin and Italian – the *Decameron* is his masterpiece – Petrarch's immediate heir was Coluccio Salutati (1331–1406). This Tuscan notary was for more than thirty years chancellor of Florence city council, and in that office introduced classical eloquence into city correspondence. He continued the quest to find hidden manuscripts and subject them to critical examination, and was himself the author of Latin works modelled on the classics of antiquity. Two of his most eminent followers, Leonardo Bruni (c. 1370–1444) and Poggio Bracciolini (1380–1459), left Florence and found jobs in the papal chancery at Rome, which, after the election of Pope Martin V in 1417, became the most important centre of humanism in Italy.

THE COUNCIL OF CONSTANCE

The Conciliar Movement, which looked for the reform of the church by the calling of a general council, was inextricably bound up with the history of the Renaissance and the expansion of humanism. While attending the Council of Constance as a papal secretary, Poggio Bracciolini found time to explore the surrounding German and Swiss monasteries for classical texts, and his searches were richly rewarded. At St Gall and elsewhere he discovered invaluable works by Cicero, Lucretius, Quintilian, Statius, Vitruvius, and other Latin authors. These were the most notable manuscript finds of the century.

The council, which was transferred from Ferrara to Florence, gave classical studies another stimulus since it was attended by several learned Greeks. Among them was Cardinal Basilios Bessarion (1403–72), the leading collector of Greek manuscripts in the fifteenth century. For the cult of ancient Rome led to the cult of ancient Greece.

One of the foremost aims of Italian humanists was to read classical Greek literature in the original. The knowledge of Greek had never entirely died out in the West, but before the fifteenth century it was confined to a mere handful of scholars in any one generation. Petrarch owned a text of Homer, but could not read it; Boccaccio tried to learn the language but made little headway. It was Salutati who most effectively championed the cause of Greek studies in Italy. Through his efforts, a professorship of Greek was created at Florence in 1396, and the post was filled the following year by Manuel Chrysoloras (c. 1355–1415), a distinguished Byzantine scholar and a diplomat brought over from Constantinople. A succession of learned Greeks occupied the position until 1480, when an Italian humanist – Angelo Poliziano (1454–94) – was appointed. By that time Greek studies were firmly established in the West.

Greek is the language of the New Testament as well as of the classics, and inevitably the humanists extended their attention from texts of profane literature to the texts of sacred literature. The pioneer in this field was Lorenzo Valla (c. 1407–57), a Roman who deserves to be called the father of modern biblical criticism. In 1444 he published a daring comparison between the Latin *Vulgate* translation and the Greek original in his *Annotations on the New Testament*.

For Valla everything was subject to the same scholarly investigation. Jerome's *Vulgate* Bible was a text to be examined on the same principles of criticism as the *Annals* of Tacitus. Four years earlier he had proved from historical and linguistic evidence that the Donation of Constantine was a forgery. In another work he mocked the methods of scholasticism. By meticulous scholarship and comparison of text with text he undermined the medieval tradition that was based on authority. In many ways Valla foreshadowed Erasmus, and his writings deeply influenced the German Reformers of the next century, being specially prized by Luther.

Other humanists were meanwhile encouraging new developments in education. For this was the age of the first humanist educators, such as Guarino of Verona (1374–1450), tutor of Leonello d'Este, Marquis of Ferrara, and Vittorino da Feltre (1378–1446), the herald of modern educational practice. In 1423 at Mantua, where he tutored the children of Gianfrancesco Gonzaga, Vittorino founded the *Casa Gioiosa* (the 'Happy House'), a school dedicated to the ideal of 'a sound mind in a healthy body' (*mens sana in corpore sano*). Its curriculum included music, philosophy, and physical training as well as the Trivium and Quadrivium of traditional medieval education. Like many other innovations of this time – such as the introduction of the clock in the home and the table-fork – the reforms in the schooling of boys initiated by these humanist educators began to be imitated far and wide, and heralded the modern world.

PLATO REVIVED

It has been well said that medieval thought means Aristotle, and Renaissance thought means Plato. The revival of Platonism in the West owes much to Petrarch, Chrysoloras and Bruni, but still more to the Council of Florence. One of the Greeks who attended it was Georgius Gemistus, later called Pletho (c. 1355–1452/4), whose life was devoted to the cult of Plato. He influenced Cosimo de' Medici (1389–1464), the banker who virtually ruled Florence, and who in turn was able to encourage Marsilio Ficino (1433–99), the Italian philosopher by whose efforts enthusiasm for Plato as a forerunner of Christ caught fire in Italy.

Ficino translated all Plato's known writings into Latin, a daunting enterprise begun in 1463 and completed in 1477. He also founded the Platonic Academy, which became the focus of the cultural life of Florence in the golden age of Lorenzo de' Medici (1449–92), called 'the Magnificent'. The most remarkable member of this Academy was Giovanni Pico della Mirandola (1463–94), who represents Renaissance thinking at its brilliant best. In his writings he sought to harmonize Plato with Aristotle, the Jewish mystic doctrines (*Kabbalah*) with Christianity, and eloquently proclaimed the dignity of men and women in the universe of God.

A NEW WORLD OF LEARNING

Neoplatonism (as this revival of Platonic thought in the context of Christianity is known) invaded the art and poetry of Florence. Examples include the paintings of Sandro Botticelli (c. 1445–1510) and the *Stanze* of the poet Poliziano. It also affected some of the Italian reformers of the sixteenth century, such as Bernardino Ochino of Siena (1487–1564), making Calvin and other Protestants suspicious of them.

Papal diplomacy and the Conciliar Movement gave many varied opportunities for social and intellectual exchange. It was not long before the Renaissance was exported from its country of origin and humanists began to multiply in France, Germany, Holland, Spain, and England. The two leading French humanists were Jacques Lefèvre d'Étaples (c. 1455–1536) and Guillaume Budé (1467–1540), whose exact and penetrating scholarship paved the way for the Reformation in their country. Of particular importance in Germany were Cardinal Nicholas of Cusa (1401–64), the foremost speculative thinker of his age, and Johann Reuchlin (1455–1522), whose *De Rudimentis Hebraicis* (1506) established the study of Hebrew in the West.

From Holland came Erasmus, the greatest of all humanists. Spain produced the *Complutensian Polyglot Bible*, a unique humanist project promoted by Cardinal Francisco Jiménez de Cisneros (1436–1517), with contributions by scholars such as Elio Antonio de Nebrija (1441–1522). In England the new learning flowered in such Christian humanists as John Colet (1467–1519), Dean of St Paul's, whose Oxford lectures on Paul's letters broke new ground. Sir Thomas More (1478–1535), the author of *Utopia*, was martyred for his Catholic constancy by Henry VIII.

Whether by cause or effect, the fifteenth century also saw the foundation of more than two dozen new universities in Europe, among them those of Alcalá, Bordeaux, Louvain, St Andrews, Tübingen, and Uppsala. The University of Wittenberg, in which Luther taught, was opened in 1502. In the wake of humanism came the founding or development of some of the greatest non-monastic libraries in western Europe, such as the Vatican in Rome, the Laurentian in Florence, and the Bodleian in Oxford.

> I wish that the Scriptures might be translated into all languages, so that not only the Scots and the Irish, but also the Turk and the Saracen might read and understand them. I long that the farm-labourer might sing them as he follows his plough, the weaver hum them to the tune of his shuttle, the traveller beguile the weariness of his journey with their stories.
>
> DESIDERIUS ERASMUS

GUTENBERG'S REVOLUTION

A completely new dimension in the history of books, scholarship, and education opened up with the invention of printing – sometimes called Germany's chief contribution to the Renaissance. The art of printing from handcut wooden blocks was invented in Asia in about the fifth century AD, and the first known printed book was produced by this means in China in 868. But Europe had to wait until the middle of the fifteenth century for the art to be rediscovered and developed. About 1445 Johannes Gutenberg (c. 1398–68) began to pioneer with movable metal type at Mainz in Germany, and – significantly – the first complete book known to have been printed in the Christian world was the Bible (1456).

Until 1462 the new art remained a closely guarded trade secret in Mainz, but in that year the city was plundered and the printers dispersed. Within two decades the invention spread north,

Erasmus monument in Rotterdam, The Netherlands
© GRAFZERO/DREAMSTIME.COM

south, east, and west: printing-presses were set up in Rome in 1467, Paris in 1470, Cracow in 1474, and Westminster in 1476. By the time Luther was born, in 1483, printing was well established throughout Europe. It was the most momentous invention since the stirrup, and a revolutionary step forward in technology. Like the invention of gunpowder (rediscovered at about the same time), the application of printing to book-production held a tremendous potential for good and evil in subsequent history.

The printing-press was very important in the early spread of the Reformation. The writings of the first German reformers – Luther and Melanchthon – reached a comparatively wide public in printed form within weeks, and were soon read in Paris and Rome. At the height of the Reformation, in the last years of Luther's life, busy printers enabled the anonymous work *Beneficio di Christo* (which more than any other book spread the doctrine of justification by faith in Italy) to sell 40,000 copies in Venice alone after its publication there in 1543.[1] But even before the Reformation, printing had helped to create a wider and more critical reading-public than had ever been known in the Christian world. It also met the new demand for reading material, with works such as the religious satires of Erasmus, which were a big commercial success. On hearing a rumour that the Sorbonne was about to condemn it, one Paris printer rushed through an edition of 24,000 copies of Erasmus' *Colloquies*. Thus printing helped prepare the way for the Reformation.

THE MODERN WAY OF SERVING GOD

Even more important in preparing the way for the Reformation was the rise of a movement called the *Devotio Moderna* ('the modern way of serving God') in northern Europe. This was a spiritual revival that began within the Catholic Church in the late fourteenth century and strongly emphasized both personal devotion and social involvement, especially in education. At the time when humanism was beginning to flower in Italy, seeds of spiritual renewal were germinating north of the Alps.

Their most industrious sower was Geert Groote (1340–84), a native of Deventer in Holland who had studied at Paris and taught at Cologne. He lived a life of self-indulgent luxury before being brought to repentance and commitment to Christ in 1374. The change in his life was total: from that time forward he devoted himself to practical piety in the service of God and man. He joined the Carthusians and spent three years in their monastery of Munnikhuizen, near Arnhem. He left the order in 1379 to undertake a strenuous travelling mission in the diocese of Utrecht, preaching with profound effect on the townspeople in Flanders, Guelders, and Holland. He had such an exalted view of Christian priesthood that he never advanced beyond the rank of deacon. At the same time, he wrote tracts against simony and the immorality of the clergy, and condemned prevailing clerical abuses so sharply that his licence to preach was revoked in 1383.

In the year of his conversion, Groote gathered a community of devout women in his house at Deventer to live the common life together, without taking the vows of a convent. Religion, he said, is to love God and worship him, not the taking of special vows. Jan van Ruysbroeck

---

[1]   The book was apparently drafted by Benedetto Fontanini (1495–1556) and completed by Marcantonio Flaminio (c. 1497–1550).

(1293–1381), the aged Flemish mystic, and Florens Radewijns (c. 1350–1400), an ordained priest with organizing genius who had studied at Prague, were both associated with him.

BRETHREN OF THE COMMON LIFE

Later a community of men, both lay and clergy (mainly like-minded friends and followers of Groote), formed around Radewijns in his Deventer house and became known as the Brethren of the Common Life (Latin, *Fratres Vitae Communis*). This was a semi-monastic group, observing the threefold rule of poverty, chastity, and obedience, but bound by no formal vow. Thus any member was free to quit the brotherhood and return to secular life if he so pleased. The Brethren did not beg for alms, like the mendicant friars, but studied to be quiet, to do their own business, and work with their own hands, according to the instruction of the apostle Paul.

When Groote died of the plague, Radewijns took over the leadership of the *Devotio Moderna* movement, and in 1387 founded its most influential house at Windesheim, near Zwolle, in Holland. Here the Brethren of the Common Life became Augustinian canons, and their constitutions were approved by Pope Boniface IX in 1395. A few years later they combined with other houses in Holland to form the Congregation of Windesheim.

They dedicated themselves not only to spiritual discipline and renouncing the world, but also to the whole process of education. They taught in the local schools and founded schools of their own. In order to support their community, they busied themselves with every aspect of book-production: writing, copying manuscripts, binding, and marketing volumes, and – with the advent of printing – operating their own press. Windesheim and its daughter-houses were soon known as hives of pious industry. In time the movement set on foot by Groote gathered momentum and spread and during the fifteenth century the Windesheim Canons set up communities in Germany and Switzerland.

Many of the Brethren of the Common Life and those educated by them left their mark on the Christian world. The foremost of these were Nicholas of Cusa and Erasmus himself. Gabriel Biel (c. 1420–95), the philosopher known as 'the last German schoolman', and the humanist Rodolphus Agricola (1444–85) were both members of the community, for the finest elements of scholasticism and humanism co-existed in the *Devotio Moderna*.

THE IMITATION OF CHRIST

Perhaps the individual who best sums up the faith of the *Devotio Moderna* is Thomas Haemerken (c. 1380–1471), better known as Thomas à Kempis, the author of *The Imitation of Christ*, the choicest devotional handbook of the Middle Ages. From the age of twelve, when he attended the chapter school at Deventer and came under the spiritual guidance of Radewijns, to the end of his long life, Thomas à Kempis was wholly immersed in the movement begun by Groote. In 1406 he became an Augustinian canon in the daughter-house of St Agnietenberg, near Zwolle, which he had entered in 1399 and where – apart from three years – he remained until he died. He wrote books, copied manuscripts, preached Christ, and counselled others. His life and works reveal the fine flower of the spirituality of the late medieval church.

The Imitation of Christ is written in Latin and divided into four parts: the first contains 'Some thoughts to help with the spiritual life'; the second 'Some advice on the inner life'; the third and longest provides 'Spiritual comfort'; and the fourth is 'A reverent recommendation to holy communion'. As its title suggests, the purpose of the book is to teach the Christian the way of perfection through following Christ's example. It began to circulate anonymously in the second quarter of the fifteenth century, and within a few decades it was read and loved throughout western Europe. Since it was first printed at Augsburg in 1471, it has appeared in thousands of editions, and is one of the most widely read books in the world.

Although it teaches justification by works, the *Imitation* focuses the mind and heart on Jesus Christ:

> *If a man knows what it is to love Jesus, and to disregard himself for the sake of Jesus, then he is really blessed. We have to abandon all we love for the one we love, for Jesus wants us to love him only above all other things. The love of creatures is fickle and unreliable, but the love of Jesus is trustworthy and enduring. The man who clings to created things will fall with them when they fall, but a man who embraces Jesus will be upheld for ever. It is Jesus whom you must love and keep to be your friend; when all else fades away, he will not leave you, nor let you perish at the end. Whether you will or no, you must one day leave everything behind. Keep yourself close to Jesus in life as well as death; commit yourself to his faithfulness, for he only can help you when everything else will fail.*

The *Devotio Moderna* conditioned many hearts and minds in northern Europe to receive the teaching of the Reformers. No great revolution, such as the Protestant Reformation, happens without rumblings and warnings. Luther had his heralds and prophets: before him came many lesser Luthers. Four of them deserve mention because their writings either anticipated the Reformer or helped form his views.

Meister Eckhart (Eckhart von Hochheim, c. 1260–c. 1327) was a German Dominican mystic whose teaching was condemned by the pope after his death. He is now recognized as the most dynamic force in the religious life of Germany before the Reformation. His pupil, Johannes Tauler (c. 1300–61), also a German Dominican mystic, was a powerful preacher who stressed human nothingness in the presence of God: his sermons helped to mould Luther's thinking at a critical stage in his spiritual experience.

John of Wesel (John Rucherat, c. 1420–81) from the Rhineland, foreshadowed the German Reformers in much of his teaching. He rejected many of the distinctive doctrines and practices of the medieval Catholic Church, and declared that the Bible alone is the ultimate authority in matters of faith. He wrote against indulgences in 1475, was tried by the Inquisition in 1479, and condemned to life confinement in the Augustinian prison at Mainz. Wessel Gansfort (1419–89), a Dutch theologian educated by the Brethren of the Common Life at Deventer, has been called the first of the biblical humanists. He, too, wrote against indulgences and took up much of the same position as Luther in attacking the pope's pretensions and denouncing church errors of his day.

THE JOURNALIST OF SCHOLARSHIP

The last and most effective forerunner of the Reformation lived long enough to be embarrassed by its challenge. Desiderius Erasmus of Rotterdam (1466–1536), the greatest humanist after Petrarch, made the Reformation almost inevitable, for (as the monks complained) he laid the egg which Luther hatched. Educated by the Brethren of the Common Life in Holland, he became an Augustinian canon in 1487, was ordained priest in 1492, but left the monastery because he felt himself unsuited to the life of a monk. In 1495 he went to study in Paris, but found the Nominalist theology of the schools distasteful, preferring the classics of antiquity and the circle of French humanists. During his first visit to England (1499–1500) he enjoyed the friendship of Colet and More, who drew him towards their own form of Christian humanism.

Back in Holland and France, Erasmus began to publish a series of best-selling satires, which ridiculed monasticism and scholasticism, contrasted the 'Old Ignorance' with the 'New Learning', and used enlightened common sense to examine the practice of Christianity. The first of these was the *Christian Soldier's Manual* (Latin, *Enchiridion militis Christiani*) and the most widely read, the *Colloquies*, which appeared in more than 600 editions. A second visit to England (1505–06) was followed by three years in Italy, which deepened his humanist sympathies and his contempt for the corruption of Rome, expressed devastatingly in his *The Praise of Folly*, written in seven days while staying with More in London.

Erasmus has been called the 'journalist of scholarship', and certainly he wrote with easy elegance and biting wit as he spread the ideals of Christian humanism. But he was also a serious editor of Latin and Greek texts. His edition of Jerome's works was a major piece of patient scholarship, but his most important contribution to the history of the church was his epoch-making edition of the Greek New Testament (the first ever published), printed at Basle in 1516 – the year before the Reformation began.

Never had official religion been at a lower ebb, or the public image of Christianity more defaced, than in the second decade of the sixteenth century. It seemed as though all opposition to the unreformed Catholic Church from within and without was dying away. The Fifth Lateran Council met in Rome in 1512 and heard the orator declare: 'Now nobody contradicts, no one opposes.' The Medici Pope Leo X ascended the papal throne in 1513 with the quip: 'Now that we have attained the papacy, let us enjoy it!' The Lateran Council ended on a note of complacent self-congratulation in March 1517. The peace of the Christian world seemed assured. But the seeds of renewal had been sown; the harvest of Reformation was at hand. In October of that same year, in an obscure province of the Empire, one roused German conscience was stung into protest – and the great revolution began.

PHILIP MCNAIR

CHAPTER 23

REFORMATION

The Reformation began on the eve of All Saints' Day, 31 October 1517. On that day Martin Luther (1483–1546), professor of biblical studies at the newly founded University of Wittenberg in Germany, announced a disputation on indulgences. He stated his argument in *95 Theses*. Though they were heavily academic, and moderate in tone, news of them spread like wildfire throughout Europe. Within a fortnight every university and religious centre was agog with excitement. All marvelled that one obscure monk from an unknown university had stirred the whole of Europe.

LUTHER PROTESTS

But the *95 Theses* were not by any means intended as a call to reformation. They were simply the proposal of an earnest university professor to discuss the theology of indulgences, in the light of the errors and abuses that had grown up over the centuries. The dealings in indulgences ('the holy trade' as it was unblushingly called) had grown

MARTIN LUTHER

More books have been written about Luther, the great German Reformer, than about any figure in history except Jesus Christ. Martin Luther (1483–1546), born in Eisleben, studied law at the University of Erfurt. In 1505 he joined a closed Augustinian friary in Erfurt, after taking a dramatic vow during a thunderstorm. Luther was ordained in 1507, and after studying theology was sent to the University of Wittenberg to teach moral theology. In 1510–11 he visited Rome on business for his order, and in 1512 became a doctor of theology and professor of biblical studies at Wittenberg.

After a long spiritual crisis, Luther finally came to understand the nature of God's righteousness. He rejected all theology based solely on tradition, and emphasized the personal understanding and experience of God's Word. Centrally, he believed justification is not by works, but by faith alone. Luther's views became widely known when he posted the *95 Theses* on the door of the Castle Church at Wittenberg, attacking the teaching behind the sale of indulgences and the church's material preoccupations.

Sculpted head of the German Reformer Martin Luther, from a statue by Theobald Stein at Frederikskirken, Copenhagen, Denmark.
© IAN DANBURY | DREAMSTIME.COM

In December 1517 the Archbishop of Mainz complained to Rome about Luther. Faced with opposition, Luther's stand became firmer; he refused to recant, confronted Cardinal Thomas Cajetan in Augsburg, and fled when summoned to Rome. In July 1519, during a into scandal. Luther did not oppose indulgences in their true and original sense — as the merciful release of a penitent sinner from a penance imposed earlier by a priest. What Luther opposed was all the additions and perversions of indulgences, which were harmful to human salvation and infected the everyday practice of the church.

Medieval people had a very real dread of the period of punishment in purgatory which was portrayed in detail by the church. They had no great fear of hell, because they believed that, if they died forgiven and blessed by the priest, they were guaranteed access through heaven's gates, whose key was held by the church. But they feared purgatory's pains; for the church taught that, before they reached heaven, they had to be cleansed of every sin committed in mortal life. Once penance was made a sacrament, the ordinary person believed (even Dante did) that an indulgence assured the shortening of the punishments to be endured after death in purgatory. The relics of the Castle Church, on whose door Luther nailed his *95 Theses*, were reckoned to earn a remission for pilgrims of 1,902,222 years and 270 days!

Luther saw that the trade in indulgences was wholly unwarranted by Scripture, reason, or tradition. It encouraged people in their sin, and tended to turn their mind

> Good works do not make a man good, but a good man does good works.
>
> MARTIN LUTHER

disputation at Leipzig with Johann Eck (1486–1543), his sharpest opponent, Luther denied the supremacy of the pope and the infallibility of church councils. He burned the papal bull which threatened his excommunication. But excommunication finally came in 1521.

Luther again refused to recant before the Diet of Worms in April 1521, unless his ideas were refuted from Scripture. For his own safety, he was seized and taken to the Wartburg Castle, under the protection of Frederick of Saxony. There he devoted his energies to translating the New Testament into German, so that the Bible might be read by all.

Eight months later, in 1522, Luther returned to Wittenberg to put a brake on the radical reformers. He set about reforming public worship, emphasizing preaching the Word, the eucharist, and congregational singing. During the Peasants' Revolt (1524–25), Luther opposed what he labelled the 'murderous hordes of peasants', and so alienated them. He rejected Zwingli's understanding of the eucharist as simply a remembrance meal rather than the real presence of Christ. In 1530 Luther approved the *Augsburg Confession* drawn up by Melanchthon. Although this led him into conflict with the Emperor, he believed the gospel must be defended whenever it was attacked. In 1537 Luther wrote the *Schmalkaldic Articles*, a doctrinal statement signed by many Lutheran theologians.

Luther's teaching and personal experience are closely linked. He always proceeds in the same way: from Scripture to personal conviction to declaration and preaching. For Luther, God's only communication with humankind is through his Word. Christ is the essence of Scripture, and in Christ the Word becomes flesh. God speaks only to those who have faith; faith is God's gift, not our achievement. Luther saw God behind everything in the world. He dismissed the problem of reconciling God's love and justice with the doctrine of predestination: God is always just. He is beyond human reason, mysterious, and inconceivable. If we could comprehend him, he would not be God.

ROBERT STUPPERICH

away from Christ and from God's forgiveness. At this point Luther's theology contrasted sharply with that of the church. The pope claimed authority 'to shut the gates of hell and open the door to paradise'. An obscure monk challenged that authority – and his contemporaries knew at once that he had touched the exposed nerve of both the hierarchy of the church and the everyday practice of Christianity. Christian Europe was never the same again.

Ordered to recant in 1520, Luther was eventually excommunicated on 3 January 1521, and finally outlawed by the Emperor Charles V at Worms in 1521. He had already had disputations with his own Augustinian order in Heidelberg in 1518, and with papal authorities in Augsburg in 1518, and in Leipzig in 1519. Luther's dramatic stand against both pope and Emperor fired the imagination of Europe.

Luther published book after book over the next twenty-five years. Those written for ordinary Christians were in powerful and vivid German. He also translated the Bible into German, which enabled people to see for themselves the truth of

> ... the maist perfyt schoole of Chryst that ever was in the erth since the dayis of the Apostillis.
>
> JOHN KNOX, ON CALVIN'S GENEVA

JOHN CALVIN

John Calvin (1509–64), the Genevan Reformer, created and systematized the Reformed tradition in Protestantism. A Frenchman, he was born at Noyon, Picardy. In contrast to Luther, Calvin was a quiet, sensitive man. He said little about his inner life; he was content to trace God's hand controlling him. He inherited from his father an immovable will, which stood him in good stead in turbulent Geneva. Calvin was always a conscientious student – at Orléans, Bourges, and the University of Paris. He soon took up the methods of humanism, which he later used 'to combat humanism'.

In Paris, the young Calvin encountered the teachings of Luther. Around 1533 he experienced a sudden conversion: 'God subdued and brought my heart to docility. It was more hardened against

John Calvin (1509–64), French humanist scholar and reformer, whose leadership of the church in Geneva, Switzerland was emulated by many Protestants in Europe.
TIM DOWLEY ASSOCIATES

such matters than was to be expected in such a young man.' He next broke with Roman Catholicism, left France, and lived as an exile in Basle. He began to formulate his theology, and in 1536 published the first edition of *The Institution of the Christian Religion* (better known as the *Institutes*), a brief, clear defence of Reformation beliefs.

William Farel (1489–1565), the Reformer of Geneva, persuaded Calvin to help consolidate the Reformation there. But Genevans opposed Calvin's efforts, and disputes in the town, together with a quarrel with the city of Berne, resulted in the expulsion of both Calvin and Farel. Calvin went to Strasbourg, where he made contact with Martin Bucer, who encouraged and influenced him. In 1539 Calvin published his commentary on the book of Romans, followed by many other commentaries. Calvin also produced a new, enlarged version of the *Institutes*. The French Reformer also led the congregation of French refugees in Strasbourg, an experience which matured him for his task on returning to Geneva.

CALVIN'S GENEVA

Calvin was invited back to Geneva in September 1541. The town council accepted his revision of the city laws, but many bitter disputes followed. Calvin tried to bring every citizen under the moral discipline of the church, and many resented such restrictions – especially when imposed by a foreigner. He now set about attaining his aim of a mature church, by preaching daily to the people.

Calvin devoted much energy to settling differences within Protestantism. The *Consensus Tigurinus*, on the Lord's Supper (1549), resulted in the German- and French-speaking churches of Switzerland moving closer together. In 1553 Michael Servetus (1509/11–53), a notorious critic of Calvin and of the doctrine of the Trinity, was arrested and burnt in Geneva. Servetus was already on the run from the Inquisition, and was regarded by all as a heretic. The Protestant reformers felt they could not afford to be seen as soft on heresy.

Wherever we find the Word of God surely preached and heard, and the sacraments administered according to the institution of Christ, there, it is not to be doubted, is a church of God.

JOHN CALVIN, IN *THE INSTITUTES*

Calvin was in a sense trying to build a more visible 'City of God' in Europe – with Geneva as a starting-point. In his later years, Calvin's authority in Geneva was less disputed. He founded the Geneva Academy, to which students of theology came from all parts of western and central Europe, and particularly France.

Calvin was the great systematizer, taking up and re-applying the ideas of the first generation of Reformers. His work was characterized by intellectual discipline and practical application. His *Institutes* have been a classic statement of Reformation theology for centuries, and he was also a careful interpreter of the Bible.

Lutheranism strongly influenced Calvin's doctrine. For Calvin, all knowledge of God is to be found solely in the Word of God. We can know God only if he chooses to be known. Pardon and salvation are possible only through the free working of the grace of God. Calvin claimed that, even before creation, God chose some of his creatures for salvation and others for destruction.

For Calvin, the church was supreme: it should not be restricted in any way by the state. He gave greater importance than Luther to the organization of the church, and regarded only baptism and the eucharist as sacraments. Baptism was the individual's initiation into the new community of Christ. Calvin rejected Zwingli's idea that the sacrament of communion was merely a symbol – but also warned against a magical belief in the real presence of Christ in the sacrament.

ANDREAS LINDT

his arguments. He published an account of each of his disputes with Rome, so that people could judge for themselves. He put the ordinary Christian on his theological feet, and his followers multiplied.

In 1529, at the Diet of Speyer, the Emperor Charles V attempted to curb Luther's movement by force. But some of the princes of the German states stood up in 'protest'; thus the movement found itself with the title 'Protestant'. From this moment the movement – which had all along been intended to reform Catholicism from within – separated off, to become known as 'the Reformation'.

In 1530, Luther put forward the beliefs of the new movement at the Diet of Augsburg. It was a cool and non-controversial explanation, peace-seeking, comprehensive, Catholic, and conservative. But Luther's movement split Christian Europe in two, and gave rise to the churches known as evangelical or Protestant. Three main traditions emerged: the Lutheran (in Germany and Scandinavia); the Zwinglian and Calvinist (in Switzerland, France, Holland, and Scotland); and the Church of England.

Lasting social, political, and economic changes followed the Reformation, and to some extent shaped it. But the Reformation was primarily a rediscovery of the gospel of God's saving work in Christ.

LUTHER'S DIAGNOSIS

In his monastery Luther had been searching for God's pardon and his peace. He faithfully obeyed his order, and observed punctiliously the spiritual techniques, yet he found himself no nearer to God. He began to see the way of the monk as merely a long discipline of religious duty and effort. Mysticism was an attempt to climb up to heaven and academic theology little more than speculation about God, his nature, and his character.

Luther found one basic error in all these techniques of finding God. Ultimately they trusted in human ability to get to God, or at least take us near enough for God to accept us. Luther now believed it was not a matter of God being far from everyone, and people having to strive to reach him, but the reverse. Humanity, created and sinful, was distant from God; God in Christ had come all the way to find us.

Luther's discovery did not represent a break with traditional doctrines. The Reformers held – as did the Roman Church – all the orthodox doctrines stated in the general creeds of the early church. But the Reformers understood these doctrines in the particular context of salvation in Christ alone. The Reformers held that the believer came into direct relation and union with Christ, as the one, only, and all-sufficient source of grace. His grace is available to the penitent believer by the power of the Holy Spirit, through the preaching of the Word of God. This did away with the need for the Virgin Mary as mediator, the clergy as priests, and the departed saints as intercessors. From Luther's rediscovery of the direct and personal relationship between Christ and the believer came three great principles of the Reformation.

AUTHORITY

Luther, and all the Reformers, believed that God had spoken to humanity, and acted on behalf of humanity, throughout history. The account of how God had dealt with people was given in Scripture. They believed God continued to speak through the words spoken to prophets and apostles. In this personal revelation, God himself spoke in love to created humanity, and renewed people heard and answered in faith.

The Reformers did not feel that they were handling and interpreting Scripture; but that God was handling them through Scripture. This is what the Reformers meant by the Word of God: the living Word speaking to them in their own situation. Beliefs and church practice could not be justified if they were other than, outside of, or apart from the Word of God. These truths could be expressed in non-biblical words, or non-biblical form, as they were in later creeds and statements of belief. But what is being expressed must be biblical truth.

The Roman Church, too, accepted the authority of Scripture, but in practice claimed that both the Bible *and* tradition were sources and rules of faith. The Roman Church also made tradition, as expressed in the decrees of popes and councils, the only permissible, legitimate, and infallible interpreter of the Bible.

The Bible was rarely read. When it was, it was interpreted at four levels – the literal, spiritual, allegorical, and anagogical (that is, its heavenly meaning). Few knew what the Bible really said or meant. Faith was regarded largely as a matter of agreeing to statements about God, the soul, grace, and other subjects. Medieval theologians had tended to place the church – in the shape of opinions of the early Fathers confirmed by popes and councils – between the believer and his Bible.

Many of the Reformers were linguists and scholars. Protestants began to produce biblical criticism, believing the Bible spoke to intellectuals of their age as well as to common people of every period. The Reformers reasserted the ancient creeds as well as formulating their own statements, and rejected only those doctrines and ceremonies for which there was no clear basis in Scripture. The Calvinists went further than the Lutherans in their opposition to traditions which had been handed down. They rejected a good deal of church music, art, architecture, and many more superficial matters, such as the use of the ring in marriage, and signs of devotional practice.

But the Reformers rejected the authority of the pope, the merit of good works, indulgences, the mediation of the Virgin Mary and the saints, and all sacraments which had not been instituted by Christ. They rejected the doctrine of transubstantiation (the teaching that the bread and wine of communion became the body and blood of Christ when the priest

Luther reads Romans

I greatly longed to understand Paul's Epistle to the Romans, and nothing stood in the way but that one expression, 'the righteousness of God', because I took it to mean that righteousness whereby God is righteous and deals righteously in punishing the unrighteous … Night and day I pondered until … I grasped the truth that the righteousness of God is that righteousness whereby, through grace and sheer mercy, he justifies us by faith. Thereupon I felt myself to be reborn and to have gone through open doors into paradise. The whole of Scripture took on a new meaning, and whereas before 'the righteousness of God' had filled me with hate, now it became to me inexpressibly sweet in greater love. This passage of Paul became to me a gateway to heaven.

MARTIN LUTHER

consecrated them), the view of the mass as a sacrifice, purgatory and prayers for the dead, private confession of sin to a priest, celibacy of the clergy, and the use of Latin the services. They also rejected all the equipment that expressed these ideas – such as holy water, shrines, chantries, wonder-working images, rosaries, paternoster stones, images, and candles.

BY GRACE ALONE

The second major principle of the Reformation was salvation by the free and undeserved grace of Christ. This came to be known as 'justification by faith only'. Protestants believed that by

THE FAITH OF THE PROTESTANTS

Careful Calvin orchestrated Protestant theology most skilfully, but fertile Martin Luther wrote nearly all the tunes. Taught by humanists to study the Bible writers' own message, Luther learned from the apostles Paul and John that God saves sinners by imparting through his Word a transforming knowledge of Jesus Christ. Believers know Christ as the divine Lover who died for their sins, who rose again to conquer 'principalities and powers', and now as mediator secures to them the gift of righteousness – pardon of guilt, acceptance as God's children, and sure hope of reward. From this faith-knowledge of Christ and his benefits flows the whole of Christian living: repentance, communion with God, and good works, all in conscious freedom from the soul-destroying necessity of earning God's continued favour by self-effort. Such was Luther's gospel of justification by faith alone, the centrepiece of Protestant theology for two centuries.

WHAT LUTHER TAUGHT

Luther affirmed the final authority of a self-interpreted Bible, and rejected non-scriptural beliefs. He taught a 'spiritual' doctrine of the church, depicting it as a serving priesthood of believers, as against the medieval idea of the church as a hierarchical institution under the bishop of Rome, administering salvation through sacraments. Here, too, all Protestants agreed.

The Lutheran churches of Germany and Scandinavia developed in isolation from the Reformed churches of Switzerland, Holland, the Rhineland, and Britain, but this was an accident of geography and politics,

rather than a sign of major theological differences. Luther taught that infants were regenerated in baptism, through infant faith. He also affirmed the 'real presence' of Christ's body 'in, with, and under' the eucharistic bread. To buttress this idea he maintained the 'ubiquity', or capacity for 'multipresence', of Jesus' glorified flesh. Lutherans followed him, but Calvin and Reformed theologians generally rejected these ideas, holding that Christ's body is 'in Heaven, and not here', and that Christ encounters his people at the communion table, not by bodily presence in the elements, but by the Spirit's presence and power in their hearts. Lutherans found this view irreverently 'low'.

CHANGES TO WORSHIP

For pastoral reasons, Luther retained much medieval ritual in worship, urging that when doctrine was sound ceremonies were 'things indifferent' (*adiaphora*), which the church was free to use or not as it thought best. Reformed leaders, however, wanted worship to be as simple and scriptural as possible, and their liturgies were plainer than those of their Lutheran counterparts. From this standpoint, the English Prayer Book was a half-way house. It came to be argued that features in worship *not* prescribed in Scripture should be seen as forbidden. This so-called 'puritan' or 'regulative' principle became the rule in Scotland, and lay behind the further purifying of worship and ministry in England for which Elizabethan Puritans unsuccessfully called.

Meantime, in Germany in 1548, two years after Luther's death, mild Melanchthon, his successor as the action of God alone, in the death and resurrection of Christ, they were called from their sin to a new life in Christ. From this proceeded the fruits of the Spirit in loving acts.

The Catholics equally believed they were saved by Christ, but believed good works parallel faith, and laid stress on the merit of good works. Protestants held that they were 'justified' – made acceptable to God – solely by Christ. Catholics modified this, placing their own good works alongside. The Protestant did not disapprove of good works, but denied their value as a condition of justification, seeing them as the product and evidence of justification.

leader, accepted an agreement (the *Leipzig Interim*) re-establishing, among other things, the Latin mass, Corpus Christi Day, and extreme unction. He claimed these were 'things indifferent'. But the fierce Matthias Flacius (1520–75) denounced him, and the Lutheran theological world was convulsed.

THE DOCTRINE OF GRACE

Melanchthon made the doctrine of grace another storm-centre in Lutheranism. Luther had stressed the sinner's total spiritual impotence, and made God's sovereign grace the sole source of faith. Now Melanchthon ascribed to fallen humanity free-will in the sense of the 'power of applying oneself to grace'. This phrase from Erasmus, which Luther had abhorred, Melanchthon explicitly approved. So my faith ceases to be God's work in me, and becomes my work. Flacius and followers attacked his position. A generation of conflict was ended by the pan-Lutheran *Formula of Concord* (1577–80), which reaffirmed the sinner's total spiritual inability and God's unconditional predestination of the elect to faith – but stated also that an external call to salvation reaches all people and that final falling from grace is possible.

Melanchthon's modification of the doctrine of sovereign grace had its Reformed parallel. Beza, Calvin's scholastic successor at Geneva, developed belief in sovereign grace into 'supralapsarianism'; the view that God decreed the fall as a means to the end of saving the elect from sin. Most Reformed theologians at the turn of the seventeenth century agreed, but Jacobus Arminius, a gifted Dutchman, and once Beza's pupil, did not. In 1610 his disciples produced their manifesto, the *Remonstrance*, affirming that election to salvation rests on faith foreseen; that Christ died for all, though only believers benefit (Beza said he died only for the elect); that grace is not irresistible; and that perseverance depends on one's own actions over and above God's help. Against this the pan-Reformed Synod of Dort (1618) formulated the so-called 'five points of Calvinism' – total depravity, unconditional election, limited atonement (that is, limited in efficacy to the elect), irresistible grace in effectual calling, and final preservation of the saints (often memorized by the mnemonic t-u-l-i-p).

Dutch Arminianism was rationalistic in spirit, and subsequently drifted into querying Jesus' full deity. Some High Church Anglicans came independently to an essentially Arminian view of grace, not from rationalism, but from deference to the Greek Fathers.

Meanwhile, Johann Arndt (1555–1621) in Lutheran Germany, and the English Puritans, following the Cambridge scholar William Perkins (1558–1602), developed an impressive devotional theology of regeneration, sanctification, and the inner life, as being what the times most needed. From this seed the later Pietist movement grew.

J. I. PACKER

EVERY BELIEVER A PRIEST

The third important Reformation principle was termed the 'priesthood of believers'. The Reformers argued that there was no precedent in the early church for the priest as mediator, and also argued that nothing in Scripture supports the secular power of the clergy. This doctrine meant there were no longer two levels of Christian, spiritual and lay. There was one gospel, one justification by faith, one status before God common to all men and women, clergy and laity. Protestants opposed the idea that authority rested in an exclusive priesthood. People were freed from their vague fear of priests in this massive liberation movement.

The Reformers held that God called people to different occupations – father or farmer, scholar or pastor, servant or soldier – and in and through his or her calling, the Christian served God. The Reformation demanded much from every Christian. Believers had the right and the duty to read the newly-translated Bible. Every lay person was expected to take a responsible part in the government and public affairs of both church and society. Such thinking eventually helped give rise to the democratic states of Europe and North America.

The Reformers sometimes used words such as the 'invisible' church, or the 'latent' church, to distinguish between the true church known only to God, and the organization visible in the world. They believed the church consisted of all those called by God to salvation.

Protestant ministers were recruited from the godly and learned. The Church of England, and large parts of the Lutheran Church, particularly in Sweden, tried to retain the outward structure and ministry of their national church. They were attacked by both conservative Catholics and radical Protestants. Calvinists held an exalted and biblical view of the church as the chosen people of God and broke away from the traditional church structures as well as the Roman ministry. In this the free churches later followed them.

GERMANY

The movement initiated by Luther soon spread throughout Germany. Luther provided its chief source of energy and vision, but received powerful academic support, notably from the brilliant and moderate young Philipp Melanchthon. Luther also

PHILIPP MELANCHTHON

Upon Luther's death Philipp Melanchthon (1497–1560), born at Bretten, near Karlsruhe, took over the theological leadership of the movement he had begun. Melanchthon taught Greek, first in Tübingen, then at the University of Wittenberg. There, in 1518, he met Luther – a decisive encounter that changed Melanchthon from a humanist into a theologian and reformer. With his gift for logical consistency and wide knowledge of history, Melanchthon's influence on Protestantism was in certain ways even greater than Luther's.

Melanchthon publicly supported Luther at the Leipzig Disputation (1519), and when Luther was away from Wittenberg, he represented and defended him. In 1521, he wrote the *Commonplaces (Loci communes)*, the first book to describe clearly the teachings of the Reformation. He also contributed to Luther's German translation of the Bible. At Marburg (1529) Melanchthon opposed Zwingli, claiming the service of holy communion was more than a memorial. He was also responsible for the *Augsburg Confession* (1530), which remains the chief statement of faith in the Lutheran churches.

Melanchthon, however, often seemed prepared to concede matters of doctrine to the Roman Catholics for the sake of peace, believing reunion was essential. The theological struggles in his own camp, with other Lutherans, deeply troubled him.

ROBERT STUPPERICH

received support from some of the princes and from the German people, but was opposed by the pope, bishops, and the Emperor.

Luther had aimed only at reform within the church. Ordered to recant in 1520, he burnt the papal bull publicly, and as a result was excommunicated by the pope on 3 January 1521. Later that same year, he fearlessly withstood the Emperor at Worms with his famous words, 'Here I stand'. Almost the whole of north Germany and nearly every German free city was on Luther's side.

Luther created and sustained the German Reformation virtually single-handed. This he achieved by an immense output of books, by fearless preaching and teaching, by putting the

GERMAN PROTESTANTISM
IN 1618

Majority denomination:
- ☐ Catholic
- ☐ Lutheran
- ☐ Calvinist and Zwinglian
- ☐ Muslim area
- — Political Boundary

0   125   250 km
0 50 100 150 miles

Bible in German into the heart and mind of every man, woman and child, and by writing many biblical hymns. The 1526 Diet of Speyer had to allow his movement free course, but another in 1529 tried to prohibit further advance. It was at this Diet that a row of evangelical princes stood their ground and resisted this legislation, giving history the word 'Protestantism'.

At the Diet of Augsburg (1530) the Protestants submitted their statement of belief. But the Catholics refused to accept it, so the Emperor ordered a recess. The Protestant princes realized that the Emperor intended to make war on Protestantism, so formed the Schmalkaldic league as a kind of defensive alliance. After several conferences designed to find some form of compromise between Catholic and Protestant, the tragic Schmalkaldic War broke out in 1547, shortly after Luther's death in 1546. The Emperor defeated the Protestant forces and imprisoned their leaders. But the Protestant Maurice of Saxony fought back successfully and by the Treaty of Passau (1552) Protestantism was legally recognized, a settlement confirmed in the 'Interim' of 1555.

Once Luther had passed from the scene, a period of bitter theological warfare occurred within Protestantism. There was controversy over such matters as the difference between justification and sanctification; what doctrine was essential or non-essential; faith and works; and the nature of the 'real presence' at the eucharist. This is the period when Lutheranism developed – something which Luther foresaw and condemned. The *Book of Concord*, which sets out what we now understand as Lutheranism, was published in 1580. It included Melanchthon's *Augsburg Confession* and *Augsburg Apology*; Luther's two catechisms and the Schmalkaldic Articles (drawn up in 1537); and the *Formula of Concord*. Some of the Lutheran theologians drove large numbers of people over to the Calvinist church through their dogmatism. The Calvinists in Germany adopted the *Heidelberg Confession* (1563) as their statement of faith.

The devastating Thirty Years' War perpetuated political strife in Germany in the seventeenth century, until by the Treaty of Westphalia (1648) the Lutherans and Calvinists won equal rights with the Catholics.

SWITZERLAND

The Reformation broke out in Zürich at the same time as in Germany, but independently of it. Its theology was similar to Luther's, except in the doctrine of the eucharist. But Huldrych Zwingli (1484–1531), the Swiss Reformer, had patriotic ideals, and determined that the discipline and worship in his church should follow a non-Roman Catholic line.

The battle of Kappel (1531), at which Zwingli was killed, brought the Reformation in Switzerland to a halt. But in 1536 John Calvin (1509–64) was unwillingly pressed to lead the cause in French-speaking Geneva. Calvin, was an exiled Frenchman whose theological writings, especially *The Institution of the Christian Religion* and his numerous commentaries on the Bible, did much to shape the Reformed churches and their confessions of faith. He developed the Presbyterian form of church government, in which all ministers served at the same level, and the people were represented by lay elders.

Calvin is often remembered for his severe doctrine of election, particularly that some people are predestined to destruction. But Calvin also set out the way of repentance, faith, and sanctification. He intended that his theology should interpret Scripture faithfully, rather than develop his own ideas.

HULDRYCH ZWINGLI

Huldrych Zwingli (1484–1531), the Swiss Reformer, died in battle against the Catholics. Educated in Basel, Berne, and Vienna, until 1516 he was vicar at Glarus, where he learned Greek, possibly Hebrew, and studied the Church Fathers. He acted as chaplain to Swiss mercenary forces at the battle of Novara (1513) and at Marignano (1515), an experience that led him to oppose the contemporary use of mercenary soldiers.

Zwingli met Erasmus in 1515 and was deeply influenced by him. After his forced transfer to Einsiedeln, he began to develop evangelical beliefs as he reflected on the abuses of the church. In 1518 he was made peoples' priest at the Grossmünster in Zurich. He lectured on the New Testament and began to reform Zurich, working carefully with the city council. In 1522 he secretly married Anna Reinhard, who bore him four children.

The Catholic bishop of Constance attempted to stop Zwingli, who overcame him in two public debates in 1523. When Zwingli won a further disputation at Berne in 1528, Basle, Gall, Schaffhausen, and Constance all joined the reform movement. After Zwingli and Luther reached deadlock in their debate over the eucharist at Marburg (1529), the Swiss reform movement lost the support of the German princes. The five Catholic Forest Cantons of Switzerland sent an army against Zurich, and Zwingli died at the Battle of Kappel.

Most of Zwingli's writings were born out of controversy. His *Commentary on True and False Religion* (1525), a systematic theology, had considerable impact upon Protestantism. Zwingli was the first Reformed theologian. He held that Christ was spiritually present at the Eucharist, and that the secular ruler had a right to act in church matters.

ROBERT STUPPERICH

The reformers Martin Luther and Huldrych Zwingli differ over the meaning of the eucharist at the Marburg Colloquy of 1529, resulting in the formation of two different Protestant confessions.
TIM DOWLEY ASSOCIATES

THEODORE BEZA

Theodore Beza (1519–1605) succeeded Calvin in Geneva as leader of Reformed Protestantism. He had been trained as a lawyer, and a book of love poetry gained him a reputation as a Latin poet. In 1544 he was secretly engaged to Claudine Desnoes, whom he later married, but they had no children. After a severe illness, in 1548 Beza went to Geneva and announced he had become a Protestant.

In 1559 Beza became the first rector of the Genevan Academy. He remained in Geneva, intimately involved in its affairs, and became Calvin's successor and one of the leading advisors to the Huguenots in France. He participated in their conferences – Poissy, 1561, La Rochelle, 1571 – and defended the purity of the Reformed faith. He produced new versions of the Greek and Latin New Testament, a source for the Geneva and King James Bibles. Theodore Beza also completed the translation of the psalms begun by Marot and wrote a biography of Calvin, *De jure magistratuum* ('The Right of Magistrates'), an important Protestant political work, as well as other political, polemical, and theological tracts.

Beza was an important figure for the Reformed churches; under his leadership Geneva became the centre of Reformed Protestantism. His political activities aimed to establish the Reformed faith throughout Europe, and particularly in France. Beza's theological method made the Reformed position more rigid.

ROBERT V. SCHNUCKER

Zwingli in Zurich and Calvin in Geneva were succeeded respectively by Heinrich Bullinger (1504–75) and Theodore Beza (1519–1605), who both kept alive the Reformed tradition. They exercised great influence in France, Holland, Germany, England, and Scotland by their teaching and by their hospitality to the many exiles from persecution in their native lands.

FRANCE

In France the pattern of reform was very different. Whereas in Germany and Switzerland there was solid support for the Reformation from the people, in France people, court, and church provided less support. As a result many of the first Protestants suffered death or exile. But once the Reformed faith had been established in French-speaking Switzerland, Calvinists formed a congregation in Paris in 1555, and more than seventy churches were represented at a national synod in Paris in 1559.

Reform took on the nature of a political movement in this hostile environment, and a series of civil wars followed. Protestants were shamelessly massacred in cold blood on St Bartholomew's Day in 1572, a blow which shattered, but did not destroy, Protestantism in France. When the Protestant Henry IV succeeded to the French throne in 1589 Protestant hopes ran high, but the French Catholics formed an alliance with the king of Spain and threatened to plunge the country in blood if Henry remained a Protestant. Henry yielded for the sake of peace and to preserve his throne (he is alleged to have said, 'Paris is well worth a Mass'), and gave up his Protestantism. Yet in 1598 he had Protestantism legally recognized, and granted the freedom to practise Reformed Christianity, under the terms of the Edict of Nantes.

The French statesman, Cardinal Richelieu, played havoc with Protestantism in the seventeenth century until finally King Louis XIV revoked the Edict of Nantes in 1685, after which French Protestants suffered bitter persecution.

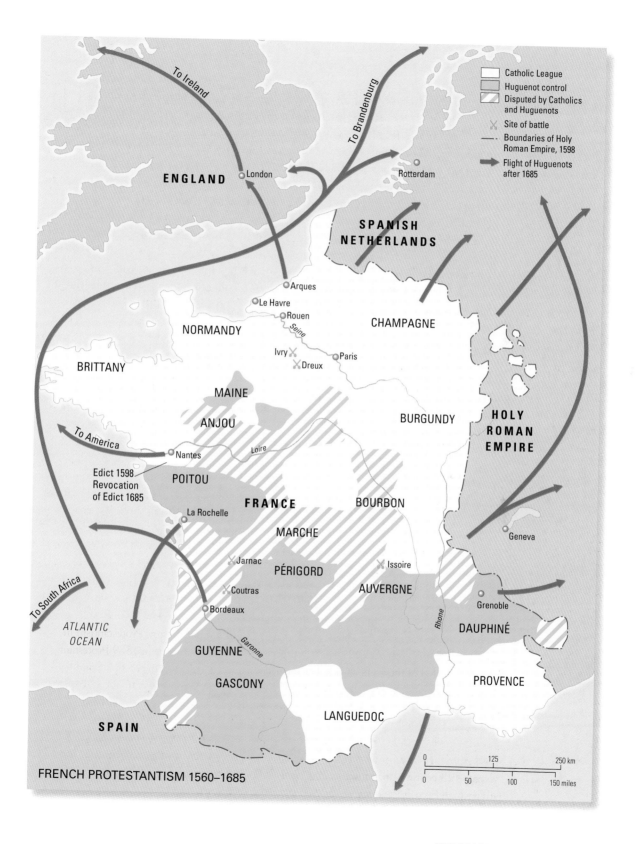

To Ireland

To Brandenburg

Catholic League
Huguenot control
Disputed by Catholics and Huguenots
✕ Site of battle
– · – · Boundaries of Holy Roman Empire, 1598
➜ Flight of Huguenots after 1685

ENGLAND

○ London

○ Rotterdam

SPANISH NETHERLANDS

○ Arques
○ Le Havre
○ Rouen
Seine

CHAMPAGNE

NORMANDY

Ivry ✕
Dreux ✕
○ Paris

BRITTANY

MAINE

ANJOU

Loire

BURGUNDY

HOLY ROMAN EMPIRE

To America

○ Nantes

Edict 1598
Revocation of Edict 1685

POITOU

FRANCE

BOURBON

○ La Rochelle

MARCHE

○ Geneva

Jarnac ✕

PÉRIGORD

Issoire ✕

AUVERGNE

Coutras ✕

○ Bordeaux

Grenoble ○

Rhône

DAUPHINÉ

To South Africa

ATLANTIC OCEAN

GUYENNE

Garonne

GASCONY

PROVENCE

LANGUEDOC

SPAIN

FRENCH PROTESTANTISM 1560–1685

0   125   250 km
0   50   100   150 miles

THE LOW COUNTRIES

In the Netherlands, reform was inspired by Luther, and people were martyred for Lutheran beliefs as early as 1523. However the reformation later came under Calvin's influence.

At this time the Low Countries were ruled by Spain. The reform movement was strongly opposed by the Emperor Charles V, and by his successor King Philip II of Spain, with the result that the reform movement developed a strong political commitment to independence. It was claimed that the Spanish Duke of Alva was responsible for the deaths of 100,000 Protestants between 1567 and 1573, and in 1584 the northern Netherlands formed a federation under William the Silent. After a long and bitter struggle, they freed themselves from both the Roman Church and the Spanish crown.

The first Reformed synod was held at Dort in 1574, and within a year the reformers founded the University of Leiden. The new Reformed Church adopted the *Heidelberg Confession* and the *Belgic Confession* as statements of belief, and drew up its own pattern of organization.

The Dutch Church now went through a bitter theological struggle concerning the nature of predestination. Jacobus Arminius (Jakob Hermanszoon, 1560–1609), professor of theology at Leiden, rejected the logical conclusions of the doctrine that the elect were determined by the sovereign will of God alone, as Calvin taught. He insisted it was possible to believe in God's sovereignty while allowing for real free will in an individual. God willed *all* to be saved – not merely the chosen. Arminius insisted that his views were biblical and not mere speculation, but his doctrines were condemned at the Synod of Dort (1618–19), tolerated later in the seventeenth century, and officially recognized in 1795.

CENTRAL EUROPE

In Bohemia, the Reformation had still earlier beginnings, under Jan Hus and Jerome of Prague. Hus's followers, the Hussites, supported Luther when the Reformation broke out, but most later became Calvinists. The cause of reform in Bohemia suffered severely during the Thirty Years' War and from the Catholic Reformation, and Bohemia was left a wilderness of desolation.

In Hungary, students of Luther and Melanchthon from the University of Wittenberg took back to their homeland the message of the Reformation in about 1524, but as in Bohemia, Calvinist theology later took hold. The first Lutheran synod took place in 1545, and the first Calvinist synod in 1557. Religious liberty was suppressed by Rudolph II, but regained by force by Prince Stephen of Transylvania, in the treaties of Nikolsburg (1621) and Linz (1645).

The Hussites, encouraged by Luther's writings, originated the reform movement in Poland. King Sigismund II Augustus (r. 1548–72) was a friend of the Reformation and corresponded with Calvin. The most distinguished Polish theologian was the Calvinist John à Lasco (1499–1560), who later went to England as a professor and helped shape the English Reformation during the reign of King Edward VI. In Poland, general understanding was arrived at between Lutherans and Calvinists by 1570, but reform was marred by dissentions created by Socinianism, the movement founded by Socinus, who denied the Trinity, the deity of Christ, his work on the cross, and that human beings are fallen. Later the reform movement was hindered by the activities of the Jesuits.

SCANDINAVIA

Two brothers, Olaus and Laurentius Petri (Olof and Lars Persson, 1493–1552, 1499–1573), both disciples of Luther, inaugurated the Reformation in Sweden. Aided by Laurentius Andreae (Lars Andersson, c. 1470–1552) they brought the evangelical theology of Luther to the Swedish Church. The courageous King Gustavus Vasa (1496–1560), who eventually delivered Sweden from the Danes in 1523, favoured Protestantism. The whole country became Lutheran, with bishops of the old church incorporated into the new, and in 1527 the Reformation was established by law. In 1593, at the Synod of Uppsala, reform was completed, when the Lutheran *Augsburg Confession* was adopted as the sole basis of faith. Sweden retained the traditional church structures and bishops, in a characteristic church-state union, and fought for the Protestant cause during the Thirty Years' War.

The Danish Church, too, went over completely to Protestantism. Danes such as Hans Tausen (1494–1561) and Jørgen Sadolin (c. 1490–1559) studied under Luther at Wittenberg and then started to preach irregularly in Denmark. A Danish version of the New Testament was produced in 1524, and King Frederick I pressed strongly for church reform, appointing reforming bishops and preachers. There was an alarming defection of Catholics and, in some places, no preaching, or a service only two or three times a year.

When King Christian III succeeded to the Danish throne in 1536, the transition to Protestantism was completed. He stripped the bishops of their lands and property at the Diet of Copenhagen (1536), transferring the church's wealth to the state. He then turned for help to Luther, who in 1537 sent Johannes Bugenhagen (1485–1558) – the only Lutheran theologian at Wittenberg who could speak the dialects of Denmark and the German border – who crowned the king and appointed seven superintendents. At the synods which followed, church ordinances were published and the Reformation recognized in Danish law. The University of Copenhagen was enlarged and revitalized, a new liturgy drawn up, a new translation of the Bible completed, and a modified version of the *Augsburg Confession* eventually adopted.

In 1536 the Reformation spread from Denmark to Norway, where the pattern was similar to that of Denmark. Most bishops fled and, as the older clergy died, they were replaced with Reformed ministers. War between Denmark and Norway worsened political and social conditions, and when Danish Lutherans went to instruct the Norwegians, they found many spoke incomprehensible ancient Norse and communications broke down.

In Iceland, attempts to impose the new Danish ecclesiastical system brought about a revolt. This was eventually quelled, the Reformation imposed, and an Icelandic New Testament published in 1540.

ENGLAND

The struggle between the old and the new lasted longer in England and Scotland than in the rest of Europe. As early as the thirteenth century an anti-papal, anti-clerical movement developed in Britain. Under Wyclif, an evangelical protest movement began, which was strengthened early in the sixteenth century when Luther's writings and English Bibles were smuggled into England.

At first the reform movement was Lutheran and supported by the older Lollard movement. But the Reformation, though religious in origin, became entangled with politics.

RELIGIOUS AFFILIATION IN
EUROPE IN 1560

Roman Catholic
Eastern Orthodox
Lutheran
Zwinglian or Calvinist
Anglican
Muslim
Hussite
✠ Anabaptists
— Political Boundary

0   250   500 km
0 100 200 300 miles

NORWAY

SWEDEN

Stockho

NORTH
SEA

BALTIC
SEA

DENMARK   Copenhagen

Konigs

Danz

SCOTLAND

Glasgow   Edinburgh

IRELAND

Dublin

York

ENGLAND ✠

WALES

London
Canterbury

Groningen ✠   Bremen Hamburg

Amsterdam ✠

Antwerp   Munster ✠

HOLY ROMAN

Magdeburg

Wittenberg

EMPIRE ✠   Zwickau

Frankfurt ✠   Prague

BOHEMIA   Brno

MORAVIA

ATLANTIC

OCEAN

Rouen   Rheims

Paris

Edict of Worms,
1521, condemns
Lutheranism

Worms   Augsburg

Regensburg

Vienna

Bud

Nantes   Tours

Poitiers

Nevers

FRANCE

Zurich   Munich

Salzburg

Peace of Augsburg, 1555,
recognizes existence
of Lutheranism

Lyons   Geneva

Milan   Venice

Bordeaux

Avignon

Toulouse

Marseilles

Modena ✠   Ferrara

Florence

ADRIATIC SEA

PAPAL
STATES

Oporto

Valladolid

Zaragoza

Madrid

Barcelona

Rome

KINGDOM
OF NAPLES

PORTUGAL

SPAIN

Toledo

Naples

Valencia

Seville

Granada

MEDITERRANEAN SEA

SICILY

REFORM AND RENEWAL

In 1534 King Henry VIII proclaimed himself the Head of the Church of England, though his quarrel with the pope was not on religious grounds, but merely because the pope would not sanction Henry's proposed divorce of Queen Catherine. Henry himself remained a Catholic; the pope entitled him 'Defender of the Faith' for a book he wrote opposing Luther in 1521, and in 1539 Henry issued the *Six Articles*, aiming to restore the traditional Catholic faith. Henry destroyed the authority of the pope and ended monasticism in England, but among his people a powerful religious movement towards reform was occurring.

Under King Edward VI (r. 1547–53), the Reformation was positively and effectively introduced, led by the Archbishop of Canterbury, Thomas Cranmer, who was supported by the scholar, Bishop Nicholas Ridley (c. 1500–55), and the preacher, Bishop Hugh Latimer (c. 1487–1555). Several European Calvinist Reformers also contributed, notably Martin Bucer from Strasbourg (1491–1551), Peter Martyr Vermigli (1499–1562) from Italy, and John à Lasco from Poland, all of whom became professors at the Universities of Oxford and Cambridge.

Queen Mary (r. 1553–58) attempted to restore Catholicism and the authority of the pope to Britain, with the help of Cardinal Reginald Pole (1500–58), an enlightened humanist, sympathetic to evangelical doctrines, particularly justification by faith. Pole had an ecumenical concern for the unity of the church, and was bold enough to censure

MARTIN BUCER

Martin Bucer (or Butzer, 1491–1551), who was born at Sélestat, Alsace, was the Reformer at Strasbourg. He had been a Dominican friar, but left the order, and in 1522 married a former nun, Elisabeth Silbereisen. He went to Strasbourg in 1523 and took over leadership of the reform.

Bucer became one of the chief statesmen among the Reformers, and was present at most of their important conferences. In an effort to unite the German and Swiss Reformed churches, Bucer tried to mediate between Zwingli and Luther. Bucer also took part in unsuccessful conferences with Roman Catholics at Hagenau, Worms, and Ratisbon. Bucer also wrote a large number of commentaries on the Bible.

Bucer resisted the Emperor's religious settlement, the Augsburg Interim. In 1549 he was forced to leave Strasbourg for Cambridge. While in England, he advised Cranmer on the *Book of Common Prayer*. He had a considerable impact on the Church of England, pointing the way towards Puritanism. He died in 1551, but his body was exhumed and burned during the Catholic reaction under Queen Mary.

ROBERT V. SCHNUCKER

Henry VIII in his book *On the Defence of the Unity of the Church* (1534–36). But Mary's inability to understand Protestantism actually did much to strengthen the movement by creating many martyrs. About 200 bishops, scholars, and other men and women were burnt at the stake, including the Cranmer, Latimer, and Ridley. Many fled to the Continent, and Mary died a despised woman.

Mary's sister Elizabeth restored and permanently established Protestantism in England during her long reign (r. 1558–1603). She faced considerable difficulties, including the threat of civil war, the theological and political opposition of the Catholic powers, the hostility of France and Spain, and doubts about her claim to the throne. Elizabeth replaced Catholic

THOMAS CRANMER

Thomas Cranmer (1489–1556) was largely responsible for shaping the Protestant Church of England. Born at Aslockton, Nottinghamshire, and educated at Cambridge University, he remained a quiet scholar until suddenly summoned to Canterbury as archbishop in 1532, following advice he had given earlier about Henry VIII's divorce. Cranmer remained archbishop throughout Henry's turbulent reign, retaining the king's respect to the end. He then piloted the Reformation through the reign of the young King Edward VI, but was deposed by Mary, and burnt as a heretic at Oxford in 1556.

Cranmer was Lutheran in his theology, well read in the Church Fathers, a gifted liturgist, and had a superb command of English. He was sensitive and brave, cautious and slow to decide, in a period of transition bedevilled by turbulence and treachery. Cranmer preferred reformation by gentle persuasion rather than by force, and, like Luther, believed firmly in the role of the 'godly prince', who had a God-given task to uphold a just society and give free scope to the gospel.

Archbishop Cranmer was responsible for the Great Bible (1538) and its prefaces, the *Litany* of 1545, and the two Prayer Books, of 1549 and 1552, and largely responsible for the Articles of the Church of England and the Homilies. He sought an ecumenical council with the Lutherans and Calvinists of Europe, but Melanchthon proved too timid. Cranmer's concern was to restore a theology based

Thomas Cranmer, Archbishop of Canterbury 1533–55.
© GEORGIOS KOLLIDAS/DREAMSTIME.COM

on the experience of the person and work of Christ. From his doctrine of Christ came Cranmer's theology of justification by faith and of Christ's presence in the sacraments.

JAMES ATKINSON

PURITANS AND SEPARATISTS

The Church of England, as established by Elizabeth I, was unsatisfactory to Roman Catholics and also to more extreme Protestants. The second group desired a fully Reformed church, more on the lines of Calvin's at Geneva. Those who worked to purify and reform the church beyond what the government had established were known as 'Puritans'.

THE FIRST PURITANS

The Elizabethan Puritans, working from within the Church of England, mostly wanted to abolish religious ceremonies thought to be remnants from Roman Catholicism – the use of the cross in baptism, the surplice, and kneeling at communion. Many of the Puritans questioned whether there was any biblical authority for bishops, and wanted instead the Reformed pattern of church government, by elders and synods, with stricter discipline.

During the first years of Elizabeth's reign, the Puritan-minded clergy and lay members of the Church of England had strong support in Parliament, and high hopes of achieving their reforms. Their leaders included Thomas Cartwright (c. 1535–1603) and William Perkins (1558–1602).

Elizabeth I was unwilling to allow changes along Puritan lines, and King James I was equally adamant against Puritans. 'I will make them conform themselves,' he threatened, 'or I will harry them out of the land, or else do worse.' The main part of the Puritan movement still survived within the Church of England, though many Puritans only marginally conformed to Anglicanism.

SEPARATISTS

In the face of these discouragements, a small separatist movement grew up alongside the main Puritan group. The Separatist Puritans were led by Robert Browne (1550–1633) and Robert Harrison (d. c. 1585). These Separatists no longer regarded the Church of England as a true church, and in 1581

> The Lord has more truth yet to break forth out of his holy Word.
>
> JOHN ROBINSON, TO THE PILGRIMS AS THEY SET SAIL FOR AMERICA.

with their followers (often called Brownists) formed an independent congregation at Norwich, in which Browne acted as pastor and Harrison as teacher. They withdrew completely from the Anglican Church, which they believed to be polluted and false, and set up their own congregation, based on a church covenant. This step marked the beginnings of the English Independent or Congregationalist movement. The English government and bishops lost patience and severely repressed the Brownists by imprisonment, harassment, and by driving them abroad to the Low Countries.

The Netherlands played an increasingly important role in the life of English dissent. As the English authorities repressed Puritanism more severely and systematically, the dissenters were often forced to find refuge abroad. The Dutch were tolerant of religious nonconformity, and allowed English refugees to come in freely. Browne and Harrison took their small church to Middelburg, in Zeeland, where it survived for a few years. Browne, however, later returned to England, where he eventually renounced his separation and resumed a ministry in the Church of England. Other leaders took over in the Separatist movement: Henry Barrow(e) (c. 1550–93), John Greenwood (d. 1593), Francis Johnson, Henry Ainsworth, John Robinson, and others.

The 'Pilgrim Fathers' led by John Robinson (1576–1625), after living in Leiden, eventually emigrated to New England. One of the Separatist groups in Amsterdam, led by John Smyth (c. 1570–1612) and Thomas Helwys (c. 1575–c. 1616), became Anabaptist.

KEITH L. SPRUNGER

POST-REFORMATION CHURCH ARCHITECTURE

At the time of the Reformation there evolved a single-room church design, reflecting the very different attitude to the clergy and to worship. Instead of emphasizing the distinctive powers of the priest in relation to the sacraments, the Reformers preached the priesthood of all believers, a view reflected in the way that they adapted the medieval buildings they inherited, and in the plans used for new churches.

Side altars were swept away, replaced by a single table, which might not even be a permanent fixture. The screen was either removed, so that the church became a single room again, or else it was made into a solid wall, and either the chancel or the nave used for worship. Sometimes the unused area was left to decay, but sometimes, as the population increased, each part was used by a different congregation.

Great importance was given to the positioning of the pulpit, so that all might see and hear the preaching of the word of God. The close relation of word and sacrament was expressed in the proximity of the Lord's table and the baptismal basin to the pulpit. These arrangements were followed in the new churches, which were built on a square or circular plan, and can be seen in the churches built in London after the Great Fire (1666), and even more clearly in the church 'meeting-houses' of seventeenth- and eighteenth-century England and New England.

HENRY SEFTON

Church leaders with Protestants, restored the church *Articles* and the Prayer Book of Edward VI, and took the title of 'supreme governor' – rather than head – of the Church of England.

As re-established by Elizabeth, the Anglican Church retained episcopal government and a set liturgy, offending many Calvinists, particularly refugees returning from Switzerland. Meanwhile Roman Catholics plotted and intrigued; every Catholic seemed a potential traitor, since the pope had ordered them to overthrow Elizabeth. Bishop John Jewel's magnificent *Apology* (1560) and the writings of Richard Hooker (1554–1600), following Cranmer's position, attempted to demonstrate that Elizabeth's church was scriptural, catholic, and reasonable. However, the early Stuart monarchs, James I (r. 1603–25) and Charles I (r. 1625–49), claimed the king received his powers directly from God, and so could not be called to account by his subjects, a doctrine known as the divine right of kings.

Following the English Civil War (1642–51), Charles I was eventually beheaded and a Commonwealth established. When King Charles II was restored to the throne in 1660, the bishops, the *Book of Common Prayer*, and the Anglican system were all re-established.

SCOTLAND

Scotland was awakened to Lutheranism by Patrick Hamilton, a student of Luther, who was burned for his faith in 1528. George Wishart (c. 1513–46) and John Knox (c. 1514–72) continued Hamilton's reforming work, but Knox was taken prisoner by the French in 1547, and forced to serve as a galley-slave. When freed, he studied under Calvin in Geneva and Bullinger in Zürich.

In 1557 Scottish Protestants covenanted to effect reformation, and wrote urging Knox to return home. Arriving in Scotland in 1559, he launched the Reformation, attacking the papacy and the mass in his sermons at St Giles Cathedral, Edinburgh. At the request of Parliament, he drew up a *Confession of Faith and Doctrine* (1560, replaced in 1647 by the *Westminster Confession*), emphasizing evangelical doctrine and urging the necessity of discipline. A General Assembly of the church was called in 1560, which settled the Reformation in Scotland. The *Book of Discipline* (1561), was followed by a new liturgy, in the *Book of Common*

Order (1564), and a translation of Calvin's *Catechism*. Knox had now consolidated the Reformation in Scotland.

IRELAND

When Henry VIII rejected the papacy in England he made the Irish do the same. However the low level of education, absence of printed books in Irish, and dearth of Irish reformers made doctrinal change virtually impossible. Under Edward VI a reformed liturgy was introduced; the English *Prayer Book*, published in Dublin in 1551, was actually the first book printed in Ireland.

Mary Tudor re-established Roman Catholicism in Ireland, deposed the reforming bishops, and punished married clergy. Queen Elizabeth subsequently restored the English liturgy, and in 1560 the Irish Parliament again repudiated the authority of the pope, and passed the Act of Uniformity which set up Anglicanism as the national religion. However, because the Reformation was imposed by the English, Protestantism became inseparably linked with foreign rule.

Under James I many Scots settled in northern Ireland (Ulster), creating a Presbyterian enclave.

THE RADICALS

Martin Luther experienced fierce opposition from radical reformers who wanted more wide-ranging changes. While he was held prisoner in the Wartburg (1521–22), Andreas Karlstadt (1486–1541) took over leadership of the reform movement in Wittenberg, setting the church in a more extreme direction. Luther believed it was necessary only to preach the Word of God, teach the Bible, and allow the Holy Spirit to create fresh ways through the old forms, for a believing church to emerge. He hoped for a reformation of doctrine and morality within an undivided church.

Inevitably he clashed with the radicals, some of whom expressed their theology in terms of the political and revolutionary aspirations of the age. This clash came to a head in the disastrous Peasants' War of 1525, which Luther bitterly opposed. The uprising was widely supported, led by the able and learned Thomas Müntzer (c. 1489–1525). During its course some 100,000 people perished, and indescribable misery followed the destruction of farms, agricultural implements, and cattle.

Luther always attempted to work with a 'godly prince', and clearly distinguished between the concerns and responsibilities of church and state. The radicals – sometimes called 'enthusiasts' (German, *Schwärmerei*) – wanted a complete spiritual reformation of the church, a programme more far-reaching than most people would accept.

JAMES ATKINSON

THE UNITARIANS

Unitarians reject the idea of the Trinity, questioning belief in the divinity of Christ and of the Holy Spirit in favour of the oneness of God, an idea found in the early church, particularly in the Monarchianist heresy. The modern Unitarian movement dates from the early sixteenth century, when Renaissance ideas combined with some extreme teaching in the Radical Reformation to produce Unitarian ideas in the minds of many individuals. Notable early Unitarians included Martin Borrhaus (Cellarius, 1499–1564), Michael Servetus and Bernardino Ochino (1487–1564). The new teaching alarmed both Catholics and Protestants: Servetus was put to death for his heresies by the Reformer Calvin in 1553.

POLAND AND HUNGARY

Two prominent centres of early Unitarianism were Poland and Hungary. The Italian Giorgio Blandrata (1515–1588) was active in Poland between 1558 and 1563, and was followed by Gregory Paulus. Unitarian congregations sprang up, known as the 'Polish Brethren'. They were formally organized in 1565, and became known as the Minor Church. After 1574, when Faustus Socinus (1539–1604) became leader, Unitarianism spread quickly. Its intellectual centre was Raców, where a Polish Unitarian declaration of faith, the Racovian Catechism, was published in 1605. During the reign of the Catholic King Sigismund III (1587–1632), a reaction set in, and the Unitarian community at Raców was suppressed in 1638. In 1658 the Unitarians were given the choice of conformity or exile: many chose exile and emigrated to Holland, Hungary, and England.

Unitarianism spread rapidly in Transylvania, where Blandrata moved in 1563. He had a strong influence on Férenc (Francis) David (1510–79), who in 1564 became bishop of the Reformed Church in Transylvania. David was also court preacher to King John Sigismund of Hungary (1540–71), who was impressed by his teaching, and in the Edict of Torda (also known as the Patent of Toleration, 1568) ordered Unitarianism to be tolerated. In 1571, along with Catholicism, Lutheranism, and Calvinism, Unitarianism was recognized as a 'received religion'.

But when John Sigismund died, severe persecution began. By the later eighteenth century, Unitarianism in Hungary was almost completely suppressed, and only revived in the early nineteenth century, when contacts were resumed with English and American Unitarians. Unitarian theology in Hungary was conservative, as it did not want to invite persecution by appearing aggressively heretical.

ENGLISH UNITARIANS

John Biddle (1615–62) is regarded as the founder of English Unitarianism, which emerged in the turbulent Civil War period, initially remaining confined to individual people. But in the rationalistic atmosphere of the eighteenth century, many English Presbyterian and General Baptist Churches began to be affected, adopting first Arian, and then Sabellian, Socinian, or full-blown Unitarian ideas. Both denominations became largely Unitarian by the second half of the eighteenth century. The liberal Anglican Theophilus Lindsey (1723–1808) left the Church of England in 1773 and opened the first self-styled Unitarian Church, Essex Chapel, in London.

Unitarianism now spread rapidly, thanks to active missionaries, the intellectual distinction of the Unitarian-controlled Warrington Academy, and the teachings of the well-known Dr Joseph Priestley (1733–1804). Unitarianism – not legally recognized in the Toleration Act of 1689 – was eventually legalized in 1813.

In the first twenty-five years of the nineteenth century, Unitarianism gradually took on the trappings and organization of a separate denomination. The British and Foreign Unitarian Society was founded in 1825, and a number of legal disputes with orthodox nonconformists ensued, threatening to deprive the Unitarians of many of their older church buildings, about a third of which claimed a seventeenth-century foundation. An Act of 1844 settled the question – largely in the Unitarians' favour – but left relations with the other nonconformists very bitter.

Meanwhile theological changes occurred in Unitarianism. Priestley and his successor, Thomas Belsham (1750–1829), found their source of authority in Scripture, interpreting the Bible in a rationalistic and optimistic way, to get around those verses which Christians had previously used to support the doctrine of the Trinity and the belief that humanity has a fallen nature. But in the 1830s James Martineau (1805–1900) and some younger Unitarians led a revolt against biblical Unitarianism and its dogmas. They advocated a less argumentative religion, with a more refined, romantic, and devotional spirituality, and located religious authority in reason and conscience rather than in a biased interpretation of Scripture. Henceforth the Unitarians were rather sharply divided into an older, 'biblical', and newer, 'spiritual', wing, with the new group well on the way to eclipsing the 'biblical' wing by 1850.

In Ireland, Thomas Emlyn (1663–1741) was prosecuted in Dublin in 1703 for denying the deity of Christ. In 1726 a Unitarian 'Non-Subscribing Presbytery of Antrim' arose out of a group of liberal Presbyterian congregations, and in 1830 the 'Remonstrant Synod of Ulster' was formed. These two Unitarian groups merged in 1835 and were – and are today – more conservative in their beliefs than English Unitarians.

NORTH AMERICA

In North America, Unitarian teaching initially arose in the later eighteenth century among New England Congregationalists. However the first to take the title 'Unitarian' was an Episcopalian, James Freeman, whose King's Chapel, Boston, became in 1785 the first Unitarian Church in the New World.

After the Revolution, Unitarianism spread rapidly, encouraged by Priestley, who fled from England to North America in 1794. Dr William Ellery Channing (1780–1842), from 1803 minister of Federal Street Congregational Church, Boston, also promoted Unitarianism. In 1816 the famous divinity school of Harvard University was founded, soon becoming the centre of Unitarian thought. In 1825 the scattered Unitarian congregations – like their counterparts in England – organized themselves into a denomination known as the American Unitarian Association, with its headquarters in Boston. A theological revolution similar to Martineau's was brought about in America by Theodore Parker (1810–60) and Ralph Waldo Emerson (1803–82), with the radicals using terms such as 'transcendentalism' and 'anti-supernaturalism' to describe their position. In England such labels tended to cause some alarm. The Bostonian Dr Joseph Tuckerman (1778–1840) and his Domestic Mission movement took a new direction in charitable work that was widely admired, and similar missions were promoted in several English cities.

IAN SELLERS

REFORM AND RENEWAL

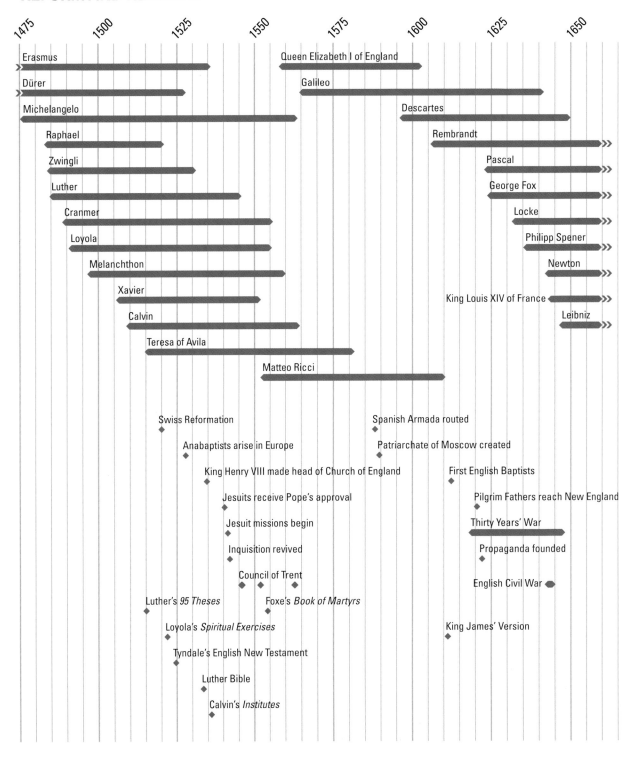

1475 1500 1525 1550 1575 1600 1625 1650

Erasmus

Dürer

Michelangelo

Raphael

Zwingli

Luther

Cranmer

Loyola

Melanchthon

Xavier

Calvin

Teresa of Avila

Matteo Ricci

Queen Elizabeth I of England

Galileo

Descartes

Rembrandt

Pascal

George Fox

Locke

Philipp Spener

Newton

King Louis XIV of France

Leibniz

Swiss Reformation

Anabaptists arise in Europe

King Henry VIII made head of Church of England

Jesuits receive Pope's approval

Jesuit missions begin

Inquisition revived

Council of Trent

Luther's *95 Theses*

Foxe's *Book of Martyrs*

Loyola's *Spiritual Exercises*

Tyndale's English New Testament

Luther Bible

Calvin's *Institutes*

Spanish Armada routed

Patriarchate of Moscow created

First English Baptists

Pilgrim Fathers reach New England

Thirty Years' War

Propaganda founded

English Civil War

King James' Version

CHAPTER 24

A FLOOD OF BIBLES
Scripture in the vernacular

Throughout the Middle Ages the Bible was known almost exclusively in the Latin translation known as the *Vulgate*. But the humanist scholars of the Renaissance period had a new concern to recover the original Hebrew and Greek texts of the Bible.

THE HEBREW TEXT

The Jews were the first to print a complete Hebrew Old Testament, at Soncino, northern Italy, in 1488. In the next few years two further editions appeared, probably from the same group of Jews. The first Christian contribution came some years later. Early in the sixteenth century the Catholic university at Alcalá in Spain produced a massive work known as the *Complutensian Polyglot*, consisting of the Hebrew and Greek (*Septuagint*) Old Testament, the Greek New Testament, and the Latin Vulgate. It was printed between 1514 and 1517, but the pope delayed authorization and it was not issued until about 1522.

Meanwhile in 1517/18, a Christian, Daniel Bomberg (d. 1549), printed the *Biblica Rabbinica* – the Hebrew Old Testament together with the Targums (paraphrases) and the rabbinical commentaries – in collaboration with a Christian Jew, Felix Pratensis (d. 1539). In 1524–25 Bomberg printed a second edition, with the aid of another Jewish scholar, Jacob ben Hayyim (c. 1470–before 1538). This edition is important, since ben Hayyim went to great pains to consult as many different Hebrew manuscripts as possible. Further editions of the Hebrew Old Testament appeared, notably from Sebastian Münster (1534/5), Robert Estienne (1539–44), and Christopher Plantin (1569–72), but these did nothing to help recover the original text.

THE GREEK TEXT

Volume 5 of the *Complutensian Polyglot*, which contains the Greek text of the New Testament, though printed in 1514, was not issued for some years, giving the Basel printer, Johann Froben (c. 1460–1527), the opportunity to be the first to publish. He persuaded Erasmus to complete his own edition of the Greek text in great haste, which resulted in many errors appearing when it was rushed through the press in 1516. Conservatives reacted with hostility, particularly since Erasmus had the effrontery to include his own Latin translation, rather than the traditional *Vulgate*. He also omitted the famous 'Johannine comma' of I John 5:7, 8 (a reference to the Trinity found in the King James Version, but in neither the original Greek nor modern translations).

Erasmus' New Testament went through many editions and was improved, though under pressure he restored the Johannine comma. The first serious attempt to produce a critical edition of the Greek New Testament, attempting to get back to the original text by comparing surviving manuscripts, was that of Simon de Colines (1480–1546), a Parisian printer, in 1534. This work was continued by his stepson Robert Estienne

(1503–59), who produced several editions from 1546, first at Paris and later at Geneva, where he fled because of his Protestant beliefs. Estienne's work was continued by Theodore Beza, Calvin's successor at Geneva, who produced a series of editions of the Greek New Testament, beginning in 1565. This text came to be known as the *textus receptus*, or universally accepted text; the attempt to get back to the original text was abandoned for some time.

THE LATIN BIBLE

The Vulgate was the authentic text of the Bible for the Roman Catholic Church, and this was confirmed by the Council of Trent in 1546. Various attempts were made by individual printers and scholars to produce a more accurate edition of the Vulgate, either by revising it against the Hebrew and Greek, or by consulting early manuscripts of the Vulgate. In 1590 Pope Sixtus V issued an official edition of the Vulgate, together with severe penalties for those who dared to alter it. But, two years later, his successor Clement VIII was forced to revise it and produce a more correct edition, which then became the standard text of the Vulgate.

TRANSLATIONS

The invention of printing allowed the Bible to be circulated more widely than ever before. With this possibility came the desire of the Reformers to make what they regarded as the Word of God available to all people in their own language. This came at a period when it was unusual to write in the vernacular, and works such as the Luther Bible contributed greatly to the growth of the European languages.

The Reformers did not accept the Old Testament Apocrypha (which is not part of the Hebrew Bible, but is accepted by the Roman Catholic Church) as inspired Scripture. But they recognized it as profitable to read, and it was included in the majority of Bibles during this period.

GERMAN

The major German translation of the sixteenth century is that by Martin Luther, upon which all the other German translations depend. Luther translated the New Testament early in 1522, in just two-and-a-half months, and the Old Testament in stages between 1522 and 1532. The first complete Luther Bible (with the Apocrypha) appeared at Wittenberg in 1534. Earlier that year it had also been translated into Low German. The Luther Bible was frequently revised, and the last revision before Luther's death (1545) later came to be regarded as the definitive version. It has been claimed that 'Luther's Bible was a literary event of the first magnitude, for it is the first work of art in German prose.'

FRENCH

No one French Bible has the exalted status of the Luther Bible. The humanist Jacques Lefèvre d'Étaples was the pioneer, with his New Testament (1523), followed by the Old Testament and Apocrypha (1528), produced together as a complete Bible in 1530. Although this translation kept close to both the text and the Latin words of the Vulgate, it was used as a basis for later translations.

WILLIAM TYNDALE AND THE ENGLISH BIBLE

William Tyndale (c. 1492–1536) is celebrated for his English translation of the New Testament. He was educated at Magdalen Hall, Oxford, and possibly later at Cambridge, and then became tutor to the family of Sir John Walsh. While living in his household, Tyndale saw at first hand the ignorance of the local clergy. To one cleric he is reported to have declared: 'If God spare my life, ere many years pass, I will cause a boy that driveth the plough shall know more of the Scriptures than thou dost.' This task became his life's work.

The bishops had banned the English Bible since 1408 because they feared the Lollards, who had their own translation, the *Wyclif Bible*. This translation had been made from the Latin *Vulgate* and was inaccurate, so Tyndale set out to make a translation from the Hebrew and Greek. He hoped to win the support of the learned bishop of London, Cuthbert Tunstall, but the bishops were more concerned to prevent the spread of Lutheran ideas than promote the study of Scripture. Instead Tyndale obtained financial backing from a number of London merchants, especially Humphrey Monmouth.

It was clear that England was no safe place to translate the Bible, so Tyndale left for Europe, never to return. By early 1525 his New Testament was ready for the press. Tyndale narrowly escaped arrest at Cologne, but managed to have the book published later the same year at Worms.

Tyndale's translation had an immense influence, and rightly earned him the title of the 'father of the English Bible'. It could almost be said that every English New Testament until the twentieth century was simply a revision of Tyndale's: some 90 per cent of his words passed into the King James Version, and about 75 per cent into the Revised Standard Version. Tyndale also translated parts of the Old Testament, including the first five books. He was unable to complete the Old Testament because he was betrayed and arrested near Brussels in 1535, and in 1536 strangled and burnt.

A. N. S. LANE

> Euangelio (that we cal gospel) is a greke word, and signifyth good, mery, glad, and joyful tydings, that maketh a mannes hert glad, and maketh hym synge, daunce, and leepe for joye.
>
> WILLIAM TYNDALE

Woodcut from Foxe's Book of Martyrs (1563) depicting the English Bible translator William Tyndale (c. 1492–1536) being burnt at the stake for heresy at Vilvoorde, near Brussels. Allegedly as he was dying he cried, 'Lord! Open the King of England's eyes!'
TIM DOWLEY ASSOCIATES

In 1535 Calvin's cousin, Pierre Robert Olivétan (c. 1506–38), produced the Neuchâtel Bible, which had been sponsored mainly by the Waldensian Church. This translation drew upon Lefèvre's, especially for the New Testament and Apocrypha. The pastors of Geneva, including Calvin and Beza, produced many revisions of this translation, and the 1588 revision became the definitive Geneva Bible.

Less influential, but no less skilful, was the translation by Sebastian Castellio (1515–63), which appeared at Basle in 1555. In 1550, a Roman Catholic based on the work of Lefèvre and Olivétan was produced at Louvain. This was revised a number of times to become, in 1578, the definitive Louvain Bible.

ENGLISH

The pioneer of the English Bible is William Tyndale, who published the New Testament (1525 and later revisions) and part of the Old Testament. Complete Bibles later began to appear: Miles Coverdale's in 1535, and the Matthew Bible in 1537. With the backing of Thomas Cranmer and Henry VIII's chief minister, Thomas Cromwell, the Matthew Bible was revised by Coverdale to become the Great Bible (1539).

During the reign of Queen Mary (1553–58) many leading Protestants went into exile. Those at Geneva determined to produce a new translation of the Bible. The New Testament and Psalms appeared in 1557, and the complete Geneva Bible in 1560. The New Testament was revised in later editions. This translation became immensely popular. The bishops attempted to undermine it with their Bishops' Bible (1568) but this never became popular. The one major Roman Catholic translation at this time is the Rheims-Douai Bible, which was translated from the Vulgate and appeared in 1582 (New Testament, Rheims) and 1609–10 (Old Testament, Douai).

King James I sponsored a new translation of the Bible, following a request by the Puritans in 1604. It appeared in 1611, and drew heavily on what was good in previous translations. This translation – the King James Version – often inaccurately called the Authorized Version, only gradually replaced the Geneva Bible, which remained popular for another fifty years.

DUTCH

Translations of parts of the Bible, and one complete Bible, were printed in Dutch in the fifteenth century. The Reformation led to an increase in such printings, but it was some time before widely-accepted versions appeared. The earliest of these was the Mennonite Bible, first printed at Emden in 1558, and later known as the Biestkens Bible, after the man who published it in 1560.

Calvinists mainly used a translation which was heavily dependent upon the Luther Bible and which first appeared in 1561–62. This was replaced in 1637 by the Statenvertaling or 'States' translation', produced at the expense of the government. This became the standard version, and was adopted by the Mennonites in the seventeenth century. The Catholics had their own translation, made by Nicolaas van Winghe in 1548 from the Vulgate. This translation, with revisions, remained in use for several centuries.

ITALIAN

Work on an Italian Bible began in the 1530s, pioneered by Antonio Brucioli (c. 1498–1566). Others followed in his footsteps. But the first Protestant Italian Bible did not appear until 1562 at Geneva, and this was only a revision of earlier translations. The greatest was that of the Italian Giovanni Diodati (1576–1649), Beza's successor at Geneva, who produced a translation of the Bible in 1603 that was revised in 1641. His translation was unchallenged until the end of the eighteenth century and remained in use much longer.

SPANISH

In Spain the Inquisition was more effective than elsewhere; as a result Bible translation took place mainly outside the country. Two translations of the New Testament appeared in the middle of the sixteenth century: those of Francisco de Enzinas (Antwerp, 1543) and Juan Perez de Pineda (Geneva, 1556). The first complete Spanish Bible was that of Casiodoro de Reina, a former monk, which appeared at Basle in 1569.

SWEDISH

Sweden early had a standard translation in the form of the 1541 version, known as the *Vasa Bible* after King Gustavus Vasa, translated by Laurentius Petri, possibly with the help of his brother, Olaus.

DANISH

In Denmark the standard translation was the Christian III Bible, published in 1550 at Copenhagen. This was revised in 1589 (Frederick II's Bible) and 1633 (Christian IV's Bible), both revisions also named after kings, indicating how far the Reformation in Scandinavia was controlled by the state.

A. N. S. LANE

CHAPTER 25

THE RADICAL REFORMATION

The Anabaptists

The Anabaptists made the most radical attempt of the Reformation era to renew the church. They did not consist of a single, coherent organization, but were a loose grouping of movements. All rejected infant baptism and practised the baptism of adults upon confession of faith. They never accepted the label 'Anabaptist' (meaning 'rebaptizer') – a term of reproach coined by their opponents – but soon discovered the term gave the authorities a legal precedent, harking back to fifth-century Roman laws against the Donatists, to persecute and execute them.

A SPLIT IN ZURICH

To the Anabaptists, however, the fundamental issue was not baptism but their growing conviction about the role the civil government should play in reforming the church. Late in 1523 intense debate on this issue broke out in Zurich, when it became clear that the city council was unwilling to make the religious changes that the theologians believed were called for by Scripture.

The Zurich Reformer, Zwingli, believed they should wait, and attempt to persuade the authorities by preaching. However, his more radical disciples believed the community of Christians should initiate Scripture-backed reforms regardless of the council. Despite continuing discussion of the matters in dispute – the mass, baptism, and tithes – the gap between the two parties widened. Finally, on 21 January 1525, the city council forbade the radicals to assemble or disseminate their views. That evening, in the neighbouring village of Zollikon, they met, baptized each other, and so became the first free church of modern times.

Despite the fact that it was illegal, the Anabaptist movement spread rapidly throughout German-speaking Europe. Unlike the other Reformers, the Anabaptists were not committed to the notion that 'Christendom' was Christian. From the beginning they saw themselves as missionaries to people who were only partly obedient to the gospel.

The Anabaptists systematically divided Europe into sectors for evangelistic outreach and sent missionaries out into them in twos and threes. Many people were bewildered by their message; and others pulled back when the cost of Anabaptist discipleship became clear; but others heard them. Mysticism, late-medieval asceticism, and the disillusionment which followed the peasants' revolts of 1524–25 had prepared the way for the Anabaptists. Almost simultaneously, Anabaptist-type groups sprang up spontaneously in various parts of Europe. By the late 1520s, Anabaptism was to be found as far afield as Holland and Moravia, the Tyrol and Mecklenburg.

ANABAPTIST BELIEFS

What did these Anabaptists believe? There was a considerable variety of opinion, ensured by their rapid growth, the diverse backgrounds of their leaders, and the absence of any ecclesiastical authority to control them. But they did attempt to agree upon a common basis. In 1527 at Schleitheim, on today's Swiss-German border, near Schaffhausen, the Anabaptists called the first 'synod' of the Protestant Reformation. The leading figure was the former Benedictine prior, Michael Sattler (c. 1490–1527), who, four months later, was burned at the stake in nearby Rottenburg-am-Neckar. The 'Brotherly Union' adopted at Schleitheim was to be a highly significant document; during the following decade most Anabaptists in all parts of Europe came to agree with the beliefs which it laid down.

By 1540 there was a body of beliefs which broadly characterized the movement. Important among these convictions was what the Anabaptists called 'discipleship': the Christian's relationship with Christ must go beyond inner experience and acceptance of doctrines, and must involve a daily walk with God, in which Christ's teaching and example shaped a transformed style of life. This meant resolutely obeying the 'bright and clear words of the Son of God whose word is truth and whose commandment is eternal life.'

The consequences of being a disciple, as the Anabaptists realized, were wide-ranging. To choose only one, the Anabaptists rejected the swearing of oaths, because of Jesus' clear command in the Sermon on the Mount (Matthew 5:33–37). For them there could be no gradation of levels of truth-telling.

A powerful Anabaptist belief was the principle of love. In their dealings with non-Anabaptists, they acted as pacifists. They would neither go to war, defend themselves against their persecutors, nor take part in coercion by the state. The love ethic was also expressed within the Anabaptist communities, in mutual aid, and the redistribution of wealth. Among Moravian Anabaptists it even led to Christian communism.

RESTORING THE CHURCH

Anabaptist beliefs about the church were particularly distinctive. They were not interested in simply reforming the church; they were committed to *restoring* it to the vigour and faithfulness of its earliest centuries. In the Scriptures they read of a church which was not a wealthy and powerful institution, but a family of brothers and sisters in Christ. It existed, not because it was recognized by some outside ecclesiastical or political organization, but because God was at work among his people.

The Anabaptists came to elaborate upon the 'congregational' view of church authority, towards which Luther and Zwingli had inclined in their earliest reforming years. In their congregations, all members were to be believers, baptized voluntarily as adults upon confession of faith. Decision-making was to be by the entire membership. In deciding matters of doctrine, the authority of Scripture was to be interpreted, not by dogmatic tradition or by ecclesiastical leaders, but by the consensus of the local gathering – in which all could speak and listen critically. In matters of church discipline, the believers were also to act corporately. They were to assist each other to live out faithfully the meaning of their baptismal commitments.

Another major Anabaptist conviction was insistence upon the separation of church and state. Christians, they claimed, were a 'free, unforced, uncompelled people'. Faith is a free gift of God, and the authorities exceed their competence when they 'champion the Word of God with a fist.' The Anabaptists believed the church was distinct from society, even if society claimed to be Christian. Christ's true followers were a pilgrim people; his church was an association of perpetual aliens.

PERSECUTION

To the established leaders of Protestant and Catholic Europe, these beliefs – and the personalities and movements which gave rise to them – were alarming indeed. The Reformers were understandably dismayed when news spread of Anabaptists interrupting Protestant sermons, or attracting the most earnest of their parishioners. They were also concerned that the Anabaptist emphasis upon life as well as belief seemed to challenge the basic Reformation principle of 'by faith alone'. In vain did the Anabaptists protest that their ethical teachings were not a means of obtaining salvation, but rather a necessary expression of the new life in Christ which resulted from salvation. In fact, the Anabaptists argued, these teachings stemmed from specific scriptural commandments.

The Reformers were not impressed by this reasoning. By 1527 they had determined to use all necessary means to root out Anabaptism, and were joined in this by the Catholic authorities. To Protestants and Catholics alike, the Anabaptists seemed not only to be dangerous heretics; they also appeared to threaten the religious and social stability of Christian Europe. In the next quarter of a century, thousands of Anabaptists were put to death – by fire in the Catholic territories, by drowning and the sword under Protestant regimes. Thousands more saved their skins by recanting.

The authorities' persecution of the Anabaptists seemed justified by the upheaval at Münster in the mid-1530s. In 1534 a group of Anabaptists who expected the millennium came to power in Münster, an episcopal city in Westphalia. When the bishop massed troops to besiege the city, these Anabaptists defended themselves by arms. As the siege progressed, still more extreme leaders gained control. Some of the Münsterite leaders claimed prophetic authority to receive new revelations. They also claimed that Old Testament ethics still applied, and thus felt justified in reintroducing polygamy. They even crowned a 'King David'.

For centuries, churches and governments exploited these excesses to make 'Anabaptism' a by-word for fanaticism and disorder. However, many of the major principles of the Münsterites – for example, the linking of church and state, the validity of Old Testament social patterns, and the right of Christians to take up arms – were more typical of the official churches than they were of other Anabaptists.

WAR NO MORE

In the aftermath of the suppression of Münster, the dispirited Anabaptists of the lower-Rhine area were given new heart by the ministry of Menno Simons (1496–1561). This former priest travelled widely, although in great personal danger, visiting the scattered Anabaptist groups of northern Europe and inspiring them with night-time preaching. Menno was unswerving in commending pacifism; as a result, his name came to stand for the movement's repudiation of violence. Although Menno was not the founder of the movement, most of the twenty-first-century descendants of the Anabaptists are called 'Mennonite'.

Anabaptists had also spread in large numbers eastwards to the Tyrol and Moravia. The early missioner who took the message eastwards along the Alps to the Tyrol was Jörg Cajacob ('Blaurock' [bluecoat], 1492–1529), the first adult to be baptized, in 1525. When the Tyrolean Catholic authorities began to persecute them intensely, many of the Anabaptists found refuge on the lands of some particularly tolerant princes in Moravia, where they founded a long-lasting form of economic community called the *Bruderhof*. In part they aimed to follow the pattern of early apostolic times, but they sought community for practical reasons too – as a means of group survival under persecution. Their communities attempted to demonstrate that commitment to others comes before self in the kingdom of God. Consolidated under the leadership of Jakob Hutter (c. 1500–36), these groups came to be known as 'Hutterites'.

With the passage of time, and under the pressure of persecution, most of the extravagant variety of views, leaders, and separate movements of Anabaptism's earliest years soon sifted out. Only three groups were able to survive beyond the mid-sixteenth century as ordered communities: the 'brethren' in Switzerland and southern Germany; the Mennonites in the Netherlands and northern Germany; and the Hutterites in Moravia.

Over the centuries, these descendants lost many of their Anabaptist characteristics. Seeking purity, they became legalistic. In the interests of sheer survival, they lost evangelistic zeal. They became known as excellent farmers, good people, and the 'Quiet in the Land'. Not until the late nineteenth century did they experience revival. During the late twentieth century Anabaptism was rediscovered as a source of renewal and a relevant historical movement. Anabaptism influences contemporary Christianity partly through the direct descendants of the Anabaptists – primarily the Mennonites, the Church of the Brethren, the Brethren in Christ, and the Hutterites – and also through their indirect descendants, such as the Baptists, and more distantly the Methodists.

JOHN H. YODER AND ALAN KREIDER

THE FIRST ENGLISH BAPTISTS

In 1608, John Smyth baptized himself in Amsterdam. He had been a fellow of Christ's College, Cambridge, but as a Separatist fled from the harsh rule of James I's England. After his death one of his associates, Thomas Helwys, led back to England a group that had split from Smyth's former congregation. They formed the first General, or Arminian, Baptist congregation in England at Spitalfields, London, in 1612.

By 1638 at the latest there were also congregations holding a Calvinistic theology in London who practised believers' baptism ('Particular Baptists'), growing out of the first congregation of English Independents, although it is not known exactly when they adopted full Baptist views. A radical look at church principles, in the Puritan manner, led first to the understanding of the church as a gathered community, then to a realization that only the baptism of believers fitted such a view.

The extent to which the early Baptists were influenced by European ideas and the thinking of the Radical Reformation is hotly contested. The links with the Dutch Mennonites in the very earliest days are clear; but it is equally clear that the English Baptist movement came out of a search among the English Separatists for the pattern of apostolic churches. They believed this could be discovered from the pages of the New Testament, and was the only pattern of church organization for all succeeding generations.

These youthful Baptist churches were hurled into the current debate about the relationship between church and state and championed their own answers to that controversy at great personal cost. They soon also became involved, to varying degrees, in the millenarian speculations of the mid-seventeenth century. Like many others, the Baptists eagerly thumbed the pages of Daniel and Revelation, seeking the signs of the times and looking for guidance about their proper Christian obedience.

At the same time parliamentary opposition to King Charles I hardened and led relentlessly to the outbreak of the Civil War, or 'English Revolution'. Cromwell's victorious New Model Army held religious opinions which differed from the state-Presbyterianism of Parliament; Independents and Baptists were dominant in the army's leadership and amongst the rank and file. Although Cromwell allowed an established church to continue, he let Baptists, Independents, Presbyterians, and non-royalist Anglicans to act as ministers in it. Those who wanted to worship apart from a state church were permitted to continue a separate existence, provided they did not disturb the peace. Some Baptists accepted office in the state church, but the majority chose to continue independently.

WHAT BAPTISTS STOOD FOR

The Baptists achieved an early peak of numerical strength and national influence during the Interregnum. But even before the Restoration their position was seriously compromised by the loss of members to more radical sects, such as the Quakers, and the adoption of the revolutionary views of the Fifth Monarchists in many places. Vavasor Powell, a committed Fifth-Monarchist, saw two alternatives, asking his congregation whether God would have 'Oliver Cromwell or Jesus Christ to reign over us?'

When these Baptist congregations claimed local independence, it was freedom from state interference they were seeking, not total competence for the local congregation. The need for mutual assistance between congregations led early to the setting up of a General Assembly amongst the General Baptists, and of regional 'associations' amongst the Particular Baptists. Both structures became important tools for expanding the work, as well as forums for discussing theological and disciplinary queries, and so for establishing a 'Baptist viewpoint'. Particular Baptist association meetings discussed such issues as the gathering of churches, believer's baptism, communion with the unbaptized, the ordination of ministers, the maintenance of the ministry, the place of the magistrate, missionary activity, liturgical usages – such as breaking bread, psalm-singing, foot-washing, and anointing the

JOHN BUNYAN

John Bunyan (1628–88) is widely known as the writer of the English classic, *The Pilgrim's Progress*. Born at Elstow, Bedfordshire, the son of a poor brazier or tinker, Bunyan served in the Parliamentary army during the English Civil War. In 1651 he encountered an Independent congregation meeting at Bedford. Despairing over his spiritual state for several years, he finally experienced assurance of salvation, joined the Bedford congregation, and began to preach successfully for them. This led to his imprisonment in Bedford jail after the Restoration (1660).

During his jail years, Bunyan's books began to appear. *Grace Abounding to the Chief of Sinners* (1666) was an account of his own spiritual pilgrimage. *The Pilgrim's Progress* (1678) is an allegory based on Bunyan's spiritual life, in which 'Christian' meets such characters as Evangelist, Faithful, Pliable, and Giant Despair during his hazardous journey from the City of Destruction until he finally enters the Celestial City. Bunyan's language is a happy mixture of homespun phrases and echoes of the English Bible, while his beliefs are shaped by his own Calvinist and Independent position. His other well-known work, *The Holy War* (1682), uses warfare images to construct another allegory.

TIM DOWLEY

> Then Mr Valiant-for-Truth said: 'I am going to my fathers, and though with great difficulty I am got hither, yet now I do not repent me of all the trouble I have been at to arrive where I am. My sword I give to him that shall succeed me in my pilgrimage, and my courage and skill, to him that can get it. My marks and scars I carry with me, to be a witness for me that I have fought his battles who will now be my rewarder.' When the day that he must go hence was come, many accompanied him to the river side, unto which as he went he said, 'Death, where is thy sting?' And as he went down deeper he said, 'Grave, where is thy victory?' So he passed over and the trumpets sounded for him on the other side.'
>
> JOHN BUNYAN, *THE PILGRIM'S PROGRESS*

sick – ecclesiastical discipline, the grounds and manner of exclusion, domestic duties and relationships.

PERSECUTION AND DECLINE

By 1660 there were roughly 300 General and Particular Baptist churches in England and Wales. The Restoration brought a quarter of a century of intermittent persecution by the state; it was not until 1687 that the churches felt able to look back on 'ye Times of our late Troubles'. The accession of William and Mary brought only limited toleration; the oppressive laws remained, though Protestant dissenters of Trinitarian faith, who subscribed to the main points of the Anglican Thirty-nine Articles, were exempted from penalty. But with toleration came tolerance for a wider range of theological views and Dissenters and Anglicans both suffered a decline in religious vitality.

On the one hand, the General Baptists, like the Presbyterians, fell prey to the spread of Arianism, which denied the divinity of Christ. By the end of the eighteenth century, many General Baptist congregations were calling themselves Unitarians or, at any rate, holding a Unitarian theology. On the other hand, some Particular Baptists, especially those who looked to the London leadership of John Gill (1697–1771) and John Brine (1703–65), overreacted against theological liberalism, tending so to stress the sovereignty of God that both individual moral action and evangelism were inhibited in what is known as 'hyper-Calvinism'.

A SLOW AWAKENING

Consequently Baptists were in no position to benefit immediately from the new life represented by the Great Awakening. But several distinct movements brought the impact of the Awakening to the Baptists. First, a group of working folk in some villages in Leicestershire who had been evangelized by one of the Countess of Huntingdon's servants came to Baptist convictions in 1755. Dan Taylor, a Yorkshire miner, converted among the Methodists, similarly came to Baptist convictions by his own study of the subject. Eventually the Leicestershire group and Dan Taylor's church, together with a few General Baptist churches that remained orthodox, formed the 'New Connexion of General Baptists' in 1770. These churches prospered in the emerging industrial communities of central England, the textile communities of Lancashire and Yorkshire, and the hosiery and lace-making areas of the east Midlands.

New life came to the Particular Baptists when, in 1785, Andrew Fuller of Kettering (1754–1815) published The Gospel Worthy of all Acceptation. He 'proved that Calvinism itself, as distinct from the 'false Calvinism' which was common in the eighteenth century, was essentially a missionary theology'. This expressed systematically the doubts that a number of ministers had about the prevailing hyper-Calvinism.

The Baptists went through a form of rebirth in the eighteenth century and their life from that time represents a debate between Puritanism and Evangelicalism. The General Baptists who opposed Dan Taylor's enthusiasm lapsed into Unitarianism; the Particular Baptists who rejected the correcting force of the Evangelical Revival, and allowed only their own members to the communion table, became the Strict Baptists.

CALL TO MISSION

Fuller completed his book in 1781, but hesitated four years before publishing it. In 1784 he was able to apply the thought of the American theologian Jonathan Edwards to the English religious scene. Others too were influenced by the Awakening. Fuller's colleague, John Sutcliffe, issued a 'Call to Prayer' to the Northamptonshire Baptists: 'Let the whole interest of the Redeemer be affectionately remembered, and the spread of the Gospel to the most distant parts of the habitable globe be the object of your most fervent requests.' Out of this renewal of Baptist life came the founding of the Baptist Missionary Society in 1792. William Carey and John Thomas became the Society's first representatives abroad. Fuller, with John Ryland of Bristol (1723–1825), John Sutcliffe of Olney, and Samuel Pearce of Birmingham, supported them at home. The message of The Gospel Worthy of All Acceptation not only revived the churches at home, it gave British Baptists a worldwide vision.

In 1812 it was agreed that a more general union of Particular Baptists was desirable, particularly, though not exclusively, to support the work of 'the Baptist Mission'. In such a way revival gave birth to mission and mission to denominational organization. But a further twenty years passed before the Baptist Union was founded.

JOHN BRIGGS

CHAPTER 26

THE CATHOLIC REFORMATION

The response of the Church of Rome to Martin Luther's *95 Theses* and his attack upon its authority is both curious and revealing. It is curious because the Roman Church seems to have been unaware of the widespread unrest among the faithful that Luther's protest represented. It is revealing in that the first response to the rumblings in northern Europe was low-key and almost nonchalant. Yet the way in which the Church of Rome reacted to Luther and his cause was to have far-reaching consequences.

LEO AND LUTHER

Leo X (1513–21), pope at the time, had other things on his mind. Leo was in many ways a typical Renaissance pope: elegant, worldly, sophisticated, intelligent, consumed with political and family ambition, more of an administrator than 'a servant of the servants of God'. An enthusiastic patron of Renaissance art and ideals, Leo aimed to advance the fortunes of his own family – the Medicis of Florence – and to increase the political power of the Papal States in central Italy, of which he was ruler. He revelled in Renaissance activities – spending a great deal of money on the arts and on gambling – while the day-to-day routine of managing the large and corrupt papal bureaucracy took much of his time and energy. All of this sapped his ability to give any kind of moral leadership over Christian Europe at a critical point in its history.

When Leo first saw a copy of Luther's Theses in 1518, he is supposed to have made two comments; probably neither of them is authentic, but both are in keeping with his known initial response to Luther. The first was: 'Luther is a drunken German. He will feel different when he is sober.' The second: 'Friar Martin is a brilliant chap. The whole row is due to the envy of the monks.' He concluded that it was probably 'only a monks' quarrel'.

Two important points emerge about the short-term response of church and papacy to Luther. First, the negative and disdainful attitude of the church towards Luther's initial pronouncements helped make the Wittenberg professor a major public figure, especially in Germany. Second, it showed the church was not aware of the significance of the threat it was facing. Indeed, the great irony and danger of the situation was that the pope was in no position to provide the kind of inspiring leadership necessary to head off Luther's challenge, nor was he able to provide a constructive channel for this new force.

Relations between Luther and the papacy deteriorated badly after 1519, as leaders of the church began to realize what Luther was actually saying. When they saw that he was calling for a spiritual authority other than the one established and accepted by the late medieval church, and for a major overhaul of the institution of the church itself – a threat to vested interests – they came to regard Luther as a 'son of iniquity'. By 1520 the die was cast. Following his reading of Luther's *Babylonian Captivity of the Church* in that year, Erasmus sadly noted: 'The breach is irreparable'. And so it was. The Diet of Worms in 1521 confirmed Luther's excommunication and declared him a political outlaw.

But through all of this there were some who remained within the church of Rome – many in high places – who readily acknowledged the truth of Luther's accusations of misplaced spiritual authority and institutional corruption. Many of these, troubled about the situation for a variety of reasons, did not leave the church. Instead, these pious individuals worked in many different ways to reform the Church of Rome from within. This large number of devout Catholics contributed to the long-term response to the Protestant challenge, now known as the Catholic Reformation. This movement was in part a direct reaction to the external threat of the Protestant movement, and in part an effort to correct internal abuses and restore genuine piety to the Roman Church.

Among the various outworkings of the Catholic Reformation were the establishment of the Oratory of Divine Love; the reform of the papacy; the founding of the Society of Jesus and several other new monastic orders; the meeting of an ecumenical council at Trent; the rejuvenation and reorganization of the Inquisition; the issuing of an 'index' of books which the faithful were not permitted to read; the resurgence of Catholic mysticism in Spain; and 'wars of religion' which led to the forced re-conversion of certain areas of Europe from Protestantism to Roman Catholicism. Each of these features helped revitalize the Church of Rome, so that by 1650 it stood at the threshold of a new era of expansion and spiritual vigour.

A SOCIETY OF REFORMERS

In 1517, the same year that Luther posted his Theses at Wittenberg, the Oratory of Divine Love appeared in Rome. An informal society of about fifty clergy and lay people, the Oratory stressed reform along liberal lines similar to the ideas of Erasmus. The group met frequently in the Church of Saints Sylvester and Dorothea for prayer, meditation, mutual encouragement, and discussions about reforming the institutional church through love and moral improvement. The society included in its ranks some of the most influential leaders in the Roman hierarchy; few of its members favoured radical doctrinal or structural changes

Among those who identified with the Oratory were Jacopo Sadoleto (1477–1547), Gian Matteo Gilberti (1495–1543), Gaetano da Thiene (1480–1547), Reginald Pole, Gian Pietro Caraffa (who later became Pope Paul IV, 1476–1559) and Gasparo Contarini (1483–1542). Of these,

GASPARO CONTARINI

Cardinal Contarini (1483–1542) was a leader of reform in the Roman Catholic church. Belonging to a leading family in Venice, he studied at the University of Padua, and became well known for his scientific studies and for defending the doctrine of the immortality of the soul against Pietro Pomponazzi. He served Venice as ambassador to the Emperor Charles V and in other important posts.

Contarini was also deeply concerned with religious reform. In 1511 he underwent a religious conversion similar to Luther's, and wrote tracts on the ideal bishop, the papacy, the sacraments, and Lutheranism. In 1535 Pope Paul III made Contarini a cardinal and the following year named him chairman of a reform commission. Contarini helped win approval for the Jesuits, and as papal legate to the Regensburg Colloquy of 1541 urged reconciliation with the Protestants, but failed to reach agreement on the sacraments. When Contarini returned to Italy, Rome refused to approve his views on justification and Luther attacked them too.

Contarini died shortly after. His life reflects – better than that of any contemporary – the political, intellectual, and religious crisis of Italy during the early sixteenth century.

JOHN P. DONNELLY

Contarini was the most deeply committed to reform on the lines of Erasmus' ideas, and the most openly sympathetic with the Protestant point of view.

Contarini was an experienced politician and diplomat, and a Christian humanist. He was a layman in 1517, but later took holy orders and was made a cardinal in 1535. He was by temperament a peacemaker and apparently shared some views with the reformers. Philipp Melanchthon, from the Lutheran camp, is often compared with him, because of their similar personalities, conciliatory natures, and humanism. Contarini influenced Pope Paul III in the direction of reform, presided over a papal reform commission, supported attempts at reconciliation with the Protestants, and advocated a return to the faith of the apostles by the church.

Perhaps Contarini's supreme attempt to bring real and lasting reform to the Church of Rome occurred in 1541 when he was a papal legate (or delegate) at the Colloquy of Regensburg. At that meeting, the last major effort was made to work out a compromise statement of theology acceptable to both the evangelical Reformers and the Roman leaders. Basing their discussions upon about twenty articles largely drawn up by Protestants, Melanchthon and Contarini hammered out a verbal statement of the doctrine of justification by faith acceptable to both men. However, they were less successful in reaching agreement on questions regarding transubstantiation and the authority of the papacy. After reaching an impasse on these and related points, Melanchthon and Contarini returned to their respective parties, only to have their views repudiated in the areas where they *had* reached agreement.

Luther adamantly refused to accept the compromise formula on faith. When Contarini returned to Italy, he was accused of heresy and associating with enemies of the church. Exhausted and grief-stricken, he died the next year, before these charges could be pressed further. The failure of Contarini and other liberals to work out a peaceful solution to the split in the church opened the way for the militant programme of the Catholic hardliners. But before the militants gained control of the papacy, the positive spiritual momentum created by the Oratory of Divine Love led to its reform.

PAPAL REFORMS

A reformed papacy made possible the vigorous programme of the Catholic Reformation. The popes most responsible for reforming the papal office were Clement VII (r. 1523–34), Paul III (r. 1534–49), and Paul VI (r. 1555–59), who had to deal with several monumental problems. For one thing, there were serious divisions among those who remained faithful to Rome over which course of action to take to meet the Protestant threat. Another difficulty facing these popes was the complex political situation in Europe at the time. For example, rulers holding a common Roman Catholic faith were often military and diplomatic rivals. The political situation was muddied further by the fact that the pope was himself the temporal ruler of the Papal States as well as the spiritual leader of the international Roman Catholic Church. Finally, those with a vested interest in a corrupt church were reluctant to give a reform-minded pope a free hand to cleanse the church of abuses.

Pope Clement VII accomplished little in the way of reform despite sincere efforts. The political manoeuvrings of the Emperor Charles V and King Francis I (1515–47) of France often put Clement in an utterly hopeless situation. Each monarch exerted enormous pressure on the pope to side with him. In the end, Clement suffered the wrath of both. An illustration of the political vice in which Clement found himself was the dilemma he faced following Henry VIII of England's request in 1527 for an annulment of his marriage to Catherine of Aragon. Henry's plea arrived in Rome at a most untimely moment: the city was surrounded by the army of Charles V, who happened also to be Catherine's nephew. In this situation, no matter what the pope decided, he had to lose. Thus, when he refused Henry's request, the first step towards the English Reformation was taken.

Perhaps the best thing Clement might have done would have been to call an ecumenical council to seek a solution to the problems besetting the church. He did in fact seriously consider such a move, but finally gave up the idea because of the political pincers in which he found himself, as the king of France and the Holy Roman Emperor struggled for supremacy in Europe. He could suggest no venue for the proposed council that was acceptable to both rulers.

POPE PAUL III

Clement made some attempts to end corruption in the church. However, his major contribution to reform was probably his recommendation that the highly gifted Alessandro Farnese should succeed him. Farnese became Pope Paul III, the most sincere reformer to mount the papal throne in the sixteenth century. Under Paul III, many positive steps were taken to correct abuses and bring about needed change. Perhaps the most outstanding of these were his appointment of reformers to the College of Cardinals, the setting up of a papal reform commission, and the calling of the Council of Trent in 1545.

Among those made cardinal by Paul III were such dedicated reformers as Contarini, Caraffa, Pole, Sadoleto (all former members of the Oratory of Divine Love – the Rome Oratory was disbanded in 1527), Pietro Bembo (1470–1547) and Jean du Bellay (c. 1493–1560). These appointments revealed Paul's determination to rid the College of Cardinals of its moral laxity and make it more international.

More important was the papal reform commission that Paul appointed in 1536. The pope named nine leading cardinals to serve on it, and made Contarini its head. Its task was to recommend reforms for the church and to prepare the way for a council. It made a wide-ranging study of conditions in the church – especially in the papal bureaucracy – and issued a formal report entitled *Advice ... Concerning the Reform of the Church*, submitted to the pope in February 1537.

The report analyzed the causes of the disorder in the church, and recommended immediate action to correct the worst offences and to remove the worst offenders. The language of the document was painfully blunt: the papal office had become too secular. Both popes and cardinals needed to give more attention to spiritual matters and stop flirting with the world. It gave concrete examples of the kind of problems which needed attention: bribery in high places, abuses of papal power, the evasion of church law by lay people and clergy alike, laxity in the monastic orders, the abuse of indulgences, and the high number of prostitutes operating in Rome itself.

Despite the opposition of a number of powerful older cardinals, Paul took action to end several of these problems. He reformed the papal bureaucracy, ordered an end to the taking of money for spiritual favours, and forbade the buying and selling of church appointments – but this amounted to only a few of the commission's recommendations. Meanwhile Protestants obtained a copy of the commission's report and published it as evidence of the corrupt state of the Roman Church.

THE COUNCIL OF TRENT

Paul III's most significant action was to call an ecumenical church council to deal with reform and the growing menace of Protestantism. After intense negotiations with the Emperor and the French king, Paul finally named Trent as the venue for the council, a compromise location. Trent is a city in present-day northern Italy, but at the time it was just inside the area of the Italian peninsula ruled by the Emperor. The French were offended by this choice, and only a handful of French church leaders attended the council.

As it turned out, Trent was the most important ecumenical council between Nicaea (325) and Vatican II (1962–65). It was to deal with the massive problems posed by the split in the church and with the renewal of the Church of Rome. In this it was only partly successful. Despite this failure to achieve all its goals, the council shaped the response of Rome to the Protestant Reformation.

The council met in three main sessions: 1545–47, 1551–52, and 1562–63. It was not a continuous meeting, but really three different gatherings attended by three different – but overlapping – groups of representatives of the Roman Church. Attendance was scanty and irregular for an enterprise of such significance. The first session opened with only four archbishops, twenty bishops, four generals of monastic orders, and a few theologians present. The largest number of delegates to attend the second session was fifty-nine. The third session was the largest, with as many as 255 at one of its meetings.

The Italians were the best represented throughout the council, with many bishops attending too from Spain and the Empire. Other areas, including France, were noticeably under-represented. It proved most difficult to bring the Spanish into agreement with the decisions of the majority; they were not only doctrinal hardliners, but also sensitive to the Emperor's wishes (Charles V, Holy Roman Emperor, was also Charles I, king of Spain), and held that councils were superior to popes – a view repulsive to the papacy. Sometimes feelings ran so high that there were physical struggles between delegates. Despite all these difficulties, the council persevered and accomplished much.

Perhaps the most interesting session of the council was the second, when a number of Protestants were present. The Emperor held back the German bishops from this session until the pope agreed to allow Protestants to attend; however, the pope did not agree to the Emperor's demand that the Protestants should also be allowed to vote. Consequently, not one leading Lutheran theologian came, nor did any Calvinists show up. However, at least three delegations of Protestants arrived late in 1551: one from Brandenburg, one from Württemberg, and one from Strasbourg. In January 1552, they were joined by representatives of Maurice of Saxony.

The Württembergers wanted to discuss their own confession of faith – not a statement imposed by the papal legate. Johann Sleidan (1506–56), a distinguished Protestant historian, led the Strasbourg delegation in maintaining their doctrinal position. They refused to compromise. When the group from Saxony arrived, the Protestants drew up a list of demands that included a chance to re-examine all decrees on doctrine previously accepted by the council. They started by declaring, in effect, that the pope was the servant of the council and not its master; but they also indicated that these points were negotiable.

Nothing came of the Protestant presence at the second session. Informal talks were held, but nothing appeared on the formal agenda concerning the points they raised. So the Protestants departed in March 1552, convinced there was nothing to be gained by remaining any longer at Trent. The inability or unwillingness of the two sides to come to some sort of understanding illustrates the width of the theological chasm between them.

CATHOLIC DOCTRINE CLARIFIED

For the Roman Church, the third session proved to be the most productive. A number of issues debated in earlier meetings were resolved. Medieval orthodoxy was reaffirmed, as it related to most of the doctrines under dispute in the Reformation. For example, transubstantiation, justification by faith *and* works, and established medieval practices connected with the mass were all upheld. The seven sacraments were once again insisted upon, and the celibacy of the clergy, the existence of purgatory, and indulgences were all reaffirmed. However, the post of indulgence-seller was abolished and abuses connected with the distribution of indulgences were condemned. In short, the council clarified and reasserted most of the doctrines of the late medieval Roman church. In addition, papal power was increased by giving the pope the authority to enforce the decrees of the council, and by again requiring that church officials had to promise him obedience.

Protestants were bitterly disappointed – though not surprised; most shared Luther's initial scepticism concerning the 'irreformability of the church'. Trent ruled out any possibility of Christian reconciliation in the immediate future. Scholastic-style definitions, with accompanying curses on anyone who did not agree with them, killed any lingering Protestant hopes of restored unity. But by elevating the papacy once more, by improving church organization, by dealing with the most flagrant of the abuses pointed out by the Protestant Reformers, and by clarifying doctrine and dogma, the Council of Trent gave the Church of Rome a clear position to uphold in the next four centuries. The work of Trent would stand the church in good stead during the wars of religion and the period of missionary expansion that lay ahead.

LOYOLA FOUNDS THE JESUITS

Present at the Council of Trent were two suave, intelligent, and highly influential members of the Society of Jesus – the new monastic order which Pope Paul III had approved in 1540. The two Jesuits, as the fledgling order soon became popularly known, were Diego Laynez and Alfonso Salmerón. The founder and leader of their order – one of the most dramatic and powerful figures in Christian history – was Ignatius of Loyola, often taken as the embodiment of the Catholic Reformation.

Loyola had been a professional soldier, but a serious wound cut short his military career. While recovering, he had time to think about his rough-and-tumble past and his future. Loyola's period waiting for God's guidance was immensely important and has been compared to Luther's monastic experience. But whereas Luther finally found peace by rejecting the traditions of the medieval church in favour of the biblical basics of primitive Christianity, Loyola finally found peace by rededicating himself to the conventions of the medieval church.

Loyola emerged from his convalescence a curious mixture of soldier, mystic, and monk. He wrote up his own spiritual pilgrimage as *The Spiritual Exercises*, the book which – with its powerful appeal to the imagination and its great emphasis on obedience to Christ and his church (meaning the Church of Rome) – provided the cornerstone for the new ascetic order that Loyola founded.

IGNATIUS OF LOYOLA

Ignatius of Loyola founded the dedicated and powerful Society of Jesus (the Jesuits). A Spanish nobleman, Ignatius was born in 1491 at the castle of Loyola, near the Pyrenees. His career as a professional soldier was ended by a leg wound in 1521, but, through reading lives of Christ and the saints while convalescing, he resolved to become Christ's soldier. He hung up his sword at the altar of Mary in Montserrat and then spent a year (1522–23) in prayer and meditation at Manresa Monastery, seeking total consecration to Christ. Here he drafted his *Spiritual Exercises*.

Between 1524 and 1534 Loyola studied at Barcelona, Alcalá, Salamanca, and Paris, preparing for service. Then he and six friends vowed to practice poverty and celibacy, to make a pilgrimage to Jerusalem (this never came off), and to devote the rest of their lives to apostolic labours, in this way initiating the Society of Jesus. 'Jesuits', as its members were called, vowed total obedience to the pope as, in effect, commander-in-chief, and under him to the general of the order. Ignatius, a fine organizer, was general till his death in 1556.

All Roman Catholic ordinands still go – at least once – through Ignatius' *Spiritual Exercises*, which form a four-week retreat programme of devotional meditations and instructions. Week one is on sin, week two on Christ's kingship, week three on his passion, and week four on his risen life, with the aim of achieving complete consecration, appealing to the will through understanding, imagination, and conscience.

J. I. PACKER

Prayer

Teach us, good Lord, to serve thee as thou deservest; to give and not to count the cost; to fight and not to heed the wounds; to toil and not to ask for rest; to labour and not to ask for any reward save knowing that we do thy will.

Through Jesus Christ our Lord.

IGNATIUS OF LOYOLA

Ignatius of Loyola (1491–1556), founder and first Superior General of the Society of Jesus – the Jesuits.
© GEORGIOS KOLLIDAS/DREAMSTIME.COM

After many initial setbacks and discouragements, Loyola finally gathered about him a small group of young men wholly dedicated to serving Christ through the Church of Rome. As the new order took shape, it bore the indelible stamp of its founder. The Jesuits were to become a new spiritual élite, at the disposal of the pope to use in whatever way he thought appropriate for spreading the 'true church'. Absolute, unquestioning, military-style obedience became the hallmark of the new society. The famous Jesuit dictum was that every member of the society would obey the pope and the general of the order as unquestioningly 'as a corpse'.

After some hesitation, Paul III gave papal approval to the Society of Jesus in 1540. The constitution of the new order insisted on a fourth vow in addition to the traditional ones of poverty, chastity, and obedience: a special oath of absolute obedience to the pope. The purpose of the society was to propagate the faith by every means at the order's disposal. Recruits for the Jesuits were to reflect Loyola's spirituality and his stress on military-style organization and obedience. They were to be of robust health, handsome in appearance, intelligent, and eloquent in speech. No one of bad character, or with even the slightest hint of unorthodox belief, was admitted.

The growth of the Jesuit order was extraordinarily rapid. When Loyola died in 1556, there were members of the society in Japan, Brazil, Ethiopia, and the coast of central Africa, as well as in nearly every country in Europe. Many had reached high positions in the church: two served as the pope's ambassadors in Poland and Ireland, while a number were professors in the largest and best universities in Europe. By 1556 the half-dozen original followers of Loyola had grown to more than 1,500.

The Jesuits' work centred on three main tasks: education, counteracting Protestants, and missionary expansion in new areas. The Jesuits provided high-quality education, and by this means upgraded the training of Catholic believers as well as winning the opinion-makers of society for the Roman Church. Their schools soon became famous for their high standards and attainments, and many individuals of the élite were won to Roman Catholicism by this means. Children were given special attention. Before long the now-familiar Jesuit saying was coined: 'Give me a child until he is seven, and he will remain a Catholic the rest of his life.'

Counter-reform was a second major Jesuit preoccupation in the second half of the sixteenth century and throughout the seventeenth. In France, in what is today Belgium, in southern Germany, and most noticeably in eastern Europe, the Jesuits led the counter-attack against the Protestants. Using almost any means at their disposal, they recaptured large areas for the Church of Rome, earned a reputation as 'the feared and formidable storm-troops of the Counter Reformation'. Only in England did their campaign fail.

JESUIT MISSIONS

The third task at which the Jesuits excelled was missionary activity in new lands. Increasingly, Jesuit priests travelled in the ships of Spain and Portugal as they sailed the seven seas in search of new colonies and new riches. Jesuit missionaries travelled to America, Africa, and Asia in search of converts, helping to counterbalance the greedy imperialism of the European merchants and soldiers. They produced scholarly accounts of the history and geography of the new places they visited; but above all they left their converts with an enthusiastic brand of Catholicism, and produced devout, tough Catholics, on their own model.

The Jesuits played a leading role in the conversion of Brazil and Paraguay. They were not as successful in Africa, where native peoples often resisted their efforts. The greatest stories of Jesuit heroism come from Asia, where the courageous Francis Xavier (1506–52) towered above the rest as the 'apostle to the Indies and to Japan'.

Xavier was born into the Spanish nobility, and was one of the original members of the Society of Jesus. Loyola early recognized that this handsome, bright, and cheerful young man would make a powerful servant of God. He became the most widely-acclaimed Jesuit missionary of all time. Xavier was appointed the pope's ambassador and sent to evangelize the East Indies in 1542, and spent three years there, followed by preaching and baptizing in present-day Malaysia, Vietnam, and Japan. His most remarkable mission was in Japan, where he established a Christian community which has survived to this day, despite numerous periods of severe persecution. Xavier died of a fever when he was only forty-six years old, while attempting to take the Christian message to China.

The Jesuits, together with the Dominicans, Franciscans, and Augustinians, led the Church of Rome in a new period of rapid overseas expansion between 1550 and 1650. By this means nearly all of Mexico, Central America, and South America, along with a large part of the population of the Philippines, and smaller numbers of people in Africa, India, the East Indies, and the Far East, became adherents of the Church of Rome.

THE INQUISITION REVIVED

The Jesuits were most active in the border areas of Europe and in the newly-discovered lands overseas. In the traditionally Roman Catholic countries such as Italy, Spain, and France, the Inquisition became the major instrument of the Catholic Reformation. The Inquisition, or Supreme Sacred Congregation of the Holy Office, as it was officially called, was not an invention of the sixteenth century. The so-called Roman Inquisition begun in 1542 was child and grandchild of the medieval and Spanish Inquisitions that had gone before it in the thirteenth and fifteenth centuries respectively.

The rejuvenation of the Inquisition as a means of reform and counter-reform was largely the work of Cardinal Caraffa. Originally a theological moderate, Caraffa became increasingly conservative as the Protestant Reformation progressed. By 1542, he was an outspoken critic of those who sought reconciliation with the Protestants and, instead, advocated fighting them with the weapons of coercion, censorship, and propaganda. It was at his urging that the new Roman Inquisition was established – 'Roman' because it was to be controlled by the papacy from Rome.

On Sundays I assemble all the people, men and women, young and old, and get them to repeat the prayers in their language. They take much pleasure in doing so, and come to the meetings gladly … I give out the First Commandment, which they repeat, and then we say all together, Jesus Christ, Son of God, grant us grace to love thee above all things. When we have asked for this grace, we recite the *Pater Noster* together, and then cry with one accord, Holy Mary, Mother of Jesus Christ, obtain for us grace from thy son to enable us to keep the First Commandment. Next we say an *Ave Maria*, and proceed in the same manner through each of the remaining nine Commandments. And just as we say twelve *Paters* and *Aves* in honour of the twelve articles of the Creed, so we say ten *Paters* and ten *Aves* in honour of the Ten Commandments, asking God to give us grace to keep them well.

FRANCIS XAVIER, JESUIT MISSIONARY, DESCRIBING HIS METHODS IN SOUTH INDIA

THE JESUITS

The Jesuits, or Society of Jesus, were founded by Ignatius of Loyola and approved by the papacy in 1540 as an order of Catholic priests depending solely on charity (mendicants).

In 1535, in Paris, Loyola and six remarkable disciples took vows of poverty and chastity, and promised to go as missionaries to Palestine. When war between Venice and the Turks blocked their passage, they began work in the north Italian cities. They gathered new recruits, sought direction and approval from Pope Paul III, and elected Loyola as their general. He devoted the rest of his life to writing the Jesuit *Constitutions* at Rome, and to directing the rapidly spreading order.

The new order had several distinctive features. It was highly centralized: all its leaders were appointed by the general, who was elected for life. The *Constitutions* imposed no religious uniform, no bodily penances or fasts, and no choral recitation of the daily liturgy. But Loyola insisted that recruits be carefully selected and arduously trained (later fifteen years' training became quite normal), and also stressed obedience and a close link with the papacy. Above all, the Jesuit was to cultivate an inner life based on meditation and Loyola's *Spiritual Exercises*; prayer was to mould him into an effective apostle.

Loyola wanted quality rather than numbers, yet the order grew rapidly. By 1556 there were more than 1,000 Jesuits – mainly in Spain, Portugal, and Italy, but also in France, Germany, the Low Countries, India, Brazil, and Africa. By 1626 there were 15,544, and during the next 130 years the Jesuits grew slowly but steadily, working in almost every corner of the globe.

In 1773 the Bourbon monarchs of France and Spain forced the pope to suppress the Jesuits, though a few survived in Prussia and Russia. In 1814 the papacy restored the Jesuits throughout the world; they reached a peak of 36,038 members in 1964, but in the unrest following Vatican II membership fell – to 19,000 by 2007.

Education quickly became the most important Jesuit emphasis; within a decade of their foundation they already had a dozen colleges. By 1626 there were 400 colleges, and by 1749 about 800, including seminaries. These schools were open to all classes of people and generally charged nothing for tuition. During the seventeenth and early eighteenth century a high percentage of the educated people of Catholic Europe passed through Jesuit schools.

Caraffa was one of the six cardinals appointed as Inquisitor General. In this capacity, and later as pope, he supported the Inquisition as the most effective means of dealing with heretics. Caraffa and his fellow inquisitors regarded heretics as traitors against God, and the foulest of criminals. It was for their own good, and for the good of the church, that they had to be sought out and dealt with by the Inquisition. If the Holy Office could not return these benighted individuals to the church, then they must be eradicated before they contaminated other immortal souls with their spiritual disease. Thus, they were to be removed from the body of Christian society in much the same way as surgeons remove cancer tissue from the human body in order to save a person's life. The Inquisition commonly used terror and torture to obtain confessions. If the death penalty was required, the convicted heretic was handed over to the civil authorities for execution, since canon law forbade the church to shed blood.

The Inquisition was used widely and effectively in Italy, except in Venice. In Spain, it was fused with the older Spanish Inquisition and produced substantial results, while in France it was modified and kept under quite close control by the French monarchs. It was not widely used in Germany, where there was no inquisitorial tradition. In England,

Jesuit education was based on the *Plan of Studies* of 1599 which purified and simplified Renaissance humanism. Jesuits insisted on pupils attending classes and a carefully planned curriculum took students forward step by step. The Jesuits used friendly rivalry instead of the rod to stimulate their students. Philosophy in their schools generally followed Aristotle, while theology was freely adapted from Thomas Aquinas, as in the system of Francisco Suarez (1548–1617). Jesuit schools were famous for their drama: moral and religious values were taught through a pageantry that rivalled early opera.

MISSIONS

Foreign missions were always the most highly regarded of Jesuit activities. Francis Xavier (1506–52), who worked in India, Indonesia, and Japan, was the first and greatest Jesuit missionary. Matteo Ricci (1552–1610) founded modern mission work in China and adapted the gospel to Chinese traditions and thought-forms. The Jesuits used their Western scientific knowledge to gain entry to court circles in Peking, yet never succeeded in converting a Chinese ruler. Robert de Nobili (1577–1656) applied Ricci's methods of adapting the gospel to the local culture in India. Isaac Joques, Jacques Marquette, and many other French Jesuits worked with mixed success among the Canadian Indians. Eusebio Kino (1645–1711) built mission stations and introduced advanced agriculture among the Indians of northern Mexico and south-western United States. Other Jesuits organized towns (Reductions, or *reducciones de indios*) to convert and 'civilize' the Indians of Paraguay and Brazil.

Loyola did not found the Jesuits in order to combat Protestantism, but this increasingly became a Jesuit goal during the sixteenth century. Several Jesuits served as papal representatives (legates) in complex negotiations to link countries such as Ireland, Sweden, and Russia more firmly to Rome. Other Jesuits served as court preachers or confessors to the Emperor, the kings of France and Poland, and the dukes of Bavaria. Peter Canisius (1521–97) from Nijmegen, in the Low Countries, and Robert Bellarmine (1542–1611) from Montepulciano, Tuscany, wrote catechisms and anti-Protestant works of theology that were influential for centuries.

JOHN P. DONNELLY

common law prevented its introduction. It was most effective where the population was still largely Roman Catholic. With wide popular support, it became a major deterrent to the further spread of the Protestant faith.

BOOKS BANNED

Associated with the concept of coercion by the Inquisition was the idea of a list of prohibited books. In fact, the practice of maintaining a catalogue of heretical and dangerous books was an old one, used in the Middle Ages with varying degrees of success. In the early sixteenth century, several theological faculties and the Holy Office itself circulated lists of books pronounced unfit for the eyes of the faithful. The first real papal 'index' of prohibited books was issued by Pope Paul IV in 1559. It was extensive, naming books, parts of books, authors, and printers.

The last major session of the Council of Trent issued the most authoritative index of prohibited books of the period. Their list – the so-called *Tridentine Index* – was handed over to Pope Pius IV (1559–65) to enforce. He published this *Index* in 1564 and called on true Christians everywhere to observe it. The *Index Librorum Prohibitorum*

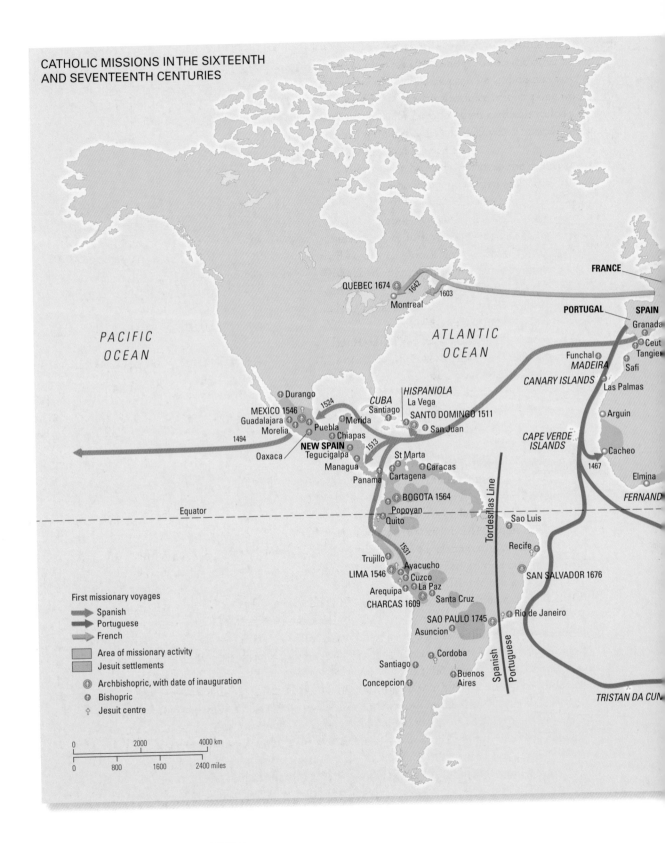

CATHOLIC MISSIONS IN THE SIXTEENTH AND SEVENTEENTH CENTURIES

PACIFIC OCEAN

ATLANTIC OCEAN

FRANCE

PORTUGAL   SPAIN

QUEBEC 1674   1642
Montreal   1603

Granada

Ceut
Tangier
Funchal   Safi
MADEIRA
CANARY ISLANDS
Las Palmas

Durango   1524   HISPANIOLA
La Vega
MEXICO 1546   CUBA   SANTO DOMINGO 1511
Guadalajara   Santiago   Merida   San Juan
Morelia   Puebla   Chiapas   CAPE VERDE
1494   NEW SPAIN   ISLANDS
Oaxaca   Tegucigalpa   1513   St Marta   Arguin
Managua   Caracas
Panama   Cartagena   Cacheo
BOGOTA 1564   1467
Popoyan   Elmina
Equator   Quito   Sao Luis   FERNAND

Trujillo   1531   Ayacucho   Recife
LIMA 1546   Cuzco   SAN SALVADOR 1676
Arequipa   La Paz
Santa Cruz
CHARCAS 1609   Rio de Janeiro
SAO PAULO 1745

First missionary voyages   Asuncion
Cordoba
Spanish   Santiago   Buenos   TRISTAN DA CUN
Portuguese   Concepcion   Aires
French

Area of missionary activity

Jesuit settlements

Archbishopric, with date of inauguration

Bishopric

Jesuit centre

0   2000   4000 km

0   800   1600   2400 miles

Tordesillas Line

Spanish   Portuguese

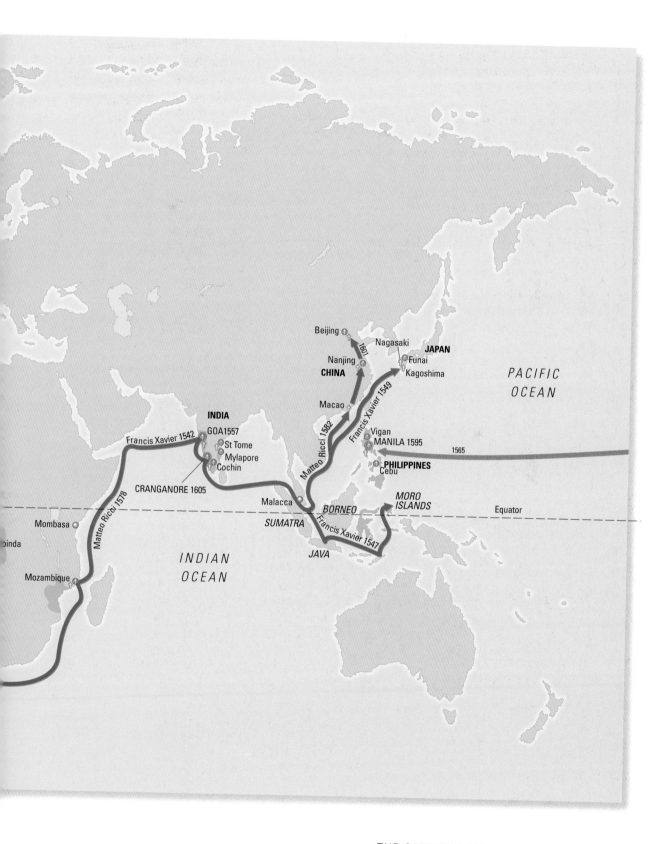

Beijing

Nagasaki

JAPAN

Nanjing

1601

Funai

CHINA

Kagoshima

PACIFIC
OCEAN

Macao

Francis Xavier 1549

Matteo Ricci 1582

Vigan

MANILA 1595

INDIA

1565

GOA 1557

St Tome

Francis Xavier 1542

Mylapore

PHILIPPINES

Cochin

Cebu

CRANGANORE 1605

Matteo Ricci 1578

Malacca

MORO
ISLANDS

BORNEO

Equator

Mombasa

SUMATRA

Francis Xavier 1547

JAVA

INDIAN
OCEAN

Mozambique

THE CATHOLIC REFORMATION

(List of Prohibited Books) censored nearly three-quarters of all the books that were being printed in Europe at the time. Almost the only books permitted were Catholic devotional literature and the Latin *Vulgate* Bible. The pope also appointed a 'Congregation of the Index' to update the list periodically. The practice of keeping up the *Index* lasted until 1966, when it was finally abolished. Both in the sixteenth century, and in the centuries following, it was largely a failure.

MYSTICS IN SPAIN

One expression of the Catholic Reformation which was not particularly welcomed by the Church of Rome was the revival of Catholic mysticism in Spain. Mysticism makes the institutional church nervous because – carried to its logical conclusion – it does away with the need for the priesthood and the sacraments. The mystic emphasizes personal religion and his or her direct relationship to God, with the ultimate goal of losing himself or herself in the essence of God. The Christian mystic usually stresses the personal reality of Christ, and seeks personal union with God through the Son. Often this ultimate union comes in a blinding flash of supreme ecstasy. In short, Christian mysticism is contemplative,

TERESA OF AVILA

Teresa of Avila (1515–82) was one of the most famous mystics of sixteenth-century Spain. Born in Avila into a Spanish noble family, as a young woman Teresa committed herself to converting the heathen and healing the division with Protestants. In 1536 she entered the Carmelite Convent of the Incarnation in Avila. Although her religious career was interrupted for a time by severe illness, she was able to return to the convent in 1540.

Teresa was persuaded of the need to reform the lax – often scandalous – condition of Spanish monasteries. Supported by wealthy relatives and friends, she founded a reformed Carmelite convent, St Joseph's (San José), in Avila, followed by sixteen more religious houses, and travelled the length and breadth of Spain inspecting monasteries, encouraging monks and nuns, and preaching reform.

Teresa was familiar with the great religious literature and epics of the Spanish Golden Age, and herself wrote an autobiography, *El Camino de Perfección* (The Road of Perfection), and *El Castillo Interior* (The Interior Castle). The theme of her best writing is the mystical life. She sought oneness with God through contemplation and prayer, which led to a profound experience and personal knowledge of God through love which she described as 'mystical marriage'. She spoke of a second conversion, and of union through love. In her *Life* Teresa describes an ecstasy – which can appear embarrassing, and even erotic – in which a seraph appeared to her carrying a spear tipped with fire. He plunged the spear into her heart, piercing to her innermost being and leaving her aflame with a great love for God. This experience, she says, was both painful and sweet beyond description, and symbolized the mystical union of the believer with God.

Teresa and her companions represent the Catholic Reformation's emphasis on emotion and religious passion.

CAROLINE MARSHALL

personal, and usually practical. Such was the case with Teresa of Avila (1515–82), the best-known of the sixteenth-century Spanish mystics.

Teresa and her devoted follower, John of the Cross, revitalized a large part of the spiritual life of Spain through their practical mysticism. Teresa was a Carmelite nun who searched for the life of perfection. Ill-health caused her great anguish and threatened her career as a nun. Finally, in the 1550s, during a period of intense prayer, she experienced the first of her many heavenly visions. She wrote of her mystical experiences, but did not stress them, because she recognized their dangers as well as their value.

Santa Teresa the mystic was also Sister Teresa the powerful figure who did not suffer fools gladly. Contemporaries admired her, describing her as single-minded, even brash. She was a good negotiator for her order, and had learned something of finance and law. She enjoyed conversations about good books, knew many people in the community beyond the confines of her convent, and liked having a good meal and a hearty laugh. She is reputed to have said, 'There is a time for penance and a time for partridge.' Nevertheless, she committed herself totally to God, and lived a life of the spirit which many wanted to follow.

Spurred on by her personal relationship with God, Teresa became the great reformer of the Carmelite Order and proved that mysticism could stimulate practical reform. Because she and John of the Cross spread Catholic mysticism throughout the country, many of the faithful experienced spiritual satisfaction. The reform of the Spanish monasteries and convents begun under Teresa also helped to head off the criticism of those religious houses in other parts of Europe which made the Protestant case for reform so compelling.

EUROPE DIVIDED

The intensity and scope of the Catholic Reformation helped set the stage for the wars of religion which broke out in many parts of Europe following the failure of the Lutherans and Roman Catholics to achieve reconciliation at Regensburg in 1541. Major fighting between the Lutheran princes and the imperial forces in the 1540s and early 1550s finally came to an end with the compromise Peace of Augsburg in 1555. The Augsburg agreement provided for the co-existence of Lutheran and Roman Catholic expressions of

JOHN OF THE CROSS

John of the Cross (1542–91) was a Spanish mystic who, with Teresa of Avila, helped found the reformed or barefoot (Discalced) Carmelite Order. Born Juan de Yepes Álvarez, John came from a noble but poor background. He joined the Carmelites at their monastery at Medina (1563) and then studied theology at the University of Salamanca. After John had been ordained a priest, Teresa of Avila persuaded him to join in the reform of the Carmelites. Later he became confessor at the Convent of the Incarnation of Avila (1572–77).

Opposition arose against the austerity and simplicity of the new Carmelite movement, which led to John's brutal imprisonment at Toledo (1578). He expressed his experience in *The Spiritual Canticle*. After escaping from prison, John spent the rest of his life in monastic administration and in elaborating his mystical theology. He was a prior on several occasions, rector of the college at Baeza, and vicar of the southern province of the Carmelite order.

During these years he wrote *The Ascent of Mount Carmel* and *The Dark Night of the Soul*, which consist of poems with commentaries, instructing the soul on how to achieve union with God. John made contact with Muslim mystics, and studied Scripture and the writings of Aquinas. These and his personal experiences are all reflected in his works. He died amidst controversy over the reform movement, but his writings influenced many later spiritual writers.

ROBERT G. CLOUSE

Christianity in Germany on the basis of 'whose the rule, his the religion' (Latin, *cuius regio, eius religio*). That is, the prince could decide the faith of his subjects.

FRANCE

In France, a series of civil wars involving both religious and political considerations raged intermittently from 1562 until 1598. The conflict was essentially between the Huguenots (Calvinist Protestants) and the Roman Catholics, with political issues often complicating the picture. Eventually, a third force appeared when the *politiques* (politically-inspired) announced it was immaterial which religion dominated France; all that mattered was the political well-being of the nation.

After much devastation, and with all parties on the point of total exhaustion, a compromise was reached by partitioning the country. This settlement, expressed in the royal Edict of Nantes in 1598, gave the Huguenots religious freedom and political control of certain parts of the country, while Roman Catholicism remained the official religion of the realm and retained by far the larger portion of the nation.

This compromise lasted on an increasingly precarious foundation until it was revoked by King Louis XIV (1643–1715) in 1685, for which the Jesuits were partly responsible. Louis' act was the signal for hundreds of Protestants to reconvert to Catholicism, and for thousands of others to flee. Many Huguenots left France in 1685 and made their way to Geneva, Germany, England, and North America. Others remained and either suffered persecution or fled to the mountains of central France to try to avoid it. Many of the Protestants who left France in the period were professional people or skilled craftsmen. Their exodus may not have crippled the French economy – as some historians in the past have claimed – but it was certainly significant both socially and economically. France lost many of its most intelligent and hardworking citizens as a result of this act of religious bigotry.

The Dutch war for independence, 1560–1618, is also an example of fighting in this period which had an important religious dimension. Along with political, economic, and racial considerations, religion was a major motivation in the Protestant Dutch struggle for independence from Catholic Spain. Likewise, the English Civil War (1642–49) involved a large element of religious conflict.

THE THIRTY YEARS' WAR

The last of the so-called wars of religion was the Thirty Years' War, 1618–48. This conflict began as essentially a religious struggle with political overtones, and ended as a basically political struggle with religious overtones – heralding the modern era.

The build-up of tension between Protestants and Catholics in Germany in the period between the Peace of Augsburg in 1555 and the outbreak of the Thirty Years' War in 1618 reflects in part the vitality of the Catholic Reformation in that area. When the Jesuit-educated Ferdinand II became Emperor and king of Bohemia, growing religious tensions came to a head. Anti-Protestant religious violence broke out in 1618, and the Bohemian nobles, mostly Protestants, appealed to the Emperor for protection and a guarantee of their religious liberties. Receiving no satisfaction, they rose in revolt.

The war began as a conflict between Calvinists and Catholics. Calvinism had not been recognized as a legal religion in the Empire in the Treaty of Augsburg in 1555, which posed

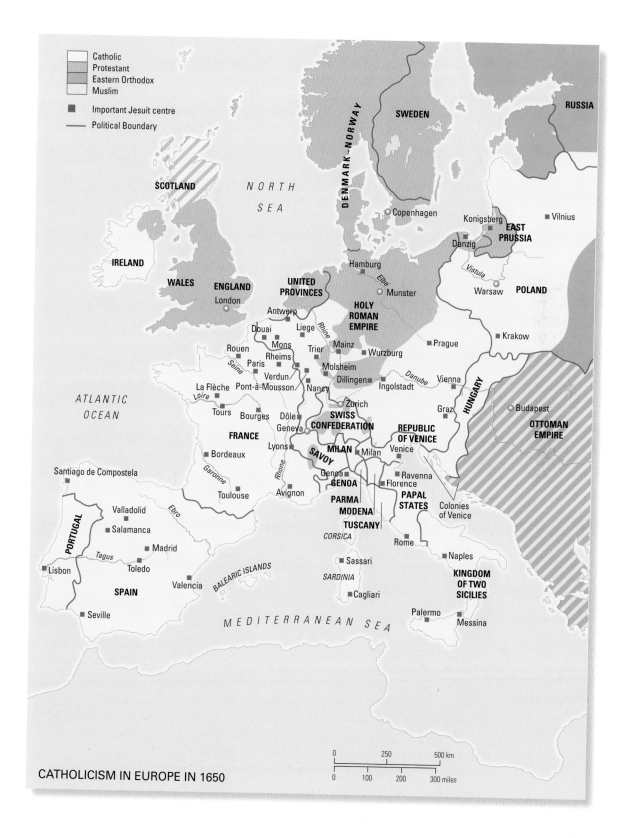

Catholic
Protestant
Eastern Orthodox
Muslim
■ Important Jesuit centre
— Political Boundary

SCOTLAND

NORTH SEA

DENMARK–NORWAY

SWEDEN

RUSSIA

○ Copenhagen

Konigsberg
■ Vilnius

EAST PRUSSIA

Danzig

IRELAND

WALES

ENGLAND
London

UNITED PROVINCES

Hamburg
Elbe

Vistula

HOLY ROMAN EMPIRE

Warsaw

POLAND

Antwerp
○ Munster

Douai
Liege
Rhine

■ Prague

■ Krakow

Rouen
Mons
Trier
Mainz
■ Wurzburg

Rheims

Seine
Paris

Molsheim

Verdun
Pont-à-Mousson
Nancy
Dillingen
Ingolstadt

Danube
■ Vienna

La Flèche
Loire

Tours

Bourges
Dôle

Zurich

HUNGARY

Graz

○ Budapest

ATLANTIC OCEAN

FRANCE

Geneva

SWISS CONFEDERATION

REPUBLIC OF VENICE

OTTOMAN EMPIRE

Lyons
SAVOY
MILAN
Milan

Venice

■ Bordeaux

Garonne

Rhone

Genoa
GENOA

Ravenna
Florence

Avignon
PARMA
MODENA
TUSCANY

PAPAL STATES

Colonies of Venice

Santiago de Compostela

CORSICA

Valladolid

Ebro

■ Salamanca

■ Madrid

Rome

PORTUGAL

Tagus

Toledo

BALEARIC ISLANDS

■ Sassari

SARDINIA

■ Naples

KINGDOM OF TWO SICILIES

Lisbon

Valencia

SPAIN

■ Cagliari

■ Seville

MEDITERRANEAN SEA

Palermo
■ Messina

0   250   500 km

0   100   200   300 miles

CATHOLICISM IN EUROPE IN 1650

a continuing problem for those German princes who became Calvinists after 1555. The situation became still more complicated when in 1618 the Bohemian nobles declared their king, Ferdinand II, deposed, and offered the crown to the Calvinist ruler of the Palatinate, one of the major German states. His acceptance of the crown of Bohemia sparked off fighting between Calvinists and Catholics all over Germany. Eventually, the German Lutherans, Danes, Swedes, and even the French became involved in the warfare in Germany.

The war dragged on sporadically for nearly thirty years. Finally, a peace was hammered out between the belligerents in a series of conferences held in the German province of Westphalia in the years 1643–48, the resultant agreements being known collectively as the Peace of Westphalia.

The war left Germany culturally, politically, economically, and physically devastated. Only the principality of Brandenburg escaped major destruction. But the peace signalled the end of the religious wars in Europe. Ironically, the treaty in essence provided for a return to the religious situation of 1529, when certain German princes and representatives of various imperial free cities made their first famous 'Protestation' on behalf of the Lutheran faith at the Diet of Speyer. All the bloodshed and misery had brought the religious settlement full circle in that tormented land. In 1648, the religious lines were broadly drawn much as they were in 1529 – and much as they remain today.

RESULTS OF THE CATHOLIC REFORMATION

What were the results of the response of Rome to the Protestant Reformation? There arose a new Roman Catholic piety and a better-defined Roman Catholic orthodoxy. The Council of Trent, and the leadership of reform-minded popes, provided a solid basis for this new piety and renewed orthodoxy. The beliefs of the Church of Rome were better understood, even by the rank and file, and differences between Roman orthodoxy and Protestant doctrine stood out more clearly.

Roman Catholic missionary expansion overseas in this period was fuelled as a response to the Protestant Reformation. Partly to make up for the loss of large areas of Europe, the rejuvenated church turned its attention to the newly-discovered lands overseas as a means of recouping its fortunes. Thanks mainly to the Jesuits and other monastic missionaries, many people in other parts of the world embraced the Roman faith during this period. Even today large numbers of people in the Americas, Africa, India, Japan, and Sri Lanka owe their affiliation to the Roman Church to the Catholic Reformation.

The political and cultural consequences of the Catholic Reformation were far-reaching. The resurgence of the Church of Rome in countries such as Germany and France kept them from becoming Protestant, as England, Scotland, and Sweden had done. The Catholic Reformation also helped Italy and Spain to retain their particular Catholic religious and cultural identities. Most important, the success of the Catholic Reformation in preventing the further spread of the Protestant faith meant that Europe developed from that time without a shared cultural base. Once again, the irony is striking: the success of the Catholic response to the Protestant Reformation eventually ended the cultural and religious unity of medieval Europe.

ROBERT D. LINDER

GEORGE FOX AND THE QUAKERS

In 1650 a judge in Derby, England, sentenced a young man to six months in jail on charges of blasphemy. The youth had claimed that Christ, the Saviour, had taken away his sin, and in Christ there was no sin. Before he was sentenced, George Fox told the judge to tremble in the fear of God. The judge knew that Fox and his followers sometimes shook with emotion at their meetings, and told him, 'You folk are the tremblers, you are the quakers.'

'Quaker' was a derisive nickname, and it stuck. The people to whom the name was applied referred to themselves as 'Children of the Light', 'publishers of Truth', or simply 'Friends' – following the words of Jesus, 'You are my friends, if you do what I command you'. Later, when dissent from the Church of England was made legal, Quakers called themselves the 'Society of Friends', as they are today.

George Fox was weary of formal religion. To him it seemed the church had given up spirituality and become a kind of public service, managed by state-appointed officials, whom Fox called 'priests' – whether Catholic or Protestant. The liturgy might vary; the system never. The church had become apostate.

George Fox went to spiritual advisers, asking them theological questions until they were uncomfortable. Then one day Christ was revealed to him in immediate experience. Later, George Fox climbed Pendle Hill, in the north of England, where he had a vision of 'a people to be gathered to the Lord'. He felt impelled to proclaim that Christ liberates people from the power of sin in their lives – and began preaching in the open air to thousands. 'Christ has been too long locked up in the Mass or in the Book,' he said, 'let him be your prophet, priest, and king.' This appealed to the people of north-west England.

A band of young men and women – the 'Valiant Sixty' – became Quaker evangelists, fanning out across England, and wherever ships would take them. Many 'seekers' joined the movement, as well as those who had previously belonged to other denominations. Three years after the Pendle Hill vision, there were 50,000 Quakers and, before the end of the seventeenth century, double that number. The movement crossed cultural barriers; servant girls took part in worship with aristocrats, such as the Scottish scholar Robert Barclay (1648–90). Early Quaker preachers sounded rather like the Old Testament prophet Amos: they proclaimed Christ as truth and let that truth stand in judgment over current evils.

BLASPHEMY?

James Nayler (1616–60), who at one time led the London Quakers, tried to illustrate the inward coming of Christ into the heart by staging a 'triumphal entry' into Bristol, complete with donkey and hosannas. This shocked townspeople and scandalized Friends. He was branded on the forehead 'B' for blasphemer, his tongue bored through with a hot iron, and he was imprisoned. This episode caused Quakers to check the 'Spirit's leadings' against what Scripture says and by prayer meetings; indeed in the eighteenth century they became very cautious.

Fox once went to Oliver Cromwell to plead for religious freedom, commending a Christian life-style that rejects military weapons in favour of the armour of the Spirit. Cromwell remarked that Quakers were people whom he could not influence, 'either with gifts, honours, offices, or places'. Quakers were imprisoned – sometimes many of them – for such offences as refusing to speak deferentially to judges, meeting in forbidden religious assembly, or refusing to pay the compulsory state-church tithe. If asked to take the oath in court, they refused on the basis of Jesus' words, 'Swear not at all …'

NORTH AMERICAN FRIENDS

In Boston, New England, a confrontation occurred between the Puritans who had left their homes in England to set up a pure Christian community and Quakers who challenged their religious exclusiveness. When banishment failed to eliminate the Quakers, Governor Endicott ordered the death penalty. Three Quakers were hanged on Boston Common (1660–61), but their deaths raised an outcry that helped pave the way for religious liberty.

As early as 1659 the Quaker John Taylor visited native Americans, urging them to turn from darkness to the light of Christ in their own hearts, beginning a long and friendly relationship with aboriginal people, some of whom later became Quakers.

John Woolman (1720–72), a modest New Jersey tailor, became convinced slavery was wrong, and campaigned to persuade fellow Quakers against keeping slaves. Through the Quakers, the conscience of others was reached; if Woolman was guest in a home where a slave worked, he would politely pay for their services, in a non-violent form of protest.

ARTHUR O. ROBERTS

CHAPTER 27

ART AND THE SPIRIT
Christianity and its cultural expression

The tensions that accompanied the transition from the Middle Ages to the early modern world were resolved in the arts, particularly in Italy, in the new approach of the High Renaissance, around 1500.

HIGH RENAISSANCE

The greatest examples of High Renaissance Roman Catholic art are to be found in Rome, in the work of Raphael (1483–1520) and Michelangelo (1475–1564) in the Vatican Palace, and above all in the new St Peter's. Most of the outstanding artists of the day contributed to what was intended to be the greatest of Christian churches. Donato Bramante (1444–1514) and Michelangelo (who designed the cupola) both took a share. In the second half of the sixteenth century, following the Catholic spiritual renewal, Giambattista della Porta (1535–1602) and Carlo Maderna (1556–1629), one of the founders of Italian Baroque, worked on the façade of St Peter's.

In Venice a similar High Renaissance took place. Titian (c. 1488/90–1576), and, in the second half of the sixteenth century, Tintoretto (1518–94) both worked there, Tintoretto's art expressing an intense Roman Catholic piety.

As the Roman Catholic Church slowly recovered from the shock of the Reformation, and gained new strength through the Counter Reformation, a new art gradually emerged, founded

The interior of St Peter's Basilica, Rome.

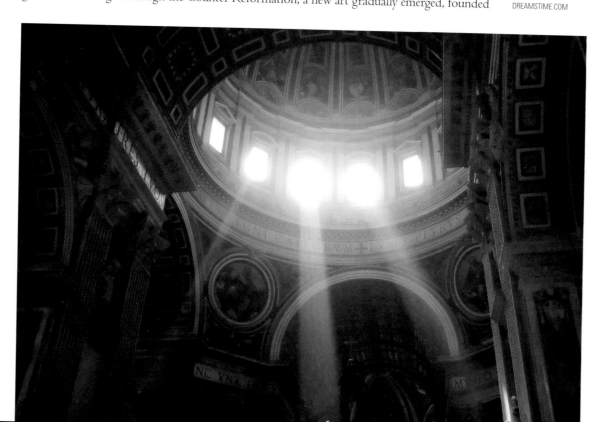

on the work of the High Renaissance, particularly that of Raphael and the Venetian artists. One of the first examples of the new style was the Gesù, the mother church of the Jesuit order in Rome, begun in 1568 by Vignola (1507–73), which set the style for many churches built in the following centuries. The Caracci brothers and Caravaggio (1571–1610), working around 1600, helped create this new style which we know as Baroque.

REFORMATION SPIRIT

Meanwhile, in Germany, Albrecht Dürer (1471–1528) pointed the way towards a new style which combined the best elements of earlier German and Flemish art with strong influences from the Italian Renaissance. Dürer's art breathed the spirit of the Reformation, a spirit found as early as 1498 in his famous series of woodcuts illustrating the book of Revelation.

Dürer's art strives to depict reality in all its aspects; he has never been equalled in the field of engravings and woodcuts, and he was also a great and prolific draughtsman and painter. Few artists have covered such a wide range of subjects: from simple animals and plants to figure studies, portraits, buildings with accurate perspective, biblical and classical stories, and even fantasy scenes and dreams. Although the painters Cranach and Holbein were also Lutheran Protestants, few other great artists came from this tradition in the following centuries; in Germany, the Protestant spirit expressed itself mainly in music.

In the late sixteenth century, Calvinist refugees from the southern Netherlands settled in Holland, where, after a while, a new art emerged, with biblical and Calvinist roots. Many churches were built in this tradition, for example by the architect Hendrick de Keyser (1565–1621) in Amsterdam, while many older churches were given new furnishings.

DUTCH ART

But Dutch Protestantism found its supreme expression in painting. After some experiment, the new art emerged around 1600 in Haarlem, quite different from the Baroque of southern Europe. The Dutch painters were mainly based in Haarlem, Amsterdam, Delft, and Dordrecht. They included world-famous masters: Frans Hals (portraits), Solomon and Jacob van Ruysdael, Jan van Goyen (landscapes), Heda and Peter Claesz (still-lifes), Brouwer and van Ostade (genre-painting), Gerard Dou (interiors), the Delft school – Vermeer and Pieter de Hoogh – and of course Rembrandt (biblical and historical themes, portraits, and etchings). These Dutch painters concentrated on depicting everyday reality in a variety of ways. Historical and biblical scenes are quite rare; their most characteristic subjects were everyday life. Rembrandt van Rijn (1606–69) was the exception, since he painted many biblical subjects.

The Dutch painters' art expressed a deep love for reality, but was not mere naturalism. Through their use of 'emblems' and other kinds of visual metaphors, their carefully constructed compositions, and their choice of subject, they were 'preaching' in their art. They pointed morals: the vanity of everything; redemption with its cosmic and human implications; the positive and negative sides to life; and the beauties of the created world. Their art was imbued with the wisdom of the Bible and of common sense.

MASTERS OF THE BAROQUE

Two geniuses appeared after 1600, both of whom used the Baroque style of Roman Catholic art of the Counter Reformation. The first was Peter Paul Rubens (1577–1640), who worked mainly in Antwerp, but also in Italy, England, France, and Spain. The altarpieces he painted are unsurpassed, portraying the Madonna and the lives and martyrdom of saints. He also painted historical and classical subjects, portraits and landscapes, and exerted an immense influence.

The second genius was the sculptor and architect Gian Lorenzo Bernini (1598–1680), responsible for some of the principal statues inside St Peter's, Rome, as well as for the great piazza in front. All later Baroque sculpture can almost be called the 'school of Bernini'. Francesco Borromini (1599–1667), another great Roman architect, worked out the inward and outward curved façades and oval-shaped plans characteristic of Baroque churches.

The Baroque is recognized as the art of the Counter Reformation, expressing the aims and serving the goals of Catholic renewal. Baroque art built on the style of the Renaissance, but added the effects of light and darkness. It can be called a 'naturalism of the supernatural', stressing that we live in an open world, where communication is possible between earth and heaven, with the Virgin and saints interceding.

The Baroque church had to overwhelm the visitor, and was designed to impress with its display of riches and power, convincing the visitor of the value, importance, and truth of the doctrines upheld. All the means of salvation had to be represented dramatically: the Madonna, the saints and revered relics, the mass, and the host. Baroque churches displayed many images, including the Trinity and Christ the Redeemer, whose suffering on the cross was often linked with the host on the altar. But, above all, the images exalted the Virgin, as Madonna, Queen of heaven, and the Immaculate Conception, assumed up into heaven. Other images portrayed the mystic fervour of the saints, whose piety and asceticism provided examples for the faithful; the great events of the Bible and of church history; and allegorical figures and scenes that spoke in more general terms of theological truth or of human and natural reality and values.

A remarkable painter, Pietro da Cortona (1596/7–1669), was at work in Rome in the mid-seventeenth century; his painted ceilings mark the final stage of the fantastic art of *sotto in su* – painting the supernatural world as seen from below. Examples in Rome include the Palazzo Barberini and Chiesa Nuova. Andrea Pozzo (1642–1709), who followed Cortona, painted the astonishing ceiling of St Ignatio, Rome, before taking this style to Austria at the end of the seventeenth century.

The other main centre of the Counter Reformation was Spain, where we also find great painters. Zurbaran (1598–1664), Ribera (1591–1652), and Murillo (1617–82) all excelled in altar pieces and religious art, and Velásquez (1599–1660) was an outstanding portraitist. But perhaps the most characteristic expression of burning Spanish piety is found in architecture, based on the examples in Rome, but amazingly developed, with a profusion of detailed statues and ornaments. This style was to spread all over the Spanish-speaking world, including South and Central America.

In eighteenth-century Italy the centre of the Baroque shifted north, where the great Tiepolo (1696–1770) painted Baroque altarpieces of unsurpassed lyrical fluency in a style that was both naturalistic and idealized.

BAROQUE IN BAVARIA

The last great flowering of Baroque Counter Reformation art was in Austria and southern Germany. The architect Johann Bernhard Fischer von Erlach (1656–1723) was working in Vienna and Salzburg early in the eighteenth century, and with his followers was responsible for the magnificent architecture of eighteenth-century Austria – which still today dictates the appearance of Vienna and other Austrian cities.

In Bavaria this style of architecture was taken to great heights by the Asam brothers, Cosmas and Egid, in their Weltenburg Abbey Church, about 1720, and by Balthasar Neumann (1687–1753) in the Basilika Vierzehnheiligen, about 1750. Johann Michael Fischer (1692–1766) also built many churches and monasteries, the most important being the basilica at Ottobeuren Abbey. The church at Wies (about 1750), designed by Dominikus Zimmermann (1685–1766), is regarded as the best example of this amazing late Baroque, or 'religious Rococo', art.

The designs were worked out very elaborately, with complex imagery carefully planned down to the smallest detail, following a scheme drawn up by a theologian. But the Baroque also had a popular, dramatic character, which extended its appeal to the masses. The Baroque church is one rich, festive whole: altars, paintings, sculptures, furnishings, organ, stucco-work, and other ornaments all contribute, with their gilding and soft but magnificent colouring. There is play with light and shade, a unity of style and content. The whole church comes to life when filled with Mozart's music performed on the organ, orchestra and choir, and packed full for a religious festival. The artists who decorated these churches remained relatively anonymous; their art was part of the whole, as they depended on one another's work.

DEATH OF AN ERA

The Counter Reformation, with its exalted piety and worship, found its ultimate expression in these Baroque churches. Yet a visitor to them will often find the body of a saint, exposed on or under the altar. Death seems to be at the centre. The whole display is intended partly to reassure us in the face of death that will surely come.

The inner spirit disappeared from this eighteenth-century Baroque art, leaving a more worldly emphasis, the beautiful forms becoming a mere façade, which may explain the sudden end of this art. Around 1780, just as the best works were completed, the tradition stopped, and nothing more was attempted in this style. Neo-classicism, with its 'rationality' and almost totally secular expression, took over. The Age of Reason and the Enlightenment had won the battle. Soon the revolutionary wars would bring about the suppression of the monasteries and closing of churches, and the Roman Catholic church lose its power.

HANS R. ROOKMAAKER

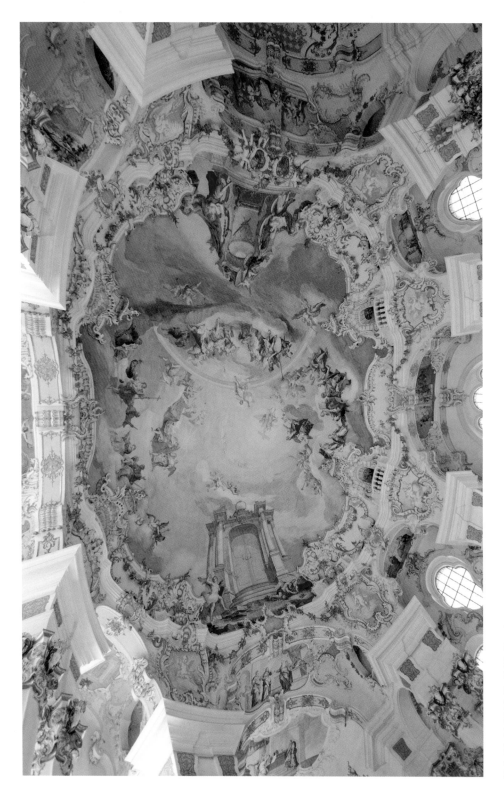

The magnificent ceiling of the pilgrimage church at Wies, south-west Bavaria, designed by Dominikus Zimmerman (1685–1766).

FURTHER READING

Diarmaid MacCulloch, *Reformation: Europe's House Divided 1490–1700*, London, 2003.
Martin Marty, *Martin Luther*, New York, 2004.
Bernard Cottret, *Calvin: A Biography*, Grand Rapids and Edinburgh, 2000.
Robert Birley, *The Refashioning of Catholicism, 1450–1700*, Houndmills, 1999.
C. R. Boxer, *The Church Militant and Iberian Expansion 1440–1770*, Baltimore, 1967.

STUDY QUESTIONS

1. Was the Protestant Reformation inevitable?

2. What was the core of Martin Luther's quarrel with the Church of Rome?

3. How did Martin Luther and John Calvin differ? Why?

4. What changes in the church did the Roman Catholic reformers demand?

5. What impact did vernacular Bible translations have upon the church?

6. Why were the first missionaries Roman Catholics?

7. How did the rise of Humanism affect the church?

8. What influence did Ignatius Loyola have upon the church?

9. How do the cultural expressions of the Reformation and Counter Reformation differ?

10. Would the Reformation have occurred without the Renaissance?

5 Reason, Revival, and Revolution

1650–1789

Summary

The Scientific Revolution of the seventeenth century paved the way for the Enlightenment of the eighteenth century, a movement which gave its name to the era: the Age of Reason. Enlightenment intellectuals believed that, through reason, they could understand and master nature, and this would lead to 'progress'.

Major Evangelical Revivals, which started in Germany and spread to Britain and North America, were partly a reaction against the speculation and moralism of Deism, and partly a response to the spiritual deadness of Protestant orthodoxy. John Wesley, George Whitefield, and Jonathan Edwards were leaders in this movement, the repercussions of which were eventually felt all over the world.

A period of political uncertainty developed during the eighteenth century, with major implications for the future of Christianity in the West. Growing hostility towards the Church in France contributed to causes of the French Revolution of 1789.

CHAPTER 28

EXPANSION WORLDWIDE
European missions

For some decades before 1650, much of Europe had been embroiled in warfare. The nations were fighting for the control of Europe – and of worldwide commerce. The powerful Habsburg rulers of Austria and Spain, usually backed by the pope, had been pitted against the kings and princes of north-west Europe, most of whom were Protestants.

THE LAST RELIGIOUS WAR

With the Peace of Westphalia (1648) an era came to an end; wars of religion now belonged to the past. A variety of churches and denominations were recognized in Europe, though religious discrimination and persecution persisted. In the same year, by the Treaty of Münster, Dutch independence was recognized. The German principalities, Denmark, and Sweden all turned away from war.

The nations which had avoided total involvement in the Thirty Years' War reaped the benefits. France, England, and the Netherlands had used the opportunity to expand their fleets, establish trading colonies overseas, and manoeuvre themselves into dominant positions in Europe. By 1650 the tide had turned in their favour. Spain – weak in armies and finance – continued to be a major colonial power, but lost the ability to keep up with her northern neighbours. Portugal's population was too small, her grip on her colonies too weak, and the colonies themselves too far-flung to protect them adequately.

Britain increased in power and influence until 1789. France's colonial growth was halted only by the first Peace of Paris (1763) when she was forced to give up some colonies to Britain. For a time the Dutch, and even the Danes, did not lag far behind. But the fortunes of Catholic Spain and Portugal steadily declined.

In the East, Christianity, whether Catholic, Orthodox, or Protestant, was on the defensive, facing Islamic Turkey's penetration into Europe. In 1529, and again in 1683, Turkish armies put Vienna under siege. The minarets to be found in Eastern Europe today witness to the Turkish occupation of much of the Balkan territories.

As Russia expanded to the east – in 1648 Russians stood for the first time on the shores of the Pacific Ocean – Orthodox missions began. These Russian missions – some state-sponsored, others voluntary – began to claim the Eastern territories for the Orthodox Church. They tended to develop in a sporadic way – but displayed apostolic simplicity and zeal, and there were many martyrs.

EUROPE COLONIZES THE WORLD

Christian missions form part of the story of European colonization; their history must be seen in that context. Friars and missionaries followed merchants and colonial administrators to remote, exotic lands; sometimes the missionaries arrived first.

Spain sustained her earlier control of the Philippines, Central and South America. In some areas she extended her control; for example on the coast of California and in the semi-arid stretches north and east of Old Mexico.

In the Caribbean and along the Gulf coast, Spain suffered losses. The British repeatedly fought Spain for the possession of Florida. French explorers also claimed this area, as they did Louisiana, which became a French territory after 1682. England occupied the Caribbean islands of Barbados and Trinidad, and in 1655 took Jamaica. To her colonies of Martinique, Guadeloupe, and Saint Christophe, France added Haiti in 1697. The Dutch, French, and English each carved out their respective Guianas on the north-east coast of South America, to form buffers between the Spanish and Portuguese colonies. One by one the islands of the West Indies — colonial jewels — were contested by the new powers. By the eighteenth century the Caribbean had become the most cosmopolitan sea in the world.

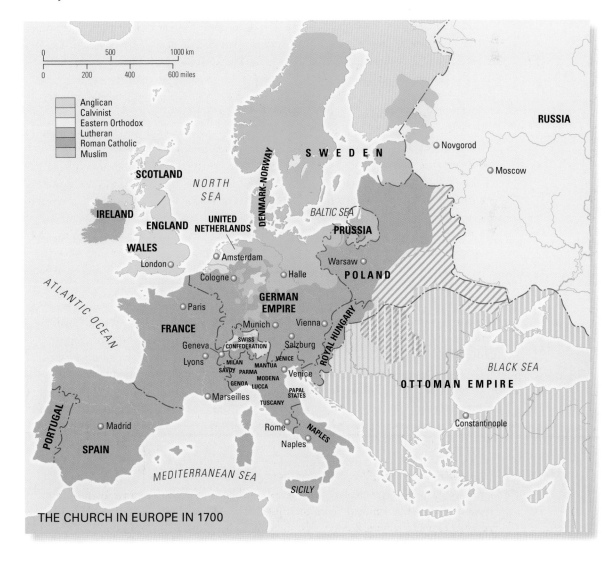

THE CHURCH IN EUROPE IN 1700

Portuguese colonies in Africa and the Far East came off even worse. As the northern colonial powers increased their shipping around the Cape of Good Hope, they established settlements on both the east and west coasts of Africa. The French, who had founded a post in Senegal in 1626, gained Madagascar in 1686, and took Mauritius from the Dutch in 1715. After 1652, the Dutch held tenaciously to the tip of Africa, and Netherlanders gradually began to colonize this area. Not to be outdone, the English settled a colony at the mouth of the River Gambia, in West Africa.

By the eighteenth century, Portugal had rivals for the rich, prized trade with India. Although she retained Goa, other European nations made their colonies in India too. The French had Surat, Calicut, Pondicherry, and Chandarnagar; the British had Bombay, Madras, and Calcutta; the Danes could be found in Tranquebar. Although in general the Dutch ignored India, they wrested Malacca from the Portuguese in 1641 and took Sri Lanka in 1655. They also increased their holdings in the Spice Islands, particularly after winning land and trade from a Javanese ruler in 1677 in exchange for military assistance.

With few exceptions, the Europeans went to Africa and Asia mainly to trade. Yet even this was opposed in China and Japan: the Manchu rulers in China cut short trade, and the Tokugawas in Japan virtually stopped it. Chinese bandits drove the Dutch from Formosa in 1661.

Not until the nineteenth century did further huge chunks of Africa and Asia come under Western domination. Meanwhile European missionaries, both Roman Catholic and Protestant, followed the trade routes, taking with them the Christian gospel.

THE 'PROPAGANDA'

Catholic missions were shaped by the new policies and organizational structures introduced by Pope Gregory XV (r. 1521–23). In 1622 Gregory founded the Sacred Congregation for the Propagation of the Faith, usually referred to simply as the *Propaganda*, in an attempt to bring Catholic missions more directly under Vatican control.

This new policy aimed to replace the patronage system, which had been used in missions since the end of the fifteenth century. Patronage had been granted by the pope to the monarchs of Spain and Portugal, giving them responsibility for Christianizing natives, establishing dioceses, and appointing clergy in their colonies. Because these responsibilities had been neglected in many instances, Gregory set up the *Propaganda*, a body of clergy charged with spreading the Catholic faith, to work in countries where the faith was either unknown or under attack from heretics.

Under the direction of its first secretary, Francesco Ingoli (1578–1649), the *Propaganda* made a series of investigations into the condition of Catholic missions. It documented many evils: rivalry between the religious orders; political interests taking priority over the spread of the gospel; and the abuse and alienation of native populations. As a result, the *Propaganda* in 1627 persuaded Pope Urban VIII (r. 1623–44) to found the College of Urban, for the training of missionaries. The *Propaganda* also found missionary recruits, gave financial aid to missions, printed liturgies and catechisms for use overseas, and requested reports from its agents to guide its work. By the time of Ingoli's death in 1649, the *Propaganda* had become the most important force in Roman Catholic expansion.

Sixteenth-century manuscript illustrating Suleiman the Magnificent (r. 1520–66) besieging Vienna in 1529, from the Topkapi Palace Museum.

The *Propaganda* made great use of the office of vicar-apostolic, which was designed to overcome the evils of patronage, and to establish bishoprics in areas not held by Spain or Portugal. The vicar-apostolic was given the full authority of a bishop, and was directly responsible to Rome. He was chosen from the non-monastic clergy, to avoid getting entangled with the religious orders. Although he was known by the name of a diocese, he was not limited to one area, and was in fact a roving missionary. The vicar-apostolic was often instructed to keep his title and mission secret until he arrived at his destination, and met the stiffest opposition from the clergy still working under the patronage system.

In 1637 Matthew de Castro, a Brahmin convert who had been an outstanding student in Rome, and Franciscus de Santo Felice were named the first vicars-apostolic. The latter was appointed Archbishop of Myra and sent to Japan, although he never arrived there. Castro was named Bishop of Chrysopolis and sent to Idalkan, an area of India free of Portuguese control, though not entirely free of its influence. The Portuguese clergy in Goa obstructed Castro's work so successfully that he was forced to give up. The *Propaganda* next sent him to Golconda, a kingdom recently taken from Portugal by the Mogul rulers of India; here Castro still met with opposition from Goa, but won a number of converts. He began training native clergy, and handed over his work to two successors – like himself Hindu converts acting as vicars-apostolic.

MISSION TO VIETNAM

The *Propaganda* turned increasingly to France for vicars-apostolic and for finances, since the French clergy were free from the ties of patronage. France's rise as a commercial power was accompanied by a growing sense of missionary obligation, fostered by widely-circulated missionary journals and accounts. Both the nobility and the clergy made generous gifts and promoted foreign missions, and organizations such as the Capuchins, the Company of the Blessed Sacrament, and the Lazarists became deeply committed to mission.

A veteran French Jesuit, Alexander de Rhodes (1591–1660), was the man mainly responsible for bringing together the *Propaganda* and French missionary concerns. He laboured in the Far East from 1623 until 1645, with about half this time spent in Macao. But de Rhodes' most effective work was done in Vietnam before 1630, and between 1640 and 1645. He quickly mastered the Vietnamese language and reduced it to writing, and also trained a group of native catechists who continued his work when he was banished from Vietnam in 1645. The catechists were organized as a celibate lay order. They showed dedication and knowledge of the faith, and were given medical instruction by de Rhodes. By the mid-seventeenth century the mission had resulted in a flourishing Vietnamese church numbering about 30,000.

When he returned to Rome, de Rhodes urged the *Propaganda* to appoint vicars-apostolic to train and ordain native clergy in the Far East. The *Propaganda* was initially cool to his idea, suggesting he should recruit missionaries in his homeland. De Rhodes found ready volunteers among his French Jesuit brothers, but desperately wanted men from the secular clergy, who could take a vow directly from the *Propaganda*. He found the priests he was looking for among a small group called the 'Good Friends', who had already committed themselves to foreign service.

'GOOD FRIENDS' IN ASIA

Out of this group grew the Society of Foreign Missions (Société des Missions Étrangères) in Paris, which in 1663 dedicated its seminary to the training of missionaries. The papacy and *Propaganda* finally accepted de Rhodes' suggestion, after prodding by the Assembly of the French Clergy in 1655. In 1658 two 'Good Friends', François Pallu (1626–84) and Pierre Lambert de la Motte (1624–79), were appointed vicars-apostolic. De la Motte was entitled Bishop of Beirut, for service in Cochin, and Pallu entitled Bishop of Heliopolis, for service in Tonkin. They were followed by Pallu's friend, Ignazio Cotolendi, who was sent as Bishop of Metallopolis to central and northern China, which included Peking.

Cotolendi died soon after reaching Asia, and the other two were strongly opposed by Portuguese clergy; but their work marked a new departure for Catholic missions in the Far East. For the first time Rome had direct rule over all areas in the Far East that were not subject to Portuguese patronage. In 1665 the first native seminary was opened in Ayutthaya, Thailand. The earlier work of de Rhodes was consolidated on a firm local basis. The future of Catholic missions seemed bright.

QUESTIONING THE INSTRUCTIONS

But in 1659 the *Propaganda* issued a set of instructions to its vicars-apostolic which touched on an issue that was ultimately to divide. The instructions dealt partly with missionary attitudes towards native culture. Until this date there had been two opposite theories on this subject. Most Catholics demanded converts should make a complete break with their ethnic culture, holding that local customs and practices were rooted in non-Christian religion and should be tested by the gospel, and cleansed of any trace of paganism. But a minority of Catholics had followed a different policy. Missionaries, such as Robert de Nobili in south India and Matteo Ricci in China, had adopted the native dress and customs, studied local literature and beliefs, and lived in the style of their adopted country.

The instructions of 1659 opted for the approach of de Nobili and Ricci. Vicars-apostolic were advised to learn the local language, and warned not to revolutionize the habits, customs, and culture of the people to whom they had been sent. The instructions claimed it was absurd to attempt to turn Asians into Europeans. The *Propaganda* felt the mission would be undermined if local customs were constantly criticized. If some things were clearly incompatible with Christianity, any changes undertaken must be gradual and gentle.

The two methods clashed most sharply in China. As the century wore on, the controversy developed into a battle between the religious orders. Vicars-apostolic found it difficult to work out exactly what the instructions meant, the debate on method became heated, and parties were formed. The *Propaganda* found itself caught between the Jesuits on the one hand and the Franciscans and Dominicans on the other.

The Jesuits had held a favoured position in China since the days of Ricci. They impressed the Chinese with such skills as clock-making, mathematics, map-making, canonry, and astronomy, and also gained access to the imperial court, where they acted as advisers to the Chinese government. When the Ming dynasty toppled, between 1644 and 1662, the German Jesuit, Johann Adam Schall von Bell (1592–1666), weathered the crisis. When the new rulers took over, he was appointed chairman of the board to regulate the Chinese calendar.

His younger colleague, a Fleming named Ferdinand Verbiest (1623–88), was befriended by the emperor, Kang Hsi, who held the Chinese throne until 1722.

A CHURCH IN CHINA

The Jesuits used their prestige to win an edict of toleration for Chinese Christians in 1692. By 1700 a flourishing Chinese church existed, with as many as 300,000 converts. But such gains had not come without a price. The Jesuits had studied Confucius and concluded he was not a Chinese god, and that Confucian temples were merely meeting-places for scholars. They decided that incense burned, and prayers offered for the dead, were not idolatry, but healthy respect for ancestors. They also claimed that Confucian terms such as *Tien* (heaven) and *Chang-ti* (sovereign lord) were Chinese names for the God of whom the Jesuits themselves spoke. The Jesuits strongly advocated that the Chinese language be used in worship, and translated the liturgy into Chinese as early as the 1660s.

Issues such as these were called into question, particularly by religious orders whose ranks were filled by Spaniards from the Philippines. The problem became known as the 'rites controversy'. Differences in the missionaries' national backgrounds, and differences between their orders, sharpened differences over the Chinese rites. Ultimately the *Propaganda*, caught in the middle, had to make a choice.

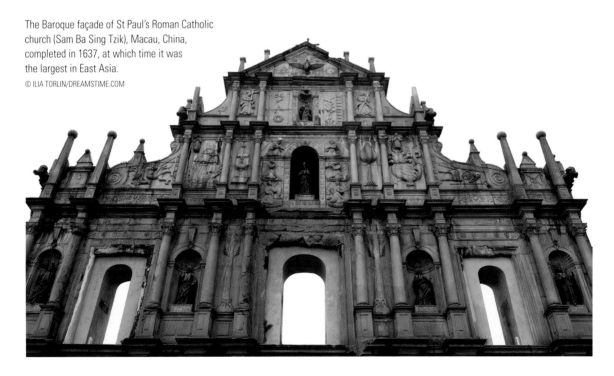

The Baroque façade of St Paul's Roman Catholic church (Sam Ba Sing Tzik), Macau, China, completed in 1637, at which time it was the largest in East Asia.
© ILIA TORLIN/DREAMSTIME.COM

Gradually both the *Propaganda* and the vicars-apostolic began to question the Jesuit approach. As early as 1684, Charles Maigrot, Pallu's successor, voiced his opposition. By 1704 Pope Clement XI (r. 1700–21) banned Jesuit missionary methods and ordered Charles-Thomas Maillard De Tournon (1668–1710), papal legate and cardinal to the East Indies, to enforce his decision. The emperor of China himself appealed to Rome, but was ignored. Angered by this, Kang Hsi, the emperor, delivered an edict forbidding evangelism. Seven years later every missionary, except a few Jesuit advisers, was expelled from China. Christians suddenly found themselves persecuted, and believers were martyred. The mission effort, which by 1684 had produced a native vicar-apostolic named Lo Wen-Tsao (Luo Wenzao, 1616–91), lost all its power. The Chinese Church shrivelled; not until the mid-nineteenth century would the Chinese Catholic Church again flourish. But the Vatican did not take this opportunity to rethink the question of missionary methods.

MISSION TO ASIA

Meanwhile the Vietnamese mission continued fruitfully, even if it never repeated the dramatic results of de Rhodes' time. In the Philippines, Spanish orders worked without interruption, impeded only by the remoteness of unreached tribes and the low level of Philippino morale.

The Philippines themselves became a base from which missions were launched to other parts of Asia. The northern and central regions of India remained closed to missionaries. But in southern India, John de Britto (1647–93), a Portuguese nobleman, used de Nobili's methods as he evangelized the lower castes. His work was short-lived, lasting only from 1685 until 1693, when he was martyred. De Britto was succeeded by the Italian Constanzo Beschi (Tamil name, Vīramāmunivar, 1680–1742), who used his fluency in the Tamil language as he built a native church between 1711 and 1742. Along India's narrow coast, the Catholic Church grew more rapidly, and by 1750 was led by many native priests and bishops. In Sri Lanka, Joseph Vaz (1651–87), a half-caste priest, proclaimed the faith with piety and dedication; despite Dutch control of the island, he founded scores of churches and made tens of thousands of converts.

The Middle East, though not impenetrable by Europeans, was not fertile mission territory. It was dominated by the Ottoman Turks, who allowed occasional French and Italian explorer-missionaries to pass through, on the old overland route to China and the northern slopes of the Himalayas. Catholic trading consuls sometimes brought Christian influence to the area, too. French missions in Persia were able to win Armenians to the Catholic faith. But such examples are exceptional; the Middle East belonged to Islam.

In Africa, Christianity had by 1789 lost the ground gained in the sixteenth and early seventeenth centuries. The Capuchin order's work on the coasts of modern Zaïre and Angola claimed more than half a million converts in the later seventeenth century. But these gains were weakened by European rivalry for Africa, by the instability of the tribes, and by the slave trade. Slaving reached its peak during this period, and undermined any chance of Christianity being planted effectively in West Africa before 1800.

French religious orders made sporadic efforts to do mission work in Madagascar. But their approach was feeble, and thwarted by native hostility. Islam was reviving in North Africa and easily withstood Roman Catholicism.

EVANGELIZING AMERICA

In Canada, Catholic Christianity grew primarily through French colonization. The church there increased from 3,000 believers in 1650 to more than 75,000 by 1763. A handful of courageous priests, such as Jean de Brebeuf (1593–1649), made early attempts to convert the Hurons and the Iroquois, but paid with their lives. In 1658 the *Propaganda* sent François de Laval (1623–1708) to New France as vicar-apostolic. Less than twenty years later, Quebec was made a diocese, and Canada no longer technically considered a mission territory by Rome. The notable expedition of the trapper Louis Jolliet and Father Marquette, begun in 1673, which led them to the Mississippi Valley, was more interested in exploration than evangelization.

The fur trade soon began to boom in Canada. Alcohol and venereal disease introduced by the Europeans first debased and then slaughtered the Indian peoples. Self-sacrificing missionary service was the exception, and the moral climate hardly conducive to the planting of a flourishing Indian Church.

In Latin America, the patronage system remained intact, despite pressure from the pope. The cross and the crown were more closely linked in this area than anywhere else in the Catholic world. The 'Council of the Indies' in Madrid continued to control important

The Cathedral of The Virgin Mary of the Immaculate Conception, Havana, Cuba, built by the Jesuits in the Baroque style – though with asymmetrical towers – between 1748 and 1777.

TIM DOWLEY ASSOCIATES

appointments in the Latin American Church. All the major religious orders — tens of thousands of priests — contributed to the almost complete, but superficial, Christianization of Latin America. Mission annals are filled with accounts of dedicated people who fought against the political and economic oppression suffered by native populations. In the mid-seventeenth century, for example, António Vieira (1608–97), a Portuguese ambassador who later entered the Jesuit order, won concessions for Brazilian Indians and blacks from the Portuguese government.

THE JESUIT EXPERIMENT

The Jesuits tried a new experiment in missionary methods in the vast, uncolonized areas of Paraguay. To protect and defend the Indians, as well as to Christianize them, the fathers gathered them into self-contained and self-sustaining villages called *reductions*. Their experiment flourished between 1650 and 1720. Natives were instructed in the basics of Christianity, and their lives organized into times for prayer, work in the fields or at trades, religious festivals, and recreation. At the peak there were approximately sixty *reductions*, involving a total of over 100,000 people. The controversial experiment collapsed in the eighteenth century, Spanish-Portuguese boundary disputes over the area and increased opposition to the Jesuit order contributing to its failure.

In Spanish North America, more permanent gains were made. After one hundred years' missionary progress among New Mexico's Indians (1580–1680), a revolt drove out the Spanish in the early 1680s. By 1692 they had retaken New Mexico and their mission centres had been rebuilt.

Meanwhile, in 1686, the Jesuit Eusebio Kino (1645–1711) entered southern Arizona, using his skills as explorer, physician, architect, and astronomer to educate and Christianize the Pima Indians of the area. In 1690, Franciscans under Damián Massanet founded short-lived missions in east Texas. Thirty years later, other Franciscans constructed six flourishing settlements along the San Antonio river. These missions were similar to the *reductions* of South America, and from this base the Catholics expanded to Texas.

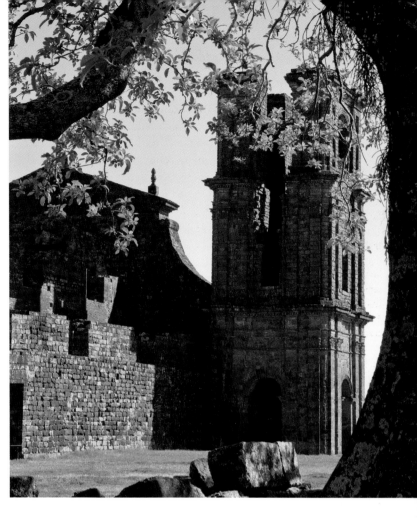

Ruins of the Roman Catholic Cathedral of *São Miguel das Missões* (St Michael of the Missions), Rio Grande do Sul, southern Brazil, built between 1735 and 1745 by Jesuit missionaries as a Reduction for the Guaraní Indians.

© ALEXANDRE FAGUNDES DE FAGUNDES/ DREAMSTIME.COM

Spanish Catholic Mission of San Xavier del Bac, outside of Tucson, Arizona, founded in 1692 by the Jesuit missionary Eusebio Francisco Kino.

In the mid-eighteenth century, Junípero Serra (1713–84), a Majorcan, erected a chain of missions along the coast of northern California. The original church buildings of many of these early missionaries still stand today. These Spanish missions all refused to train local Indian clergy.

By 1789 Catholic missionaries had traversed the globe and organized about sixty dioceses outside Europe. In the Americas and parts of Asia, they founded a Catholic Church that still survives today. The missionaries experienced policy differences, friction between rival orders, political tensions, and obstacles of travel and climate. But they were people with faith, vision, and dedication.

COLONIES AND COMPANIES

Protestant Christianity expanded during this period along two different – but not unrelated – lines. The first approach rested on the assumption that all the citizens of a nation formed the Christian church of that country – a view of society later undermined by religious dissent. But it shaped missions of two types during the early part of this period. The first type of mission worked through the national trading companies; the second type through the overseas colonies of European emigrants. Both the companies and the colonies were chartered by the crown; thus both bodies were expected by the state to promote the form of Protestantism practised in the homeland.

The second approach used by Protestants was through voluntary societies and denominations, which regarded mission as their duty. A number of societies were formed specifically to evangelize peoples outside Western Europe, their vision fuelled by movements such as Pietism in Germany and the awakenings in England and America. In time, denominations such as the Moravians and the Quakers became directly involved in spreading Christianity overseas. The missionary vision is clearly set out in the hymns of Nicolaus Zinzendorf, Isaac Watts, Charles Wesley, and John Newton.

A survey of Protestant missionary work needs to begin by looking at the trading companies and European colonies. In London, Amsterdam, and Copenhagen, the boards of trading companies faced the problem of whether they should attempt to Christianize the peoples they contacted through their trading ventures. The Dutch East India Company, and for a time the British East India Company, ordered their chaplains to engage in native evangelism; the other companies ignored or resisted missions. Later the British East India Company prohibited mission work in India, afraid of disrupting their good trade relations. In the late eighteenth century, the British public became outraged at the inhumane policies of colonial governors such as Robert Clive (1725–74) and Warren Hastings (1732–1818). The company was forced to change its policy and send out chaplains such as the Scot Claudius Buchanan in 1796 and Henry Martyn in 1805.

THE DUTCH GO EAST

The Dutch East India Company had been established in 1602, and supported the training of twelve men at a missionary training centre in Leiden from 1622 to 1633. Although the college collapsed for lack of finance, the company continued to support mission work. Its chaplains in South Africa, Sri Lanka, and the Malay archipelago were paid a sum of money for every native converted and baptized. The company filled missionary posts, established schools, and encouraged Bible translation and the pastoral care of converts. An interesting relationship developed between Classis Amsterdam and the Dutch East India Company. The Classis, a regional division of the Dutch Reformed Church, controlled the theological education and ordination of the chaplain-missionaries while the company paid their salaries.

The results of the Dutch work were often superficial, but most of the Calvinist churches founded still exist today. By 1800 a native church, estimated at 200,000, existed in the East Indies. The New Testament was translated into the Malay language by 1688, and the entire Bible by 1734. The Dutch tried unsuccessfully to root out Portuguese Catholicism in Sri Lanka, founding a network of schools, and translating the Bible into the native dialects of the island. In 1690 they opened two seminaries for training Sinhalese catechists and teachers, and by the mid-eighteenth century there were well over 300,000 Protestants on Sri Lanka. In South Africa, minister-chaplains concentrated their evangelism on Dutch and Huguenot refugees. Some slaves were baptized and instructed in the faith and formed a small, local church.

The fortunes of the Dutch East India Company waned after 1750, and the number of missionary-chaplains fell. The company was disbanded in 1798.

PRAYING TOWNS

The best example of Protestant expansion through colonies is in Puritan New England. When Charles I (r. 1625–49) granted the Massachusetts Bay Company a charter as a colony, the document contained a clause concerning missions:

> The people from England may be so religiously, peaceably, and civilly governed, as their good life and orderly conversation may win and incite the natives of the country to the knowledge and obedience of the only true God and Saviour of mankind, and the Christian faith.

In the 1640s, Thomas Mayhew Sr (1593–1682) took the gospel to Martha's Vineyard, an island just off the coast of Massachusetts, a work that was continued by the next four generations of Mayhews. About the same time, John Eliot (c. 1604–90), a Puritan minister at Roxbury, Massachusetts, began to evangelize the Native Americans of the Pequot tribe, gathering New England Indians into 'praying towns', where he taught them trades, agriculture, and academic subjects. Eliot believed he had to civilize the Native Americans before he could Christianize them, so he mastered their language, into which he translated the Bible by 1663. Eliot was familiar with Catholic missionary methods, and seems to have borrowed some of his ideas from the Jesuits. He sent several Native Americans to Harvard College for training as pastors. In 1675, there were two dozen Native American evangelists at work, fourteen 'praying towns', and about 4,000 Christian Native Americans. However in that year war between the Native Americans and the colonists virtually destroyed his work.

News of Mayhew's and Eliot's work reached England through printed reports known as the *Eliot Tracts*, which generated interest that led to the formation of the 'Society for the Propagation of the Gospel in New England' in 1649 – the first Protestant missionary society. This organisation supported the work of both Eliot and Mayhew, and continued to finance Native American missions until the American Revolution, when it channelled its resources into missions among Canadian tribes.

European colonists on the Atlantic coast and in the Caribbean began to evangelize Native Americans and blacks early in the eighteenth century. Previous pioneers included Roger Williams (c. 1603–83) in Rhode Island, Swedes in Delaware, and Quakers throughout the colonies. But Europeans did not colonize the New World for the express purpose of evangelizing non-Christians, although some contemporary writers suggested that they should do so.

A BURNING FIRE

Towards the end of the seventeenth century an evangelical piety began to appear among Protestants, crossing denominational and political boundaries. Protestants again emphasized the importance of personal conversion, holy living, and the need to tell non-Christians about Christ's saving work. They believed that the entrance of Jews and Gentiles into the church, and the kingdom of Christ, would fulfil promises in the Bible.

English Puritans and dissenters, and Dutch Calvinists, had practised this form of piety early in the seventeenth century. Philipp Spener's *Pia Desideria* (1675) gave it a new name and new direction, in the form of German Pietism. It caught fire among some Anglicans in

THE FIRST ENGLISH MISSIONS

A revolution took place in English preaching during the later years of the seventeenth century – largely brought about by John Tillotson, Archbishop of Canterbury 1691–94 – and it changed from theological interpretation and magnificent eloquence to moral argument and practical simplicity. One effect of this was that 'groups of serious men' formed voluntary societies for religious and social purposes, influenced by some of the great preachers in London. Both the Society for Promoting Christian Knowledge (SPCK) and the Society for the Propagation of the Gospel (SPG) owe their foundation to the initiative of a small group of lay people and clergy, under the leadership of Dr Thomas Bray (1656–1730).

Bray was rector, first of a parish in Warwickshire, then in London, and was concerned by 'the gross ignorance of the Christian religion' which was so prevalent. In 1696 he drew up a plan for 'a Protestant Congregation or Society' to work in a similar way to the *Propaganda* of the Roman Catholic Church. In 1698, with four laymen, Bray set up the SPCK, whose objects were

> 'to promote and encourage the erection of charity schools in all parts of England and Wales; to disperse, both at home and abroad, Bibles and tracts of religion; and in general to advance the honour of God and the good of mankind by promoting Christian knowledge both at home and in the other parts of the world by the best methods that should offer'.

During the first half of the eighteenth century, the SPCK gave much of its attention to education, helping to found charity schools, where poor children were given an elementary education and religious instruction. The SPCK also published books and tracts, encouraged the formation of libraries for the clergy, corresponded with Protestant churches on the continent of Europe, assisted Protestant refugees, and provided religious books for settlers in the American colonies.

When the SPCK had become active in so many fields, Bray decided to found a separate society to engage in overseas mission. Started in 1701, this was the Society for the Propagation of the Gospel (SPG), whose object was to provide an Anglican ministry for British people overseas, and to evangelize the non-Christian subjects of the British monarch. It had a more official position within the Anglican Church than the SPCK, being authorized by the English clergy in Convocation and incorporated by royal charter.

In 1699 Bray had made a brief visit to Maryland as the Bishop of London's representative (Commissary), having become aware of the weakness of the Church of England in the American colonies. As a result, the society concentrated at first on raising money to provide 'a sufficient maintenance for an orthodox clergy' to care for the spiritual needs of the colonists. But in 1710 the SPG agreed to concern itself also with the 'conversion of heathens and infidels', and during the eighteenth century its missionaries worked in the North American colonies, Canada, and the West Indies. The SPG was the first missionary society of the Church of England.

LEONARD W. COWIE

the early eighteenth century, in the Great Awakening, and burned in virtually every church in the American colonies. Wherever it appeared it generated a practical interest in mission.

In Britain, Thomas Bray (1658–1730) adopted the use of the society for Christian missions. He was appointed Commissary for the colony of Maryland by the Bishop of London in 1695. Bray recruited evangelists for the colonies and collected funds to establish parish libraries, and out of these efforts grew the Society for Promoting Christian Knowledge (SPCK) in 1698.

Bray next helped to found the Society for the Propagation of the Gospel in Foreign Parts (SPG), in 1701, a society with specifically missionary aims. During the eighteenth century it supported several hundred men working among British colonists, Native Americans, and blacks in North America and the Caribbean. In 1709 the Scottish SPCK was founded. All three agencies, together with the older New England Company, supported missionaries who had a zeal sparked by evangelical piety.

THE DANES DEPART

Much of the religious fervour of the eighteenth century began in Germany. Spener, and after him August Francke (1663–1727), founded several projects and institutions in Halle which provided a stream of foreign missionaries. When King Frederick IV of Denmark (r. 1699–1730) wanted missionaries for his colony in Tranquebar, he found them among the Pietists in Halle. Bartholomäus Ziegenbalg (1682–1719) and Heinrich Plütschau (1678–1747) responded to his appeal in 1705, marking the beginnings of the Danish-Halle mission.

These two missionaries arrived in India the following year, but met harsh criticism from Lutherans in both Denmark and Germany, whilst the Danish governor of Tranquebar opposed them too. Plütschau died five years later, but Ziegenbalg continued the work for fifteen years. Their example aroused wide interest in missions in Europe. They concentrated on educating children, translating the Bible into the native language, preaching a gospel of personal conversion, and training a local clergy – all of which became hallmarks of evangelical Protestant missions.

In 1714 a royal authority was established in Copenhagen, guaranteeing missionaries official Danish sanction and support in further areas. Hans Egede (1686–1758) started a missionary colony in Greenland in 1722, while other missionaries went to the West Indies. By 1800 Halle had contributed approximately sixty people to the Danish-Halle enterprise.

The English also became involved in the Danish-Halle mission. Anton Wilhelm Böhme, a former student of Francke, persuaded the SPCK to support Danish-Halle missionaries in British holdings in India. These evangelicals from Germany used Anglican Church practices, and ministered to British troops in India for decades, despite their links with Halle and Copenhagen. One of the most successful of these missionaries was Christian Friedrich Schwartz (1749–98), who served with such distinction that, upon his death, the Rajah of Tanjore (Thanjavur) erected a marble monument in his memory.

The most significant missionary movement arising directly from Halle Pietism was the work of the Moravians. In Copenhagen in 1731, Count Zinzendorf met two Eskimo converts from Greenland and a West India Christian, who pleaded with him for missionaries. When he returned home to Herrnhut, Zinzendorf inspired the Moravians to respond to this appeal.

MORAVIAN MISSIONS

Within thirty years, the Moravians had begun missions in at least ten countries. By 1740 they had reached the Virgin Islands, Greenland, Surinam, the Gold Coast (West Africa),

North America, and South Africa. Their self-sacrifice, love, and total commitment to evangelization are unparalleled in the history of missions. Despite the group's small size, the Moravians sent out hundreds of missionaries in the eighteenth century – and inspired countless others.

One notable Moravian missionary is David Zeisberger (1721–1808). He was educated at their centre in Bethlehem, Pennsylvania, and then worked among the Iroquois and Delaware Native Americans. He followed the Iroquois when European colonizers pushed their tribe into eastern Ohio, where he founded several Native American settlements, which were later ruthlessly exterminated by white colonists during the American Revolution. But wherever the Moravians went with the gospel, their loving spirit, strong faith, and commitment conveyed such an attractive example of Christianity that hundreds of converts were made. One historian has estimated that the Moravian missions achieved more in this period than all the Protestant efforts before them.

THE ENGLISH AWAKENED

Meanwhile in England and the American colonies the awakenings created new evangelistic efforts. In 1741–42 the Scottish SPCK sent Azariah Horton (1715–77) and David Brainerd (1718–47) to work among the Native Americans. Brainerd's diaries and journals long outlived his short, ascetic service, inspiring later missionaries such as William Carey and Henry Martyn. Thomas Coke promoted Methodism in the West Indies towards the end of the eighteenth century, and is remembered for giving the Methodist movement a commitment to evangelize the non-whites.

By the last quarter of the eighteenth century, Protestant expansion was led largely by movements arising out of the new piety. Instead of kings and trading companies, voluntary societies – organized specifically for promoting Christianity – now sponsored missions. The Moravians pointed forward to the nineteenth and twentieth centuries, when mission came to be regarded as the duty of each denomination. The heroic examples and literature associated with eighteenth-century Protestant missions formed the basis for the numerically greater achievements of the next 150 years.

RUSSIA

Christian expansion in this period cannot be recorded solely in terms of Western Christianity. The Eastern churches were intimidated and repressed by Islam, but the Russian church contributed to missionary outreach. Czar Peter the Great, whose reign began in 1682, encouraged the expansion of Christianity into his eastern territories as part of his overall policy.

Filofei Leshchinskii, Metropolitan of Tobolsk, 1702–9, gained the Czar's permission to promise tax concessions to new Christians. He gained 40,000 converts, and planted about 300 new churches in western Siberia, but this work declined after his death in 1727. In the early 1700s Peter excused from military service men of the middle Volga region who were baptized as Christians. But the Christianization of tribes in this area was not completed until the mid-eighteenth century, by Bishop Luka Konashevich.

In 1720 Peter the Great campaigned to raise religious and moral standards among both clergy and people, but missionary efforts remained sporadic and were often politically motivated. In 1721, as a result of the *Ecclesiastical Regulation*, the Russian Orthodox Church in effect became a section of the imperial bureaucracy.

Some missionary work may have been achieved by the Russian diplomatic delegation in Peking, and there was also mission work among the Kalmucks, and missions to eastern Siberia and the peninsula of Kamchatka. But the poor state of Russian Orthodoxy, the political situation, and the geographical vastness and ethnic diversity of Russia all tended to discourage missionary outreach. It is amazing that as much Christian expansion occurred as did in Russian territories.

Compared with what followed in the nineteenth century, Christian expansion between 1650 and 1800 was limited. But from its achievement the next generations of mission leaders gained inspiration and guidance. The missionary vision did not pervade the Christian West as in the next century, but issues such as the relationship between Christianity and indigenous culture, the need to train local Christian leaders, and the importance of translating the Bible were grappled with by Protestants, Orthodox, and Roman Catholics. In this era, their Christian faith became global.

JAMES A. DE JONG

REASON, REVIVAL, AND REVOLUTION

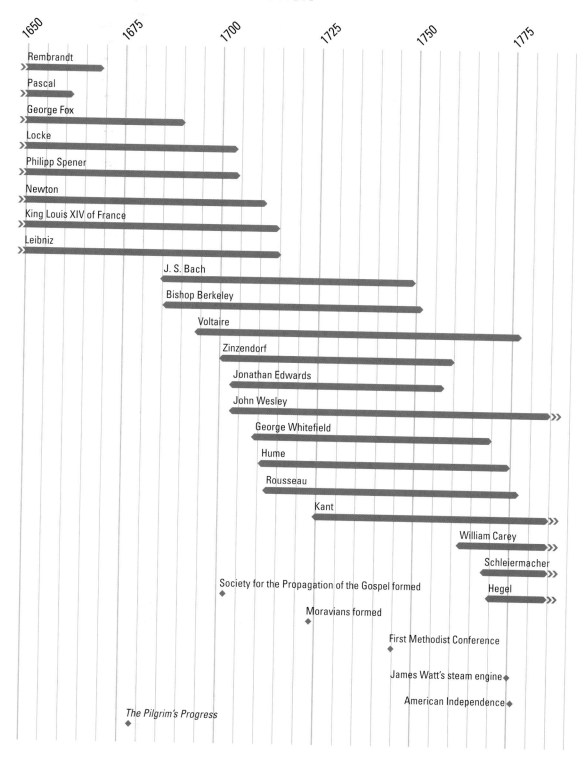

1650   1675   1700   1725   1750   1775

Rembrandt

Pascal

George Fox

Locke

Philipp Spener

Newton

King Louis XIV of France

Leibniz

J. S. Bach

Bishop Berkeley

Voltaire

Zinzendorf

Jonathan Edwards

John Wesley

George Whitefield

Hume

Rousseau

Kant

William Carey

Schleiermacher

Hegel

Society for the Propagation of the Gospel formed

Moravians formed

First Methodist Conference

James Watt's steam engine

American Independence

The Pilgrim's Progress

CHAPTER 29

AWAKENING
The Evangelical Revival and the Great Awakening

In many of the English-speaking churches the Age of Reason became the Age of Renewal. In the 1730s and 40s, the tide of rationalism was stemmed, and dead formalism suppressed, as a rebirth took place with its roots in both European Pietism and English Puritanism. In Britain the movement was known as the Evangelical – or Methodist – Revival; in the North American colonies as the Great Awakening. The latter began in Northampton, Massachusetts, under Jonathan Edwards in 1734 – which preceded the conversions of both George Whitefield and the Wesley brothers, and can be regarded as feeding the Evangelical Revival in Britain – and came to fruition in New England between 1740 and 1743, the time of Whitefield's visit.

THE FIRST AMERICAN PROTESTANTS

Successive waves of immigrants from Britain and Europe had come to the east coast of North America. All but one of the thirteen English colonies had Protestant beginnings, and most of the newcomers were Calvinists. Calvinism in its most direct form was carried across the Atlantic by the Scots and the Dutch, who set up both Presbyterian and Reformed churches. The early settlers also brought the modified Calvinism of the English Puritans and Separatists, whose beliefs were to have a notable influence. Groups tracing their origin to other Reformation movements – Dunkers, Lutherans, Moravians, and Mennonites – came later and in smaller numbers.

The earliest American Protestants were Anglican. In 1607 a community was set up at Jamestown, Virginia, with Robert Hunt (c. 1568–1608) acting as chaplain. But Anglicanism was never popular either in Virginia or in the other colonies. The church authorities failed to provide a bishop for New England, which weakened the Episcopalian Church during the colonial period.

The Congregational churches, together with the Presbyterians, formed the largest group in the English colonies. American Congregationalism arose from a merging of Separatists and Puritans. The Pilgrim Fathers who disembarked at Plymouth, New England, in 1620, were Independents who had already left the English national church to seek ecclesiastical asylum in Holland. The much larger group who migrated from 1628 onwards were Puritans in the strict sense of the term: those who desired reform from within the Anglican Church. Driven from England by repressive measures during the reign of Charles I, they settled in Massachusetts. The Separatists and Puritans eventually joined forces, and in 1648 expressed their agreement in the 'Cambridge Platform' – the charter of American Congregationalism.

THE PRESBYTERIANS ARRIVE

Presbyterianism first appeared in America in the form of the Dutch Reformed Church. In 1626 the Dutch East India Company founded a colony on the Hudson River, renaming

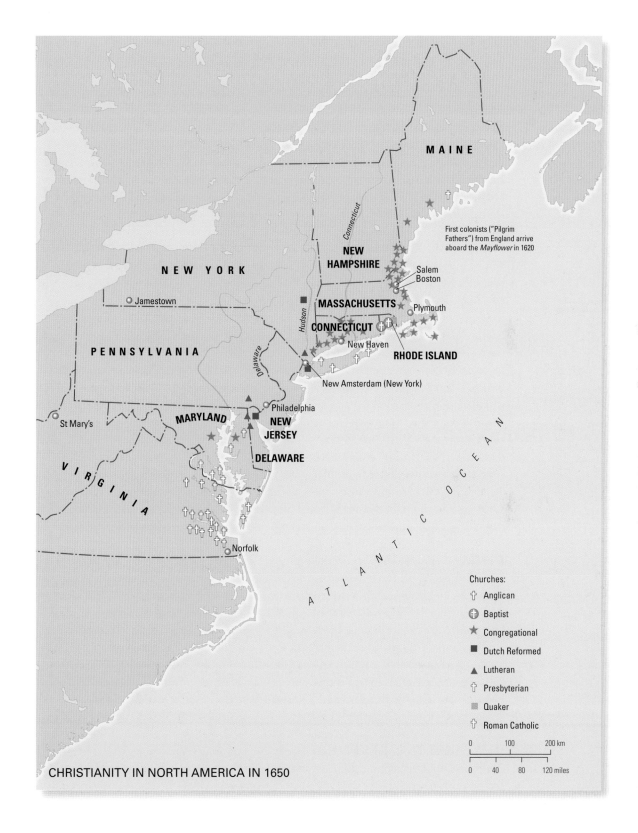

MAINE

First colonists ("Pilgrim
Fathers") from England arrive
aboard the *Mayflower* in 1620

NEW YORK

NEW
HAMPSHIRE

Salem
Boston

Jamestown

MASSACHUSETTS

Plymouth

CONNECTICUT

PENNSYLVANIA

New Haven

RHODE ISLAND

New Amsterdam (New York)

St Mary's

Philadelphia

MARYLAND

NEW
JERSEY

DELAWARE

VIRGINIA

Norfolk

ATLANTIC OCEAN

Churches:

† Anglican

✠ Baptist

★ Congregational

■ Dutch Reformed

▲ Lutheran

† Presbyterian

■ Quaker

† Roman Catholic

0		100		200 km

0	40	80		120 miles

CHRISTIANITY IN NORTH AMERICA IN 1650

Manhattan Island as 'New Amsterdam'. Two years later a minister was appointed, and the Dutch Reformed Church continued to flourish after the colony was handed over to England, in 1664. By 1700 the church held a strong position in New York.

The form of Presbyterianism that was to play a particularly prominent part in American Christianity came from Britain, founded by Francis Makemie (1658–1708), who was commissioned by an Irish presbytery to work in the American colonies. Churches were planted in Maryland as early as 1683, and in 1706 the presbytery of Philadelphia was formed, with Makemie as its moderator. He encouraged many Scottish and Irish Presbyterians to seek refuge in America from oppression under the Stuarts. From 1710, the flow of immigrants increased dramatically, after England imposed economic sanctions on Ireland.

AMERICAN BAPTISTS

American Baptists trace their ancestry to a congregation at Providence, Rhode Island, first gathered in 1639 by Roger Williams, a Separatist from London, who had been ejected from the Puritan colony in Massachusetts Bay. Most of those making up the first congregations were English or Welsh Baptists, who already shared Williams' beliefs. The Baptists grew slowly until after the Great Awakening. Meanwhile the Quakers launched their 'holy experiment' in Pennsylvania in 1681.

In 1690 the population of the colonies – some 250,000 – was almost exclusively British. But European Protestants had begun to arrive – Huguenots and Mennonites, as well as the Dutch Calvinists – a movement that intensified at the opening of the eighteenth century, when there was a large-scale influx of German Lutherans, most of them fleeing persecution in the Palatinate. When William Penn invited them to his colony, Pennsylvania, they crossed the Atlantic in thousands. By the middle of the eighteenth century there were 70,000 Germans in Pennsylvania alone, and almost 200,000 in North America as a whole, comprising Moravians, Dunkers, and Schwenkfelders as well as Lutherans. These German settlers, some of whom had already been touched by the Pietist movement, introduced a new element into American Christianity, hitherto dominated by the Calvinist tradition.

FORMAL RELIGION

By the beginning of the eighteenth century, the American churches had been overtaken by paralysis. The evangelical enthusiasm of the pioneering generation of colonists had not been maintained. The development of commerce, and the accompanying increase in wealth, bred a materialism that blunted the keen edge of Protestant witness. The fervour of the fathers was not reproduced in their children.

The Puritan ideal of a society ruled by God faded from view. Previously believers had been obliged to assent to a church covenant to qualify for church membership; now this was seriously compromised. The 'Half Way Covenant' of 1662, promoted by Solomon Stoddard of Northampton, Massachusetts (1643–1729), allowed the children of uncommitted parents to be received in baptism, whereas previously only those who could testify to a conversion experience were admitted as members. Now any 'persons not scandalous in life' could be included. Moral respectability – rather than spiritual rebirth – had become the criterion.

A Presbyterian Synod held at Boston in 1679 discussed 'the necessity of reformation', and described the evils that had 'provoked the Lord to turn His judgments on New England'. For the next thirty years, zealous ministers bemoaned the worsening situation, and called on their congregations to repent. In 1727, an earthquake that disturbed much of New England and neighbouring provinces was interpreted as a sign of God's judgment. There was a temporary rush to the churches – but little lasting improvement. Something more than reform was required, and by the 1730s people were calling for revival. It began in Northampton in 1734.

There had already been early signs elsewhere. The German, Theodorus Jacobus Frelinghuysen (1692–1747/8), a minister in the Dutch Reformed Church, was revived by Pietism in his homeland and while in Holland studying. When he arrived in America, he was shocked by the lifeless orthodoxy of his denomination, and launched a campaign of evangelism and reform. In 1720 he embarked on a mission in the Raritan Valley, New Jersey, where his impassioned preaching produced many conversions, but earned the disapproval of the Amsterdam church authorities, who still controlled the American congregations. By 1726 revival was spreading to the Presbyterian churches of the district.

In the same year, the Irish-born Gilbert Tennent (1703–64) was ordained as a Presbyterian minister and placed at New Brunswick, where he was influenced by Frelinghuysen and brought revival to his own denomination. Tennent saw signs of revival among his congregation, composed mainly of Ulster refugees. He followed Whitefield as one of the great itinerant figures of the Awakening, provoking scandal with his sermon 'On the Dangers of an Unconverted Ministry'.

JONATHAN EDWARDS

One further local revival is regarded as inaugurating the Great Awakening. It occurred in Northampton, under Jonathan Edwards, and had a profound effect not only elsewhere in America, but in Britain too, through the circulation of Edwards' account of what happened, his *Narrative*. Edwards followed his grandfather, Solomon Stoddard, as pastor of the Congregational church at Northampton, but found the people 'very insensible of the things of religion.' In 1734, Edwards preached a series of sermons on justification by faith, and towards the end of December 'the Spirit of God began extraordinarily to set in'. The revival grew and 'souls did as it were

There was scarcely a single person in the town, old or young, left unconcerned about the great things of the eternal world. Those who were wont to be the vainest, and loosest; and those who had been most disposed to think, and speak slightly of vital and experimental religion, were now generally subject to great awakenings. And the work of conversion was carried on in a most astonishing manner, and increased more and more; souls did, as it were, come by flocks to Jesus Christ. From day to day, for many months together, might be seen evident instances of sinners brought out of darkness into marvellous light, and delivered out of a horrible pit, and from the miry clay, and set upon a rock with a new song of praise to God in their mouths.

This work of God, as it was carried on, and the number of true saints multiplied, soon made a glorious alteration in the town; so that in the spring and summer following, *anno* 1735, the town seemed to be full of the presence of God: it never was so full of love, nor of joy, and yet so full of distress, as it was then. There were remarkable tokens of God's presence in almost every house. It was a time of joy in families on account of salvation being brought unto them; parents rejoicing over their children as new born, and husbands over their wives, and wives over their husbands.

JONATHAN EDWARDS, *A FAITHFUL NARRATIVE OF THE SURPRISING WORK OF GOD*

JONATHAN EDWARDS

Jonathan Edwards (1703–58), whose name is inseparably linked with the Great Awakening, was born in Connecticut, New England, the son of the local pastor. He was a precocious child, fluent in Latin, Greek, and Hebrew at thirteen. At sixteen, while at the Collegiate School of Connecticut (afterwards Yale), he worked out a speculative philosophy on Being that anticipated the thinking of the British philosopher, Bishop Berkeley. Edwards graduated head of his class in 1720, then studied divinity and, after a short period as a Presbyterian minister in New York, became a senior tutor at Yale in 1724.

In 1727 Edwards had an experience that gave him a new awareness of God's absolute sovereignty, and of his dependence on God, which he described in his *Personal Narrative* (1739). In 1727, too, he became the associate pastor of the Congregational church at Northampton, Massachusetts, where, in 1735, and under his preaching, came the Awakening. Edwards described and analyzed in minute detail what happened, believing it was a genuine work of God, expressing itself in both mental and physical excitement.

Edwards was dismissed from his pastorate in 1750, after a long controversy about admitting unbelievers to the church ordinances – especially the Lord's Supper – and then went as a missionary to the frontier hamlet of Stockbridge, preaching to the Housatonic people and white settlers. Edwards produced his most important work at Stockbridge, *Freedom of the Will* (1754), in which he denies that human beings are free to choose, a view that fitted with his Calvinistic doctrines of election, predestination, and the fallenness of humanity in every aspect.

In January 1758 Edwards reluctantly became President of the College of New Jersey, Princeton. But, after being inoculated against smallpox, he died of the disease. His arguments for a clear, Calvinistic position delayed the liberal theology that was to dominate New England in the nineteenth century. Unusually, he brought together evangelistic zeal and a powerful intellectual curiosity.

HOWARD J. SAINSBURY

come by flocks to Jesus Christ'. 'The town never was so full of love, nor of joy, and yet so full of distress, as it was then,' Edwards declared. The effect was felt in the surrounding area and even in neighbouring Connecticut. Although the excitement in Northampton subsided within a couple of years, Edwards was convinced something had started that would have widespread repercussions.

GEORGE WHITEFIELD

When the Awakening reached its peak in 1740, Northampton was again a centre, and Edwards important; but now the major figure was George Whitefield. Converted in 1735, Whitefield had been a pioneer in the English Revival. He arrived in New England in September 1740 for his second visit to America, and set off on a six-week tour that resulted in the most general awakening the American colonies had experienced.

In Boston, the crowds soon grew too large to be accommodated in any of the churches, so Whitefield took to the open air – as he had done previously in England. He preached his farewell sermon to a congregation estimated to number 20,000, and, before leaving, invited Gilbert Tennent to Boston 'to blow up the divine fire lately kindled there'. The revival continued in Boston for eighteen months, thirty 'religious societies' were formed,

GEORGE WHITEFIELD

George Whitefield was an outstanding preacher during the Revival. Born in Gloucester in 1714, he was educated at Pembroke College, Oxford, where he became associated with the Wesleys and others in the 'Holy Club'. Converted in 1735, he was ordained deacon in 1736, and set sail for Georgia the following year. In America, he engaged in a variety of charitable and church work, returning to England briefly between 1738 and 1739 to be ordained priest, and to collect money for his new orphanages and schools. On this visit he first discovered his talent for open-air evangelism and made contact with Howell Harris and the Welsh revival. He returned to Georgia, and in 1740 his Calvinistic form of Methodism came into sharp conflict with the Wesleys' Arminianism, opening up a breach that was never healed.

Returning to England in 1741, Whitefield embarked on a round of missionary tours that took him huge distances and were to continue almost to the end of his life. He paid fourteen visits to Scotland, on the second of which, in 1742, he helped at the Cambuslang revival; visited America seven times; and travelled all over England and Wales. Whitefield became closely associated with the Welsh Calvinistic Methodists, and toured South Wales several times with Howell Harris. He preached in many chapels owned by the Countess of Huntingdon, whose preachers' college at Trevecca he opened in 1768. George Whitefield died in America in 1770.

Whitefield is generally thought of as a fervent persuader, who left others to build churches out of his converts. Certainly his letters to Wesley, and his entrusting the care of his English societies to Harris in 1749, show his lack of interest in the administrative task of raising and caring for infant churches. But he founded the English Calvinistic Methodist Connexion, whose first conference met in 1743, and which boasted important London chapels, such as Moorfields and the Tabernacle, Tottenham Court Road. These churches, known as 'the Countess of Huntingdon's Connexion', mainly in the south and west of England, kept up a separate existence, until absorbed into Congregationalism in the nineteenth century.

Whitefield centred his theology on the English Puritan themes of original sin, justification by faith, and regeneration. Sometimes he was militantly Calvinist, but he preached with a passion to convert. 'Calvinistic Methodist' was a term with real meaning when applied to him.

His preaching was dynamic and compelling; he spoke with fervour, yet in a style plain, unadorned, and often colloquial. His physical bearing commanded attention, while the range of his voice was astonishing. Anglican pulpits were often barred to him: his open-air services were often interrupted, and he was a favourite target for anti-Methodist propaganda. In many ways, Whitefield's work complements that of Wesleyan Methodism – though in some respects he was a forerunner of the Wesley brothers: for example, in his choice of Bristol as a base for evangelism, in publishing a magazine, founding a school, daring to preach in the open air, and summoning a conference of preachers.

IAN SELLERS

churches were packed, and services were regularly held in homes. A similar tale was told as Whitefield continued his triumphal journey.

Within three years around 150 churches were affected by the Awakening, not only in New England, but also in New York, New Jersey, Pennsylvania, Maryland, and Virginia. In the latter colony, revival started in Hanover County under William Robinson (d. 1746), paving the way for the outstanding preaching of Samuel Davies (1723–61), and the growth of the

Presbyterian Church there. The Baptists began to expand too, through such evangelists as Daniel Marshall (1706–84) and Shubal Stearns (1706–71). Devereux Jarrett (1733–1801) also attempted to arouse the established church, but it proved largely unresponsive.

The Awakening was not impelled solely through the campaigns of itinerant preachers. One effect of Whitefield's visits was to rouse the ministers. 'The reason why congregations have been so dead,' he explained, 'is because dead men preach to them.' During the Awakening 'dead men' came alive and themselves revived their people.

Renewed churches began to show a novel concern for evangelism, and missionary enterprise was stimulated. David Brainerd, a product of the revival, became the apostle to the Native Americans. As the movement gained support – or provoked opposition – parties tended to polarize. Denominational barriers were broken down, and a new spirit of co-operation prevailed among those sympathetic to the Awakening. Higher education was encouraged; as a result of the revival, major institutions such as Princeton College opened. Spiritual liberation paved the way for political liberation, and contributed indirectly to the American Revolution.

GERMAN PIETISM

On the continent of Europe revival had its source in the Pietist movement, cradled in the early seventeenth century Dutch Reformed Church. It was probably Theodore Untereyk (1635–1693) who introduced it to Germany, where it flowered in the Lutheran Church, breathing new life into a country exhausted by the Thirty Years' War. This was an age of Protestant scholasticism, when the insights of the Reformers had hardened into rigid formulas. Reacting to this barrenness, one writer, Heinrich Müller (1631–75), described the font, the pulpit, the confessional, and the altar as 'the four dumb idols of the Lutheran Church'. In contrast, the Pietist revival re-emphasized the importance of the

PIETISM IN EUROPE

Influence of Pietism

RUSSIA

Pietist mission to Greenland

Bergen

Pietist mission to Lapps of northern Norway

SCOTLAND

SWEDEN

Influence of Francke on Peter the Great
Moscow

IRELAND

ENGLAND

DENMARK-NORWAY

Returnees from Siberian prisons, c. 1720, spread Pietism in Sweden

Swedish students of Francke

PRUSSIA

WALES

Jacobus Arminius (1560–1609)

Johann Arndt (1555–1621)

Academic centre of Pietism

Oxford

London

UNITED PROVINCES

John Wesley (1703–91): "Aldersgate Street Experience"

Amsterdam

Brunswick

Berlin

POLAND

Herrnhut
Count Nikolaus von Zinzendorf (1700–1760): founds colony of Moravian Brethren

Leiden

Rhine

Elbe

GERMAN EMPIRE

Halle

Leipzig

August Francke (1663–1727)

Moravian Brethren influence

Dresden

HUNGARY

Poltava

Battle of Poltava (1709): Swedish prisoners-of-war sent to Siberia where pietistic movement begins

George Whitefield and John Wesley return from America influenced by Pietism

FRANCE

Philipp Spener (1635–1705): forms "assembly of piety," 1669

Frankfurt

Prague

Augsburg

Danube

OTTOMAN   EMPIRE

SWISS CONFEDERATION

new birth, personal faith, and vital Christian experience as a spur to effective mission.

Philipp Jacob Spener (1635–1705), a Frankfurt pastor, was a central figure. He wanted to recover Luther's appeal to the heart, and set up house-meetings for prayer, Bible study, and the sharing of Christian experience. August Herman Francke, professor of Hebrew at the University of Leipzig, founded a Bible school, which led to an awakening among undergraduates and citizens. When he was appointed to Halle in 1692, he made that city a centre of Pietist influence, founding a poor school, an orphanage, and other institutions.

Pietism restored the vitality of the German Church, although it had weaknesses which opponents were not slow to expose. Some adherents left Lutheranism to join or form other denominations. Others – such as Paul Gerhardt (1607–76), Joachim Neander (or Neumann, 1650–80), and Gerhard Tersteegen (1697–1769) – were inspired to write new hymns, many of which were translated by the Wesleys and widely used in England during the Evangelical Revival. Pietism also stimulated a missionary concern that became a prominent feature of the revival both in Britain and America. Through Spener's godson, Count Nikolaus Ludwig von Zinzendorf, Pietism made its impact on the Moravian community, by which route too Pietist influence reached England.

PHILIPP SPENER

Philipp Jacob Spener (1635–1705) was the founder of Lutheran Pietism. Having studied history and theology in Strasbourg, he was appointed a senior member of the Lutheran clergy in Frankfurt in 1666. In his sermons Spener stressed the value of a life of devotion, rather than correct dogma. He began to hold devotional meetings – known as *Collegia pietatis* ('schools of piety') – which quickly multiplied and formed a basis for the Pietist movement.

In 1675 Spener published his *Pia Desideria* ('Holy Desires'), a plan to remedy spiritual decay he saw in the church at every level. He believed the reason for this decay was the absence of a true, living faith. Spener sought to promote Bible-reading, put into practice the doctrine of the priesthood of all believers, and shift the emphasis from the theory to the practice of Christianity. *Pia Desideria* was completely in line with Lutheran theology, except for Spener's belief that there will be a millennium on earth. In spite of this, he could not prevent the separation of Pietists from the Lutheran Church, and the persecution of Francke's group of Pietists in Leipzig. In 1691, Spener moved to Berlin – where the state was more tolerant – and he was able to secure positions in church and academic life for Pietist friends, most importantly at the University of Halle, which by the time of his death had become the centre of Pietism.

IAN SELLERS

THE MORAVIANS

The Moravians were the spiritual descendants of Jan Hus. Driven from their homeland during the Thirty Years' War, they were scattered throughout Europe and lost many members. However some remained, holding services in secret, and praying for the rebirth of their Church of the United Brethren. In 1722 a little company of Moravians settled in Saxony, on Zinzendorf's Berthelsdorf estate, led by an itinerant carpenter named Christian David (1690–1722), a convert from Roman Catholicism, who 'burned with zeal like an oven'. Since the estate lay on the *Hutberg*, or 'Watch Hill', the new community

NIKOLAUS VON ZINZENDORF

The key figure in the renewal of Moravianism in the eighteenth century was a Lutheran nobleman, Count Nikolaus Ludwig von Zinzendorf (1700–60), whose father died when Nikolaus was only six weeks old. Brought up by his grandmother – a friend of Spener and a devotee of Pietism – Zinzendorf was sent to Francke's grammar school at Halle, where, with five other boys, he founded 'the Order of the Grain of Mustard Seed', pledged to 'love the whole human family' and spread the gospel. Zinzendorf went on to study law at the universities of Wittenberg and Utrecht.

On a grand tour of Europe in 1719, he was moved by a painting in an art gallery at Düsseldorf: Domenico Feti's *Ecce Homo*, showing Christ wearing the crown of thorns, with an inscription reading: 'All this I did for you. What are you doing for me?' Zinzendorf now offered himself for Christ's service.

In 1722 he brought about the settlement of a company of Moravian refugees on his estate at Berthelsdorf. With schoolfriend Friedrich von Watteville (1700–77), and pastors Andreas Rothe and Melchior Schäfer, he subscribed to the 'Covenant of the Four Brethren', which sought to promote world-wide evangelization. After the founding of the Moravian Church at Herrnhut in 1727, Zinzendorf emerged as leader, and was consecrated bishop in 1737. He travelled extensively in Europe, visiting England, and also went to North America.

Zinzendorf was a leader of many talents – pastor, teacher, theologian, missionary, hymnwriter, liturgist, and administrator. He was a pioneer of ecumenism, indeed the first to employ the term 'ecumenical' in its modern sense: his aim was to unite all Christians in evangelism.

A. SKEVINGTON WOOD

was called *Herrnhut* ('The Lord's Watch'). It became a haven for Protestant refugees from all parts of Germany, as well as from Moravia and Bohemia; and included not only the United Brethren, but also Lutherans, Reformed, Separatists, Anabaptists, and Schwenkfelders.

It seemed unlikely that people from such an assortment of traditions could co-operate, but in May 1727 the community agreed to accept an apostolic rule, drawn up in 42 statutes: it was no longer to be a hive of sectarians, but a united congregation.

At a communion service on 13 August 1727 they were:

so convinced and affected that their hearts were set on fire with new faith and love towards the Saviour, and likewise with burning love towards one another; which moved them so far that of their own accord they embraced one another in tears...

The Moravians now became 'the vital leaven of European Protestantism'.

There are clear links between the renewed Moravian community and the Evangelical Revival in England. A London bookseller named James Hutton (1715–95) became the first English member of the Moravian Church, and was to play a leading role in the English Revival. In his house met the religious society from which both the Moravian and the Methodist witness in England sprang. Other similar groups soon appeared, some of which attracted German exiles. In the period of intense evangelization produced by the Revival, the Moravians were particularly active.

It was also a Moravian leader who steered John Wesley towards his conversion in 1738. The Wesley brothers first met a group of Moravian missionaries on a voyage to Georgia, and were greatly impressed by their spirituality. Another Moravian, Peter Böhler (1712–75), counselled John Wesley as he searched for assurance of salvation. When Wesley wanted to consider the implications of his revolutionary experience, it was to Herrnhut that he went. Many features of the Moravian community were taken up by the Methodist societies: for example the love feast, the watch night, and the class meeting. Wesley soon parted company with the London Moravians and took a line of his own – but he owed an incalculable debt. Wesley and Whitefield were themselves major figures in the Revival, but much of its inspiration can be traced back to the Moravians.

ANGLICAN DECAY

The Anglican Church of the eighteenth century – though not so black as it has sometimes been painted – stood in urgent need of revitalization. Several causes had contributed to its decline. The seeds of decay had been sown in the previous century, when Anglicans had developed a fear of extremes – both Roman Catholic and Puritan – that resulted in a moderation that frowned on passionate convictions of any kind.

The political situation also helped to stifle spirituality. King George I and his son were both indifferent to Christianity. Sir Robert Walpole, Prime Minister for twenty-one years, openly aimed to put a stop to the progress of Christianity. The cynicism of the age was reflected in a rumour that there was 'a bill cooking up … to have 'not' taken out of the commandments and clapped into the creed'.

The collapse of personal faith led to a slide in moral standards. Although orthodox theologians scored an intellectual victory in the fight against Deism, so defending the central doctrines of Christianity, the new life in Christ they were intended to encourage was no longer in evidence. Wesley spoke candidly of the irreligion of his time: 'What is the present characteristic of the English nation? It is ungodliness … Ungodliness is our universal, our constant, our peculiar character.' The hymn-writer Isaac Watts regretted 'the decay of vital religion in the hearts and lives of men', while the philosopher, Bishop Berkeley, declared that morality and religion in Britain had collapsed 'to a degree that was never known in any Christian country'.

REVIVAL REACHES WALES

It is usual to regard the Revival as running from 1738 to 1742, but – as in America – there were earlier signs of it. They first appeared almost simultaneously at Talgarth and Llangeitho, Wales, in the summer of 1735. Howell Harris (1714–73), a schoolmaster at Talgarth, had been moved by reading books published by the SPCK, and was converted at a communion service on Whitsunday, 1735. He witnessed to his new experience and soon gathered a small society of fellow believers, which formed the beginnings of the Welsh Calvinistic Methodist Church. Although not ordained, Harris began to preach in private houses. People were transformed; the district was transformed; and further societies were started – the Welsh Revival had begun. Meanwhile, Daniel Rowland (1713–90), curate of Llangeitho, had been spiritually awakened through a sermon. His own preaching in turn brought about an awakening in his parish. Harris and Rowland met, and from that point worked together for the spiritual welfare of Wales.

In the year of the Welsh Revival, 1735, George Whitefield was converted. The son of a Gloucester innkeeper, he had once hoped to become an actor. Instead, he was ordained as an Anglican clergyman and became the impassioned orator of the new movement. Whitefield was the pioneer in England; his converts in London and Bristol in 1737 were the first of the

Great Awakening. It was he who started field-preaching, who first recruited lay preachers, and who first travelled to and fro as 'one of God's runabouts' – as he described himself. He was also the first to make contact with both the American and Scottish awakenings.

THE APOSTLE OF ENGLAND

With the strange 'warming' John Wesley experienced on 24 May 1738, the movement received its most vital stimulus. The dapper little Oxford scholar was transformed into the 'apostle of England'. On 1 January 1739, a remarkable love feast was held at Fetter Lane, London, at which were present the Wesleys, Whitefield, and Benjamin Ingham (1712–72), who was to become an outstanding evangelist among the Moravians. John Wesley recorded in his *Journal*:

> *About three in the morning, as we were continuing instant in prayer, the power of God came mightily upon us insomuch that many cried out for exceeding joy and many fell to the ground. As soon as were recovered a little ... we broke out with one voice, 'We praise Thee, O God, we acknowledge Thee to be the Lord'*

This experience confirmed that the Awakening had come, and launched the campaign of extensive evangelization that sprang from it.

The eighteenth-century Revival in England developed through various channels: the Moravian mission, led by men such as Ingham and Cennick; the Calvinistic mission, in which Whitefield was the key figure; the Wesleyan mission, which produced the societies that were eventually to evolve into the Methodist Church; and the movement within the Church of England, which gave rise to 'Anglican Evangelicalism'. At first, all caught up in the spiritual renewal were dubbed either 'Methodists' or 'Evangelicals', irrespective of their church membership. But gradually the Evangelicals were recognized as a party within the Church of England, seeking to achieve their aims within its existing framework.

METHODISTS

What Charles Wesley described as 'the harmless nickname of Methodist' was originally applied in 1729 to a group at Oxford University also known as the 'Holy Club'. This group was led by his brother John, and aimed to encourage a disciplined method of spiritual improvement. Members pledged themselves to have regular private devotions, and to meet each evening to read the Bible and pray. Several labels were invented for them by mocking undergraduates – Enthusiasts, Bible Moths, Sacramentarians – but 'Methodist' was the one that caught on.

John Wesley traced the 'first rise' of Methodism to these years; the second stage, he explained, was in 1736 when 'the rudiments of a Methodist society' appeared in Georgia. Then, in 1738, Wesley helped to reframe the rules for an Anglican society that met in Fetter Lane, London. All this came before his revolutionizing conversion.

A NEW SOCIETY

When – as a result of his conversion – John Wesley became 'an apostle to the nation', he was soon faced with the problem of caring for the converts. To meet this need, the Methodist organization was called into being. Wesley found similar societies already

JOHN AND CHARLES WESLEY

The Wesley brothers were partners in evangelism, and in the care of the Methodist societies. Both were powerful preachers, but each also made his own special contribution: John (1703–91) was the organizer and administrator of a rapidly expanding movement, Charles (1707–88) the 'sweet singer' of Methodism, whose hymns are a legacy to the worldwide church.

John and Charles were born at the rectory at Epworth, Lincolnshire. Their father, Samuel Wesley, was a staunch high churchman; Susanna Wesley, their mother, a remarkable woman whose influence on her sons was exceptionally strong. After attending different schools, both went up to Oxford University. While John was away from Oxford for a period, serving as his father's curate, Charles started the Holy Club; on his return, John took over as leader. It was Charles who guided the devotional reading of George Whitefield before his conversion.

In 1737, the Wesley brothers sailed for Georgia to undertake a mission on behalf of the Society for the Propagation of the Gospel. Charles acted as secretary to the governor of the colony, James Oglethorpe. During the voyage to America and in Georgia, the Wesleys encountered Moravian Christians. Dissatisfied with the result of their mission, they returned to England in 1738.

Both brothers were influenced by the Moravian Peter Böhler. Within three days each had a vital Christian experience – Charles on Whitsunday, and John on 24 May, 1738, when his heart was 'strangely warmed', at a meeting in Aldersgate Street, London, as a passage from Luther's *Preface to Romans* was read. It proved to be the turning-point of the Evangelical Revival.

The Wesleys were convinced that, at all costs, the people of Britain must hear the good news of salvation. While others might confine themselves to their parishes, the Wesleys believed their call was to travel from place to place, preaching in churches whenever pulpits were made available to them. But more often, as opposition grew, the only possibility was to go to the marketplace or the common, so the crowds might hear. The result was that the working classes were drawn to Christianity.

In 1749 Charles Wesley married Sarah (Sally) Gwynne, made his home in Bristol, and for twenty years supervised the Methodist society that met at the New Room there. He moved to London in 1771, and shared the preaching at City Road Chapel. Charles has been described as the most gifted and untiring hymn writer that England has known: he produced more than 7,000 sacred songs and poems. Hymn singing made a huge contribution to the Evangelical Revival: the songs – which had at least as great an effect as the sermons – expressed the joys of Christian experience and taught the truths of Scripture. John Wesley called the *Methodist Hymn Book* of 1780 'a little body of experimental and practical divinity'.

John Wesley's *Journal* is a classic of terse, shrewd, and revealing comment, and records evangelizing journeys covering more than 250,000 miles. Wesley virtually invented the religious tract, and also edited the *Christian Library*, which brought a rich selection of theological and devotional books within reach of the non-specialist reader. He also pioneered a new type of publication – the monthly magazine. His printed sermons, along with his expository *Notes on the New Testament*, form the doctrinal standard of the Methodist Church.

A. SKEVINGTON WOOD

operating in Bristol, but in London he was pressed to devise one of his own, for those who had heard his outdoor preaching at Moorfields. When numbers increased to about a hundred, Wesley noted their names and addresses, intending to visit them in their homes.

Statue of John Wesley (1703–91) in the churchyard of St Paul's Cathedral, London, near Aldersgate. The bronze, cast in 1988, is based on a plaster model by Samuel Manning the Elder (1825).

TIM DOWLEY ASSOCIATES

'Thus, without any previous plan or design, began the Methodist society in England – a company of people associating together to help each other work out their own salvation.' The early successes of the Methodist preachers are to be explained both by the carelessness of many Anglican clergymen, and the fact that the Church of England had very little strength in the industrial towns and cities.

Methodism, then, began not as a church or a sect, but as a society that was born – and expected to remain – within the Church of England. From the start, Wesley assumed Methodists would attend Anglican services and sacraments; he himself had no desire to leave the Anglican Church, despite the opposition he met, especially in the early years of his ministry. He consistently advised his people to stand by the Established Church.

The title 'United Society' was probably borrowed from the Moravians, and indicated that – even though societies multiplied throughout a county – they were regarded as one body. By 1743 Wesley was referring to the 'United Societies' in the plural; they were soon organized into a Connexion. Only after his death did the Methodist Church emerge.

The parent society in London was gathered late in 1739, and met in a disused cannon-foundry which remained the headquarters of Methodism until the opening of City Road Chapel in 1778. This society included 'voluntary bands' – select groups of up to ten Christians supervised by a leader. Existing religious societies restricted membership to those already attached to the Anglican Church, or in full communion with it – such as the Moravians. Wesley refused to impose any such ecclesiastical test, and opened his new society to Nonconformists too. This openness was a mark of Methodism from the outset.

In 1742 the class meeting was introduced; it turned out to be of 'unspeakable usefulness', as Wesley recognized. The name was simply the English form of the Latin *classis*, division, and carried no overtones of school. The classes were larger in size than the bands, and involved every member of the society. Their original purpose was to encourage Christian stewardship, since each member gave a penny a week to the funds. Then Wesley realized that the leaders were 'persons who may not only receive the contributions, but also watch over the souls of their brethren'. The class system secured discipline, as well as providing fellowship and pastoral care.

A NATIONWIDE MOVEMENT

Wesley took another step in 1743, when he drew up a common set of rules for all his societies; for Methodism was by then a nationwide organization. In 1744 the first Conference was held to consider 'the best method of carrying on the work of God' throughout the land. The Connexion was arranged in a series of circuits, or preachers' rounds. The earliest printed list of circuits, published in 1746, included seven: London, Bristol, Cornwall, Evesham, Yorkshire (covering six other counties), Newcastle, and Wales.

These circuits were placed under the control of Assistants (that is, assistants to Wesley himself), who were recruited from the more experienced travelling preachers (or itinerants). They were responsible 'in the absence of the [parish] Minister, to feed and guide, to teach and govern the flock', and to lead the team of preachers (or Helpers) in the circuit. From the beginning, the oversight of Methodism was entrusted to the Assistants (later called Superintendents), although their authority was always subject to that of Wesley and the Conference.

The Assistants were sometimes backed up by a limited number of Anglican clergymen who were prepared to devote part of their time to itinerating for Wesley. Of these the most notable was John Fletcher of Madeley, Shropshire (1729–85). In addition to the travelling preachers (clergy and laymen), others on the spot shared in proclaiming the gospel as local preachers (laymen – and, in a few cases, laywomen).

Preachers and members alike were committed to what Wesley referred to as 'our doctrines'. The basic theological conviction of the Methodists was 'that justification by faith is the doctrine of the Church as well as of the Bible'. To this they added a specific emphasis that salvation is for all, and a stress on the assurance of the Holy Spirit and scriptural holiness.

> I fear, wherever riches have increased the essence of religion has decreased in the same proportion. Therefore I do not see how it is possible, in the nature of things for any revival of true religion to continue long. For religion must necessarily produce both industry and frugality, and these cannot but produce riches. But as riches increase, so will pride, anger and love of the world in all its branches.
>
> JOHN WESLEY

Whitefield disagreed with Wesley's belief that salvation is for all, and went his separate way; but the two men kept in touch, and helped one another from time to time. From 1741 on, the 'Arminian Methodists' allied with Wesley, and 'Calvinistic Methodists' followed Whitefield.

Methodism spread rapidly and much of England was covered within ten years. Ireland, first visited by Wesley, in 1747, became another stronghold. In Wales, the Calvinistic Methodists prevailed, except in some English-speaking areas. Only in Scotland did Methodism fail to gain much ground, although it left a mark on the Presbyterian Church.

METHODISM IN AMERICA

Methodism in America owed its beginnings to immigrants from Ireland. Robert Strawbridge (d. 1781), a Methodist local preacher from Drumsna, Ireland, settled at New Windsor, Maryland, where he opened his log cabin for services and formed a society in 1768. Soon he began to evangelize the district, and further societies were started. About the same time, another local preacher from Ireland, Philip Embury (1729–75), arrived in New York and joined the Lutheran Church. In 1765 his cousin, Barbara Heck, prodded him to start preaching again and he began a Methodist society there. Another Methodist, the British army officer Thomas Webb (1724–96), also lent a hand, sending Wesley an account of what was happening and appealing for help.

The major figure in the founding of American Methodism was Francis Asbury (1745–1816), from Handsworth, near Birmingham, who had been apprenticed to an iron-smelter before joining the ranks of Wesley's itinerant preachers. In 1771 Asbury responded to another call for help in America, and went on to urge his colleagues in America to press to the frontiers in their evangelism. During the Revolutionary War, when Wesley's other preachers returned to base in England, Asbury alone remained.

In 1784 Wesley appointed Asbury and Thomas Coke (1747–1814) joint superintendents for America. Contrary to his wishes, the title of 'Methodist Episcopal Church' was adopted by the Christmas Conference in Baltimore, and Asbury and Coke were made bishops. This amounted to a declaration of independence; American Methodism now stood as a separate body.

LEAVING THE CHURCH OF ENGLAND

When he set apart Coke for service in America, Wesley authorized him to ordain Asbury. The two superintendents were then to ordain presbyters from among the American preachers. Later, Wesley broke with Anglican practice, by himself laying hands on men who were to minister in Scotland and overseas as missionaries. Shortly before his death, he began to make similar provision for areas in England where the Methodists could not receive the sacraments. These steps inevitably hastened the departure of his followers from the Established Church, although Wesley insisted to the end that he did not aim at separation.

A legal *Deed of Declaration* in 1784 ensured that, on Wesley's death, his authority would pass to the Methodist Conference, represented by one hundred of its members. In 1787, Methodist preaching-places were licensed under the Toleration Act, and in 1795 Methodism seceded from the Anglican Church, as set out in a document called the *Plan of Pacification*. By the close of the century the Methodist Church was ready to spread across the world.

ANGLICAN EVANGELICALS

Cornwall was the cradle of Anglican Evangelicalism, and Samuel Walker of Truro (1714–61) emerged as its leader. James Hervey (1714–58), whose books attempted to bring the evangelical message to polite society, began his ministry in the west of England before moving to the English midlands. The scholarly William Romaine (1714–95) was the first evangelical with a parish in London. Henry Venn (1725–97) at Huddersfield, and William Grimshaw (1708–63) of Haworth, were significant evangelical leaders in the north. John Berridge's (1716–93) parish at Everton, Bedfordshire, was the scene of a local awakening in 1759; while John Newton, the slave-trader turned preacher and hymn-writer, was curate of Olney, Buckinghamshire. The Anglican Evangelicals witnessed particularly effectively at the universities of Oxford and Cambridge.

Selina, Countess of Huntingdon, was a patroness of the Revival. When evangelical preachers were banned from other pulpits, she found them a place in her domestic chapels and drawing-rooms, and made possible the preaching of the gospel to the aristocracy. In 1768 she founded a theological training college at Trevecca, South Wales. She was compelled by law to register her chapels as 'nonconformist meeting-houses' in 1779, when they became known as 'the Countess of Huntingdon's Connexion'.

REVIVAL IN SCOTLAND

The impact of the Evangelical Revival on the Scottish national church was more marked than in England and Scottish Presbyterianism radically altered. A debate about patrons had drained the energies of the Scottish Church, leaving it incapable of facing the challenge of theological scepticism. John Simson (1668–1740), Professor of Divinity in Glasgow – a 'New Licht' theologian – was accused of teaching heretical views about the person of Christ, similar to those of the English deists, whilst one of his students, Francis Hutcheson (1694–1746) – who became a founding father of the Scottish Enlightenment – set out to 'put a new face upon theology in Scotland'. Hutcheson's ideas, known as 'Moderatism', reduced Christianity to a system of morality that offered little hope to those who wanted assurance of salvation. Ministers were more concerned about culture than conversions, and dismissed with derision their heritage.

THE SECEDERS

A group of objectors, led by Ebenezer Erskine (1680–1754) of Stirling, set up an independent presbytery, and in 1740 were forced to leave the national church, though they insisted they were only withdrawing from 'the prevailing party', not from the church. The 'Seceders' – or Secession Church – gained some support, and their breakaway might have spread; but revival broke out in the parish of Cambuslang in 1742.

There had already been stirrings of revival in Easter Ross and Sutherland, in the north of Scotland. John Balfour (d. 1752) of Nigg emerged as a leader of the movement in the northern Highlands, which reached its peak in 1739. This was before Whitefield crossed the border, though he is often regarded as the bringer of revival to Scotland. As in America, he sowed the seed on prepared soil. Whitefield was first invited to Scotland in 1741 by the Seceders, but when he refused to confine his activities to their churches, they disowned him. He soon found an opportunity to work in the Church of Scotland.

THE CAMBUSLANG WORK

The revival of 1742, led by William McCulloch – known as the 'Cambuslang Work' – was already under way when Whitefield visited Cambuslang, near Glasgow, during his second Scottish tour, and shared in two momentous open-air communion services. Revival quickly spread to the surrounding area. Another outbreak soon occurred at Kilsyth, when the minister, James Robe (1688–1753), began a series of sermons on the new birth in 1740.

Cambuslang and Kilsyth were the highlights of the Scottish Revival. When the excitement subsided, the benefits remained. The Evangelical party – mocked as 'Zealots' and 'High-flyers' by their opponents – took over from the moderates and shaped the outlook of the church.

THE IMPACT OF THE AWAKENING

What were the effects of the eighteenth-century Awakening? Nominal members of the church were turned into active Christians. Many thousands, who before had made no claim to be Christians, had become committed believers. The clergy were reformed, and set new and high standards of pastoral care. The revival was not confined to the Anglican Church; Nonconformists shared in the renewal.

The Awakening led to the creation of agencies aimed at promoting Christian work. Foremost among these were the missionary organizations that multiplied at the close of the century: the Baptist Missionary Society (1792), the London Missionary Society (1795), and the Church Missionary Society (1799). In 1786 the Wesleyan Conference approved the plan of Thomas Coke to take the gospel to India, and took on the task of overseas extension.

It was not only missionary societies that owed their inspiration to the Revival. Both the Religious Tract Society (1799, now the United Society for Christian Literature) and the British and Foreign Bible Society (1804) sprang from the Revival. Christian education gained a new dimension with the introduction of Sunday schools, started in 1769 by a Methodist, Hannah Ball (1734–92), and then developed and popularized by Robert Raikes (1736–1811), an Anglican layman. The Church of England Sunday School Society was founded in 1786 by William Richardson (1745–1821), evangelical vicar of St Michael le Belfrey, York; and the Sunday School Union was founded in 1803. The Sunday school movement in Britain marked a step towards free education for all.

SOCIAL JUSTICE

The Revival also encouraged a passion for social justice. The campaign to banish slavery from British colonies was led by people of evangelical convictions. In 1767 Granville Sharp (1735–1813) fought a case in the law courts to ensure that a slave should be freed whenever he set foot on British territory. Thomas Clarkson (1760–1846) submitted a prize-winning essay on slavery in 1785, while still at St John's College, Cambridge, where he had been influenced by evangelicals. It was Clarkson who persuaded William Wilberforce to take up the issue of slavery in Parliament.

Wilberforce himself had experienced conversion while on a tour of Europe with Isaac Milner (1750–1820), 'the Evangelical Dr Johnson', who became President of Queens' College, Cambridge. John Wesley published his *Thoughts on Slavery* in 1774, and only four days before his death penned a now-famous letter to Wilberforce urging him to 'go on, in the name of God, and in the power of His might, till even American slavery (the vilest that ever saw the sun) shall vanish away before it'.

Wesley also advocated prison reform, and encouraged John Howard (1726–90) in his crusade for reform. Wesley had a practical concern for the poor, and contributed personally to their relief, as well as raising funds. Through his societies, clothing was distributed, food provided for the needy, and dispensaries set up to treat the sick. In London, one Methodist meeting-room was turned into a workshop for carding and spinning cotton. Other jobs were created for the unemployed.

A lending bank was opened by Christians in 1746; legal advice and aid was made available; and widows and orphans were housed. This Christian concern for the under-privileged led to the birth of the Benevolent or Strangers' Friend Societies in 1787, which quickly established themselves as agencies of poor relief, and bridged the gap until finally the state took over. The Evangelical Revival made Britain aware of its social obligations.

A. SKEVINGTON WOOD

HYMNS AND CHURCH MUSIC

For two centuries after the Reformation there was no book of hymns for use in the Church of England. Metrical psalms were often sung, especially those included in *The Whole Book of Psalms* (1562), collected by Thomas Sternhold (1500–49) and John Hopkins (d. 1570), and often known as the 'Old Version'. In 1696 the popular *New Version of the Psalms of David*, by Nahum Tate (1652–1715) and Nicholas Brady (1659–1726), was published. To this collection we owe such paraphrases as, 'Through All the Changing Scenes of Life' (Psalm 34) and 'As Pants the Hart for Cooling Streams' (Psalm 42). Both books continued in use until about 1870, while *The Scottish Psalter* (1650) is still used by Scots Presbyterians.

In 1623 George Wither (1588–1667) published his *Hymnes and Songs of the Church*, in an attempt to stimulate hymn singing as well as psalmody, but it had little success. It was not until late in the seventeenth century that hymns began to be written more widely, as Baptists pioneered their use in congregational worship.

WATTS AND DODDRIDGE

Isaac Watts (1674–1748) gave a huge boost to the movement for using 'man-made' hymns – as distinct from the inspired hymns (mainly psalms) in Scripture. His best-selling *Hymns and Spiritual Songs* appeared in 1707, followed by *Divine Songs* for children (1715), and *The Psalms of David* (1719), in which he made 'David speak like a Christian' – for example, transforming Psalm 72 into the missionary fervour of 'Jesus Shall Reign Where'er the Sun'. In more than 600 hymns – many still sung – Watts expressed wonder, praise, and adoration, covering the range of Christian experience. Another dissenter, Philip Doddridge (1702–51), composed about 370 hymns, including 'O Happy Day' and 'O God of Bethel'. The staunch Calvinist Augustus Toplady wrote 'Rock of Ages', which first appeared in a magazine article calculating the National Debt in terms of sin.

> When I survey the wondrous Cross
> On which the Prince of Glory dy'd,
> My richest Gain I count but loss,
> And pour Contempt on all my Pride.
>
> Forbid it, Lord, that I should boast
> Save in the Death of Christ my God;
> All the vain things that charm me most,
> I sacrifice them to his Blood.
>
> See from his Head, his Hands, his Feet,
> Sorrow and Love flow mingled down;
> Did e'er such Love and Sorrow meet?
> Or Thorns compose so rich a Crown?
>
> His dying Crimson like a Robe
> Spreads o'er his Body on the Tree,
> Then am I dead to all the Globe,
> And all the Globe is dead to me.
>
> Were the whole Realm of nature mine,
> That were a Present far too small;
> Love so amazing, so divine
> Demands my Soul, my Life, my All.
>
> ISAAC WATTS

A MOVEMENT BORN IN SONG

Overshadowing all other eighteenth-century hymnwriters were the Wesley brothers. *A Collection of Psalms and Hymns* (1737) was compiled by John Wesley and published in Charleston, South Carolina. He later edited several hymnals for the Methodists, notably the definitive *Collection* (1780), which contained many of his brother Charles' hymns and his own paraphrases from German writers such as Zinzendorf.

Methodism, like Lutheranism, was 'born in song'. Charles Wesley's hymns are marked by a constant note of praise – for example 'O For a Thousand Tongues to Sing', 'Rejoice, the Lord is King', 'And Can it be that I Should Gain', and 'Jesu, Lover of my Soul'. Watts and Doddridge freely paraphrased Scripture; Charles Wesley in addition paraphrased the *Prayer Book*, and versified Christian doctrine and experience, creating hymns that are still sung at all the major Christian festivals. Although the Wesleys popularized congregational hymn singing in Britain, early Methodism lacked a really outstanding composer. Their tunes were borrowed or adapted from many sources, particularly German.

In 1779 the fiery, converted slave-trader John Newton (1725–1807) and the gentle, retiring, melancholic poet William Cowper (1731–1807) produced a hymn-book for the village of Olney, Buckinghamshire, where they lived. Newton wrote such hymns as 'Glorious Things of Thee are Spoken' and 'Amazing Grace!'. Cowper was more inward-looking; even his hymn of assurance, 'God Moves in a Mysterious Way' had its 'fearful saints' dreading the storm-clouds.

AMERICAN HYMNS

The earliest book known to have been printed in English in the British North American colonies was *The Whole Booke of Psalms, Faithfully Translated into English Metre* (1640), compiled by, among others, John Eliot and Richard Mather, which became known as the *Bay Psalm Book* as it was used by the Massachusetts Bay Colony. American hymns of the eighteenth century were similar to English hymns of that period. Hymns of only two of their authors are still in regular use: Samuel Davies – 'Great God of Wonders, All thy Ways' – and Timothy Dwight (1752–1817) – 'I Love thy Kingdom, Lord'. Davies was President of the New Jersey Presbyterian College, Princeton; Dwight President of Yale.

LUTHER AND CALVIN

In countries where Luther's influence was strongest, a great tradition of singing by choir and congregation was laid down. A treasury of organ music, largely based on the melodies from chorales, reached its peak in the genius of Johann Sebastian Bach (1685–1750), whose many cantatas written for different periods in the church's year include the *Christmas Oratorio*. His most ambitious works were the *Mass in B Minor* and *St Matthew Passion*.

Church music developed differently in countries dominated by Calvin's teachings. The *Genevan Psalter* (1562), a volume of metrical psalms in French, with music edited by Louis Bourgeois (1510/15–61) and others, was translated into German and Dutch and for a long time was the only tune-book of the Reformed

Statue of Johann Sebastian Bach (1685–1750), outside the Thomaskirche, Leipzig, Germany, where he was Cantor from 1723 until his death.
© UWE BUMANN/DREAMSTIME

churches in continental Europe. Unaccompanied unison singing was the rule except in Holland, where the organ continued in use.

England and Scotland followed Geneva's lead. Each psalm was 'lined out' – that is, each line in turn was first read by a precentor before being slowly sung by the congregation – a practice necessary when few could read and books were expensive.

Roman Catholics in Europe revived hymns in the sixteenth and seventeenth centuries. The French diocesan prayer books of 1675–1800 provided admirable tunes, modified from plainsong.

Engraving of George Frideric Handel, composer of *Messiah* and many other oratorios.

© GEORGIOS KOLLIDAS/DREAMSTIME.COM

Glorious things of thee are spoken,
Zion, city of our God!
He whose word cannot be broken
Formed thee for his own abode.
On the Rock of Ages founded,
What can shake thy sure repose?
With salvation's walls surrounded,
Thou mayst smile at all thy foes.

Saviour, if of Zion's city
I, through grace, a member am,
Let the world deride or pity,
I will glory in thy name:
Fading is the worldling's pleasure,
All his boasted pomp and show,
Solid joys and lasting treasure
None but Zion's children know.

JOHN NEWTON

ANTHEMS

Although metrical psalms long prevailed in parish churches, in Anglican cathedrals choirs began to sing anthems. Henry Purcell (1659–95) wrote fine anthems, especially 'Thou Knowest, Lord, the Secrets of Our Hearts'. The church music of George Frideric Handel (1685–1759) consisted mostly of passions, Latin psalms, and cantata-like anthems. He also wrote a number of oratorios for performance in secular venues – above all *Messiah*. Franz Josef Haydn (1732–1809) followed with *The Creation*, and Felix Mendelssohn (1809–47) with *Elijah*. With some exceptions, little memorable music appeared in England for church choirs before the end of the nineteenth century.

JOHN S. ANDREWS

CHRISTIANITY AND THE RISE OF MODERN SCIENCE

The years between 1500 and 1700 saw not one but two profound upheavals in Western thought. In religion Luther, Calvin, Zwingli, and Knox were replacing a human-centred view of the world with a God-centred one. In science Copernicus, Galileo, Brahe, Kepler, and Newton were replacing a universe centred on the earth with one centred on the sun. A religious reformation and a scientific revolution went hand in hand.

The search for causal connections between the Protestant Reformation and the rise of modern science has involved historians in a complex debate. Essentially, the debate has been between two points of view: first, that religion gave decisive encouragement to science; and second, that both religion and science were spurred by another factor, such as social and economic developments. There is distinct and plausible evidence that Protestantism gave rise to modern science.

THE PROTESTANT CONTRIBUTION

There is considerable evidence of specific Protestant contributions to the 'scientific revolution'. A Lutheran prince, Duke Albrecht of Prussia, subsidized the publication of the astronomer Nicolaus Copernicus' *De revolutionibus* (1543); Andreas Osiander, a Lutheran theologian, arranged for its printing and wrote its preface; Joachim Rhaeticus, a Lutheran mathematician and professor at the Reformer Melanchthon's Wittenberg University, supervised the printing; and Erasmus Reinhold, another Wittenberg professor, supported Copernicus' teaching in his astronomic tables.

The great astronomers Tycho Brahe (1546–1601) and Johannes Kepler (1571–1630) were both devout followers of Luther. Michael Maestlin, a Lutheran pastor, edited Kepler's *Prodromus* (1596), which led the author to the principles of planetary motion that bear his name. David Chytraeus (1530–1600), a Lutheran

theologian, dealt with the new star of 1572 in his commentary on Deuteronomy, published a book on the comet of 1577, and discussed these phenomena in letters to Brahe. Johannes Fabricius (1587–1616), a Lutheran layman, first observed sunspots and the rotation of the sun, and Georg Samuel Dörffel (1643–88), a Lutheran pastor, first demonstrated that comets may move in a parabola.

During the seventeenth century, followers of Calvin took the lead in advancing the cause of science. Philip van Lansberge (1561–1632), a Reformed minister and renowned astronomer, became the keenest supporter of Copernicus in the Netherlands. His fellow-countryman Isaac Beeckman (1588–1637), a scientist and strict Calvinist, was an early defender of the atomistic philosophy.

THE ROYAL SOCIETY

Meanwhile, in England the Puritan movement produced men such as Henry Briggs, Henry Gellibrand, and John Wilkins, who devoted themselves to discovery and learning. Briggs and Gellibrand were professors at Gresham College, London, which was strongly Puritan. There, in 1645, the German Calvinist Theodore Haak (1605–90), inspired by the Moravian educator J. A. Comenius (1592–1670), commenced informal gatherings, which in 1661 became the Royal Society of London. Seven of the ten scientists who formed the nucleus of those meetings were Puritans. In 1663, 62 per cent of the members of the Royal Society were clearly Puritan by origin, at a time when Puritans were only a small minority in England. After the Restoration of 1660, Puritan interest in science was encouraged in the dissenting academies, educational institutions for Nonconformists which emphasized scientific disciplines and experiment.

Other evidence that Protestantism encouraged the rise of modern science comes from statistics con-

Johannes Kepler, German mathematician and astronomer.
©GEORGIOS KOLLIDAS/DREAMSTIME.COM

cerning the religious inclinations of scientists. Protestants seem to have been relatively more numerous among scientists than in the population at large. For example, 90 per cent of the foreign members of the *Académie des Sciences* in Paris between 1666 and 1883 were Protestants; yet in the same period Protestants made up only 40 per cent of the population of Western Europe outside France. Similar statistics elsewhere point in the same direction.

Historians have tried to interpret this evidence by pointing out aspects of Protestantism that may have encouraged science. Lutherans taught that Christ was 'really present' in nature as well as in the eucharist. Calvinists stressed that believers would do good works to confirm that they are among the 'elect'.

Protestants in general supported free enquiry and the freedom of the individual. The best-known interpretation of the rise of modern science in the seventeenth century stresses the role of the so-called Puritan ethic: the demand that nature should be studied systematically, rationally, and experimentally for the glory of God and the good of humankind.

WAS THE SCIENTIFIC REVOLUTION PROTESTANT?

Such theories face numerous problems. For example, the terms 'Protestant', 'Puritan', and 'Calvinist' do not mean exactly the same, and their meanings changed over time. Doing good works could easily have been a motive for scientific activity among Protestant groups whose doctrines were not Calvinistic. The 'glory of God' and the 'good of humankind' were not concepts unique to Puritans, or even to Protestants. Both occur, for example, in the writings of Ignatius of Loyola.

Thus, although it is widely held that Protestantism encouraged the birth of modern science, there is little agreement as to *how* it was involved. Some historians believe the Protestant emphasis on the priesthood of all believers significantly nurtured the growth of the scientific spirit. However, modern science cannot be traced simply to Protestant origins: Roman Catholic scientists did important work throughout the sixteenth and seventeenth centuries. Thomas Sprat gave no specifically Puritan or Protestant basis for science in his important *History of the Royal Society* (1667). The Royal Society, which had many Puritans as early members, was in fact open to men of every denomination. So also, it seems, was the scientific revolution.

JAMES R. MOORE

CHAPTER 30

REASON AND UNREASON
The rise of rationalism

The seventeenth and eighteenth centuries were an era of conflict, during which reason vied with unreason, though at the end of the day there was no agreement. There was at the same time also a retreat from reason. Some had a horror, not only of secular thinkers, but also of those in the church who set out their doctrines in a rational way. To the Pietists, what mattered was the personal devotional life. To the Quakers, even reformed theology, with its stress on the Bible and the ordered worship of the community, went too far; what mattered for them was the 'inner light' of the Spirit.

In everyday language, rationalism means everything is to be judged by reason. Bound up with this is the idea that, when this is done, belief in God and the supernatural will be swept away; we shall be left with nature and hard facts. But in the seventeenth century rationalism was not necessarily hostile to belief in God. There were various rationalist systems of thought, but common to all was belief in the rationality of the universe, and the power of reason to grasp it.

Engraving of the French philosopher and mathematician René Descartes (1596–1650).

© GEORGIOS KOLLIDAS/ DREAMSTIME.COM

DESCARTES

The first of the great rationalists was René Descartes (1596–1650), a mathematician of the first rank and a Roman Catholic, whose ideal in philosophy was to think rationally from first principles. He lived at a time when modern science was beginning to transform our view of the world, but this in itself presented a problem. Science relies on the evidence of our senses – what can be touched, seen, and measured – but how do we know that our senses can be relied upon? To answer this, Descartes turned to the formula: *Cogito ergo sum*, 'I think, therefore I am'.

Descartes was attempting to devise a philosophy that would answer the sceptics of his time. The 'New Pyrrhonists' (named after the ancient philosopher Pyrrho) were students of classical scepticism who applied the arguments of ancient scepticism to the great questions of their own day in the fields of science, religion, and philosophy, and who made doubt the basic principle in philosophy. When Descartes, too, resolved to doubt everything that he possibly could, he was playing the Pyrrhonists at their own game. He readily saw that there was one thing that he could not doubt: the fact that he was doubting. And if he was doubting, he must actually exist in order to doubt. In other words, 'I think, therefore I am.'

The formula *Cogito ergo sum* was not exactly new. It had been used by Augustine in answering the sceptics of his day. What was new was Descartes' use of it as the first principle of his philosophy, from which he went on to prove the existence of God, and to show that God – being good – would not allow us to be deceived in the right use of our minds and senses.

> What a vast distance there is between knowing God and loving him!
>
> BLAISE PASCAL

BLAISE PASCAL

Blaise Pascal (1623–62), one of the great thinkers of the West, excelled as mathematician, physicist, inventor, writer, and religious thinker. He was born in Clermont-Ferrand, France, and at an early age made original contributions to geometry and the calculus, and later worked on the theory of probability. At nineteen Pascal invented the first workable calculating machine, using a system of rotating discs – the basis of arithmetical machines until modern times. In physics, 'Pascal's Law' stated the principle that makes possible all modern hydraulic operations.

In 1654 Pascal had a 'second conversion', as the result of a mystical vision. He inscribed the details of his experience on a piece of parchment that he sewed into his coat. Pascal and his sister had become associated with the Jansenists in 1646, and in 1657 he published his *Provincial Letters*, a work of irony and satire written to support the Jansenists' demand for a re-emphasis on Augustine's doctrine of grace in the Catholic Church.

About 1658, Pascal set out to prepare an *Apology for the Christian Religion*, which was never completed. He left only a series of remarkable notes, later published as *Pensées (Thoughts)*, a classic of literature and apologetics, which puts the case for vital Christianity, against the rationalism of Descartes and the scepticism of the French writer Montaigne (1533–92).

Pascal wrote that God can be known through Jesus Christ by an act of faith, itself given by God. People's need for God is made evident by their

Blaise Pascal (1623–62), French mathematician and philosopher.
© GEORGIOS KOLLIDAS/DREAMSTIME.COM

misery apart from God. God may be known only by faith, though there is plentiful evidence to support belief: fulfilled prophecies, miracles, the witness of history, the self-authentication of Scripture. 'The heart has its reasons, which the reason does not know,' wrote Pascal.

PAUL BECHTEL

Although Descartes is widely regarded as the first modern philosopher, he took over the medieval proofs of the existence of God. He adapted Anselm's 'ontological argument': just as the sum of the three angles of a triangle equalling two right angles is included in the very idea of a triangle, so the existence of God is included in the idea of God. Descartes also took over Aquinas' 'cosmological argument', which argued back to a first cause. But whereas Aquinas had used the world to show the existence of God, Descartes used God to argue for the validity of our perceptions of the world.

From that day to this, philosophers have argued over *Cogito ergo sum*. Some have seen it as an attempt to deduce the existence of a person from the fact of thinking. But if so, it is like the rabbit in the conjuror's hat: the rabbit has to be there to begin with. The premise of the argument already contains the conclusion. However, the argument is best seen as an affirmation of personal existence. Some things in life cannot be doubted – even by the doubters – among them the fact that we exist. It is a basic, irremovable intuition.

Pyrrhonian scepticism left its mark on many thinkers of the age, including the sceptical Scottish philosopher David Hume. But, attracted as he was to scepticism, Hume pronounced thorough-going Pyrrhonism to be unworkable. Meanwhile Blaise Pascal produced a Christian answer to it in France, and in Holland Spinoza turned rationalism into a form of pantheism.

SPINOZA

Whereas Descartes remained an orthodox Catholic, Baruch Spinoza (1632–77) came of Jewish stock. His parents had migrated to Holland, which in the seventeenth century was a haven of toleration for intellectual refugees. But Spinoza soon found himself in conflict with his own Jewish rabbis, and was expelled from the synagogue for his unorthodoxy. In 1663 Spinoza published a testament of Descartes, set out in geometrical fashion; his posthumously published *Ethics* took the same form.

Spinoza has been described by turn as a hideous atheist and as God-intoxicated. In fact, he was a pantheist who combined features of both. He emphatically denied the existence of God over and above the world; at the same time, he believed there was only one substance – God, or nature. All reality is the manifestation of God: whether we say God or nature we are really talking about the same thing. To speak of God emphasizes the cause; to speak of nature emphasizes the end product.

Spinoza's pantheism was not the same as that of the later Romantic poets, although some of them drew intellectual inspiration from it. Rather, it was an elaborate system worked out in a geometrical manner from what he alleged were self-evident first principles. Whether it was as rational as Spinoza imagined is another matter. The first principles might have been clear definitions, but philosophers now recognize it is not enough to start with a clear definition, unless there is something that actually corresponds with it.

The rationalists made a double mistake. On the one hand, they thought that, if their first principles were rational enough, they were sound. On the other hand, they thought it was enough to proceed by rationally deducing one point from another. But in both instances – as the British empiricists pointed out – reality is not known by reason alone. Our knowledge has to be based on our experience of it.

LEIBNIZ

The third great thinker in the rationalist tradition was the German Protestant, Gottfried Wilhelm Leibniz (1646–1716), whose scientific work earned him honorary membership of the Royal Society in England. His view of reality was different again: he held that the universe is made up of an infinite number of *monads*, or simple substances without parts that are eternally active. These *monads* form an ascending series, from the lowest, which is next to nothing, to the highest, which is God. Leibniz used the ontological argument to prove the existence of God – the original, simple substance from which all others come.

BRITISH EMPIRICISM

Rationalism dominated continental European philosophy, but in Britain empiricism was the most significant philosophical movement. The term derives from the Greek word for experience. Though they had many differences, the empiricists all stressed the part played by experience in knowledge. In this they were reacting to, and correcting, European rationalism. The three leading British figures were Locke, Berkeley, and Hume.

LOCKE

John Locke (1632–1704) studied medicine at the University of Oxford in the heyday of the Puritans, but when the Commonwealth collapsed and Charles II was brought back as king, Locke found it prudent to live in Holland. He wrote various books on politics and apologetics, but his main philosophical work was *An Essay Concerning Human Understanding* (1690).

> The existence of one God is according to reason; the existence of more than one God contrary to reason; the resurrection of the dead, above reason.
>
> JOHN LOCKE, *AN ESSAY CONCERNING HUMAN UNDERSTANDING*

Locke pictured the human mind as a blank sheet (*tabula rasa*). Locke stated that there is only one way it get ideas and knowledge: through the experience of the senses. Reason has its part to play in judging ideas, and in interpreting the data fed to it by the senses. But reason cannot operate independently. It is what we see, touch, taste, hear, and smell that provides the basis of all knowledge.

If this is so, then Christian faith must likewise be based on experience. The world around us points to its origin in a wise, loving, and all-powerful God. The gospel is vindicated by the way in which Old Testament prophecy is fulfilled by Jesus and by the miracles that he performed. Miracles are like the credentials of an ambassador; they are proof of his authority. Because we accept the miracles of Jesus, we can trust the truth of his teaching about God. There are some things which accord with reason (for example, the existence of God). Other things are contrary to reason (for example, the existence of more than one God). But there are also things that are above reason (for example, the resurrection of Jesus). There are grounds for believing it, but human reason just cannot grasp it.

BERKELEY

George Berkeley (1685–1753), who went to Bermuda to establish a missionary college for the evangelism of America, was later made bishop of Cloyne in Ireland. Like Locke, he was interested in the problem of knowledge, but gave it a novel twist. He claimed that to exist means either to perceive or to be perceived; in other words, all reality is in the mind. It is not material.

Few thinkers have followed Berkeley in his non-material position. Dr Johnson's reply was to kick a stone and remark: 'Thus I refute Dr Berkeley.' But Berkeley would not have regarded this as a refutation; for all it would mean was that, in his mind, Dr Johnson was performing the act of kicking the stone. Most thinkers have viewed Berkeley's position as too improbable to be taken seriously. It makes the objects we perceive hollow; there is nothing behind them.

Berkeley's argument contains a novel proof of the existence of God. The continued existence of objects requires the continued existence of God, in order that he can perceive them and thus give them reality. On the other hand, it is not clear whether the objects that we perceive are the same as the objects that God perceives.

HUME

Both Locke and Berkeley believed in God. In Britain scepticism began with David Hume (1711–76), in his lifetime perhaps best known for his *History of England*. Hume's sceptical thought was embodied in such works as *A Treatise of Human Nature* (1739–40), *An Enquiry Concerning Human Understanding* (1748), and *Dialogues Concerning Natural Religion* (1752, published posthumously, in 1779).

Hume's scepticism extended to the whole range of human knowledge. He claimed it was impossible to demonstrate the existence of the soul or self, or whenever we look into ourselves we see only some feeling of pleasure or pain, but never the *self* as such. Hume also questioned the logic of speaking about cause and effect, insisting that all we can see is one event following another. We do not see the cause as such, but only the sequence of events.

In religion, he cast doubt on the old proofs for the existence of God, pronouncing the idea of a first cause to be useless. Miracles violate the laws of nature, and are therefore improbable. For, since 'a firm and unalterable experience' has established the laws of nature, the proof against miracles is as complete as any proof can be.

Hume has influenced many thinkers, from Kant in the eighteenth century to the logical positivists in the twentieth, and has become a kind of patron saint of scepticism. But how valid were his arguments? There is a sense in which what Hume says about the self is true. It cannot be seen directly, like an arm, a leg, or even a brain. But this is not the same as saying that Hume gets rid of the self altogether, for, when we try to look into ourselves, the self is active as the organizing subject of the action. In other words, in order to refute the self as an object, Hume has to make use of the self as a subject. What the argument shows is something of the peculiar nature of the self.

Similarly, Hume did not dispose of the idea of causation. The whole of our everyday experience of things – and the whole fabric of modern science – rests upon the principle that when certain things always follow other things under given conditions, it is proper to say that one causes the other. The idea of a law of science depends on the fact that things do not just happen at random, but that some things are causes and other things are effects. It was this very thing that Hume appealed to in his rejection of miracles.

Some of Hume's criticism of the arguments for the existence of God were just. A cause cannot be wholly known from its effect, and the first cause is hidden from us by myriads of other causes. Moreover, if we have an argument for God's existence from causation and another from design, we need another argument to show that the God in each case is one and the same. And we need a further argument to show that this God is the same as the God of Christian faith.

But to say all this is only to spotlight certain flaws in the way in which the existence of God has been argued. It does not settle once and for all whether God exists – still less does it settle the question of who God is.

Hume's critique of miracles made some telling points, but it was far from watertight. For when Hume talked about 'a firm and unalterable experience' establishing the laws of nature, he omitted to ask, 'Whose experience?' If we take a sample selection of experience only from those who have no experience of miracles, then we are bound to conclude that miracles have not been experienced. But if we include evidence of contrary cases, we cannot say that miracles are automatically ruled out. They may be unusual and contrary to common experience, but we cannot rule them out on the grounds that they are at variance with all experience.

DEISM

Rationalism and empiricism were by no means the only intellectual movements of the period. In its own day, Deism provoked much discussion, and – like both rationalism and empiricism – became increasingly hostile to the Christian faith. Today the word Deism suggests the 'absentee landlord' view of God – a God who originally made the world, but ever since has left it to its own devices. But the original Deism of the Englishman Lord Herbert of Cherbury (1583–1648) was an attempt to demonstrate the rationality of religious belief in God without appealing to the special revelation of the Christian faith.

This argument was taken a step further in such books as John Toland's *Christianity Not Mysterious* (1696) and Matthew Tindal's *Christianity as Old as the Creation* (1730), which argued that Christianity is really the religion of nature. Admittedly, the Christian faith includes certain beliefs that go beyond natural religion, such as the incarnation of God in Jesus Christ, but these were explained away as the work of superstitious priestcraft.

British Deists also attacked arguments based on fulfilled prophecy and miracles. Anthony Collins (1676–1729) claimed that the Old Testament prophecies did not really fit Jesus, and Thomas Woolston (1668–1733) wrote a series of bitter discourses on the miracles of Jesus, culminating in an attack on the resurrection, which he claimed was a fraud perpetrated by the disciples, who had in fact stolen the body of Jesus. Something of a martyr for his beliefs, Woolston was tried for blasphemy and sentenced to a year's imprisonment and a fine of £100. Unable to pay, he spent the remainder of his days in prison.

But there were less savage ways of replying to Deism. Thomas Sherlock (1678–1761), a bishop and best-selling Christian writer, took his cue from Woolston's trial to write *The Trial of the Witnesses of the Resurrection of Jesus* (1729), in which he put the New Testament witnesses in the dock. His book went on reprinting into the nineteenth century. Another opponent of Deism was Bishop Joseph Butler (1692–1752) whose *Analogy of Religion* (1736) argued that the evidence of nature and the testimony of the Christian faith both pointed in the direction of supernatural religion.

ROUSSEAU

Deism spread to the continent of Europe, where it again provoked a great debate. Among the thinkers who called themselves deists were Rousseau and Voltaire. Jean-Jacques Rousseau (1712–78) was a Frenchman of many talents: in turn a Protestant, a Catholic, and a deist. He invented a new system of musical notation, wrote an opera, several novels, and numerous studies of education and politics. Something of an enigma, Rousseau never ceased emphasizing human dignity, yet his own personal relationships were mean and sordid. His educational theories have left a lasting mark on modern progressive education, yet he deposited his five illegitimate children in an orphanage.

Rousseau was not unaware of his own shortcomings, and of those of the society around him, but blamed them all on civilization. People, if left to themselves, are noble and good. Rousseau's educational ideal was to keep children away from the corrupting influences of society and let them learn naturally what they want to learn. His ideal was the 'noble savage'. The child will naturally ask questions, and, if treated wisely, will virtually teach him- or herself.

Another of Rousseau's ideas that had far-reaching consequences was the 'social contract', expounded in his book of the same name (1762). In England, the divine right of kings had been overthrown by those who held that kings were bound by law and were not above the law. If they broke the law, they could be deposed. In France and other European countries, the divine right of kings was still maintained.

Rousseau put forward instead a radical and secular theory of government that has profoundly influenced revolutionary thinking ever since. Neither the laws nor the government of a state are appointed by God; they are based on the general will of the people governed. Society is based on a social contract to which its members consent. This contract is designed to combine individual freedom with just government in the interests of the majority. Such thinking paved the way for the American Declaration of Independence in 1776, and for the French Revolution in 1789.

VOLTAIRE

In religion, Rousseau claimed that he rejected the dogmas of the church and brought everything 'to the bar of conscience and of reason'. He professed faith in a Being behind all beings, whom he could feel, but who was a mystery lying beyond all rational thought. The god of the Frenchman François-Marie Arouet (1694–1778), alias Voltaire, was constructed on similar lines. God is to be adored and served – not argued over or made the object of institutional religion. Voltaire attacked the church with remorseless wit; he saw nothing in it but deceit and corruption.

Like Rousseau, Voltaire lived a colourful life, turning his hand to all kinds of literature. His major philosophical work was his *Philosophical Dictionary*, which consisted largely of articles he had written for Diderot's *Encyclopedia*. The latter work – intended to be a complete review of the arts and sciences – proved to be a powerful revolutionary force. Between 1751 and 1780, 35 volumes of the *Encyclopedia* appeared, expressing free thought, Enlightenment ideas, and revolutionary change.

LESSING

The work of the English deists was also known and discussed in Germany, where it resulted in a demand for an enlightened re-evaluation of the church and its teaching, and of culture and philosophy. One of the leading 'enlightened' thinkers was the dramatist and amateur theologian, Gotthold Ephraim Lessing (1729–81). While serving as librarian to the Duke of Brunswick at Wolfenbüttel, Lessing published the notorious *Wolfenbüttel Fragments*, claimed to be ancient documents found in the duke's archives. In fact they were the work of the recently deceased Hermann Samuel Reimarus (1694–1768), who took up the deists' view of Jesus, claiming the resurrection was a fraud invented by the disciples, who merely wanted to continue their easy way of life.

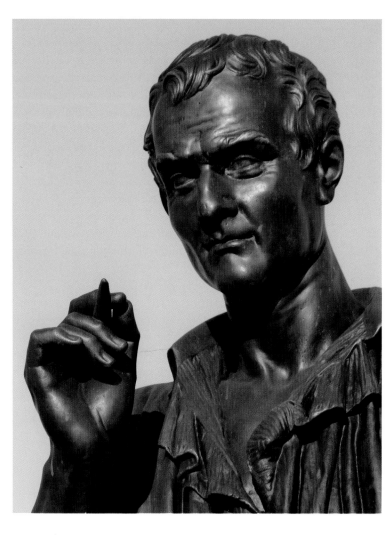

Bust of Jean-Jacques Rousseau by James Pradier, 1835, Rousseau Island, Geneva, Switzerland.
©ELENA DUVERNAY/ DREAMSTIME.COM

In the controversy that followed publication, Lessing tried to appear to sit on the fence, while pouring fuel on the fire as fast as he could. He argued that religion was not true because the apostles taught it; they taught it because it was true. He wrote that 'The accidental truths of history can never become proof for the necessary truths of reason.' Both points were in fact truisms. We cannot prove that two and two make four by appealing to history. But history does not give the same kind of truth as mathematics. Therefore Lessing was unwilling to base faith on history. At best history might embody truths; it does not provide the basis for truth.

In his play, *Nathan the Wise* (1779), Lessing expressed his ideas through the parable of the three rings: There was once a ring that gave its owner the gift of being loved by God and people. The owner of this ring had three sons whom he loved equally dearly. To resolve the dilemma of who should receive the ring upon his death, the owner had two exact replicas made. The three sons quarrelled as to which of them had the true ring, but a wise judge told them each to behave as if they possessed the authentic ring. Their behaviour would show which had the gift of being loved by God and people.

The three sons represent Judaism, Christianity, and Islam. Lessing's point is that the truth of religion cannot be settled by appeals to history. All religions are relative, and will be superseded one day by a universal religion. In the meantime, the enlightened person realizes all this, and proceeds to live according to good sense, in tolerance and harmony.

One of the difficulties about this enlightened position is that it assumes all religions are saying more or less the same thing, and that what happened in history is either relatively unimportant or unknowable. The enlightened thinkers imagined that they had superior knowledge – or that what they did not know was not worth knowing.

KANT

Enlightened thought reached its climax in the philosophy of Immanuel Kant, whose ideas dictated the course of much nineteenth-century philosophy and theology. For Kant, the human race's emergence from a self-imposed immaturity represented enlightenment. It was humanity come of age, casting aside all outside authorities, and bringing everything to the bar of human reason. The motto of enlightenment was, said Kant, *Sapere aude* – 'Dare to be wise!'

Although Kant wrote this some time after the American Declaration of Independence, those who framed the Declaration were strongly inclined in the same direction. They were not prepared to renounce God altogether – indeed, they appealed to God as the ultimate source of justification for the liberties they demanded. But their political philosophy had much in common with Rousseau. (The principal author, Thomas Jefferson (1743–1826), was a deist at heart, and owed much to English and French political theory.)

The appeal to self-evident truth to justify the basis of the Declaration had an ancestry that went back to Descartes:

> *We hold these truths to be self-evident, that all men are created equal, that they are endowed by their Creator with certain unalienable Rights, that among these are Life, Liberty and the pursuit of Happiness. That to secure these rights, Governments are instituted among Men, deriving their just powers from the consent of the governed. That whenever any Form of Government becomes destructive of these ends, it is the Right of the People to alter or to abolish it, and to institute new Government, laying its foundation on such principles and organizing its powers in such form, as to them shall seem most likely to effect their Safety and Happiness.*

Congress shall make no law respecting an establishment of religion or prohibiting the free exercise thereof.

FIRST AMENDMENT, *US CONSTITUTION*

The ideals which led to the separation of the United States of America from Great Britain came back into a French setting in the Statement of Human and Civil Rights agreed by the revolutionary French National Assembly in 1789, which also contains references to God though perhaps less strongly.

THE BREAK WITH RELIGION

Be that as it may, the two respective governments broke with religion. The First Amendment to the American Constitution (1791) laid down that there should be neutrality in religion: it allowed free speech and right of assembly, but laid down that 'Congress shall make no law respecting an establishment of religion'. The Constitution rejected all religious tests for office-holders, and the United States of America was the first modern secular state. Christianity (and other religions) flourished in America because of — or, some would say, in spite of — the neutral position of the government and Constitution.

In France it was different. It soon became clear that the liberties granted to all in the Statement did not extend to the church. 'Liberty, Equality, Fraternity' did not include those who had supported the old regime. For a time the church was outlawed, and a 'religion of reason' was introduced. But, although the religious orders were suppressed and church property was confiscated, the Catholic Church was too strong to be crushed.

FREEMASONRY

When Napoleon came to power, a 'Concordat' was negotiated in 1801 by which the church surrendered its former property, and the state undertook to subsidize the clergy. In the often bitter relations of church and state, Freemasonry played a crucial part. The Catholic Church and Freemasons were deadly rivals, an antagonism that was by no means confined to France. Many of the enlightened people who wanted to escape from the old ways and find a new outlook, guided by reason and humanity, were enthusiastic Freemasons. Figures as diverse as Lessing, Mozart, and George Washington were Freemasons.

QUIETISM

Alongside those who stressed the role of reason, others sought meaning and reality elsewhere. In seventeenth-century France the Quietists, such as the Spanish priest Miguel de Molinos (c. 1628–97), mystic Madame Guyon (1648–1717), and Archbishop François Fénelon (1651–1715), condemned human effort, believing that, to attain perfection, people must be passive, so far abandoning themselves to God that they do not even care for their own salvation. This state can be reached in prayer, and when it is truly achieved, sin is impossible. Temptation may come, and even compel the Quietist to perform actions which would be sinful in others; but because they no longer have wills of their own, the actions are not sins. Quietism was condemned by Pope Innocent XI in 1687.

Jansenism, another seventeenth-century movement within the Roman Catholic Church, was also condemned. It was named after Cornelius Jansen (1585–1638) whose work, *Augustinus* (1640), revived a form of Augustine's theology. Jansen claimed it is impossible to obey God's commandments without special grace; at the same time, it is also impossible to resist God's grace. Thus logically, humanity is a victim of natural or supernatural determinism, its actions determined either by nature or grace.

Jansenist teachings were accompanied by a harsh, moral rigorism. They were first condemned by Pope Innocent X in 1653, although the Jansenists claimed they had been condemned for ideas they did not in fact hold. In 1668 they were persuaded to modify their position. Final condemnation came in the bull *Unigenitus* issued by Pope Clement XI in 1713, after which many French Jansenists found refuge from persecution in the Netherlands.

COLIN BROWN

THE REASONABLENESS OF CHRISTIANITY

Beginning with the speeches of Peter and Paul in the book of Acts, Christians have engaged in apologetics, defending their faith from hostile attacks, and commending it through argument to unbelievers. In giving 'a reason for the hope' that is in them, Christians have often appealed to natural theology, looking for a basis in innate or 'natural' human reason for accepting specific theological beliefs. Origen, Anselm, and Aquinas are among the better-known apologists who used natural theology in their arguments.

NATURAL THEOLOGY

At no time in history was natural theology more widely used to defend the Christian faith than in the eighteenth century. At no time did it seem so important to make Christianity appear 'reasonable'. There were three main causes for this. First, Descartes, Spinoza, and Leibniz had exalted reason and doubt in building their influential philosophies. Second, Isaac Newton in his *Principia Mathematica* (1687) had set out laws that appeared to prove that the universe was divinely ordered, encouraging the belief that human enquiries into nature, unaided by Scripture, could demonstrate the power and wisdom of the Creator. Third, a century of appalling religious conflicts – the Thirty Years' War in Germany, the persecution of Jansenists and Huguenots in France, the English Civil War – had created a thirst for tolerance and a desire to find doctrines on which everyone could agree.

'The reasonableness of Christianity' – the title of John Locke's revolutionary book, published in 1695 – became the central theme of theology for more than a century. The fundamental truths of the Christian religion were claimed to be few and simple, intelligible to the plainest of people. The immense size of the universe, the stability of its bodies, and the simplicity of its laws; the position of the earth, the usefulness of its resources, and the variety of its inhabitants; and the detail, order, and symmetry of every form of life – all witnessed clearly to God's existence, his wisdom and goodness, his purposes, providence, and power. They witnessed, in other words, to a God of whom it was probable that a special revelation had been given. And this revelation – the Bible – confirmed that Christianity was basically reasonable.

From the outset, the English specialized in using natural theology in apologetics. The 'Cambridge Platonists' – among whom were Ralph Cudworth, Henry More, and John Wilkins – made important contributions in the last decades of the seventeenth century. Their followers, the so-called 'Latitudinarians' – including Edward Stillingfleet, Bishop of Worcester, and John Tillotson, Archbishop of Canterbury – wrote in a rather more rationalistic manner. In 1691 Robert Boyle (1627–91), a chemist and natural theologian, founded a lectureship 'for proving the Christian Religion, against notorious Infidels, viz. Atheists, Theists, Pagans, Jews, and Mahometans....' The Boyle Lectures continued for many years.

But the natural theologians so neglected the teaching of the Bible that in time some came to argue that its distinctive doctrines were either superfluous or false. They claimed that the parts of the Bible that agree with natural theology are simply unnecessary; the parts that contradict natural theology – the myths, miracles, and priestly mumbo-jumbo – are untrue. The Christian religion consists solely of what nature and reason teach unaided: belief in the worship of God, the repentance of sin, the practice of virtue, and the expectation of punishment and rewards after death.

Those who held such views were known as deists. Their number greatly increased in England and continental Europe during the first half of the eighteenth century. John Toland, the author of *Christianity Not Mysterious* (1696), was patronized by German nobility. Lord Bolingbroke, a witty and frivolous popularizer, won the admiration of Voltaire. And when Anthony Collins and the 'doubting Thomases', Woolston, Morgan, and Chubb, published their free-thinking works, Matthew Tindal gave deists everywhere a new 'Bible': his *Christianity as Old as the Creation* (1730).

Orthodox Christians responded to the deists in various ways. Many continued with ever more detailed elaborations of natural theology, particularly using the argument from design. In England, John Ray's *Wisdom of God Manifested in the Works of Creation* (1691) passed through numerous editions, while in France, Abbé Pluche and J. B. Bullet produced similar works between 1730 and 1770. Meanwhile, in Germany the arguments were taken to extraordinary lengths by J. A. Fabricius in his *Water-Theology* (1734), and by F. C. Lesser in his *Stone-Theology* (1735), *Insect-Theology* (1740), and *Shell-Theology* (1744).

Other Christians chose to defend the Bible by first showing that its authors were reliable and honest, and then using the evidence of miracle and prophecy to show that orthodox beliefs were reasonable. The older work of the Dutch jurist Hugo Grotius (1583–1645) was useful in this regard. The controversy also produced some classics of its own – for example, Thomas Sherlock's *Trial of the Witnesses of the Resurrection* (1729), and Nathaniel Lardner's 14-volume masterpiece, *The Credibility of the Gospel History* (1727–55). The literature on 'Christian evidences' grew and remained in fashion until the mid-nineteenth century.

The deists were best combated by writers who questioned and reinterpreted the role of 'reason'. In *The Case of Reason* (1731), William Law (1686–1761) showed it was false to suppose that God always behaves according to strictly human rationality. Bishop George Berkeley, in *Alciphron* (1732), argued that God's ideas, not matter, are what really exist; therefore all beliefs which separate the human reason from the divine are faulty. Joseph Butler (1692–1752) all but ended the controversy with his famous *Analogy of Religion* (1736), in which he argued that reason justifies only probable inferences about the world; and that both nature and revelation are beset with difficulties that make inferences about them merely probable. Therefore both natural and revealed religion can be accepted on the same grounds as from the same Author.

The difficulties that Butler highlighted could become the grounds for *denying* the divine authorship of both nature and the Bible – but this was not yet so obvious as it would be later. The sceptical philosopher David Hume had little effect upon his own century; his *Dialogues Concerning Natural Religion* appeared only after he died, in 1777. Similarly Kant's critical philosophy, contained in his *Critique of Pure Reason* (1781) and *Critique of Practical Reason* (1788), influenced the nineteenth rather than the eighteenth century. Writers of natural theology, cautioned by Butler, continued to follow the lines laid down in the deistic controversy, their work culminating in the most popular apologetics texts ever written: William Paley's *View of the Evidences of Christianity* (1794) and *Natural Theology* (1802).

JAMES R. MOORE

CHAPTER 31

THE RUSSIAN CHURCH: 1500–1900

The alliance between the Russian Church and the state, which was close from the time of Prince Vladimir's conversion in 988, became especially strong after 1500. As the sixteenth century opened, controversy raged within the church regarding its role in society. On the one hand, Nil Sorsky (or Nilus of Sora, c. 1433–1508), leader of the Russian medieval movement, called on the church to minister to society from a position of poverty, independent of secular, political concerns. On the other hand, Joseph Volotsky (or 'Joseph of Volokolamsk', 1439/40–1515) wanted church and state united, with the rich church supporting, and supported by, the ruler. Nil's supporters were known as 'Non-Possessors'; Joseph's as 'Possessors'.

VICTORY FOR THE POSSESSORS

For obvious reasons, the state favoured the Possessors and severely persecuted the mystical Non-Possessors, but in doing so it created fateful consequences for the Russian Church. The intense devotional emphasis of Nil and his 'Transvolga Hermits' receded into the background; following Joseph, the church became a wealthy landowner, holding as much as one-third of all property in Russia.

In line with the claim of 'Moscow, The Third Rome', the prince of Muscovy assumed the title 'Czar', a variation of 'Caesar'. Ivan IV, the Terrible, (r. 1533–84) was the first ruler to be crowned formally as successor to the Roman emperors, 'Czar of all the Russians'. Consistent with the theory that assumed there could be only one Christian emperor, the Russians asserted that Moscow deserved to have a patriarch, the highest office in the Orthodox Church. Consequently, in 1589, the head of the Russian Church was raised to the rank of patriarch, equal to the patriarchs of Antioch, Alexandria, Jerusalem, and Constantinople.

TIME OF TROUBLES

The first decades of the Moscow patriarchate coincided with a period of political disorder in Muscovy. The dynasty came to an end with the death of Ivan IV's son. Russia plunged into the terrible 'Time of Troubles' (1598–1613), which ended with the election of the Romanov royal house. The patriarchs played a leading role in shepherding Russia through the chaos; Patriarch Germogen (or Hermogenes, c. 1530–1612) inspired national unity in the worst years of the troubles, until he was murdered by the Polish conquerors of Moscow. His successor, Filaret (r. 1619–33), father of the first Romanov Czar, Michael, completely dominated his weak son. The patriarch called himself 'The Great Sovereign', and sat on the throne beside his son, signing state papers jointly with the Czar. Thus the Russian Church and state became as one.

Material concerns sorely sapped the spiritual vitality of the Russian Church. Several sensitive, devout young men became disturbed by this, and soon a circle of 'Zealots of Faith' formed around Michael's son, the future Czar Alexis (r. 1645–76). Travelling throughout the land, they called clergy and lay people alike to sincere spiritual devotion. Although united by the desire to see error and corruption rooted out of the church, the circle of Zealots was soon broken by disputes over the way to correct the abuses.

SCHISM

When Alexis became Czar, he arranged for the election of his fellow-Zealot, Nikon, as patriarch in 1652. Nikon immediately used the power of his office to order changes in the forms of ritual which, he thought, the Russians employed wrongly. For example, he declared that the sign of the cross must be made with three fingers raised, not two – as had been the Russian Practice; the three-fold *Alleluia* was to be sung in worship, not the two-fold.

Nikon's former associates objected that his reforms were not what was needed to purify the church. They called, instead, for reform of the moral and spiritual laxness that had crept in at all levels of the church, from parishioners to bishops. Moreover, they accused Nikon of introducing further error into the church, rather than correction. Led by the archpriest Avvakum (1620/1–82), they rejected Nikon's liturgical reforms. When the patriarch used the power of the state to enforce his changes, the Russian Church split into two parts. Avvakum and his followers were imprisoned and exiled; from prison, Avvakum wrote his *Autobiography*, a landmark in Russian literature that deserves a place second only to Augustine's *Confessions*.

When Avvakum was finally burned at the stake in 1682, the schism was complete. Large numbers of ordinary believers, who had been spiritually awakened by the fervent preaching of the Zealots, readily followed their leaders into openly opposing the official church. Thousands of these 'Old Ritualists', or 'Old Believers', died in fires lit either by state agents or by themselves. They were ready to die because they believed the end of the world was near: the liturgical changes clearly demonstrated to them that this was the case. Was not Moscow the third, and last, Rome? If it deserted Orthodoxy – that is 'true worship' – had not the reign of Antichrist begun? To understand the extreme reactions of the schismatics, it is important to remember that the Russians attached great significance to the external forms of worship.

Russian liturgical practices had diverged from those in the Orthodox churches that lay under the political sway of the Ottoman Empire. Nikon declared that the Greeks – not the Russians – had preserved the original, and therefore correct, forms of worship. Moreover, he reckoned that if Russian practice was made to conform with that of the subjugated churches, it would allow the Russians to lead all Orthodoxy, and perhaps even permit Russia to liberate the suppressed peoples.

St Basil's Cathedral, on Red Square, Moscow, also known as The Cathedral of the Protection of Most Holy Theotokos on the Moat and Pokrovsky Cathedral, was built by Ivan the Terrible between 1555 and 1561. The church was confiscated and later secularized by the Soviet Union, and in 2012 remained the property of the Russian Federation.

TIM DOWLEY ASSOCIATES

THE MOST HOLY SYNOD

The schism profoundly weakened the power of the church over against that of the state. When Patriarch Nikon attempted to claim the title of 'Great Sovereign', as his predecessors had done, Czar Alexis had him removed from office to ensure that the church remained under the state. Alexis' son, Peter the Great, abolished the office of patriarch altogether in 1721, replacing the patriarchate with the Most Holy Synod. The Synod consisted of a board of bishops, which supervised church affairs, and which was, in turn, supervised by a secular government official, the Procurator General, appointed by the Czar.

The Russian Orthodox Church thus became little more than a government department for the remaining 200 years of the existence of the Czarist state. The 'Ecclesiastical Regulation' creating the Synod obliged any priest who discovered, in the confessional, evidence of treason or anti-government plans, to pass on such information to the police.

Peter's innovations made significant changes in Russian religious life, confirming Old Ritualists' suspicions that Antichrist ruled in Russia. As a result, some Old Believers withdrew into communities of like-minded believers. Because of their discipline, frugality, and industry, these communities soon became prosperous, helping create the basis of Russian economic development and expansion to the north and east. Some Old Believers concluded that, under the rule of Antichrist, the succession of the true priesthood had ceased on earth. Thus the schismatics divided into 'priestly' and 'priestless' groups, both of which continue to exist to the present. Peasant revolts in Russia, notably that led by Yemelyan Pugachev (also known as the Cossack Rebellion, 1773–74), were fuelled by Old Ritualist opposition to the Czarist state and church.

The Synodal church, by pressing its claim as leader of Orthodox Christianity, became an instrument of Russian imperialism. Under Catherine the Great (r. 1762–96), the treaty ending Russia's aggressive war against the Turks in 1774 recognized the Czar's right to intervene in the internal affairs of the Ottoman Empire on behalf of the Orthodox subjects of the Sultan.

As a result of Peter the Great's innovations, a split appeared in the official Orthodox church between the upper, 'black' clergy, bishops, and monks, and the lower, 'white' parish clergy. The former, who sometimes received lavish support from the state, became enmeshed in politics; the latter were frequently extremely poor, compelled to earn their living through working in the fields, or charging fees for the sacraments and prayers. Generally they were poorly educated, and were obliged to report social discontent to the state. As a result, the Russian clergy gained a miserable reputation.

The church suffered yet further at the hands of the state when Catherine ordered that church and monastery lands should become state property. The church thereby lost most of its property to the state and, subsequently, over three-quarters of its annual income.

In these circumstances, Russian society became a fertile field for the growth of sectarian movements. Many Russians sought satisfaction for their religious needs outside the church, which they felt to be unspiritual – even hostile to their interests. Some turned to mystical Protestantism and Freemasonry. Opposition to Orthodoxy also often assumed bizarre forms: *Khlysty* ('Flagellants'), *Skoptsy* ('Castrates'), *Dukhobors* ('Spirit-Wrestlers'), and *Molokans* ('Milk Drinkers').

Bishop Mercury celebrates the Russian Orthodox liturgy in the Vysokopetrovsky Monastery, Moscow, probably founded in the 1320s.
© ALEKSEY ANASHKIN/ DREAMSTIME.COM

RUSSIAN DEVOTION

It is perhaps surprising that religious devotion could survive in Russian Orthodoxy. Nevertheless, the church can point to such leaders as Tikhon Zadonsky (Tikhon of Zadonsk, 1724–83) and Seraphim of Sarov (1759–1833). Tikhon's humility and wisdom have been immortalized in Dostoevsky's portrait of Father Zosima in *The Brothers Karamazov*. Seraphim revived monasticism in Russia as a source of godly advice and aid for ordinary Russian believers. The most notable outpost of spirituality in Russia was the famous hermitage of Optino, to which, among thousands of other pilgrims, the great writers Gogol, Dostoevsky, and Tolstoy travelled. There was a great revival in the nineteenth-century Russian Church, accompanied by a mushrooming of church-backed educational institutions, and by a new enthusiasm for missionary work, particularly in China, Japan, and North America.

The devout Czar Alexander I sponsored the creation, in 1812, of the Russian Bible Society, which began to translate the Scriptures into the ordinary Russian language. Although the Society's work was temporarily interrupted by Nicholas I's prohibition of the circulation of Russian Scriptures, after 1863 the Scriptures became widely available to the Russian people.

It was also in the nineteenth century that two of Russia's greatest original religious thinkers appeared – both laymen. Alexis Khomyakov (1804–60) put forward a doctrine of Christian community that suggested religious authority rested in the entire body of the church, rather than in the papacy or the Bible. Vladimir Solovyov (1853–1900) proclaimed the idea of 'godmanhood', that God and man were united through spiritual participation in the incarnated *Logos*. Both men viewed Russia as God's appointed teacher for the world, pointing the way to the ecumenical unity of all Christians.

PAUL D. STEEVES

FURTHER READING

Meic Pearse, *The Age of Reason: From the Wars of Religion to the French Revolution 1570–1789*, Oxford, 2006.

W. R. Ward, *The Protestant Evangelical Awakening*, Cambridge, 1992.

E. Gordon Rupp, *Religion in England 1688–1791*, Oxford, 1986.

Owen Chadwick, *The Popes and the European Revolution*, Oxford, 1981.

STUDY QUESTIONS

1. How did Jesuit missionaries evangelize?

2. In what ways did Pietists contribute to the Awakening?

3. One historian has argued that the rise of Methodism helped prevent an English revolution. Do you agree?

4. What were the causes and results of schism in the Russian church?

5. Why did Christian missions expand in this period?

6. What impact did the Age of Reason have upon the church?

7. What was the legacy of John and Charles Wesley respectively to the church?

8. Why do so many well-known hymns date from this period?

9. Assess the influence and importance of Jonathan Edwards.

10. Is it useful to defend Christianity as 'reasonable'?

6 Cities and Empires

1789–1914

Summary

The French Revolution saw Christianity publicly displaced from French society. Although it did not achieve the permanent removal of Christianity from the nation, it created an atmosphere of instability. Revolutionary movements throughout Europe sought to repeat the success of their French counterparts, creating serious difficulties for the Catholic Church in many parts of Europe, especially Italy.

There was a surge of Protestant missionary activity from Britain during the closing years of the eighteenth century. The Baptist Missionary Society, the London Missionary Society, and Church Missionary Society all played a major role in planting Christianity in Africa, India, and Oceania. American missionary societies also played important roles in establishing Christianity in various regions of the world, especially Korea.

The churches of late nineteenth-century Europe and the United States could not ignore the sweeping new problems caused by the rapidly spreading Industrial Revolution, and particularly the rapid rise in the numbers of workers crammed into the newly industrialized cities of such countries as Britain, France, and Germany. One major response to these problems was socialism and Marxism.

Science and religion seemed to draw further apart with the publication of Charles Darwin's landmark works, dividing Christians between those who accepted his views and their implications and those who rejected them. Similarly, the new geology and the wider application of scientific methods to society also created new tensions. During the 1840s, the German philosopher Ludwig Feuerbach (1804–72) argued that the idea of God was simply a projection of the human mind.

CHAPTER 32

EUROPE IN REVOLT
Church and State in the Nineteenth Century

At the end of the eighteenth century revolution was in the air. In 1776, the North American colonists declared their independence from Britain. A dozen years later, revolution erupted in France, shattering a monarchy ruling by divine right. These events set the scene for the spread of revolution in Europe in the nineteenth century. The horrors of the French Revolution, and the destructive wars that followed it, also fuelled a strong conservative reaction. Much of the nineteenth century was characterized by the battle of ideas between these forces.

A second revolutionary force transformed the economy of much of Europe. This was the Industrial Revolution, which began in Britain late in the eighteenth century, and spread to Germany and France in the nineteenth century. Industry attracted working people into the growing urban centres, and as a result many injustices appeared, often leading to strong demands for political reform or revolution. These social changes also helped popularize nationalism, the belief that a country should be defined by the cultural or linguistic make-up of its people, rather than by the extent of an empire's conquests.

During this period of immense change, the church often found itself at the centre of the war of ideas. Many church leaders sought to resist the changes – or ignore them – while others embraced them; but eventually Christianity was forced to confront the new world and adapt to it.

TO THE BASTILLE!
On 14 July 1789, a Parisian mob attacked the great prison of the Bastille, a hated symbol of oppressive rule. The storming of the Bastille is today remembered as the totemic event of the French Revolution, but the consequences were felt throughout Europe, by state, church, and people for much of the century that followed.

The French Bourbon monarchy had derived its strength from an autocratic system of government known as absolutism, in which the king ruled alone, without the Estates General (the French parliament) which had not sat since 1614. As Louis XIV (1638–1715) is famously said to have remarked, 'l'état, c'est moi' ('I am the state'). Aside from the monarchy, the church was the most important institution in France, a country where Catholicism had an official monopoly on faith, and where religious dissent was violently suppressed. Privileged insiders – wealthy members of the nobility, senior churchmen, and a few others – administered the state largely in their own interests, imposing punitive taxation on the poor whilst frequently avoiding it themselves. By the 1780s, France was in crisis. Huge debts had been incurred to fund foreign wars, including – ironically – support for the American colonists in their own fight for liberty. France was broke, and her people impatient for change.

During the eighteenth century, much that had previously been taken for granted, including both absolutism and religion, came under attack from thinkers of the

Enlightenment. Voltaire (1694–1778) argued fiercely for political and religious liberty. After visiting Britain, he wrote favourably of 'the only people on earth who have been able to prescribe limits on the power of kings'. In 1763 he published the *Traité sur la tolérance*, a plea for tolerance of religious minorities, in response to the notorious, brutal execution of Jean Calas, a Toulouse Calvinist convicted of murdering his son, apparently to prevent his conversion to Catholicism, despite strong evidence pointing to suicide.

The Enlightenment thinkers were not writing only for the privileged few; many of their ideas were widely disseminated. Perhaps as much as one third of the population of France at this time could read, and there was nothing to stop these people from reading aloud to the other two-thirds. Many *philosophes* were persecuted for their efforts (Voltaire himself spent time in the Bastille), and though much of their work was officially banned, it was impossible to prevent the spread of books and journals printed across the border in the Netherlands or Switzerland. This was not simply a threat to the French state, but also to the Catholic Church, which had traditionally enjoyed considerable power over education and public information.

THE CONSTITUTIONAL REVOLUTION

Unable to deal with France's problems alone, Louis XVI (r. 1774–92), was in 1789 finally forced to call the Estates General, which had traditionally sat as three houses: the clergy, the nobility, and the Third Estate (everyone else). A majority of the clergy representatives elected in 1789 were ordinary parish priests, many of whom sympathized more with the peasantry than with their bishops. Some of these priests joined the Third Estate representatives in breaking away to establish themselves as the National Assembly, sitting as a single united chamber, which the king had little choice but to recognize. Soon nobility was abolished and the Declaration of the Rights of Man – which guaranteed freedom of conscience and of religion – was established. The tenets of the old order were fast being wiped away.

The extensive lands of the church were soon taken into public ownership, to provide the state with much needed funds and, later, monastic institutions were abolished. In July 1790, the Assembly passed the Civil Constitution of the Clergy, which redrew diocesan boundaries, almost halved the number of bishops, and insisted that priests – at all levels – must be elected by the people. Most controversially, priests were also required to swear an oath of allegiance to the French Constitution rather than to the pope. Since 1516 French kings had enjoyed the right to appoint bishops, and since the 1680s Gallicanism – the doctrine denying papal power over temporal matters, and insisting on the right of church councils to contradict the pope – had been widely accepted in France, yet these new changes were extremely divisive. Nearly half the priests of France refused to take the oath, and many fled the country. The issue became one of the major causes of rebellion against the revolution in conservative regions such as the Vendée and Normandy.

THE TEMPLE OF REASON

This internal opposition to the revolution became significant, and a wave of paranoia swept the revolutionary leadership. Figures such as the warmongering Jacques-Pierre Brissot (1754–93) hoped that war with Catholic Austria – a dangerous external threat – would unite the country and silence dissidents. As war dragged on, the regime – now led by the radical Jacobin faction — began to pursue threats real and perceived with increasing ferocity. The king himself was sent to the guillotine in January 1793, and during the Reign of Terror of 1793–4 thousands of others were executed.

During the Terror, attempts were made to obliterate Christianity in France. A new calendar was introduced, which dated years from the start of the Republic rather than from the birth of Christ, and which did not provide for Sundays. Priests — whether they had taken the constitutional oath or not — were considered particularly suspect, and a large number were compelled to renounce their orders. In many areas churches were desecrated, and in Paris, the Cathedral of Notre Dame was renamed the Temple of Reason. In the spring of 1794, a new patriotic religion — the Cult of the Supreme Being — was introduced by the Jacobin leader, Maximilian Robespierre (1758–94), who argued that this bizarre, institutionalized Deism was inspired by Rousseau, though it is doubtful whether the *philosophe* would have approved.

Before long, others fearing — literally — for their heads, deposed Robespierre, bringing the excesses of the Terror to an end. Until Napoleon Bonaparte (1769–1821) seized power in 1799, France remained virtually ungovernable.

A POWERLESS POPE?

One of Napoleon's first acts was to restore normal relations with the papacy. It was clear that the revolution had been undermined by its persecution of the church, which still retained huge support in the country at large, and Napoleon was happy to take advantage of this to help consolidate his power. Under the new concordat with Pius VII (r. 1800–23), Napoleon secured grudging assent to the revolution, in exchange for state payment of the clergy. He undermined his new favour with the Catholic Church however by subsequently introducing state payment for Protestant ministers.

Equestrian statue of Napoleon Bonaparte by Emmanuel Frémiet, Laffrey, France.
© ELENA DUVERNAY/ DREAMSTIME.COM

Napoleon's imperial ambitions took him to war with much of Europe during the first decade of the nineteenth century. In December 1804, Pius VII reluctantly presided over Napoleon's coronation as emperor at Notre Dame. After the pope had anointed the new emperor, Napoleon placed the crown on his own head, in an act designed to humiliate the pontiff. Relations with the Vatican remained tense, as Pius refused to acknowledge Napoleon's temporal supremacy over the Papal States. The emperor responded by occupying Rome and having the pope arrested; the pope countered by excommunicating him, and was then moved more or less at Napoleon's whim between Savona, Florence, Grenoble, Avignon, and Nice. These indignities continued until 1814, when Pius was finally restored to the Vatican.

After Napoleon's final defeat in 1815, the Catholic Church was in turmoil and needed to re-establish itself in Europe. The papacy was determined to reassert orthodoxy and its own authority against both the forces of Enlightenment and those who sought to diminish Rome's position within the church. The Jesuits, suspended in 1773, were revived in 1814 to play their part in this work. At the same time, there was a revival in Ultramontanism (literally, 'beyond the mountains'). Ultramontanists recognized the authority of the pope in Rome and the southern side of the Alps, and were militantly loyal to the pope as the supreme authority in matters of faith and practice. Throughout the nineteenth century a struggle persisted in the French Church between Ultramontanists and the Gallican nationalists.

In Germany similarly, a Catholic party stood for the equivalent of Gallicanism, but was there known as Febronianism, arising from the writings of the Bishop of Trier, Johann Nikolaus von Hontheim (1701–90). Writing in 1763, under the pseudonym of 'Justinius Febronius', he argued that the keys of the kingdom of God had been committed to the entire church, not only to Peter and his successors. Consequently church councils, not the pope, were the primary source of authority.

> Without the pope there can be no church, without the church no Christianity, and without Christianity no religion and no society …
>
> LAMENNAIS

Despite these divisions, Ultramontanism gained ascendancy in most Catholic countries. The Ultramontane party in France was eloquently represented by the 'three prophets of traditionalism': Joseph de Maistre (1754–1821), Louis de Bonald, and Hugues Felicité Robert de Lamennais. De Maistre experienced the invasion of Savoy by the revolutionary French, which awakened in him a strong spirit of conservatism. His Ultramontane ideas are most clearly set out in *Du pape* ('On the Pope', 1819), where he argued that society required a central authority to achieve cohesion, and that two pillars of such authority were the papacy and the monarchy.

ROUTES TO RENEWAL

The Enlightenment, and the confusion of the Revolutionary Wars, provoked a new wave of popular pietism in much of Europe. At the same time, many of the continent's monarchs felt that their only hope lay in reasserting their divinely-ordained rule and the authority of the church.

At the Congress of Vienna in 1815, the great powers settled the borders and governments of the new Europe. The map they drew – dominated by empires and ancient royal dynasties – showed their desire to carry on as though the Revolution had never happened. In the same way, Russia, Prussia, and Austria formed a new 'Holy Alliance' to control international relations by 'the sublime truths which the Holy Religion teaches'. In reality, the alliance was a reactionary bloc determined to preserve a deeply conservative vision of Christian statehood, if necessary by repressive means.

One inevitable result of this new/old Europe was that in many areas, long-established religious communities were treated as unwelcome minorities. Much of Poland, for example, was officially a kingdom – albeit one with the Russian Czar as king – with a parliament, the *Sejm*, containing seats for Catholic clergy. The *Sejm* was, however, suspended for much of the 1820s, and the kingdom was formally subsumed into Russia after an uprising in 1830–31. The Jesuits had been expelled from Russia in 1820 and the Polish Catholic Church was now permitted no contact with Rome.

Between 1815 and 1848 a series of popular religious awakenings occurred throughout Protestant Europe. The awakening (*Réveil*) in French-speaking Europe had its origins in Geneva, in the ministry of the Scot, Robert Haldane (1764–1842). In Denmark, Nicolaj F. S. Grundtvig (1783–1872) initiated a pietistic movement by openly opposing liberal theology. Revival in Sweden resulted from the ministry in Stockholm of a Scottish Methodist preacher, George Scott (1804–74). In Norway the awakening was largely a lay movement, connected with Hans Nielsen Hauge (1771–1824). These revival movements were not directly related to each other, and mainly involved lay Christians.

In Prussia, concerns about a number of popular independent sects led to rigorous government surveillance. Friedrich Wilhelm III used the tercentenary of the Reformation in 1817 to decree the union of the Lutheran and Reformed Churches, in the hope of arresting the development of such sects, and to provide a united front against rationalism. By the 1830s, though, he had simply provoked opposition from Lutheran and Reformed alike, leading to a schism in Lutheranism. Many of these 'Old Lutheran' communities emigrated to Australia and North America.

During this period, the cultural movement known as Romanticism became dominant in most of Europe. In part a reaction to the Enlightenment and the excesses of the French Revolution, and in part in response to growing industrialization, Romanticism stressed beauty, passion, and humanity's union with nature. The movement was later to exert a strong influence on emerging nationalist movements in many countries. In France, François-René de Chateaubriand's *Génie du christianisme* ('Genius of Christianity', 1802) presented a powerful argument for Christianity, based on the aesthetic values of the religion.

GOD AND THE PEOPLE

In spite of the strength of Ultramontanism, between 1815 and 1848 the Catholic Church was never free from conflict with political liberals. Some now sought to reshape the church in a context compatible with the emerging liberal nationalism. Lamennais, for example, gradually moved away from his earlier hopes for an alliance between Ultramontanism and royalism, and now used his newspaper *L'Avenir* (founded 1830) to promote freedom from the state for the church. *L'Avenir* rejected the divine right of kings and advocated popular sovereignty. Pope Gregory XVI (r. 1831–46) condemned the teachings of Lamennais and *L'Avenir* in his encyclical *Mirari Vos* (1832).

The Catholic Church's most significant tensions with liberalism arose during the Italian *Risorgimento* (literally, 'resurrection'), between 1815 and 1870. This issue was complicated because of the pope's continued dual role as both spiritual leader and as secular ruler of the Papal States in central Italy, part of a patchwork of small states ruled by rival dynasties. Any moves towards either unity or liberalism in Italy were quickly and thoroughly suppressed by the papacy, Austria, and France. Around 1820, a force of dedicated democratic revolutionaries, the *Carbonari*, appeared in Italy, stirring up small uprisings in Sardinia, Naples, and Piedmont, put down each time by Austria. Giuseppe Mazzini (1805–72), one of their leaders, and his compatriots swore to unify Italy on the basis of 'God and the people'.

In Spain too, the Catholic Church allied itself to conservatives. In 1833, the reactionary *apostolicos* – an alliance of the church and nobility – opposed the accession of the infant Queen Isabella II (1830–1904), refusing to accept female succession, and instead backed the claim of her uncle Carlos (1788–1855). Numerous attempts at liberal reform were quickly overturned, and in 1843 General Ramón Narváez seized power and came to a settlement with the Catholic Church.

THE BARRICADES CRUMBLE

1848 is remembered as one of Europe's most turbulent years, with revolutionary uprisings taking place in numerous countries. The previous year there had been a brief civil war in Switzerland, when seven Catholic cantons (states) seceded from the Swiss Confederation after liberals protested at the reassertion of the church's role in these areas. These rebels were quickly defeated, and in 1848 a new constitution was introduced, giving all men the vote and guaranteeing freedom of religion.

In France, barricades were thrown up in the streets of Paris in February 1848, a provisional government proclaimed a republic, and King Louis Philippe fled to England. Presidential elections at the end of 1848 resulted in victory for Napoleon's nephew, Louis Napoleon (1808–73), who soon dissolved the legislature, and in 1852 proclaimed himself Emperor Napoleon III. The short-lived Second Republic came to an abrupt end.

In Prussia meanwhile, Friedrich Wilhelm IV (1795–1861), who many had hoped would be open to political reform, rejected a written constitution presented to him in 1847, declaring he would never 'allow a scribbled sheet of paper to intervene like a second Providence between our God in heaven and this land of ours'. In March 1848, street fighting erupted in Berlin; the king soon lost his nerve and promised immediate concessions. Representatives attended an assembly in Frankfurt that published its 'Declaration of the Rights of the German People' in December, guaranteeing freedom of religion for dissenters, including the Old Lutherans and nonconformists. However, as in France, the revolution was not to be long-lasting: by 1850 most of the new institutions had vanished, and in 1851 the 'Declaration of Rights' was annulled.

In Austria, the government initially went on the offensive in 1848, with troops shooting dead a number of protesters in Vienna. This only inflamed the situation, and soon the emperor bowed to the inevitable, dismissed his arch-conservative chancellor, Prince Klemens von Metternich (1773–1859), and introduced some modest social reforms. This was perhaps the most important symbolic victory of 1848, for Metternich had been one of the key figures in establishing the reactionary mindset of post-1815 Europe.

A barricade thrown up during the Paris rising of 1848, the 'Year of Revolutions'.
ILLUSTRATED LONDON NEWS

BLESS ITALY

In Italy, the revolutionary impetus of 1848 had a much more direct bearing on the church. On his accession, Pope Pius IX (1846–78) made some significant reforms in the Papal States, and was initially taken by many to be a liberal with Italian nationalist sympathies. 1848 brought new constitutions to the northern states of Piedmont and Tuscany, Naples in the south, and the Papal States. In the north-east, a revolt in Venice forced out Austrian troops and a republic was declared, while much of Lombardy also rose against Austrian rule. When the pope prayed 'Bless Italy, Great God, and preserve her with thy most precious gift of faith', many took this as support for a united Italy.

When other northern states – Piedmont especially – showed willingness to support the Venetians against Catholic Austria, the pope quickly recoiled, and in April repudiated entirely the idea of a united Italy, instructing Catholics to remain loyal to their existing rulers. This announcement was greeted with such anger in Rome that Pius was forced to flee in disguise to Gaeta, in the Kingdom of Naples, and a short-lived republic was proclaimed in Rome.

POPE PIUS IX

Pius IX (1792–1878), who enjoyed the longest papacy in history, did much to strengthen the doctrinal supremacy of his office. Baptized Giovanni Maria Mastai-Ferretti, he was ordained to the priesthood in 1819, consecrated Archbishop of Spoleto in 1827, became a cardinal in 1840, and served as pope from 1846. While he was pope, the papacy endured a humiliating loss of temporal power, and Pius' earlier supposed liberalism soon vanished.

Although he lost much ground on the political side, Pius IX strengthened the doctrinal position of the papacy, being firmly in favour of Ultramontanism. He strengthened the papacy by re-establishing Catholic hierarchies in England (1850) and the Netherlands (1853), and concluding favourable agreements (concordats) with Russia (1847), Spain (1851), and Austria (1855).

In 1854 Pius proclaimed the immaculate conception of the Virgin Mary, according to which she was purified from original sin before her birth. The *Syllabus of Errors*, issued in 1864 in connection with the papal encyclical, *Quanta Cura*, list heresies and threats to the church in reaction to political liberalism, democratic ideas, rationalism in theology, and anti-clericalism.

Pius IX summoned the first Vatican Council to meet in Rome (1869–70), where his position was strengthened by the declaration of papal infallibility when speaking *ex cathedra* on faith and morals. 276

Contemporary engraving of Pope Pius IX (1792–1878), whose long reign as pope started in 1846.
© GEORGIOS KOLLIDAS/DREAMSTIME.COM

Italian bishops attended – but only 265 from all the other European countries – creating a built-in majority in favour of Ultramontanism. Pius IX enthroned tradition: he once rebuked a dissenting bishop: 'Tradition; I am tradition.'

WAYNE A. DETZLER

The Austrians soon reasserted their authority in northern Italy, and early in 1849 the pope called on the Catholic powers for help. Louis-Napoleon of France, keen to win the support of Catholics in his own country, and concerned that Austria might now come to dominate Italy, sent a force which – after some bloody fighting – retook Rome. By the time the pope returned in 1850, it was clear he had lost any liberal sympathies he might once have possessed.

Popular support for Italian unification was now so strong, especially in the north, that there was little the pope could do effectively to oppose it in the long term. Piedmont now cultivated French support, and in 1859 the two went to war with Austria, and succeeded in

> Tradition; I am tradition.
>
> POPE PIUS IX

capturing Lombardy. Most of the other northern states – including much papal territory – now united under Piedmontese leadership. In the south, the adventurer Giuseppe Garibaldi (1807–82), who had been instrumental in forming the Roman republic of 1848, succeeded in overthrowing the Bourbon monarchy in Naples, and Piedmont soon united with this territory. Venetia followed in 1866, and in 1870 Italy took advantage of the outbreak of war between France and Prussia to capture Rome itself, finally ending the papacy's temporal rule in Italy.

Pius IX refused to negotiate with the Italian state, which in response unilaterally redefined papal rights in the Law of Guarantees of 1871. The pope's person was declared inviolable, he was granted an annual income and full diplomatic rights, and was allowed to retain possession of the Vatican, the Lateran, and Castel Gandolfo. Pius refused to recognize this law, declined the financial grant, and went into voluntary exile in the Vatican, where the popes remained until 1929, when Mussolini agreed to the more favourable Lateran Treaty.

ERRORS

The events of 1848–50 had instilled in Pius IX a profound fear of the contemporary world; just as the European leaders of 1815 had tried to reverse the changes of the revolutionary era, the pope now reacted to the onslaught of liberalism by trying to turn back the clock. Alongside this, he reacted to the decline in his political power by emphasizing his spiritual role. In 1853, Pius issued the papal bull *Ineffabilis Deus*, which set out the doctrine of the immaculate conception: that, from the moment of her conception, Mary was free of original sin. This laid a solid foundation for the veneration of Mary and, at the same time, strengthened the spiritual authority of the pope himself.

A decade later, Pius issued the encyclical *Quanta Cura* (1864), together with the *Syllabus of Errors*, an all-inclusive list of errors of the modern world. Though the *Syllabus* stemmed from the need to give direction to the church in dealing with the realities of a unified Italy, it set Catholicism against developments that were increasingly dominating Europe. The *Syllabus* condemned the emergence of political liberalism, and denied that the church could – or should – reconcile itself to it. In addition, the supremacy of the Catholic Church over other denominations and over secular law was restated, while Catholics were denied the right to dispute papal authority, and civil marriages were forbidden. Bible societies – which the Catholic Church had long condemned for publishing Scripture without Church-approved commentaries – and liberal Catholics – such as Lamennais – were lumped together for condemnation in the same clause as socialists, communists, and secret societies.

In 1869 Pius went further, with the opening of the First Vatican Council. This proved to be the ultimate showdown between Ultramontanism and conservative Catholicism and Gallicanism, Febronianism, and liberal Catholicism. Gallicans maintained that church councils – such as Vatican I itself – held supreme authority within the Catholic Church; but at Vatican I, the Ultramontanists triumphed, when the doctrine of papal infallibility was adopted on 13 July 1870. This taught that the pope is infallible when speaking *ex cathedra* on matters of faith and practice. Those who opposed the doctrine outright, or as being ill-timed, formed a small minority, but mostly accepted the majority view. The German church historian Ignaz von Döllinger (1799–1890) refused to withdraw his arguments against papal infallibility and was excommunicated. The French government sent a formal protest against the doctrine, while in Britain, Prime Minister W. E. Gladstone – a high-church Anglican close to many English Catholics – lamented that 'for the first time in my life, I shall now be obliged to talk about popery'. In Germany, the political response was to be more extreme, with the initiation of the *Kulturkampf* ('culture struggle').

Pius IX's successor, Leo XIII (r. 1878–1903), made some tentative steps towards reconciling liberalism with Catholic teaching, in the 1888 encyclical *Libertas Praestantissimum*. In this, Leo reminded Catholics of their duty to uphold 'just' civil law, and conceded 'it is not of itself wrong to prefer a democratic form of government, if only the Catholic doctrine be maintained as to the origin and exercise of power'. In spite of moderating steps such as this, the papacy mostly remained in the reactionary mindset of the *Syllabus of Errors* until well into the twentieth century.

THE IRON CHANCELLOR

In 1862, Otto von Bismarck became Chancellor of Prussia, putting him at the head of the North German Confederation. Bismarck, a conservative, hoped to unite liberal nationalism with his own politics to create a united Germany under Prussian direction. After neutralizing Austria as a rival for this in the war of 1866, Bismarck took advantage of war with France in 1870 to unite the various north German states and – after defeating the French – had Wilhelm I of Prussia proclaimed Emperor of Germany.

In the years that followed, Bismarck – a committed Protestant from a Protestant state – needed to pursue internal unity in a new German Empire, whose population was 35 per cent Catholic. Prussia had always had Catholic subjects, especially in its eastern – Polish – territory; however states such as Bavaria were overwhelmingly Catholic, and had traditionally looked toward Catholic Austria rather than Protestant Prussia. Bismarck had a deep distrust of Catholicism, especially as a political force, which was exacerbated by Vatican I's declaration of papal infallibility.

Otto von Bismarck (1815–98), conservative German statesman, and author of the anti-Catholic *Kulturkampf*.
ILLUSTRATED LONDON NEWS

Within the new Germany, the Catholic Centre Party became a significant electoral force, apparently confirming his fears.

Confident of both conservative Protestant and liberal support, Bismarck, together with his education minister Adalbert Falk (1827–1900), undertook an anti-Catholic programme known as the *Kulturkampf*. The roots of this campaign can be found in the 1830s, when Archbishop Droste-Vischering (1773–1845) of Cologne was imprisoned by Friedrich-Wilhelm III for refusing to sanction marriages between Catholics and Protestants. In the 1870s, however, Bismarck went much further. In 1871 he abolished the Catholic bureau in the Prussian Ministry of Education and Public Worship, while priests who pursued an openly political agenda were liable to prosecution. In time, all trainees for the priesthood had to complete a state-authorized curriculum prior to ordination. The Jesuits were expelled from Germany in 1872, education was taken entirely under state control, and civil marriage was made compulsory.

Many in Germany – Catholic and Protestant – had been disturbed by the pronouncement of papal infallibility, and Döllinger had enjoyed considerable support and sympathy when he rejected the doctrine. Now, though, many Catholics came to believe that *Kulturkampf* was the greater threat, and most united behind a pope who in the 1875 encyclical *Quod Nunquam* reminded the faithful that the law of God was higher than the law of Prussia. Between 1871 and 1874, support for the Centre Party doubled; *Kulturkampf* had simply alienated a large part of the population. By the early 1880s, Bismarck had quietly abandoned the programme, realizing he had more in common with the conservative tendencies of southern Catholics than with northern liberals and socialists.

Even in Austria, liberals who controlled the government were determined to amend the relationship between church and state. The Church in Austria was governed by the *Concordat* of 1855, which reserved to the church power over all ecclesiastical matters as well as matrimonial questions. It also stipulated that the education of young Catholics, whether in state or private schools, had to conform to Catholic doctrine. During the 1860s, a number of laws restricting the church were passed, civil marriage was introduced, and Protestants were made equal in law. The *Concordat* itself was scrapped in 1874.

FRANCE BREAKS WITH THE CHURCH

In the late nineteenth century, France was rapidly secularized. In 1870 Napoleon III withdrew his troops from Rome to meet the Prussian threat at home, giving much fuel to his Catholic critics. After defeat by Prussia, the Third Republic was proclaimed, and initially ruled by a National Assembly in which conservatives with monarchist sympathies held a majority. In 1871, radicals and socialists in Paris revolted and established the Paris Commune, which attempted to establish a secular social-democratic republic, until it was defeated by government forces. During its brief existence, the Communards behaved rather like their Jacobin predecessors, desecrating and looting church property, and imprisoning priests. Many, including Georges Darboy, the Archbishop of Paris, were executed. As after the Revolution of 1789, there was initially a conservative reaction coupled with support and sympathy for the church – but this proved short-lived.

One of the most conservative Catholic figures in France at this time was Louis Veuillot (1813–83), editor of the strongly Ultramontanist *L'Univers* (1843–60, 1867–74). When he criticized Napoleon III in 1860 for deserting the pope, the paper was shut down. Veuillot was obsessed with the unrealistic dream of reversing the changes that had occurred since 1789, and wished to bring education under church control. Though *L'Univers* was enthusiastically read by rural, conservative Catholics, it did nothing to stem the rising tide of secularism in France, or reverse the French Church's detachment from the reality of the new politics. Until 1892 the pope himself remained wedded to the idea of a Bourbon restoration.

By the end of the century, anticlericalism had become a significant force in French politics. Though the church was still governed by the *Concordat* of 1801, which guaranteed state payment of clergy, new reforms gradually diminished the church's role in public life. In addition to reforms such as allowing businesses to open on Sunday, education was increasingly taken under state control. Jules Ferry (1832–93), the education minister, made primary education compulsory between 1879 and 1881, but entirely secularized schools at this level.

The legal status of all religious institutions in France was reformed in 1901, with passage of the Association Law, under which every religious body was required to register with the state. No member of an unregistered association was allowed to teach in a French school, and any congregation could be closed simply by government decree. About 615 congregations registered, but 215 did not, among them the Jesuits and Benedictines. Emile Combes, prime minister from 1902 to 1905, used the Act to close 13,904 schools by 1904.

In 1905 came the final break between church and state in France, when the Separation Law was passed, finally repealing the *Concordat* of 1801. All state funding of religious bodies now ended, and church buildings became state property, to be held in trust by 'associations of public worship'. Pope Pius X (r. 1903–14) declared the law null and void, and called on Catholics to disobey it, but anticlerical feeling in France was now so strong that this stood no chance of achieving anything.

INTO THE TWENTIETH CENTURY

For much of the nineteenth century, the Catholic Church largely ignored the industrialization and urbanization of Europe, or was actively hostile; Gregory XVI, for example, had such a hatred of railways that he forbade their construction in the Papal States. But in an urbanized continent, in which Marxism was increasingly gaining an audience, the church was forced to pay some attention to the social consequences of industry. In his encyclical *Rerum Novarum* (1891), Leo XIII encouraged the establishment of Catholic workers' associations, to provide an alternative to socialist trade unions. He condemned socialism, maintaining that any reforms had to take place in the context of the private ownership of property, but at the same time recognized that employers had a responsibility to provide a fair wage and ensure good living conditions. One of the consequences of *Rerum Novarum* was the emergence of Christian Socialist movements that became significant political parties in many countries during the twentieth century.

Leo XIII also encouraged individual Bible study, made a friendly approach to the Church of England in his 1895 apostolic letter *Ad Anglos*, and improved diplomatic relations with Washington, Tokyo, and Moscow. However, while much of the Protestant world was exploring ecumenism – leading to events such as the innovative

World Missionary Conference in Edinburgh in 1910 – Catholicism maintained an uncompromising stance of superiority, and in 1896 declared Anglican orders invalid.

Leo's successor, Pius X (1903–14), sought to emphasize the role of the liturgy in the church. In 1904 he launched a revival of the Gregorian chant, preferring simplicity to the grand – even bombastic – music of European Catholicism of this era. He revised the breviary of prayers in 1911, and – crucially – reemphasized the importance of the eucharist, insisting that Catholics should receive it more frequently – at least once a week – than was common at the time.

Yet in other respects Pius continued the reactionary tendencies of his predecessors. In 1904 he broke off diplomatic relations with France over the anticlerical laws. He also condemned modernist theology, which sought to reconcile Christianity with new developments in philosophy and science, and ruthlessly suppressed those with modernist and liberal tendencies within the church.

AFTERMATH

At the outbreak of World War I in 1914, the churches of Europe were profoundly different from 1789. Christianity had been forced to confront the changes wrought by new ideas in philosophy and science, and by changes in the political world. Belief in God was no longer taken for granted, and subjects – citizens – were no longer prepared to do as they were told. The Catholic Church, having spent much of the century refusing to accept change, was – by emphasizing the pope's spiritual role – beginning to understand it could no longer claim a monopoly on belief or morality. Protestantism, too, had change forced upon it. Many of the state churches of northern Europe had to face a diminution in their role, and in some cases a detachment from the state. Neither Protestantism nor Catholicism was any longer able simply to impose itself on the people, or suppress opponents. Above all, Christianity – and belief in general – had now become a matter for the individual not for the state.

WAYNE A. DETZLER
REVISED BY DANIEL GUY

CITIES AND EMPIRES

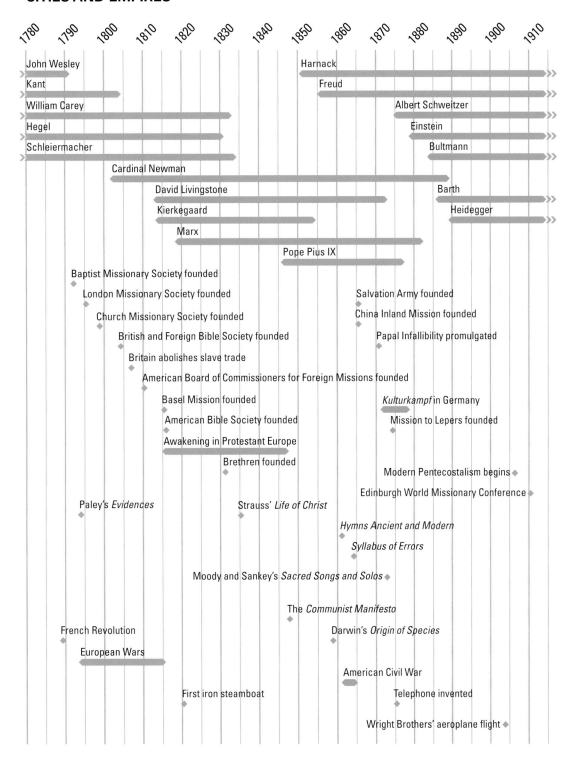

1780 1790 1800 1810 1820 1830 1840 1850 1860 1870 1880 1890 1900 1910

John Wesley

Kant

William Carey

Hegel

Schleiermacher

Cardinal Newman

David Livingstone

Kierkegaard

Marx

Pope Pius IX

Harnack

Freud

Albert Schweitzer

Einstein

Bultmann

Barth

Heidegger

Baptist Missionary Society founded

London Missionary Society founded

Church Missionary Society founded

British and Foreign Bible Society founded

Britain abolishes slave trade

American Board of Commissioners for Foreign Missions founded

Basel Mission founded

American Bible Society founded

Awakening in Protestant Europe

Brethren founded

Salvation Army founded

China Inland Mission founded

Papal Infallibility promulgated

Kulturkampf in Germany

Mission to Lepers founded

Modern Pentecostalism begins

Edinburgh World Missionary Conference

Paley's *Evidences*

Strauss' *Life of Christ*

Hymns Ancient and Modern

Syllabus of Errors

Moody and Sankey's *Sacred Songs and Solos*

The *Communist Manifesto*

Darwin's *Origin of Species*

French Revolution

European Wars

American Civil War

First iron steamboat

Telephone invented

Wright Brothers' aeroplane flight

CHAPTER 33

THE FIRST INDUSTRIAL NATION
The Industrial Revolution and the British Churches

A schoolboy once despatched the Industrial Revolution in one sentence when he wrote: 'About 1760 a wave of gadgets swept over England.' The process was much more complicated than that. In the mining industries – iron and coal – important innovations came in the later seventeenth century, whilst in other industries technological change did not come until the twentieth century. In fact, the pattern seems to be one of gradual development rather than revolution. Often hesitant and uncertain innovations were introduced into the manufacturing processes at different times in different industries, even in differing parts of the same industry.

AN INDUSTRIAL REVOLUTION?
But the term 'Industrial Revolution' still had much relevance. Contemporaries clearly perceived the revolutionary spirit of the age. Eric Hobsbawm concludes:

> *By any reckoning, this was probably the most important event in world history, at any rate since the innovation of agriculture and cities. And it was initiated by Britain.*

The Industrial Revolution was not a change imposed from above, but something which emerged from below, from the daily work of provincial England. The British Industrial Revolution was revolution by consent, at least by manufacturers and their financiers. It was stimulated by the expanding market represented by the increasing population of the eighteenth century, which in general managed to protect its purchasing power. But at the same time the early capitalists of the textile industry – first silk and then cotton – were driven to make technical innovations to make up for a scarcity of appropriate labour.

Each industry had its own technical breakthroughs, but of most universal significance was the improved form of steam engine produced at the Boulton and Watt factory in Birmingham. At last the manufacturer had a source of power independent of climate and season, both of which had until this time limited the power available from wind- and water-mills. With the development of the canal system, and later the railway system, the old limitations on the geographical location of industry were also removed.

The use of steam power changed the working situation of many Englishmen. An engine was expensive to purchase, and set a minimum scale and efficiency of enterprise below which it failed to provide the hoped-for profits. It offered little to the small manufacturer, but strengthened the slow movement towards purpose-built factories. The Industrial Revolution brought capital, power, and labour together under the one roof of the factory.

THE TYRANNY OF THE MACHINE
British agriculture was unable to employ the expanding population gainfully. Industrialization meant jobs for the victims of bad harvests and destitution – but they

did not often see it in this way. They hated the new factories. It was not the long hours or low wages they objected to; they were used to toiling day after day for a mere pittance. Nor were urban slums much worse than rural slums, and old agriculture depended on the employment of women and children as much as new industry.

The real tyranny was the substitution of the rhythm of nature in the daily lives of the people. Over against the irregularity of life in Old England, with its loose discipline, and pace of work determined by night and day, sowing and harvest, had to be set the precision, the discipline, and the regularity of the factory world. God's sun was now hid in the heavens and in its place was the factory clock and bell, symbols of human time as against divine time. Within the factory the emphasis was on precision, scrupulous standards of care, and the avoidance of waste. The greatest industrial sin was drunkenness, which so cheerfully challenged all the values of the new capitalist system.

Industrial capitalism then put forward a new morality which had much in common with the social values praised by the Evangelical Revival. The great potter Josiah Wedgwood (1730–95) sought a lifestyle for his workers that had much in common with that seriousness of life often attributed to Evangelicalism.

SAVED FROM REVOLUTION?

The Evangelical Revival witnessed not only a renewal of evangelistic activity, but also renewed concern for Christian morality. The nineteenth-century historian W. E. H. Lecky, although himself a free-thinker, credited it with bringing about:

> a great moral revolution in England: it planted a fervid and enduring religious sentiment in the midst of the most brutal and most neglected portions of the population, and whatever may have been its vices or its defects it undoubtedly emancipated great numbers from the fear of death and imparted a warmer tone to the devotion, and a greater energy to the philanthropy of every denomination both in England and the Colonies.

Lecky went on to suggest that a major reason why Britain was saved from the ravages of a revolution similar to that in France was this new religious commitment. This idea was taken over by the French historian, Élie Halévy (1870–1937):

> We shall explain by [the Evangelical Revival] the extraordinary stability which English society was destined to enjoy throughout a period of revolution and crises; what we may truly term the miracle of modern England, anarchist but orderly, practical and businesslike, but religious, and even pietist.

What Halévy saw as providential, left-wing historians have labelled as a conservative prop for an economically oppressive society. Other historians have suggested that Evangelical and Methodist strength in England was too small either to prevent revolution, or to act as a widespread 'opiate'.

There is little precise evidence of the extent and class nature of church attenders in Victorian England. England's first census of church attendance was recorded in 1851. The deduction was made that roughly 30 per cent of those who could have attended service on census Sunday did not do so. Dissenting churches were found to be roughly as strong as the Church of England, in fact stronger in urban England. Church absenteeism was highest in the new industrial towns of the north.

CHURCHES FOR INDUSTRIAL ENGLAND

One consequence of industrialization was the emergence of an urban society in England, particularly in the midlands and the north. Alongside William Blake's 'dark Satanic mills' there emerged towns such as Dickens' Coketown, 'a town of machinery and tall chimneys, out of which interminable serpents of smoke trailed themselves for ever and ever, and never got uncoiled'.

The Church of England was particularly slow to respond to the new situation, and found it difficult to do so. An act of Parliament was needed for a new parish to be created, which was both time-consuming and costly. As a consequence the Church of England found itself unable, until the 1840s, to respond to the new industrial England. The new urban masses consequently grew up very often beyond the care of the Church of England. There was no room for them in church, and all too often no clergy to care for their spiritual needs.

Methodism did not face the same difficulties. With its simple, barn-like preaching-places, its itinerant ministers, and its local preachers, it was admirably designed to go where the Established Church was unable to go. Other dissenters, too, expanded into the towns and cities of industrial England, and engaged in missionary work there with some success. But there always remained many more people beyond, in the unreached jungle of 'darkest England', as General Booth described it.

Part of the difficulty was that the churches were dominated by the concept of class. Many congregations became middle-class preserves, though the working classes were not all non-church goers. Different denominations appealed to different classes – the Wesleyans and Congregationalists tended to attract the middle classes, whilst the Baptist 'Tabernacle' and the Primitive Methodist 'Bethel' were more likely to have a largely working-class congregation.

The parish church all too often represented 'the Tory Party at prayer'. In the 1830s, for example, the protest movement called Chartism found little support in the Established Church. Chartists frequently marched on the parish church and required the vicar to preach on some congenial text, such as: 'Go to now, ye rich men, weep and howl for your miseries which are coming upon you' (James 5:1). The rebuff they got from all the churches led them to establish separate Chartist churches in certain areas, for many of the Chartist leaders of the 1830s and 1840s were Christians.

REACHING THE WORKING CLASSES

How to evangelize the working classes was an ongoing problem, partly because the children of working-class Christians tended to join the middle class. There was something bourgeois about Christian ethics in practice: gone was the old expenditure on drink; new priorities included the family, self-improvement, and Sunday School education. So there came to be a distinction between 'chapel' or 'prim working class' and the 'brute working class' of the back alleys.

The bustling city of London in the late nineteenth century. Capital of the first industrial nation and centre of an empire, the city's teeming slums challenged the resources of the Victorian church.
ILLUSTRATED LONDON NEWS

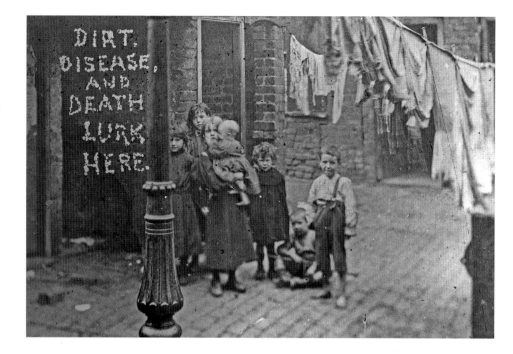

One organization that attempted to keep in touch with the working classes was the Pleasant Sunday Afternoon (PSA) Movement, formed in the 1880s, with the motto 'Brief, Bright and Brotherly'. Its meetings were for men only, and were held on Sunday afternoons, so that men would not feel ashamed to attend in their working clothes. The Sunday afternoon programme was part entertainment, part evangelistic, and partly concerned to address political topics, with some of the early Labour leaders frequent speakers. In the twentieth century the PSAs became the basis of the international Brotherhood Movement. The Salvation Army, too, came into being to serve the working classes. 'We can't get at the masses in the chapels,' claimed Catherine Booth, so she and her husband opened their own Christian Mission in the East End of London.

THE SALVATION ARMY

William Booth, founder of the Salvation Army, had a varied previous career. He had preached for the Wesleyans, the Wesleyan Reformers, and then the Methodist New Connexion, by whom he was ordained in 1858 after being disciplined the previous year for his irregular itinerant ministry. He stayed within the New Connexion for only three years before again becoming an irregular itinerant.

In 1865 the Booths began their own Christian Mission in a tent in Whitechapel, London – a venture that gradually grew into the Salvation Army – to the irritation of many churchmen. Even Lord Shaftesbury, in old age, concluded that the Salvation Army was a trick of the devil, who was trying to make Christianity ridiculous. Others, less Christian, retaliated against this new military presence more violently: in 1882, for example, 642 Salvation Army officers – including women – were assaulted, and sixty army buildings damaged. Much of this opposition was undertaken by a 'Skeleton Army' which parodied Booth's activities, and was supported by brewers who opposed the Army's teetotalism as a threat to their trade.

The Salvation Army was concerned about spiritual rather than material conditions. Booth spoke out against attempts to deal with great social difficulties as though they were simply due to lack of bricks and mortar. The first thing to do to improve the condition of the wretched was to get at their hearts. The Salvation Army was not engaged in a fight, in the first place, against bad conditions and oppressive political philosophies, but – as its title suggests – with salvation.

Booth was authoritarian in his attempt to achieve results, and gained control of the Mission in 1877 by what was virtually a military coup. After this, the military emphasis was developed, with uniforms, corps, citadels, and the magazine *The War Cry*. Booth offered his followers not only a force with which they could identify, but also a task to which they were committed. The Army was perhaps the only Christian movement to reach the wavelength of the masses in the nineteenth century; they alone understood the principles of mass communication and, in particular, the techniques of religious advertisement.

To begin with, the Salvation Army continued traditional revivalist evangelism, adding its own military slant, which fed the appetites of an increasingly jingoistic nation. But Booth's friendship with J. B. Paton (1830–1911), a Congregationalist theologian concerned with social problems, and W. T. Stead (1849–1912), editor of the *Pall Mall Gazette*, led him to wider concerns. It was widely believed that Stead was the ghost-writer for Booth's *In Darkest England and the Way Out* (1890), of which *The Methodist Times* exclaimed, 'Here is General Booth turning Socialist.' The book was designed to show that 'the submerged tenth' in England were as much in slavery as certain African tribes.

The Salvation Army today is a worldwide movement. At its centenary meeting in London in 1965 General Frederick Coutts outlined its twin aims:

William Booth (1829–1912) founder and first General of the Salvation Army, addresses his 'troops'.
SALVATION ARMY

If we refer to our evangelical work and also to our social work, it is not that these are two distinct entities. . . . They are but two activities of the one and the same salvation which is concerned with the total redemption of man.

VARIETIES OF METHODISM

The Booths had found themselves unable to reach the masses from a position within mainstream Methodism. In the nineteenth century the Wesleyan Methodists, led by Jabez Bunting (1779–1858), became a staid, respectable denomination. It had not always been so. Even in the early 1800s, the Home Office feared leaving education in industrial areas to Methodists, 'a set of men not only ignorant but of whom I think we have of late too much reason to imagine are inimical to our happy Constitution'.

Wesleyan Methodism imposed upon itself in the nineteenth century a 'no politics' rule, and until the late 1880s it was suspicious of open political discussion. But Methodism had its own non-conformity, where this restraint was missing. For example, the Staffordshire Primitive Methodists produced several Chartist leaders. Involvement in chapel affairs made them into natural community leaders; they learnt organization, how to speak in public, and how to deal with people. The local preacher could step readily from the pulpit to the political platform.

As a result, the Primitive Methodists had a close connection with the Trade Union movement. John Wilson, the leader of the Durham miners, was converted at the age of thirty-one at a Primitive Methodist Class Meeting. This conversion experience led on to a search for education, enrolment as a local preacher, an office within the Miners' Union, and election to Parliament in 1885, as one of the earliest Labour MPs. Many other Labour leaders, especially in the north-east of England, had a similar story.

THIS WORLD – OR THE NEXT?

One of the great debates in the nineteenth century concerned the relationship between a Christian's citizenship in this world and that in the other world. Lord Shaftesbury (1801–85), the evangelical social reformer, told a Social Service Congress at Liverpool in 1859:

When people say we should think more of the soul and less of the body, my answer is that the same God who made the soul made the body also. . . . I maintain that God is worshipped not only by the spiritual but by the material creation. Our bodies, the temples of the Holy Ghost, ought not to be corrupted by preventable disease, degraded by avoidable filth, and disabled for his service by unnecessary suffering.

Christians with similar views were much offended at the end of the eighteenth century by slavery – that 'odious traffic in human flesh' which William Wilberforce had attacked in a precocious letter to a Hull newspaper in 1773. British trade was reckoned at the time to depend so much on slavery that intense opposition arose to the Abolition Committee set up in 1787.

So great was the protest that it provoked Wilberforce into developing a new style of political opposition, in the form of pressure-group politics. The Abolition Committee was convinced of the need to acquire information about the operation of slavery in practice.

WILLIAM WILBERFORCE

William Wilberforce (1759–1833) is best known for his campaign against the slave trade. Educated at St John's College, Cambridge, during a continental tour in 1784–85 Wilberforce read Philip Doddridge's *Rise and Progress of Religion in the Soul*, and subsequently underwent a spiritual crisis. He emerged as a believer in 'real Christianity', centred on Christ's redeeming work. He later contrasted this with nominal religion in his influential book *A Practical View of the Prevailing Religious System of Professed Christians* (1797).

In 1784 Wilberforce became MP for Yorkshire, a seat he retained until 1812, when he moved to a safe seat, held until he retired from Parliament in 1825. His conversion gave Wilberforce the dynamic to lead the campaign against the slave trade, which he had abominated since the age of fourteen. From 1789 on, he frequently moved parliamentary resolutions against the British slave trade. After its formal abolition in 1807, he pressed for the enforcement of the ban, and for European agreement to prohibit the trade.

As leader of the 'Clapham Sect' of parliamentary Evangelicals, Wilberforce also helped to open India to missionaries in 1813, and to protect travelling evangelists in Britain from government interference. In his concern to preserve constitutional order, Wilberforce supported repressive statutes between 1795 and 1819 – but was in favour of moderate parliamentary reform, relief for boy chimney-sweeps, and Jeremy Bentham's 'model' prison. Wilberforce influenced prominent politicians quietly and per-

Engraving of the English politician William Wilberforce (1759–1833), leader of the movement to abolish the slave trade.
© GEORGIOS KOLLIDAS/DREAMSTIME.COM

suasively – particularly his friend William Pitt, Prime Minister in the periods 1783–1801 and 1804–6. He used his charm, tact, and eloquence in a political life to which he was convinced that he had been called by God.

DAVID W. BEBBINGTON

The widespread deployment of popular propaganda stimulated public opinion right across the country with petitions, supported by numerous signatures, dispatched to influence the judgment of ministers and MPs.

This pressure had to be kept up for twenty years, before the slave trade was finally abolished in 1807. The emancipation of slaves within the British Empire did not come until 1833 – and indeed rather later than that because of the introduction of the unjust apprentice system, which kept plantation blacks in semi-slavery – after a long campaign led by Fowell Buxton, who was aided by indignant missionaries on the spot who described the part played by slavery in dehumanizing the life of blacks in Africa, the Caribbean, and North America.

WHITE SLAVES

1833 also saw the first effective Factory Act passed by Parliament. It has often been suggested that Wilberforce and his associates, the 'Clapham Sect', were only concerned with black slaves overseas, and not with the white slaves of industrial England. This is unfair. Wilberforce was in fact one of the few to complain that the ineffective Factory Acts of 1802 and 1818 did not go far enough. The specialists in the industrial problem were, however, the Yorkshire Evangelicals, such as Wilberforce's friend, Thomas Gisborne, Richard Oastler of Huddersfield, Parson Bull of Bierley, Michael Sadler, MP, their parliamentary spokesman, and John Wood, a Bradford textile manufacturer.

Wood put the issue to Oastler in 1830 in terms of the earlier campaign against the slave trade:

> You are very enthusiastic against slavery in the West Indies: and I assure you there are cruelties practised in our mills on little children, which, if you knew, I am sure you would strive to prevent.

Within a few months Oastler had written his famous letter to the *Leeds Mercury* entitled 'Yorkshire Slavery'. These Yorkshire campaigners constantly regretted the lack of support from dissenters and the more pietistic of their fellow Evangelical Anglicans, who appeared content to leave the plight of the depressed to the operation of so-called 'natural laws'.

As time went by, there emerged a proliferation of philanthropic activity, based on a perilously fragile 'social theology'. Some Christians argued that the campaign for social righteousness was essential to a proper gospel ministry, whilst others saw social action as little more than a device for securing a working-class hearing for the gospel. Part of the problem was an inadequate theology of the secular and of community.

A CHRISTIAN SOCIAL ORDER?

It is doubtful whether the activities of the 'Christian Socialists' added up to very much. The novelist Charles Kingsley (1819–75) set out their responsibilities attractively in his novel *Alton Locke* (1850). The Christian Socialist co-operative workshops were weak in organization, unduly idealistic about the contribution of labour, and only lasted a short while. However, Christian Socialists did good work in securing a better legal framework within which workers' organizations could develop, and in fostering workers' education.

The ideas of F. D. Maurice (1805–72), their principal thinker, were to have a tremendous influence on Anglican thought about the secular world in the twentieth century, partly due to the solid work of the Christian Social Union, founded in 1889, with Brooke Foss Westcott (1825–1901), the Cambridge New Testament scholar, later Bishop of Durham, as its first president. In England this tradition came to its climax in the work of William Temple, Archbishop of Canterbury, 1942–44. Temple had deep insights into the nature of Christian worship, and a commitment to evangelism; he constantly exercised prophetic judgment on the social situation. William Temple kept both this world and the next in equal focus.

A BATTERY OF SOCIETIES

From the 1790s, the churches began to found overseas missions. At home a whole galaxy of home missionary agencies also sprang up. The sense of crisis in Europe emphasized the urgency of the times, and brought to birth a range of agencies 'making for the prospect of a popular evangelical church'. Accordingly, there developed itinerant societies, the great urban Sunday schools, an undenominational Christian press, and a great battery of Bible, tract, and missionary societies. These organizations formed a pattern of Christian progress, seeking to capitalize on the evangelistic opportunities that seemed to be afforded by the turmoil of society. Such a movement, like society, seemed to be getting out of control as the social tensions of the early nineteenth century increased. In consequence the 'undenominational evangelicalism' of the 1780s and 1790s was short-lived, and by the 1800s was challenged by the assertion of 'denominationalism' – new to both the Church of England and dissent.

The leaders of the Oxford Movement were alarmed at what they took to be the liberal tendencies of modern thought. In particular, they were worried by liberal reform of the church by a Parliament whose members, since 1828, did not need to be Anglican, and who, since 1829, did not need to be Protestant. Furthermore, with the first rumblings of biblical criticism in Germany, the Bible appeared to them an uncertain authority. Accordingly they placed their faith in the church itself, as represented by the apostolic succession of the bishops, the sacraments, and priestly office.

Nonconformists also felt the tensions involved in the relationship between church and evangelism. Victorian Nonconformity blended Puritan tradition, which promoted the faith of the family in which the children of believers were nurtured on the scriptures and brought up within the life of the local church, and revival evangelism, with its zeal to bring to faith all manner of people, regardless of their social status and lack of knowledge of gospel truths. This revivalist strand was reinforced by the experience of the revival of 1859, and later by the visits of American revivalists such as D. L. Moody and Ira D. Sankey, and R. A. Torrey and C. M. Alexander.

CHAPEL CULTURE

From the 1840s onwards, most city churches boasted a cluster of satellite missions in the poorer areas of the city. These mission halls were often far more than preaching stations, and provided their respective areas with a kind of all-purpose relief station, complete with clothing societies, penny banks, tontine clubs, soup kitchens, and other agencies. They paralleled the many-sided activities of the institutional church of the suburbs, which apparently provided a total 'chapel culture' for its adherents.

In church and mission alike it was possible to forget the true nature of the church. Amidst a welter of activity, the idea of the church was increasingly confused and altered. The old Puritan concept of the covenant community gave way to a Christian presence, represented by a range of Christian societies engaged in various aspects of the missionary task. In the late nineteenth century, people's concerns broadened, and many agencies

THE OXFORD MOVEMENT

The Oxford Movement within the Anglican Church aimed at making real the clause in the Creed, 'I believe in one holy catholic and apostolic church.' The movement – also known as the Tractarian Revival – had its roots in the High Church movement of the seventeenth century, from which the 'Tractarians' derived their interpretation of the doctrine of apostolic succession. They believed it was wrong to recognize the ministers of non-episcopal churches.

The Oxford Movement also looked back to the church of the first four centuries, which they believed placed more emphasis on the authority of the tradition of the church than on that of the Bible. They shared with seventeenth-century Anglicans a sacramental attitude towards nature and the world, and the belief that only the best is good enough for God, which made them pay careful attention to church furnishings and services. They were also influenced by the Romantic Movement. Some feared a second French Revolution might cross the Channel, bringing atheism and democracy with it, and sweeping away the God-given authority of the king and the bishops.

All this is found in John Keble (1792–1866), a country clergyman with poetic gifts, and an early leader of the movement. He firmly believed in tradition, in the catholic, apostolic church and its apostolic ministry. He preached in his assize sermon (1833) that the government had no right to suppress bishoprics in Ireland or England, and opposed the Reform Bill of 1832. But above all he was a sacramentalist; his hymnal, *The Christian Year* (1827), shows that feeling and emotion are central to Tractarianism. In its own way, the Oxford Movement was as much a revival as the Evangelical Movement which preceded it.

BEGINNINGS

The Oxford Movement began in Oriel College, Oxford, which had the highest academic reputation among the colleges. Keble was a Fellow from 1811 to 1823, and joined J. H. Newman, E. B. Pusey (1800–

82), Hurrell Froude (1803–36) and Robert Wilberforce (1802–57) to form the initial group. Events in the late 1820s and early 1830s made this group determined to declare themselves publicly. In 1828, the restrictive Test and Corporation Acts were repealed, which meant a better deal for dissenters. In 1829, Roman Catholic emancipation became law, which improved the position of Roman Catholics. In 1830 the disestablishment of the Church of England seemed a distinct possibility. Keble and his friends asked: 'If the church is disestablished … on what grounds has it a right to be heard, over against the Roman Catholics on the one hand and the dissenters on the other?' Their answer was that the Church of England is nearer the purity of the early church than the corrupt Church of Rome; and that it was a true church because Anglican clergy were episcopally ordained and visibly within the apostolic succession, as dissenting ministers were not.

Soon after Keble's assize sermon, the group set out to show that the church was completely separate from the state. Newman, Keble, and Froude published their views in a series of *Tracts* setting out the nature of the church. The first, by Newman, claimed that the church's authority was guaranteed by its apostolic descent. More influential than the tracts were Newman's sermons, Keble's poetry, and Pusey's scholarship.

As support for the Reformation grew stronger among Evangelicals, a Romeward wing formed among some of the younger Tractarians. Newman's *Tract 90* was an attempt to keep this group in the Church of England, by showing that the Anglican Thirty-nine Articles could be interpreted in a Catholic sense. This caused a furore, and the Bishop of Oxford forbade the publication of further tracts. In 1845 Newman was received into the Church of Rome, followed in 1851 by Robert Wilberforce and Henry Manning.

A MEDIEVAL REVIVAL

The original Tractarians showed no special interest in ritual. Two Cambridge undergraduates, John

Mason Neale (1818–66) and Benjamin Webb (1819–85), started a society to revive interest in church architecture, the internal arrangement of churches, and medieval ritual. Clergy influenced by the movement went on to work in east London, Leeds, and other industrial areas. These 'Anglo-Catholics' believed that, to reach scarcely literate congregations, Catholic truth required Catholic ritual. Stewart Headlam (1847–1924) founded the 'Guild of St Matthew' in 1877 to link Christian Socialists and Anglo-Catholics. Charles Gore (1853–1932) edited the critical essays in *Lux Mundi* in 1889, which led an increasing number of Anglo-Catholics to accept biblical criticism. Robert Aitken and G. H. Wilkinson broke away from Keble's restrictions on popular preaching and conducted evangelistic missions. Though no bishop was appointed from the Tractarians until 1854, the successors of the Oxford Movement dominated the Anglican Church in England for the first half of the twentieth century.

Anglo-Catholics have stressed the church, ministry, and sacraments. The doctrine of apostolic succession has been a stumbling-block in the way of reunion with non-episcopal churches. Controversy has arisen over the sacraments of baptism and the eucharist, and made the whole Church of England put more emphasis on the sacraments. The Tractarians' main lasting contribution is in worship, where they restored a sense of reverence. They restored to Anglicanism such features as religious communities, retreats, pilgrimages, the sacrament of confession, the reading of devotional books, and a pattern of disciplined prayer and regular communion for ordinary Christians.

MICHAEL HENNELL

of the church became more concerned to offer a social gospel than the old dogmatic one. The Christian minister was becoming an organization man rather than a pastor of the local body of Christ. He was the mechanic who cared for a great, streamlined machine, powerfully tooled up for evangelism and social redemption. But sometimes large congregations, gathered together in great solid temples of middle-class respectability, possessed neither the common life of the meeting-house nor the urgent concern to rescue the lost. Instead they seemed to perpetuate themselves by some self-justifying principle. Church-building programmes increased in every decade of the century, and many full churches, both in city centres and in the suburbs, were presided over by princes of the Victorian pulpit. An impression of progress and advance was often conveyed, whereas in fact the churches were failing to keep pace with the expanding population.

CHURCH VERSUS CHAPEL

The 1810s and 1820s saw the end of the easy eighteenth-century co-existence of church and chapel. The revival of hostility led to the fierce campaign for the repeal of the restrictive Test and Corporation Acts, which achieved success in 1828. Even after repeal, many irritants remained for Nonconformists: first the need

THE BRETHREN

From time to time in the history of Christianity, movements have arisen which refuse any special title, and strive to recapture the outlook and beliefs of the church in its earliest days. One such movement which emerged in Britain early in the nineteenth century also arose in Switzerland, Germany and other European countries. Dubbed 'Plymouth Brethren' because Plymouth was prominent in the early days, Brethren have always tried to avoid any distinctive label. The founding fathers were mainly Anglican evangelicals who felt that the Evangelical movement was not going far enough. There were also Nonconformists who deplored certain features of Nonconformity in their day.

The founders shared a deep concern at the divided state of the church. They wanted their simple communion service to be a means of fellowship for Christians, irrespective of denomination, expressing the priesthood of all believers and therefore needing no priestly order. They also shared an expectation that Christ would soon return and an insistent appeal to Scripture, and renounced the possessions, pleasures, and status of this world. Their earliest leaders held strongly Calvinistic doctrines, and were often enthusiastic evangelists. Soon they developed a distinctive form of worship and church life.

From the start there were two different emphases. John Nelson Darby (1800–82) and others believed that the church was in ruins, as at the end of other 'dispensations' of God's dealings with men and women. The assemblies were not to be set up with elders and deacons, but simply to be groups of people separated from the world, awaiting Christ's return. Later these 'exclusive' assemblies declined into authoritarianism.

The other grouping, simply known as Christian Brethren (or 'open' Brethren), developed into a small – but influential – nonconformist group. As the result of emigration and a strong missionary emphasis, Brethren are to be found in most parts of the world. They are relatively numerous in Argentina, Zaïre, Zambia, southern India, Singapore, and New Zealand.

The most distinctive emphasis of the Brethren is that the ministry and gifts of the church are distributed to all believers, and the service of worship and communion is led by different members of the congregation. Full-time pastors are rare, though they became more common; full-time evangelists and Bible teachers travel widely. What also distinguishes the Brethren is that there is no church government beyond the local church. Agencies may be set up for particular functions, such as financing missions and church-building, or setting up a Bible college, but there is no hierarchy or centralized organization. Local churches are free to apply the teaching of Scripture in the light of contemporary needs and the local situation – though in practice the inbuilt conservatism of any grouping results in widely-recognized common practice.

HAROLD H. ROWDON

to secure validity for nonconformist marriages and funerals, then the campaign to repeal church rates, which were finally abolished in 1868. The ancient universities were bastions of Anglican power, and a campaign to open them to nonconformists achieved most of its aims by 1871.

The campaign for the outright disestablishment of the English Church, shorn first of the minority churches in Ireland, 1869, and Wales, 1920, ceased to concern late Victorian nonconformists — and indeed in the next century an Established Church came to be seen as a protection for all people of all faiths, against the onward march of an increasingly forceful

C. H. SPURGEON: 'PRINCE OF PREACHERS'

Charles Haddon Spurgeon (1834–92) was a celebrated Victorian Baptist preacher, whose father and grandfather were independent ministers. Spurgeon was converted while listening to a Primitive Methodist local preacher in January 1850, subsequently baptized, and became a Baptist village-preacher in Cambridgeshire. In 1854 – before his twentieth birthday – he became Baptist pastor at New Park Street Chapel, Southwark, London.

Spurgeon quickly gained fame for his directness in preaching – which seemed to some to border on irreverence. But the power of his sermons led to many conversions. He drew vast congregations to Exeter Hall, London, and – to the scandal of some – to the Surrey Gardens Music Hall, when his own chapel was being extended. From 1861 until 1891, Spurgeon preached in the specially-erected Metropolitan Tabernacle, which seated 6,000. Associated with the Tabernacle were a Pastors' College, which trained nearly 900 men before Spurgeon's death, a Colportage Society for distributing Christian literature, an orphanage, and the monthly magazine *The Sword and the Trowel*.

Spurgeon gloried both in being a Calvinist – although he warmly supported Moody and Sankey – and a Baptist. But he left the Baptist Union during the 'Downgrade Controversy' of 1887, claiming some Baptist ministers were relaxing their grasp of vital doctrines. Spurgeon injected his playful humour, common sense, and gift for epigram into all his numerous works, which included an extended commentary on the Psalms, *The Treasury of David*

Contemporary illustration of the Victorian Baptist preacher Charles Haddon Spurgeon (1834–92), sometimes known as the 'Prince of Preachers'.
TIM DOWLEY ASSOCIATES

(1870–85). His sermons were published weekly until 1917: he was the most popular and greatest preacher of his age.

DAVID W. BEBBINGTON

secularism. But the fight between church and chapel over the nature and control of primary education festered on until the outbreak of World War I. This campaign did little credit to either side, but deprived several generations of English children of elementary education, for which all the labours of the Sunday schools of both sides hardly compensated.

Early Victorian nonconformist movements tended to concentrate on the negative campaign of disestablishment. But the Free Church movement of the 1890s was more missionary-minded. It did not campaign so much against the Establishment as for the gospel, and employed 'Gipsy' (Rodney) Smith (1860–1947) for a time as its full-time evangelist. It also reflected certain solid achievements concerning unity among the Free Churches. In 1856 a number of Methodist groups came together in the United Methodist Free Church; Presbyterian union was achieved in 1876; and in 1891 the New Connexion of General Baptists finally united with the Particular Baptists.

But at the end of the nineteenth century the rift between church and chapel in English society still ran very deep. It was not simply 'the chapels of the industrial revolution confronting the churches of the rural squirearchy'; urban Anglicanism and rural dissent were equally part of the conflict. 'Church' meant not only bishops, parishes, and the *Book of Common Prayer*, but also deference to 'the Establishment' in both church and state. 'Chapel' stood for two forms of dissent: the older, more loosely organized, congregational Christianity, principally of the Baptists and Congregationalists; and the newer, more centrally organized, Evangelicalism of the various brands of Methodism. Chapel religion had made such advances in the early nineteenth century that Nonconformists became increasingly ambitious to secure equal rights with Anglicans in what was becoming a pluralist and a largely secular state.

PROTESTANT VERSUS CATHOLIC

Only slowly in Victorian England did Catholic-Protestant antipathy decrease. From Stuart times onwards, it had been easy to rouse a popular mob to campaign under the banner of 'no popery'. The most dramatic occasion was the Gordon Riots in 1780, when a mob under Lord George Gordon held the city of London in terror, demanding the repeal of a moderate Act of Catholic Relief.

Catholic emancipation increased Protestant suspicions in 1829, and a further anti-Catholic outburst occurred in the 1840s, when the British government increased its grant in support of the Roman Catholic Maynooth College seminary in Ireland. The climax of anti-Catholicism came in 1850, when the re-establishment of the Roman Catholic hierarchy in England was regarded as a 'papal aggression' against Protestant England. John Kensit and the Protestant Truth Society in the 1890s provided a further focus for Protestant feelings, though their concern was initially about the growth of ritualism within the Church of England. The contest was violent, and Kensit himself was fatally wounded in a religious riot in Liverpool in 1902.

Throughout the period, anti-catholicism was fed by fictional literature, dating back to M. G. Lewis's *The Monk*, the original horror novel – spine-chilling and suspenseful, in 1796. Even in the midst of a most moral society, pornography was permissible as long as the perversity was perpetrated by Catholics – preferably by monks and nuns. Books in the traditions of *The Female Jesuit or the Spy in the Family* (1851), *The Awful Disclosures of Maria Monk* (1836), and *Geralda, The Demon Nun*, continued to appear up to World War I. Catholicism was portrayed as un-English, priest-ridden, and ruled over by a capricious but all-powerful pope. The word of a Roman Catholic could not be relied upon, and the work of the Jesuits was a byword for sinister duplicity. The growth of Catholic sentiment within the English Church formed part of the same problem. It was worriedly discussed in the highest councils of state. Dr Arnold, the headmaster of Rugby School, said: 'I look upon a Roman Catholic as an enemy in his uniform, I look upon a Tractarian as an enemy disguised as a spy.'

JOHN HENRY NEWMAN

John Henry Newman (1801–90) was a leader of the Oxford Movement, and later a cardinal of the Roman Catholic Church. His father, an Evangelical banker, sent him to a private school at Ealing, where at sixteen he had a conversion experience. Newman was never a typical evangelical; from his reading he gained 'a zealous faith in the Holy Trinity', yet he seems never to have believed in justification by faith. Newman went up to Trinity College, Oxford, in 1817 and in 1822 was elected a Fellow of Oriel. Ordained in 1824, four years later he was made vicar of St Mary's, Oxford.

Newman's views changed rapidly under the influence of friends, chief of them Hurrell Froude, who 'made me look with admiration towards Rome and … dislike the Reformation'. In the winter of 1832–3 Newman and Froude went on a tour of the Mediterranean, during which Newman wrote his poem *Lead, Kindly Light*. They were back in Oxford in time for Keble's assize sermon in July 1833.

Newman immediately became the leader of the Oxford Movement, by his sermons in St Mary's, by the 24 *Tracts for the Times* which he wrote, and by his books. Newman tried to show that the Church of England had steered a middle way between Roman Catholicism and Protestantism, but gradually became convinced that the only true successors of the early Christian theologians were in the Roman Catholic Church. He wrote Tract 90 in 1841 to show that the Thirty-nine Articles can be interpreted in the spirit of the Catholic Church – which created an uproar. The Bishop of Oxford forbade Newman to publish further tracts. The Anglican-Lutheran alliance, which resulted in setting up a bishopric in Jerusalem, further alarmed Newman about the Protestant leanings of Anglicanism. In 1843 he resigned from St Mary's, after preaching a sermon on 'The parting of friends'. Two years later, in 1845, he was received into the Roman Church, and almost immediately published his important 'Essay on the Development of Christian Doctrine'.

Statue of Cardinal John Henry Newman (18901–90), outside Brompton Oratory, London.
© BASPHOTO/DREAMSTIME.COM

After ordination in the Roman Catholic Church, Newman was appointed head of the Oratory of St Philip Neri, Birmingham. In 1864 he responded to an attack by Charles Kingsley with his famous *Apologia Pro Vita Sua*. The following year he wrote the poem *The Dream of Gerontius*, which contains the text of the hymns 'Firmly I Believe and Truly' and 'Praise to the Holiest in the Height', and which was memorably set to music by Edward Elgar (1900). In 1870 came the *Grammar of Assent*, which defended religious belief. He was made a cardinal in 1877 and died in 1890; Pope Benedict XVI announced his beatification in 2010.

MICHAEL HENNELL

CATHOLIC PRIORITIES

Part of the problem was that a racial question was bound up with the religious question. Anti-catholicism thrived on the threat to employment posed by Irish immigrants. This same migration of labour presented problems to the Catholic hierarchy. Should they use their new-found freedom to build splendid cathedrals – or should they first provide for urban migrants? Priority had to be given to pastoral provision for the faithful. Under Cardinal Nicholas Wiseman (1802–65), the Catholic hierarchy was successfully re-established and Catholic life in England was accepted as respectable.

Gently guided by Cardinal Henry Manning (1808-92), the three distinct strands of English Catholicism – the old Catholic families, the Irish, and the converts – were slowly integrated into one community, and moved forward to make a positive impact on English society. Manning lent his support to Joseph Arch (1826–1919), a Primitive Methodist, in his agricultural unionism; served on the royal commission on the housing of the poor; and in 1889 mediated in the London dock strike. He did not forget his own Evangelical background, and tried to get his clergy to engage in missions, to conduct open-air services, and to be more missionary-minded.

WORLDWIDE VISION

In 1846 interdenominational cooperation was promoted through the founding of the Evangelical Alliance. In part a rebirth of the popular ecumenism of the 1780s and 1790s, it also sought to promote 'an enlightened Protestantism against the encroachment of Popery and Puseyism and . . . the interests of a Scriptural Christianity'. It was an international movement, though differences over the issue of slavery prevented the founding of an American branch until 1867.

Two years prior to the founding of the Evangelical Alliance, George Williams (1821–1905), a London draper, had founded the first branch of what was to become the Young Men's Christian Association, an international organization for evangelism amongst young men. Lay, interdenominational, and worldwide in character, it represented one of many initiatives bringing Christians of differing traditions closer together.

In 1895, the World Student Christian Federation brought together the various university interdenominational Christian Unions. Under such influences, many of the ablest young men of late Victorian Cambridge offered for missionary service overseas. Both their university and their missionary experience argued against the denominational straitjacket that had emerged in Victorian England. It was in order to produce a strategy to surmount denominational barriers in promoting world evangelization that the delegates went to the first World Missionary Conference at Edinburgh in 1910. Whatever their meaning in Europe and North America, most denominational differences meant little or nothing in the rest of the world. The Edinburgh Conference of 1910 is considered by many to mark the founding of the modern ecumenical movement, leading up to the establishment of the World Council of Churches in 1948.

JOHN BRIGGS

THE EVANGELICALS

Three groups emerged from the Evangelical Revival in the eighteenth century: the Methodists, who separated from the Church of England after Wesley's death; the Calvinists, successors of Whitefield and the Countess of Huntingdon; and the Evangelical Anglicans, of whom the key figures were Samuel Walker of Truro, Henry Venn of Huddersfield, and John Newton of Olney.

The Methodists believed Christ died for all, and that some might attain Christian perfection in this life. The Calvinists, led by Thomas Haweis (1732–1820), believed Christ died only for the elect, and stressed that human nature was fallen in every aspect (total depravity). The Anglican Evangelicals believed Christ died for the whole world; they also believed in total depravity, and shared with both the other groups the assurance that their sins were forgiven. They also held that – through Christian missions – the whole world would eventually come to faith in Christ, at which time Christ would return and the millennium would begin.

These were the beliefs of the group of influential Evangelicals who became known as the Clapham Sect – founder members of the Church Missionary Society, the British and Foreign Bible Society, and the Religious Tract Society. They drew away from the Calvinists and nearer to the Methodists, as they emphasized that salvation was for the world, and not just for the elect. On the other hand, they rejected Wesley's doctrine of Christian perfection, and also strongly supported the parish system, objecting to the tendency of Methodists to set up their own churches in Evangelical parishes.

A MORAL REVOLUTION

Wesley had begun a revolution in morals and behaviour among the working classes, a revolution that spread to other classes at the beginning of the nineteenth century through the writings of William Wilberforce and his friend Hannah More (1745–1833). She wrote simple moral tales, in homely English, and her tracts were distributed by door-to-door salesmen very cheaply, circulating in huge numbers. Many were also read at court and by the upper classes.

For the privileged classes Wilberforce wrote his book, *A Practical View of the Prevailing Religious System of Professed Christians in the Higher and Middle Classes in this Country contrasted with Real Christianity*. In it he commented on the increase of prosperity, the growth of new cities, the splendour and luxury of the age, and the decline of religion, manners, and morals. He reminded the rich of their duties to the poor, and claimed that the only remedy for the selfishness that their wealth encouraged was to turn from their nominal Christianity to the real Christianity to be found in personal commitment.

7,500 copies were sold in six months, and few books have been more influential. The 'reformation of manners' for which Wilberforce had campaigned took place before his eyes. Cock-fighting and bull- and bear-baiting died out through lack of support, and bookshops selling 'dirty' books had to close down for lack of customers. Within the first twenty years of the nineteenth century a complete change came over the social habits of Britain: 'Victorianism' had arrived – twenty years before Victoria came to the throne. The old upper classes, together with the new wealthy classes, became less frivolous and more conscious of their responsibilities. Some of the coarseness and cruelty that had marred eighteenth-century life disappeared.

RESPECTABILITY

All was not gain. The cult of respectability was not the same as Christianity, and hypocrisy replaced corruption as the typical sin of the age. The Evangelical magazine, *The Record*, is full of advertisements such as this one for a coachman: 'High wages not given. A person who values Christian privileges will be preferred'. Privileges doubtless meant permission to attend church and family prayers.

Evangelicals believed neither in democracy nor in trade unions. The French Revolution had frightened them away from such radical ideas. The Evangelicals were willing to do all they could for the poor – but not to allow them to do it for themselves.

Most Evangelicals observed Sunday strictly, but the Victorian Evangelicals were strictest of all. The Lord's Day Observance Society was founded 1831, and numerous letters and articles in *The Record* protested against Sunday opening of parks, museums, and zoological gardens. For six years, the Evangelical minister at Cheltenham managed to prevent all passenger trains stopping there on a Sunday.

Evangelical societies made it their business to supply Evangelical ordinands and endow Evangelical parishes where they might serve. The most important patronage trust was that begun by John Thornton and taken over by the Revd Charles Simeon (1759–1836). When Simeon died, the Simeon Trust had the right to nominate the clergy to twenty-one Anglican positions, mainly in large towns such as Bradford and Derby. By 1820, one in twenty of the Anglican clergy were Evangelical; by 1830 it was one in eight.

NEW PATTERNS AND PARTIES

Evangelicals gained high office only slowly. Henry Ryder became Bishop of Gloucester in 1815; Charles Richard Sumner Bishop of Winchester in 1827; and John Bird Sumner (1780–1862) Archbishop of Canterbury in 1848. These three men produced a new style for bishops, much simpler in their life-style than their predecessors. They visited all parts of their dioceses, and took more care over confirmations and ordinations. Their example was followed in the 1850s by the 'Palmerston bishops', mostly appointed on the advice of the Evangelical Lord Shaftesbury.

Evangelical ranks divided from the 1820s. Edward Irving (1792–1834) convinced many Evangelicals that they were far too optimistic about the conversion of the world; in fact, the day of judgment was at hand, and Christ's second coming would precede the millennium. He believed missionary societies were deceiving the elect by talking of the conversion of the world. Irving was later deposed from the ministry of the Church of Scotland, and became associated with the foundation of the Irvingite, or Catholic Apostolic, Church.

At the same time the Calvinist, Robert Haldane (1764–1842), won his campaign – against Simeon – to prevent the apocrypha from being included in Bibles published by the Bible Society. Haldane's nephew, Alexander, a young London barrister, shared his uncle's views. When the younger Haldane became the chief owner of the twice-weekly *Record* in 1828, he propagated these strong ideas, giving strict Calvinism a foothold again in Anglican Evangelicalism. *The Record* also adopted Irving's views on biblical prophecy and the millennium.

The Record was ultra-conservative in politics and theology, its strongest condemnation reserved for sabbath-breakers and Roman Catholics. The 'mainstream party' continued the tradition of Simeon and the Clapham Sect, and among its leaders were Edward Bickersteth and John Venn. Their journal, which stressed loyalty to the church, was the monthly *Christian Observer*, started in 1802. Despite theological differences, there was no open rift. 'May Meetings' were held in Exeter Hall, London, every year, and were able to accommodate every kind of evangelical society – and every kind of evangelical.

MICHAEL HENNELL

CHAPTER 34

A CRUSADE AMONG EQUALS
Revivalism, Abolition, and Evangelism in the USA

American Protestantism had always been associated with a frontier, which gave it a distinctive flavour. During the nineteenth century, the United States experienced geographical and political expansion, moralistic crusades, laissez-faire individualism, and a cataclysmic Civil War. The more dynamic denominations took the opportunity to share the hopes of the buoyant democracy – but they also had to cope with the resulting social adjustments. Nineteenth-century Protestantism responded to the geographical and social differences it met across the country with two merging forces: Christian revivalism and democratic nationalism. The stage was set for 'a crusade among equals', as a second Great Awakening.

REVIVALISM
By 1800 there were manifestations of a second Awakening. Lyman Beecher (1775–1863), a Congregational-Presbyterian minister, and Timothy Dwight, president of Yale, initiated a crusade that was to continue for seven decades. The Presbyterian James McGready (1763–1817), and the Methodist circuit-rider Peter Cartwright (1785–1872), carried the torch of revival to the frontier, where they popularized the holding of 'camp meetings'. In 1801 Presbyterians and Methodists staged the Cane Ridge meeting in Kentucky, and Baptists joined Methodists in carrying the Awakening over the mountains into the Old Southwest, forming an 'Evangelical United Front'.

These early nineteenth-century revivals put the principle of churches being supported freely by their members (voluntarism) before liturgy, democracy before orthodoxy, and emotion before intellect. By crossing denominational barriers, they enabled the churches to reach the masses. They made the camp meeting a social institution that supported the politics, spirit, and mood of American expansion to the West. Revivalism emphasized the work of man in salvation – but also the doctrine of the sovereignty of God – and was approved of as a missionary movement both at home and abroad. The idea of a personal encounter with God, preached at revival meetings, gave them a democratic character. The belief that America was being visited by God linked politics and religion. The writer Emerson noted that Europe extended to the Alleghenies – but America lay beyond; which was as true of American religious history as it was of its political history.

Most Protestants were initially sympathetic to the revival movements in the West, although the Methodists and Baptists were more actively involved in this work. Both groups were equally comfortable on the frontier – though they differed over education for the clergy, and on the doctrines of the eternal security of the believer, free will, and grace. Methodist circuit-riders such as Francis Asbury inspired many a boy to feel called to preach as he listened to the gospel in a barn or tavern.

By 1855 the Methodist Church numbered over a million and a half members, and formed the largest Protestant denomination in the United States. The Baptists appealed

D. L. MOODY: MASS EVANGELIST

Dwight L. Moody (1837–99) was the most noted evangelist of his age, though life did not give him a promising start. He was one of nine children born to a Unitarian family in Northfield, Massachusetts. His father died when he was four, leaving the family in a struggling financial position. With little schooling, Moody left home at seventeen to work in his uncle's shoe shop in Boston. There he was converted through his Sunday school teacher, Edward Kimble. But his request for membership of the Congregational Church was initially turned down because of his ignorance about the Christian faith.

Moving to Chicago in 1865, Moody became a successful businessman and an active worker in Plymouth Congregational Church. Every Sunday he filled four pews in the church with those he had recruited. He also successfully recruited members for the Sunday school, and at the age of twenty-three founded his own Sunday school, which he served as administrator and recruiter rather than teacher. Soon he devoted himself to Christian work full-time, speaking at Sunday school conventions, preaching to troops, establishing his own church, and serving as the president of the YMCA.

But it was Moody's tour of Great Britain between 1873 and 1875 that launched his career as a renowned evangelist. It started unpromisingly, but by the time he returned to America he was a preacher of international fame. He had already teamed up with and singer Ira D. Sankey, and Harry Moorehouse had taught him how to preach. When he left England, it was to devote his life to conducting revival campaigns. He was never a polished preacher, but the style and organization of his campaigns were to have a long-term influence on mass-evangelism.

In his last years, Moody established two schools and a regular summer Bible conference at Northfield. In 1886 he founded the Chicago Evangelization Society, known today as the Moody Bible Institute.

D. J. TIDBALL

The American evangelist Dwight L. Moody preaching in 1875 at London's Agricultural Hall, Islington. His song-leader Ira D. Sankey is next to him, seated at the harmonium.
MOODY BIBLE INSTITUTE

particularly to the lower middle classes; their untrained and unpaid farmer-ministers would gather a few families around them and organize a church, before moving westwards to spread the revival fire. Second in size to the Methodists, the Baptists numbered more than a million by 1855.

This 'crusade among equals', which multiplied the 'sects', alarmed the Unitarian-Universalist Association, whose most illustrious member was a defector from Congregationalism, Ralph Waldo Emerson. But the Methodists and Baptists stoutly defended their orthodoxy – emphasizing their trust in the Bible as the Word of God, and faithful observance of the sabbath.

AN ARMY OF CRUSADERS

The 'crusade among equals' was conducted in the social arena, too. Every Protestant denomination participated in social action during the twenty-five years before the Civil War. Issues such as women's rights, temperance, prison reform, public education, world peace, and the abolition of slavery thrust American Christians into a multitude of crusades. The evangelistic campaigns of Charles Grandison Finney (1792–1875), and the founding of hundreds of church-linked parish schools and colleges, were other signs of Protestant social concern. Anti-Freemasonry, millennialism, spiritualism, Mormonism, and communalism claimed their adherents, while the churches crusaded against sabbath-breaking, the theatre, duelling, prostitution, alcohol, immigration, slums, and, most strongly, Roman Catholicism and slavery. As the century progressed, the denominations became less sophisticated and ordinary Christians played a more important role. There was more emphasis on love and social concern.

Charles Grandison Finney (1792–1875), leader of the American Second Great Awakening, abolitionist, and 'Father of Modern Revivalism'.
TIM DOWLEY ASSOCIATES

The most militant Protestant crusade was against its oldest rival, Roman Catholicism. Hatred of Catholics, and of foreigners, had been growing steadily in the United States since the seventeenth century, and in the nineteenth century popular Protestantism joined with democratic nationalism to produce 'Native Americanism'. For example, in 1830 the American Bible Society urged Protestants to unite against Catholic influence in the West. The Society pledged to get Bibles into every schoolroom in the country, in order to combat Catholic efforts to throw Scripture out of the classroom. The American Home Missionary Society was dedicated to 'the general welfare of society and the West', and the American and Foreign Christian Union sought to 'diffuse and promote the principles of religious liberty … both at home and abroad, wherever a corrupted Christianity exists'. During the Mexican-

American War of 1846 it was rumoured there were popish plots to poison US soldiers. In many people's minds, preaching the gospel and purifying the government had come to mean the same thing.

THE CIVIL WAR

American slavery had always been opposed by humanitarians both inside and outside the church. In 1817 the American Colonization Society put forward a plan to send freed black people to Liberia, and within four years this won the backing of the leaders of every major Protestant denomination in the USA. Unfortunately this did not solve the problem.

A decade later, Christians from all parts of the United States began to use the Bible either to attack or to defend slavery. The churches split over this issue. Northern seminaries became hotbeds supporting the abolition of slavery. The evangelist Charles Finney – though no radical – supported the abolitionist cause. In 1845, Southern Methodists declared themselves independent, and the Southern Baptist Convention was organized. After 1860 ministers both north and south encouraged their young men to serve in their respective armies.

During the American Civil War (1861–65) Northern chaplains visited the battlefields and hospitals, and received payment of $100 a month from Congress. Both sides prayed for victory. Julia Ward Howe wrote the 'Battle Hymn of the Republic' in 1861, to explain that God was 'trampling out a vintage where the grapes of wrath were stored' and that God's truth (the Northern cause) was marching on. The Confederates answered with a prayer to the same God: 'Lay Thou their legions low, roll back the ruthless foe; Let the proud spoiler know, God's on our side.'

The surrender of the southern armies brought no reconciliation between the churches of the North and South. Northern churches tended to look upon the southern churches as needing evangelization, along with the freed slaves. Most blacks became Baptists or Methodists, because they felt freer to express their emotions in those denominations. After the Civil War, southern Christians failed to admit the wrong of slavery, and to pledge their loyalty to the Union, because they were committed to the southern cause.

In the post-war decades the 'new frontier' was more urban than rural. American claims to be fulfilling her 'manifest destiny' stretched beyond the continent in imperialist expansion. The day of the crusade among equals was past.

JANETTE BOHI

HYMNS AND CHURCH MUSIC AFTER 1800

In the Church of England, hymn-singing was long considered to be illegal. In 1819 Thomas Cotterill, a Sheffield vicar, was charged by a church court for using a hymnbook in services. This test case led to hymn-singing being more or less legally accepted in the Church of England. Cotterill's book contained many hymns by James Montgomery (1771–1854), a radical Sheffield journalist who wrote 'Prayer is the Soul's Sincere Desire', and 'Stand Up and Bless the Lord'.

In 1827 Bishop Reginald Heber's *Hymns* was published; its literary merits and the authorization it secured from the bishops did much to extend the use of hymns in the Church of England. The collection included Heber's missionary hymn, 'From Greenland's Icy Mountains', as well as Dean Henry Milman's 'Ride On! Ride On in Majesty'.

The Oxford Movement revived interest in early Greek and Latin hymns. J. M. Neale translated and adapted many early Christian and medieval hymns, also writing some originals, including 'Good King Wenceslas'. *The Christian Year*, an anthology by John Keble, was first published in 1827, and by 1867 had run through over 100 editions. Some of his hymns are still sung today, among them 'New Every Morning'. The Oxford Movement's emphasis on personal devotion comes over in F. W. Faber's hymn, 'Souls of Men, Why Will Ye Scatter'; but Victorian sentimentality all too easily took over.

There were many women hymn-writers in the nineteenth century. Some of the best-known children's hymns were written by Mrs C. F. Alexander (1818–95), who set out basic Christian beliefs in such hymns as 'All Things Bright and Beautiful', 'Once in Royal David's City', and 'There is a Green Hill Far Away'. Among other women hymn-writers were Charlotte Elliott (1789–1871) – 'Just As I Am' – and Sarah Adams (1805–48) – 'Nearer, My God, to Thee'. Catherine Winkworth (1827–78), the finest translator of German hymns after John Wesley, put into English, 'Now Thank We All our God'.

Between 1800 and 1880, 220 hymnbooks appeared in the Church of England alone. *Hymns Ancient and Modern* (1861) came out of the Oxford Movement; but its wide selection of hymns finally made it popular with Anglicans of all parties. It was revised again and again, and by the end of the nineteenth century far outstripped its main rivals, the *Hymnal Companion* (1870) and *Church Hymns* (1871). Total sales of all editions are now well over 150 million. The only collection anywhere near as popular was the *Methodist Hymn Book*, which was revised in 1876.

NORTH AMERICA

American religious music was less inhibited. The folk tradition of the Baptists in the south and the singing-school movement produced simple, but distinctive, congregational music. Revivals in Kentucky in between 1797 and 1805 inspired spirituals, full of longing for release from slavery, such as 'Swing Low, Sweet Chariot'.

Many American hymns of the nineteenth century, however, reflected a literary, but liberal or Unitarian outlook. This is particularly true of *Hymns of the Spirit* (1864), compiled by Samuel Johnson and Samuel Longfellow, brother of the poet. One of Johnson's hymns expressed his opposition to dogma: 'City of God! How broad and far/Outspread thy walls sublime!' Similar writers included Oliver Wendell Holmes senior (1809–94) – 'Lord of All Being, Throned Afar'; William Merrill – 'Rise Up, O Men of God'; and Edward Sears – 'It Came Upon the Midnight Clear'. One of the most popular of these hymns still sung today is 'Dear Lord and Father of Mankind', taken from a poem by the Quaker John Greenleaf Whittier (1807–92). By contrast, Ray Palmer (1808–87), author of 'Jesus, These Eyes Have Never Seen', wrote in a spirit of Christ-centred devotion.

In 1870 Dwight L. Moody and Ira D. Sankey began to collect hymns for their evangelistic campaigns. It has been said that fewer people listened to the works of Bach during the entire nineteenth century than heard Sankey sing in 1875. Moody and Sankey's *Sacred Songs and Solos* grew from a six-penny pamphlet (1873) to a book of 1,200 pieces (1903). Its restricted subject-matter and mass appeal were ideal for revival meetings, but less suitable for ordinary congregations – though some of the hymns – such as Elizabeth Cleophane's 'There Were Ninety and Nine' – were taken into standard hymn-books. This collection introduced the tunes of the music-hall into the churches, and brought story-telling into the hymns. The most prolific contributors were Fanny J. Crosby, Philip P. Bliss, Frances Ridley Havergal, and David W. Whittle.

MUSIC IN BRITAIN

Many new hymn-tunes were written in the nineteenth century, but they were often too concerned with harmonic part-writing and chord sequences. John Bacchus Dykes and Sir John Stainer (1840–1901) wrote many tunes for *Hymns Ancient and Modern*, which gave each hymn its own 'proper' tune. It was not the first book to do so; but it made this common practice. Dykes wrote *Nicaea* for 'Holy, Holy, Holy', and *Lux Benigna* for 'Lead, Kindly Light,' and had a remarkable gift for writing memorable and singable melodies. Stainer's compositions, particularly his oratorio, *The Crucifixion*, still remain popular with church choirs. Sir Joseph Barnby, a well-known choral conductor, and editor of five hymnals, wrote more than 200 hymn-tunes, including *Laudes Domini* for 'When Morning Gilds the Skies'.

Samuel Sebastian Wesley (1810–76), Charles Wesley's grandson, was an influential cathedral organist, who composed fine anthems – such as *The Wilderness* – and many hymn-tunes, doing much to improve the music of the church. It was the poet Robert Bridges (1844–1930) who in his *Yattendon Hymnal* (1895–99) set a new high standard in tunes and words for hymns, reacting against the rather cloying tunes of Dykes and Barnby. German chorales and old psalm-tunes, rediscovered by Bridges and others, were gathered into *The English Hymnal* (1906) by Ralph Vaughan Williams (1872–1958). He contributed strong tunes of his own, such as *Sine Nomine* and *King's Weston*, and also adapted folk melodies for it.

During the second half of the nineteenth century the Free Churches, though still heavily influenced by Watts and Wesley, shaped their hymn-books along the lines of *Ancient and Modern*. They gave a lead Anglicans could not ignore in getting the entire congregation to sing.

In Scotland, until the mid-nineteenth century, only psalms were sung. When hymns were introduced, they mainly used English tunes. On the other hand, the Evangelical Revival released a stream of haunting tunes in Wales.

In the second half of the nineteenth century, English Roman Catholics involved their congregations in hymn-singing. F. W. Faber, one of their most prolific authors, aimed at providing the Catholic Church with a hymn-book which would do for their services what Wesley and Watts had done for Protestant worship. Later in the century there was a revival of authentic plainsong – 'Gregorian chant' – a vast repertory of unharmonized music, intended for the use of trained choirs singing the Roman liturgy.

JOHN S. ANDREWS

CHAPTER 35

A WORLD COME OF AGE
Science and philosophy challenge Christianity

The Victorian era was an age of authority and conformity, but also an age of doubt and seething discontent. The seeds of doubt that had been sown by the rationalists of the seventeenth century, and nurtured by the sceptics and deists of the eighteenth century, came to full flower in the nineteenth century. The whole fabric of Christianity was called into question, as science, philosophy, and history were all called upon to show that the Christian faith no longer had a valid basis.

A SOPHISTICATED APE?

Were human beings really sophisticated apes? That is what the theory of evolution seemed to be saying. But more important was the reasoning behind it, which suggested that the world was not the work of a wise, loving Creator who had planned everything. Instead, all plant and animal life had evolved naturally, and the fittest had survived. God was an unnecessary hypothesis.

The idea of evolution was not exactly new. It had its advocates from the ancient Greek philosopher, Anaximander, right down to Darwin's own grandfather, Erasmus Darwin (1731–1802). In the 1830s, Charles Lyell had published *The Principles of Geology*, in which he argued that the present state of the earth's surface had been brought about by a long and gradual development, and some strata contained the remains of sea creatures that had been deposited over many centuries, fossils that dated back an almost incalculable length of time. In 1844 the idea of evolution was extended from geology to the whole of animal life in *The Vestiges of the Natural History of Creation*, published anonymously by Robert Chambers. But the crisis came to a head with the publication of Darwin's *The Origin of Species* in 1859.

Charles Darwin (1809–82) had studied medicine at Edinburgh and theology at Cambridge – but neither with conspicuous success. In the 1830s he sailed as a naturalist on *HMS Beagle* on a survey expedition to South America, and then for years pondered his theories. At last he was stung into action when he received a manuscript from Alfred Russell Wallace (1823–1913) outlining ideas similar to his own. They published a joint paper, which paved the way for Darwin's masterpiece.

The creation story in Genesis chapter 1 tells how God created the world in six days and rested on the seventh. The evolutionists were now saying that the world had evolved over millions of years, possibly from a single prototype being. To explain how life had developed, Darwin set out the principle of natural selection or – more bluntly – the survival of the fittest. In order to survive, he said, plants and animals have to prey upon each other. To cope with their environment, they have to develop new capacities. Where such capacities become a permanent feature, a new species evolves.

Darwin's work met with a mixed reception. Darwin himself was not free from nagging doubts. At the meeting of the British Association in Oxford in 1860, the

Statue of the English naturalist Charles Darwin (1809–82), author of *On the Origin of Species*.

© IAN KEIRLE/ DREAMSTIME.COM

Bishop of Oxford, 'Soapy Sam' Wilberforce (1805–73), treated his audience to a display of sarcastic wit, ridiculing the new ideas. But the bishop found more than his match in T. H. Huxley (1825–95), who took the stance of a humble scientist and persuasively argued the case for evolution. In the following years it was Huxley, as much as anyone, who gave the evolutionary theory the stamp of scientific orthodoxy.

Huxley also coined the word 'agnosticism'. Many -isms claimed definite knowledge of all kinds of things; Huxley wanted a word to express the state of not knowing. Rather than adopt the point-blank denial of God of the atheist, Huxley said he just did not know – and was not in a position to know. In *The Origin of Species* Darwin had left room for belief in the Creator; in its sequel, *The Descent of Man* (1871), he was more openly agnostic. But in spite of everything, when Darwin died, he was duly buried in Westminster Abbey.

Public reaction to the theory of evolution ranged from outright hostility to wild enthusiasm. All kinds of people tried to jump on the bandwagon, using 'evolution' to justify whatever they happened to believe. Karl Marx declared that Darwin had provided the biological basis for communism, while American capitalists such as Andrew Carnegie and J. D. Rockefeller appealed to 'evolution' to justify the growth of big business.

A MONSTROUS ERROR?

Among Christian leaders, C. H. Spurgeon pronounced the theory of evolution a monstrous error, which would be ridiculed before another twenty years. Others were cautiously in favour. Frederick Temple (1821–1902), who later became Archbishop of Canterbury, was fairly typical of this attitude: he held that the concept of evolution left the argument for an intelligent Creator and Governor of the earth stronger than ever. The world was not just a series of accidents. The old argument from design to belief in God could be restated in a dynamic way.

At first sight the idea of evolution seemed flatly to contradict the book of Genesis. For centuries Christians had read Genesis chapter 1 as if it had been a newspaper account of what happened, step by step. Many Bibles were printed with marginal notes stating that the world was created in the year 4004 BC, the date worked out by Archbishop James Ussher (1581–1656). After Darwin, many continued in these beliefs – but others began to ask whether their reading had been too literal. Could it not be that, in describing the origin of the world, Genesis used a certain amount of symbolism, just as the last book of the Bible uses symbolism to describe the cosmic events of the end of the world? Since the habit of reading Genesis I literally – and often at the expense of Genesis 2, which tended to be ignored – was deeply ingrained, it was inevitable that the battle should rage over creation *versus* evolution. It was equally inevitable that many people should exchange an uncritical view of creation for an equally uncritical view of evolution.

A WORLD COME OF AGE

The debates on science and religion occupied centre stage in mid-Victorian England. Meanwhile, a debate of no less significance was taking place in the universities of Germany throughout the nineteenth century. Already, before the opening of the century, Immanuel Kant (1724–1804) had flung down the gauntlet. Previously, philosophers had held that God's existence could be proved by various rational arguments. Kant swept all these away – or at least he thought he had. In addition, he argued that the human mind was equipped to grapple only with the objects that we see around us, which exist in time and space. Once we try to think about any kind of reality that might lie beyond the objects in time and space, we land ourselves in all kinds of contradictions. Therefore it is impossible to think coherently about God. If God is to play any part at all, it is in the area of morals. There God is necessary – if there is to be any kind of after-life where virtue can be rewarded. Religion is useful for the simple and uneducated; but it can never be a substitute for philosophy. We should not do good because God says so; we should do good for its own sake. Human reason is our only authority and guide.

Kant regarded his philosophy as a second Copernican revolution – which is rather ironical. Copernicus had inaugurated a new era, by teaching that the earth is not the centre of the universe; instead, it rotates around the sun. Kant's philosophical revolution took humanity as its starting-point. It began by setting out the scope and limitations of human knowledge. This approach was revolutionary – though Kant was merely completing a process begun by Descartes over a century before. But the irony is that Kant was doing the opposite of Copernicus: he was placing humankind in the centre of his universe, and making everything else rotate around us.

It is often the case with philosophers that what they hand out as a solution is only the old problem in another form. Certainly Kant put his finger on numerous weaknesses in the old approach of philosophy to religion. But to reject the old-fashioned proofs for the existence of God is simply to see the flaws in the logic of particular arguments; it leaves unanswered the question of whether God can be known in some other way. To say that our minds think in terms of time and space is not the same as saying that we can have no insight into what lies behind our existence in time and space.

If we recognize that God is not an object of time and space, but that our language is geared to think in terms of time and space, it is inevitable that our language about God uses a great deal of symbolism. When Jesus said that the kingdom of God was like this or that, he was drawing on picture language to convey truths that could not be put in any way but by symbols. Humans do not have direct access to God; knowledge of him is always mediated by events, experiences, and words. Kant began a continuing debate on how we should think of God in the light of our existence in time and space, the limitations of the human mind, and the nature of our language.

FRIEDRICH SCHLEIERMACHER

The German theologian Friedrich Schleiermacher (1768–1834) was born into a clergy family and received a strict pietistic upbringing – against which he rebelled. In later life he described himself as a pietist again – but a pietist of a higher order. As a young professor at Halle, Schleiermacher witnessed the Napoleonic invasions. He later went to Berlin as professor at the newly-founded university.

The work of Schleiermacher's later years has to be seen against the background of the rise of Prussia. With the defeat of Napoleon, a new Prussia emerged which became the foundation of the new Germany. Schleiermacher was tireless as a patriotic preacher, and keenly commended uniting the Protestant Church in Germany, as part of the programme for national renewal.

It has been said that Schleiermacher did not found a school of thought, but an era. He was the first great theological thinker after Kant, and in effect accepted Kant's prohibition on metaphysical speculation. Schleiermacher was also a pioneer of biblical criticism – steering a middle way between secular philosophy and orthodox Christianity, by taking religious *experience* as his starting-point.

Schleiermacher saw the essence of religion in experience, and the essence of experience in the believer's sense of absolute dependence. He made this in turn the key to every other Christian doctrine. God is that on which we feel dependent; sin is a failure of our sense of dependence. Christ is the man who was utterly dependent upon God in every thought, word, and action – a dependence that added up to an existence of God in him. Christ's mission was to communicate this sense of dependence to others.

COLIN BROWN

GOD A 'WORLD-SPIRIT'

In the meantime, the attempt to outflank Kant was a major preoccupation of nineteenth-century thinkers. In theology, Schleiermacher looked for a new approach, which accepted Kant's criticisms of the proofs for the existence of God and his strictures on the limitations of human thought. His answer lay in basing theology on religious experience.

The 'Absolute Idealism' of philosophers such as G. W. F. Hegel (1770–1831) was partly an attempt to outflank Kant, but also an attempt to provide an alternative understanding of God to that of orthodox Christianity. Instead of starting with the individual 'I', the Idealists began with the absolute 'I': all reality is the manifestation of the Absolute Spirit. God does not exist over and above the world – as in Christian orthodoxy – but is the 'world-spirit' that is to be found in the depths of the world-processes. The world is a manifestation of God.

The end product of all this was a dynamic pantheism. These different philosophical approaches left their mark on the way in which Jesus Christ is understood. In the writings of Kant and in liberal Protestant theology, Jesus appears as an enlightened teacher of moral religion. In Schleiermacher and Hegel, Jesus appears as the supreme manifestation of the divine Spirit among men and women, and as the agent of the divine being in achieving the oneness of God and humanity.

When Hegel died in a cholera epidemic, his followers split into two camps. The right wing was concerned to preserve the teachings of their master, more or less as he had left them. The left wing consisted of revisionists and malcontents, who ended up by standing Hegel's philosophy on its head.

Ludwig Feuerbach (1804–72) had studied under Hegel. But whereas Hegel regarded all reality as the outworking of the Absolute Spirit, Feuerbach told his readers this 'spirit' was none other than nature. He could agree with Schleiermacher that the essence of all religion is a sense of absolute dependence; but he believed that on which humanity depends and feels dependent is simply nature. God is a projection of our own nature, which has been purified and freed from all limitations. Theology is simply anthropology, and the knowledge of God is nothing other than the knowledge of ourselves. Feuerbach protested that he was not so much an atheist as an 'antitheist'.

MARX

Another one-time devotee of Hegel, Karl Marx (1818–83) was born in the Rhineland to Jewish parents who became Lutherans. A student of philosophy, Marx became a journalist after leaving university, but soon fell foul of the authorities on account of his political views. Marx was expelled from Germany in the year of revolutions, 1848, and found a haven in London, and a supporter in Friedrich Engels. In London he divided his time between stirring up agitation, and gathering evidence in the British Museum for what he intended to be the grand indictment of the capitalist system, *Das Kapital* (1867).

Karl Marx (1818–83), author of *Das Kapital*.
ILLUSTRATED LONDON NEWS

By this time Marx had rejected not only Hegel, but Feuerbach too: neither the Absolute Spirit nor nature was the basis of reality. The basis of reality was to be found in matter. The history of the human race, then, is the history of how people are related to material things. According to Marx, history is moving relentlessly forward in the direction of the communist society. Up to this point, all history is the history of class struggle. When the communist society is reached, private property will be a thing of the past, and the state itself will manage everything. The political programme had already been announced by Marx and his patron, Engels, in *The Communist Manifesto* (1848). The authors called upon the downtrodden proletariat to unite in revolution, to overthrow the existing order and usher in the new society.

GOD IS DEAD

An atheist with a more individualistic approach was Friedrich Nietzsche (1844–1900). Whereas Marx was the prophet of communism, Nietzsche was adopted as a prophet of their new order by the Nazis in the 1930s. Nietzsche regarded himself as a prophet of the death of God, and a spokesman for liberated humanity. Since God is dead, humanity must go it alone, making up our own rules and values as we go along. Virtues prized by Christianity must be discarded, as they tend to preserve the weak and ailing. What is needed is a reassessment of all values, and a will to impose new values on others – whether they want them or not.

The most important of more recent events – that 'God is dead', that the belief in the Christian God has become unworthy of belief – already begins to cast its first shadows over Europe.

FRIEDRICH NIETZSCHE

A thinker who saw clearly the dangerous way in which political, and even church, systems were developing was the Danish writer Søren Kierkegaard (1813–55), in his lifetime little known beyond the borders of his native Denmark. Only in the twentieth century, as his writings began to be translated, did his significance come to be appreciated. Kierkegaard had a horror of systems, and was acutely aware of the danger of trying to manipulate God. He believed we must never forget God is *other*; that he exists on a different plane, and in a different way, from humans. It is therefore folly to try to prove his existence by rational arguments. To be known directly is the mark of an idol – not the living God.

God is known as he makes himself known. He does so in Jesus Christ. But because he takes on human form and speaks to us in human words, God comes to us in Christ *incognito*. We can know him – but only in faith. The faith that counts is one that is willing to put all at risk for God, and lead a life of personal discipleship. Such was Kierkegaard's answer to the totalitarian schemes of idealist philosophy and of church politics.

THE BIBLE UNDER FIRE

In the nineteenth century, the Christian faith also found itself challenged by history, in the guise of biblical criticism. If the truth of the Bible could be shown to be doubtful, then there would be nothing left on which Christian faith could stand. As the nineteenth century wore on, the Old Testament came increasingly under fire. It was widely assumed that the patriarchs Abraham, Isaac, and Jacob were mythical figures, or perhaps titles of tribes associated with particular names, and many questioned whether Moses had ever lived.

The most influential critic, the German Julius Wellhausen (1844–1918), held that Hebrew religion had developed from primitive stories of nomadic times to the elaborate, institutionalized ritualism of the centuries before the birth of Jesus. He claimed to find various sources behind the Old Testament law, which he dated to different stages in the history of Israel. Scholars of this outlook saw the Old Testament as a patchwork of pieces that owed their shape and texture to external influences.

But the central issue of biblical criticism concerned the figure of Christ. The quest for the 'historical Jesus' – the supposed picture of Jesus as he really was, behind the theology of the New Testament – dates back to the English deists in the eighteenth century. Among the early German writers in this tradition was H. S. Reimarus (1694–1768), who saw Jesus as an earnest Galilean teacher, who met an untimely end because he got his earnest moral teaching mixed up with the idea that the kingdom of God meant the setting up of a new political state in which God was King. After the crucifixion, he said, the disciples put out the story that Jesus had risen from the dead and would come again. The whole thing was a fraud, committed for material gain.

Another writer who took a sceptical view was David Friedrich Strauss (1808–74). In his famous *Life of Jesus* (1835–36), Strauss dismissed all the supernatural and messianic elements in the Gospels as myth. In Catholic France, J. E. Renan's *Life of Jesus* (1836), and in Protestant England J. R. Seeley's *Ecce Homo* (1865), both took a more positive view of the historical contents of the Gospel stories – but both tried to eliminate the supernatural, and reduced Jesus merely to a magnetic teacher.

Perhaps the most notorious of the nineteenth-century critics was Strauss's former teacher, F. C. Baur (1792–1860), who worked on the assumption that there had been a great conflict in the early church between Peter, whose party stood for a strictly Jewish attitude to the law, and Paul, whose party held a more liberal Greek approach, which set little store by the law and Jewish ritual. On this basis, Baur set about deciding which books of the New Testament were genuine, dismissing as later productions those which did not appear to reflect this supposed conflict. Thus, only four of Paul's letters could be regarded as genuine: Romans, Galatians, and 1 and 2 Corinthians.

NEW LIGHT ON THE BIBLE

But not all nineteenth-century biblical scholarship was destructive. Among the positive gains was the less spectacular, but steady, work of reconstructing the text of the Bible from ancient manuscripts, such as the *Codex Sinaiticus*, which was discovered in a monastery on Mount Sinai. The discovery of new texts, and the development of the scientific study of manuscripts, confirmed the essential accuracy of the texts on which older translations of the Bible, such as the *King James Version* (1611), were based. Prominent in New Testament research were the Cambridge scholars B. F. Westcott, F. J. A. Hort, and J. B. Lightfoot. Westcott and Hort's Greek text of the New Testament surpassed all earlier versions.

The exploration of the language and background history of the New Testament threw fresh light on what the Bible was actually saying. Lightfoot's study of early Christian literature after the New Testament period disproved Baur's late dating of the New Testament books, for it showed that the New Testament must already have been written by the end of the first century.

Archaeology too confirmed the accuracy of a great deal of the information given in the Bible. This can readily be seen, for example, in the writings of Sir William Ramsay (1851–1939), whose study of the geography and archaeology of the Roman Empire supported the picture painted by Luke in the Acts of the Apostles. If Christianity is a historical religion, based on events which happened in history, these events are open to the historian to investigate.

COLIN BROWN

CHAPTER 36

OUTPOSTS OF EMPIRE
The nineteenth-century missionary explosion

Of all the transformations of Christianity that have taken place since 1789, perhaps the most remarkable is the shift of its geographical and cultural centre of gravity. In 1789, an observer from Mars might well have assumed Christianity to be the tribal religion of the white, Caucasian, peoples. With a few exceptions – readily explained by historical circumstances – all the Caucasians of Europe and their descendants in the New World professed Christianity. With a few more exceptions, explained by survival or conquest, no one else did. Such an observer might have had doubts about the survival of Christianity in Europe. Had the recent revival in Protestant areas come too late to stem the tide of rationalism which was producing – in both Catholic and non-Catholic areas – a non-religious interpretation of life? But at least he could not doubt that Christianity was identified with Europe and the Europeans.

If the Martian next returned to Earth in 2000, he would find Christianity a world religion, firmly established in every continent, among people of the most diverse and disparate origins and cultures. It was still growing, and most rapidly in the southern continents – especially tropical Africa and Latin America – and receding only amongst the Caucasians – to whom 200 years before it seemed confined.

Between the Martian's two visits fall events which transformed the relations of East and West, and of North and South: the Industrial Revolution, the rise and fall of the European empires, and the missionary movement. The relation between these is highly complex, and cannot be explained by any single theory. What is certain is that not only the world, but also the church, was changed out of recognition as a result.

By 1789, Europeans knew the outline map of the world much as it is today, except for some tentativeness about Australasia and the larger Pacific islands. They knew very little of the interior of any of the continents except their own, if we leave the Middle East and India out of the account. Scientific concerns – it was a self-consciously investigatory age – and commercial interests – the quest for both raw materials and markets – prompted greater curiosity about these continents. An important minority also wished to spread the Christian gospel.

MOTIVES FOR MISSION

On the whole, Protestant thinkers were slower than others to recognize the implications of new discoveries of lands and peoples. When Roman Catholic controversialists asked where were the Protestants' missions, a common orthodox reply was that it was presumptuous to apply to oneself Christ's missionary commission, which was addressed only to apostles. The English explorer Captain James Cook (1728–79) believed it was unlikely that the faith would ever be preached in the islands he discovered, since it could never be worth anyone's while financially. Devout Anglican churchmen, shocked at the prevalence of

Presbyterianism and vice in the American colonies, had in 1701 formed the Society for the Propagation of the Gospel. Among the founders, committee, and clergy there were those with a vision for evangelizing neighbouring peoples. But, with rare exceptions, the SPG in the eighteenth century was essentially concerned with the English overseas.

It was in North America that the crucial experience came: there the line connecting Puritan missionary endeavours with the Evangelical movement never quite broke. Two strands led to a new Protestant world vision. One was prophetic: the thought of the earth 'filled with the knowledge of the Lord, as the waters cover the sea' (Habakkuk 2:14). Jonathan Edwards, for instance, believed this biblical prophecy was near fulfilment. The other strand is evangelical; the sense of God's command to preach the gospel, which broke through theological rigidity and habits of sanctified self-interest. In America, these impulses led to a renewed concern for native Americans. In Britain, with no neighbouring non-Christian peoples, but now awake to regions overseas, the same thoughts – often coming from American sources – produced a concern for the evangelization of the world.

BELIEF INTO ACTION

A new organization – the missionary society – turned prophetic conviction into action. A remarkably wide spectrum of churches and denominations was involved. The tiny Moravian community was the acknowledged leader, not only in time, but also in numbers of missionaries in proportion to its membership, and the lengths to which they were prepared to go. Moravian missionaries in the West Indies even sold themselves into slavery.

By the 1790s Calvinistic Baptists, Arminian Methodists, impeccable Anglican churchmen, and ardent dissenters and seceders in England and Scotland were seeking to 'use means for the conversion of the heathens' (William Carey's phrase). But, with the rarest exceptions, such interests reached only those touched by the Evangelical Revival; for the first two or three decades of the missionary movement, interest in missions was restricted to the Evangelicals.

This is hardly surprising. The Evangelical Revival revolutionized preaching and its objectives. Earnest churchmen, who regarded the clergyman's task as being to nurture the seed of faith planted at baptism in virtually all members of his parish, could not easily adjust to the thought of preaching the gospel in a tribal society. People who inherited a rigid doctrine of predestination, in which God inscrutably made up his elect, saw no reason to concern themselves with why there were evidently no elect in India or China. But the Evangelicals saw preaching as calling sinners to God through faith in Christ. They felt a personal responsibility to do this, and saw no difference in principle between 'baptized heathen' in Britain and non-Christian peoples overseas.

Only in the 1820s and 1830s did interest in overseas missions become a regular feature of British church life generally, due partly to the success of the Evangelicals in influencing English and Scottish life. Many of their values were adopted outside their circle – in particular, the idea of Britain as a Christian nation, with Christian responsibilities overseas, took root.

Bishoprics were established in India and elsewhere (none had ever been established in pre-colonial America). The Society for the Propagation of the Gospel enlarged its operations to those of a genuine missionary society. In Scotland, moderate churchmen joined with Evangelicals to promote missions, strongly educational in character, under the umbrella of the General Assembly of the Church of Scotland.

SOCIETIES FOR MISSION

In the eighteenth century it was taken for granted that there were only three forms of church government: episcopal, Presbyterian, and independent (or congregational). The supporters of each claimed to be following the Bible, and all the main arguments on each side were well known. But as the conviction of the responsibility to spread the gospel worldwide began to dawn on British Christians at the end of the century, it became clear that none of these forms of church government enabled the church to embark on a world mission. The Church of England, with its hierarchy of bishops, had at this time no central organization; nor, by definition, did the independent churches. The Church of Scotland, the only large Presbyterian Church, did discuss in 1796 whether to appoint a committee or take a collection for missions. They voted to approve the principle – and prevent anything being done in practice. The friends of world mission were driven to find another form of machinery: the voluntary society.

ORGANIZING FOR MISSION

The voluntary society was still a relatively undeveloped type of organization. The Church of England had two well-established societies – the Society for Promoting Christian Knowledge and the Society for the Propagation of the Gospel – but these had royal charters and the approval of the bishops. Political pressure-groups of this time operated through loose 'association' and not societies. In fact, when William Carey wrote his book, *An Enquiry into the Obligations of Christians to use Means for the Conversion of the Heathens* (1792), he asked: what would a trading company do? From this, he proposed the formation of a company of serious Christians – laymen and ministers – with a committee to collect and sift information, and to find funds and suitable men.

The voluntary society, of which the missionary society was one early form, was to transform the nineteenth-century church. It was invented to meet a need rather than for theological reasons, but it undermined all the established forms of church government. In the first place, it made possible ecumenical activity: churchmen and dissenters or seceders, isolated from church business, could work together for defined purposes. It also altered the power base in the church, by encouraging lay leadership. Ordinary Christian men – and later women – came to hold key positions in the important societies. And again, the best societies made it possible for many people to participate.

All these features appeared early in the history of missionary societies. The London Missionary Society adopted in 1796 its 'fundamental principle that our design is not to send Presbyterianism, Independency, Episcopacy or any other form of church government … but the glorious gospel of the blessed God to the heathen'. One of the founders called for 'the funeral of bigotry'. Ordinary Christian people held responsible office in missionary societies at a time when such responsibilities would have been unthinkable elsewhere in the church.

The enthusiast who collected a penny a week from members of his local missionary society auxiliary, and distributed the missionary magazine, was fully involved in the work of the society. It was through the work of such people that missionary candidates came forward. The American missionary Rufus Anderson (1796–1880) wrote in 1834: 'It was

WILLIAM CAREY

William Carey (1761–1834), an English Baptist, devoted most of his life to taking the Christian gospel to India. Born at Paulerspury, Northamptonshire, the son of a parish clerk and schoolmaster, he was converted in 1779, and baptized as a believer in 1783. After some local preaching, Carey became pastor of Moulton (1786) and then Harvey Lane, Leicester (1789), Baptist Church. He was deeply influenced by the theology of Jonathan Edwards, which supplied an impetus to mission.

In 1792 Carey published *An Enquiry into the Obligation of Christians to use Means for the Conversion of the Heathen*, arguing that Christ's great commission to 'preach the gospel to every creature' still applied to all Christians. The same year, in a sermon at Nottingham, he urged Christians to 'expect great things from God' and 'attempt great things for God'. As a direct consequence, in October 1792, the Baptist Missionary Society was founded: the first foreign missionary organization created by the Evangelical Revival.

Carey and his family sailed to India the following year. In 1799 he was joined at Serampore, near Calcutta, by two fellow-Baptists, Joshua Marshman (1768–1837) and William Ward (1769–1823), and for the next quarter-century the three men organized a growing network of mission stations in and beyond Bengal. In the years up to 1824, Carey supervised six complete and twenty-four partial translations of the Bible, as well as publishing several grammars, dictionaries, and translations of Eastern books. Although some of his early translations were hurried and stilted, his work was an immense achievement for a largely self-educated pioneer.

Carey achieved much in various areas. He initiated mission schools, conceived the idea of Serampore College, founded the Agricultural Society of India (1820) to promote agricultural improvements, and took a leading part in the campaign for the abolition of widow-burning (*sati*), which succeeded in 1829. Carey's devotion to India – which he never left – and his practical wisdom are shown in his encouraging Indians to spread the gospel themselves.

DAVID W. BEBBINGTON

not until the present century that the evangelical churches of Christendom were ever really organized with a view to the conversion of the world.' They became organized by means of the voluntary society.

THE 'SOCIETY' IS INVENTED

By the 1780s, many Christians in all denominations were feeling that the signs of revival in Protestant countries foreshadowed an extension of gospel preaching to the whole world. It was a group of Baptists from the English midlands who first formed an effective organization, as The Particular Baptist Society for the Propagation of the Gospel, later the Baptist Missionary Society.

The London Missionary Society – at first called simply The Missionary Society – also began in regional gatherings for prayer. But the leading figures, men such as John Love (1757–1825) and David Bogue (1750–1825), were – unlike William Carey – prominent figures in their denominations. Most were Independents, but some were churchmen or Presbyterians: and it was proposed to form a society which would ignore denominations. The scale was much greater than that of the Baptists; soon after its formation in 1795, the society sent a party of more than thirty missionaries to the Pacific. Despite its ecumenical intentions, the LMS soon became an overwhelmingly Congregational society, partly because other denominational societies were formed.

In Scotland, the refusal of the 1796 General Assembly closed the door to any official church mission. This left friends of mission in the Church of Scotland free to join with members of the secession churches in local societies, modelled on the LMS. Societies in the smaller towns could only collect funds; but the Glasgow and Edinburgh (later the Scottish) Missionary Societies sent out their own missionaries. Scotland also contributed many missionaries to serve the LMS.

THE BIBLE SOCIETIES

In December 1802 Thomas Charles, a Calvinist minister from Bala, North Wales, attended a committee meeting of the Religious Tract Society (RTS) in London, to urge the society to produce a Welsh Bible. The Tract Society did not regard Bible distribution as part of its job, so Joseph Hughes, a London Baptist, suggested that a new agency be formed to provide Bibles, both for Britain and for other countries throughout the world.

On 7 March 1804, the British and Foreign Bible Society (BFBS) was established 'to encourage the wider circulation of the Holy Scriptures, without note or comment', its governing committee composed of fifteen Anglicans, fifteen Nonconformists and six foreign members. Sympathetic societies soon appeared throughout the United Kingdom – in Glasgow (1805), Edinburgh (1809), and Dublin (1806). Societies in Canada (1807), Australia (1817), and New Zealand (1837) followed.

Prince Galitzin, Czar Alexander I's Minister for Foreign Religions, backed the setting up of a Russian Bible Society (1813), but this was subsequently banned by Czar Nicholas I, in 1825. BFBS missionary Robert Pinkerton (1780–1859) established committees at Amsterdam, Elberfeld, Hanover, Berlin, and Dresden in rapid succession; while another missionary, John Paterson (1776–1855), toured Scandinavia, setting up societies in Norway, Sweden, and Denmark. Most of these European agencies flourished, with financial support from the BFBS.

Roman Catholics also enjoyed the support of the BFBS. Soon after its founding, the BFBS sent funds to support the Bible translation work of Bishop Michael Wittmann (1760–1833) of Regensburg. The BFBS also backed Leander van Ess (1772–1847), professor of theology at Marburg, whose German translation of the New Testament was published in 1807.

For its first two decades, the Bible Society's operation was unclouded by conflict. But in 1825 the German Bible societies applied for permission to include the Apocrypha in their Bibles. The BFBS refused, and as a result the Germans separated from the London Committee. The Scottish societies also separated themselves from the BFBS, holding that the BFBS had been tardy in refusing to print the Apocrypha. In 1831, after the BFBS refused to introduce a doctrinal test that would exclude Unitarians, the Trinitarian Bible Society was formed.

Despite these divisions, the BFBS expanded continuously. In 1907, the society reported that – since its founding – more than 200 million Bibles, Testaments, and portions of Scripture had circulated.

AMERICA

In 1808 the Philadelphia Bible Society was formed. A year later similar societies appeared in Connecticut, Massachusetts, New York, and Maine. In 1814, Samuel John Mills Jr (1783–1818), an American missionary, journeyed throughout the frontier territories of the United States, and discovered the

DENOMINATIONS MOBILIZE

These developments presented strict Anglican Evangelicals with a problem: they felt the need for missions as much as their dissenting brethren, but did not believe the SPG was suited to gospel-preaching. On the other hand, they wanted to retain denominational boundaries, and ruled out participation in the LMS, under its mainly dissenting leaders. Crucial discussions took place in an Evangelical club, the Eclectic Society, and in 1799 the Church Missionary Society for Africa and the East was formed, its first committee mostly consisting of little-known London clergymen. The Anglican hierarchy acquiesced but gave no approval. Only when the society had proved itself – many years later – did prominent churchmen recognize it.

John Wesley was very conscious of the transatlantic dimension of Methodist work, including the West Indies, to which preachers were regularly sent, and which by 1790 had been made a separate Methodist province. Thomas Coke, to whom Wesley gave much responsibility in his last years, was anxious to extend Methodist missions on a world scale. He published a plan for a society as early as 1784, and tried several times to get the Methodist Conference to approve an extension, but met financial objections. Coke worked towards forming local auxiliaries, and by 1814 these were recognized by the Conference. In 1818 the Methodist Conference brought together the auxiliaries in a Methodist Missionary Society, of which eventually every member of the Methodist Church was automatically a member.

It was twenty-eight years after the 1796 Assembly debate that the Church of Scotland took direct responsibility for missions, and commissioned its first missionary Alexander Duff (1806–78). By that time Evangelical and moderate could

need to provide Bibles for the settlers. In 1816 the American Bible Society (ABS) was founded in New York City, with its early efforts devoted to providing Bibles for the pioneers who were opening up the West, European immigrants flooding into the country, and Native Americans.

In 1835 the British Baptist missionary William Pearce (1794–1840) applied to the ABS for aid in printing a Bengali Testament, intending to use the word 'immerse' for 'baptize'. When this was refused by the ABS, the American Baptists withdrew to form the American and Foreign Bible Society (1836).

The ecumenical movement of the first half of the twentieth century influenced the Bible societies. During the 1930s, the possibility of joint activity was explored, though such moves were interrupted by World War II. The major Bible societies met in 1946 at Haywards Heath, England, and formed the United Bible Societies (UBS), consisting of Bible Societies from many countries worldwide. Anxious to avoid the Western centres of London and New York City, the UBS set up regional offices in Nairobi, Mexico City, Singapore, and Bassersdorf, Switzerland (later Brussels), each office housing specialists in Bible translation, production, and distribution. Within a decade, Bible circulation increased by more than 400 per cent.

WAYNE A. DETZLER

agree on this, and the stress on education – which was to be so important for Scottish missions – possibly first arose from their agreement. When the church was split by the 'Disruption' in 1843, the missionaries all joined the Free Church. The Church of Scotland had to begin anew recruiting missionaries.

In North America, the presence of neighbouring non-Christian peoples – the Native Americans – meant the missionary challenge was always present, if not always taken up. Native American missions had first stimulated British missionary societies. In turn, the example of the British Societies led to American societies patterned on the LMS, the first being the New York Missionary Society in 1796. In 1810, the first society specifically designed for worldwide mission was founded: the American Board of Commissioners for Foreign Missionaries.

In Holland the voluntary society began almost as early as in Britain, the inter-denominational *Nederlandsch Zendelinggenootschap* being founded in 1797.

EUROPE CATCHES THE VISION

On the rest of the European continent, the missionary seminary came earlier than the missionary society; but in the years following the Napoleonic Wars missionary societies sprang up. The religious societies of German Pietism were especially fertile soil: a missionary visit to the Deutsche Christentumsgesellschaft – founded in 1780 – produced missionary societies in Bremen (1819), Hamburg (1822) and elsewhere, which merged to form the North German Missionary Society in 1834. Berlin had its missionary society for Prussia from 1824, and the Rhineland its own society from 1828. From 1815, Basle formed the focus of Protestant missionary interest in Switzerland, southern Germany, southern France, and the Austrian Empire; its roll of missionary recruits was long and its seminary influential. French Protestants had formed the Paris Mission by 1822.

As in Britain, the ecumenical impulse was strong in the early days, but tensions between Lutherans and Reformed eventually split the North German Mission. In its early days, the Basle Mission required those of its missionaries who served with the Church Missionary Society to become Anglicans, those serving in the Danish territory, Lutherans, and so on.

Denmark, which was still a minor maritime power, with interests in West Africa and the West Indies, founded its missionary society in 1821. For various reasons, major societies did not emerge in the other Scandinavian countries until late in the century.

COMMON-SENSE MISSIONARIES

The founders of the early British societies clearly did not expect many missionary recruits from among ministers, or from the normal sources of supply of ministers. William Carey – a self-educated cobbler turned minister – is an exception. Most of the early recruits were craftsmen or tradesmen, who would have been unlikely to obtain ordination for the home ministry. The first enthusiasm of the LMS – that spirituality and common sense were qualifications enough – was damped by the disasters that overtook many of their early missionaries. 'Culture shock' took a heavy toll, and a few years' experience was enough to show the importance of preparing missionaries. Though many LMS candidates had little formal education, their training – superintended originally by David Bogue – was impressive. Much early LMS study on languages and tribes is strikingly scholarly.

The greatest recruiting difficulties were met by the CMS, since their principles required the use of ordained men as missionaries — and at first very few came forward. This difficulty was eased by co-operation with continental seminaries. Many missionaries from Germany and other continental European countries served the CMS with distinction. Of the first twenty-four CMS missionaries, seventeen were German, and only three were ordained Englishmen.

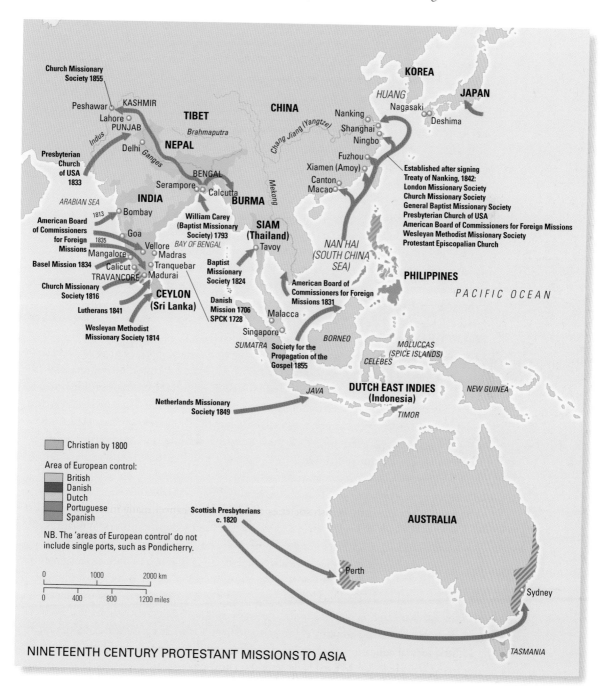

NINETEENTH CENTURY PROTESTANT MISSIONS TO ASIA

Things changed when English bishops became more favourable to the society, and as the society became more rooted in the parishes. By mid-century the importance of 'native ministers' was also becoming recognized, and an increasing number served on the staffs of missionary societies. The CMS Niger Mission, begun in 1857, was entirely African staffed.

In the last third of the century, missionary recruitment expanded enormously, largely due to the effects of the 1859 revival, the Keswick Movement, and other forces. The universities were particularly involved: the 'Cambridge Seven' – ex-Cambridge undergraduates who set out for China in 1885 – were only the first of hundreds who followed. These decades – the period of high imperialism – not only produced many more missionaries, but a different type of missionary.

The same influences were at work in America, where students had been important in the missionary movement from the beginning. In 1886 the Student Volunteer Movement was founded, which led in turn to the Student Volunteer Missionary Union, and later the Student Christian Movement. In the last two decades of the century a series of conferences were held under titles such as 'Make Jesus King', and 'Students and the Missionary Problem'. The numbers of volunteers, together with the technical and political developments of the age, led to the prospect of 'The evangelization of the world in this generation'. World War I entirely transformed the situation: but by the time European manpower was reduced, the great African-led mass-movements had begun.

The forces which produced new supplies of candidates also created new forms of society, which maintained the voluntary society principle, but were directed to particular areas – for example, the China Inland Mission (1865) and the Qua Iboe Mission (1887). Others met particular needs, such as the Mission to Lepers (1874).

FOLLOWING THE FLAG?

The birth of the missionary societies had nothing to do with the protection of British interests abroad. The earliest missions were in fact associated with traditionally radical groups, such as the Baptists, and supported by people with known revolutionary sympathies, such as the Haldane family in Scotland. This caused some to believe that they were basically subversive, to which was added the fear that missionary preaching would offend Hindus and Muslims, upset a volatile situation in India, and harm British trade. The semi-official Honourable East India Company, through which British administration and trade was exercised, was not initially well-disposed towards William Carey and his colleagues, who had to sail in a Danish ship and work from Danish territory.

The situation altered through the changes in British life brought about by the Evangelicals. Charles Grant (1746–1823), who had been radically converted in India, rose to the highest position in the Company. When the Company's charter came up for renewal in 1813, the Evangelicals of the Clapham Sect, briefed by Grant, denounced some aspects of its policy. Not only did the Company not promote the gospel, not only did it hinder missionary work; it positively profited by means of the temple tax and similar institutions for idolatry. Britain should awake to its Christian responsibilities, abolish the tax, and – by appointing a bishop and all other means – stand up for the Christian faith.

The outcome was a qualified victory for the Evangelicals. Temple tax was abandoned, and later administrations felt free to intervene against certain Indian religious customs, such as *sati* (widow burning). Bishops were appointed, and the system of government chaplains reformed and enlarged. Missions were, with occasional exceptions, unhindered, and often favoured. But anything approaching an official mission to India was carefully avoided. This attitude towards missions remained characteristic of government policy throughout the nineteenth century.

Grants to missions by colonial governments were tied to specific projects, particularly grants-in-aid for education. The largest extension came after World War I, when the colonial powers, especially the British, came to recognize a wider responsibility for education than previously. The cheapest and most efficient way of putting this into practice was to develop a system of funding education by means of grants to the missions.

Nineteenth-century Evangelicals soon stopped asking for 'official' backing for missions. They continued, however, to claim that the British owed a debt to Africa on account of the slave trade, and to India on account of the wealth derived from it. What was required was the best that Britain could give in return. Apart from India, there was little appetite in Britain in the first half of the nineteenth century to acquire new overseas territories, and in the 1840s there were plans to abandon as many as possible of such expensive 'luxuries'.

The missionary societies fought to keep overseas concerns before both the public and the government. They persuaded a reluctant government to fund a philanthropic expedition to the Niger in 1841, to develop agriculture and undercut the slave trade. They lobbied for British support for the little African state of Abeokuta, when it was threatened with destruction by its powerful slave-running neighbour, Dahomey. There was little thought of acquiring territory for Britain in all this: it was a call for Britain to use its power and influence on behalf of justice, and freedom from slavery.

THE SCRAMBLE FOR AFRICA

When Britain and other European powers moved into the high imperial period and annexed large sections of territory, the missionary interest on the whole went along with it. Sometimes it seemed the best way to deal with an unsatisfactory situation. For instance, Scottish missionaries in Malawi begged for a British protectorate, lest Portuguese misrule spread from Mozambique and increase war and slavery. When the protectorate was actually set up, the same missionaries were soon protesting about British maladministration. John MacKenzie (1835–99) sought a British protectorate for Botswana, to stop Cecil Rhodes' British South Africa Company acquiring it.

Sometimes the factors that influenced the great powers in 'the scramble for Africa' also influenced the missionaries: Protestant missionaries feared annexation by a Catholic power, and vice versa. Sometimes annexation was seen as opening up to Christian influences territories closed until then; rightly so – for 'closed' areas knew that to admit one sort of white man would ultimately mean admitting them all. European overrule, in Africa at least, was seen by most people as inevitable. Except for some American missions, there was little sign of missionaries opposing in principle the spread of imperial rule.

But relations between missions and colonial governments were not always smooth. Missions were often critical of government actions, while governments were often nervous of missionary activities. This nervousness sometimes extended to excluding missionaries altogether. The Muslim-ruled provinces taken into Northern Nigeria by the British contained many millions of non-Muslims, who had been conquered in holy wars (*jihads*). The British governed them by 'indirect rule', which insulated some of these provinces from missionary activity and ensured they became completely Muslim.

The most notable casualties of the age of imperialism were – especially in Africa – the indigenous educated leaders. Most were Christian, brought up under Christian influences, who under earlier conditions had been trained for responsibility. It is not surprising to find such people – for example, James Africanus Beale Horton (1835–83), Bishop James 'Holy' Johnson (c. 1836–1917), Joseph Ephraim Casely Hayford (1866–1930), and the many-sided Afro-Caribbean, Edward Wilmot Blyden (1832–1912) – leading early nationalist and pan-African thought. They made their case by appealing to the Christian faith.

The nationalist movement evolved into the independence movement. Many of the new leaders not only derived from Christian schools the education that made them effective, but also – even when they were critical of existing missionary institutions – drew their inspiration – and their criticisms – from Christian teaching. In India, where Christians made up only a tiny proportion of the population, the Christian colleges often contributed much to the agitations of the 1920s and 1930s. That many of the missionaries sympathized strongly with the national aspirations of their students is very apparent. In fact, some of the bitterest modern critics of missions have been white settlers.

The relation between missions and colonial expansion is complex. Sometimes missions preceded the flag, sometimes they followed it. But one thing is clear: if missions are associated with the rise of imperialism, they are equally associated with the factors which brought about its destruction.

ABOLISHING SLAVERY

In the 1790s, the Evangelical was marked out as much by a desire for the abolition of the slave trade as by an interest in missions. Inevitably, the two causes marched together.

The Sierra Leone colony was founded by the enterprise of the Evangelical 'Clapham Sect', most of whose members also supported the missionary societies. The colony had three aims: to provide a haven for freed slaves; to prove that economics did not dictate the need for the slave trade; and to be a base for missionary operations in Africa. After the abolition of the British slave trade in 1807, the colony (its capital significantly called Freetown) became the centre to which intercepted slave-ships from all over West Africa were diverted, and their miserable cargoes of slaves landed. From this source came a people who were to be vital for the spread of Christianity in West Africa. By the time of the emancipation of the slaves in British territories (1834), opposition to slavery had become a normal British reaction, just as interest in mission had become part of church life.

But acts of Parliament did not end the slave trade. In the 1830s abolitionists were still led by an Evangelical, Sir Thomas Fowell Buxton (1786–1845). They reflected sadly that more slaves than ever were now crossing the Atlantic, and that West Africa was being depopulated by the trade and the wars that it encouraged. Buxton, like Wilberforce before him, believed that an economic institution could only be countered by an economic initiative. It burst upon him one day that the solution for Africa lay in developing its own resources: Africa would be reborn by the Bible and the plough.

A SUBSTITUTE FOR SLAVERY

So came to birth the doctrine of the 'Three Cs' – Christianity, commerce, and civilization. The basic idea was that the interests of all three lay in the same direction. Christianity and slavery were irreconcilably opposed. The most effective way of combating the slave trade was to provide an attractive commercial substitute. The development of the export of raw materials from Africa, instead of the export of labour, would in turn involve developing in Africa commercial agriculture and the appropriate technologies – 'civilization', in fact, as Buxton understood it.

These ideals inspired the Niger Expedition of 1841, forced by Buxton upon the reluctant British government. Three specially designed ships, with hand-picked crews, sailed up the River Niger, with instructions to make anti-slavery treaties, set up model farms, and survey the possibilities for technological and commercial development. Some months later the expedition limped back, its ranks decimated by fever, and little of significance achieved. Buxton was discredited; except in the eyes of the missionary representatives, all that had been proved was that European residence, and consequently 'civilization', was impossible in inland Africa.

But those with missionary interest continued to argue that 'Christianity, commerce, and civilization' stood together. In a modest way, the Church Missionary Society was able to prove the effectiveness of the 'Three Cs' in its Yoruba mission, not many years after the Niger Expedition. Old chiefs were soon saying that the mission-sponsored cotton industry brought more benefits than all the slave trade.

Porch of the slave house, Goree Island, Dakar, Senegal.
©CARLOS MORA/
DREAMSTIME.COM

DAVID LIVINGSTONE

David Livingstone, the missionary and explorer, was born in Blantyre in the industrial west of Scotland in 1813, to poor and godly parents. At ten years of age, he began work in a cotton mill, with a book propped up on the machine. By this means, and through night classes, he built up some general education. Converted, and convinced he had a missionary calling, Livingstone studied medicine in Glasgow and London, and theology in England. He was not a promising student – awkward, dour, and heavy.

From 1841 until 1856, Livingstone served under the London Missionary Society, starting in South Africa, under the celebrated Robert Moffat (1795–1883), whose daughter he married. But David was soon going into uncharted territory, laying the foundation for missions, building relationships, acquiring a knowledge of the geography, transport possibilities, movement of peoples, and the horrible facts of the slave trade.

Nineteenth-century illustration of the medical missionary and explorer David Livingstone (1813–73). Livingstone was badly mauled by a lion in Africa in 1844.
TIM DOWLEY ASSOCIATES

Livingstone's remarkable travels between 1851 and 1856 included his walk across Africa from west to east – recorded in *Missionary Travels and Researches in South Africa* (1857) – and first established his legendary reputation. His committee, however, was not convinced of the missionary relevance of such travels, and, when he returned to Africa in 1858, it was to lead a British government expedition to explore the River Zambesi – which he called 'God's highway into the interior'. The expedition did not prosper: Livingstone failed in his objects, his wife died, and his enthusiasms were questioned. But he was soon back, this time without European companions. Landing in Zanzibar in 1866, he continued his quests in the East African interior with incredible endurance, until his death in 1873. His African companions carried his body back to the coast, and he was buried in Westminster Abbey.

As an explorer, Livingstone ranks with the greatest. He walked further – across what is now South Africa, Botswana, Zambia, Mozambique, Malawi, Tanzania, and Eastern Zaire – and recorded better than most of his contemporaries. He held to his early belief in the ultimate unity of all truth, biblical and scientific. But a mastering motive for his journeys was that they could help drain 'the open sore of Africa' – the Arab slave trade.

Livingstone was convinced that the slave trade had to be countered with an economic substitute, to lessen its attractiveness. Trade and developed agriculture – accompanying the gospel – could do this. His relations with Africans were excellent; his failures mostly with Europeans. Though technically a missionary for only half his thirty years in Africa, Livingstone saw all his work in the context of a providential plan, in which gospel-preaching, the increase of knowledge, and the relief of suffering marched together. The Anglican Universities Mission to Central Africa owed its inspiration to this Scots independent, through a speech in Cambridge in 1858. After his death, the Church of Scotland and the Free Church of Scotland opened Central African missions which reflected his ideals and breadth of vision.

ANDREW F. WALLS

The Atlantic slave trade was killed by moral, political, and economic factors. Attention next turned to the East African slave trade, which was operated by Arabs and Swahili peoples, and sometimes favoured by the Portuguese. The British government directed pressure mainly on the Sultan of Zanzibar. But the doctrine of the 'Three Cs' found its last and greatest prophet in David Livingstone, whose journeys were based on the conviction that the Arab slave trade could be strangled by alternative commerce.

The other main areas directly affected by slavery were the West Indies and, to a lesser extent, South Africa. The West Indies had been one of the earliest targets for missions, but the slave-owners there were deeply hostile to missionary activity, whether evangelistic or educational. Missionaries were generally instructed by their home committees not to attack slavery publicly, nor to encourage dissidence among the slaves. This did not prevent the prosecution or maltreatment of anti-slavery missionaries, such as the Baptist William Knibb (1803–45) in Jamaica, or the London Society's John Smith (1790–1824), who died in prison in Demerara while under sentence of death. Missionaries such as Knibb, and stories such as Smith's, provided much of the evidence used by abolitionists in their campaign in Britain.

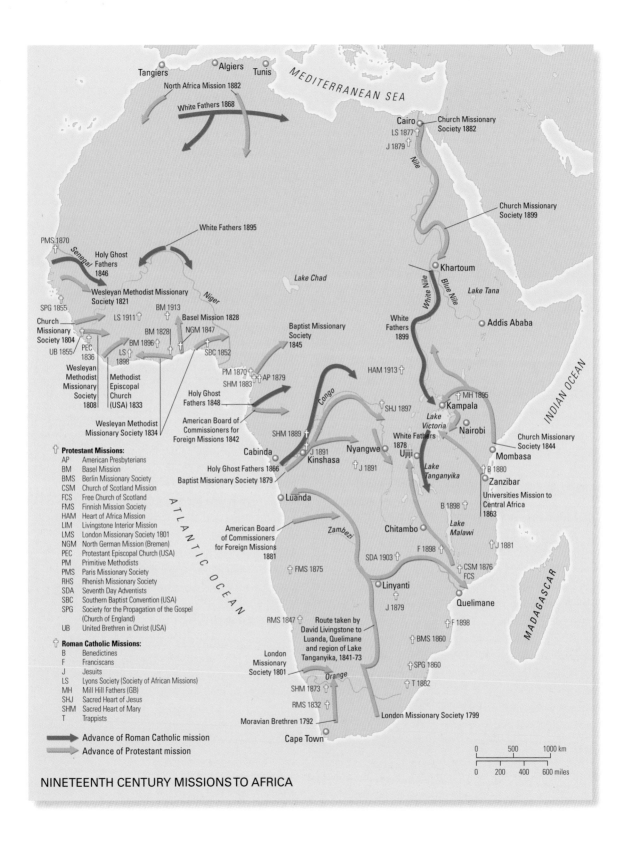

Tangiers Algiers Tunis

MEDITERRANEAN SEA

North Africa Mission 1882

White Fathers 1868

Cairo ○ Church Missionary Society 1882
LS 1877 †
J 1879 †

Church Missionary Society 1899

White Fathers 1895

PMS 1870 †
Senegal

Holy Ghost Fathers 1846

Lake Chad

Khartoum

White Nile · Blue Nile

Lake Tana

Wesleyan Methodist Missionary Society 1821

Niger

SPG 1855 †
LS 1911 † · BM 1913 †
Basel Mission 1828

Church Missionary Society 1804 †
BM 1828 · NGM 1847
BM 1896 †
UB 1855 †
PEC 1836 †
LS 1898 †
SBC 1852

White Fathers 1899

Addis Ababa

Wesleyan Methodist Missionary Society 1808
Methodist Episcopal Church (USA) 1833

Baptist Missionary Society 1845

HAM 1913 †

MH 1895 †

Wesleyan Methodist Missionary Society 1834

PM 1870 † AP 1879
SHM 1883

Holy Ghost Fathers 1848

Congo

SHJ 1897 †

Kampala

Lake Victoria

Nairobi

Church Missionary Society 1844

American Board of Commissioners for Foreign Missions 1842

SHM 1889 †

White Fathers 1878

Nyangwe
Ujiji

Mombasa

Zanzibar

† **Protestant Missions:**

AP   American Presbyterians
BM   Basel Mission
BMS   Berlin Missionary Society
CSM   Church of Scotland Mission
FCS   Free Church of Scotland
FMS   Finnish Mission Society
HAM   Heart of Africa Mission
LIM   Livingstone Interior Mission
LMS   London Missionary Society 1801
NGM   North German Mission (Bremen)
PEC   Protestant Episcopal Church (USA)
PM   Primitive Methodists
PMS   Paris Missionary Society
RHS   Rhenish Missionary Society
SDA   Seventh Day Adventists
SBC   Southern Baptist Convention (USA)
SPG   Society for the Propagation of the Gospel (Church of England)
UB   United Brethren in Christ (USA)

Cabinda ○
J 1891 † Kinshasa
Holy Ghost Fathers 1866
Baptist Missionary Society 1879

J 1891 †

Lake Tanganyika

Universities Mission to Central Africa 1863

B 1898 †

Luanda ○

American Board of Commissioners for Foreign Missions 1881

Zambezi

Chitambo

Lake Malawi

J 1881 †

† **Roman Catholic Missions:**

B   Benedictines
F   Franciscans
J   Jesuits
LS   Lyons Society (Society of African Missions)
MH   Mill Hill Fathers (GB)
SHJ   Sacred Heart of Jesus
SHM   Sacred Heart of Mary
T   Trappists

FMS 1875 †

SDA 1903 †

F 1898 †

CSM 1876 †
FCS

Linyanti

J 1879 †

Quelimane

RMS 1847 †

Route taken by David Livingstone to Luanda, Quelimane and region of Lake Tanganyika, 1841-73

F 1898 †

London Missionary Society 1801

BMS 1860 †

Orange

SPG 1860 †

SHM 1873 †

T 1882 †

RMS 1832 †

London Missionary Society 1799

Moravian Brethren 1792

Cape Town ○

MADAGASCAR

➡ Advance of Roman Catholic mission
➡ Advance of Protestant mission

0   500   1000 km
0 200 400 600 miles

NINETEENTH CENTURY MISSIONS TO AFRICA

HUDSON TAYLOR

A Yorkshireman, converted at seventeen, James Hudson Taylor (1832–1905) went to China in 1853 as a missionary with the Chinese Evangelization Society. The shortcomings of the support system of the society – and possibly the influence of Brethren thinking – made him cut his links with the CES. He continued in China as an independent missionary, until ill health forced him home in 1860. He then completed his medical training, and in 1865 founded the China Inland Mission – the first truly interdenominational foreign mission, and the prototype of the 'faith' missions that were to play a prominent part in world evangelization during the nineteenth century.

Hudson Taylor's concern was to bring the gospel to every unevangelized province of the Chinese Empire, now open to Westerners. Anxious not to divert funds from other missions, he resolved never to appeal for financial support. The example of the Brethren evangelist and orphanage director,

George Müller (1805–98), made him determined to rely on prayer to bring in supplies, and on careful administration to conserve them. This 'faith principle' did not rule out appeals for prayer, or for specific numbers of missionary recruits.

Hudson Taylor made several innovations to the mission practice of his day. He was prepared to accept candidates who had no college training, and required his missionaries to identify with the national peoples by, among other things, wearing Chinese dress. He was determined not to locate ultimate control of mission operations at home, insisting that the work be directed on the spot. He himself had earlier suffered from the home-controlled system. At the same time, Hudson Taylor recognized the need to keep Christians at home fully informed, and by his writing and preaching made a great impact.

HAROLD H. ROWDON

The slaves avidly embraced Christianity. They were not always passively obedient: the leaders of the slave revolt of 1831–32 were Jamaican Baptists. When emancipation came in 1834, the chapel bells were run all through the islands. Only afterwards did the Anglican Church, until then on the side of the owners, have a chance to spread in the black community.

CHRISTIANITY, COMMERCE, AND CIVILIZATION

By the middle of the century, the belief that the interests of 'Christianity, commerce, and civilization' were in harmony brought some missions into actual trading. The Basle Mission developed the idea of trade as a means of self-support in the Gold Coast (modern Ghana) and elsewhere. The Church Missionary Society developed cotton growing in Yorubaland (Nigeria), introduced machinery to process the cotton, provided facilities for training the technologists to maintain the machinery and, with the help of a sympathetic Manchester merchant, arranged an export trade for it.

Later in the century, the alliance of Christianity and commerce turned sour. Merchants complained of unfair mission competition, missionaries complained of the evil example of nominally Christian European traders, and alcohol became increasingly important in trade. Travellers reported that the effects of alcohol were just as bad as those of the slave trade in those areas open to trade, and contrasted this with the sober Muslim areas. Mission theory at home was veering away from involvement in trading institutions and towards 'direct' evangelism, and the CMS abandoned its institutions associated with trade. However, the

The 'Lammermuir Party' of British missionaries, who in 1866 sailed to China with James Hudson Taylor, founder of the China Inland Mission, aboard the tea-clipper *Lammermuir*. The largest group of Protestant missionaries yet to arrive in China, it included nine unmarried women.
OVERSEAS MISSIONARY FELLOWSHIP

'African churches' which split from the CMS in the 1890s continued to involve themselves in agriculture and trade.

The missions came into direct conflict with trading interests in China. The attempts by Western powers to force the opium trade on China were opposed vigorously by missionaries. Marshall Broomhall (1866–1937) of the China Inland Mission constantly wrote against opium trading and government indecision.

MISSION EDUCATION

From the first, missions were involved in education. Protestantism was a religion of the Book: Christian growth without Bible reading would be unthinkable. Also, in many situations, education was the most attractive aspect of the package on offer. For example, in India, Western education opened up a new intellectual world and, from the 1830s, positions in the administration. In Africa and the Pacific, literacy offered access to the powers that the Europeans displayed. Perhaps no invention has a more revolutionary effect on any society than writing. At any rate, young people came to learn – and stayed to pray.

One early result was that peoples in some mission areas became more literate than some levels of Western society. The American mission presses provided the Hawaiians with a wider range of literature than was available in rural America. Freetown, Sierra Leone, had a grammar school in 1845, and a girls' grammar school in 1865. By 1876, Fourah Bay College was affiliated to the University of Durham in England, which made it possible for Africans to take arts and theology degrees in Sierra Leone. The satirical magazine, *Punch*, suggested that Durham would soon affiliate to the London Zoo – an anecdote that illustrates the important fact that, in some matters, missions were out of step with contemporary Western opinion. From earliest days the missionaries believed that – given the same opportunities – Africans and Pacific islanders would perform equally well with Europeans. In general, this conviction weathered the nineteenth-century theories that the races had different inherent abilities.

Literacy led to a demand for higher education, and in English-speaking areas the English grammar school became the model. Missionary suggestions that subjects such as Greek were unnecessary in Africa were brushed aside: African schools must have all that British schools had. Government officials often suggested that agriculture and technical subjects were as important as the academic, but they could not dim the attractiveness of the grammar school, or seriously modify it. The Scottish missions in central Africa achieved perhaps the most successful marriage of academic, technical, and agricultural education.

Only at the end of the nineteenth century did Roman Catholic missions seriously rival Protestants in education. But when they did intervene, it was on a massive scale, using the primary school as an instrument of primary evangelization.

EDUCATION IN INDIA

India, with its ancient literary heritage, contrasted strongly with the pre-literate societies. Certainly missionaries from the beginning taught in schools attended by low-caste people. But when Alexander Duff (1806–78) arrived in India in 1830, he decided to work by means of higher education in English. His decision was based on his idea that truth is a unity: the teaching of science, philosophy, and Christian doctrine would undermine the foundations of Hinduism.

Duff was assisted by the ferment already proceeding among young Hindu intellectuals, who were disillusioned with old corruptions, rebelling against old institutions, and already influenced by Western rationalists. When the East India Company decided in 1835 to replace Sanskrit and Persian with English as the language of administration, the prospects for his work were further improved. Duff received support from the Hindu liberal Ram Mohan Roy (1774–1833), and eminent converts such as Krishna Mohan Banerjea (1813–85) carried on his work.

The 'Scots colleges' became an important part of missionary operations in India, offering high academic standards and recruiting missionaries of academic calibre for their staff. But most of their students remained non-Christian, and Hinduism did not crumble, as Duff had hoped. He lived long enough to see the emergence of biblical criticism in Britain and the Bengal Renaissance in India. By the end of the century, Western-educated Hindus were turning weapons forged in the West against the Christians.

SAMUEL AJAYI CROWTHER

Samuel Crowther (c. 1806–91) was the outstanding African Christian leader of his time. Born in the Egba group of the Yoruba people, in what is now Nigeria, he was captured by slave raiders when he was aged about fifteen. But the slave ship was intercepted by a British warship, and Ajayi was taken to Sierra Leone, where he was converted and baptized, taking the name Samuel Crowther.

Outstanding at school, and a foundation pupil of Fourah Bay College, Crowther became a teacher for the Church Missionary Society, and a pioneer of Yoruba services in Freetown. He was one of two CMS representatives on the 1841 Niger Expedition, and became convinced that the evangelization of inland Africa must be carried out by Africans. Ordained in London in 1843, he was appointed to the new mission in his own Yorubaland. Among the first converts were his long-lost mother and sister.

Crowther achieved much as evangelist, translator, and negotiator, and impressed many, including Queen Victoria, when he visited England. He led the new Niger Mission in 1857, and in 1864 became the first African Anglican bishop. His all-African staff operated over hundreds of miles of the Niger territories. His last years were clouded by controversy concerning alleged indiscipline in his staff.

ANDREW F. WALLS

When the modern missionary movement began in the 1790s, its activists had nothing but the prophecies of the Bible and the conversion of a few hundred American Indians to support their endeavour. By 1910, the church had changed out of recognition, and was now rooted in every continent. The change had come almost imperceptibly. Carey and his colleagues were in India seven years before baptizing their first convert, and disasters abounded. Of more than thirty enthusiastic London missionaries who sailed to the South Seas in 1795, only a handful survived the physical, mental, and spiritual strains placed on them.

AFRICAN MISSIONARIES

We have seen how 'Clapham Sect' enterprise founded the Sierra Leone colony. 1,100 people of African descent were brought there from America in 1792, to form a 'province of freedom' in Africa. They came as Christians, bringing their own churches and preachers with them. To these people were added the 'recaptives', rescued from slave-ships after 1809 – uprooted, disorientated people from all parts of West Africa. It was from these that the first mass movement towards Christianity in modern missionary history took place. Sierra Leone became a self-consciously Christian community, and a literate one. Many missionaries died in the 'White Man's Grave' of Sierra Leone, and as the demand for missions moved to other areas –particularly to India – fewer missionaries went to Sierra Leone.

But Sierra Leone Christians found their way back to their original homelands as traders. On their initiative, the Anglican and Methodist Yoruba missions were begun in Nigeria in the 1840s. When these African missionaries arrived, they found the church already there. When most people were deducing from the failure of the Niger Expedition that it was impossible for Europeans to reside in inland Africa, the missionary representatives, James Frederick Schön (1803–89) and Samuel Ajayi Crowther (c. 1809–91), were arguing that Africans must be Africa's evangelists. They pointed to Sierra Leone, where there was a firmly planted church of people who already spoke the various languages of West Africa. Over the next half century, the tiny Christian population of Sierra Leone produced dozens of ministers, missionaries, catechists, and agents for the rest of West Africa, and particularly the Niger territories. Dozens more Sierra Leone Christians, as traders, clerks, or workmen, first introduced the Christian faith to other places. The United Free Methodists even sent two Sierra Leonean missionaries to Kenya in the 1880s, and Bishop Crowther once planned a Sierra Leone mission to the Congo.

The Sierra Leonean was often regarded as a 'black European' – in dress, speech, and customs. If this was true – and in fact Sierra Leone produced a distinctive *African* literary culture – it was a missionary advantage in the period of the 'Three Cs'. African peoples, who did not divide life into 'culture' and 'religion', met the Western and Christian way of life as a single package: the fact that they met it embodied in black people was crucial. There were twenty-six members in the first CMS mission to Yorubaland; most of them were from Sierra Leone. It was often the 'angry young men' – impatient with the old ways of old men – who responded most readily to the gospel: they took on a total way of life.

The people most likely to distinguish between 'secular' and 'religious' aspects of missionary activity lived in those areas used to Western traders. The Scottish Calabar Mission knew that some of their African hosts were interested in reading solely for trading purposes.

Ludwig Nommensen (1834–1918), the German Lutheran missionary to Sumatra, with his wife and daughter. He built an indigenous Batak church and translated the New Testament into the Batak language.
VEREINIGTE EVANGELISCHE MISSION

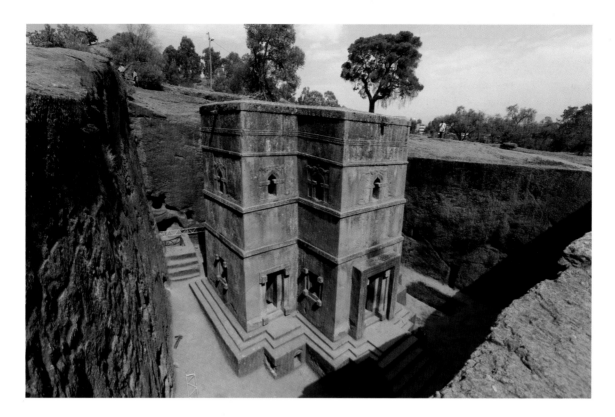

Orthodox Ethiopian rock-cut Church of St George, Lalibela.

© FEIJE RIEMERSMA/ DREAMSTIME.COM

Here, and elsewhere, a good deal of missionary activity was aimed at reforming local institutions — especially human sacrifice — and moving the whole community in a Christian direction, as well as forming churches.

At the beginning of the missionary movement, there was no reason to expect that one people would respond more readily than another. Practical considerations led missionaries to go first to India, certain Pacific Islands, Sierra Leone, the West Indies, and the Cape of Good Hope. China was impenetrable, except for certain ports, until mid-century, and Japan until later still. By mid-century, too, it was plain that in India more Christians came from among Hindus than from among Muslims, and more from among the tribal peoples than from either.

By the end of the nineteenth century it was clear that, although Christians in India, China, and even Japan were a significant part of the world church, it was in Africa and the Pacific that the most dramatic changes had occurred. Hinduism and Buddhism, which was hardly recognized at the beginning of the nineteenth century, had not collapsed — indeed both were adapting to the impact of Western culture. Islam had almost wholly resisted Christian mission. It was from among the world's tribal peoples that most Christians were coming; and in the African grasslands a race with Islam promised to follow.

> I am not reaping the harvest; I can scarcely claim to be sowing the seed; I am hardly ploughing the soil; but I am gathering out the stones. That, too, is missionary work; let it be supported by loving sympathy and fervent prayer.
>
> DR ROBERT BRUCE WRITES OF THE SLOW PROGRESS OF THE GOSPEL IN PERSIA (IRAN)

THE ANCIENT CHURCHES

One other feature of the early missionary societies had proved disappointing: the attempt to work for revival in the ancient churches of the Mediterranean, the Middle East, Ethiopia, and India. Despite temporary encouragement in all these places, only in India was effective contact made between Protestant Christians and Orthodox, Nestorian, and Monophysite churches.

A SECOND ROMAN CATHOLIC MOVEMENT

The first Roman Catholic missionary movement had almost burnt out when the Protestant movement began; the second came in imitation of the Protestants. The intellectual centre was in France, the Catholic power with strongest overseas commitment. New missionary orders were formed: the White Fathers (1868), the Congregation of the Holy Spirit (founded in 1679, but renewed in 1848), and the Society of the Divine Word (1875). Like the Protestants, the Catholic supporters of missions identified themselves with anti-slavery agitation, in which the great Cardinal Charles Lavigerie (1825–92) was particularly prominent. Rivalry with Protestant missions was intense, and in the period of the 'Scramble for Africa' became entangled with politics. Catholic missionaries – who were often French – were assumed to favour French colonial policies, and Protestant missionaries those of Britain. In many areas which the French annexed, such as Indo-China, the only important Christian presence was Roman Catholic.

A WORLD CHURCH?

Throughout the Victorian era – and long beyond it – overseas missions were taken for granted in the European churches, and were supported by all sections of the church. The Evangelicals and Anglo-Catholics provided the greater part of the interest, funds, and personnel. A small but significant 'liberal' missionary movement developed in the early twentieth century, with a more sympathetic approach to other faiths, and a stress on Christian service. Only rarely did doctrinal differences split missionary societies. Until at least the middle of the twentieth century, children in Christian homes and Sunday schools were reared on stories of 'missionary pioneers'.

World War I damped the dream of the 1890s of the evangelization of the world in one generation. But when it broke out, the church was already more international than at any previous period of its history. The nineteenth-century missionaries, and the societies which called and directed them, were a major factor in transforming Christianity into a world church.

A. F. WALLS

FURTHER READING

David Bebbington, *Evangelicalism in Modern Britain: A History from the 1730s to the 1980s*, London, 1989 and later eds.

Michael Burleigh, *Earthly Powers: The Conflict Between Religion and Politics from the French Revolution to the Great War*, London, 2005.

Owen Chadwick, *The Secularization of the European Mind in the Nineteenth Century*, Cambridge, 1975.

Brian Stanley, *The Bible and the Flag: Protestant Missions and British Imperialism in the Nineteenth and Twentieth Centuries*, Leicester, 1990.

STUDY QUESTIONS

1. What impact did the Industrial Revolution have upon the church in Britain?

2. Why did revivals play a vital part in religious life in the USA?

3. Compare and contrast the influence of William Wilberforce and David Livingstone.

4. Why and how did France become a secular state?

5. What was the importance of the non-denominational Christian society in this period?

6. Did missionaries 'follow the flag'?

7. What was the impact of science and philosophy on the church?

8. What is Evangelicalism? How did it impact the nineteenth-century church?

9. How did Pius IX react to the loss of temporal power?

10. Why was education integral to Christian missionary activity?

7 A Century of Conflict

1914–2001

Summary

At the turn of the twentieth century, many Christians believed the kingdom of God – or at least a better world – was at hand. Two world wars, followed by fifty years fearing a third one, buried those hopes of human perfectibility.

The Russian Revolution of 1917 led to the establishment of the world's first explicitly atheist state, while the dictatorships in Italy, Germany, and Russia challenged Christianity in the inter-war period.

World War II had a devastating impact on Christianity, with the deliberate direction of war against civilians, and the indifference of leaders in the Christian West to the sufferings of the Jews. The defeat of Nazi Germany in 1945 led to Eastern Europe coming under Soviet influence and the state adoption of anti-religious policies. With the fall of the Berlin Wall in 1989, Christianity – especially in its Orthodox forms – experienced a renaissance in these countries.

The Pentecostal movement, begun in 1901 in the USA, held that Christians could experience the supernatural power displayed by the apostles. The Pentecostal movement spread rapidly worldwide, becoming the fastest growing Christian movement, both within its own churches and within the traditional denominations. It was particularly popular in the Third World, notably in Latin America and among the African Independent churches.

Christianity is now primarily a faith of the developing, rather than developed, world. The implications of this massive shift from the West to the developing world signal a new phase in the history of the Christian church, with momentous implications for the future.

CHAPTER 37

AN AGE OF IDEOLOGY

The eminent historian Arnold Toynbee suggested that the great world religions had been replaced in modern times by three post-Christian ideologies – nationalism, communism, and individualism. All three are equally impersonal and dehumanizing.

The progress of secularization in the nineteenth century, aided by Marxism, Darwinism, and positivism, chipped away at the Christian underpinnings of Western thought. The liberal tradition, rooted in Christianity and the Enlightenment, emphasized freedom, but classical economics and social Darwinism reduced liberalism to a self-serving, highly competitive individualism. Social radicalism drew from these sources also, but the scientific, materialist socialism of Marx sharply departed from the liberal humanism of earlier thinkers. Out of the American and French Revolutions and the Romantic Movement emerged nationalism, an ideology of tribal exclusivity, which eventually became identified with militarism, imperialism, and racism.

The three new ideologies – nationalism, communism and individualism – took on the character of religious faiths in the twentieth century. Each made ultimate demands – patriotism, class struggle, or secular humanism; each had its sacred symbols and ceremonies, inspired writings, dogmas, saints, and charismatic leaders. Only by grasping the nature and extent of the challenge these ideologies presented can the Christian response be understood.

As the world entered the twentieth century, both liberal humanists and the supporters of social Christianity proclaimed that a better world – or the kingdom of God – was at hand. But others questioned whether science supported such a belief in progress, suggesting that the evils of the Industrial Revolution and urbanization far outweighed the benefits. The new ideologies were as pessimistic as they were optimistic about the destiny and nature of man. Marx made man a reflection of property-relations, Darwin the survival of the fittest, and Freud an unknown libido. Self-control and freedom of choice did not really exist. There was no future to look forward to – only despair.

THE FIRST TOTAL WAR

Prior to 1914, the movement for international conciliation had made considerable advances. Peace societies existed in several countries, and a number of international congresses attempted to give direction to the cause. The secular, humanitarian, and liberal outlooks found in the continental European societies complemented the Christian anti-war views of English and American peace groups. They expected that institutions would emerge to settle disputes between nations, and such bodies as the Permanent Court of International Justice at The Hague, and the Carnegie Endowment for International Peace were formed. The American Secretary of State, William Jennings Bryan (1860–1925), a prominent churchman, tried to negotiate 'cooling-off treaties' to deter countries from rushing hastily into war.

In spite of these well-meaning efforts, international tensions rose steadily, fuelled by an escalating arms race and imperialistic confrontations abroad. It took only a spark to ignite

496   A CENTURY OF CONFLICT

the tinder-box of Europe – the assassination of the Crown Prince of Austria-Hungary in Sarajevo on 28 June 1914. The armies marched joyously off to war, naïvely assuming that in a few weeks they would win a glorious victory which would solve all the pressing problems their countries faced. What in fact followed was a stalemate. The so-called civilized peoples of the West engaged in an unparalleled carnage, which annihilated a significant part of a generation. Liberal humanism proved inadequate for the times as the sudden unleashing of the pent-up emotions of war shattered the optimism of peace advocates.

For the first time, the world knew 'total war'. It was fought on land, sea, and air. Industry was regimented to maintain a constant flow of weapons. Governments directed the economic life of their countries, strictly controlling industrial output, food production, and allocation of labour and raw materials. Through naval blockade and submarine warfare each side tried to throttle the economy of the enemy.

Governments restricted the activities of civilians. Civil rights were curtailed to combat subversion at home. Those who questioned the war were pressured to conform. Censorship was used to stop the spread of news helpful to the enemy and to strengthen morale. Instilled in the people was a sense of solidarity, singleness of purpose, and the conviction that they were engaged in a righteous crusade. Church leaders on both sides reinforced this belief. British liberal writers, in particular, hammered home the idea that it was a 'holy war' against tyranny, despotism, and militarism. On the other hand, Christian groups worked to relieve suffering in the war-torn areas, and to aid prisoners-of-war and wounded soldiers.

Allied propagandists slanted news reports and exploited such German blunders as the sinking of the *Lusitania* and the execution of nurse Edith Cavell, thereby winning the sympathy and cooperation of influential people in the United States, especially in church circles. They took a moralistic and ideological view of the war that ruled out any negotiated peace based on re-establishing the balance of power. When the idealist President Woodrow Wilson (1856–1924), son of a Presbyterian minister, brought the USA into the war, he made it clear that the total defeat of the Central Powers was necessary to enable the creation of an entirely new world. The overthrow of the Russian autocracy in March 1917 further strengthened the idea of the war as a struggle between democracy and authoritarianism. Neither side obtained a breakthrough, but then the radical Marxist Bolshevik faction led by Lenin overthrew the moderates in November 1917 and took Russia out of the war. The Germans now poised for a knockout blow on the Western Front, but the resources of the USA precluded a German victory. The Central Powers collapsed, revolution swept their countries, and Germany formally surrendered on 11 November 1918.

PEACE AND PUNISHMENT

At the Paris Peace Conference which followed, the mood was one of nineteenth-century nationalism: the desire for national self-determination and security against Germany. Some of the statesmen, and many churchmen, wanted to overcome future conflicts and tensions by supra-national organization and by strengthening international law. But their hopes were dismissed in favour of power politics, nationalist fervour, and fear of Bolshevism spreading into Europe. The delegates felt compelled to settle scores with their principal foe, Germany, and the final Treaty of Versailles had the appearance of a dictated peace. The peacemakers also constructed a firewall to contain the Bolshevik menace by permitting the creation of several new states in eastern Europe.

The settlement with Turkey was significant because, during the war, the Allies had promised independence to the sultan's Arab subjects. However, Britain and France had agreed secretly to partition the Ottoman lands among themselves, and Britain had also promised in the Balfour Declaration of 1917 to support the establishment of a Jewish national home in Palestine. What followed was the creation of internationally guaranteed mandates: British ones in Palestine and Transjordan, and French ones in Lebanon and Syria. Tensions mounted among Arabs, Jews, and Europeans in the Middle East.

A further difficulty facing the conferees was the semi-autonomous Orthodox minorities in Ottoman Turkey. Massacres of Armenians before, and Greek minorities after, the war had aroused passions in the West. But Turkish nationalists bitterly resented the terms agreed to in Paris and, led by Mustafa Kemal Atatürk (1881–1938), forced a revision of the treaty in 1923. Kemal then brought Turkey into the twentieth century by secularizing the state and reducing the influence of both Islam and the Christian minorities.

Finally, the peace settlement created the League of Nations – a worldwide organization for the preservation of peace, proposed by Wilson. He believed that in the new order, openly arrived at agreements would guarantee the political independence and territorial integrity of all states. The League would provide the peace settlement with a moral foundation and the means for correcting defects in the treaties.

The inter-war period saw great changes. For one thing, the 'civil war of the West', as some call it, had undermined Europe's pre-1914 world position. The new industrial giants, the United States and Japan, were now finding places in the imperial sun. Great Britain was under pressure to relax its hold over Ireland, India, and the Middle East, while the Statute of Westminster (1931) accorded the white dominions – Canada, Australia, New Zealand, South Africa, and Ireland – legal equality with Britain in the Commonwealth. Colonial nationalism in North Africa and South-east Asia undermined France's effort to promote cultural assimilation in its possessions.

The war shattered the economies of the western countries, and a whole generation of potential leaders perished on the battlefields. The democratic nations broadened the base of political participation, including the vote for women, but were plagued by unemployment and inflation. Socialist agitation and demands for welfare intensified. Left-wing parties, such as the British Labour and German Social Democratic parties, now participated in governments. Democratic socialism fitted well with the rapid advance of secularism in the post-war decade. Protestant and Catholic churches alike proved unable to hold the allegiance of younger people, and the more progressively-minded channelled their energies into secular ideologies.

Although it began with high aspirations, the League of Nations failed to prevent aggression and preserve peace. From the outset the United States refused to join, while Germany and Soviet Russia were excluded. For this reason the Bolsheviks regarded it as a capitalist plot to overthrow communism in Russia, and the Germans saw it as a weapon for keeping their country down. The member states rejected any infringements of their sovereignty, while the major disarmament and political agreements of the interwar years were negotiated outside its framework. The League did promote co-operation in the technical and economic spheres, and guaranteed religious and missionary freedom in the former German and Turkish territories placed under its mandatory supervision.

THE NEW MENACE

The most deadly challenge facing democracy in the interwar period was totalitarianism. A much-debated political concept, such regime is distinguished by such features as an official ideology that covers all vital aspects of human existence and looks towards a perfect state of mankind; a single, mass party led by a dictator or small group who are dedicated to the ideology, and which controls most aspects of life; a political police using sophisticated scientific and psychological techniques, directed against all 'enemies' of the regime; a monopoly over the mass media and education; and the systematic use of propaganda to manipulate and control the public. Totalitarian governments tightly regulate the economy and all means of armed combat, but also aim at a social revolution that will produce a new type of human, without any sense of individual freedom. Totalitarian governments challenged the Christian church, and it responded in a variety of ways.

Right-wing versions of totalitarianism are popularly known as 'fascism'. They counter personal frustration and alienation as well as social and economic tensions by stressing class unity and reaffirming traditional values. Fascist movements glorify the national entity – defining it in terms of national mission, imperial greatness, the racial or folk community, or the state itself. Other distinctive features of fascism are some sort of civil religion, anti-rationalism, elitism, and an emphasis upon the values of struggle, action, violence, courage, and self-sacrifice. Private property and capitalist enterprise are permitted, but tightly controlled.

Fascism appeared first in Italy, as a response to the frustrations of the war and ensuing economic crisis. Benito Mussolini (1883–1945), a former socialist journalist and army veteran, founded the Fascist Party in 1919, gained power in the legendary 'March on Rome' (1922), and exploited nationalist discontents and the spectre of Bolshevism. Police supervision, terror, censorship, and propaganda characterized his regime. His 'Corporate State' had a façade of economic democracy which mainly benefitted large industrialists and landowners.

Mussolini achieved a reconciliation between the Roman Catholic church and the Italian state, ending the antagonism dating from 1870. Cardinal Achille Ratte (1857–1939), elected Pope Pius XI in 1922, had experienced first-hand the Bolshevik attack on Poland in 1920, and was a bitter foe of both communism and traditional liberalism. He was willing to overlook the more unsavoury aspects of the fascist regime in Italy in order to solve the so-called 'Roman question'.

Although Mussolini himself was outspokenly anti-clerical, he saw the political advantages of coming to terms with the pope in the Lateran Agreements of 1929. The papacy gave up its territorial claims in Italy, recognized the Italian ruling dynasty, agreed to keep out of politics, and permitted state approval of nominations to bishoprics. Fascist Italy in turn recognized the Vatican City as an independent, sovereign state with the pope as its ruler, compensated the papacy for revenues lost because of the seizure of Rome in

1870, established Catholicism as the 'sole religion of the state', extended canon law rules to marriage matters, allowed religious instruction in secondary schools, and gave legal standing to Catholic religious orders and associations.

SENT BY PROVIDENCE

Pius XI praised the Italian dictator as a 'man sent by providence'. But Mussolini's view of state superiority, and his cynical attitude towards the church, soon led to a cooling of relations. In the encyclical *Quadragesimo anno* (May 1931), Pius XI criticized the corporate state, and a month later, in *Non abbigmo bisogno*, he denounced the fascist crackdown on the lay organization Catholic Action. Mussolini then backed off and agreed to permit Catholic Action's continued existence, but under severe restrictions.

Italian churchmen gave their blessing to overseas ventures such as the conquest of Ethiopia and intervention in the Spanish Civil War (1936–39). Criticisms of fascism were restricted to specific matters where the state competed for the religious loyalty of Catholics, rather than on broad philosophical, humanitarian, or theological grounds.

Ties also existed between Roman Catholicism and fascist-type movements in other parts of Europe. Examples include the 'clerical-fascist' state of Engelbert Dollfuss (1892–1934) in Austria, Francisco Franco's *Falangist* regime in Spain, the 'New State' of the Jesuit-trained António Salazar (1889–1970) in Portugal, and the 'Arrow-Cross' party of Ferenc Szálasi (1897–1946) in Hungary. The anti-democratic royalist Charles Maurras and his Action Française commanded a wide following among Catholics in France and Belgium, but its influence diminished after papal condemnation of the leader's basically atheist views in 1926.

German National Socialism (Nazism) also fed upon disillusionment with the war, resentment over the peace, fear of communism, and the economic crisis. Adolf Hitler (1889–1945), the Austrian-born leader of the movement, was named chancellor of the German Republic on 30 January 1933. Within two years he achieved greater control over the state than Mussolini, who was legally subordinate to the Italian crown.

The basic Nazi organizational idea was the absolute unity of the German people with its leader (*Führer*), and implementing the leadership principle in the political, economic, and social structures of the country. Through extensive regulation and economic planning, a system of state capitalism replaced the autonomy of capital and industry. By integrating all the various competing classes and interest groups into the nation, the Nazis sought to form an ideal super-community. They set in motion a significant social revolution, but were unable to win the full allegiance of the army and churchmen, while the support of workers and rural villagers was only lukewarm.

Ideologically, National Socialism was similar to Italian fascism, but its distinctive trait was a utopian anti-modernism that rejected the assumptions underlying the Enlightenment and glorified a primitive, idealized past portrayed in Wagnerian operas and ancient Germanic sagas, where the complexities of modern life had no place. The concern with race was central to Nazi ideology. The *völkisch* thinkers provided the emphasis on 'people', 'soil', and 'blood' – the idea that Germans possessed a series of traits bound up with their *Heimat* (homeland) that set them apart from others. Foreign persons, ideas, and institutions were considered corrupting, especially those identified with Jews. Pseudo-anthropologists set out a 'science' of race, which distinguished between superior and inferior human types. Social Darwinism supplied the idea of struggle between groups and nations, in which the stronger peoples would dispossess and destroy the weaker.

A 'CULTURE-DESTROYING RACE'

Drawing upon these ideas, Nazi theoreticians developed their barbaric doctrine of anti-Semitism. To regain the lost innocence of the past, they argued it was necessary to purge the present of its impurities. The 'Jew' was the source of all modern evils: the 'culture-destroying race' that gave the world both capitalism and Marxism. Hitler declared that even the Christian faith was a Jewish plot: 'The heaviest blow that ever struck humanity was the coming of Christianity. Bolshevism is Christianity's illegitimate child. Both are inventions of the Jew.' Since the 'culture-creating' Aryan race was engaged in a life-and-death struggle, the eradication of the Jewish race would be the act of social purification necessary to restore the uncorrupt past.

Another key concept was space: the master race needed more room to live (*Lebensraum*). By acquiring space in Russia and Eastern Europe, Hitler intended to end German dependence on imported foodstuffs and raw materials. There German colonists could settle on the land, away from the defiling influence of the cities, and this simple yeomanry would provide an inexhaustible reservoir of warriors for future conflicts. Racial purity supplemented by cultural purity would restore health to Germany.

The Nazi Führer Adolf Hitler (1889–1945) poses in combative stance.
ILLUSTRATED LONDON NEWS

The Nazis deprived German Jews of their rights as citizens, and encouraged them to emigrate through boycotts, expulsion from their jobs, and constant harassment. When the German armies overran Eastern Europe, which had a much larger Jewish population, anti-Semitism became much more brutal. In Russia Nazi death-squads liquidated many thousands of Jews on the spot, while in Poland Jews were herded into urban 'ghettos' and forced to live in appalling slum conditions. The infamous concentration camps, originally created to break the spirits of Nazism's opponents, had acquired even more ominous meaning for the Jews. In 1940–41 a series of new camps were created in Poland, of which the best known are Auschwitz and Treblinka. Here the Nazis put into operation the 'final solution', the extermination of the entire Jewish population of Europe. Men, women, and children were transported to these 'death factories', and in a cold-blooded, calculated manner beaten, starved, shot, worked to death, utilized in medical experiments, and gassed. Known today as the 'Holocaust', the number of Jewish deaths caused by all these measures is estimated at six million.

The plight of Christians under the Nazi regime was also precarious. Born and reared a Catholic, Hitler abandoned whatever Christian principles he had for the secular philosophies of the day, though he never formally cut his ties with the church, nor was he excommunicated. National Socialism was a new faith which appealed to the millions of Germans who longed for national regeneration. Hitler's distaste for the church was primarily political; he envied the power Catholicism had over its adherents, but despised Protestantism for its lack of unity and authority. However, he courted both Protestant and Catholic support during his rise to power by emphasizing the nationalist aspects of his programme, and by claiming to support the church's position in the state.

The German defeat and revolution in 1918 had stunned the Protestant church leaders. They were cool towards the new republic, which they regarded as dominated by socialist and Roman Catholic politicians. The Weimar Constitution of 1919 provided for separation of church and state, thus removing the threat of government control of the church. But the churches retained a privileged legal status, continued to receive state subsidies, and kept their traditional role in education.

Since churchmen sympathized with the anti-republican right wing, they were won over to the 'national movement' as conditions deteriorated after 1929. Many Protestants overlooked the anti-Semitic and pagan side of Nazism, and praised Hitler's anti-communism and call for 'positive Christianity'. Hitler cleverly held in check the anti-Christian radicals such as Alfred Rosenberg, so as not to alarm church leaders. The 'German Christian' movement that arose in the 1930s even formed a pro-Nazi party within the church.

REGENERATION THROUGH NAZISM?

Conservative churchmen felt that, if Nazism were treated with understanding, it would outgrow its faults – such as racism – and bring about national regeneration. Many Protestants welcomed Hitler's overthrow of democracy in 1933 as a first step toward replacing the 'Marxist' republic with 'Christian' rulers. His 'pro-moral, pro-family' stance was also appealing. He emphasized the importance of child bearing and women's role in the home: he would eliminate pornography, prostitution, and homosexuality. Although some in the Catholic hierarchy were uneasy about Nazism, they shared the Protestants' outlook.

Hitler's policy toward the churches after January 1933 was purely pragmatic. Realizing the power they possessed, he did not want to launch another conflict like the *Kulturkampf* of the 1870s, but assumed that, in time, the outdated Christian faith would die out. The Catholic bishops welcomed the new regime, the Catholic Centre Party voted for the measure in March 1933 allowing Hitler to rule by decree, and the Centre and Catholic trade unions 'voluntarily' dissolved themselves a few days later. In return, the *Führer* agreed to a concordat with the Vatican which guaranteed Catholics freedom to profess and practise their religion, and the independence of the church. The treaty reaffirmed diplomatic relations with the Holy See and the clergy's legal status, regularized the appointment of bishops, protected the Catholic educational system, continued public funding of the church, permitted pastoral care in the army, prisons and hospitals, and forbade all political activities by the clergy.

The concordat greatly increased the prestige of Hitler's regime. By it the church sanctioned the liquidation of the religious (confessional) political parties, and the exclusion of the clergy from politics. It was a milestone in the consolidation of the totalitarian state. Many churchmen feared that open conflict with the regime might jeopardize those privileges still protected by the agreement. The Nazis violated the concordat almost from the very beginning, while it gave the church no protection from attacks. At the same time it undermined the developing Catholic resistance.

A movement swept the Protestant church in 1933 calling for the unification and 'nationalization' of the provincial churches (*Landeskirchen*) with a single '*Reich*-bishop' at its head. This seemed in line with Hitler's policy of bringing all groups under the total control of the *Führer* and the state. The 'German Christians' secured the election of Ludwig Müller, a fervent Nazi, and also restructured the church along Nazi lines, by introducing the *Führer* principle into church government and adopting the 'Aryan paragraph', which provided for dismissal of all people of Jewish origin from church staffs. Hitler, however, took little notice of these steps, and rejected the 'German Christians'' idea of a National Socialist state church. He felt that the church's sole function was to cater for benighted people who still had religious needs. Any church – even a Nazified one – could divide people's loyalties and might be a limitation to his power.

Hitler listened increasingly to anti-Christian Nazis who called for the elimination of both the 'German Christians' and their opponents in the church. After 1934 Nazi support for the 'German Christians' waned, although many continued to occupy church posts. They became even more extreme in their claims that the Nazi movement represented the true fulfilment of Christianity, but lost all power and influence, especially after the church was placed under a secular Ministry of Church Affairs in 1935.

KARL BARTH

Born in Basel, Switzerland, Barth was trained in Protestant Liberalism, against which he reacted during World War I, believing his teachers had been misled in claiming divine support for a war they said was in support of German culture. In his commentary on Romans, Barth argued that God, as revealed in the cross of Jesus, challenges any attempt to ally God with human cultures, achievements, or possessions.

In 1934, as the German Protestant church tried to come to terms with Hitler's regime, Barth was largely responsible for the *Barmen Declaration*, which argued that the church's allegiance was to the God of Jesus Christ and should resist other 'lords', such as the *Führer*, Adolf Hitler. Barth was forced to resign from the University of Bonn for refusing to swear an oath to Hitler and returned to his native Switzerland.

Barth's theology is summed up in his *Church Dogmatics*, regarded by some as one of the most important works of twentieth-century theology. When a reporter once asked Barth to summarize his theology, he replied: 'Jesus loves me, this I know, for the Bible tells me so.' After World War II, Barth co-authored the *Darmstadt Statement* (1947), an expression of German guilt and responsibility for the Third Reich and for World War II.

TIM DOWLEY

First they came for the socialists, and I didn't speak out because I wasn't a socialist.
Then they came for the unionists, and I didn't speak out because I wasn't a trade unionist.
Then they came for the Jews, and I didn't speak out because I wasn't a Jew.
Then they came for me, and there was no one left to speak for me.

MARTIN NIEMÖLLER

THE CHRISTIAN CHURCH AND THE JEWS

At first, Christians were regarded as a Jewish sect by both Jews and Gentiles, which led to opposition and persecution of the church by the Jewish authorities, who objected to its doctrines and to the admission of Gentiles without their accepting the Law. After the Jewish revolts against Rome (AD 66–74, 132–35), most Christians dissociated themselves from the Jews. Jewish Christians' refusal to support the revolts caused them to be regarded as national enemies, and from this time few Jews converted to Christianity.

Increasingly, Christians came to regard Jews as deliberate haters of the good. When the church became recognized by Constantine, legal discrimination against Jews increased, and they were gradually deprived of all rights. In the centuries that followed, Jews were exposed to harassment, frequent expulsions, and sometimes massacre – one of the worst examples of which occurred during the First Crusade (1096–99). The Jews were banished from England in 1290, from France in 1306, 1322, and finally in 1394. Often the Jews were given the choice of accepting Christianity or banishment. In Spain, the massacres of 1391 led many 'Marranos' to accept Christianity, though often only in name. The Inquisition investigated – with its terrors – the genuineness of their faith. Eventually all Jews were expelled from Spain in 1492. Throughout this period in Europe, contacts between Christians and Jews were minimal. Jews were often forced to wear distinctive dress, and to live in separate streets or districts (ghettos).

The Renaissance and Reformation brought a few of the more learned and liberal to revise their opinions of Judaism and the Jews. But even Martin Luther made bitter and despicable attacks on them. Jews were allowed to settle in Holland in 1598, in Hamburg in 1612, and in England – unofficially – in 1656.

From 1354, Poland was the chief centre of European Jewry. As the country grew weaker, the Jews were increasingly subjected to the hatred of the Roman Catholic Church and the hostility of the people. When, after 1772, Poland was partitioned, most Polish Jews found themselves under either Roman Catholic Austria or Orthodox Russia. Economic pressure and Russian massacres – the 'pogroms' of 1881–1914 – sent nearly two million Jews from eastern Europe, mainly as emigrants to the United States.

The Enlightenment of the eighteenth century brought a new attitude towards Jews. In opposing traditional Christianity, many thinkers also attacked Christian ideas about Jews, which led to the complete emancipation of French Jews during the French Revolution (1790). By 1914, emancipation had occurred throughout Europe, as far as the frontiers of Russia and the Balkans.

THE GERMAN CHURCH DIVIDES

Christ has come to us through Adolf Hitler ... We know today the Saviour has come.

PASTOR LEUTHEUSER

The increasing encroachment of the Nazi state on religious matters alarmed so many in both churches that a *Kirchenkampf* (church-struggle) followed. In September 1933 Pastor Martin Niemöller (1892–1984) formed a Pastors' Emergency League to combat 'German Christian' ideas. In the following year his group repudiated Müller and set up an alternative church government structure, known as the Confessing Church. Its theological basis was spelled out in the Barmen Declaration of May 1934. Largely written by Karl Barth, the Declaration called the German church back to the central truths of Christianity, and rejected the totalitarian claims of the state in religious and political matters.

The Barmen Declaration was not intended as a political protest, and the Confessing Church did not plan to spearhead resistance to Nazism. It was a theological document,

But political acceptance for Jews did not remove deep-rooted prejudice, which came to a head in 1879 when the German Wilhelm Marr (1819–1904) founded the Anti-Semitic League. Anti-Semitism found its ultimate expression in Adolf Hitler's 'Final Solution', in which about six million Jews – one third of world Jewry – perished. Even in the USA, where the Jews had never been discriminated against, anti-Semitic feeling increased.

The first missionary concern for Jews since the early days of the church was shown by the Moravians and German Pietists in the first half of the eighteenth century. Jewish missions were started in the Church of England in 1809, in the Free Churches in 1842, and in Scotland in 1840. From Britain, this movement spread rapidly to other Protestant countries, especially to Norway. The Jewish mass exodus from Eastern Europe to America resulted in missionary work there too. Some Roman Catholics also sought to evangelize among Jews.

Since 1939 and the Nazi Holocaust, Christians have tended to stress understanding, the removal of prejudices, and dialogue rather than a direct missionary approach, although there is little evidence that Anti-Judaism is disappearing.

H. L. ELLISON

The Swiss Reformed theologian Karl Barth (1886–1968). SCM PRESS

directed against the heretical distortions of the 'German Christians'. Church leaders repeatedly affirmed their loyalty to the state and congratulated Hitler on his political and foreign policy moves. Because Luther had supported the ruling power, the Confessing Church did not set itself up as a rival church, but simply defended the orthodox Christian faith against innovations.

Harassed by the Gestapo, and repudiated by most Protestant leaders, the Confessing Church led a perilous existence. Its very presence was an embarrassment to the Nazis, and its witness to Christ's Lordship over the world implicitly challenged Hitler's totalitarianism. A few adherents, such as Dietrich Bonhoeffer, were conscious of their political responsibility, and reluctantly became involved in the anti-Hitler resistance. But the conservatism and nationalism of most Germans deterred them from standing up publicly for democracy and individual rights. After the war, Niemöller and other surviving leaders of the Confessing Church declared their guilt for failing to speak out against the Nazi regime.

THE 'NEW HEATHENISM'

The German Catholics, too, wanted to uphold the state and retain their privileged status, but soon were drawn into the church struggle. The Nazis gradually, but methodically, destroyed the network of Catholic organizations in Germany, and clamped down on the Catholic press and schools. In vain churchmen expressed alarm over the spread of 'new heathenism' and increasing restrictions on their work; finally they turned to the Vatican for help.

Accordingly, Pius XI drafted the encyclical *Mit brennender Sorge* ('With deep anxiety') of 14 March 1937, the first significant church document to criticize Nazism directly. Smuggled into Germany, it was read on Palm Sunday from every Catholic pulpit. The encyclical protested against the oppression of the church, and called upon Catholics to resist the idolatrous cult of race and state, to stand against the perversion of Christian doctrines and morality, and to maintain their loyalty to Christ, his church, and Rome. Hoping to keep the door open to reconciliation, the pope condemned the excesses of Nazi doctrines, without denouncing the regime's totalitarianism as such.

Hitler was furious, but avoided a break by treating it with silence. Knowing that he had the support of the German Catholic laity, Hitler simply stepped up the pressure on church activities and clergy. The Nazis dealt severely with dissent in the lower ranks, but were reluctant to move against high dignitaries, such as Bishop Galen of Münster, whose attack on the euthanasia programme in August 1941 aroused such public indignation that Hitler had it suspended.

THE COMMUNIST CHALLENGE

Communism, the left-wing variety of totalitarianism, generally arose in poorer, less developed nations. Communist systems are similar to those on the right in that they possess a dictatorial, charismatic leadership; a centralized, bureaucratic party whose members comprise the 'elite' of the new order; rigid discipline and ruthless terror, with a secret police and concentration camps; the use — and even glorification — of violence to achieve the regime's goals; a stereotyped negative image of the 'class' enemy; propaganda and censorship to condition and direct the public mind; indoctrination of youth; strict control of the economy; and hostility to all organized religion.

Communist ideology emphasizes the working classes (the proletariat), revolution as the means for social change, and the utopian ideal of a classless society. V. I. Lenin (1870–1924), the principal theorist of totalitarian communism, regarded his work as a logical development of Marxist historical and dialectical materialism, and formulated a doctrine of the party and the nature of revolution that would ensure the ultimate victory of the proletariat.

According to Lenin, the party must be a small, tightly-knit organization that instils political consciousness into the masses, and leads in the struggle for power — even to the point of actually seizing power on behalf of the workers. The party organs represent the masses' interests, but no deviation is permitted from the party 'line' — the tactics and strategy developed by the leadership. Lenin believed the workers and peasants in Russia could together overthrow the czarist regime and establish a revolutionary dictatorship that would direct the country's economic development and create the classless society.

Following the March 1917 revolution that replaced czarist rule, Lenin's Bolsheviks identified with the popularly elected councils (soviets) that rivalled the provisional government of the new republic, and seized power in a coup in November, allegedly on behalf of the soviets. As he began putting his theories into practice, his enemies struck back, leading to a bitter civil war and intervention by the Western Allies. Leon Trotsky (1879–1940) saved the day by raising a 'Red Army', which defeated the 'Whites' after two years, and left the Russian Bolsheviks (now called communists) more hostile than ever to the Western capitalist countries.

Proceeding from Trotsky's theory of 'permanent revolution' – that the Russian venture could not succeed unless revolution occurred in other countries as well – the Bolsheviks in 1919 created the Communist International (Comintern) to coordinate the world revolutionary movement. Although that year communist regimes briefly held sway in Hungary and Bavaria, and popular hysteria (the 'Red Scare') against leftists swept the United States, the world revolution never got off the ground.

When Lenin died in 1924, a bitter struggle for Soviet leadership raged between Trotsky and the ambitious Joseph Stalin (1879–1953), resulting in the latter's victory by 1927. As a boy, Stalin had studied for the priesthood at the Orthodox seminary in Tiflis, but abandoned religion for Marxist materialism. He realized that, in the immediate future, any hope of spreading revolution beyond Russia was futile, and he countered with his own doctrine of 'socialism in one country'. Russia must be transformed into a highly industrialized state on the basis of its own resources, so it could compete with – and resist the aggression of – the capitalist nations.

The First Five Year Plan (1928) laid the basis for the totalitarian control of the country's economic and social life. The collectivization of agriculture was decreed, and the prosperous peasants (the *Kulaks*) who resisted were wiped out. The capital generated in the agricultural sector was diverted to heavy industry, and though wages were depressed and the production of consumer goods low, Russia was transformed into an industrial nation.

Stalin also concentrated heavily on education and youth organizations to win over the younger generation to the new order, and the party exercised a dictatorship over all aspects of life and thought in the Soviet Union, as the country had been renamed in 1922. He held that the strengthening of the state was necessary so long as the capitalist encirclement of the country prevailed. An even more brutal and ruthless dictator than his counterpart in Germany, the moody, suspicious Stalin utilized secret police terror and labour camps to suppress the slightest dissent and to eliminate all potential rivals, including his old Bolshevik comrades who were executed after the spectacular Moscow trials in 1936–38.

OPIATE OF THE PEOPLE

Central to Marxist-Leninist ideology is hostility to Christianity – and all religion. Its adherents claim that the existing socio-political order determines all phenomena – including religious beliefs. Religion is false consciousness, an illusory reflection of the world resulting from class divisions. It will die a natural death once communism is established. This explains the struggle of Soviet Russian communists against religion. Since the party embodied the ideals of Marxism-Leninism, it could not allow some part of visible reality to remain outside its scope. Institutional religion was a reactionary social force that impeded progress towards the classless society, and had to be smashed. As Christianity was an alternative world-view, it threatened the power and prestige of the Communist party. At the same time, Christians could not accept a secularized version of their own understanding of history – that humanity is moving towards a final perfect end, the coming of Christ. The Marxist-Leninist emphasis on violent class struggle also challenged Christian values, thus making a *modus vivendi* between them essentially impossible. Bolshevism and Christianity were ideologically incompatible.

The Russian Orthodox Church had long been subservient to the state, but pressure for reform had been mounting. Although the Czar was in theory the head of the church, he appointed the Procurator of the Holy Synod, who actually governed the church. Although more and more churchmen believed that the conditions of workers and peasants must be improved, only a tiny group of radical priests regarded socialism as a solution. Because various scandals and personal interference by the imperial couple in church matters undermined Nicholas II's position among Orthodox leaders, they welcomed the March Revolution and sided with the provisional government.

In August 1917 an All-Russian Council (*Sobor*) of the church was convened. This conservative body challenged revolutionary public opinion by reintroducing the long-abandoned patriarchal system of church government. When the Bolsheviks seized power, they confiscated church lands, cancelled state subsidies for the church, legalized civil marriage, and nationalized the schools.

Patriarch Tikhon (1865–1925) responded in February 1918 by excommunicating the government leaders. Church officials organized resistance and called for restoration of the monarchy. The Bolshevik Council of People's Commissars immediately decreed the separation of church and state. It recognized the equality before the law of all religious groups, and permitted them freedom of worship 'so long as they do not disturb public order or interfere with the rights of citizens'. It disestablished the Orthodox Church, and banished every vestige of religion from state and public schools. All church property was nationalized. The state kept revenue-producing lands, and leased church buildings used for worship to their congregations. Religious bodies were denied the rights of a person in law, which placed them in an extremely vulnerable legal position in the years to come.

The regime surrounded the church with an ever-tightening network of administrative and police controls. When famine spread through Russia in 1922, the government confiscated church treasures for humanitarian relief purposes. Patriarch Tikhon denounced this as sacrilege and urged the faithful not to submit. The authorities in turn arrested him, freeing him only after he recanted his 'anti-Soviet actions' and declared his loyalty to the regime.

A schism occurred when a group of parish clergy formed the 'Living Church' (Renovationists), which opposed the monastic-episcopal basis of the patriarchal church, and adopted a pro-Soviet position. In 1923 the *Sobor* accepted the reforms of the Living Church, cut all counter-revolutionary links, assured the government of its unconditional loyalty, and recognized the separation of church and state and the nationalization of church property. But neither this surrender, nor later expressions of Soviet patriotism, restored the church to official favour or healed its divisions. At the same time, Protestant groups such as the Baptists and Mennonites enjoyed considerable freedom in these early years.

LEAGUE OF THE GODLESS

From the beginning, the Bolsheviks sponsored atheist endeavours, culminating in the creation in 1925 of the League of Militant Godless, which spread anti-clerical propaganda and promoted 'cultural enlightenment' by stressing science and materialist philosophy. The League produced anti-religious films, plays, radio talks, and literature, sponsored lectures and exhibits, and established museums of atheism.

Although the first constitutions of 1918 and 1925 guaranteed 'freedom of religious and anti-religious propaganda', the Stalinist Law on Religious Associations (1929) placed strict limits on the activities of churches in Russia. They could not engage in social, charitable, or educational work, hold prayer, Bible study, women's or young people's meetings, or even give their members material aid. They were free only to worship, and were deprived of any influence on society.

Meanwhile, the state had unlimited power to control religious bodies. It required every congregation to be registered, and the registering authority could exclude individuals from elected church councils. All extraordinary meetings and religious conferences required special permission, and local officials could close a church if they deemed the building was needed for some public purpose. Removed was the right of 'religious propaganda,' which crippled the evangelistic efforts of the non-Orthodox bodies. From this point only public worship was tolerated.

The 1930s were years of intense persecution. Thousands of clergy were imprisoned or liquidated during the collectivization of agriculture and Stalin's purges. The new Soviet constitution of 1936 granted the clergy voting rights — previously they were classified as an 'exploiting element' and disenfranchised — but the 'servants of religion' continued to be second-class citizens, constantly harassed by the secret police as 'clerico-fascists'.

By 1939 the Russian Orthodox Church as an institution was on the verge of disintegration, while the rigid application of anti-religious laws, atheistic propaganda, and Stalinist terror also ravaged the Lutheran, Baptist, and Evangelical Christian communities. Large numbers of Russian Mennonites emigrated to the Americas in the 1920s, and those who stayed behind suffered along with the rest. Similar treatment was meted out to Roman Catholics, Old Believers, Uniate (Greek rite) Catholics — and even Jews and Muslims.

ROME VERSUS MOSCOW

The persecution of Christians contributed greatly to the revulsion against the Soviet regime in the West. The Roman Catholic Church was most alarmed about events there; Moscow regarded it as the ally of capitalism, reaction, and fascism — a major obstacle to world revolution. In 1930 Pope Pius XI called for a worldwide day of prayer, and celebrated a mass of expiation on behalf of suffering Christians in Russia. Anglican and German Lutheran churches joined in the protest. The Soviet response was to form Militant Atheists International to combat the Vatican. But when Hitler began persecuting Catholics, the Soviets backed off, declared fascism to be the main enemy, and adopted the 'united front' policy with Catholic anti-fascists.

Viewing the Soviet anti-religious campaign with deepening concern, Pius XI issued on 18 March 1937 the encyclical *Divini Redemptoris*, condemning the 'errors of communism'. He criticized the spread of communism into Spain and Mexico, expressed sympathy for the Russian people, and offered the doctrines of the Catholic Church as the alternative to communism. To counter Stalin's 'popular front' policy, the pope declared that 'communism is intrinsically wrong, and no one who would save Christian civilization may collaborate with it in any undertaking whatsoever'. Coming only four days after his encyclical criticizing Nazi Germany, the Vatican had sided with persecuted believers in the totalitarian countries.

CHRISTIANS AND WORLD WAR II

The determination of the German and Italian dictators to engage in expansion brought Europe ever closer to the brink of war. A militaristic clique imposed a fascist-style regime in Japan which made common cause with the European 'Axis' powers. In August 1939 Stalin concluded a non-aggression treaty with Hitler that opened the way for the German invasion of Poland and the launching of World War II; but two years later Hitler abruptly turned on his erstwhile friend. President Roosevelt prevailed over isolationist sentiments in the United States to undertake preparations for war, and the December 1941 Japanese attack on American and British possessions in the Pacific set the stage for the greatest conflict in history. Meanwhile, Stalin signed a neutrality agreement with Japan that lasted until 1945.

During the 1930s, Christians in the United States were divided in their attitudes toward the totalitarian dictatorships. Some were so staunchly anti-communist that they backed fascist-type movements. Even Hitler found favour with a number of Christians, and one leader was reported to have commended him for building 'a front line of defence against the Anti-Christ of Communism'. On the other hand, the agonies of the depression pushed many clergy towards the left. Liberal Christians denounced the evils of capitalism, called for social reform, and embraced Roosevelt's policy of a 'New Deal'. Some were active socialists – for example the Presbyterian minister Norman Thomas – but very few actually joined the Communist party, or approved of events in the Soviet Union.

Although torn by ideological and organizational divisions, the American peace movement grew during the 1930s, and provided considerable support for isolationist policies. Liberal Christians were heavily involved in the peace societies, but some came to see a vast difference between the totalitarian threat and the pre-1914 situation, and argued for American participation in the widening struggle. Outraged by what they called short-sighted pacifism, Reinhold Niebuhr (1892–1971) and others founded in 1941 the journal *Christianity and Crisis* that challenged church people to reject neutralism and accept the necessity of intervention.

With the outbreak of World War II, churchmen in the various countries pledged loyalty to their regimes. But in comparison with 1914, the commitment was more tentative, and a crusading air not so evident. In the West the peace movement rapidly collapsed, and the churches supplied military chaplains for the pastoral care of servicemen. The rights of the minority of religious conscientious objectors were usually – but not always – respected, while the historic peace churches and liberal pacifist organizations were left alone.

German Protestant and Catholic leaders alike publicly urged their people to back the war effort, and the Russian churches enthusiastically supported the 'Great Patriotic War'. In 1941 most Christians in Japan had, under government pressure, united into one church, the *Kyodan*, which, after Pearl Harbor, urged believers to 'promote the Great Endeavour'.

Although German church officials remained conciliatory towards the Nazi state, this failed to ease the suffering of Christians. Hitler's closest advisers systematically worked towards the 'final settlement' in church-state relations, where the churches would be subordinated to the 'new order', the clergy stripped of all privileges, and Christianity left to suffer what Hitler called 'a natural death'. In the occupied areas of Europe priests and pastors, as well as devout laypersons, were treated as common criminals. Thousands were executed or sent to concentration camps, though war-time exigencies and the need for popular support kept the Nazis from eradicating religion in Germany itself. But what lay ahead was dramatized in the Warthegau, the model territory in Poland, where the Nazis proceeded to wipe out the institutional church.

To bomb cities as cities, deliberately to attack civilians, quite irrespective of whether or not they are actively contributing to the war effort, is a wrong deed, whether done by the Nazis or by ourselves.

BISHOP GEORGE BELL OF CHICHESTER

GERMANS RESIST HITLER

However, a small minority of clerics and laymen in both denominations opposed the Nazis. The Kreisau Circle, led by Count Helmuth von Moltke (1907–45), met regularly at his estate to discuss the spiritual and other problems that would confront Germany once Hitler was gone. These men were not directly implicated in the assassination attempt of 20 July 1944 but were still tried and condemned. Count Klaus von Stauffenberg, who planted the bomb, was a Catholic, but the hierarchy itself offered no encouragement to him or to other conspirators. The execution of Jesuit Father Alfred Delp and Pastor Dietrich Bonhoeffer illustrated National Socialism's implacable hostility to Christianity.

By and large, however, the churches' resistance was meagre. They were mainly concerned with individualistic personal faith, traditional submission to the state, and a conservative outlook that rejected all left-wing proposals for social and political reform, and enabled them to accept the Nazis' claim to be the only alternative to communism.

In later years, Christian activists in the United States and other countries drew inspiration and ideas from the German experience in the struggle for social justice in their own lands. In post-war Germany the memory of the church conflict led to a revitalization of the role of ordinary Christians, acceptance of political and social responsibility as a Christian duty, and the total rejection of any pseudo-religious glorification of the nation. Recognizing that unity in Christ binds together Christians of every nation and race, they now took an active part in the ecumenical movement. Conscious of their own deeply-rooted anti-Semitism, many churchmen openly confessed guilt for the horrors that overtook their Jewish compatriots, and gave their backing to the new state of Israel.

STALIN'S UNEXPECTED ALLY

The situation in wartime Soviet Russia was quite different. Stalin came to realize the value of the church's contribution to public morale, and how it could help integrate the territories acquired during the war and promote Soviet foreign-policy views in the future. He allowed the patriarchal church to revive, reduced the level of atheist propaganda, and somewhat relaxed the rigid application of the 1918 and 1929 laws. The church could re-establish its hierarchical organization, collect funds, and give some private religious instruction to children. In 1945 the Orthodox Church and other religious groups regained corporative legal status, including the right to possess property and produce liturgical objects. It now enjoyed the most favourable position since the civil war, but was still closely supervised by the state. Special bureaucratic agencies were created to maintain liaison between the government and the various churches, draft regulations on religion, and ensure that the laws were enforced.

The Roman Catholic Church clearly recognized the difficulties that the deepening tensions in Europe posed, and in March 1939 chose an accomplished diplomat, Cardinal Pacelli, as Pope Pius XII. Deeply committed to bringing peace to the world, he held no illusions about either Soviet communism or Nazism, both of which he detested, but his efforts to avert conflict and lessen suffering in occupied areas were unsuccessful. The problem of how to overcome the sin of war while ministering to those overwhelmed by the catastrophe seemed insoluble. A forceful denunciation of Nazi crimes might only increase Nazi atrocities and result in still more suffering. Yet if he said nothing, the reputation of the Vatican as the guardian of moral and spiritual values would be shattered.

WHY THE POPE WAS SILENT

The debate over why Pius remained silent about German aggression, and especially the murder of millions of Jews, continues. Critics argue that if he had spoken out vigorously, and threatened to excommunicate all Catholics involved in carrying out the 'final solution', the Jewish massacre could have been averted. But if had done so, he would have lost the allegiance of German Catholics, and the institutional church throughout occupied Europe might have been crushed. To preserve that seemed more important than saving Jewish lives. Moreover, Pius did not want to undermine the struggle against Russia; he regarded communism as a greater evil than National Socialism.

Pius' defenders argue that his stance of strict neutrality put him in a position to negotiate reconciliation, and to avoid lending any religious support to the conflict. He also realized that most German Catholics supported Hitler, and that anti-Semitism had so infected them that they were unlikely to respond to papal efforts to counteract Nazi Jewish policies. Further, it was difficult to obtain solid information on crimes against Jews, and practically impossible to spread this to a sufficient number of Germans. Finally, a Catholic call to action against the central tenet of National Socialism would most certainly have been regarded as high treason, and dealt with in a brutal, summary fashion. World War II presented the pope with an irresolvable crisis of conscience.

The Protestant ecumenical movement also found itself in an awkward position because of the war. The 1938 Madras conference of the International Missionary Council observed that a militant 'new paganism' had arisen which demanded religious devotion from its followers. But, fearful that believers in the Soviet Union, Axis countries, and Japanese-occupied lands in Asia would suffer retaliation, no specific national sins were pinpointed or condemned. After 1939 the IMC assisted the 'orphaned missions' of Germany and other European countries in Africa and Asia to continue functioning. It demonstrated that a Christian world fellowship, transcending nation and denomination, was possible. Other ecumenical groups concentrated on international relief efforts, caring for war prisoners and refugees, and maintaining contacts between churches on both sides.

World War II had a devastating impact on Christianity, both physically and morally. Thousands of church buildings were destroyed, and untold numbers of clergy and faithful believers were killed, persecuted, or uprooted from their homes. The level of violence escalated, with the use of armoured vehicles, incendiary and carpet bombing, long-range rockets, and atomic weapons, all of which together snuffed out the lives of millions.

The deliberate direction of war against civilian populations, indifference to the sufferings of Jews and other minorities, development of a military-industrial complex, and the alliance of the Western democracies with the totalitarian Soviet Union were moral issues of paramount concern to Christians and led many to question whether a 'just war' could any longer be possible. They suggested that any Christian endorsement of war only led to its intensification. Although some Christians were involved post-war in attempts to bring nations and churches together in community – the United Nations (1945) and the World Council of Churches (1948) – the coming of the Cold War frustrated their work.

POST-WAR EUROPE

After the war, a complex and lengthy process of European integration took place. The Maastricht Treaty (1993) expanded the European Common Market (1957), later the European Economic Community, into the European Union. The newly reconstituted areas of Eastern Europe quickly sought membership. Many members adopted a common currency – the euro – but the problems in several countries of economic underdevelopment and separatist movements undermined full integration. The EU is a fully secular organization, although separation of church and state is not mentioned in the founding documents, and progress did occur in the area of human rights and religious liberty.

The basic document in this regard is the Universal Declaration of Human Rights, adopted by the United Nations General Assembly on 10 December 1948. Crucial to religious freedom is Article 16 which states:

> Everyone has the right to freedom of thought, conscience, and religion; this right includes freedom to change his religion or belief, and freedom, either alone or in community with others, and in public or private, to manifest his religion or belief in teaching, practices, worship, and observance.

A similar stance was taken in the founding document of the Organisation of Security and Cooperation in Europe (Helsinki Final Act, 1975). The Council of Europe, founded in 1949, focussed on matters of legal standards, human rights, democratic development, and cultural cooperation. It adopted the European Convention on Human Rights and Fundamental Freedoms (1950, 1953), which in turn established a European Court of Human Rights. Its provision recognizing freedom of religion is worded similarly to that in the UN Declaration on Human Rights. The Vatican II conciliar document *Dignitatis Humanae* (1965) also affirmed the right of the person to 'religious freedom', including that all are free from coercion by any individual, social group, or human power to act in a manner contrary to one's own beliefs.

IDEOLOGIES IN CONFLICT

After 1945, a rift opened between the victors, and the United States – as leader of the Western democracies – took the initiative through a 'containment' policy to counter Soviet expansion. This process, however, became confused with communism as a political doctrine, especially after China was 'lost' in 1949. Communism anywhere – whether at home, in Europe, or in the Third World – was now viewed as a threat to American national security. The 'witch-hunts' of Senator Joseph McCarthy and others were aimed at domestic subversion, while foreign economic and military aid and a string of defensive alliances with independent countries around the world were designed to counter possible communist exploitation of their weakness. Direct military intervention also occurred, particularly in the Korean and Vietnam conflicts. The United States was committed to resisting communism everywhere, until eventually the development of the H-bomb and long-range ballistic missiles made armed conflict between the superpowers unthinkable.

Although the Cold War started as a political rivalry, it rapidly took on an ideological dimension. Both sides in the polarized world received support from their Christian populations. In a messianic manner, the Soviets preached the doctrines of

BILLY GRAHAM

William Franklin 'Billy' Graham is the most successful Christian mass evangelist in history. Born on a dairy farm at Charlotte, North Carolina, USA, on November 7, 1918, he was converted in an evangelistic campaign in 1934. He graduated from Wheaton College, Illinois, in 1943, married Ruth Bell (1920–2007), daughter of a veteran missionary to China who bore him five children, and was employed as the first evangelist of the Youth for Christ movement.

In 1947 Graham was named president of Northwestern College, Minneapolis, and two years later rose to national prominence during a Los Angeles evangelistic campaign that received extensive media coverage. In 1950 he assembled a group to form the Billy Graham Evangelistic Association, and initiated a radio programme, *The Hour of Decision*. Resigning the college presidency in 1952, he devoted his life to holding evangelistic rallies ('crusades') in cities throughout the world, most of which were televised to widen their impact.

Possessing a warm, winsome personality, Graham used modern mass communications and organization to put across a simple, Bible-centred gospel message. He emphasized individual decisions for Christ and careful follow-up to integrate the new believers into churches. Although at first a staunch anti-communist and American nationalist, the mature Graham gained world-wide respect for his ecumenical vision, rejection of racial discrimination, global awareness, and sense of social concern. Not only did he preach on all six continents, including the former Soviet Union and China, but many presidents and heads of state regarded him as a friend and welcomed his counsel. In his later years, however, he was drawn into political controversies and Republican Party endeavours that brought him heavy criticism.

Graham authored thirty books, including several best-sellers, his organization produced over

The audience at a Billy Graham evangelistic crusade in New Jersey, eastern USA, September 1991.
BILLY GRAHAM EVANGELISTIC ASSOCIATION

a hundred evangelistic films, and a mass circulation magazine *Decision* was launched in 1960. He played a leading role in inaugurating the periodical *Christianity Today* in 1956, and sponsored the World Congresses on Evangelism in Berlin (1966), Lausanne (1974), and Manila (1989), as well as the Amsterdam Conferences for Itinerant Evangelists (1983, 1986, and 2000). He also founded a research centre on evangelism and missions at Wheaton College, a training school for Christian workers in Asheville, North Carolina – 'The Cove' – and a library at Charlotte.

In failing health, Graham retired from active ministry in 2005 and his son Franklin assumed leadership of the BGEA. Billy spent his remaining years in rela-tive seclusion at his mountain home outside Montreat, North Carolina. Throughout his life he was the recipient of innumerable awards and honours from governmental and private agencies at home and abroad. He conducted more than 400 crusades in 185 countries, and estimates are that his audience numbered at least 2.2 billion people, with 3.2 million responding to his call to receive Christ as Saviour.

RICHARD V. PIERARD

communism and the necessity of freeing peoples oppressed by 'imperialists'. At the same time, by installing friendly regimes on their borders, they secured Mother Russia against another attack from the West, like those in 1914 and 1941.

Russian Orthodox leaders meanwhile sought to bring churches in other countries under their jurisdiction. Orthodox representatives travelling abroad invariably proclaimed the current Moscow 'line' on world issues, and praised conditions in the Soviet Union. They were especially active in the Soviet-sponsored peace campaigns. With the emphasis on 'peaceful co-existence' following Stalin's death in 1953, the Orthodox Church participated in ecumenical affairs, and finally joined the World Council of Churches in 1961, as did the Russian Baptists, who resumed their place in the Baptist World Alliance.

The West reacted with the counter-ideology of anti-communism. The basic assumption was of a universal communist conspiracy controlled by Moscow, which masterminded all revolutionary unrest in the world. Anti-communism was, particularly, an American response to the East-West stalemate after World War II, and the frustration resulting from America's inability to spread the virtues of liberal democracy to all nations. It also sprang from the anxieties of people whose traditional values had been uprooted by the social changes of the war years — the extreme mobility of American life that shattered their sense of security, the demands of minorities for equality, and the impersonality of bureaucratized society. Communism — the ideology that seemingly clashed with the basic elements of 'Americanism' as a secular faith — was regarded as the source of these problems. The 'American way' was hard work and rugged individualism; 'compromise' with this global adversary was an inconceivable alternative to 'victory'.

The Vatican too was extremely critical of communism. Pius XII excommunicated Catholics involved in communist activities, openly denounced persecution, backed resistance efforts by East European Catholics, and called upon the faithful in Italy to reject the party. Similarly, most American Catholics — Senator McCarthy was one — were hostile to the 'foreign' ideology.

Even more fervent in its support of anti-communism was the conservative Protestant community in America. Communism was regularly condemned from pulpits of the land. The interdenominational National Association of Evangelicals and American Council of Churches urged forceful action to halt the spread of the 'red menace'. Funds flowed into the coffers of those religious groups of the radical right that exposed alleged conspirators and reaffirmed the traditional values they regarded as both American and Christian, singling out for attack internationalist and social-activist liberal churchmen and ecumenical bodies. Although American Christian anti-communism remained strong well into the 1960s, the easing of the Cold War, the liberalizing currents flowing from the Second Vatican Council, and the quest for East-West *détente* undermined the impact of what had become an outdated ideology.

New forces were shaping world politics. First was the recovery and growing independence of Western and Central Europe. Second was the disintegration of the monolithic communist bloc, as a result of the Sino-Soviet rift and the increasing assertiveness of the leaders of Moscow's East-European 'satellites' and communist parties elsewhere. A third factor was the demise of colonialism and the emergence of Africa, Asia, and Latin America in the world arena. World revolution was redefined as a quest for economic and racial equality with the white nations of the northern hemisphere. Finally, the mutual balance of terror caused a decline in the importance of nuclear weapons in the world power balance. They were not used in settling political disputes and were of no value in guerrilla wars.

THE MARXIST CHALLENGE

In addition to the resurgence of traditional religions and the rise of new religions, other political and social challenges faced Christianity that had enormous religious implications. Among these were Marxism, ethnic and religious strife, and civil religion.

As World War II ended, the Chinese communist leader Mao Zedong (1893–1976) resumed his struggle for control of China with Chiang Kai-shek's *Kuomintang* (Nationalists). Mao's forces were finally victorious in 1949, and established the People's Republic of China. Believing that Christianity was tied both to Western colonialism and to Vatican and American anti-communism, Mao's government expelled all foreign missionaries, liquidated church organizations, and subjected believers to intense persecution. This reached its peak in the 'cultural revolution' of 1966–71. There was also a resurgence of nationalism that led to a split with its Soviet ally, and the end of monolithic communism. However, after China's *rapprochement* with the United States, its admission to the United Nations, and the death of Mao, the more stringent aspects of the regime began to relax.

Out of the Chinese Revolution came a new variant of Marxism known as Maoism. Mao emphasized the peasantry rather than the proletariat as the social basis of the revolution. He regarded the party as a people's democracy, where the peasantry, workers, petty bourgeoisie, and intellectuals would unite in a revolutionary organization. The tactics for obtaining power were those of guerrilla warfare and disciplined action, which chipped away at the existing order. Finally, Mao stressed Chinese nationalism, and blamed feudalism and imperialism for the country's desperate plight.

China was an outstanding example of an underdeveloped country, but under Mao's communist rule it made enormous strides in eliminating hunger, creating an industrial base, and building a military machine. This was a model for revolutionary action that could be imitated and implemented elsewhere.

The Chinese claimed to be the ally of the world's impoverished nations, and tried to win their allegiance in a struggle of the poor against the rich, thus making Marxism an instrument of class warfare between rich and poor countries, rather than economic classes within nations. Both Maoism, and the recently developed Christian variety of Marxism, the theology of liberation, appealed to revolutionary leaders in Africa, Asia, and Latin America.

Mao Zedong (also transliterated as Mao Tse-tung; 1893–1976), Chinese communist revolutionary and founding father of the People's Republic of China, photographed as a young man.
ILLUSTRATED LONDON NEWS

The brightly-coloured steeple of a Christian church in a village near Beijing, China.
© CHEN LIRONG/ DREAMSTIME.COM

In the late 1970s, China began orienting itself more towards the West. External business interests invested heavily, tourists flocked in, teacher and student exchanges multiplied, the transfer of Hong Kong from British control took place in 1997, and in the new century China became the second largest industrial power in the world. Especially noteworthy was the resurgence of Christianity. The regime allowed churches to re-open, and the faith expanded so rapidly that the country seemed to be on the verge of a major revival. The brutal suppression of the student protest movement in June 1989 temporarily put political, economic, and religious progress on hold, but gradually the democratization process resumed and the economy boomed.

Meanwhile, in communist Europe, organized religion was subjected to varying degrees of restriction. All religion was rooted out in Albania, which professed to be the world's first truly atheistic state. Churches in Bulgaria and Romania worked under severe restraints, while the other Soviet bloc countries permitted substantial religious activity, although churches were hardly a welcome feature.

In 1959 the level of persecution in the Soviet Union intensified considerably, and the Russian Baptists split over whether they should continue to submit to state regulation of religious activity. The determination of Soviet believers to practise their faith, and the pressures of world opinion, made a return to the excesses of the Stalin era impossible. Although the church laboured under severe constraints for the next few years, it was clear by the 1980s that times had changed. The pressure of world opinion produced some moderation

PERESTROIKA AND GLASNOST

A few outspoken religious figures were permitted to emigrate, and Billy Graham, the prime symbol of Western Evangelicalism, visited and preached. When Mikhail

Gorbachev (b. 1931) assumed power in 1985, he proclaimed the new policies of *perestroika* and *glasnost*, and pressures on the churches were further relaxed. Christian prisoners in labour camps were freed, Bibles were allowed in the country, closed churches reopened, regulations restricting religious education were modified, and Christian leaders could attend international gatherings.

In Poland the level of religious freedom was relatively high for a communist state. The overwhelming majority of the people identified with the Roman Catholic Church, which provided the spiritual and ideological backing for the *Solidarnösc* (Solidarity) movement, which in 1989 formed the first non-communist government in Eastern Europe since the imposition of the peoples' republics in the immediate post-war years.

The regime of the (East) German Democratic Republic waxed hot and cold towards Christianity. Its constitution guaranteed a substantial level of religious freedom, and university theological faculties, religious publishing houses, and a large number of churches existed. But practising Christians suffered discrimination in employment, and the regime provided substitute rituals and activities to woo young people away from the church. Then, in 1978, the head of state and church leaders reached an understanding which allowed the churches more freedom of action. They, in turn, agreed to function as 'the church within socialism'; that is, to minister within the system.

In 1989, when it became clear that the Soviets would not interfere in the internal affairs of the bloc countries, a wave of grassroots uprisings swept Eastern Europe. Following the Polish example, first Hungary, and then East Germany, Czechoslovakia, Bulgaria, Romania, and Albania replaced their communist regimes with democratic ones. Christians were visible in all of these efforts, especially in the GDR, where churches served as gathering points for those disaffected with the system, and the church leadership negotiated with state officials and counselled the populace to moderation and non-violence.

The client states now went their own separate ways, East and West Germany reunited, and the demands of the constituent nationalities for freedom forced far-reaching changes in the Soviet Union. The result was the dismantling of the entire communist system, and the country's dissolution into over a dozen separate states. Yugoslavia also disintegrated into competing national entities, and a bloody civil war ensued in the 1990s; while Czechoslovakia split into two parts. Resurgent nationalism lay at the root of most conflicts, but religion was a central factor too. The old anti-religious laws were scrapped, and the traditional churches sought to regain their former power. They competed with evangelical missionary agencies and new religions from the West, and before long the existing churches were pressing for restrictions on the newcomers.

RACIAL TENSIONS

The second problem, ethnic and racial strife with religious overtones, was most serious. Both in South Africa and the United States, relations between blacks and whites reached a critical stage in the 1960s. Most white church leaders supported the South African apartheid – separate development – policy, but their country became an international outcast because of it. The programme consisted of laws requiring racial classification and identity cards, residential separation in the cities, the formation of remote reservations euphemistically labelled 'homelands', separate public amenities and accommodation, and racial discrimination in employment. Suffrage was for whites only. The regime had virtually unlimited police and judicial power to enforce these regulations, and imprisoned, tortured, and even murdered alleged violators. The World Council of Churches' Programme to Combat Racism fought apartheid in the 'white redoubt' of southern Africa during the dark days of the 1970s.

South African Christians played the leading role in the struggle against apartheid. Individuals such as Alan Paton (1903–88), Archbishop Desmond Tutu (1931–), Beyers Naudé (1915–2004); groups such as the South African Council of Churches, the Christian Institute and African Enterprise; theological declarations such as the *Kairos Document* (1985) and the *Kabare Statement* (1987), were acclaimed for their bold criticism of the system. Various churches in the country, especially charismatic ones, provided models of integrated life, and by 1990 even the mainline churches were speaking out against apartheid. As more and more Christians withdrew their support from the system, and international economic and political boycotts left South Africa isolated, apartheid was dismantled and multi-racial democratic rule was established, with the first free election in 1994. The heroic Nelson Mandela became the first president. Assisting in the process of reconstruction was the Truth and Reconciliation Commission, in which Christian leaders played a key role.

In the United States, racial segregation was deeply rooted in the churches. The black church came into existence largely as response to their exclusion from white congregations, and the Civil Rights movement had a significant Christian dimension. The black church was the one social institution that enabled ex-slaves to survive in a racist society. Some white Christians, realizing their own complicity in racism, joined with African-Americans in the quest for justice. The outstanding figure in this movement was the Rev. Martin Luther King, Jr, and many other Civil Rights activists came from the ranks of black and white clergy. Although legal integration was achieved, overcoming the social and economic gaps between the races has proved to be more elusive.

In the Middle East and Northern Ireland, both ethnic and religious differences contributed to tensions. The founding of Israel in 1948 came after thirty years of strife between Palestinian Arabs, Jewish immigrants, and the British. Israel received solid support from West European and North American Christians, partly from a sense of guilt over the Holocaust, and partly because many saw the return of the Jews

Desmond Tutu (1931–) South African social rights activist and first black South African Archbishop of Cape Town.
© KOMELAU/ DREAMSTIME.COM

to Palestine as the fulfilment of biblical prophecy. On the other hand, Orthodox Christians sided with the Palestinians against Israel, so it was not solely a Muslim-Jewish controversy. As tensions between the Israelis and Palestinians mounted, conservative Evangelicals in the West unconditionally backed Israel alongside Jewish extremists who demanded a religious state and the expulsion of the Palestinians. More liberal church leaders called for a political

MARTIN LUTHER KING

Martin Luther King, Jr, the black Civil Rights leader, was born in 1929 in Atlanta, Georgia, where both his father and grandfather had been ministers of Ebenezer Baptist Church. King attended Morehouse College, Crozer Theological Seminary, and Boston University, and in 1953 married Coretta Scott.

In 1955, while King was a pastor in Montgomery, Alabama, a black woman, Mrs Rosa Parks, refused to move to the black section of a racially-segregated bus and was arrested. The young minister was suddenly thrust into the leadership of the bus boycott that followed, achieved the de-segregation of the buses, and was then propelled into world prominence as a crusader for social justice. As president of the Southern Christian Leadership Conference, King gave dynamic leadership to the Civil Rights movement, which gained more for black people than they had achieved in the previous three centuries.

The key to King's success was his Christian commitment. Brought up in the black Evangelical tradition, and influenced by the social gospel movement, he saw Christianity as a force that could transform not just the individual but the whole of society. His unique combination of the message of Jesus, to love your enemies, and the non-violence of Gandhi, gave a philosophy and a strategy to the Civil Rights movement. The use of non-violence as a means of achieving social justice in a violent society appealed to both blacks and whites.

During the thirteen years he led the Civil Rights movement, King won victory after victory, without once resorting to violence. His message to his white opponents was: 'We shall match your capacity to inflict suffering with our capacity to endure suffering.

Martin Luther King Jr Memorial, Washington DC, USA.
© RICHIE LOMBA | DREAMSTIME.COM

We will meet your physical force with soul force. Do to us what you will, and we shall continue to love you …' His message and method became world-famous, and in 1964 he was awarded the Nobel Peace Prize. An assassin's bullet ended the life of Martin Luther King, Jr in 1968, at the age of 39.

WESLEY A. ROBERTS

solution. Although violence seemed to be the way of life in the region, agreements in 1978 between Egypt and Israel, and in 1993 between Israel and the Palestine Liberation Organization, held out some hope of peace; but ongoing border conflicts, and the support of Middle Eastern Islamic states for the Palestinians, undermined any lasting settlement.

Deepening tensions in the Middle East was the overthrow of the unpopular regime in Iran of the American client Mohammad Reza Pahlavi by Islamic militants under Ayatollah Ruhollah Khomeini (1902–89). The Iraqi leader Saddam Hussein (1937–2006) defeated Iran in a bloody border war, and invaded oil-rich Kuwait in 1990. A UN coalition organized by the United States drove him back. But terrorism, as well as anti-Israel sentiment, was on the rise, culminating in the 11 September 2001 attack on the United States, orchestrated by the terrorist group al-Qaeda and Osama bin Laden. America responded by attacking bin Laden's support bases in Afghanistan, and assaulting Iraq in 2003, on the pretext that Saddam had weapons of mass destruction. These conflicts raged for years and undermined American moral standing and economic stability.

In Northern Ireland the differences were more historical and ethnic than religious. Protestant and Catholic leaders alike roundly denounced the violence perpetrated in the name of religion, and in the 1990s truces were arranged that scaled down the level of violence. The situation did much to harm to all Christian groups.

CIVIL RELIGION

A third threat to Christian vitality was 'civil religion'. Also known as public religion, or civic deism, it is a group of commonly-accepted religious sentiments, symbols, and concepts which serve to undergird the state and help secure popular allegiance. An elaborate matrix of beliefs, flowing from a nation's historic experience, it generally blurs religion and patriotism. Whether or not civil religion is identified with a particular denomination or faith, it is enlisted in the patriotic cause of enhancing national identity. Examples include Japanese Shinto, the white Afrikaner's sense of being chosen by God, Islamic Shi'ism in Iran, and the North American understanding of being a 'nation under God'.

In the American context, the Declaration of Independence and the Constitution were the 'sacred documents' and the president the 'high priest'. The God of civil religion was a unitarian deity, whose name was invoked on public occasions. State schools became the vehicles for inculcating and celebrating the national faith. The country's wars were 'righteous conflicts', and the 'American Way of Life' was seen as synonymous with God's way. The extensive use of public religion in recent years reveals how enticing it was, especially to committed Christians who loved their country and who believed it had been set apart by God as a 'Christian nation'. It remains as a serious hindrance to integrating immigrant groups and ameliorating ethnic and racial tensions.

Despite these challenges, Christianity has remained vibrant and growing. Old structures have crumbled, traditional approaches have been discarded, and new ideas accepted. Western hegemony in the church has been replaced with a shared responsibility with the peoples of the 'non-Western' or 'majority world' for proclaiming the gospel.

RICHARD PIERARD

A CENTURY OF CONFLICT

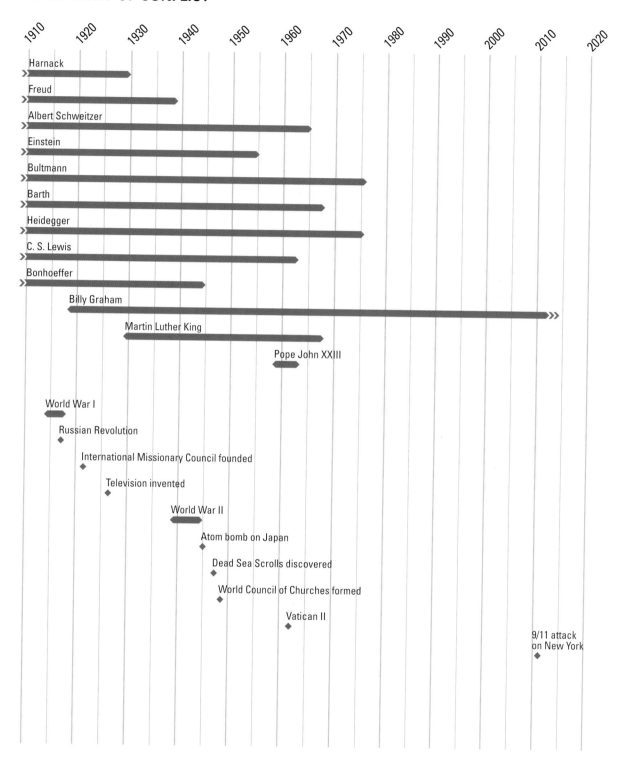

1910 1920 1930 1940 1950 1960 1970 1980 1990 2000 2010 2020

Harnack

Freud

Albert Schweitzer

Einstein

Bultmann

Barth

Heidegger

C. S. Lewis

Bonhoeffer

Billy Graham

Martin Luther King

Pope John XXIII

World War I

Russian Revolution

International Missionary Council founded

Television invented

World War II

Atom bomb on Japan

Dead Sea Scrolls discovered

World Council of Churches formed

Vatican II

9/11 attack
on New York

CHRISTIANS, WAR, AND PEACE

Throughout Christian history, most believers assumed warfare is the business of sovereigns. For the ordinary subject, citizen, or soldier this left only one choice: obedience. Some Christians have gone beyond automatic obedience and developed three distinct approaches.

Underlying the ensuing Crusades – and countless similar conflicts during the following centuries – were characteristic assumptions. Crusaders go into battle for a religious – or ostensibly religious – cause. Since their enemies stand for the forces of evil, they must be defeated totally; there can be no compromise between righteousness and wickedness. Ideally, the enemy is vanquished by honourable means; but if you hate an enemy who embodies error, and attack indiscriminately, that is excusable in the circumstances. Over the centuries the crusader's enemy has ranged from Muslims, to Catholics or Protestants, French revolutionaries, Germans or the Allies, and Communists.

JUST WAR

Older than the crusade, though by no means so popular, is the second approach: the 'just war'. Although this idea was rooted in Roman Stoic philosophy, in the late fourth century Ambrose and Augustine formed the just war into a Christian approach to the problem of warfare. Thomas Aquinas, the Spanish Dominican Francisco de Victoria (c. 1492–1546), and the Dutch Protestant Hugo Grotius (1583–1645) developed it further.

The just war theory has come to provide a series of criteria by which the permissibility of war in a particular situation can be weighed. Some of these criteria concern the origins of war: Is there a just cause – for example, a clear injury which needs to be redressed? Has every reasonable attempt been made to achieve redress without bloodshed? Will war be declared by a legitimate authority? Other criteria concern the way in which the war is fought: Is it to be waged solely by legitimate and moral means? Is the damage which is likely to be incurred by the war less grievous than the prior injury? Is success likely? If the answers to these questions are 'Yes', one may justly declare war. Unfortunately this will entail killing – though Augustine claimed this does not clash with loving the enemy. What really matters are the intentions of the combatants' hearts.

Although these criteria for the just war may seem clear, in practice they have often proved difficult to apply. For instance, Augustine's assumption that, in any conflict, justice will lie mainly on one side is clearly wrong. In any event, it is rarely clear who has the insight and objectivity necessary to decide what 'justice' means in a given situation. In practice, decisions about the meaning and application of 'justice' have almost always been made by the interested parties in a dispute – and they in turn have used the criteria of the just war to justify wars in which they were already engaged.

In the heat of battle, it is difficult to ensure that solely moral and legitimate means are used. The Christian warrior has often been overcome by exhaustion or over-excitement, and atrocities have been inevitable. One British observer commented on excesses of the Battle of the Somme (1916): 'If you start a man killing, you can't turn him off again like an engine.'

PACIFISM

The third, and oldest, Christian approach to war is pacifism. Early Christians combined a simple obedience to the words of Jesus – 'Love your enemies' (Matthew 5:44); 'Put your sword back in its place' (Matthew 26:52) – with a genuine international spirit – Christians 'love all men as their brothers'; 'Christ is also among the barbarians'. In practice, the early Christians were not as strictly pacifist as some of the theologians' writings might indicate. By the third century, Christians were serving in the Roman legions. Some soldiers left the army upon their conversion to Christianity; following his conversion in 339, Martin of Tours exclaimed, 'I am Christ's soldier; I am not allowed to fight.'

After the triumph of the Emperor Constantine in the early fourth century, Christian pacifism withered rapidly. In 392, the Emperor Theodosius declared Christianity to be the sole legal religion in the Empire; and in 416 all non-Christian troops were purged from the Roman army. Only a few monks and mendicants remained pacifists, until the Waldensians in thirteenth-century Italy, and the Czech Brethren in the fifteenth century, revived pacifism.

During the Protestant Reformation, the Anabaptists were the first to revive pacifism. Many of their emphases echoed concerns of some early church theologians. Nations would go on warring, but 'the regenerated do not go to war'.

In mid-seventeenth century England, pacifism appeared among the Quakers – the Society of Friends – who committed themselves to struggle in a loving and non-violent way against the 'powers of darkness'. By the end of the seventeenth century, the nature of the Quaker witness to peace had begun to change. Humanitarian concerns became predominant: war's unreasonableness, its economic waste, and its injury of the innocent. Friends could now appeal to people whose ethics were based on different grounds from their own.

In the 1920s and 1930s, yet another variety of Christian pacifism developed, that of the liberal Protestants. World War I – still a recent and vivid memory – gave liberals an arsenal of anti-war arguments. But they also felt confident that humanity could come to rational solutions of international disputes by peaceful means, particularly through new political instruments, such as the League of Nations. A liberal slogan advocated the 'renunciation of war as an instrument of national policy'. By their political activities, the liberals hoped to put an end to political boundaries and nation-states. Instead, the rise of Adolf Hitler and other dictators put an end to liberal pacifism as a popular movement.

NON-VIOLENT ACTION

Since World War II, many Christian pacifists have adopted techniques of non-violent action to obtain specific political goals. Leaders such as Martin Luther King Jr popularized non-cooperation, boycott, and public demonstration as a means of protest. Advocates of non-violent action point out that these techniques – unlike violence – do not dehumanize or alienate the adversary.

Pacifism has generally been espoused by only a minority of Christians, who have therefore tended to retreat from involvement in the world – indeed, persecution has often forced them to withdraw. Pacifists have also been accused – sometimes justly – of enjoying the benefits of society without contributing to its defence. Yet pacifism has generally been a movement of suffering. In the 1970s, Christian conscientious objectors suffered in Soviet and Spanish prisons. Finally, many pacifists have believed in human perfectibility, at times unwilling to face the extremity of human sin – which has given their thought an aspect of unreality.

ALAN KREIDER AND JOHN H. YODER

CHAPTER 38

AN AGE OF ANXIETY
Theological thinking in troubled era

The twentieth-century and the beginning of the twenty-first saw an astonishing diversity of theological thinking, from the speculative thought of liberalism to radical new approaches and painstaking biblical scholarship.

The most important and influential theologian in the first decade of the twentieth century was Adolf von Harnack of Berlin (1851–1930). Christian doctrine, he believed, developed largely under the influence of Greek thought. The essence of Christianity lay in three central truths that he found in the teaching of Jesus: the fatherhood of God, the brotherhood of man, and the infinite value of the individual human soul.

The roots of Harnack's Liberalism lay in the theology of Albrecht Ritschl (1822–89). Ritschl was suspicious of the role of doctrine – rather than experience – as an authentic source of truth. Harnack communicated his ideas to a vast readership in his book, *What is Christianity?* (1900). He was deeply concerned to commend the teaching of Jesus as something relevant to men of his own day. For this reason, he especially stressed the role of Jesus as a liberator who released men from legalism, and showed them the presence of God and the way of love.

Harnack's influence declined when thinkers began to call attention to the basic weakness of Liberalism as a whole. The whole teaching of Jesus cannot be reduced to three general truths, nor can the whole gospel be reduced to certain elements in the teaching of Jesus.

America too had many exponents of an optimistic and humanist kind of Christian liberalism. What came to be known as the 'social gospel movement' had theological roots in Ritschl's Liberalism. The most famous theologian of the social gospel was Walter Rauschenbusch (1861–1918), whose major work was *A Theology for the Social Gospel* (1919). He claimed that all theology must stem from the central idea of the kingdom of God, believing that when Jesus spoke about the kingdom this meant, not the community of the redeemed, but the transformation of society on earth – social reform and political action. Rauschenbusch himself called on the church to ally with the working class to transform the social order.

Rauschenbusch's approach began to lose momentum when two difficulties were spotlighted. First, it is doubtful whether Jesus himself understood the kingdom of God in this way at all. Second, the gospel contains much more than this one particular aspect. But his emphasis on the social gospel was also a reaction against pietism, which was growing in the churches.

THE ESSENCE OF CHRISTIANITY?
Harnack's attempt to find the essence of Christianity in the teaching of Jesus was immediately criticized by the French scholar, Alfred Loisy (1857–1940). As a Roman Catholic, Loisy saw the essence of Christianity in the ongoing faith of the church, rather than exclusively in the teaching of Jesus.

But Loisy was also a modernist. He insisted that the truth of Christianity is something living, and is constantly re-shaped by the present; it is not a once-for-all deposit of truth from the past. He also argued that the Gospels do not report reliably the teaching of Jesus, but express the faith of the early church. He concluded that Harnack's Protestant Liberalism could have no historical basis. The Roman Catholic Church officially condemned Loisy's work because of its disturbing implications.

In Britain, one notable cause of controversy was R. J. Campbell's *The New Theology* (1907), which almost completely removed any distinction between God and man, and made the incarnation no more than the supreme example of God's indwelling a human being.

The vacuum left by Liberalism is illustrated by the reaction of the Scottish theologian, P. T. Forsyth (1848–1921). Forsyth began as a Liberal, but gradually became disillusioned with what he saw as its shallowness. He discovered the truths, emphasized by Evangelicals, of the centrality of the cross and the power of grace. He comments, 'I was turned from a Christian to a believer; from a lover of love into an object of grace.'

IS THE BIBLE UNIQUE?

One group of scholars began to try to shed light on biblical and Christian thinking by comparing similar or parallel features in other – usually ancient – religions. Many of these scholars, especially in the first two decades of the twentieth century, claimed that biblical and Christian thought were by no means as unique as had been supposed. One of the main leaders of this 'history of religions' school was the German, Hermann Gunkel (1862–1932), who examined ancient Babylonian myths in his attempt to shed light on biblical ideas about the beginning and end of the world.

The work of the 'history of religions' school was not simply destructive, for biblical material cannot be viewed in isolation, as if there were no cultural interaction between the biblical writers and the wider world of their day.

A startlingly different approach from the prevailing liberal view of the kingdom of God was adopted by Johannes Weiss (1863–1914) and by Albert Schweitzer (1875–1965). Weiss argued that in the teaching of Jesus the kingdom of God referred, not to a human society or to human activity, but to the sovereign rule of God breaking in

ALBERT SCHWEITZER

Albert Schweitzer (1875–1965), who was born in Kaysersberg, Germany, achieved fame as a theologian, philosopher, musician, and missionary doctor. As a theological scholar, he wrote *The Mystery of the Kingdom of God* (1901), an outline of Christ's life, and *In Quest of the Historical Jesus* (1906). From 1915 onwards Schweitzer proposed 'reverence for life' as the solution to the world's problems. 'Being good is to preserve life, to promote life, to raise life to the highest level that it can attain. Being evil is to destroy life, to injure life, to suppress life which could attain a higher level.'

Schweitzer felt compelled to become a doctor and help preserve life. His medical work at Lambarene in the Cameroons, to which he devoted thirty-five years – broken by only occasional visits to Europe – made his message clear to the whole world, as did his pleas for world peace and his warnings, from 1957 onwards, against the atomic bomb. In 1953 he was awarded the Nobel Peace Prize.

Schweitzer also made an impact as an interpreter of J. S. Bach; his tours giving organ recitals led to theoretical discussion of musical problems. Schweitzer's autobiographical writings, *On the Edge of the Primeval Forest* and *Memoirs of Childhood and Youth*, made him and his work internationally well-known.

F. W. KANTZENBACH

upon history. It was God's supernatural intervention as King, acting in judgment and grace, in accordance with the expectations of Jewish apocalyptic literature.

Schweitzer developed this idea to argue that Jesus was wholly dominated by an expectation of the imminent end of the present world order, and that he attempted to force the arrival of this end by his death. Schweitzer's approach, although it contained elements of truth, was too extreme to be taken seriously. In fact, neither Weiss nor Schweitzer succeeded in showing the credibility or relevance of Jesus to later generations.

FUNDAMENTALISM

In America, the movement protesting against liberal theology became known as 'Fundamentalism'. Fundamentalists believed not only in the verbal inspiration and infallibility of the Bible, but also in a whole series of Evangelical doctrines published around 1909 under the title of *The Fundamentals*. The writers included such men as B. B. Warfield (1851–1921), H. C. G. Moule (1841–1920), and James Orr (1844–1913), who emphasized the substitutionary death of Christ on the cross, the reality of eternal punishment, and the need for personal conversion.

In later years the term 'Fundamentalism' came to denote an unduly defensive and obscurantist attitude, which was anti-scholarly, anti-intellectual, and anti-cultural. For this reason, many conservative theologians who might be regarded as heirs of the original Fundamentalists disown the label today.

KARL BARTH

The twentieth century has produced few theologians of greater stature and importance than Karl Barth (1886–1968). For twelve years Barth served as a pastor in Switzerland. During the anguish and suffering of World War I, Barth became increasingly convinced that Liberal theology was bankrupt. He saw in the Bible 'a strange new world' which spoke of God and of the 'otherness' of God; a world which is utterly different from our world. His viewpoint owed much to the writings of Luther and Calvin, but much more to the nineteenth-century religious thinker Søren Kierkegaard.

> The Gospel falls upon man as God's own mighty Word, questioning him down to the bottom of his being, uprooting him from his securities and satisfactions, and therefore tearing clean asunder all the relations that keep him prisoner within his own ideals in order that he may be genuinely free for God and for his wonderful new work of grace in Jesus Christ.
>
> KARL BARTH

Barth's protest against Liberalism broke upon the world with the publication of his now-famous commentary on Romans, in 1919 and 1922. Its themes were the sovereignty of God, God's grace and revelation, and human finiteness and sinfulness. God is wholly other. Christianity is not 'religion' at all: it is God's sovereign and revealing word, to which people can only respond.

Barth argued that, since God cannot be grasped by any single set of human concepts, we can speak about him only by the dialectical method of statement and counter-statement, of 'yes' and 'no'. Barth also taught that God's Word stands over against us and judges us. In the tradition of the Reformation, we stand 'under' God's Word. Barth also argued that Christianity is a matter of revelation, not of our religious aspirations. Any point of contact between God – who is wholly other – and us lies solely in God's revealing Word. Barth's later work stressed the Trinity and Christology. After 1945, the influence of Barth's theology began to wane, and to give way to the influence of Rudolf Bultmann. However, even today Barth's theology still has its champions. In Scotland, Thomas F. Torrance (1913–2007) was one such champion.

Another figure closely associated with Barth is the Swiss theologian Emil Brunner of Zurich (1889–1965), who represented a more restrained form of Barthianism. The Swedish bishop Anders Nygren (1890–1978) also shared Barth's emphasis on the distinctiveness of the Christian faith over against other religions.

IMMORAL SOCIETY

During the 1930s and 1940s the most important theologian in America was probably Reinhold Niebuhr (1893–1971). For thirteen years, until 1928, he was a pastor in Detroit and, like Barth, he found Liberalism and moral idealism inadequate for the pastoral problems that he faced. In the tradition of much American theology, he was particularly concerned with social and political ethics, but took a more positive approach to the Bible. He was influenced by Kierkegaard and Barth, but criticized their failure to talk adequately about ethics.

In his first major work, *Moral Man and Immoral Society* (1932), Niebuhr reacted against liberal theology and the optimistic humanism of the social gospel movement. He argued that, because of the evil in people and in society, Christian political action called not simply for love, but for an attempt to give each group within society enough power to defend itself against exploitation by other groups. Although relations between individuals might be a matter of ethics, relations between groups were a matter of politics. Niebuhr himself took an active part in politics, and founded the Fellowship of Socialist Christians. *Moral Man and Immoral Society* showed that self-interest more deeply and subtly marks societies. Sin can be disguised as actions 'for the sake of the family', or especially 'for the sake of the nation'.

In his later work Niebuhr criticized equally both the Liberal and Marxist views of human nature, and wrote *The Nature and Destiny of Man* (1941–43). He stressed that the final answer to the human problem lay beyond history, in the love of God and the cross of Christ. But Christians must not seek to evade their real human nature and real human tasks by opting out of the politics and power-struggles of the twentieth century.

Reinhold's brother, H. Richard Niebuhr (1894–1962), also criticized Liberal theology. According to American Liberalism, he ironically remarks: 'A God without wrath brought men without sin into a kingdom without judgment through the ministration of a Christ without a cross.'

JESUS: HISTORY OR FAITH?

The German Rudolf Bultmann (1884–1976) probably had more influence on twentieth-century theology than any other thinker. His early work, *The History of the Synoptic Tradition* (1921), came to very sceptical conclusions about the historical reliability of the Gospels as reports of facts, and was extremely pessimistic about the extent of our historical knowledge of Jesus.

Bultmann used the method of 'form criticism', which assumes that much of the biblical material circulated in oral forms before it was committed to writing. It also holds that every 'form', or type of material in the Gospels, reflects a typical situation in ancient Israel or the earliest churches. Bultmann argued that the situations behind the 'forms' of the gospel were often those of preaching, argument, or teaching – but hardly ever that of historical reporting. The Gospels reflected the theology of the earliest churches, rather than the facts about Jesus.

Bultmann inherited the Liberal belief in the priority of experience and ethics over doctrine. It was easy for him to conceive of the earliest churches as proclaiming the risen Christ of their own experience, rather than being concerned mainly with historical facts about Jesus of Nazareth. It will come as no surprise that in his book *Jesus and the Word* (1934) Bultmann wrote, 'We can now know almost nothing about the life and personality of Jesus.' He even argued that this is a positive advantage to genuine Christian faith. Jesus – Bultmann believed – must not be located in the realm of facts and objects, and made to fit in with categories which describe the everyday world. He is not the Jesus of history, but the Christ of faith and present experience.

From the first, many questioned Bultmann's position. Why is such a sharp division between history and experience necessary? What becomes of the biblical emphasis on Christ's taking flesh and living a real flesh-and-blood life? Was the resurrection of Christ a historical event in the sense of being a factual event? Bultmann rejects this possibility. Finally, many of Bultmann's arguments based on form criticism are also questionable. In 1974 Graham Stanton, in *Jesus of Nazareth in New Testament preaching*, convincingly attacked Bultmann's assumption that new converts would not seek to know about the deeds and character of Jesus.

A WORLD OF MYTH?

Bultmann's historic essay on myth in the New Testament appeared in 1941, and gave rise to an extensive debate which has still not ended. Bultmann believed that the New Testament embodied a pre-scientific view of the world, which he called a 'mythical' outlook. When its message is communicated today it should be translated into non-mythical terms ('demythologized').

Although the gospel must be demythologized, Bultmann insists this in no way reduces its power to save people. He writes: 'The purpose of demythologizing is not to make religion more acceptable to modern man … but to make clearer to modern man what the Christian faith is.' Bultmann is not simply a Liberal theologian; on the matter of presenting people with the challenge and offence of the cross, he stands nearer to Barth and Kierkegaard than to Liberalism.

Bultmann's proposals have met with some very hostile criticisms. The United Evangelical Lutheran Church of Germany condemned his entire position. His left-wing and right-wing critics join in making one common criticism: once Bultmann starts to demythologize, how can he know where to stop? His chosen stopping-point appears to be arbitrary. Bultmann has affected the churches, partly by undermining confidence about the right way to use the Bible, and partly by increasing suspicions about the reality of God's active engagement with the world.

CAN WE TALK ABOUT RELIGION?

Positivism is the philosophical doctrine that all valid knowledge comes through the methods of the sciences. The French positivist philosopher Auguste Comte (1798–1857) claimed there were three stages in the evolution of human thought. Early mankind thought largely in theological terms, seeing the gods as responsible for events. Next, humanity reached the speculative or metaphysical stage, with better explanations, but still not based entirely on fact. Finally, humanity has arrived at the positive stage, and sees that all claims to knowledge must be tested by scientific fact. This scientific knowledge is positive knowledge, which no longer depends on superstition or speculation.

Replies to positivism came from many philosophers and philosophical theologians. They argued that the decision to restrict all knowledge to scientific observation was a personal decision and not a logical necessity.

The most striking version of positivism in the twentieth century came in the philosophical doctrine known as logical positivism. In Britain, the climate for logical positivism was prepared early in the century by the reaction against philosophical idealism led by G. E. Moore (1873–1958) and by Bertrand Russell (1872–1970), and particularly by Moore's defence of 'common sense' realism in philosophy.

In 1936 A. J. Ayer (1910–89) published his famous book, *Language, Truth, and Logic*. He argued that statements which cannot be checked or verified by observation through the physical senses are not so much false or undemonstrable as simply meaningless. Religious statements – such as 'God is love' – were held to be 'non-sense'. Ayer stated his arguments so well that his book had an enormous influence.

Replies came from various thinkers, including the philosopher F. C. Copleston (1907–94), the theologian E. L. Mascall (1905–93), and the philosopher of religion Ian Ramsey (1915–72), who later became Bishop of Durham. What was the logical status, it was asked, of Ayer's own principle of verification? It was neither a tautology, nor could it be checked by scientific observation, so it would exclude itself as a 'meaningless statement'. Partly in response to this criticism, the area of debate moved from verification – how can a statement be checked as true? – to falsification – how can it be shown to be false?

MARXISTS AND NEO-MARXISTS

Since the 1920s, Marxists in France, Italy – and more recently Latin America, and Africa – have increasingly dissociated themselves from the repressive regime of Soviet communism. Stalin's status as an interpreter of Marx is challenged, and increasingly emphasis is laid on Marx's earlier writings, in which Marx was more concerned with human nature and alienation than with materialism as such. Under capitalism, he argued, labour is alien to us, because we do not work for ourselves. We are de-personalized into a mere tool of production for someone else's gain. We need to be liberated and restored to true dignity.

This approach of Neo-Marxism, developed by the German Ernst Bloch (1885–1977), has contributed to the Christian theology of hope, and especially to the thinking of Jürgen Moltmann in the 1960s. Neo-Marxism has also inspired much of the theorizing about liberation in the Third World, and is closely connected with recent theologies of revolution in Latin America.

THE URGE TO COMMITMENT

It is difficult to define existentialism in general terms, for existentialist philosophers are themselves partly making individual protests against generalization and abstract thinking.

The father-figure of existentialist thought is the Danish thinker Søren Kierkegaard (1813–55), who stressed the importance of first-hand practical decision and involvement, as against mere intellectual assent to abstract truths. He attacked nominal Christian orthodoxy that was not personally committed. It is personal decision – rather than abstract reason – which brings a person into relationship with God. This idea was taken up both in Barth's earlier writings and by Bultmann.

German existentialist philosophers include Karl Jaspers (1883–1969), and especially Martin Heidegger (1889–1976). Heidegger stresses the relativity of knowledge: we cannot view reality as a detached observer outside history. Heidegger also declared: 'The person is not a thing, not a substance, not an object.' Whereas 'things' exist, in the sense of having certain fixed properties, people exist in the sense of having intentionality, or possibilities, for the future. A person can be open to the future and cease to be an 'object', by breaking out of the conventions and mere 'everydayness' of the crowd. In this way he or she may achieve authentic existence. Heidegger had enormous influence in Europe, especially in Germany.

Existentialism is most widely known in France through the writings of Jean-Paul Sartre (1905–80). Like Kierkegaard and other existentialists, he investigated such experiences as anguish, dread, and the prospect of death, and reasserted individualism. Sartre's thought is militantly atheistic; because God is neither (in Sartre's sense) a person nor a thing, 'the idea of God is contradictory'. 'God' is a weapon used by society to impose its moral values on the individual. But existentialism is not necessarily always anti-Christian. Kierkegaard wrote as a Christian, criticizing nominal Christianity; Jaspers opposes the exclusive claims of Christianity, but is sympathetic with religious belief.

The Viennese philosopher Martin Buber (1878–1965) wrote from the perspective of a strong Jewish faith, yet is also regarded as a major existentialist thinker. There is, he said, a sharp contrast between our relationship to objects which we observe (the I–it relation) and our relationship to a personal 'Thou' who addresses us (the I–Thou relation). God must not be changed into an 'it' by being regarded as a mere object of thought or experience. Gabriel Marcel (1889–1973), writing as a Roman Catholic, insists that no human person is to be reduced to a mere 'case' or number.

LANGUAGE AND LIFE

One of the most original thinkers in twentieth-century philosophy was Ludwig Wittgenstein (1889–1951), who was born in Vienna, but went to England in 1908. When the war came in 1914, he joined the Austrian army, and carried about with him in his rucksack the notebooks on logic that provided the basis for his great work, the *Tractatus Logico-Philosophicus* (1918). In the first part of this work, he sets out statements about the relation between language and the world. The most famous part of this work is his picture theory of meaning: 'A proposition is a picture of reality.' Elements of the world correspond with elements of language in such a way that 'the totality of true thoughts is a picture of the world'. Propositions depict facts, but values are higher than facts. The riddles of life, Wittgenstein believed, went beyond the limits of thought and language; the attempt to *speak* about it resulted in confusion.

After 1929, Wittgenstein became increasingly dissatisfied with this way of looking at the problem, and developed a different approach. He examined the relation between uses of language and the particular 'surroundings' which gave them currency and meaning. Wittgenstein used the term 'language-games' to stress that 'only in the stream of thought and life do words have meaning'. Confusions arise when uses of language are examined 'outside a particular language-game'. Wittgenstein therefore aimed to make observations about particular uses of language in their concrete settings in life, not in the abstract. For example, he shed light on language about expecting, intending, understanding, and believing.

Wittgenstein's methods inspired the movement known as linguistic philosophy. Some philosophers, including Antony Flew (1923–2010) and R. B. Braithwaite (1900–90), were influenced both by positivism and by the methods of linguistic philosophy, and attacked certain aspects of language in religion. Thinkers such as Copleston and Mascall defended traditional views, claiming that analogy had a valid place in religious language.

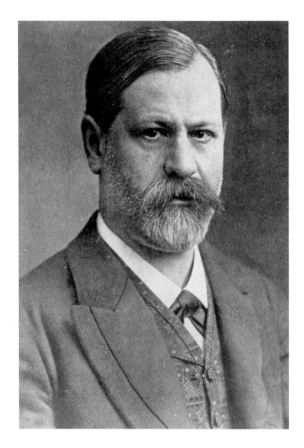

Sigmund Freud (1856–1939), founding father of psychoanalysis.
ILLUSTRATED LONDON NEWS

AN OBSESSIONAL NEUROSIS?

Sigmund Freud (1856–1939) is without doubt one of the most influential figures of the twentieth century. The whole of modern psychology is influenced by his work, even if only certain psychologists still regard themselves as belonging to his school of thought. His influence on popular ideas about religion can hardly be exaggerated.

Psychological disorders, Freud believed, can often be cured by probing the unconscious, to release repressed wishes into self-knowledge. One important way of gaining access to the unconscious is through dreams, which are repressed wishes in disguise. Repressed urges often take the form of sexual desires. In psychoanalysis, a patient is encouraged to talk freely about his dreams, feelings, attitudes, and mental associations, in the hope that these will bring aspects of the unconscious to light.

Freud was an atheist, and was deeply influenced by the positivism of Comte. His theories about religion rest on the positivist claim that all knowledge comes through the sciences. He described religion as 'the universal obsessional neurosis of humanity'.

Neurosis is a conflict between different parts of the mind that results in stress or anxiety. One part of the mind clamours for the gratification of desires that another part represses. Freud argued that part of the mind – the 'superego' – tries to repress by projecting, or 'externalizing', the figure of the human father into that of God. The father who gave life

> Religion is an attempt to get control over the sensory world in which we are placed, by means of the wish-world, which we have developed inside us as a result of biological and psychological necessities.
>
> SIGMUND FREUD

and protection, but also enforces laws, becomes the God who creates and sustains, but also gives commands. For Freud, 'God' is a device conjured up by the mind to cope with its own inner tensions. This figure also comforts and supports the mind when tensions arise from suffering, guilt, or disappointments in life. 'The face which smiled at us in the cradle, now magnified to infinity, smiles down upon us from heaven.'

Christian thinkers have reacted to Freud's claims in several ways. They have pointed out that Freud's theories about religion owe more to philosophical speculation than to scientific observation: they are theories which cannot be proved. Some have also argued that – on the basis of Freud's theories – his own hatred of his Jewish father might be said to account for his own repression of God into his unconscious.

Some Christian thinkers, especially in America, have been more concerned to apply some of his psychological insights in Christian pastoral counselling. Pastoral psychology, and what is sometimes called 'clinical theology', attempt to relate the more positive aspects of modern psychology to questions about Christian growth and maturity. The difficulty that faces this movement is that psychiatrists still argue over the value and validity of the different approaches in psychology. In a different context, towards the end of the twentieth century Paul Ricoeur (1913–2005) and Hans Küng both criticized Freud for his positivist views, and also pointed to more positive aspects for Christians.

A WORLD COME OF AGE

Dietrich Bonhoeffer (1906–45) put forward the idea of religionless, or 'worldly', Christianity. In his earliest works, he argued that the church is concerned not with religious ideas, but with Christ. In *The Cost of Discipleship* (1937), he argued that the Sermon on the Mount is not to be shelved on the pretext that it sets out an impossible ideal, intended only to convict men of sin. He argued, like Barth, that we do not meet God on our terms, but at the cross. The standard way of preaching justification by faith to bourgeois congregations, Bonhoeffer insisted, makes for 'cheap grace'. Grace comes only when people step out and follow Christ in costly discipleship.

In 1945 Bonhoeffer was executed, but after his death passages from his prison letters were published. In them, Bonhoeffer attacks that 'religion' which calls God in, either as a psychological crutch in moments of need, or to explain otherwise inexplicable phenomena. Too often God is seen as the source of comfort, helping people in moments of stress or insecurity. Evangelists even try to make people feel guilty or insecure in order to make them turn to God. Bonhoeffer called this 'an attempt to put a grown-up back into adolescence'. The world today has 'come of age'. 'God is teaching us that we must live as people who can get along very well without him.' This does not mean atheism: it means rejecting the way of 'religion'. God's reality is revealed in Christians serving their fellow human beings in a costly and positive way amidst life as it is. The pattern for this, Bonhoeffer believed, was Christ Jesus. Jesus Christ was 'there only for others'. 'Being there for others' is what really points to the reality of God.

GOD AND THE ULTIMATE

The main aim of Paul Tillich (1886–1965) was to relate Christian faith to secular thought. In his intellectual autobiography, *On the Boundary* (1966), he writes of how he wished to make connections between theology and philosophy, religion and culture, Lutheranism and

DIETRICH BONHOEFFER

Active in the Anti-Hitler resistance movement, the German Lutheran clergyman Dietrich Bonhoeffer was hanged by the Nazis at Flossenbürg on 9 April 1945. Born in 1906, Bonhoeffer studied theology at Tübingen, Berlin, and Union Theological Seminary, New York City. When Hitler came to power in 1933, Bonhoeffer joined the anti-Nazi pastors in the German 'church struggle'. In 1935, he was appointed head of the Finkenwalde Confessing Church Seminary, which was closed by the government in 1937.

In 1939 Bonhoeffer rejected the possibility of a job in America, convinced he should face the difficulties ahead with the Christians in Germany. During World War II Bonhoeffer – forbidden to preach or publish – served as a double-agent on Admiral Canaris' military intelligence staff. Using his ecumenical contacts, especially his friendship with George Bell (1883–1958), Bishop of Chichester, Bonhoeffer vainly sought the British government's support for the anti-Hitler conspirators. His arrest in 1943 arose from his involvement in smuggling fourteen Jews to Switzerland.

Bonhoeffer left a rich legacy of books – *Sanctorum Communio*, *Act and Being*, *The Cost of Discipleship* and *Life Together* – as well as letters, papers, and notes published after his death by his friend and biographer, Eberhard Bethge. These include *Letters and Papers from Prison*, *Ethics*, and six volumes of collected writings. A seminal thinker, who refused to retreat from the harsh realities of his day, Bonhoeffer challenged Christians to reject complacent, undisciplined faith and life. His writings focussed on Jesus Christ, 'the man for others', and on the nature of Christian community. In his prison letters – the most popular of his works – Bonhoeffer explored pathways of future church renewal. Exposing the negative side of institutional religion, Bonhoeffer called for mature faith in the God of weakness and suffering in 'a world come of age'.

Bonhoeffer's thought and example continue to influence both conservatives and liberals in Protestant, Catholic, and secular circles. His ideas have sparked and shaped diverse movements, including ecumenism; death of God theology; liberation theology; Christian resistance to war and to oppressive political regimes; and traditional tributes to Christian discipleship, heroism, and martyrdom.

RUTH ZERNER

socialism, and between German and American thought. He was born in Germany and taught at five German universities; but with the rise of Hitler he moved to the United States.

Tillich's *Systematic Theology* (1951, 1957, and 1963), attempts to offer theological answers to secular questions. Questions about reason, being, and existence are matched by answers about revelation, God, and Christ. He probed into human anxieties about fear and death, and into experience of emptiness, meaninglessness, and guilt. In his attempt to come to grips with the questions asked by secular people, he used the resources and vocabulary of existentialist philosophy and depth-psychology.

It is infinitely easier to suffer in obedience to a human command than to accept suffering as free, responsible men. It is infinitely easier to suffer with others than to suffer alone. It is infinitely easier to suffer as public heroes than to suffer apart and in ignominy. It is infinitely easier to suffer physical death than to endure spiritual suffering. Christ suffered as a free man, alone, apart, and in ignominy, in body and in spirit, and since that day many Christians have suffered with him.

DIETRICH BONHOEFFER, *LETTERS AND PAPERS FROM PRISON*

Tillich is particularly concerned with the problem of the 'Ultimate', which must be located only in God. Unbelievers may imagine that they have thought about God and rejected him, when all the time they have never encountered the Ultimate at all. 'It is not *he* whom we reject and forget, but some distorted picture of him.' Tillich does not like to say that God 'exists'; for to ascribe ordinary existence to him is to view him as one object among others in the everyday world. The only way of encountering the Ultimate, Tillich believes, is through experience. His method is to start 'with the experiencing of the holy' and advance 'to the idea of God'. 'God' becomes almost a 'feeling of the holy'. Critics comment that, in Tillich's thought, an ultimate God has become merely any experience which 'feels' ultimate.

Tillich helped to initiate dialogue between theology and secular thought – including existentialist philosophy, depth-psychology, and political and cultural movements. But he also led many to challenge the authority of theological creeds and church structures. Tillich raised questions about what we mean by the personality of God, and whether God may still be conceived of in traditional terms at all. Symbols to describe God effectively, Tillich urged, may well change from age to age.

THE BIBLE AND SCHOLARSHIP

Between the early 1940s and early 1960s, the biblical theology movement arose. It stressed that the various books of the Bible proclaimed what was basically a single message, and attempted to single out what was most distinctive to the Hebrew or biblical outlook. The Bible was seen as the continuous unfolding to faith of God's saving acts in the sacred history of Israel and the church.

A great exponent of this salvation-history (German, *Heilsgeschichte*) theme in New Testament studies is Oscar Cullmann (1902–1999), who declared his aim was 'to determine what is central in the Christian proclamation'. He finds this distinctive theme in the biblical view of time and history. The particular claim of the Bible is that the key to all history lies in the salvation-history of Israel, Christ, and the church. It sees history as linear, not cyclical, which points both to the unrepeatable uniqueness of God's acts, and to the importance of history's future goal. Today, while the biblical theology movement is still valued for its insights, it is also perceived as overstressing the unity of the Bible – or even its uniformity – to the extent that it implies a flat uniform landscape.

Patient and solid work on biblical commentaries also proceeded steadily. Old Testament commentaries were produced by the German scholars Martin Noth, A. Weisser and Gerhard von Rad; important New Testament commentaries by Vincent Taylor, C. K. Barrett and F. F. Bruce appeared in Britain. In America, the biblical theology movement was represented in the fields of Old Testament archaeology and history by G. E. Wright, John Bright and, less directly, W. F. Albright.

All this activity enriched the life of the church, but three kinds of criticism have been levelled against it. First, it was claimed that the variety of the Bible was lost from view. Second, James Barr (1924–2006) and others argued that there were sometimes faults in the linguistic methods of the movement. Third, it often failed to pay attention to the relations between theology and history, and between the ancient text and the modern reader (the questions of interpretation or 'hermeneutics'). What was the relevance of the Bible? By 1970 the biblical theology movement had gone out of favour, although its influence was still felt.

THE NEW QUEST

Criticism arose among Bultmann's own former pupils, who attempted to pay more attention to Jesus as a figure of history than Bultmann did. This movement became known as the 'new quest of the historical Jesus', and its leaders include Ernst Käsemann (1906–98) of Tübingen, Günther Bornkamm (1905–90) of Heidelberg, and Ernst Fuchs (1903–83) of Marburg. Käsemann insisted that the earthly history of Jesus must be taken seriously, as part of the truth of the word made flesh.

The stress on the unity of the Bible represented by the biblical theology movement was replaced by a stress on its diversity. In research on the Gospels this was linked with a new interest in the technique known as 'redaction criticism': the study of how each individual Gospel-writer or Gospel-editor ('redactor') shaped the material that came to him in such a way as to reveal his own special theological interests.

Redaction criticism of the Gospels became widespread in the second half of the twentieth century, but it encountered two main difficulties. It is difficult to prove just how free the gospel writers felt themselves to be to re-shape material in their own interests. Secondly, there are many competing theories about what precisely these interests are. Nonetheless, redaction criticism, form criticism, and literary criticism (or theories about sources) remain standard tools in both Old and New Testament studies.

The practical effect of all this is to see the Bible as containing not one theology, but many theologies. Israel and the New Testament churches, it is argued, did not simply hand down fixed doctrines that came to them from the past, but interpreted the word and deeds of God afresh for themselves. On this basis, some have argued that it is less 'biblical' to look back to a fixed body of doctrine, than to state anew what God is for the present. This has opened up new questions about biblical authority, and the relation between the Bible and tradition.

In the 1980s, three further developments occurred in biblical scholarship. First, there was an increasing emphasis on theories of interpretation, or hermeneutics (discussed below). Second, in 1977, E. P. Sanders (b. 1937) made an influential attack on the traditional view of Paul (often called the 'Lutheran' view) in which we begin with consciousness of sin and then move on to the remedy of divine grace. Sanders reversed this process. Moreover he questioned whether the Reformation emphasis on 'justification by faith' was really the central message of Romans and Galatians, rather than God's promise to the Jews and the relation between Jews and Gentiles within the church. He defined Judaism not as suggesting 'works-righteousness', but as 'covenantal nomism', and described his approach as 'the new perspective on Paul'. James Dunn and Terence Donaldson have broadly defended this approach from the 1980s to today, but Seyoon Kim (2002) and many others have strongly attacked it. Tom Wright (N. T. Wright) adopts what might be called the mediating position, which he calls 'Fresh Perspectives' on Paul. Third, new developments underlined the importance of sociology. One example of this approach is the research of Gerd Theissen (b. 1943) into the Gospels and Pauline churches.

Behind these developments – of interpretative models and sociology of knowledge – lies an important conviction. The New Testament message concerns specific situations, people, and communities. It is not simply a collection of thoughts or ideas divorced from time and social realities.

ARCHAEOLOGICAL FINDS

From 1929 onwards, a series of vital discoveries was made at Ras Shamra, Syria, the site of the ancient city of Ugarit. The material found shed new light on the myths and religious practices of the Canaanites. In addition, inscriptions from excavations at Mari, on the River Euphrates, shed new light on the history of the Near East from the time of the early patriarchs to the conquest of Canaan. These finds mean that the biblical narratives are generally regarded as more reliable than was fashionable some years earlier. But some archaeological discoveries – such as the excavations at Jericho in the 1950s – posed new problems. Israeli archaeologists particularly have contributed increasingly to our knowledge of biblical times.

The discovery at Nag-Hammadi, Upper Egypt, in 1945 of numerous so-called Gnostic texts (for example the Gospel of Thomas) raised fresh questions about the religious environment of the New Testament.

The discovery in 1947 of the famous Dead Sea Scrolls occurred by accident. A Bedouin boy was searching for a lost sheep among the caves of Qumran, just north-west of the Dead Sea, when he came upon several jars, about two feet (60 cm) tall, containing leather scrolls wrapped in linen cloth. He had stumbled upon part of an extensive library of scrolls that belonged to a monastic-like community of Jews living in the first century BC and in the time of Christ, which had been hidden at the time when the Romans suppressed the Jewish Rising of AD 70.

By 1949, several hundred writings were recovered from this source. What most caught the popular imagination was the find of copper scrolls, which had become so oxidized that they could only be deciphered by treating them and cutting them into thin strips. For theologians, the most important were the scrolls of the Old Testament text and commentaries, 1,000 years older than previously known texts, and scrolls describing the life of the community itself, which shed light on one type of Judaism in the time of Christ. These and other discoveries helped to encourage a biblical scholarship which used the Bible itself as a source-document of historical evidence, and used other evidence to shed light on its setting and meaning.

HONEST TO GOD

In 1963, J. A. T. Robinson (1919–83), then Bishop of Woolwich, published the paperback, *Honest to God*, asking: 'How does one preach the gospel today?' For his answer he drew on Bultmann's ideas about myth and demythologizing, on Tillich's notion of God as the ground of our being, and on Bonhoeffer's comments about religionless Christianity. Why did *Honest to God* have such an explosive impact? In simple, often autobiographical, language Robinson succeeded in familiarizing a massive readership – more than a million copies were sold – with ideas that were almost unknown outside the lecture-room. Here was an English bishop expressing what many regarded as radical ideas.

What caught people's imagination was his rejection of the notion of a God 'up there'. Robinson also made it clear that traditional teaching on prayer left him cold. Thousands who for years had never opened a Bible claimed to gain reassurance from finding their doubts and problems shared by a bishop. But Robinson failed to show how the very different ideas that he called into play could be combined in a consistent and positive way. The book is better at raising questions than at answering them. Many serious scholars attacked Robinson's work, including the then Archbishop of Canterbury, Michael Ramsey

(1904–88). Ian Ramsey, Professor of the Philosophy of Religion at Oxford University, showed that Robinson had misunderstood the nature and function of religious language, which regularly used symbols, or what Ramsey termed 'models and qualifiers'.

VATICAN II

The Second Vatican Council (1962–65), originated at the initiative of Pope John XXIII (1958–63), had two aims: the renewal of the church and the promotion of Christian unity. The Council ushered in a new era in Roman Catholic thought, and showed a new openness to many theological questions, including dialogue with Protestant churches, and even with non-Christian religions. Its findings were classified under such headings as: the sacred liturgy – including the administration of Holy Communion and 'concelebration', social communication, the constitution of the church, ecumenism, the pastoral office of bishops, renewal, the training of priests, Christian education, non-Christian religions, revelation, and the laity. All this re-defined the church, its worship, and its place in mission to the modern world.

About 2,000 attended the congregation of the Council, with roughly one third of the bishops from Europe, one third from the Americas, and one third from the other continents. More than 200 theologians served as consultants, and there were nearly 100 non-Roman Catholic observers. After the death of Pope John, Pope Paul VI presided, from September 1963.

The conclusions (or 'constitutions') were four: on liturgy (*sacrosanctum concilium*); on the church (*lumen gentium*); on revelation, scripture, and dogma (*Dei verbum*); and on the church in the modern world (*gaudium et spes*). The work on the church gave authority to the Pope in accord with the bishops; an individual bishop is not infallible as such. *Dei verbum* insisted that revelation is the self-communication of God, mediated through both Scripture and Tradition. The decree on ecumenism included a declaration on religious liberty. The Roman Church now became committed to serious ecumenical discussions, rather than simply opposing other traditions. One fruit of this was the Pontifical Biblical Commission's *The Interpretation of the Bible in the Church* (1994), which commended almost all the methods of biblical interpretation used in Protestant churches.

Another theologian closely associated with the post-Vatican spirit was the Jesuit, Karl Rahner (1904–84). He was influenced partly by the existentialism of Heidegger, and stressed that divine grace can be fully understood only when it is experienced in practice; yet he endorsed traditional Catholic doctrine and its claim to be universal truth. Rahner's thought is marked by this two-sidedness. He asserts that only through Christ and the church can salvation become real to people. On the other hand, he believes that 'the people of God' extend outside the Roman Catholic Church and the other churches to include the whole of humanity. The church, Rahner declares, must be open to the outer world, which means drawing a distinction between nominal church membership and a genuine commitment to Christ.

Other Roman Catholic theologians who made crucial contributions at Vatican II were Yves Congar (1904–95) of France, and the Swiss theologian Hans Küng (b. 1928). Congar contributed decisively on the church, tradition, revelation, mission, and ecumenism. Küng – the youngest and probably most 'progressive' of the theological consultants – was already influenced by Karl Barth, and critical of much in Roman belief and practice. In

1979 Pope John Paul II withdrew Küng's Catholic licence at Tübingen, where he was then appointed Ecumenical Professor by the university.

It is impossible to exaggerate the influence of Vatican II on ordinary Roman Catholic life, worship, and practice. In effect, it marked its entrance to the modern world.

GOD IS DEAD

In the 1960s, the headline-catching 'death of God' movement appeared. The slogan 'the death of God' was used in several different ways. In 1963 Paul van Buren (1928–98) declared that the *word* 'God' is dead. Using well-worn arguments of logical positivism and positivist brands of linguistic philosophy, he insisted that language about God had no meaning. He also drew on Bonhoeffer's hints about 'religionless Christianity'.

The most uncompromising writer on the death of God was the American, Thomas J. J. Altizer (b. 1927). He draws his inspiration from Nietzsche, Hegel, and William Blake, and asserts that God died when Christ died on the cross. Altizer ends in an obscure kind of mysticism: God is dead, but somehow he is represented by Jesus.

Harvey Cox's *The Secular City* (1966) has been described as the Bible of post-liberal American theology. The secular city is seen as a fulfilment of God's purposes, since it provides people with fuller lives. 'God comes to us today in the event of social change.' Cox (b. 1929), too, frequently quotes Bonhoeffer. Cox's attitude, however, changed; in 1995 he wrote *Fire from Heaven*, which expressed cautious – even grudging – admiration for Pentecostalism.

It would also be a mistake to imagine that secular theology dominates the American scene. Conservative writers such as Edward Carnell, Bernard Ramm, and G. E. Ladd stress the importance of the Bible as the source of revealed truth, and their outlook speaks for millions of American Christians. Unlike the American Fundamentalists of a previous generation, Ladd (1911–82) uses the tools of biblical criticism. This does not mean criticizing the Bible, he insists, but paying attention to the historical particularity of the biblical text. Moreover millions of ordinary Christians in America, especially in the largely Baptist 'Bible Belt' of the Southern states, continue to hold the Bible and orthodox faith in high esteem.

EASTERN ORTHODOXY

Meanwhile, alongside the two great traditions of Christianity – the Roman Catholic and the Protestant – a third, namely the Eastern Orthodox Church, has developed since the earliest years. Although the Orthodox Church in Russia and in Greece accords special value to the Church Fathers of the East, it would be a mistake to assume that no significant development occurred after the death of the Eastern Fathers.

Thought flourished in the nineteenth century, especially in the metaphysical system of Vladimir Soloviev (1833–1900), who drew on Hegel, and to a lesser extent on F. W. Schelling and Dionysius. Alexei Khomyakov (1804–60) developed the concept of *sobernost*, or solidarity, partly in contrast to the more authoritarian tradition of Roman Catholicism and the more individual tradition of much Protestantism. In the first part of the twentieth century Sergei Bulgakov (1871–1944) stressed economics and the human task of shaping the material world, but rejected a sharp dualism between matter and spirit.

The two dominant theologians of the twentieth century are Vladimir Lossky (1903–58), representing the Russian Orthodox Church, and John Zizioulas (b. 1931), the foremost theologian of the Greek Orthodox Church. Other important figures include Georges Florovsky (1893–1979), and, in Britain, Kallistos Ware (b. 1934). Lossky was an émigré from Russian Marxism who established the Brotherhood of St Photius in Paris; he remained loyal to the Patriarchate of Moscow, and was critical of Bulgakov.

From 1938 onwards, Lossky expounded the contrast between person and nature. He read deeply the mystic Meister Eckhart, and in 1944 published *The Mystical Theology of the Eastern Church* (translated into English in 1957), in which he argues, 'individual and person mean opposite things'. The 'individual' belongs only to nature, caught up in a chain of cause and effect. The individual blocks itself off defensively from all that is not self, and becomes like the self-contained 'ego' of Descartes. By contrast, 'person' opens itself to God and to others, in love, communication, and mutuality. Thereby it mirrors the nature of God as self-giving, and engaged with the world. This principle can be seen pre-eminently in the Holy Trinity, in which the Father, the Son, and the Holy Spirit work together in loving engagement with one another. Lossky re-mints the word '*perichoresis*' or the 'inter-penetration of persons', which he drew from the Eastern Fathers – an idea he expounds further in his book, *The Image and Likeness of God* (English, 1974).

A further key theme in Lossky is his notion of 'deification' – not in the sense of human beings 'becoming God', but in the sense of attaining, by grace, a likeness to, and participation in, God. This is broadly parallel with 'sanctification' in the Western Church. Again, the term is drawn from the fourth-century Eastern Fathers, sometimes signifying the ascent of the human soul to God, although with a strongly moral dimension. Athanasius said: 'Christ became man in order that we might become divine'. This notion of 'deification' remains central in both Russian Orthodoxy (Lossky) and the Greek Orthodox Church (Nikos Nissiotis, 1924–86).

The most influential figure in the Greek Orthodox Church today is John Zizioulas (b. 1931), whose most widely-read book is *Being as Communion* (English, 1997). He states: 'God is a relational Being: without the concept of communion it would be quite impossible to speak of the being of God.' He continues: '"God" has … no true being, apart from communion.' Zizioulas is strongly concerned with the nature of the church – especially the problem of '*how* to relate the institutional with the charismatic' – and the work of the Holy Spirit with Christ. Zizioulas lays immense emphasis on the Holy Spirit, as does Nissiotis. For Nissiotis, the doctrine of the Holy Spirit is the heart of Christianity; while Zizioulas actually writes: 'There is, so to say, no Christ until the Spirit is at work.' The Holy Spirit 'constitutes the very identity of Christ'. Both Zizioulas and Nissiotis also regard the Eucharist as central to all communal Christian worship, of which an important part remains the *epiklesis*, or invocation, of the Holy Spirit.

FEMINIST THEOLOGY

Feminist theology arose in the USA in the 1970s, following in the wake of a concern addressed in wider society, especially about the use of power to oppress women, to regard them as 'the other', and to impose upon them expected or conventional roles. Kate Millett's *Sexual Politics* (1969) and Germaine Greer's *The Female Eunuch* (1970) provide examples. In theology, Rosemary Radford Ruether (b. 1937) defined feminism as the promotion of the full humanity of women.

Most strands of feminism appeal to hermeneutics. Elisabeth Schüssler Fiorenza (b. 1938) attacked 'the dogma of value-neutral detached interpretation', and many feminists regard 'women's experience' as a necessary preliminary understanding of biblical texts. But there are huge variations within feminism. Mary Daly's *Beyond God the Father* (1973) is in general viewed as post-Christian. Some feminists stress the distinctive difference of women; others stress their interchangeability with men.

Phyllis Trible (b. 1932) works in Old Testament Studies. In *God and the Rhetoric of Sexuality* (1978), she sees 'the image of God' as the possession of men and women co-jointly. In *Texts of Terror* (1984) she 'retrieves' the role of Hagar in Genesis, 'trapped in a circle of bondage'; of Tamar, the victim of rape in 2 Samuel; and the daughter of Jephthah in Judges, sacrificed by an impulsive vow. The Book of Ruth not only exhibits Ruth's courage and loyalty, but also exposes 'the presuppositions of a patriarchal culture'.

Elisabeth Schüssler Fiorenza is more extreme. She writes 'The place of divine revelation and grace is not the Bible … but the *ekklesia* (church) of women and the lives of women' (*In Memory of Her*, 1983). She urges 'women's self-affirmation, power and liberation from patriarchal alienations', and advocates a 'women-church'.

Feminist theology began as a movement for social justice, like liberation theology. But whether – also like liberation theology – the basic point has now been made, is widely debated. Afro-American women often prefer the term 'Womanist', as against perceived middle-class, white, academic women, and often urge wider concerns.

WOLFHART PANNENBERG

Wolfhart Pannenberg (b. 1928) should be ranked among the most eminent and learned theologians of the twentieth century and up to today. He overshadows Bultmann, and is at least comparable with Barth, Küng, and Moltmann in stature. He studied theology at Heidelberg, after earlier interests in Marx and Nietzsche. Gerhard von Rad and Hans von Campenhausen encouraged his deep concern for history, which then marked him as a serious alternative to Bultmann. Pannenberg became Professor at Mainz (1961) and then at Munich (1967 to retirement).

His concern for history appeared in *Revelation as History* (1961). Pannenberg saw God as the God of all history (von Rad) and of promise (Zimmerli), and wrote, 'History is the most comprehensive horizon of Christian theology.' This concerns not only Israel and the Church ('salvation-history'), but also all God's dealings with the world (universal history). He also argued, 'Natural events in the history of a people have no meaning apart from the connections with the traditions and expectations in which men live.' Hence the historicity of the resurrection of Christ – which is fundamental for Pannenberg – must be seen against the background of apocalyptic expectation and the sure testimony of witnesses.

In his work on Christ, Pannenberg wrote, 'In dealing with Jesus we are dealing with God himself.' Jesus 'binds history into a whole', and history 'receives its light from him'. Against Bultmann, he argued 'Faith or trust presupposes a knowledge'; it is not merely a subjective conviction. Equally, in contrast to Martin Kähler, and perhaps Barth, he insisted in starting out with the history of Jesus, that is, 'from below'. He argued that if the tomb of Jesus had not been empty, and thus no witnesses to the resurrection, the preaching of Jesus 'could not have been maintained in Jerusalem for a single day'.

Pannenberg expounds his main themes in his three-volume *Basic Questions in Theology* (1970–73). The truth of God, he writes, 'must prove itself anew', and meaning is determined by 'the horizons of the future'. But his great masterpiece is his three-volume *Systematic Theology* (1988, 1991, and 1993). The first volume concerns God; the second, humankind and Christ; the third, the church and the future, or eschatology. He places a firm emphasis on the Holy Trinity: New Testament narrative shows how every significant act, including the birth and baptism of Jesus, involves the Father, the Son, and the Holy Spirit. He comments, 'All sonship [i.e. Christ's and ours] rests on the Holy Spirit'. Although he is one with the Father, Jesus also distinguishes himself from him.

On humankind, Pannenberg points out that we are destined for fellowship with God. Hence the breaking and disruption of the relationship can most profoundly be described as 'misery'; 'misery is the lot of those who are deprived of the fellowship with God that is the destiny of human life.' 'Sin' is *not merely an act*, but a *state of being*, as the biblical vocabulary implies, and Augustine expounded. But Christ came as someone 'who does something for others'. There is no sufficient reason for replacing such terms as 'representation', 'atonement', or 'substitution' for others, merely because many have failed to be educated in the history and proper meaning of these terms. Jesus did not die for his own sins, but for ours; Jesus accepts us 'as sinners'.

In the third volume, Pannenberg contrasts the church with the Kingdom of God. The church contains failures, but 'points beyond itself' to the kingdom, or reign, of God, in which there is perfect obedience. God's future is 'the final horizon of the definitive meaning' of all things. Even the significance of our lives 'can be measured only at the end of our lives'.

Jürgen Moltmann (b. 1926) is another leading theologian of the late twentieth century. As a prisoner of war in Britain, he came to faith through the realization that in 'the death of all my mainstays', nevertheless, according to Psalm 139, 'If I make my bed in hell, you are there.' He reflected 'God is with those who are broken in heart'; 'nothing is shut off from God'. He returned to Germany after the war determined to study theology. He was influenced by Luther's theology of the cross, and by eschatology and promise in Arnold van Ruler (1908–70).

Moltmann's best-known classic, *Theology of Hope*, appeared in 1964 (English, 1967). His message was based not only on biblical themes, but also on the political signs of the times: Vatican II, the Medellín Conference in Latin America, and Alexander Dubček's 'socialism with a human face'. He urged practical action, writing 'Faith, whenever it develops into hope, causes not rest but unrest.' Presumption and despair negate hope: the first by anticipating God's 'yes'; the second by anticipating God's 'no'. Horizons of hope are not static, but capable of enlargement. The resurrection of Christ annihilates the 'nothingness' of death. In the early years, Moltmann collaborated with Pannenberg, with whom many of these ideas are shared.

Moltmann then produced a succession of major and influential writings. *The Crucified God* (German, 1972; English, 1974) asked: 'What does Jesus' suffering and death mean for God himself?' At the time, he saw signs of the fading of hope in human affairs: the invasion of Czechoslovakia, the Vietnam War, and the assassination of Martin Luther King. God himself, however, has experienced pain; God is present in human suffering. He also writes, 'The suffering of abandonment is overcome by the suffering of love.' He states,

'Even Auschwitz is taken up into the grief of the Father, the surrender of the Son, and the power of the Spirit.' He then wrote *The Church and the Power of the Trinity* (1975).

Moltmann's systematic theology begins with the doctrine of God, in *The Trinity and the Kingdom of God* (German, 1980; English, 1981). Here he writes: 'The New Testament talks about God by *proclaiming in narrative* the relationship of the Father, the Son, and the Holy Spirit.' For example, God 'sends' the Son, who is anointed by the Holy Spirit. At the baptism of Jesus, the Father declares his love, and the Spirit descends visibly upon Jesus. More especially, the Father raises Jesus from the dead through the Holy Spirit, as Paul states in Romans. We must not simply ask, 'What does God mean to me?' but also 'What do I mean for God?' He adds, 'A God who cannot suffer cannot love.'

God in Creation (English, 1985) expounds an ecological doctrine of creation. God manifests himself in 'making, measuring, maintaining and perfecting the world.' God created the world 'out of love'. Next, in *The Way of Jesus Christ* (English, 1990), Moltmann, like Zizioulas, traces the beginning of Jesus' earthly life to the Holy Spirit: he is endowed by the Spirit throughout his life.

The Spirit of Life (English, 1992) urges the avoidance of undue individualism, and appeals to 'experience'. The Spirit is the creative power of God, who enables God's people to perform assigned tasks. The Spirit inspires prayer, and reproduces the filial attitude of Jesus, whereby we cry 'Abba, Father' — the special word used by Jesus. Personhood is always 'being-in-relationship'.

Finally, in *The Coming of God* (German, 1995; English, 1996), Moltmann discusses the 'Last Things', or eschatology. Weiss and Schweitzer offered a false dawn: we must face up to the deadliness of death. If we mourn, 'the greater the love, the deeper the grief'. But most of the book concerns the resurrection of the dead, the transformation of the world, and the glory of the heavenly Jerusalem. We find our completion in God.

It is not surprising that Moltmann's influence is incalculable. Many clergy and ordinands, on the brink of disillusion and doubt, have found fresh vision and life from reading Moltmann's works. He has more recently produced *Sun of Righteousness Arise* (2010) and *Ethics of Hope* (2012), as well as many other works.

THE THIRD QUEST OF THE HISTORICAL JESUS

Although the term 'Third Quest' is widely used, it is difficult to define since it holds no firm conclusions in common. It broadly reflects the period from 1980 to the present, but even this is disputed. In practice the term marks it off from the 'First Quest' of the nineteenth century, culminating in the scepticism of Albert Schweitzer; and from the 'New Quest' of several former students of Bultmann, of whom the leaders were Ernst Käsemann (1906–98), Günther Bornkamm (1905–90), and Ernst Fuchs (1903–83). Whereas Bultmann had claimed that we can know almost nothing about the earthly life of Jesus, except for his call to disciples, his message of the Kingdom of God, and his crucifixion, Bornkamm argues that the actions of Jesus implied certain characteristics about his life.

Like the First Quest and New Quest, the Third Quest stresses the historical context — rather than theology — of the life of Jesus. Many argue that the first significant writer on the Third Quest was Ben F. Myer (1927–95), whose book *The Aims of Jesus* (1979) drew on 'critical realism' — which denotes the theory of knowledge of Bernard

Lonergan (1904–84). Meyer advocates 'a hermeneutics of generosity', in contrast to 'the hermeneutics of suspicion' that had marked so much New Testament scholarship since the Enlightenment. He examined the historical background of Jesus in Judaism, but with far more positive results than hitherto.

In stark contrast to Meyer, Robert Funk (1926–2005) founded the 'Jesus Seminar' at the Society of Biblical Literature in 1985. Its leading lights were James M. Robinson (b. 1924) and John Dominic Crossan (b. 1934) – a Irish-American scholar with interests in postmodernism – and between 100 and 200 scholars met annually. Crossan suggested that Jesus was an illiterate Jewish peasant, who taught a 'Wisdom' cluster of aphorisms (or pithy one-liners) akin to those of Greek Cynic philosophy. Jesus, according to Crossan, advocated free healing and common eating. Crossan's conclusions were broadly shared by F. G. Downing and Burton Mack, but were strongly attacked by Dale Allison and N. T. (Tom) Wright. The Jesus Seminar had reduced the authentic sayings to a third of the sayings of the Gospels, but Allison and Wright strongly argued otherwise.

Some include in the Third Quest Anthony E. Harvey, Marcus Borg, and E. P. Sanders – but a dozen such scholars might be mentioned. Of special note is N. T. Wright (b. 1948) and his book *Jesus and the Victory of God* (1996); James D. G. Dunn (b. 1938) and his book *Jesus Remembered* (2003); and Richard Bauckham, and his book *Jesus and the Eyewitnesses* (2006). This last establishes the importance of testimony in the Gospels. All three British scholars mounted a counter-blast to the excessive scepticism of the Jesus Seminar.

NARRATIVE
One of the special advances in theology in the late twentieth- and early twenty-first century has arisen out of an attention to narrative. The first step was the realization that narrative served theology in three ways: it did justice to the account of people's anecdotal testimonies; it provided a literary form in which very personal traits could emerge, from

Main entrance to Auschwitz Birkenau concentration camp, Poland.
©EWA MAZUR/ DREAMSTIME.COM

personality to eccentricity and creativity; and it did justice to vast stretches of the Bible, such as Luke-Acts or even Jonah, which were written primarily in the form of narrative. It also appealed to children and to a very broad readership. Indeed, during the 1980s it became virtually a fashion to turn as much of the Bible as possible into 'story'.

This touches only the surface of narrative, however. At least two scholars investigated narrative in a deeper, and more sophisticated, way. The first was Paul Ricoeur (1913–2005), a highly distinguished French philosopher, who happened also to be a Protestant Christian. His work included the human will, symbol, metaphor, narrative, and hermeneutics – or interpretation. In the area of narrative, he wrote a magisterial three-volume work, *Time and Narrative* (French, 1983–85; English, 1984–88).

The second was Gérard Genette (b. 1930), whose subject was not theology, but French literature. His most influential book was *Narrative Discourse* (1980), which drew on the work of Vladimir Propp and others on folk tales, but made special advances on narrative and time. Genette showed that many narrators make extensive use of such devices as 'narrative time', which is different from chronological time or clock-time. Most detective stories rely on flashbacks, variations of speed, and so on – and so does the Bible. The Gospels, for example, use narrative-time in different ways. Mark begins in his first eight chapters at a very fast pace; he slows down in the middle chapters; and recounts the suffering and death of Jesus virtually in slow motion. Thereby he shows that the whole narrative of the life of Jesus points to the cross, which gives it its meaning.

Attempts to fit the chronology of the different Gospels together often ignore the dimension of narrative-time, such as John's use of flashbacks and flash-forwards. Paul Ricoeur shows that the reporting of bare facts contributes only one function of narrative. Following Augustine, he stresses the importance of expectation, attention, and memory. But whereas Augustine represents the aspects of discordance (a seemingly random succession of events), Aristotle expounded the unifying logic of a temporal plot (*récit*). The plot is what organizes – and makes sense of – the succession of events in a narrative.

These are not the only thinkers to contribute to our understanding of narrative. In the *Art of Biblical Narrative* (1981), Robert Alter (b. 1935), a Jewish American literary scholar, showed that differences in the Old Testament accounts of the same event, which do indeed differ, may not be due to the use of contradictory sources. For example, in the accounts of the anointing of David as king, one account gives succinctly the involvement of divine choice and decree; the other, longer, account (which includes the Goliath story) tells it from the point of view of 'the hurly-burly' of everyday life.

HERMENEUTICS

In one sense hermeneutics – understood as rules of interpretation – has always been with us. The Stoics used hermeneutics in the interpretation of Homer, and Rabbi Hillel formulated 'seven rules' in relation to the Old Testament. But from the early nineteenth century, Friedrich Schleiermacher showed that the 'art' of interpretation needed to draw on biblical studies, philosophy, linguistics, and other disciplines.

Wilhelm Dilthey developed this in the direction of sociology at the beginning of the twentieth century, and then decisively Martin Heidegger, Rudolf Bultmann, Hans-Georg Gadamer (1900–2002) and Paul Ricoeur developed the discipline in the second half of the twentieth century and beyond. Interpretation, they all argued, does not depend on some illusory and 'objective' standpoint outside history, but begins with the historical situatedness (*Geschichlichkeit*) of the interpreter. Every interpreter is conditioned by his or her own place in history (including education, gender, class, and outlook), just as the text itself arrives from its own place in history. Gadamer, especially, called this beginning from within a 'horizon'. This is different from an immovable 'presupposition', for horizons expand and move, as we move.

A text may 'speak back', to correct or enlarge a horizon. Indeed, these four thinkers used a special term to describe this process. We begin with a 'preliminary understanding' of the text (German *Vorverständnis*, literally 'pre-understanding'), but our horizon becomes more adequate through 'the hermeneutical circle' of dialogue with the text, and further experience and reflection. Some have spoken of the 'Two Horizons' of the text and interpreter; hermeneutics has become the art of bringing them together. Gadamer called this a merging or fusion of horizons.

Such merging or fusion remains, however, an *aim*; it seldom – if ever – happens totally in a short space of time. That is why yet another thinker, Hans Robert Jauss (1921–97) insists that meaning is always 'unfinished', in the sense that a later generation may appreciate what we have missed. He has urged the importance of 'Reception Theory', namely comparing and assessing how different generations may often expect different things from the text.

Hermeneutics does not leave behind more traditional questions. For example, whether a text may have one meaning or many may depend on the genre to which the text belongs. If the text reports, or gives a factual account, it has one meaning; but if its genre is that of symbol, metaphor, or poetry (or even prophecy), it is likely to have more than one meaning.

Many thinkers have drawn particular tools from history, the sociology of knowledge, linguistics, and other areas, to shed light on biblical interpretation. For example, some use 'speech-act' theory, drawn from linguistics.

SPEECH-ACT THEORY

Among the newer movements in biblical studies, mention should be made of the use of Speech-Act Theory, drawn from the field of the philosophy of language and linguistics. John Austin (1911–60), its modern pioneer, defined speech-acts (strictly illocutionary acts) as 'performance of an act *in* saying something' (*How to Do Things with Words*, 1962). Typical examples include naming a ship in saying 'I name this ship …'; or marrying a wife in saying, 'I take you …'; or baptizing a candidate in saying, 'I baptize you …'; or opening a library in saying, 'I open …'.

This approach has been applied fruitfully to biblical studies, for the utterance of speech-act depends heavily on the authority and status of the speaker, and the circumstances of the utterances. Thus, when Jesus said, 'Your sins are forgiven you', this becomes an *act* of forgiveness, because Jesus has the status and authority to forgive sins. To say 'I repent' becomes an *act* of repentance if the speaker is repentant and sincere; otherwise it remains only empty words.

Speech-act theory has been developed and applied in more sophisticated ways by Donald Evans, John Searle, and many others. It was in embryo anticipated by the Reformer

William Tyndale, who argued that the Bible not only talked about healing, forgiveness, and liberation, but also conveyed acts of forgiveness, healing, and liberation. Work in Biblical studies has been carried out in 1995 by Nicholas Wolterstorff, and since 1980 and after 2000 by Anthony C. Thiselton, Richard S. Briggs, and many others.

THE HOLY SPIRIT AND THE HOLY TRINITY

Until the 1970s, there was widespread neglect of the theology of the Holy Spirit. There were exceptions, the most obvious being Pentecostalism – which has vastly increased in global numbers – and the first embryonic attempts of the Renewal Movement in the 1960s and 1970s. Other exceptions include Karl Barth, who argued in 1932 that the theology of the Holy Spirit is inseparable from that of the Father and the Son, and that the doctrine of the Trinity should be the starting-point of our Christian theology. He wrote, 'The Holy Spirit guarantees man what he cannot guarantee himself'; he is the 'yes' to God's word (*Church Dogmatics*, vol. 1). In volume 2 he wrote that the Holy Spirit opens our blind eyes.

Pentecostalism continued largely on the basis of the teaching of Charles F. Parham (1873–1929) and William J. Seymour (1870–1922) in the first decade of the twentieth century, and led later to the founding of the Assemblies of God in 1913, and of the Elim Fellowship in 1933.

The Swiss scholar Eduard Schweizer (1913–2006) and the British theologian Geoffrey Lampe (1912–80) wrote – in 1960 and 1977 respectively – thorough biblical and Patristic surveys emphasizing the prophetic role of the Holy Spirit, as well as his empowerment of Jesus. John V. Taylor wrote *The Go-Between God* (1972), in which he argued that the Holy Spirit excludes the notion of 'it all depends on me'. James D. G. Dunn gave serious attention to Pentecostal claims in *Baptism in the Holy Spirit* (1970), in which he also claimed (against most Pentecostals) that in Paul the Holy Spirit is given to *all* Christians, not just to some.

Meanwhile the Renewal Movement began to take hold in mainline churches. Initially such leaders as Dennis Bennett (1917–91) in America and Michael Harper (1931–2010) in England, who were not theologians, took an uncompromising line, which split many local churches. Emphasis was laid on prophecy and tongues, perhaps without due regard to scholarly accounts of these phenomena.

Later the movement began to mellow. Such mainline theologians as Yves Congar, the Roman Catholic theologian, and Jürgen Moltmann, from the Protestant side, expressed broad sympathy with their aims. Congar's three volumes, *I Believe in the Holy Spirit* (1983), provided a judicious discussion of Renewal. But he argued, 'All experience has to be checked, tested, and proved authentic', and also warned that Renewal cannot and should not 'be extended to the whole Church', because its style of meetings 'is not acceptable to everyone'.

Moltmann, similarly, cautiously approved many signs of life, but with some reservations. In his crucial book *The Trinity and the Kingdom of God* (1981), he wrote: 'The New Testament talks about God by proclaiming in narrative the relationship of the Son and the Spirit.' The Father 'sends' Jesus Christ; Jesus is anointed by the Holy Spirit. The Persons of the Trinity work together in all God's acts of creation and redemption. The Spirit should be honoured, but not separated from God. The Christian is inspired by the Spirit to cry the prayer of Jesus, 'Abba, dear Father'.

During the 1980s 'house churches' sprang up in the Renewal Movement, and were often called 'new churches' in the 1990s. In 1983 the Renewal Movement began to use the term 'third wave' or 'neo-charismatic', under the leadership of C. Peter Wagner (b. 1930) and others. On one side 'Baptism in the Spirit' was associated with conversion, rather than with a 'second' blessing. On the other hand, prophecies and 'casting out demons' became more pronounced. In the 1990s, many traditional Christians expressed consternation at the 'Toronto Blessing', when such phenomena occurred.

Meanwhile Pentecostals began for the first time to embrace serious scholarship. Gordon Fee wrote *God's Empowering Presence* (1994), mainly on Paul's letters, and Roger Strongstad and Robert Menzies wrote on *Luke-Acts* (1984 and 1994). Fee, firmly a Pentecostal, no longer accepted classic Pentecostalism's view of 'Baptism in the Holy Spirit'. Scholarly enquiries were also undertaken by Amos Yong, Veli-Matti Kärkkäinen and Frank Macchia, with ecumenical interests.

Both Pentecostals and the Renewal Movement continued to stress 'miracles'. Mainline scholars did not universally approve this term, as implying a 'dualist', or two-storey, view of God's action. They also argued that the final phase of the Kingdom of God was still in process of fulfilment, and that it would anticipate God's timing to 'expect' miracles on a regular basis before the End.

Debate continues in the twenty-first century. Michael Welker (b. 1947), surprisingly, appeals to post-modernism to approve patterns of pluriformity. Tom Smail and Jim Purves question many of the excesses of the Renewal Movement (1995 and 2004). Most important of all, Eugene F. Rogers Jr develops Moltmann's narrative approach to the Holy Trinity in *After the Spirit* (2005 and 2006). He writes: 'The baptism of Jesus is ... an inter-Trinitarian event.' In this event 'the Spirit bears witness to the love between the Father and the Son ... The Father expresses his love in 'This is my Son, the beloved'. The Spirit acts creatively in Jesus.'

The narrative approach to the Trinity not only gives us the New Testament way of explaining the Trinity, it also avoids all such abstract analogy as clover leaves, shamrocks, or playing with numbers. In the fourth century, Gregory of Nazianzus and Gregory of Nyssa had insisted that the threefold nature of the Trinity had nothing to do with numerals. Numerals, they said, measure the quantities of 'things' or created beings; but God cannot be quantified in this way. The Holy Trinity stands above everything in creation, including angels and human beings.

ANTHONY C. THISELTON

CHAPTER 39

PENTECOSTALISM AND THE CHARISMATIC MOVEMENT

Pentecostalism belongs to that stream within Christianity that places a personal experience of the Holy Spirit high among the marks of a Christian. In contrast, the Catholic has normally tended to 'channel' the Spirit through bishop and sacrament, and the Protestant through the Bible. The most important figure within this stream in previous centuries was John Wesley. Indeed Wesley – whose own heart was 'strangely warmed', who emphasized the inner 'witness of the Spirit', and taught that sanctification was a second work of grace, distinct from, and following, justification – might well be called the great-grandfather of Pentecostalism. From the early Methodists the stream runs directly through the Holiness movement of the nineteenth century. In camp meetings and 'higher life' conventions, holiness teachers proclaimed the 'second blessing' of sanctification as a cleansing of the heart from all sin, and sometimes called it 'the baptism of the Holy Ghost'.

ABLAZE WITH THE SPIRIT

Towards the end of the nineteenth century, three significant developments in the USA heralded the emergence of Pentecostalism as such. Increasing opposition to holiness teaching within the older denominations, particularly Methodism, resulted in the formation of several distinct holiness churches. Belief in baptism in the Holy Ghost and fire as a *third* blessing became increasingly widespread. And there was also a renewed interest in spiritual gifts, particularly healing.

The decisive step was taken at the turn of the century in Topeka, Kansas, where the doctrine was first formulated that 'speaking with other tongues' was the initial evidence that a person had received the baptism with the Holy Spirit. 'Other tongues' was generally understood as the Holy Spirit speaking through a person's speech organs in a language he or she had not previously known. This teaching began to gain scattered support in the southern states of the USA during the early 1900s.

But it was the revival that began in Azusa Street, Los Angeles, in 1906, which really forged the link between Spirit-baptism and tongues. This three-year-long meeting was the launchpad of twentieth-century Pentecostalism, as hundreds of Christians from all over North America, and then from Europe and the Third World, visited Azusa Street and took its message back with them. The fire spread quite rapidly, resulting in the formation of many new churches. Most of the Holiness groupings were also influenced, and either split over the new teaching on tongues, or became Pentecostal in doctrine.

A FOURTH STRAND IN CHRISTIANITY

In the century since Azusa Street, Pentecostalism has spread throughout the world. It is important to realize that Pentecostalism is neither a denomination nor a Protestant sect. In fact, it represents a fourth major strand of Christianity – alongside Orthodoxy, Roman Catholicism, and Protestantism – and is composed of many denominations.

The largest Pentecostal denominations in the USA include the Assemblies of God, the Church of God in Christ – the largest black denomination – the Church of God, and the Pentecostal Holiness Church. In Europe, Pentecostalism is strongest in Scandinavia, and in Italy has more adherents than all the Protestant groups put together. In Britain, it remained a movement within the older denominations for some years. The Apostolic Church – predominantly Welsh – began in 1916, and the Elim Alliance, and Assemblies of God established themselves in the early 1920s. When many people emigrated from the Caribbean in the 1950s, West Indian Churches of God organized themselves separately from the more established British groups. Pentecostalism grew in Russia and China, too, while elsewhere in Asia the most significant advance was in Indonesia.

The most striking spheres of Pentecostal influence, however, are Latin America and Africa. In many Latin American countries, Pentecostalism is the largest non-Catholic grouping. The most striking examples are Brazil, where Pentecostals have been estimated to number forty million, and Chile, where about fifteen per cent of the population is reckoned to be Pentecostal. In West Africa, Zaïre, and southern Africa there are large independent churches which have derived much of their inspiration from Pentecostalism.

WHAT PENTECOSTALS BELIEVE

Pentecostalism is, for the most part, wholly orthodox in its beliefs as far as the major Christian doctrines are concerned. The only exception is the 'Jesus Only' churches in the USA, who hold a modalist view of God and baptize in the name of Jesus only. The largest of these churches is the United Pentecostal Church, with worldwide membership of around three million.

The one other major theological split within Pentecostalism concerns the question of whether baptism in the Spirit is a second or third work of grace. Almost all the Pentecostal pioneers simply tacked a belief in Spirit-baptism, as a third work, on to the Holiness belief in sanctification, as a second work of grace. But in the years after 1910, there was increasing support for the doctrine that sanctification is part of Christ's 'finished work' on the cross, and so part of conversion. The Pentecostalism rooted in North America is split about fifty-fifty on this issue. A number of Pentecostal churches also regard footwashing as being as obligatory as baptism and the Lord's Supper.

Pentecostalists tend to see Christ in four roles: as Saviour, Baptizer in the Spirit, Healer, and soon-coming King. A distinctive dogma is that tongues are the initial physical sign of Spirit-baptism (though some of the early pioneers were not so insistent on this). Healing evangelists have played a significant role in Pentecostalism's expansion, and teaching on healing often includes the unfortunate doctrine that all illness is the result of sin or lack of faith. Belief in demon possession is also general, and exorcism regularly practised. The conviction that the second coming of Christ is at hand has caused strains between the generations – but the continued growth of Pentecostalism has constantly revitalized this hope.

Pentecostal worship is patterned on the model given in I Corinthians, chapters twelve to fourteen. The spiritual gifts mentioned there are regularly regarded as the norm, and spoken contributions in a service are usually understood as a 'prophecy', or 'words of wisdom'. Services are not necessarily without a structure, and there is usually a leader or pastor at the front. Worship in older (white) Pentecostal churches has often become stereotyped, and in practice little different from that of many Protestant churches. One result of the increasing importance of a minister was the formation of the Full Gospel Business Men's Fellowship International (FGBMFI) in 1952, by Demos Shakarian (1913–93), an organization of ordinary Christians which has done much to spread Pentecostal ideas all over the world.

WHO ARE THE PENTECOSTALS?

For most of its existence, Pentecostalism has been rigidly fundamentalist and anti-intellectual. It was not until the 1950s at the earliest that Pentecostal theological students began to move in significant numbers into non-Pentecostal seminaries in the USA. In the early decades it drew its support almost entirely from the poorer classes of society, and made the sort of impact in the twentieth century that Methodism made in the eighteenth, and the Salvation Army in the nineteenth centuries. From the beginning, blacks have played a significant role in the development of Pentecostalism, and for nearly twenty years Pentecostal churches were among the most inter-racial organizations in the USA. Pentecostals have generally given little consideration to social issues but have strict ethical standards. Some of the newer churches in Africa and Latin America are developing a concern for social issues.

Their phenomenal growth has been due in large part to the enthusiastic vitality of their experience of the Spirit, the appeal of their spontaneous style of worship – in which all can participate in their own way – the absence of a caste of clergy and of a priestly hierarchy, and the insistence that all members must share their faith with others. For the most part Pentecostals in the Third World have not had to labour under church structures and forms imposed from North America and Europe, which has made possible an indigenous growth which can hardly be rivalled in the history of Christian expansion. On the other hand, the Pentecostal churches have been remarkably divisive – as is clearly seen in the fragmentation of Afro-Caribbean Pentecostal sects in Britain.

A storefront Hispanic Pentecostal church in Brooklyn, New York, USA.
© VALENTINO VISENTINI/ DREAMSTIME.COM

PENTECOSTALS WORLDWIDE

The growing influence of Pentecostalism on world Christianity has been marked by several significant developments. In the early 1950s, leading figures in the World Council of Churches began to recognize Pentecostalism as genuinely Christian – indeed as a 'third force' within Christianity. About the same time, David du Plessis (1905–87), then Secretary of the Pentecostal World Conference, believed God was calling him to make contact with the World

Council. Following this, he became an ambassador extraordinary for Pentecostalism within ecumenical circles, and exercised a widespread influence.

In the early 1960s, Pentecostal teaching and experiences began to penetrate significantly the older Protestant denominations, starting with Anglo-Catholics in California. This neo-Pentecostalism caused strains within many congregations, but neo-Pentecostals have for the most part remained within their original denominations, functioning mainly in prayer groups and conferences.

In the second half of the 1960s, this emerging Charismatic movement spread rapidly among the drop-out generation, who were disillusioned with a society that justified the Vietnam War. The 'Jesus Movement' caught attention for only a short time, but made a lasting impact on that generation. More significant was the development of Catholic Pentecostalism, which within a few years became one of the significant forces within Roman Catholicism, supported by Cardinal Suenens of Belgium (1904–96) and a significant number of bishops.

The acceptance of Pentecostalism by the leaders of the World Council marked the first time that more traditional Christianity genuinely welcomed this enthusiastic brand of faith and worship as a valid and important expression of Christianity. Previously, such forms of Christianity were either persecuted, or only able to flourish outside the organized church.

The Charismatic movement increasingly broke down many of the barriers and misconceptions on both sides. Initially it operated at a very personal level; but when the first Roman Catholics became involved, in 1967, the movement entered what has been called its corporate phase. As the movement developed its own understanding of the nature of the church, difficulties arose within the mainstream churches, resulting in the formation of some new denominations — although the term 'denomination' was denied by the new groups. For example, in Great Britain house churches and the restorationist movement began. By the 1980s the Charismatic movement had moved into its global phase, with ever increasing influence in most world communions, particularly in Latin America. By the mid-1980s more than 100 Anglican bishops were active in renewal, and in France there were almost one million charismatics within the Roman Catholic Church.

In some places the movement has produced schism and tension, and fostered an immature intellectualism and unhealthy emphasis on authority. But — at its best — it has led to a renewal of confidence, a re-energizing of lay authority, an enlivening of worship, a new emphasis upon the church as community, and the offering of a new basis for unity between Christians. It has spread across all the traditional groups in society and church life; and Catholic Pentecostalism, particularly, has drawn in a calibre of scholarship, and a respect for authority, sacraments, and tradition that was missing from classic Pentecostalism. In the 1960s, neo-Pentecostals were content to take over Pentecostal theology in large measure, and gave speaking in tongues a Pentecostal prominence. But the widening of the Charismatic movement since the 1960s has brought with it a questioning of the classic Pentecostal categories, a desire to formulate the theology of the 'Pentecostal experience' more carefully, and a renewed concern to let the life of the Spirit be expressed in new forms of community.

JAMES D. G. DUNN

AFRICAN INDEPENDENT CHURCHES

For some centuries Christianity as a world religion has been divided into three main traditions, Protestant, Roman Catholic, and Orthodox; to these should now perhaps be added a substantial African development of Christianity. This African strand has been given a variety of titles: indigenous, separatist, prophetic, messianic, millennial, Zionist; but these terms were either too wide or too narrow to describe the movements which – while remaining recognizably Christian in intention – have abandoned any connection with the mission-founded churches. Here we will call them 'African independent churches'.

These African independent churches are a recognizable new form of the Christian tradition. But they are also part of a wider series of new religious movements in tribal societies in Africa, the Americas, and the Pacific, which result from Christian and other Western influences interacting with tribal culture to produce something new to both. The African independent churches must not be too sharply distinguished from other forms of African Christianity; some of the factors that make them popular are common African features, which can often be traced within mission-founded African churches.

Independent churches occur widely in West, East, Central, and Southern Africa. There are, however, great differences in the extent of their influence, both between nations, and between peoples and areas within the same nation. They rarely occur where Christians are few, or where Christianity has only recently arrived.

The independent churches differ widely in style, organization, and attitudes. One classification divides between 'Ethiopian' churches, which assert African and reject European leadership, but keep the 'shape' of the church much as before, and 'Zionist' churches, which are charismatic, and seek the fulfilling of a Zion of their own – for these churches perhaps the description 'prophet-healing' would be better. It is impossible to guess sensibly at total membership, though it is many millions; and many people belong to both a 'mainline' church, out of loyalty or respectability, and to an independent church, for their deepest needs.

WHY INDEPENDENT CHURCHES?

In trying to understand the origins of the independent churches, we must distinguish between immediate causes – events which lead to a break with older churches or missions – and underlying causes – which produce conditions where a break becomes likely.

Five underlying causes can be isolated:

An Ethiopian Orthodox priest holding a metal cross, Addis Ababa, Ethiopia.
© JANTHONJACKSON/DREAMSTIME.COM

- The desire to be free of foreign domination in the church. Some of the oldest 'Ethiopian' churches arose from such a desire. In the 1880s and 1890s, West African Christians felt that the missionary societies were going back on their principles of self-governing, self-supporting, self-propagating churches. As a result they created the African Church, the Native Baptist church, and others. Elsewhere, the feeling that missionary leaders did not understand important local institutions, such as ancestor veneration or marriage, has encouraged this desire for freedom.
- Conditions produced by white dominance. No country has been more marked by these movements than South Africa, where the feeling among Africans of dispossession, the lack of other outlets for leadership, the effects of the migrant labour system in separating men from their families, and strict controls on black residence and movement produced the commonwealths of Isaiah Shembe (1870–1935) and Engenas Barnabas Lekganyane (c. 1885–1948), and other attempts to build 'Zion which is our home'.
- The effects of mass movements. Between 1910 and 1930, African evangelists with little or no official church status led mass movements towards Christianity. Many who obeyed the call of Prophet William Wadé Harris (c. 1860–1929) to abandon fetish joined the 'mainline' churches, but the 'Harriste' churches of the rest are still important in Ivory Coast. Sam(p)son Oppong (c. 1884–1965) in Ghana, and Walter Matitta (1885–1935) in Lesotho, were also men whom the missions had to recognize as very influential, but who did not meet the missions' formal requirements for 'native ministers'. None of these movements were themselves independent churches, but they produced the conditions for them.
- Religious revival. Simon Kimbangu (1887–1951), a young Baptist catechist, led a revival movement which in 1921 began to alarm the Belgian Congo government. He was sent to jail for life; but the church bearing his name now claims five million members in Congo-DRC. Another church of similarly extensive membership is the Church of the Lord (Aladura) found throughout West Africa. Immigrant communities in Europe and North America took their church with them. In 1928, Joseph Ayo Babalola (1904–59), a steamroller driver, received a call to preach and gave a new impetus to revival in western Nigeria. The preaching of the catechist Garrick Braide (1882–1918) brought thousands into the Anglican Church in the Niger delta; his dismissal took thousands out into the Christ Army and other churches.
- Quest for a wider salvation. In traditional African society, healing is closely linked with religion, and Africans asked whether faith in Christ was not equally effective. The 1918 influenza epidemic in particular posed this question acutely for African Christians. Kimbangu, Babalola, and Braide were all healers attended by vast crowds, and healing remains a feature of many independent churches today.

WHAT DISTINGUISHES INDEPENDENT CHURCHES?

The independent movements are usually Bible-centred, and occur most readily where the whole Bible is available in the local language. These churches seek direct continuity with the New Testament period, and claim to display the power and gifts of that period: often prophecy, revelation, and healing – less frequently the gift of tongues. They also often continue traditions of healing, or the work of mediums, from pre-Christian religion and culture.

These movements combine ritualistic elements – such as robes, ceremonies, a hierarchy of apostles and prophets – with charismatic ones – such as spontaneity, dancing, and ecstasy. In Western Christianity, these two elements are found in different types of religion; but African society is both ordered and spontaneous.

The independent churches reflect the concerns most pressing to local people, concerns that were not necessarily those selected by missionaries. A few have emphasized polygamy, but many do not regard monogamy as essential, except for churches such as the Kimbanguists. But independent churches take witchcraft and the evil produced in the community by hatred – the essence of witchcraft – very seriously. They are frequently accused of being mixtures of Christian and traditional elements – syncretistic – and undoubtedly many of them are. But many of the churches are radical, requiring a complete break with features of the old religion – witchcraft, charms, and fetish – which are maintained among nominal members of older churches, as well as a break with tobacco, alcohol, and gambling.

Like other religious movements, the independent churches have a history; they change and develop. They may move closer to, or further from, biblical Christianity; and become inspired less, or more, by religious, economic, or political factors. Some also represent splits from European Catholicism or the ancient Orthodox churches.

The independent churches are immensely diverse; some have expressed political protest or nationalist sentiment, others are quietist and non-political. Some are large and highly-structured, others small and localized. Some have developed doctrinal peculiarities: the concern with 'power' sometimes makes the Holy Spirit more prominent than the Son. But theology is rarely important for them, and most do not consciously wish to break with the central Christian doctrines. The independent churches want to be part of a wider fellowship of churches – several have joined the World Council of Churches – but fear a take-over.

It is helpful to think of the independent churches as Africa's Anabaptists. Profusion of variety, the eccentricity of their wilder manifestations, and a spirituality and radical Bible-centredness are essential to them at their best. They are a response to Christianity in African terms, 'a place to feel at home'; and also a witness to the fact that here there is no 'abiding city'.

A. F. WALLS

CHAPTER 40

THE ARTS IN THE CHRISTIAN WEST

Ever since the fourth century, the shape of civilization in the West has been heavily influenced by Christianity. Art is no exception. No account of history in the last sixteen centuries is possible without an understanding of the Christian contribution. It is ordinarily a shaky business to insist that a factor such as religion has a direct effect on particular political, economic, or social events in history, but Christianity and art were causally linked between the fourth and the twentieth centuries. Even the 'post-Christian' art and literature of the last 200 years in the West emerges from Christian roots – and often involves a more or less conscious repudiation of Christian categories, and an attempt to forge new forms, free of Christian influence.

It is natural that Christianity should have affected art deeply. Christianity is rooted in history: its central events occurred in the times of public figures such as Caesar Augustus and Pontius Pilate. Christianity proclaimed not a retreat from real, historic, human existence and experience, but rather the redemption and glorification of that existence and experience. The very foundations of Christianity are the doctrines of creation and incarnation, so Christianity robustly celebrates human flesh, created in the image of God, made the habitation of the incarnate God, and redeemed for the vision of God at last.

The human imagination, reflecting on this view of things, was roused to shape and express its vision in visual, musical, narrative, and dramatic forms. However, there is no single common thread in the art of the Christian West over sixteen hundred years. What, for example, does medieval Chartres Cathedral, France, have in common with Sir Christopher Wren's seventeenth-century London churches? Or the icon of the Virgin of Vladimir in Russia with a painting by Rembrandt (1606–69) of the holy family? Or medieval plainsong with the twentieth-century French composer Olivier Messiaen (1908-92)?

There is an enormously wide range of expression in Christian art, resulting from the central paradoxes of the Christian faith – paradoxes that arise when the human imagination attempts to function on the frontier between time and eternity, between the transcendent and the immanent, and between the spiritual and the material. Theological language staggers on this borderline; the arts have similar difficulties.

IMAGES

This has meant that Christians have always differed about the arts. Although official church councils in both East and West before the year 1000 proclaimed that Christian image-making was permissible, many Christians have a lingering distrust of such images. They fear that by having an image of the thing before them, vision and devotion might attach themselves to the image, and fail to press on to the thing for which the image stands. This viewpoint was maintained by the image-rejecting 'iconoclasts' in the Orthodox Church for hundreds of years, with fluctuating success, and has always been alive in some part of the church. Some Protestant traditions show a similar trend, playing down the visual.

Christians vary widely over what sort of imagery is appropriate. For example, in depicting the annunciation, one artist would try to capture the idea of mortal flesh being hailed by God's splendour, by depicting the Virgin Mary (our flesh) crowned with gold (raised to glory by the promise of redemption), sitting under gilded arches, and approached by a shining, winged creature. This is the visual expression of a theological concept – and one that was widespread in the Middle Ages. Another artist, wishing to suggest the apparently unfavourable way in which the drama of the gospel was played out on the stage of history, showed the Virgin as a very ordinary young woman in ordinary surroundings. The difference between the two paintings arises not so much from a difference in the two artists' doctrines, as from their contrasting ways of approaching the subject.

Christian artists have also had to ask whether they should paint 'religious' subjects (annunciations, nativities, crucifixions, and saints' lives), or celebrate ordinary human life, without tackling these religious topics. Christian art from the early centuries up to the Renaissance tended to choose the first option. However, medieval artists, far from ignoring ordinary life, brought the whole of everyday life into service. We find tiny farming scenes decorating the borders of devotional books, and, in cathedrals and churches, wooden carvings of craftsmen at work. On the other hand, with the cultural and theological shift of emphasis in the fifteenth and sixteenth centuries, we find such Northern artists as Rembrandt, Vermeer (1632-75), van Ruysdael (c. 1628-82), and Cuyp (1620-91) busy celebrating ordinary domestic, community, and professional life.

Engraving of a self-portrait by Rembrandt van Rijn.

LITERATURE

When we consider the relationship of Christianity with literature – poetry, fiction, essays, and drama – some of the same questions come up. For the first few centuries of Christianity, most Christian writing was in the form of theology. There were also poetical paraphrases of the Bible, for example the Old English *Genesis*, *Exodus*, and *Daniel* (formerly attributed to the Anglo-Saxon poet Caedmon). Up to the time of the Renaissance, the writing of sermons by such men as Isidore of Seville (c. 560-636), Bede, Alcuin, and Rabanus Maurus (c. 780-856), owed much to Augustine of Hippo, who rigorously subordinated considerations of style to the service of truth and moral instruction.

Western writers were hampered by an austere sense of the moral uses of poetry, and an almost paralyzing worry about the laws of rhetoric. Despite this, Western writing did flourish, in prose, poetry, history (Bede; Gildas, 500-570; Geoffrey of Monmouth, c. 1100–c. 1155), sermons (Gregory; Ailred of Rievaulx, 1110–67; John of Salisbury, c. 1120–80), and lyric (Caedmon and Cynewulf), up to the thirteenth-century peak in Dante Alighieri (1265–1321), and, in England, to *Piers Plowman*, *Pearl*, *Patience*, and the writing of the mystics, including Richard Rolle, Lady Julian of Norwich (c. 1342–c. 1416) and the author of *The Cloud of Unknowing* in the fourteenth century. All writers, whatever their talent, were officially Christian during these centuries. Their works – Chaucer's poetry, for example – are wrought with Christian assumptions, implicit or explicit.

Although the fifteenth and sixteenth centuries are often thought of as the period when the Western imagination broke free of Christian dogma and began to assert its autonomy, consciously non-Christian literature does not appear widely until well into the eighteenth century. This is not to say that all literature before that was religious in its concerns: Shakespeare, Rabelais, Cervantes, and a hundred others were not writing Christian drama and fiction. But the Christian view of the universe was still generally

C. S. LEWIS

Clive Staples Lewis (1898–1963) became the most popular defender of orthodox Christianity in the English-speaking world in the mid-twentieth century. Lewis was born in Belfast in 1898, and brought up in the Christian faith – a faith he lost before he reached his teens. He was educated at Malvern College, England, and then privately under a tutor, whose atheism had such an influence on him that by the time Lewis went up to Oxford University in 1917 he described himself as an unbeliever.

Lewis took a triple first at Oxford, and was elected to a fellowship in English at Magdalen College, a post he held until 1954, when he became Professor of Medieval and Renaissance English Literature at Cambridge. He wrote a number of works of literary criticism.

After a long intellectual battle, Lewis was converted to Christianity in 1931. Gifted with a rich imagination and a reasoning mind, his conversion triggered off a variety of creativity. His international bestseller, *The Screwtape Letters* (1942), won him the reputation of being able to 'make righteousness readable', and he wrote many other works of theology and fantasy with theological dimensions. Lewis achieved further fame as a preacher, debater, and effective 'apostle to the sceptics'. Believing, as he said, that 'all that is not eternal is eternally out of date', he was essentially orthodox and admired by Christians from all branches of the church.

A jovial and saintly man, he could have amassed a fortune, but following his conversion he regularly gave two-thirds of his income to charities. Between 1950 and 1956, Lewis published seven much-loved fantasies about his invented world of Narnia, beginning with *The Lion, the Witch and the Wardrobe*. Lewis also wrote an autobiography, *Surprised by Joy*, which traces the story of his conversion.

WALTER HOOPER

accepted, and provided the moral backdrop against which these authors wrote. In fact the Christian and the classical Greek moral imagination have more in common with each other than either has with the modern. Since the Enlightenment, people have attempted to begin afresh, to shape human communication and culture on the assumption that humankind is autonomous.

CHURCH AND STAGE

By the end of the ancient world, drama had reached such a low point that it could only be viewed with alarm and disgust by the church. Christianity was assumed to be – and was – anti-theatre, for some hundreds of years. Before the year 1000, however, short dramatic elements called *tropes* were introduced into the church's liturgy. One of the earliest and most familiar of these was the *Quem Quaeritis* ('Whom seek ye?'), sometimes known as *Visitatio sepulchri* ('Visit to the tomb'), from the Easter service, in which monks took the parts of the women and the angel at the tomb. As time went on, more and more of the gospel story was dramatized, so that by the fourteenth century we find long, elaborate play-cycles of biblical history being staged by the craftsmen of such English cities as York and Chester.

The most productive period in English drama followed in the sixteenth century, with Shakespeare at its peak, though little explicitly Christian expression was coming from the theatres. Since that period, there has been a widespread feeling in the church that, although drama ought to be a useful method for portraying Christian interpretations of existence, it is not easy to arrive at an understanding between church and theatre. T. S. Eliot (1888–1965), in *Murder in the Cathedral*, *The Family Reunion*, and other plays, came as close as any author to writing drama that is at one and the same time good and specifically Christian, yet his attempt was not an unqualified success. The problem, as always, is the difficulty of depicting the mysteries of grace, which are central to any Christian handling of human experience, in artistic forms.

WESTERN MUSIC

Of all the arts, that most unambiguously celebrated and nourished in the Christian West has always been music. No one knows, of course, just what Western music would have sounded like without Christian influence; but from the hymns of the early church, through plainsong, motet, oratorio, and modern hymnody, we find the Christian imagination expressing its response to existence.

THOMAS HOWARD

CHAPTER 41

ORGANIZING FOR UNITY

Ecumenism, in the twentieth-century sense, began in a shared concern for evangelism in the Student Volunteer Movement, a forerunner of the Student Christian Movement. There was also a concern to recover shared denominational heritage. There had already been reunions in Scotland at the turn of the century, and the merging of two Methodist groups in England to form the United Methodists a few years later. But the new incentive ran across denominations, and led to a dynamic discovery of a much wider oneness in Christ, which in part already existed.

The movement was first organized at the International Missionary Conference held at Edinburgh in 1910, under the chairmanship of John R. Mott (1865–1955), with the task of surveying the world mission of the non-Roman churches. Over 1,000 delegates from all over the world encountered each other across the denominational divides, and three main movements arose as a result of this conference.

First, the International Missionary Council was formed in 1921, the result of the work of the Continuation Committee from the Edinburgh Conference. The IMC met at Jerusalem in 1928, and at Madras in 1938. When the World Council of Churches was formed in 1948, the IMC did not participate directly; however, when the IMC met in Ghana in 1958 its assembly voted to merge with the World Council of Churches, which occurred at the New Delhi Assembly of the WCC (1961).

The second outcome of the Edinburgh Conference was the 'Faith and Order' Movement. Bishop Charles Henry Brent (1862–1927), of the Protestant Episcopal Church in the USA, returned from Edinburgh with a vision for the union of the churches, and with a strong desire to see the doctrinal problems faced squarely. He persuaded his own church to issue in 1912 an invitation to 'all churches' to join in this endeavour. Planning was delayed by World War I, but from a preliminary meeting in 1920 grew the first World Conference on Faith and Order at Lausanne in 1927, which had an even wider membership than the original Edinburgh Conference, and included some Eastern Orthodox delegates. The next meeting was held at Edinburgh in 1937, where proposals for a 'World Council of Churches' were received from the Life and Work conference at Oxford. The Faith and Order conference accepted these proposals, and worked towards forming the WCC.

The third strand originating from Edinburgh, Life and Work, took shape in the period after World War I, when much reconstruction was needed. Archbishop Nathan Söderblom of Uppsala (1866–1931) was fired by the concept of churches uniting in service to the world, and his initiative led to conferences at Stockholm in 1925, and at Oxford in 1937. At the Oxford conference, proposals were drawn up to unite with Faith and Order, and become one 'World Council of Churches'. When this was accepted by Faith and Order, at Edinburgh in the same year, an exploratory meeting was held at Utrecht in 1938. A 'World Council of Churches in process of formation' established headquarters in Geneva. World War II held up progress, but the WCC was inaugurated in Amsterdam in 1948.

The World Council has now held ten full Assemblies: at Amsterdam (1948), Evanston, USA (1954), New Delhi (1961), Uppsala (1968), Nairobi (1975), Vancouver (1983), Canberra (1991), Harare (1998), Porto Alegre, Brazil (2006), Busan, Korea (2013). At New Delhi the IMC merged with the WCC, and for the first time the Orthodox churches were fully represented, and some Pentecostalist churches were also involved. At Uppsala and Nairobi the Roman Catholic Church was represented by 'participating observers'.

Whilst the WCC, and the various national councils of churches, still has a concern with doctrine, it has also assumed a growing political role, increased by the addition of non-European members. One cause of tension was the special fund connected with the 'Programme to Combat Racism' which supported black 'freedom fighters' and guerrilla movements in Southern Africa, though without supplying arms.

ROME CHANGES COURSE

The Roman Catholic Church itself changed in its approach to ecumenism. In the first half of the twentieth century the nearest it came to treating non-Catholics as anything other than heretics was at the Conversations at Malines (1923–27). These were unofficial talks between a few Anglicans (mostly extreme Anglo-Catholics) and a few Roman Catholics, conducted with the knowledge of the pope and the Archbishop of Canterbury. Pius XI finally brought them to a halt.

It was not expected that the Church of Rome would hold an 'Ecumenical Council' of its own. The last, Vatican I (1870), had declared that when speaking *ex cathedra* in his own person, the pope was infallible, even without the backing of a council. This view was confirmed when in 1950 Pius XII, without the backing of a council, defined and enforced the doctrine of the bodily assumption of the blessed Virgin Mary into heaven. This decree both showed that councils were now unnecessary, and also increased the distance between the Church of Rome and other churches.

The surprise came when Pius XII's successor, John XXIII, announced that he would call a council. He called on non-Roman Catholics to seek 'that unity for which Jesus Christ prayed'. The council, Vatican II (1962–65), fully achieved his purpose. There were no infallible pronouncements; instead the council worked out a series of advisory, pastoral, disciplinary, and exemplary documents. A new climate of relationships arose, shared worship followed, and genuine ecumenical dialogue was joined. Intercommunion began, along with shared ministerial training, a 'Common Bible', and doctrinal agreements with other denominations reached by joint commissions.

The Roman Catholic Church still stands outside the World Council of Churches. The Orthodox are fully involved in ecumenical dialogue, although their doctrine of the church severely limits the recognition they can give to other churches. However, in the last quarter of the twentieth century, both Roman Catholics and Orthodox engaged in theological dialogue with other world communions, notably the Anglicans, Lutherans, Methodists, and Reformed.

EVANGELICALS AND UNITY

Evangelicalism has largely been suspicious of ecumenical dialogue, and even more so of ecumenical action. The call to live in organic unity with all believers has been in tension with a concern for doctrinal purity for the sake of the gospel. Evangelicalism has a

POPE JOHN XXIII

John XXIII was born Angelo Giuseppe Roncalli near Bergamo, Italy, in 1881 and died in 1963. His parents were tenant farmers, but scholarships enabled him to attend seminaries at Bergamo and Rome, where he was ordained in 1904. After serving in World War I, he filled administrative posts at Rome until appointed papal nuncio, and in 1953 Cardinal Patriarch of Venice. His energy, charity, and ability to get on with people of all persuasions marked out his early career.

Roncalli's election, at the age of seventy-six, in the difficult conclave which followed the death of Pius XII in 1958, suggested he would be a caretaker pope. Instead, he began a new age in the Roman Catholic Church. He issued eight encyclicals. *Mater et Magistra* (1961) updated papal social teaching, insisting that co-operation between individuals and social groups, rather than national or class struggle, is the basic principle of social order, and stressing for the first time the duty of developed nations to aid emerging nations by technological means. *Pacem in Terris* (1963) argued that peace flows from right order, that all nations are equal in dignity, and that co-operation and trust must replace the arms race. John XXIII urged reconciliation during the world political crises over Berlin, Cuba, and Algeria. He elevated many clergymen from developing nations to the posts of bishop and cardinals, sought closer ties with Eastern Orthodoxy, sent representatives to the World Council of Churches, and set up the Vatican Secretariat for Promoting Christian Unity.

The aim of all his work was to update the church, '*aggiornamento*'. Accordingly he created a commission to revise canon law. The peak of his achievement was the Second Vatican Council (1962–65), which he called to improve the pastoral work of the church. Once the council opened, the pope intervened rarely, but liberal bishops took courage from his stand. Whether John XXIII was responsible for shaping post-Vatican II Catholicism is doubtful. His actions before and after becoming pope show him swinging between conservatism and liberalism. His personal spiritual notes, published posthumously as *Journal of a Soul*, reveals a deep, but traditional, piety. His peasant background and appearance tended to obscure his wide learning. Although he discouraged the cult of personality, his kindliness and wit made him a charismatic and popular pope.

JOHN P. DONNELLY

built-in tendency towards separation, traced in history from the Anabaptist and other radical groupings of the Reformation, through the Pilgrim Fathers, Puritans, Baptists, and Quakers in the seventeenth century, to the Methodists of the eighteenth century, and the Brethren movement of the nineteenth century. In the twentieth century, the church saw the formation of the Pentecostals and 'Restorationist' or house churches. The charismatic movement and the rise of the house churches tended to draw adherents away from the historic, mainstream churches into more exciting, yet more uniform, groupings. Charismatics would claim that a shared experience of the Holy Spirit has a uniting power across the denominational divide, and exposes a longing for spiritual union without which structural renewal is sterile.

There are other divisive tensions within the world's churches. There is a traditional split between those who are doctrinally conservative and those who are more liberal. For some the divide is political – churches differ, for example, over how to resist dictatorial governments. For others the tension lies in their own organization and structures: for example, some churches do not view the ordination of women as conformable to the Bible or their own tradition. There is also the constant issue of the position of the Christian church on non-Christian religions, which are now found in strength in the Western world, as well as in Africa, India, and Asia.

Organic union between denominations has been achieved. Perhaps the most notable have been the creation of the united Churches of South India (1927), North India (1970), Pakistan (1970), and Bangladesh (1971). In 1972 in Great Britain, Congregationalists joined Presbyterians to form the United Reformed Church, and added the Churches of Christ to their union in 1982.

The concern of the Orthodox Church for Christian unity, the emergence of the Church of Rome as a partner in ecumenical discussions, and the impact of the charismatic movement, have totally changed ecumenical relationships.

COLIN BUCHANAN

CHAPTER 42

AN AGE OF LIBERATION

When we survey the expansion of Christianity in the twentieth century, three historical facts of particular importance emerge. First, the modern missionary movement had its base in the West at a time when, as a result of the Industrial Revolution, the West had become politically and economically dominant. Second, missionaries carried not only Christianity, but also values and perspectives typical of Western society and associated with modernity: a naturalistic worldview. Finally, missionary work contributed to the disruption of order in traditional non-Western societies, and brought a new desire for development. A revolutionary situation was created, which eventually led to liberation.

These facts are basic to understanding the role that Christianity has played in the modern search for national liberation, and also the challenge to the church that the current revolutionary mood presents. The church today has to face the demands of an age of liberation that its missionary thrust has been largely responsible for ushering in.

A WORLDWIDE CHURCH

As a result of the work of the voluntary missionary societies – established first in Western Europe, and then in the United States – the 'younger churches' in the non-Western world bore the hallmarks of their origin, and depended heavily on foreign leaders for many years. Even so, they vividly demonstrated that the Christian faith is for all people. By the end of the nineteenth century, there were only a few regions where the Christian gospel had not been preached, and a few countries – such as Afghanistan, Tibet, and Nepal – remained closed to missionaries. A worldwide Christian community had been created.

Four distinct factors contributed to the missionary movement responsible for this dramatic change.

- In the first place, Protestant missions were rooted in the Evangelical Awakening of the eighteenth century. The Awakening emphasized personal conversion and holiness of life, an emphasis that in turn became one of the characteristics of the 'younger churches' of the non-Western world.
- Second, 'the great century' of missions saw amazing achievements both by Protestants and by the Roman Catholic Church. Various countries in Europe – especially France and Belgium, and later Holland and Ireland – became the base of Roman Catholic missions.
- Third, missionary advance coincided with the heyday of Western imperialism. The modern mission movement cannot be understood in isolation from political, economic, and cultural imperialism.
- Finally, the modern missionary movement – particularly in its Protestant form – was initially a revolutionary force. It confronted the traditional societies of the non-Western world with a message of freedom and a 'modern' outlook that challenged the old values. In many lands, missionaries were pioneers in various fields of human endeavour, particularly in higher education and medicine. In some cases their efforts were rewarded by the emergence of an educated Christian elite which had an influence out of all proportion to its numbers.

The first World Missionary Conference, held in Edinburgh in 1910, heralded the situation that the church was to attain in the twentieth century. The conference took place at a time when a combination of forces was beginning to threaten the destruction of Christianity in the countries of Western Europe which until then had been the basis of its expansion. Throughout the nineteenth century, the development of science and technology, followed by industrialization, urbanization, and the disruption of traditional patterns of society, had been producing a revolution that was accompanied by a growing secularization of life and the abandonment of faith by millions of European Christians. Edinburgh marked the end of an epoch, but also pointed towards a new age – the age of liberation – when the worldwide movement that had taken shape through missionary work was to come into its own. It pointed to the displacement of Christianity from its traditional centre, which was entering a so-called 'post-Christian' era, to a new one in the world beyond Europe.

THE EVANGELIZATION OF THE WORLD IN THIS GENERATION

Of more than 1,200 representatives at Edinburgh, only seventeen came from the 'younger churches': eight from India, one from Burma, three from China, one from Korea, and four from Japan. Latin America was completely omitted, for it was regarded as a Christian continent. Although the church had by then become a global fellowship, it reflected a church colonialism that paralleled contemporary political colonialism. In line with the recommendations of the organizing committee, each participating missionary society – the delegates represented missionary societies rather than churches – sent some of its 'leading missionaries' and 'if practicable, one or two natives'.

The Edinburgh Conference demonstrated a growing interest in missionary work among Christians in Western Europe and the United States, and the remarkable influence of the Student Volunteer Movement. The vision of the SVM was summed up in the watchword, 'The Evangelization of the World in this Generation', which had helped numerous students to feel a responsibility for world missions. But it also threw into relief a problem that for many years remained unsolved, at least for a large portion of the missionary movement: resistance on the part of missions to establishing truly indigenous churches – 'self-governing, self-supporting, and self-propagating', according to Henry Venn's dictum.

THE CHURCHES MULTIPLY

World War I marked a new stage in the modern revolutionary age, and in the history of Christianity. Having reached its peak of world power, Western Europe began to experience a decline that culminated in the liberation of its colonies. Meanwhile, the process of secularization, which had gained ground during the nineteenth century, accelerated so greatly that it became doubtful whether Christianity would survive in what was traditionally called Christendom.

Paradoxically, in the non-Western countries where, in 1914, Christians were still very small minorities, the churches – particularly the Protestant churches – began to display an unexpected vitality. But soon they had to face the same revolutionary forces that Christianity had helped to create, and that the West had faced and spread to the rest of the world during the nineteenth century. After 1914, these revolutionary forces continued to mount, until they formed the greatest challenge that Christianity had yet faced.

Although in Europe many observers claimed that the post-Christian era had arrived, Christianity continued to advance in the rest of the world. In the United States, church membership continued to rise in proportion to the growth in population. Missionary interest grew so strong that, by the time the USA had become a world power, it had also become the headquarters of the Protestant missionary movement, and began to contribute greatly to Roman Catholic missions. By 1973, seventy per cent of all Protestant missionaries in the world – and an even higher proportion of the total cost of the missionary operation – was estimated to originate from North America. Christianity influenced the institutions of the nation. Each US President after Jimmy Carter claimed to be a Christian, and the Moral Majority Movement tried to make a clear connection between Christian values and the American way of life, which President Reagan especially decked in evangelistic terms.

But by far the most amazing numerical growth of the church in the twentieth century took place in the Third World.

ASIAN EXPANSION

In Japan, where the centenary of the re-launching of Roman Catholic missions and the beginning of Protestant missions was celebrated in 1959, the results were not very impressive in terms of numbers. Yet after 1914 the percentage of Christians – more than half of them Protestant – increased faster than the population. At the early stages, Christianity appealed chiefly to the intelligentsia; but then, with the influx of North American missionaries after 1945, it began to attract people of lower income. In 1914, there were more than 100,000 Roman Catholics in Japan, growing to 500,000 in 2010. In 2010 there were over 555,000 Japanese Protestants.

In Korea – the 'hermit kingdom' – in 1914 there were approximately 80,000 Roman Catholics and 96,000 Protestants. Despite political problems caused by empire-building nations in the years between World War I and World War II, the number of Christians continued to increase remarkably. After World War II and the invasion of South Korea by North Korea in 1950, Christians – like the rest of the population – suffered greatly. But once the armistice was signed, in July 1953, Christianity began to flourish in the South, encouraged by the efforts of North American missionaries. It is estimated that Roman Catholic and Protestant Christians now number fifteen million, out of a population of forty-eight million, and that there are some 50,000 Protestant churches. However, in North Korea, as in China, the organized church has faced great difficulties.

In a few countries of South-East Asia and the fringing islands, the rate of church growth since World War II surpassed that of the population. For instance, in Indonesia, the number of Christians increased from four million in 1964 to eleven million in 1970, the greatest growth being registered in northern Sumatra, East Java, Kalimantan (Borneo), and the islands of Nias and Timor, where thousands of Muslims were converted to Christianity. In 2010 there were 37 million Christians out of a population of 232 million. In Myanmar, Buddhism was declared the state religion in 1961, and the 'Burmese way to Socialism' – established by a military government in 1965 – did not allow the presence of foreigners. In spite of this, Christianity was said to be growing in such a way that by 1972 a new church was being organized every week. Ten years later there were over 7,000 congregations, amounting to nearly two million Christians, and in 2010 four and a half million Christians. Since World War II, the number of Christians has also multiplied in Cambodia, Hong Kong, and Taiwan.

In addition various countries that had traditionally remained closed to missionaries from abroad changed that policy, noticeably the Himalayan kingdoms of Bhutan, Sikkim, Nepal, and the Tibetan refugee kingdom on the Indian border. The first church in Bhutan was organized in 1970, with P. S. Tingbo as its pastor. Meanwhile, in the subcontinent of India, restrictions were placed on the entrance of missionaries in the years that followed independence (1947), but this resulted in an unprecedented growth of the national leadership in the church. Christianity, represented by the Syrian Orthodox Church, or Mar Thoma (the oldest Christian community, claiming to have originated with the apostle Thomas), Catholicism and Protestantism, gained ground, especially among the underprivileged and the animistic tribes on India's northern frontiers. By 2010 the Christian population was over seventy million. Afghanistan, perhaps the largest unevangelized nation in the world, remained closed to the gospel.

In the Pacific, some tribes in Papua New Guinea were practically unaware of the existence of the white man until the middle of the twentieth century. But missionaries representing fifteen different Protestant organizations and several Roman Catholic orders entered the island, and today the great majority of the population – 95 per cent, according to recent estimates – claim to be Christian, the greater number of them Protestant.

ADVANCE IN AFRICA

There was a startling advance of Christianity in Africa, with an increased rate of church growth after World War II, when a large number of African nations were becoming independent.

From the nineteenth century on, thousands of Africans had been educated in mission schools, frequently subsidized by the colonial governments. For both Protestant and Catholic missionaries, education had been so common that it could be claimed that for most African Christians the mission school was the door to the church. After World War I, great stress had been laid – particularly by the Roman Catholics – on building up a complete educational system, from primary to university levels. By the early 1920s, in British Africa alone, there were about 6,000 mission schools, compared with 100 government schools.

With the coming of independence – in the 1950s and 1960s for most African countries – the new governments increasingly took control of mission schools. Yet the number of Christians continued to increase – although growth varied from country to country – and in some areas the educated class returned to the churches. A revival movement, which had begun in Ruanda-Urundi in 1935, influenced the life of the churches in Uganda, Kenya, and Tanzania. African independent churches proliferated right across the continent south of the Sahara, notably in South Africa, Nigeria, Zaire, Ghana, and Kenya. By 2010 there were 38 million Christians in South Africa, 62 million in Congo-DRC (formerly Zaire), 81 million in Nigeria, 28 million in Uganda and 24 million in Tanzania. By denomination, in Africa there were some 165 million Roman Catholics, 150 million Protestants, 100 million independent Protestants, 50 million Anglicans, and 46 million Orthodox, and 21 million unaffiliated.

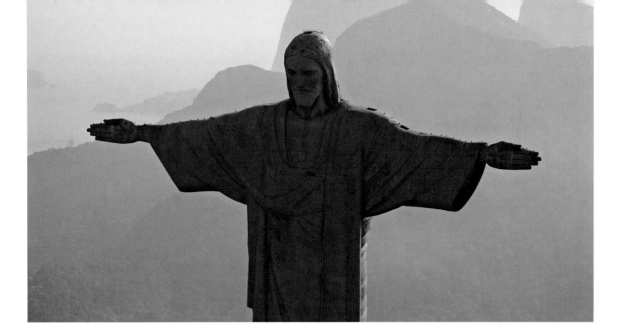

LATIN AMERICAN GROWTH

In Latin America – regarded for centuries as a Christian continent – Protestantism grew at an astonishing rate during the first three-quarters of the twentieth century. In 1914, Protestant Christians were a minority of 500,000, often persecuted by the official church; by 1975 there were more than twenty-five million, with nearly fifteen million of these in Brazil alone. In 2010 there were 61 million Protestants, 41 million independent Protestants, and 422 million Roman Catholics. One Latin American writer claimed this is 'the only area in the world where a Christian church is growing more rapidly than the population' (Emilio Castro). The greatest growth was among the Pentecostals, who made up over 60 per cent of the Protestant total, and the Seventh-Day Adventists. Among Roman Catholics, the great new development in the 1980s was the 'base communities', of which tens of thousands exist, especially in Brazil. Poor people study the Bible in the light of their own experience of oppression, and find it comes to life.

By 1975 more than 3,000 Third World missionaries – mostly Asian – were also at work abroad. The great new fact of the century was an exploding worldwide Christian movement, advancing mainly among the masses of the non-Western world, and with a growing concern to make disciples among all nations.

OBSTACLES TO GROWTH

The expansion of Christianity outside Europe during the twentieth century is undoubtedly impressive. But there are still many largely unevangelized areas, particularly the Muslim countries of the Near East, the Middle East, and North Africa, but also within countries with a growing percentage of Christians. For instance, in the state of Himachal Pradesh, India, only one in a thousand is a Christian.

When the Communists took over China in 1949, there were fewer than one million Protestants, and about two million Roman Catholics. Stories of a persecuted church circulated which, along with government disinformation, led many to believe the church had

Statue of *Cristo Redentor* (Christ the Redeemer), Rio de Janeiro, Brazil, created by Paul Landowski.
PHOTODISC

virtually died out under the strains of the Cultural Revolution. However, when in 1979 churches began to open again for worship, they were filled to overflowing; far from dying out, the church had grown remarkably. In 2010 it is estimated there were 30 million Protestants, 21 million Roman Catholics, and 55 million independent Protestants. The Roman Catholic Church is split between the government approved Catholic Patriotic Association and a persecuted church loyal to the Vatican. Protestantism embraces both the officially recognized Three-Self Patriotic Movement and the House Church movement. In some places the house churches are simply extensions of the Three-Self movement, but elsewhere they embrace those who would not wish to be so associated. In 1989, the Three-Self organization courageously gave vocal support to the students' agitation for greater democracy.

RELIGION REVIVES WORLDWIDE

The phenomenal growth of the church in the last several decades is part of a much wider revival of religion taking place all over the world. Evidence of this revival includes the way occultism and Asian religions have come to flourish in the West; the resurgence of Islam in Africa, Malaysia, and Pakistan; the revival of Buddhism in Thailand, Vietnam, Cambodia, Burma, and Sri Lanka; of Hinduism in India; and of Shintoism in Japan; the vitality of Spiritism – and especially of *Umbanda* – in Brazil; and of the *Sokka Gakkai* in Japan. Fundamentalist movements have flourished: Islamic, Jewish in Israel, Protestant in North America, and Roman Catholic in Spain's 'Opus Dei'. If it is true that 'The Industrial Revolution has become a kind of irresistible bulldozer forcing a way for Western civilization into the non-Western areas of the World', it is also true that in this 'globalized world' – bewitched by the achievements of Western civilization – people continue to search for answers to their deep existential questions.

It is significant that the greatest growth of the church in the twentieth century took place among animistic peoples, and among the deprived classes in the cities. Contemporary mass movements to Christianity in the Third World – like other flourishing religious movements — seem to be both a result of the impact of Western civilization upon traditional societies, and a reaction against it.

The revolution that the West has brought to the values and lifestyle of millions in the rest of the world can hardly be exaggerated. To cope with this revolution, many people are turning to religion — but not mainly to Westernized Christianity, with its bad associations from colonial times. They are turning either to an resurgent ancient religion — sometimes championed by nationalistic political leaders who use it to create a new national identity — or to a 'native' version of Christianity — sometimes strongly nationalistic and tolerating ancient ideas and customs — that takes into account aspects of human life that the Western Church left out. In Africa, for instance, the independent churches are said to attract around 450,000 people a year from the traditional churches, both Roman Catholic and Protestant; in Latin America, Pentecostalism — 'the only Christian movement with real indigenous roots,' according to many observers — is the least dependent upon foreign personnel and finance. If the survival of Christianity is not in doubt in the Third World, the survival of churches founded by Western missionaries and soaked in Western culture certainly is.

In any event, the church in the Third World is threatened by a number of problems.

CHRISTIANITY AND CULTURE

Some Western missionaries have labelled as 'syncretism' legitimate efforts to express Christianity through indigenous cultural patterns, all too easily assuming that the new churches have to pattern themselves on models imported from abroad. Undoubtedly one reason for the proliferation of 'indigenous' Christian movements is many missionaries' lack of cultural sensitivity.

However, some of the mass movements with a high rate of numerical growth may be no more than 'baptized heathenism'. For many people in the Third World, Christianity has become a symbol of modernity, alongside which non-Christian views and customs are allowed to survive. For example, in New Guinea and other areas, new Christians followed a 'cargo cult', constructing installations on the seashore in the hope that God — the 'higher power' they supposed had sent the white man and the many material objects that had arrived by sea and air — would make them rich. In Africa, the practice of polygamy and witchcraft, and the use of charms and fetishes, often co-exist with outward acceptance of the Christian faith. In some areas of Latin America, adherence to Christianity does not necessarily imply a complete break from Spiritism.

TOO MANY DENOMINATIONS?

A more common problem is what may be called the 'over-denominationalism' of the church in the Third World. In Africa alone, approximately 100 new 'independent' groups are founded every year, and the same trend is present in Asia and Latin America. Denominational allegiance is one of the major hindrances to mission in the Third World.

But it must be remembered that in 1900 there were 61 Western missions working in China, a number that increased to 92 by 1913. From the beginning, the church in non-Western countries has been split by imported divisions. The younger churches of Africa, Asia, and Latin America have in turn produced their own divisions, often brought about by individualistic leaders who have little or no concern for the unity of the body of Christ.

Western missionaries took to the Third World not only the Christian gospel, but also a Western naturalistic outlook. They carried a world-view in which disease and disaster were explained in terms of the natural law of cause and effect, and the supernatural restricted to a small area of human experience. They stressed technological responsibility for the natural world, rather than interdependence with the environment, and brought with them a sharp division between the sacred and the secular, according to which secular matters lay outside the orbit of religion.

The result of such missionary work, conditioned by Western secularism, was churches in which a sharp separation was taken for granted between the sacred and the secular – and therefore between the church and the world, faith and works, religion and daily life. An Asian author states that, as a result, the churches in Asia 'are living spiritually and socially in what are called mission compounds, 'Christian ghettoes' of their own creation, inward-looking and concerned with themselves'. An African has said that the church there is 'suffering from a conservatism which makes it look like a relic of medieval European Christianity, deposited here and left to rust and rot away'. For such reasons the leaders of the new nations are increasingly rejecting Christianity as irrelevant to practical life.

Isolation from society is a matter of deep concern to Christians who observe the church in the light of the radical social, political, and economic changes taking place in the developing countries. They claim that, if the churches that have emerged out of the Western missionary enterprise are more interested in their numerical growth as religious institutions than in the meaning and practice of Christian discipleship in a revolutionary situation, the future of Christianity in the Third World is in question.

THE CHINESE EXPERIENCE

Such concerns are illustrated by the struggle of the Chinese Church since the Communist takeover of China in 1949, when all foreign missionaries were required to leave the country. By that date, a Protestant Church of less than a million and a Roman Catholic Church of some two million strong had developed as the fruit of patient missionary endeavours, but concern was essentially restricted to personal salvation, and thus Chinese Christianity up to that time failed to make any mark upon the structures of Chinese society.

The years of 'The Great Leap Forward', of Mao Zedong's Red Guards, and of the Cultural Revolution that followed, all put the church under great pressure. In 1951, denominational Christianity was replaced by the Three-Self Patriotic Movement, which – whatever its faults – represented a genuinely Chinese form of church organization, independent of mission boards in the West. In 1967, the formation of a Catholic Patriotic Association sought to nurture a continuing Catholicism independent of Vatican control, but not all Roman Catholics accepted this, and so a split occurred. Similarly some Protestants – especially those associated with local house churches – were not prepared to work within the Three-Self Movement, with its search for a church which would be self-supporting, self-administering, and self-propagating. They judged the movement to be too closely associated with the state, though the Three-Self Movement, along with other Christians, suffered in the years of persecution.

The church, in fact, more than survived, emerging in 1979 stronger and more Chinese. A woman who had been a church-worker before the Cultural Revolution testifies to how, before the Cultural Revolution, 'my only contact with those outside the church was as objects of evangelization. It seemed I always assumed a higher status.' But eight years working in a factory enabled her to find a new identity with ordinary factory workers and their needs, providing both opportunities for practical service, and a place to confess her faith from within the community of workers.

So, when the churches reopened in 1979, there were many new believers and seekers anxious to attend. The church had more than doubled in numbers; some suggest it had grown even faster. In subsequent years, the Anglican Bishop Ting Kuang-hsun (b. 1915) and other leaders of the China Christian Council began to travel extensively abroad, conferences were held, institutions reopened, and Bibles were printed. The constitution of 1982 provided for the rights of religious believers, with the proviso that they should be free of foreign control.

Post-Mao China found itself in desperate need of modernization, and the need for outside help to aid that process was reluctantly agreed by an ageing leadership. But with economic modernization and the opening up of education overseas to Chinese students, the demand for greater democratization developed. This burst through the system on the occasion of Mikhail Gorbachev's visit to Beijing, in the summer of 1989, when large numbers of students defied the security forces by gathering in force in Tiananmen Square. In this they had the support of the leadership of the China Christian Council, and at first it looked as if their peaceful protests might prevail; but the security forces were apparently only biding their time before taking action.

The most urgent question confronting the churches in the Third World today is whether Christianity has anything to say to the millions of people struggling against poverty and social injustice, and searching for liberation and development. However, the tendency to reduce the gospel to a 'spiritual' message, and fail to be concerned for social righteousness, seem to be constant features of Christianity in the Third World, as they have been of Christianity in the West for several centuries.

A WESTERN GOSPEL

During the heyday of Western political imperialism, which came to a close in 1914, few missionaries could have suspected that their alliance with the world powers would in time become a danger to them, and an embarrassment to the younger churches that resulted from their work. Most missionaries simply took it for granted that Western prestige and power should be used in the service of Christ – as they were – though some courageously opposed aspects of their own governments' colonial policies. But it is indisputable that missionary work was done from a position of political and economic power, and with an assumption of Western racial and cultural superiority.

World War I did much damage to the image of the 'Christian West', an image that was completely shattered by World War II. Within a few years, the age of Western political imperialism was brought to an end, giving way to an age marked by the liberation of 'new nations'. This change resulted immediately in a resurgence of nationalism and traditional values; several countries, notably India, were closed to foreign missionaries. It looked as if circumstances would force the 'young churches' to depend completely on their own leaders and finance.

But American Protestant missions – almost wholly dependent on American personnel, leadership, and finances – grew in numbers during the same period. For the Western missionary movement, the age of liberation had hardly dawned. Many Christian churches, institutions, and movements in the Third World continued to live in a 'colonial' situation, heavily dependent on foreign resources, and therefore subject to foreign control. Despite the progress made towards genuine independence, Christians in the developing countries were caught in a situation in which economic and cultural imperialism had hardly been broken, even though its outward appearance had changed.

The mentality of colonial dependence also lingers in the 'younger churches'. An African writer said: 'The church in Africa has for too long been very missionary minded, but only in terms of receiving missionaries and depending on them.' The missionary movement has been slow to recognize the importance of partnership in Christian work; Christianity is still commonly regarded as a Western religion, and the Christian mission still generally identified with a white face.

PARTNERS IN MISSION

The church has become a worldwide community, its emergence as such coinciding with the emergence of a 'global consciousness' – the sense shared by a large part of humanity that they belong to one world, and that all nations share a common destiny. The 'parity' between older and younger churches was brought to the fore – as never before – at the Second World Missionary Conference, held at Jerusalem in 1928. At the next World Missionary Conference, in Madras in 1938, the emergence of a worldwide Christian community was reflected by the presence of delegates from nearly 50 countries, many of them from the non-Western world. This conference also insisted that mission and the creation of indigenous churches must be closely linked. But it was at the enlarged meeting of the International Missionary Council, held at Whitby, Canada, in 1947, that the church was confronted with the need to break down the distinction between older and younger churches, and face its global responsibility: '... emphasis centred upon missionaries as agents of the church universal whose responsibilities, like those of their national colleagues with whom they should be on a par, would be determined by their training and ability.' Yet many of this council's recommendations have still not been put into practice many years later.

This reluctance by missions to heed the call to partnership – even in the post-colonial situation – explains the call for a moratorium by the Commission on World Mission and Evangelism of the World Council of Churches at its assembly at Bangkok in 1973. It recommended that mission agencies consider stopping sending funds and personnel to particular churches for a period of time, as 'a possible strategy of mission in certain situations'. The debate that followed, especially among conservative Evangelicals, was characterized by more heat than light. The All-Africa Conference of Churches turned up the heat by adopting the moratorium at its meeting at Nairobi the same year, adding: 'Should the moratorium cause missionary agencies to crumble, the African Church could have performed a service in redeeming God's people in the Northern Hemisphere from a distorted view of the mission of the church in the world.' However, the International Congress on World Evangelism, at Lausanne in 1974, recognized in its Covenant that 'a reduction of foreign missionaries may sometimes be necessary to facilitate the national church's growth in self-reliance and release resources for unevangelized areas.' By the time of the follow-up conference in Manila in 1989, these truths had become common ground in the Evangelical movement.

After the Lausanne Congress, at which a number of critical issues had been brought up – mainly by Third World speakers – it became increasingly clear that even the most traditional missionary agencies could no longer avoid the issue of world partnership in the Christian mission. The Lausanne Covenant claimed that 'a new missionary era has dawned' and that 'a growing partnership of churches will develop and the universal character of Christ's church will be more clearly exhibited.' In 1976 executives from the North American Evangelical Foreign Missions Association and the International Foreign Missions Association – who together controlled one third of the Protestant missionaries in Latin America – met representatives of the Latin American churches, in Quito, Ecuador. Frank discussion of such painful realities as 'the ecclesiological crisis, the phenomenon of dependence, and the too-frequent failure to reach true brotherly interdependence' showed that changes were taking place in the relationship between the 'younger churches' and missionary agencies.

LEADING THEIR OWN PEOPLE

At the same time, parallel progress was made by the Roman Catholic Church. Already in his encyclical, *Maximum Illud* (1919), Pope Benedict XV had admitted that, in some regions where the Catholic faith had been present for centuries, there were no indigenous clergy except those of a lower order, and they had not produced 'bishops to rule them, or priests capable of making a deep impression on their fellow-citizens'. It took several years for this situation to be altered. The first six Chinese bishops were consecrated there in 1926; an Indian in 1923, a Japanese in 1927, an Annabite and a Sri Lankan in 1933, a Korean in 1937, and an African not until 1939. In the following years, however, a rapid multiplication of bishops, archbishops, and even cardinals occurred in the Third World. The attitude towards foreign missionaries was summarised by the Association of the Members of the Episcopal Conferences of Eastern Africa (AMECEA) at its 1973 meeting in Nairobi: foreign missionaries were needed to support and to train national leaders, and their presence showed the universality of the church. The movement from missionary paternalism to partnership in mission was painfully slow; but by the mid-1970s it had become clear the process was irreversible.

TOTALITY OF HUMAN LIFE

The greatest challenge that confronts the church is applying Christianity to practical life in a world plagued by poverty, social injustice, racial discrimination, oppression, and driven by secularism and materialism.

Among Protestants, there is evidence of a growing concern to bridge the separation between religion and life, evangelism and social action, although a number of missionary strategists continue to emphasize the numerical growth of the church, applying techniques derived from North American industry and commerce. Within Roman Catholicism, Vatican II opened the windows of an old church structures.

C. RENÉ PADILLA

FURTHER READING

Jeremy Morris, *The Church in the Modern Age*, London, 2007.
Philip Kennedy, *Twentieth Century Theologians: A New Introduction*, London, 2009.
Ian Breward, *A History of the Churches in Australasia*, Oxford, 2001.
Grant Wacker, *Heaven Below: Early Pentecostals and American Culture*, Cambridge, MA, 2001.

STUDY QUESTIONS

1. Why was there a strong movement towards Christian unity in the twentieth century?

2. World War I or World War II: Which had the most damaging impact on the church in the West? Why?

3. How did the Protestant church in Germany respond to the rise of Nazism?

4. In what ways did the church in the developing world develop distinctively?

5. What was the effect of Pentecostalism and the Charismatic Movement upon the church in the twentieth century?

6. How and why did Christian missions change during the twentieth century?

7. What is secularism and how did it impact the church?

8. Compare and contrast the contribution of Billy Graham and C. S. Lewis to twentieth century Christianity.

9. Did Marxism have a legitimate contribution to make to Christianity?

10. What were the main challenges confronting the church in the late twentieth century?

8 Epilogue

A New Millennium

Today, Christianity is primarily a faith of the developing, rather than developed, world. Although European and American missionaries planted Christianity in regions such as Asia and Africa, these are now largely self-sufficient. The phenomenal growth of Christianity across the southern continents in modern times is unprecedented; millions in Latin America, Africa, and Asia embrace it. The advent of huge migrations from the southern continents into Europe and North America is resulting in the appearance of 'Southern' forms of Christianity in great urban centres of the Western world, where they often become the largest and most dynamic Christian communities.

The growth of non-Western churches in contexts characterized by ongoing dialogue with other faiths holds the promise that fresh insights into the meaning of Christ and his salvation will emerge from these new heartlands during the twenty-first century. Non-Western churches are overwhelmingly churches of the poor, in a world shaped by economic globalization.

Eastern Orthodoxy has resurfaced in Russia and other East European nations since the collapse of Communism. The movement of Christianity eastwards has often been an untold story, but its significance will increase as China moves centre stage in world history. Christianity is again in a missionary situation in the West, as Christendom fades into secularism.

A new phase in the history of the Christian church has begun, with momentous implications for the future.

CHAPTER 43

PRESENT AND FUTURE
The church in an ever-changing world

The leaders of the Enlightenment in the eighteenth century, the positivists of the nineteenth century, and orthodox Marxist thinkers in the twentieth century all agreed on one thing. They believed that advances in scientific understanding would give birth to a world in which religion would die at the hand of an ever more confident secularism.

With the emergence of the new, almost entirely man-made, environment of the city-dwellers of the late twentieth century, old moral landmarks seem to have been supplanted. Society is less conscious of its roots and its direction. Pluralist in culture, it operates on essentially pragmatic and empirical considerations: does it work, and how does it fit with our experience? 'Computers,' as a Russian scientist remarked, 'know no morality, only mathematics'.

Over against this 'scientific secularization', popular superstitions – such as luck, fate, and astrology – continue to command support, even in technological societies. Nonetheless, churches continue to grow and to develop new ways of attempting to be relevant to human needs. Alongside this, there is a resurgence of other world faiths, which raises the question of how different religions can live together in the modern world. The Christian church has to consider to what extent dialogue is a legitimate aspect of mission.

Western historians, although confident about the inevitability of secularization, nonetheless now have to learn how to spell Ayatollah and al-Qaeda. Others involved with global politics have to distinguish different traditions within Islam, to understand a world that stretches from Nigeria to Indonesia. Students of anthropology stress the similarities between all fundamentalisms, noting the significance for international relations of such religious intransigence. In fact, no one can hope to understand the modern world without a thorough mastery of the nature of religious belief and practice. Religion is very much alive – which is not to deny the decline in church membership and attendance in the 'Christian West', with the 1960s identified as the critical decade in this respect.

WORLD IN TURMOIL

Early in the twenty-first century, on the morning of 11 September 2001, the security of the Western world was severely challenged, when nineteen militant Islamic fundamentalists associated with al-Qaeda, using hijacked passenger aircraft, carried out a series of attacks on targets of iconic significance in the USA. Two aircraft were flown into the twin towers of the World Trade Center in New York City, causing both to collapse within two hours, and giving little hope of survival for those working above the points of impact. A third aircraft was flown into the Pentagon in Washington, whilst a fourth plane, intended to crash into Washington's Capitol Building, fell to the ground in Pennsylvania, after some of the passengers attempted to overcome the hijackers. Altogether just short of 3,000 people lost their lives that morning, including the nineteen hijackers.

The United States responded to these attacks by launching the so-called 'War on Terror', invading Afghanistan to depose the *Taliban*, which had harboured al-Qaeda. This military engagement was to cause further loss of life to America and her allies, not to mention innocent civilians caught up in the conflict, in more than ten years of warfare. Given this history, it has sometimes been difficult to distance Islam as a world faith from the violence of those who promote *jihad*, or holy war.

A different kind of conflict began in December 2010, when the so-called Arab Spring spread across North Africa and the Middle East, forcing from power authoritarian rulers in Tunisia, Libya, Egypt, and Yemen, and challenging rulers in Syria and Bahrain. In this process, those rulers deriving their strength from minority Islamic groups – such as President Assad of Syria, with his Alawite base in a predominately Sunni country – were particularly vulnerable. Nor did secular governments fare very well, while Islamic parties often succeeded, leaving questions as to how – once in power – they would treat Christian minorities.

RACE AND NATIONALITY

A largely post-colonial world still faces many problems associated with race. In the last decades of the twentieth century, this was clearly focused in the struggle against apartheid in South Africa, where the Dutch Reformed Church finally abandoned its attempts to underpin the doctrine of apartheid with theological argument. But for many years it failed to use its influence with sufficient urgency to hasten the coming of a government that would effectively reflect the multi-racial nature of South African society. Other Christians and churches understood the Bible to insist that all people are God's creatures and require equal respect, seeking an end to injustice, and accepting the personal cost demanded by their Christian discipleship.

In the changing world of the former Soviet Union, ethnic diversity presented major problems. This was seen both in the southern and central Asian republics, and in the north, where old Baltic nationalisms became vocal – though by the end of the Cold War many ethnic

The Crystal Cathedral, Garden Grove, Southern California, USA, founded by Robert H. Schuller in 1955. The reflective glass building was designed by Philip Johnson. In 2012 the building was sold to the Roman Catholic Church for use as a Roman Catholic cathedral.
© DEVIN070205CHEN/DREAMSTIME.COM

Russians were resident in the newly-independent republics. Ethnicity is a worldwide phenomenon. There is, for instance, Basque separatism in Spain, and the demands of the Hungarian minority in Romania. In Asia, similar ethnic questions strain the peace, with the Kurds ill-used by several different states. Tamils have revolted and been repressed in Sri Lanka, and Tibetans continue to resent government from Beijing. Religion is often at the heart of a people's culture, and in many places ethnic divisions have been reinforced by credal divisions in a variety of political power struggles: Christian against Muslim in Nigeria and in the Lebanon; Sikh against Hindu in India; Muslim verses Muslim in the Gulf; and Christian versus Christian in Northern Ireland.

Elsewhere the moral issue of racial integrity and ethnic rights is seen in the land-claims of the North and South American Indians, and those of the Maoris and Aborigines in Australasia. Such claims are made by indigenous peoples all around the world, who have seen their best land taken over by settlers from overseas. This is the mirror image of the plight of the world's refugees: exiled from their own land, they have increased vastly in number and range in the later twentieth and early twenty-first century.

Although migration may provide the solution for a few individuals, the problems of an unjust international order leave many peoples without hope. Third World debts, the arbitrary pressures of international commodity prices for primary products, and the fact that every year in Third World countries more days' work are needed to secure the same technological necessities, leave many communities without reasonable hope of orderly economic development. In the short term, all these factors present problems of survival for the Southern poor, and in the longer term challenge the stability of East and West, North and South.

At times the power of the nation state has been questioned. In Eastern Europe, in the late 1980s people's power became a formidable agent for large-scale changes. Elsewhere, the elected government has been shown to be the pawn of a well-entrenched military cadre. On the one hand, we witness the inability of the authorities in arguably the most powerful nation on the earth to intervene effectively against the arbitrary action of hostage-takers, hijackers, and other terrorists, or to force a determined aggressor to implement peace terms. On the other, the weakest nations know well that many a transnational company wields more effective power than they can ever hope to employ.

At another extreme, the late twentieth century saw the emergence of extra-national organizations deploying immense influence over sovereign states. The most obvious example is the European Economic Community, the nature of whose powers has been hotly contested. Meanwhile, central bureaucracies in many countries do not allow their citizens meaningful participation in the decision-making crucial to their future welfare.

THE END OF COMMUNISM?

Within Russia, China, and the Eastern bloc, questions were raised as to the viability of the Communist system of production. Working for the state, or for the future advance of Communism, was no guarantee of a well-motivated work force; some more immediate incentive to secure adequate effort seemed to be required. This called for basic changes, not only in the economic, but also in the political sphere, and so, in Russia, President Mikhail Gorbachev advocated both *glasnost* (openness) and *perestroika* (restructuring).

These new strategies not only revolutionized domestic policies, but also placed the Soviet Union in the forefront of those advocating drastic reductions in nuclear weaponry. It made Russia a much less certain agent – both in capacity and desire – in exporting her revolution overseas, though this did not put an end to her hostility to NATO-type alliances and foreign policy. But it did point to the end of balanced superpower politics in the twenty-first century. Military success often seemed to elude the superpowers: Russia had its Afghanistan – later also to entrap the Western powers – and the USA its Vietnam.

Within the Warsaw Pact countries, economic difficulties prompted both economic and political change in Hungary in the late 1980s, while in 1989 Poland appointed its first non-Communist prime minister since 1948. Again the dynamics of change need to be noted: the Polish free trade union, *Solidarnösc*, was founded in 1980, banned a year later, but by the end of the decade was sharing in government. Dramatic changes at an alarming and unanticipated pace also brought about peaceful revolutions in East Germany, Czechoslovakia, and Bulgaria, though in Romania changes were only secured with considerable loss of life.

Changes however have not all been in one direction. Moscow witnessed armed insurrection on its streets, while several East European countries used the ballot box to re-elect governments of the left. In Russia the election and re-election of the ex-KGB officer Vladimir Putin, with a large measure of popular support, re-established authoritarian one-man leadership, working in close relationship with the Moscow Patriarchate – the Patriarch referred to the Putin era as 'a miracle of God' – to reinforce Russian identity, but to the disadvantage of religious minorities.

In 1989, *glasnost* and *perestroika* made it possible for the Central Committee of the World Council of Churches to meet in Moscow and to be received at a reception by the Soviet Prime Minister. One of the then younger leaders of the Russian Church, Archbishop Kirill of Smolensk and Kaliningrad (b. 1946), confessed that, when he first became involved in the ecumenical movement, many of the programmes of the World Council of Churches seemed to be of little relevance. But involvement in them, he said, had provided him with an enviable education, equipping him to understand the critical needs of the Soviet Union post-*perestroika*. Since 2009 Kirill has served the Russian Church as Patriarch; his ecumenical experience now tempered by national and local ecclesiastical demands.

The churches in many parts of Eastern Europe have experienced new opportunities for re-establishing themselves: churches have been reopened, seminaries re-established, and the churches have again developed their own newspapers and radio programmes, while the secular press now carries stories about their charitable works. Opportunities for Christian witness have become widespread amidst such profound change: the Bible is a much sought-after book, and people have found that the Christian conscience speaks powerfully to many contemporary questions in Russian society.

In Poland and the German Democratic Republic, both the Roman Catholic and Protestant churches played a significant part in encouraging change: they offered an ideological alternative to a Communism which no longer commanded popular support. But the ending of Communism did not remove all difficulties; economic chaos and the exclusiveness of some state churches still made Christian witness difficult, especially since the authorities did not always find it easy to distinguish between self-established churches with significant national support and sectarian external groups, most often financed from North America.

WITHIN THE CHURCHES

Christian churches themselves have been the focus of changes as radical as those influencing other aspects of society. In many respects the centre of gravity within Christendom is moving from Europe and North America to Latin America and Africa – what the historian Philip Jenkins calls 'The New Christendom'. The phenomenal growth of indigenous Third World churches has almost reversed the situation faced by the European and American missionary societies at the end of the last century: missionaries are now coming from the developing world to Europe and North America, alongside their diaspora congregations now permanently present in large numbers in all the great cities of the developed world.

In the West, the historical structures of the mainstream denominations have been challenged by a number of movements, variously described as charismatic, restorationist, and communitarian. Their emphases are not wholly new, but are in part a recovery of earlier movements. The new charismatic awareness looks back to earlier revival movements; the house churches find continuity with the Brethren movement of the nineteenth century; and the focus on community, with Christians sharing together in all aspects of life – not just worship, evangelism, Christian education, and service – has its roots within the Anabaptist tradition.

These new movements have not always been easy for the established churches to accept, especially when they seem to exhibit a spiritual buoyancy that the older churches lack. However, almost all churches – especially those which are more traditionally and hierarchically organized – have developed greater freedom as they have been forced to accept diversity of outlook. This is partly the result of a new pluralism, seen in a diversity of versions of the Bible, varieties of liturgy, and widespread adoption of new hymns and music. The weakening of older denominational forms of Christianity in the West does not entirely represent overall decline, but partly a transfer of allegiance to these newer forms of churchmanship.

Where tradition finds itself in conflict with pluralism, difficulties often arise. For example, at the 1988 Lambeth Conference the provinces of the Anglican Communion differed over the ordination of women to priests' orders. The consecration of the Reverend Barbara Harris the following year as the first woman bishop of the Episcopal Church in America was soon followed by the appointment of the first woman diocesan bishop in New Zealand. Both produced predictable reactions. Those opposing this change came from both extremities of church tradition, including some Anglo-Catholics and some Evangelicals. Questions were posed not only about the role of women in the church, but also about the nature of authority within a worldwide communion.

The ordination of women produced widespread theological debate, with churches reacting differently to the issue. For some, a woman cannot be a priest; they take as their models the Old Testament priesthood and the twelve male disciples of Jesus. Others place no special emphasis on the nature of priesthood, but believe the Bible does not allow women into positions of authority. Yet others have no theological objection, but instead stress the removal of divisions in Christ, and have moved ahead for several generations, ordaining suitable candidates and appointing them at all levels of leadership throughout their churches. Concern has also been expressed over the language used in liturgy, and attempts made to use more inclusive phrases, in order to remove what many see as over-dependence on male images and words.

The Church of England's 1992 vote in favour of ordaining women was bitterly contested. Whilst some argued for equality and for releasing gifts for mission, others passionately believed the traditional apostolic faith was being compromised. Some left to join the Roman Catholic Church, which in the Papal Encyclical *Veritatis Splendor* reinforced its commitment to traditional teaching. Debate about the consecration of women as bishops within the Church of England was heightened in 2011 by the Pope's creation of the Personal Ordinariate of Our Lady of Walsingham, which offered Anglo-Catholic priests and people a new home within the Roman Catholic Church, whilst retaining a special Anglican identity, thus continuing the 'uniate' offers made by the Roman Catholic Church over the years, namely an offer to retain certain practices – for example the service of married priests – as long as loyalty to the Vatican is subscribed.

No less divisive between Anglican provinces in the northern and southern hemispheres were attitudes to the celebration of gay marriage in church, and the ministry as priest or bishop of those living in an openly gay relationship. Rev. Gene Robinson (b. 1947), elected Bishop of New Hampshire, USA, in 2003, was the first priest in an openly gay relationship to be ordained bishop in a major Christian denomination. Such issues – rather than questions of doctrine – threatened the unity of the Anglican Communion in the early decades of the twenty-first century.

CHURCH AND SOCIETY

In the United States of America in the 1980s, conservative Christians began to play a major part in politics, securing the White House for Ronald Reagan on two occasions, for George Bush Snr as Reagan's successor, and later for his son, George W. Bush. To this end Jerry Falwell (1933–2007), a fundamentalist Baptist preacher, founded the Moral Majority Movement, which was supposedly concerned to protest against the liberal trend of American politics. However, the definition of what was moral was largely personalist, and did not embrace issues of structural injustice that concerned many other Christians. High-profile television evangelists secured vast followings, which – in some instances – they exploited in a fashion shown to be corrupt in the American courts. Most often they preached an other-worldly gospel that put its silent voice behind support for the *status quo*.

Among Evangelicals, often criticized in the past for caring only for the soul and not the body, there were calls to think seriously about the radical ethical demands made by a biblical faith. Many became actively engaged in combating structural evil within the contemporary world, and their writings and example have been widely influential in changing Evangelical attitudes all around the world. Lack of consensus as to the nature of Christian ethics made Christians less influential in society than they might otherwise have been.

Evangelicals have developed a more aggressive critique of society, and of the structural injustices of the international economic order. The Lausanne Congress of 1974 was an important landmark in successfully reintegrating social action and evangelism. At a second

Congress in 1989, in Manila, delegates acknowledged the imperative for 'the whole church to take the whole gospel to the whole world'. The Filipino Jovito Salonga (b. 1920) told those assembled,

> *We achieve spirituality when we are out there in the busy streets or in the crowded market place, among the oppressed and the poor, identifying ourselves with the lowliest of them and struggling with them for a free, open society where the weak shall be strong and the strong shall be just.*

A similar emphasis has come from Mortimer Arias, a Latin American bishop, who advocates 'holistic' evangelism. At the same time, many agencies with ample funds – often from North America – still preach an other-worldly, sectarian gospel, little related to the day-to-day conditions of their listeners.

Evangelicalism developed a new confidence after World War II. This was partly a reflection of its growing strength of numbers, partly because of the success of its evangelism, and partly through the impact of its scholars, who won such respect that the movement could no longer be classed as anti-intellectual. In many parts of the world, the movement was also influenced by 'church-growth' principles emanating from Fuller Theological Seminary, Pasadena, California, whose leaders stressed the need to perceive growth in more than numerical terms. Evangelicalism must now be distinguished from its right wing, fundamentalism, which remains exclusive, denying the validity of the faith of other Christians, and pietistic, often opposing the findings of broader theological scholarship.

VARIETIES OF FAITH

Pentecostalists are close cousins to Evangelicals, but they now represent a new strand in Christian history. Through charismatic renewal, the influence of Pentecostalism extended out beyond traditional Protestant circles to include Anglo-Catholics, Roman Catholics, and some Orthodox. Although some remained suspicious of charismatic influences, many congregations found their worship enlivened, with a new sense of participation by the whole church membership, rather than reliance on a single minister or leader. Together they have discovered a new unity with Christians in traditions which previously seemed very distant from their own.

The state churches of Northern Europe remain strong, at least from the viewpoint of official statistics, with impressive budgets largely provided by church taxes. Church buildings are beautifully maintained and ecclesiastical headquarters offer a wide range of services, and the activities of the churches continue to make media news. But church attendance has seriously declined; young people are noticeably absent, regardless of stringent pre-confirmation discipline. Successive *kirchentags* (German national church conferences) and meetings at Taizé (a French monastic community, whose devotion to liturgical reform and Christian unity inspired many to renewed commitment) capture the imagination of a wide range of people in a way that the routines of parish life do not. Elsewhere, the legacy of various movements of pietistic revival is to be found in the existence of fellowship organizations that exist as a kind of church within the church.

VATICAN II

The Second Vatican Council (1962–65) was a watershed in Roman Catholic history. It divided the years of Catholic Reformation exclusiveness from the new, more open, co-operative stance legitimized under Pope John XXIII's benign rule. After the council there was greater emphasis upon the church as the whole body of all the baptized – lay and ordained. The church was seen as God's pilgrim people, commissioned to serve his mission in the world. The liturgy was modernized and offered in the vernacular, and the Bible accorded a more significant place in Catholic life. Many, however, regretted the passing of the old order and found the new world threatening and uncertain.

Pope John Paul II (1920–2005), the Polish Pope, and the first non-Italian to sit on Peter's throne since 1523, gave high visibility to the papal office by his worldwide travels. Parts of the church in Europe, North America, and Latin America pressed for further reforms regarding the role of women in the church and the possibility of ministry by married clergy, whilst some wanted to accept new emphases in theology. However, Pope John Paul's personal judgment was for the most part exercised in a conservative direction. Meanwhile the pressures of contemporary culture led to both monks and nuns forsaking their orders, and parish priests leaving the priesthood. Such pressures put strains on recruitment to both the priesthood and to monastic life. John Paul II's successor, the German theologian, Cardinal Joseph Ratzinger (r. 2003–2013), formerly Prefect of the *Sacred Congregation for the Doctrine of the Faith*, who took the name Benedict XVI, through his scholarship and office reinforced these conservative emphases in a church which was troubled by the revelation of many cases of child abuse.

Visitors to St Peter's Basilica, Rome, walk in front of a huge image of Pope John Paul II (r. 1978–2005).

© MILESFOTO/ DREAMSTIME.COM

WORLD COUNCIL OF CHURCHES

There has been a tendency for the Protestant world to divide between Evangelicals and ecumenically-committed Christians. However, there are significant overlaps between these groups, although many Evangelicals remain opposed to organizational links with non-evangelicals.

The World Council of Churches seeks to be a vehicle to express the common mind and conscience of its member churches yet, at the same time, to give prophetic leadership. These functions are not easy to combine, and tensions arose over some aspects of the council's work. In particular, some expressed reservations over the Programme to Combat Racism, and more especially that programme's special fund of separately donated gifts, from which grants were made to various protest agencies for their humanitarian activities. When challenged about this, Archbishop Desmond Tutu (b. 1931) – himself a Nobel Peace Prize Winner – asked why Bonhoeffer was regarded as a saint for trying to kill Hitler, while black South Africans who took up arms against an apartheid-supporting regime were labelled terrorists. In retrospect, the council's role in the anti-apartheid movement has come to be seen as an important chapter in Christian obedience, not least appreciated by thousands of black South Africans as offering solidarity in the bleak years of white sovereignty.

Another area of concern has been the injustices suffered by many women in the modern world, which has led to the coining of the phrase 'the feminization of poverty'. Although many churches are committed to working for a better deal for women in society, others reinforce the prejudices of secular society by their own exclusive structures. Patriarchal traditions, long accepted as the order of things, are now challenged by feminist theology, sometimes strident, but frequently deriving from a biblical basis. Many have become aware of the hurts caused by the older exclusiveness, and consequently take greater care over the wording of hymns, the translation of the Bible, and the revision of liturgies. They seek to avoid thought-forms that suggest male dominance, and use inclusive language wherever possible.

THIRD WORLD CHURCHES

A post-colonial world is also in many respects a post-missions world, in so far as missionary societies now look to work in partnership with national churches rather than perpetuate any form of missionary imperialism. Ideally this partnership extends to sharing of resources of all kinds – personnel, finance, and education – and in both directions. But, in truth, the imperialism of those who provide the financial support often still determines which projects are funded and which are not.

There has been a move from focusing funds on immediate aid to investing resources in long-term development, with the aim of increased self-dependency, or at least the strengthening of production processes, so that the developing country improves its trading position and thereby its bargaining power in the world market.

The national churches of the developing world now enjoy complete autonomy of jurisdiction. However, in many places they are challenged by 'independent' churches, which deliberately reject the legacy of Western missions and mission culture. African independent churches, for example, are still growing fast, claiming a more complete relevance to African culture and thought.

Independent churches are to be found all over the African continent – some are relatively small and local, while the largest, such as The Church of The Lord Aladura (Praying) and the Kimbanguists, spread across national boundaries in West Africa and have growing branches in the capitals of the West. Similar movements are to be found in other parts of the world, and their theology reaches across a broad spectrum. For example, some indigenous Pentecostal churches in Latin America exercise an acute social conscience, while others emphasize millenarian and otherworldly views. The growth of the church in China is part of the same story. It is clear that, after the missionaries had been expelled from that country, the church became far more Chinese. Not only did the church survive in China; it grew remarkably, though its evangelistic faithfulness and its willingness to criticize the ruling political system still represents costly witness.

LATIN AMERICA

Latin America has made its greatest impact on Christian thinking as the home of liberation theology, an approach was initiated by Catholic theologians such as Gustavo Gutiérrez (b. 1928), Juan Luis Segundo (1925–96), José Miranda (b. 1946), and the Boff brothers. Liberation theologians affirm that theology is not something to be isolated in a university or seminary, but rather to be 'done', as theory is put into practice – and that practice should then be allowed to inform and revise the theory. In this way the key inter-connecting word for the Latin American theologian becomes *praxis* – that is, theology hammered out in terms of its relevance to the everyday experience of ordinary people, and then used to illuminate their situation and provoke significant action.

There is, they say, in the Christian gospel a bias to the poor. In developing countries, Protestantism tended to create a modernizing elite, but liberationists are concerned about justice for the poorest groups in their society. Because of their emphasis on *praxis*, theological education is undertaken in the community, rather than separate from it in some academic ivory tower. More contentiously, the liberation theologians have found Marxism a useful tool for social analysis, helping them to understand the ills of their society. But they make a clear distinction between analysis and cure: Marxist social science provides a

Women worship at a Catholic church in China.
©LILIZHOUFOX/
DREAMSTIME.COM

valuable diagnostic instrument, but Marxist politics are not necessarily seen as the solution to Latin American problems. Nevertheless, liberation theologians are widely condemned by a middle-class society, which in Latin America is capable of labelling quite centrist democratic programmes as Communist.

These theological emphases have divided the Roman Catholic Church in Latin America. Some leaders have taken up the new thinking, while others have bitterly opposed it, and made life difficult for priests who introduce it into their ministry. But the radically reshaped Catholic Church in Latin America has shown itself unwilling to be bound by church bureaucracies. New life broke out at local level, in what have been called 'grass-root' or 'base communities'. Here, often without any priestly superintendence, lay people gather around the Bible, and seek to apply its guidance to all aspects of their daily living. In so doing, the Latin American poor have found a new way of affirming their own dignity. Leonardo Boff (b. 1938) describes such groups as 'a resurrection of the church', while others have seen them as critical agencies of change 'from the bottom upwards'. In areas of profound shortages of clergy, lay participation has been further advanced by the widespread appointment of 'Delegates of the Word', lay ministers who supplement the ordained ministry.

With appropriate amendments and developments, the radicalism of liberation theology has been made available to Protestant audiences through the writings of José Miguel Bonino, among others. An evangelical response is found in the work of C. René Padilla (b. 1932), Orlando Costas (1942–87), and Emilio Nuñez; and creative thought within the Latin American Theological Fraternity has been one influence that has led to a renewal of evangelical social thinking around the world.

CONTEMPORARY THEOLOGIES

Liberation theology is but one attempt to relate theology to people's personal circumstances. The vitality of theology early in the twenty-first century is seen in the many attempts to contextualize theological truth to a particular problem or situation. This problem is not new: many of the so-called classic theologies were in their day contextual theologies, building bridges between biblical revelation and the dominant philosophical culture of the time. But because the world of theological discourse was so much smaller, the divergences of history, and the dependency on prevailing cultures were less apparent. The perceived need for theology to become indigenous to many very different specific cultures has produced the variety we see today: theologies of liberation, of the poor, of suffering; feminist theology, black theology, African theology, and *minjung* theology (meaning, 'of the mass of the people') from Korea. Even this list is not exhaustive.

The danger is that coherence can be lost in the search for vitality and relevance: so there is a search for a way in which to contain all this liveliness within the coherence of the biblical and trinitarian faith of the church. This underlines two basic ways of regarding theology: one is to see theology as a *task*, which the professional theologian undertakes in order to clarify the mind of the church; the other to see theology as *something given*, that is, the truth about God and his purposes for creation graciously revealed to those who will receive it. On this second understanding, to engage in theology is to move on to ground where 'we have to remove our shoes'.

JUSTICE, PEACE, AND THE INTEGRITY OF CREATION

In 1990 in Seoul, South Korea, the World Council of Churches organized a major convocation on Justice, Peace, and the Integrity of Creation, attempting to bring together the major aspects of a practical programme of Christian discipleship. They were seeking a commitment to peace over against all that destroys or puts life at risk. But they sought peace with justice – for the biblical concept of peace is understood not simply an absence of violence, but a concern for wholeness of life for all humanity. To these themes of peace and justice they added a third: the integrity of creation – a thoroughgoing working out of God's creation mandate to those created in his image. A mandate given in the context of a world which, rather than the result of random accident, is God-created, and to be respected as such.

God's plan of redemption is seen as not just for the human race, but for the whole created order, which today appears to be as much under threat from human agency as the weakest members of human society seem to be from their fellows. Christians now feel they need to add to the traditional list of social injustices sins against creation: the 'greenhouse effect', the devastation of the world's forests, the production of acid rain, the pollution of the seas, the exhaustion of finite resources, and an unbridled biotechnology which – unless subjected to proper disciplines – does not always provide the improvement of life it promises. With reduced tension between the superpowers, the threat of nuclear holocaust may have retreated; but the disposal of nuclear waste and the stability of nuclear plants remain major problems awaiting resolution.

Christians believe the cause of this crisis is essentially theological. Taken together, the Enlightenment and the experience of industrialization led humanity to believe that material progress was the goal of society. Given this, humanity had a right – even a duty – to dominate and exploit creation. Thus a secular worldview was legitimized that made no reference to the creator or his purposes in creation. Creation was instead viewed 'as a receptacle for raw materials which are only given value through exploitation'. Since such a philosophy increasingly puts the world itself at risk, Christian thinkers called for a reassessment of the exploitative ethic and the worldview that underlies it. This gives new relevance to the biblical theology of creation and human alienation from both the created order and its creator. It is socially urgent, because of the appalling destitution suffered by the poor in many parts of the world. It is also vital for coming generations, threatened with the legacy of a polluted and denuded cosmos.

Within such a programme lies an evangelistic strategy, through which people of all ages and all classes are alerted to the demands and the hope of the Christian gospel. The Bible speaks of a good creation destroyed by human sin, of a God who is passionately concerned for peace and justice for all his creation, of a world redeemed by the sacrificial death of God's only Son. The death of Jesus can put into reverse the processes of sin, both for creation and for individual men and women. Thus, as the structural problems of a threatened creation are positively addressed, the personal needs of individuals to be reconciled to their creator God become revealed.

JOHN BRIGGS

FURTHER RESOURCES ON THE HISTORY OF CHRISTIANITY

Diarmaid MacCulloch, *A History of Christianity: The First Three Thousand Years*, London, 2009

Owen Chadwick, *A History of Christianity*, London, 1995

Adrian Hastings ed., *A World History of Christianity*, Grand Rapids, 1999.

Eamonn Duffy, *Saints and Sinners: A History of the Popes*, 3rd ed., New Haven and London, 2006.

Sheridan W. Gilley and W. J. Shiels, *A History of Religion in Britain: Practice and Belief from Pre-Roman Times to the Present*, Oxford, 1994

Mark Noll, *A History of Christianity in the United States and Canada*, Grand Rapids, 1992.

Adrian Hastings, *The Church in Africa, 1450–1950*, Oxford, 1994.

Tim Dowley, *Christian Music: A Global History*, Oxford/Minneapolis, 2011.

QUESTIONS ON SECTION 8

1. What might the worldwide church look like in 2050?

2. In what ways are Christians of the Third World impacting the church worldwide?

3. How has post-imperialism affected the church in the West?

4. Is the papacy still central to the Roman Catholic church?

5. How are mass communications influencing Christianity?

QUESTIONS ON SECTIONS 1–8

1. In what ways has the church interpreted Jesus' command in Mark 16:15?

2. Describe five major turning points in the history of the church.

3. Why has Christianity divided into so many different churches and denominations?

4. Do scandals and corruption in the story of the church negate its message?

5. Are the historic Christian creeds of importance to today's church?

GLOSSARY

The terms include some that do not appear in this book but are included to give additional information to readers. Cross-references are indicated thus: CHURCH.

A

Abraham, Isaac, and Jacob The three PATRIARCHS who are remembered in the Jewish liturgy as the original recipients of God's promise and blessing.

Absolute, The Term for GOD or the divine often preferred by those who conceive of God predominantly in abstract or impersonal terms.

Acolyte Person who performs minor duties in a CHURCH, e.g. lighting altar candles.

Adonai see YHWH.

African Independent Churches African churches which have risen in the past 150 years and offer a synthesis of Christianity with traditional indigenous religions. Many have prophetic or charismatic founders, and emphasize spiritual healing and communication with ancestors. Some have been a focus of nationalistic aspirations.

Agape Greek word for 'love' that has come to express the Christian understanding of God's love which does not depend on any worthiness or attractiveness of the object of his love. Christians are taught to demonstrate this love to each other in the Christian FELLOWSHIP, and to others.

Albigensians The CATHARS of southern France who flourished in the late twelfth and early thirteenth centuries. Their theology was a DUALISM that has been compared with that of the MANICHAEANS, although they were probably unconnected. They saw CHRIST as an ANGEL whose teachings had been corrupted by the Catholic clergy.

Al-Hallaj (d. 922) Sufi MYSTIC who was crucified because of his confession 'I am the real,' which was taken as a claim to divinity. He considered JESUS OF NAZARETH as the supreme example of human deification and at his death forgave his enemies in imitation of the passion of Jesus.

Almsgiving The giving of free gifts, usually of money, to the poor.

Altar Table used to celebrate the eucharist, usually situated at the east end or front of the church.

Alternative spiritualities Contemporary private, non-institutional forms of belief and practice that focus on 'the self', 'nature', or simply 'life', and look with suspicion on traditional authorities, sacred texts, churches, and hierarchies of power.

Angels Spiritual beings who in JUDAISM and CHRISTIANITY act as the messengers of GOD. They have two primary functions: to worship God, and to support and encourage human beings.

Anglican churches Worldwide groupings of churches which recognize the primacy among equals of the ARCHBISHOP of Canterbury. They include both CATHOLIC and REFORMED elements, and retain BISHOPS.

Animism A term formerly used to describe pre-literary religions, dropped because its meaning – 'spiritism' – was felt to be misleading.

Aphrodite Greek goddess of love and patroness of beauty and sexual attractiveness. Her cult was imported from the Near East. The Romans identified her with VENUS.

Apocalyptic Genre of writing in CHRISTIANITY and JUDAISM, concerned with hidden truths, pointing to the ultimate triumph of faith and the judgment of nations. Daniel and Revelation are examples in the BIBLE.

Apocrypha Historical and wisdom writings found in the Greek version of the Hebrew scriptures, but excluded from the CANON of the HEBREW BIBLE. The ROMAN CATHOLIC CHURCH and EASTERN ORTHODOX churches accept its authority, but PROTESTANT churches distinguish it from inspired SCRIPTURE.

Apollo A major god of both Greeks and Romans, though Greek in origin. He is sometimes seen as the sun and is the patron of the arts (especially music), or prophecy, of divination, and of medicine.

Apologists Title of early Christian writers who used reason to defend and explain the faith to non-believers.

Apostle 'One who is sent' – name for the twelve original followers of JESUS OF NAZARETH, also PAUL. The 'apostolic age' is a time of great authority for the Christian CHURCH.

Apostles' Creed A statement of faith used by Western CHRISTIAN churches, and often repeated in services. Introduced during the reign of Charlemagne (c. 742–814).

Apse Semi-circular recess at the east end of a CHURCH where the ALTAR is located.

Aquinas, Thomas (1225–74) DOMINICAN theologian and philosopher whose teachings form the basis of official ROMAN CATHOLIC THEOLOGY. He taught a fundamental distinction between faith and reason, asserting that God's existence can be proved, but that the doctrines of the TRINITY and the INCARNATION are revealed and must be accepted on FAITH.

Archangel Highest level in the hierarchy of angels.

Archbishop BISHOP who has authority over an ecclesiastical province made up of several DIOCESES.

Archetypes Term invented by C. G. JUNG to describe the concepts held in common by different people at different times and in different places. He believed the concept of GOD was the archetype of the self, and that it was the object of each individual to discover it.

Arianism Fourth-century Christian HERESY of Arius, who denied the divinity of CHRIST, claiming that the SON OF GOD was created, not eternal. It was condemned at the Council of Nicea (325) but flourished until the Council of Constantinople (381).

Aristotle (384–322 BC) Greek philosopher and scientist who taught on every branch of knowledge valued in his time. His work is characterized by acute observation, close reasoning, and orderly exposition. His work was rediscovered in the Middle Ages and laid the basis for the theology of Thomas AQUINAS and for the Humanism of the Renaissance.

Artemis Greek goddess and patroness of virginity, hunting, archery, and wild animals. At Ephesus, in Asia Minor, she was worshipped as the mother goddess.

Arthur Legendary hero of Celtic Britain who may have originated as a Romano-British chieftain. His legends were gradually worked into a Christian framework in which he became the medieval ideal of a Christian king.

Asceticism Austere practices designed to lead to the control of the body and the senses. These may include FASTING and MEDITATION, the renunciation of possessions, and the pursuit of solitude.

Ashkenazim One of the two main cultural groups in JUDAISM that emerged in the Middle Ages. Their tradition is from Palestinian Jewry, and they live in Central, Northern, and Eastern Europe. See also SEPHARDIM.

Athanasius (296–373) BISHOP of Alexandria who strongly resisted the teachings of ARIANISM, and developed the Christian doctrines of the INCARNATION and the TRINITY.

Athena One of the great Greek goddesses. She is the patroness of war, of the city of Athens, and of many crafts and skills. Her Roman counterpart is Minerva.

Atonement Reconciliation between God and humanity required because of the absolute holiness of God and the sinfulness of men and women. As human beings are incapable of achieving atonement, it is a work of God's GRACE, through the death of JESUS CHRIST, for human SIN.

Augustine (354–430) BISHOP of Hippo in North Africa who was converted to CHRISTIANITY from the teaching of the MANICHAEANS. He stressed the absolute GRACE of GOD in men and women's SALVATION and the depravity of human beings through ORIGINAL SIN.

Augustus Title of the first Roman emperor, formerly known as Octavian, who ruled 31 BC – AD 14. He pacified and unified the empire, thus facilitating the later spread of CHRISTIANITY. While he was still alive he was declared a god, and after his death worshipped throughout the Empire.

Austerity Ascetic practice in which one exercises self-restraint or denial, for example, the restriction of food during a FAST.

Averroes *See* IBN RUSHD.

B

Baptism The SACRAMENT of entry into the Christian CHURCH. By washing in water in the name of the TRINITY, it symbolizes the person's identification with CHRIST's death and resurrection, in dying to sin and being raised to new life. In the case of infants, promises are made on behalf of the child for later CONFIRMATION.

Baptism in the Holy Spirit *See* PENTECOSTALISM, GLOSSOLALIA.

Baptist churches PROTESTANT churches emphasizing the BAPTISM of adult believers by total immersion.

Baptistery Building or pool used for baptism, or place in a CHURCH where baptism is performed.

Barth, Karl (1886–1968) Swiss CALVINIST theologian who reacted against Liberal Protestantism in theology and declared theology's central theme to be the WORD OF GOD.

Basilica Large, oblong hall with double colonnades used for judicial or trade purposes, adopted for CHURCH use.

Benedict (c. 480–550) Monk and reformer who wrote a Rule of monastic life which has been followed by MONKS and NUNS of the Western Church ever since.

Bible The book of CHRISTIANITY, comprising the Hebrew OLD TESTAMENT and the NEW TESTAMENT which, Christians believe, together form a unified message of God's SALVATION.

Bishop The senior order of ministry in the Christian CHURCH, with authority to ordain PRIESTS. Many REFORMED CHURCHES do not have bishops.

Blavatsky, Helena Petrovna (1831–91) Founder in 1875 of the Theosophical Society, who claimed to have received the 'ancient wisdom' after seven years in Tibet being taught by various MAHATMAS. She wrote books defending SPIRITUALISM and various OCCULT teachings.

Book of Mormon Sacred SCRIPTURE of MORMONISM which was revealed to Joseph SMITH. It describes a conflict between two branches of a family that had emigrated under divine guidance from JERUSALEM to America in 600 BC. The Mormons regard it as the completion of the biblical revelation.

Breviary Liturgical book containing instructions for the recitation of daily services as followed by the Christian clergy, MONKS and NUNS of the Western Church, with the proper hymns, psalms, and lessons for each service.

Brighid Celtic goddess of poetry, prophecy, learning, and healing. She was absorbed into Irish Christianity as St Brighid, whose feast day coincides with a Celtic spring festival.

Buber, Martin (1878–1965) Austrian-Jewish theologian whose religious roots were in Hasidism. He believed the central task of Jews was to build up God's kingdom on the basis of the Jewish belief in an essential dialogue between God and humanity. He influenced Christian spirituality and social teaching.

C

Calvin, John (1509–64) French theologian who organized the REFORMATION from Geneva. He emphasized JUSTIFICATION BY FAITH and the sole authority of the BIBLE, and in particular that each person's eternal destiny was decided irrevocably by God, and only those destined for SALVATION would come to faith. (*See also* PREDESTINATION.)

Calvinism PROTESTANT theological system developed by and after JOHN CALVIN, emphasizing PREDESTINATION, ELECTION, and ORIGINAL SIN.

Canon Authoritative collection of Christian scripture comprising the accepted books of the Old and New Testaments.

Cardinal Member of a college of ordained high officials in the ROMAN CATHOLIC Church who, since 1059, have elected the POPE. Cardinals are appointed by the pope.

Catacomb Underground burial place sometimes used by early Christians as place of refuge during persecution. The most extensive are in Rome.

Catechism (1) Instruction on Christian faith; for example, instruction in question and answer form given to those preparing for BAPTISM or CONFIRMATION. (2) A popular manual of Christian DOCTRINE.

Catechumen Candidate in training for Christian BAPTISM.

Cathars Members of a medieval heretical Christian SECT which flourished in Germany, France, and Italy before suppression in the thirteenth century. (*See also* ALBIGENSIANS.)

Catholicism CHRISTIANITY as practised by those who emphasize a continuous historical tradition of faith and practice from the time of the APOSTLES to the present day.

Chalice Cup or bowl used to contain wine for use in the EUCHARIST.

Chancel Eastern section of a CHURCH used by the choir and PRIEST and containing the ALTAR. Originally separated by a screen from the NAVE.

Chant Type of singing in which many syllables are sung on a single note or a repeated short musical phrase. Jews and Christians chant the PSALMS. The repetitive nature of chanting can aid MEDITATION.

Chantry Endowed chapel reserved for prayers for the soul of its founder.

Charismatic movement Renewal movement in CATHOLIC and PROTESTANT churches stressing the work and manifestation of the HOLY SPIRIT in the life of the CHURCH and of the individual believer.

Chasuble Sleeveless vest worn by the PRIEST while celebrating MASS.

Christ Greek word for MESSIAH. First applied to JESUS OF NAZARETH by his followers, who believed him to fulfil the hopes of ISRAEL, it later became more a proper name of Jesus than a title.

Christadelphians Christian SECT founded by John Thomas (1805–71) in the USA, which claims to have returned to the beliefs and practices of the original DISCIPLES. They accept the BIBLE as infallible, and are particularly interested in the fulfilment of prophecy. They reject the doctrines of the TRINITY and INCARNATION and have no ordained ministry.

Christian Follower of JESUS OF NAZARETH, the CHRIST; a member of the Christian CHURCH.

Christianity Religion based on the teachings of JESUS OF NAZARETH, the CHRIST, and the significance of his life, death, and RESURRECTION.

Christian Science Christian SECT founded in the USA by Mary Baker EDDY in 1866. It began with a small group fathered 'to reinstate primitive Christianity and its lost element of healing'.

Christmas The festival of the birth of CHRIST celebrated in Western Christendom on 25 December (which is not necessarily the date believed to be the actual date of his birth). The date suggests that it was intended to replace the Roman festival of the birth of SOL INVICTUS in the fourth century .

Christology Teaching about the nature of the person of CHRIST.

Church (1) The community of all CHRISTIANS, seen in the NEW TESTAMENT as the 'body of Christ', of which he is the head. (2) Building used for Christian WORSHIP. (3) A local group, organized section, or 'denomination' of the church (1).

Church of Jesus Christ of Latter-day Saints *see* MORMONISM.

Civil religion Religion as a system of beliefs, symbols, and practices which legitimate the authority of a society's institutions and bind people together in the public sphere.

Communion *See* EUCHARIST.

Conciliar process The decision making of the CHURCH through the resolutions of specially convened COUNCILS or SYNODS in which the will of CHRIST is revealed to the gathered body. Since the second VATICAN COUNCIL, member churches of the WORLD COUNCIL OF CHURCHES have pledged themselves to work towards a common stand on important issues.

Confirmation Christian rite involving the laying on of hands on those who have been baptized, with prayer for the gift of, or strengthening by, the HOLY SPIRIT. It is often the sign of becoming a communicant member of the CHURCH. In ORTHODOX churches it is performed at BAPTISM. ROMAN CATHOLICS are confirmed at about seven years of age. Other churches that accept confirmation offer it at puberty or later.

Congregationalists *see* INDEPENDENTS.

Conversion A moral or spiritual change of direction, or the adoption of religious beliefs not previously held.

Coptic Church The Church of Egypt, a more or less tolerated minority in Egypt since the coming of ISLAM in 642. The church is MONOPHYSITE.

Councils of the church *see* ECUMENICAL COUNCILS.

Counter-Reformation The revival and reform of the ROMAN CATHOLIC CHURCH as a reaction to the REFORMATION. Its reforms included those of the Council of Trent (1562–63).

Covenant A bargain or agreement. In JUDAISM the chief reference is to that made with MOSES at SINAI: GOD, having liberated his people from Egypt, promises them the land of ISRAEL and his blessing and protection as long as they keep the TORAH. This confirms the earlier covenants with ABRAHAM and with Noah. With the defeat of the Kingdom of Judah in 586 BC, Jeremiah's prophecy of a new covenant written on the people's hearts came into its own. In the Christian NEW TESTAMENT the sacrificial death of JESUS OF NAZARETH marked the sealing of a new covenant between God and the new Israel, the Christian CHURCH, which completes and fulfils the old covenant.

Cranmer, Thomas (1489–1556) ARCHBISHOP of Canterbury under Henry VIII who helped overthrow papal authority in England and created a new order of English worship in his *Book of Common Prayer* of 1549 and 1552.

Creation The act of GOD by which the universe came into being. Hence it also refers to the universe itself. In JUDAISM and CHRISTIANITY, creation is usually thought of as being *ex nihilo*, from out of nothing that existed before.

Creation Spirituality Initiated in 1977 by the Dominican theologian Matthew Fox (b. 1940), it is critical of traditional CHRISTIANITY, which is described as the 'Fall–Redemption' tradition, emphasizing original sin and the fundamental badness of humanity and the created order. Creation spirituality speaks of 'original blessing', and seeks to provide a life-affirming celebration of humanity and CREATION, drawing liberally on the mystical traditions – particularly Christian MYSTICISM – NEW AGE thought, INDIGENOUS SPIRITUALITIES, and eco-spiritualities.

Creed Formal statement of religious belief. In CHRISTIANITY, the two creeds used most commonly today are the APOSTLES' CREED and the NICENE CREED.

Crusades The military expeditions undertaken by Christian armies from Europe from the eleventh to the fourteenth centuries, intended to liberate the Holy Land from ISLAM.

Cynic Follower of the eccentric Greek philosopher Diogenes (c. 400–325 BC), who taught people should seek the most natural and easy way of life, ignoring conventions. Some historians believe JESUS OF NAZARETH may have been influenced by the radical lifestyle and pithy wisdom of the cynics.

D

David King of the Israelite tribes c. 1000–962 BC, who united them and extended their territory. A musician and poet, to whom a number of psalms in the BIBLE are ascribed. The belief is common to JUDAISM and CHRISTIANITY that the MESSIAH would be a descendant of David.

Deacon Junior minister in the Christian CHURCH. The word means 'servant', and the deacon's functions originally included the distribution of ALMS to the poor.

Dead Sea Scrolls Sacred writings of a breakaway Jewish SECT discovered in 1947 at Qumran, on the western shore of the Dead Sea. The several scrolls and fragments include much of the HEBREW BIBLE, as well as hymns, treatises, and rules for the life of the sect. Many scholars identify the sect with the ESSENES.

Death of God theology Radical American movement of the 1960s seeking to reconstruct Christianity on the basis of atheism. Its tenets were that God had 'died' in human experience, but that it was still possible to be a follower of JESUS OF NAZARETH. Later developments of Death of God theology are NON-REALISM, and an attempt to blend Christian teaching with Buddhist rejection of a personal God.

Deists Followers of a movement for natural religion which flourished in seventeenth-century England. They rejected the idea of revelation and held that the Creator did not interfere in the workings of the universe.

Demiurge Term used in GNOSTICISM to describe the creator god, seen as wilful, passionate, and ignorant. His CREATION is a cosmic disaster which traps in material existence the divine sparks that emanate from the true God.

Demonology Teaching about the demonic and all forms of personified evil.

Devil Term generally used to describe an evil spirit. In CHRISTIANITY the devil (SATAN) is the personification of evil who is permitted to tempt and accuse human beings within the overall providence of GOD.

Diaspora The spread of the Jewish nation, the dispersion from the land of ISRAEL, partly as a result of war and exile, partly as a result of travel and trade.

Diocese District under the control of a BISHOP, normally sub-divided into PARISHes. In the Eastern Church, the area controlled by a PATRIARCH.

Dionysus Greek god of wine and of liberation, a dying and rising god identified with OSIRIS. In the late Hellenistic world (*see* HELLENISM) the cult of Dionysus became an important MYSTERY RELIGION.

Disciples The original followers of Jesus in the NEW TESTAMENT, but also all Christian 'followers' throughout history.

Doctrine A religious teaching or belief which is taught and upheld within a particular religious community.

Dominicans Order of FRIARS founded in the thirteenth century by Dominic de Guzman, devoted to study and preaching.

Dualism (1) The belief that reality has a fundamentally twofold nature. Opposed to Monism, it describes the belief that there is a radical distinction between God and the created world. (2) The belief that there are two fundamentally opposed principles: one of good, the other of evil. (3) The belief that the mind and the body are fundamentally different yet act in parallel.

E

Easter The festival of the RESURRECTION of CHRIST, the greatest and oldest festival of the Christian CHURCH. Its date is fixed according to the paschal full moon and varies from year to year.

Eastern Orthodox Churches Family of self-governing churches looking to the Ecumenical PATRIARCH, the Patriarch of Constantinople, as a symbol of leadership. (*See also* GREAT SCHISM.)

Ecclesiology Teaching about the CHURCH.

Ecumenical councils Assemblies of Christian BISHOPS whose decisions were considered binding throughout the Christian church. These ended with the GREAT SCHISM, though the ROMAN CATHOLIC CHURCH has continued to assemble councils into the twentieth century. The most important of the Ecumenical Councils were held at Nicaea (325, condemning ARIANISM), Constantinople (381), Ephesus (431, condemning NESTORIANISM), and Chalcedon (451, concerning the INCARNATION OF CHRIST).

Ecumenical movement Movement for the recovery of unity among the Christian Churches dating from the Edinburgh 'World Missionary Conference' of 1910 and today focussed in the WORLD COUNCIL OF CHURCHES.

Eddy, Mary Baker (1821–1910) American spiritual teacher and founder of CHRISTIAN SCIENCE. She believed orthodox CHRISTIANITY had repressed CHRIST's teaching and practice of spiritual healing, and that healing was not miraculous but a natural expression of the divine will. She founded the First Church of Christ Scientist in Boston in 1879; it remains the mother church of Christian Science. She wrote the authoritative work of the movement – *Science and Health with Key to the Scriptures* – and founded the newspaper the *Christian Science Monitor*.

Elder An officer of the church in the PRESBYTERIAN and INDEPENDENT CHURCHES. Teaching elders also deal with pastoral care; ruling elders help in church government and administration.

Election God's choice of ISRAEL to be his people as expressed in the COVENANT at Mount SINAI, and manifested in the gift of the land of ISRAEL. In Christian THEOLOGY, the concept is widened to include GENTILE converts to CHRISTIANITY who spiritually inherit the promises made to the PATRIARCHS and to MOSES.

Enlightenment Eighteenth-century European movement of philosophy and science which stressed the supremacy of reason over REVELATION and tradition.

Epicureanism Philosophical school founded by Epicurus (341–270 BC) and holding an atomic theory of the universe. It teaches that the gods are irrelevant to human life, the chief end of which is happiness.

Epistle (1) Letter in the NEW TESTAMENT to a Christian community or individual, usually from one of the APOSTLES. (2) Letter on DOCTRINE or practice addressed to a Christian community in post-apostolic times.

Eros Greek god of love, Cupid to the Romans, the son of APHRODITE. In the Christian era 'cupids' became angelic beings symbolizing divine benevolence and compassion.

Eschatology Teaching about the 'last things'. In Christianity this includes discussion of the end of the present world order, the SECOND COMING/PAROUSIA, the final JUDGMENT, PURGATORY, HEAVEN, and HELL.

Esoteric Word meaning 'inner', suggesting something (e.g. a knowledge or a teaching) that is available only for the specially initiated and secret from outsiders, and perhaps even from ordinary believers.

Essenes Jewish group which withdrew to live a monastic life in the Dead Sea area during the Roman period. Most were celibate and they stressed the importance of ASCETICISM. They also performed EXORCISMS and rites of spiritual healing. Many scholars believe the DEAD SEA SCROLLS were the scriptures of an Essene community.

Eucharist ('thanksgiving') The central act of Christian worship instituted by CHRIST on the night before his death. It involves sharing bread and wine, which are sacramentally associated with the body and blood of Christ. (*See* SACRAMENT.) In

PROTESTANT churches often called COMMUNION or the LORD'S SUPPER.

Evangelicals CHRISTIANS of all denominations who emphasize the centrality of the BIBLE, JUSTIFICATION BY FAITH, and the need for personal CONVERSION. In Germany and Switzerland, the term refers to members of the LUTHERAN as opposed to the CALVINIST churches.

Evangelism The preaching of the Christian GOSPEL to the unconverted.

Exile (1) The period between 597 BC and around 538 BC when leading JEWS from the former Jewish kingdoms were held in captivity in Babylon. (2) The condition of Jewish life in the DIASPORA, away from the land of ISRAEL.

Exodus The flight of the people of ISRAEL from Egypt under the leadership of MOSES.

Exorcism Removal of SIN or evil, particularly an evil spirit in possession of someone, by PRAYER or ritual action.

Extreme unction The ROMAN CATHOLIC SACRAMENT of anointing a person with consecrated oil in their final hours.

F

Faith Attitude of belief, in trust and commitment to a divine being or a religious teaching. It can also refer to the beliefs of Christianity, 'the faith', which is passed on from teachers to believers.

Fall of Jerusalem The capture of JERUSALEM and the final destruction of the TEMPLE OF JERUSALEM by the

Roman general Titus in AD 70 at the end of a revolt which broke out in AD 66.

Family Federation for World Peace and Unification Another name for the HOLY SPIRIT ASSOCIATION FOR THE UNIFICATION OF WORLD CHRISTIANITY, commonly known as The Unification Church, or, after the name of the founder, the 'Moonies'. It was founded in Seoul, South Korea, in 1954 by Sun Myung MOON.

Fasting Total or partial abstinence from food, undertaken as a religious discipline. In JUDAISM and CHRISTIANITY it is a sign of mourning or repentance for SIN.

Fellowship The common life of Christians marked by unity and mutual love, a creation of the HOLY SPIRIT.

Feminist theology A movement developed first in the USA which uses the experience of being female in a male-dominated society as a basis for critical reflection on Christian thought, tradition, and practice.

Font Vessel, usually made of stone and situated at the west end of the NAVE of a CHURCH, that contains the water used for BAPTISM.

Francis of Assisi (1182–1226) Founder of the Franciscan monastic order who lived by a simple rule of life, rejecting possessions, ministering to the sick, and having a special concern for nature.

Franciscan *see* FRANCIS OF ASSISI.

Freemasonry Originally a religious brotherhood of English masons founded in the twelfth century. In the sixteenth century it spread to the European mainland where in ROMAN CATHOLIC countries it became associated with Deism (*see* DEISTS). In the UK and USA today, it is a semi-secret society which retains certain mystical symbols and ceremonies. Members are committed to a belief in GOD as 'the great architect of the universe', symbolized by an eye.

Friar Member of one of the MENDICANT orders founded in the Middle Ages.

Friends, Society of *see* QUAKERS.

Fundamentalism The doctrine that the BIBLE is verbally inspired, and therefore inerrant and infallible on all matters of DOCTRINE and history. The bases of fundamentalism were set out in twelve volumes, *The Fundamentals*, published between 1910 and 1915.

G

Gabriel An ARCHANGEL named in both the Old and New Testaments. In the GOSPEL of Luke he foretells the births of John the Baptist and Jesus.

Gentile Person who is not a JEW.

Glossolalia Expression in unknown tongues by people in a heightened spiritual or emotional state, used to express WORSHIP to GOD and prophetic messages.

Gnosticism Movement of ESOTERIC teachings rivalling, borrowing from, and contradicting early CHRISTIANITY. Gnostic sects were based on MYTHS that described the creation of the world by a deluded DEMIURGE, and taught a way of SALVATION through *gnosis* – 'knowledge' of one's true divine self. Gnostics contrasted their 'knowledge' with FAITH, which they considered inferior.

God The creator and sustainer of the universe; the ABSOLUTE being on whom all that is depends.

Good Friday The Friday before EASTER, kept by the CHURCH as a holy day, sometimes including FASTING, penance, and witness, in memory of the crucifixion of Jesus CHRIST.

Gospel (1) One of the four accounts of the 'good news' about Jesus in the NEW TESTAMENT. (2) The Christian message, proclamation of 'good news', referring especially to Jesus' teaching about the KINGDOM OF GOD and to the preaching of the CHURCH about Jesus. (3) The ritual reading of a set portion from the Gospels (1) in the context of the EUCHARIST. (4) A partial account of the life and teaching of Jesus, usually ascribed to a New Testament figure, but rejected by the CHURCH as heretical.

Gospel of Thomas Syriac text of a collection of sayings of Jesus discovered at Nag Hammadi in Egypt in 1947. It has many parallels with the sayings of Jesus in Matthew and Luke, and some scholars consider it to be as authentic as the canonical GOSPELS. Its teaching is GNOSTIC.

Grace (1) Unmerited favour, especially in the divine SALVATION of the unworthy.

Christians believe that nobody receives salvation because he or she deserves it, but only by God's grace. (2) A prayer or blessing before a meal.

Great Schism The SCHISM declared in 1054 between the Eastern and Western Christian churches resulting from disagreements over the POPE's claim to supremacy, and over the doctrine of the HOLY SPIRIT.

Gregory of Nyssa (c. 330–395) Christian theologian who helped develop the doctrine of the TRINITY and expounded the BIBLE as a spiritual path leading to the perfect contemplation of GOD.

Ground of Being Phrase used by German-US theologian Paul Tillich (1886–1965) to describe GOD. It stresses the immanence of God as depth or ground, rather than his TRANSCENDENCE as CREATOR.

H

Hades Greek name for the underworld, the abode of the dead. In the SEPTUAGINT version of the HEBREW BIBLE it translates as *sheol*. In Christian usage it is sometimes used for the interim abode of the departed as distinguished from HELL, the abode of the damned.

Hamartiology Teaching about SIN.

Heaven In CHRISTIANITY the dwelling of GOD, and the ultimate home of the saved, regarded both as a place and a state.

Hebrew The (Semitic) language of the ancient

people of ISRAEL, and of the HEBREW BIBLE.

Hebrew Bible The Jewish SCRIPTURES which comprise the Books of the Law (see TORAH), the PROPHETS, and the WRITINGS. According to tradition, the CANON was fixed at the Synod of Jamnia, or Yavne, c. AD 100.

Hell Realm where the wicked go after death. In CHRISTIANITY, it is total separation from GOD.

Hellenism The adoption of Greek language, culture, philosophy, and ideas, particularly around the Mediterranean, from the time of Alexander the Great (356–323 BC). It was the dominant cultural influence during the rise of CHRISTIANITY.

Heresy The denial of a defined, orthodox doctrine of the Christian faith. The word means 'chosen thing', and refers to the heretic's preference for an individual option over the consensus of the CHURCH .

Hermeticism Mystical movement based on a collection of Egyptian scriptures from the first to third centuries . The writings drew on Greek and Eastern ideas, and were ascribed to Hermes Trismegistus (thrice-great HERMES).

Herzl, Theodor (1860–1904) Leader of the Zionist movement (see ZIONISM) who argued that a national homeland for the JEWS was a necessity. He travelled widely raising support from Christian governments for the Zionist cause, and convened the First Zionist Congress in 1897 which formulated a political programme for the return to Palestine.

Heterodox Holding an unorthodox DOCTRINE; heretical.

High Priest Traditional head of the Jewish priesthood and organizer of TEMPLE worship. His function was to enter the Holy of Holies and offer sacrifice on the DAY OF ATONEMENT. The office ceased at the destruction of the Jerusalem Temple in AD 70.

Hijrah ('going forth') The migration of MUHAMMAD from MECCA to Medina in AD 622, the decisive event for the development of ISLAM. In Medina, Muhammad established himself as a religious and political leader, and organized his followers as an Islamic community. The MUSLIM *Hijri* calendar counts years 'after *Hijrah*'.

Hillel Pharisaic Jewish teacher of the first century AD, known for his humane and lenient interpretations of the TORAH.

Holiness The sacred power, strangeness, and otherness of the divine. In the BIBLE, the term has moral implications and refers to God's purity and righteousness as well as to that which invokes awe. Believers are called to reproduce God's holiness in their own lives, with the help of the HOLY SPIRIT.

Holocaust (from the Latin BIBLE's word for 'whole burnt offering') The name given to Hitler's extermination of six million Jews in the Nazi death camps in Europe from 1941–45. The Holocaust is also referred to by many Jews as the *Shoah* (catastrophe).

Holy Communion Name widely used by ANGLICANS and some other PROTESTANTS for the Christian EUCHARIST.

Holy Spirit The third person of the Christian TRINITY. In the BIBLE, the Holy Spirit is the instrument of divine action, and is portrayed as fire or wind. The Holy Spirit is the source of FAITH and new life in the believer and the CHURCH, bestowing spiritual gifts, guidance, and holiness.

Holy Spirit Association for the Unification of World Christianity *see* FAMILY FEDERATION FOR WORLD PEACE AND UNIFICATION.

Homoiousios (of like substance) Term used, for example at the Council of Seleucia (359), to define the Son as 'of like being' with – or 'similar to' – the Father, a view associated by ATHANASIUS and his followers with Arius and ARIANISM.

Homoousios (of one substance) Term used in the NICENE CREED to describe the orthodox Christological relationship between the Father and the Son, holding that JESUS CHRIST was of one substance with – 'the same as' – GOD.

House churches/New churches Networks of CHARISMATIC, non-denominational churches which started in the 1960s. Members claim they are restoring the conditions of the primitive church, which met for worship in members' houses. See RESTORATIONISM.

Humanism A cultural and intellectual movement of the Renaissance resulting from the rediscovery and study of the literature, art, and civilization of ancient Greece and Rome.

Hymn A sacred song sung in the context of communal worship; a PSALM of communal praise.

I

Icon A likeness of a divine figure or SAINT, painted on wood or inlaid in mosaic, and used in public or private devotion.

Iconostasis Screen covered in ICONS and containing two doors separating the sanctuary from the NAVE in Eastern churches.

Incarnation The Christian doctrine that GOD became human in Jesus CHRIST, so possessing both human and divine natures.

Incense Sweet-smelling smoke used in worship, made by burning certain aromatic substances.

Inclusive language A response to feminism that tries to eradicate the assumption in speech and writing that maleness is more normally human than femaleness. Churches adopting it modify their HYMN, LITURGY, and BIBLE translations.

Independents/ Congregationalists CHRISTIANS who uphold the authority and independence of each local CHURCH, claiming this system to be the earliest form of church order.

Index of prohibited books The official list of books which members of the ROMAN CATHOLIC CHURCH are forbidden to possess or read, first issued in 1557. The *Index* was abolished in 1966.

Indigenous religions The preferred term for religions that are sometimes referred to as 'primal', 'tribal', 'traditional', 'primitive', and 'non-/pre-literate' religions. Indigenous religions are often developments of the traditional religions of tribal and aboriginal cultures.

Indulgence The remission by the Christian church of a period of correction in PURGATORY.

Inquisition Papal office for identifying heretics, founded by Pope Gregory IX, and staffed by the Franciscan and Dominican religious orders. Torture became an approved aid to interrogation in 1252.

Intercession Prayer offered on behalf of others by a believer on earth or by a SAINT in HEAVEN; supremely the work of CHRIST, who intercedes for men and women before GOD.

Islam (infinitive of the Arabic verb 'to submit') Teachings derived from the QUR'AN, which is the revelation to MUHAMMAD, a religion of submission to the will of Allah.

Israel (1) Name given by GOD to Jacob the PATRIARCH and hence to his descendants, the 'people of ISRAEL'. (2) The land promised by God to Abram (ABRAHAM) in the early traditions of JUDAISM. (3) The Northern Kingdom of Israel, which seceded from Solomon's kingdom in 922 BC, and was destroyed by the Assyrians in 722 BC. (4) The modern state of Israel, founded in Palestine as a Jewish state in 1948.

J

Jehovah's Witnesses
Christian SECT founded in the 1870s by C. T. RUSSELL. It propagates its own version of the BIBLE (*The New World Translation*), which it regards as inspired and inerrant, and stresses the imminent return of CHRIST. Members are pacifists, and are forbidden to have blood transfusions.

Jerome (c. 342–420) Translator of the BIBLE into Latin (the 'Vulgate' version) who also wrote many commentaries on the text.

Jerusalem Fortified city captured by DAVID in c. 1000 BC which became the capital of the people of ISRAEL and has remained the focus of Jewish religious aspirations and ideals. It is a holy city for CHRISTIANS because of its association with the passion, death, and RESURRECTION of JESUS OF NAZARETH.

Jesus of Nazareth Teacher, PROPHET, and worker of miracles in first-century Palestine, and founder of Christianity. He taught the coming of the KINGDOM OF GOD with forgiveness and new life for all who believed. His claims to be the promised MESSIAH (or CHRIST) roused opposition from the religious authorities, and he was put to death by crucifixion. After his death, his followers claimed he was risen from the dead and seen alive by many. CHRISTIANS, members of his CHURCH (1), believe him to be fully divine and fully human, and await his promised SECOND COMING, which will bring the fulfilment of the Kingdom of God.

Jihad ('striving') A much-misunderstood concept, *jihad* is the relentless fight against worldliness. Muslims are exhorted to wage holy war only in their defence.

Judaism The religion that developed from the religion of ancient ISRAEL and is practised by the JEWS. It is an ethical MONOTHEISM, based on the revelation of GOD to MOSES on Mount SINAI and his giving of the Law (*see* TORAH).

Judgment The divine assessment of individuals and settling of their destinies. Christianity teaches that judgment is based on the individual's response to CHRIST.

Juno Roman goddess, counterpart of the Greek HERA, and wife of JUPITER.

Jupiter/Jove Principal god of the Romans, identified with the Greek Zeus.

Justification by faith The PROTESTANT belief that SALVATION is achieved by repentance and FAITH in JESUS OF NAZARETH.

K

Kabbalah Jewish mystical tradition which flourished in the teaching of two schools: a practical school based in Germany which concentrated in PRAYER and MEDITATION; a speculative school in Provence and Spain in the thirteenth and fourteenth centuries.

Kingdom of God The rule of GOD on earth. JESUS OF NAZARETH proclaimed the arrival of the kingdom in himself. Christians share in the kingdom now, and it will be completed and fulfilled at his SECOND COMING.

Kook, Abraham Isaac Rabbi (1868–1935) First Chief Rabbi of the Holy Land. He believed the ZIONIST movement to be essentially religious, and that the restoration of ISRAEL was necessary for the REDEMPTION of the world.

Koran *see* QUR'AN.

L

Laity (from Greek *laos*, 'people') The non-ordained members of a religious community (see ORDINATION), or those with no specialist religious function.

Lares Roman agricultural spirits who were worshipped at crossroads and in the home as household gods.

Latter-Day Saints, Church of Jesus Christ of *see* MORMONISM; SMITH, JOSEPH.

Lent A forty-day period of FASTING and penitence before EASTER, originally a period of training and examination for those who were BAPTIZED at Easter.

Liberation Theology Originating in Latin America, associates SALVATION with the political liberation of oppressed peoples. Its insights have been used by black Christians and feminists to understand sexism and racism. Marked by a stress on the challenges to social action in the BIBLE, especially the prophetic books and the NEW TESTAMENT, and the reality of the KINGDOM OF GOD as a coming event.

Limbo According to Roman Catholic doctrine, the dwelling place of souls (e.g. of unbaptized children) excluded from HEAVEN but not subjected to HELL or PURGATORY.

Liturgy ('public service') (1) Any regular prescribed service of the Christian

Church. (2) The EUCHARIST, especially in ORTHODOXY.

Logos Greek for word or principle. In STOICISM it identified the principle of reason, immanent in nature. Speculations about the logos were developed by the Jewish philosopher PHILO OF ALEXANDRIA. The Prologue to St John's GOSPEL identifies CHRIST with the pre-existent logos of GOD.

Lord's Supper Name for the Christian EUCHARIST favoured by the Protestant reformers, who saw the eucharist primarily as a memorial of CHRIST's death.

Luther, Martin (1483–1546) Founder of the German REFORMATION. He held people could be justified before GOD only by FAITH in JESUS CHRIST, not by any 'works' of religion. Thus, the 'mediating' role of the priest and church are unnecessary.

Lutheran Churches Churches in Scandinavia, other parts of Western Europe, and the USA which follow Luther's tradition of theology and liturgy.

M

Maccabees The family and supporters of Judas Maccabeus. They were the forerunners of the ZEALOTS in fighting a holy war against alien rulers.

Magic The manipulation of natural or supernatural forced by SPELLS and RITUALS for good or harmful ends.

Maimonides, Moses (1135–1204) Jewish philosopher who lived in Spain and later Egypt and attempted a synthesis of Aristotelian and

biblical teaching. He listed the Thirteen Principles of belief that have been treated in JUDAISM as a creed and are found in the Jewish Daily Prayer Book.

Mandaeans Members of a GNOSTIC sect teaching REDEMPTION through a divine saviour who has lived on earth and defeated the powers of darkness.

Manichaeans Followers of Mani (c. AD 216–276), a Persian teacher whose strict ascetic system was designed to release the divine spark trapped in every person by the wiles of SATAN. Their teaching influenced AUGUSTINE.

Mars Roman war god, regarded as second only to JUPITER.

Martyr ('witness') Title originally applied to Christians who died, rather than renounce their faith, during times of persecution. Now applied to anyone who dies for a religious belief.

Martyrion Church that contains the relics of martyrs, or marks the site of the grave of a martyr.

Mary, the mother of Jesus Because of her role in the divine plan of SALVATION, Mary is honoured by Christians and venerated by ROMAN CATHOLIC and EASTERN ORTHODOX Christians. The GOSPELS describe her as divinely chosen to be the mother of the Saviour. ROMAN CATHOLIC churches have attributed an intercessory role to Mary, and developed other doctrines concerning her nature.

Masoretes A group of Jewish scholars from the Babylonian and Palestinian

schools who from the seventh to the eleventh centuries supplied the text of the HEBREW BIBLE with vowel points and divided it up into sentences and paragraphs.

Mass Name for the Christian EUCHARIST, derived from the words of dismissal. The standard ROMAN CATHOLIC term, it emphasizes the sacrificial aspect of the rite.

Mecca Holy city of Islam, in Saudi Arabia, the birthplace of MUHAMMAD.

Meditation Deep and continuous reflection.

Mendelssohn, Moses (1729–86) German Jewish rationalist philosopher who translated the PENTATEUCH into German and encouraged Jews to become more involved in European culture.

Mendicants Members of preaching orders forbidden to own common property. Not tied to one monastery or controlled by the bishops, in the Middle Ages they begged or worked for a living.

Messiah ('anointed one') A HEBREW word referring to the person chosen by GOD to be king. (1) After the end of the Israelite monarchy it came to refer to a figure who would restore ISRAEL, gathering the tribes together and ushering in the KINGDOM OF GOD. Modern Jews are divided as to whether the messiah is a symbolic or a representative figure, and whether the founding of the Jewish state is a prelude to his coming. (2) In the Christian NEW TESTAMENT, JESUS OF NAZARETH is described by messianic titles, e.g. messiah, CHRIST, 'the King', 'the One who Comes'.

The account of Jesus' entry into JERUSALEM is deliberately phrased in messianic terms. Jesus himself was cautious about claiming to be messiah, probably because of its political overtones.

Methodist Churches Churches deriving from those which joined the Methodist Conference, first established in 1784 by John WESLEY. They are now spread worldwide, promoting EVANGELISM and social concern.

Midrash A method of exposition of HEBREW texts designed to reveal the inner meaning of the TORAH. The method was originally oral; the most important midrashim were recorded and written down.

Minister (1) A lay or ordained Christian who has been authorized to perform spiritual functions (ministries, literally 'service') in the CHURCH. (2) General title for any member of the clergy, especially those of PROTESTANT denominations.

Miracle An event which appears to defy rational explanation and is attributed to divine intervention.

Mishnah A compilation of Jewish oral teachings undertaken by Rabbi Judah HaNasi c. AD 200. It quickly became second in authority only to the HEBREW BIBLE and formed the basis of the TALMUD.

Missal Liturgical book containing all that is said or sung throughout the year at the celebration of the MASS, with appropriate directions.

Mission Outreach to the unconverted.

Missionaries, Christian
Those who propagate
Christianity among people
of another faith.

Mithra An important figure
in ZOROASTRIANISM. To the
Romans he was the god
Mithras of MITHRAISM. (*See
also* SOL INVICTUS.)

Mithraeum A cave-like
sanctuary housing a statue
of MITHRA slaying the bull.

Mithraism Religion of
MITHRA which flourished
throughout the early Roman
empire. Popular among
soldiers, it stressed courage
and endurance. (*See also*
SOL INVICTUS.)

Moderator MINISTER of the
PRESBYTERIAN CHURCH appointed
to constitute and preside over
one of the courts governing
the life of the church.

Mohammed see MUHAMMAD.

Monk Member of a male
religious community living
under vows that usually
include poverty, chastity, and
the wearing of a distinctive
form of dress.

Monotheism The belief
that there is one supreme
GOD, who possesses all the
attributes and characteristics
of divinity.

Moon, Sun Myung (1920–
2012) Korean businessman
and founder of the FAMILY
FEDERATION FOR WORLD PEACE
AND UNIFICATION. He claimed
to have authoritative visions
of Jesus.

Moonies see FAMILY
FEDERATION FOR WORLD PEACE
AND UNIFICATION.

Monophysitism Fifth-
century DOCTRINE that asserts
CHRIST had one divine
nature, and rejects the
orthodox teaching about the

INCARNATION OF CHRIST agreed
at the ECUMENICAL COUNCIL of
Chalcedon.

Moravians PROTESTANT PIETIST
Christians who continued the
simple ideals of an earlier,
mid-fifteenth century group,
the Bohemian Brethren or
Unity of the Brethren. After
Count Nikolaus Ludwig
von Zinzendorf allowed
Moravian refugees to live
on his land in 1722, they
became particularly active
MISSIONARIES.

Mormonism Unorthodox
Christian SECT founded
in 1830 in the USA on
the basis of the visionary
experiences of Joseph SMITH.
Under its second leader,
Brigham Young (1807–77),
the Mormons journeyed to
found Salt Lake City (1847),
where they developed into a
strong MISSIONARY community.
Mormons accept the BIBLE
and the BOOK OF MORMON
and some other revealed
writings. The Mormon
Church, officially the 'Church
of Jesus Christ of Latter-day
Saints', has about 14 million
members, half of them in the
USA and Canada.

Moroni see SMITH, JOSEPH.

Moses The father of JUDAISM
who received the TORAH from
GOD on Mount SINAI, having
led the people of ISRAEL
out of captivity in Egypt.
The first five books of the
Hebrew BIBLE are traditionally
ascribed to him.

Muhammad (c. AD 570–632)
PROPHET and APOSTLE of
ISLAM, whose message – the
QUR'AN – claims to sum up
and complete the previous
revelations to the Jews and
Christians. Muhammad saw
the expansion of ISLAM in
terms of military conquest
and political organization

and was outstandingly
successful as a commander
and ruler.

Muslim 'One who submits'
to the will of God, a follower
of ISLAM.

Mystery religions Cults
based on ancient MYTHS
which flourished in Greece
and the Roman Empire.
Initiates went through a
secret ceremony in which
they identified with the
divinity at the centre of the
myth, and experienced
SALVATION and the assurance
of immortality.

Mystic One who seeks
direct personal experience
of the divine and may
use PRAYER, MEDITATION or
various ascetic practices to
concentrate the attention.

Mysticism The search for
direct personal experience
of the divine, leading to
union with God's love and
will.

N

Native American Church
Religious organization of
Native Americans founded
in the 1880s. It teaches
a synthesis of native
religion and Christianity.
Its rituals include the
ceremonial use of peyote,
a cactus containing the
hallucinogenic substance
mescaline.

Nave In traditional church
architecture, the main part of
the building, running west to
east from the front door to
the SANCTUARY.

Near-death experience
Visionary sequence of events
occasionally reported by
those resuscitated. Features
include a sensation of being
out of body, a journey

down a long tunnel, the
appearance of a being of
light who is sometimes
identified as CHRIST or an
ANGEL, and a flashback of
one's past life.

Neo-Platonism Religious
and philosophical movement
from the third to the sixth
centuries AD. It used the
teachings of PLATO as a
basis for ascetic practices
and mystical experience.
Its principal architect was
PLOTINUS.

Nestorianism CHRISTIAN
HERESY that claimed that two
separate persons, human
and divine, existed in the
incarnate CHRIST (as opposed
to the orthodox view that
GOD assumed human nature
as one person in Christ).
Although condemned in AD
431, it continued to flourish
in Persia. A few groups of
Nestorians survive in the
present day.

New Age With roots in
particularly THEOSOPHY, the
term refers to alternative
spiritualities that emerged
in the mid-1960s principally
on the west coast of the
USA and spread throughout
North America and Europe.
The movements are
characterized by a concern
to realize the spiritual
potential of the individual
self, which is often believed
to be divine. Also common
is the belief that – as we
move from the astrological
age of Pisces into the age of
Aquarius – we are witnessing
a spiritual renaissance, a
New Age of non-hierarchical,
non-patriarchal, eco-friendly
self-spirituality. Their
teachings claim to revive
ancient mystical traditions
of East and West, and
emphasize healing, a healthy
and balanced lifestyle, and

expansion of self-awareness through meditation and personal counselling.

New Testament The second division of the Christian BIBLE, comprising the GOSPELS, the Acts of the Apostles, the Revelation of John, and various EPISTLES.

Nicene Creed The fullest version of the orthodox Christian CREED, compiled to counter Christological heresies in the fourth century.

Non-realism Movement arising from DEATH OF GOD theology which claims that religious doctrines refer only to human sources of value, and do not refer to objective reality.

Numen In Roman religion, the divine power suffusing nature. From this concept Rudolf Otto developed the idea that the root of religion was a sense of holy power which he termed the 'numinous'.

Nun A member of a religious community of women. Nuns live under vows, usually including poverty and chastity, and often the wearing of a distinctive form of dress.

O

Occult Teachings, arts, and practices concerned with what is hidden and mysterious.

Old Catholic Churches A group of national churches which have separated from Rome. Since 1932 they have been in communion with the Church of England.

Old Testament The HEBREW BIBLE as the first part of the Christian BIBLE.

Omnipotence All-powerfulness.

Omniscience Simultaneous knowledge of all things.

Option for the poor Decision of Latin American churches, following Medellín Conference of 1968 and Puebla Conference of 1978, to adopt the tenets of LIBERATION THEOLOGY by insisting that God chose the poor and willed social justice.

Ordination Rite in the Christian CHURCH by which chosen individuals are authorized as MINISTERS of the WORD OF GOD and the SACRAMENTS.

Origen (c. AD 184–c. 254) Theologian who tried to present biblical CHRISTIANITY using the ideas of HELLENISM. He believed that all creatures would eventually be saved, a view condemned as heretical in AD 553.

Original sin The SIN of Adam and Eve, the first human beings, in eating from the forbidden tree in the Garden of Eden, thus expressing disobedience to GOD. In Christian teaching, the consequence is seen as separation from God; human creatures inherit Adam and Eve's fallen state, resulting in the need for SALVATION.

Orthodoxy CHRISTIANITY as practised by the Eastern Churches after the GREAT SCHISM. Orthodox Christians are found mostly in Eastern Europe, the Balkan States, and Russia.

Ottoman Empire (1453–1918) The empire of the Ottoman Turks who were converted to ISLAM. It stretched from the Middle East to the Balkans, and at its height to the frontiers of Austria, but went into slow decline in the eighteenth century.

P

Pagan/Paganism The word 'pagan' (from the Latin *pagus*, literally 'from the countryside' or 'rural') was first used in a religious sense by the early Christians to describe the non-Christian GENTILE religions. It is now used to refer to a range of nature-venerating religious traditions, such as Wicca, Druidry, and the 'Northern Tradition'.

Pan Arcadian fertility god, patron of shepherds and herdsmen, usually portrayed with goat's horns and legs.

Pantheism The belief that all reality is in essence divine.

Parish Area under the pastoral and administrative care of a clergyman.

Parousia *see* SECOND COMING.

Passover Seven-day Jewish festival marking the Israelites' deliverance from Egypt (*see* EXODUS). Since Talmudic times (*see* TALMUD) the festival has begun with a service in the home where unleavened bread, wine, and bitter herbs symbolize the joys and sorrows of the Exodus. There is then a meal and the evening concludes with PSALMS and HYMNS which look to God's final redemption of ISRAEL.

Paten Dish or plate that holds the bread used in the EUCHARIST.

Patriarch (1) in JUDAISM and CHRISTIANITY, refers to the founders of the faith, such as ABRAHAM, ISAAC, AND JACOB. (2) Head of one of the EASTERN ORTHODOX CHURCHES. The Ecumenical Patriarch of Constantinople is a figurehead for Orthodox Christians.

Paul APOSTLE of CHRISTIANITY who established new churches throughout Asia Minor and Macedonia. Originally a PHARISEE, he was converted by a vision of CHRIST on the road to Damascus. He wrote several New Testament EPISTLES.

Penance One of the seven SACRAMENTS recognized by the ROMAN CATHOLIC CHURCH.

Penates Spirits or gods who protected the Roman household and family.

Pentecost (1) Hellenistic name for Jewish harvest festival, fifty-two days after PASSOVER. More usually called *Shavuot* or the Festival of Weeks. (2) Christian festival marking the coming of the HOLY SPIRIT upon the APOSTLES, fifty days after EASTER. The second most important Christian festival, it commemorates the beginning of the CHURCH (1).

Pentecostal churches Churches which have formed from a renewal movement which started in the USA in the early 1900s. They teach the experience of 'baptism in the HOLY SPIRIT', which shows itself in speaking in tongues (*see* GLOSSOLALIA) and other 'spiritual gifts'.

Peter APOSTLE and close follower of JESUS OF NAZARETH, from whom he received the name Peter, meaning 'rock' in Greek. He was a leader among the early APOSTLES. Tradition asserts he was martyred in Rome.

Pharisees Jewish anti-nationalistic party that emerged in the time of the MACCABEES. They believed GOD was universal, and taught the individuality of the soul and the RESURRECTION. They prepared the way for the survival of JUDAISM after the FALL OF JERUSALEM in AD 70.

Philo of Alexandria (c. 25 BC – AD 40) Jewish philosopher who tried to reconcile Greek philosophy with the Hebrew SCRIPTURES. His commentaries used allegorical devices to penetrate the meaning of scripture. His speculations were widely studied by the early Christians.

Pietist Someone with strong feelings of religious devotion; it originally referred to an important seventeenth-century Lutheran reform movement in Germany.

Pilgrimage A journey to a holy place, undertaken as a commemoration of a past event, as a celebration, or as an act of PENANCE. The goal might be the location of a MIRACLE, revelation, or THEOPHANY, or the tomb of a hero or SAINT.

Pilgrim Fathers PURITAN Christian group who left England for America in the Mayflower in 1620, and founded the colony of Plymouth, Massachusetts.

Plato (c. 427–347 BC) Greek philosopher and pupil of SOCRATES. He taught the theory of Forms or Ideas, which are eternal prototypes of the phenomena encountered in ordinary experience. Above all is the Form of the Good, which gives unity and value to all the forms. Plato also taught the immortality of the soul.

Plotinus (c. AD 205–69) Philosopher and author of NEO-PLATONISM whose speculations influenced early Christianity. He dealt with the relationship between the world and the soul, and blended Platonic teaching with oriental mysticism. His teachings influenced AUGUSTINE.

Polytheism The belief in, and worship of, a variety of gods, who rule over various aspects of the world and life.

Pontifex High priest of Roman religion, and member of a guild of priests whose president was the *pontifex maximus*. From the fifth century, the title was applied to Christian BISHOPS, usually the POPE.

Pontius Pilate Roman procurator of the province of Judea AD 26–36, under whose authority JESUS OF NAZARETH was crucified. Some Eastern Orthodox traditions assert he killed himself out of remorse.

Pope BISHOP of Rome, Vicar of CHRIST, and head of the ROMAN CATHOLIC Church, regarded as the successor of PETER. Since the First VATICAN COUNCIL, his pronouncement on matters of faith and doctrine issued *ex cathedra* have been regarded as infallible.

Prayer The offering of worship, requests, confessions, or other communication to GOD publicly or privately, with or without words; often a religious obligation.

Predestination The doctrine associated with CALVIN that claims God has determined the fate of all creatures: eternal damnation or eternal reward has already been decided for every individual.

Preferential Option for the Poor *see* OPTION FOR THE POOR.

Presbyter ('elder') Term for a Christian minister used in the NEW TESTAMENT interchangeably with BISHOP. Later it was held that the authority of the presbyter (from which comes 'PRIEST') derived from the BISHOP.

Presbyterian Churches REFORMED CHURCHES whose teachings and order of worship reflect CALVINISM. They are governed by a pyramid of elected, representative courts.

Priest A Christian MINISTER, the term deriving from PRESBYTER.

Propaganda Sacred Congregation for the Propagation of the Faith, a ROMAN CATHOLIC body concerned with MISSION in non-Christian countries. It dates from the COUNTER-REFORMATION, and is now known as the Congregation for the Evangelization of Peoples.

Prophet One who speaks for, or as a mouthpiece of, GOD. The Old Testament prophets were social and religious reformers of ISRAEL and Judah and of the people of God in EXILE. They proclaimed God's prospective judgment of Israel, recalled the people to obedience to God, and some offered hope of a future vindication.

Prophets, The The second division of the HEBREW BIBLE, including the histories and the prophetic books.

Protestantism Christian faith and order as based on the principles of the REFORMATION. It emphasizes the sole authority of the BIBLE, JUSTIFICATION BY FAITH, and the priesthood of all believers. Since the nineteenth century it has also embraced liberal trends which have stressed the subjective side of religion.

Province District over which an ARCHBISHOP has jurisdiction; a territorial division of the Jesuits, Templars, and other religious orders.

Psalm A sacred song or poem. The Book of Psalms in the BIBLE provides the basis for much Jewish and Christian worship.

Pulpit Raised wooden or stone stand in a church from which the PRIEST or preacher delivers the sermon.

Puritanism Reform movement within Elizabethan and Stuart PROTESTANTISM.

Purgatory In ROMAN CATHOLIC teaching, the temporary state of punishment and purification for the dead before their admission to HEAVEN. Its existence was denied by the PROTESTANT reformers.

Q

Quakers Members of the Religious Society of Friends, deriving from a PURITAN group which formed around George Fox in the 1650s. They have no SACRAMENTS and no ordained ministry. Instead authority derives from the 'inner light of the living Christ' in each believer.

Qur'an The central sacred text in ISLAM – the Muslim holy SCRIPTURE.

R

Rabbi ('my master') Jewish religious teacher and interpreter of the TORAH.

Rabbinic Judaism The religion of the RABBIS who – beginning from the second century – expanded the interpretation of the TALMUD and produced authoritative codes of laws, responses, views, and judgments.

Radical Theology Term sometimes used for theology committed to left-wing politics, or that tends towards NON-REALISM.

Rastafarianism Religious and political movement centred in the Caribbean. It is a cult of Ras Tafari, better known as Haile Selassi, Emperor of Ethiopia (1930–74). Many Rastafarians are distinguished by keeping their hair in dreadlocks, and by their use of cannabis in worship. Some prefer the term Rastafari Movement.

Reader Person who reads prayers in CHURCH.

Redemption God's saving work of buying back or recovering what is his. In JUDAISM it refers to the restoration of ISRAEL; in CHRISTIANITY to the ransoming of sinners from the power of SIN and death.

Reformation The movement within Western CHRISTIANITY between the fourteenth and the

seventeenth centuries which led to the separation of the PROTESTANT churches from Rome. The main issue was the authority of the POPE, but doctrinal issues such as the precise meaning of the EUCHARIST and the authority and accessibility of SCRIPTURE were also important.

Reformed Churches Churches which inherit the CALVINIST PROTESTANT tradition, including PRESBYTERIANS, INDEPENDENTS, CALVINISTIC METHODISTS, and CONGREGATIONALISTS.

Relics Bones or remains of SAINTS, venerated and accredited with miraculous powers.

Renunciation Giving up ownership of material possessions.

Reservation of the sacrament The practice of retaining part of the consecrated bread of the EUCHARIST for the COMMUNION of the sick.

Restorationism Movement to restore the CHURCH to a pristine state in which the KINGDOM OF GOD is established through a charismatically ordained ministry. Restorationists see themselves as EVANGELICALS and PENTECOSTALISTS, but with a new edge to their commitment. Many HOUSE CHURCHES promote a Restorationist theology.

Resurrection (1) The Christian belief that JESUS OF NAZARETH was raised from death by GOD the Father, who thus vindicated him as MESSIAH and revealed his defeat of death and SIN. (2) The raising of all the dead for JUDGMENT, as taught in JUDAISM and CHRISTIANITY.

Roma The personification of the city of Rome, worshipped by the Romans as a goddess.

Roman Catholic Catholic CHRISTIAN who recognizes the authority of the POPE, the Bishop of Rome.

Rood Christ's cross; a cross or crucifix, especially at the entrance to a church CHANCEL.

Rosh Hashanah The Jewish New Year, celebrated as the anniversary of CREATION. The LITURGY is penitential in tone, and looks forward to the KINGDOM OF GOD and the MESSIAH. The blowing of the ram's horn *shofar* proclaims God as king of the universe.

Rosicrucianism Mystical system founded in seventeenth-century Germany and based on an account of a secret brotherhood founded 'to improve mankind by the discovery of the true philosophy'. Several societies came into being based on this originally fictitious 'Meritorious Order of the Rosy Cross', with its private language and magical alphabet.

Russell, C. T. (Charles Taze) (1852–1916) US Bible scholar who started a periodical called *Zion's Watchtower* after being influenced by speculation about the return of CHRIST. This grew into the JEHOVAH'S WITNESSES movement.

Russian Orthodox Church The principal church of Russia since AD 988.

S

Saadia Ben Joseph (892–940) Head of the Jewish academy at Susa in Babylon. He defended the doctrine of the oneness of GOD against the Christian TRINITY.

Sabbath (*Shabbat*) Jewish day of worship and rest, lasting from Friday sunset to Saturday sunset.

Sacrament 'an outward and visible sign of an inward and spiritual grace' (*Book of Common Prayer*). REFORMED CHURCHES count only BAPTISM and the EUCHARIST as sacraments, both being instituted by CHRIST. Roman Catholic and Orthodox Churches add CONFIRMATION, marriage, ORDINATION, PENANCE, and EXTREME UNCTION (the anointing of the sick).

Sadducees Aristocratic Jewish party which emerged in the time of the MACCABEES. They rejected the oral law and doctrines such as the RESURRECTION. They were nationalists and collaborated with the Romans to ensure the survival of the Jewish state. The party collapsed after AD 70.

Saint (1) Holy person or dead hero of faith who is venerated by believers on earth and held to be a channel of divine blessing. The PROTESTANT reformers rejected the practice of devotion to saints. (2) In the NEW TESTAMENT and some Protestant churches, a term for any believer.

Salvation In the BIBLE, deliverance of God's people from their enemies, and especially from SIN and its consequences, death and HELL; hence also the whole process of forgiveness, new life, and final glorification for the believer.

Sanctuary A place consecrated to GOD, a holy place, a place of divine refuge and protection. Also, the holiest part of a sacred place or building. Historically, a holy place where pursued criminals or victims were guaranteed safety.

Sanhedrin Jewish supreme council of seventy which organized religious life during the period of independence following the revolt of the MACCABEES.

Satan In the BIBLE, the personification of evil, identified with the DEVIL.

Satanism Sometimes referred to as 'devil-worship'.

Saturnalia Roman festival of Saturn, a mythical king of Rome, which began on 17 December. A time of banquets and present-giving, some of its characteristics were transferred to the festival of CHRISTMAS.

Schism A deliberate division or split between Christians that disrupts the unity of the CHURCH.

Scribes Officials who organized the religious life of the Jewish community after the EXILE of 586 BC.

Scripture Writings which are believed to be divinely inspired or especially authoritative.

Second Coming/Parousia The personal second coming of CHRIST which, Christians believe, will be a time of JUDGMENT and the full inauguration of the KINGDOM OF GOD.

Sect A group which has separated itself from an established tradition, claiming to teach and practise a truer form of the faith, and often critical of the wider tradition it has left. For example, the JEHOVAH'S WITNESSES and the SEVENTH-DAY ADVENTISTS are sectarian Christian organizations.

See Office of BISHOP of a particular DIOCESE; bishop's throne.

Sephardim One of the two main cultural groups in JUDAISM which emerged during the Middle Ages. Sephardic JEWS lived in Spain and Portugal, and their traditions go back to Babylonian Jewry.

Septuagint Greek version of the Hebrew scriptures produced by Jews in Alexandria, completed in 132 BC. Often abbreviated as LXX.

Seventh-Day Adventists Christian SECT which emerged from a number of nineteenth-century groups stressing the imminent return of CHRIST. In line with Saturday being the original seventh day of the Judeo-Christian week, they observe Saturday as the SABBATH. They accept the BIBLE as infallible and require a lifestyle of strict temperance.

Shema The Jewish confession of faith, recited in the morning and evening service. '*Shema*' is the opening word in HEBREW of the confession: 'Hear, O Israel, the Lord our God, the Lord is One …'

Sin (1) An action which breaks a divine law. (2) The state of rebellion against GOD which, in Christian

teaching, has been the human condition since the Fall of Adam and Eve and their expulsion from the Garden of Eden.

Sinai, Mount Mountain in the south of the Sinai peninsula where GOD revealed himself to MOSES and gave him the Ten Commandments.

Smith, Joseph (1805–44) Founder of MORMONISM who claimed to be the recipient of a divine revelation in the form of golden plates inscribed in ancient languages. With the help of the ANGEL Moroni, he translated these, and they became the basis of the BOOK OF MORMON. Ordained PRIEST by the heavenly messenger, he founded the CHURCH OF JESUS CHRIST OF LATTER-DAY SAINTS in 1830.

Sol Invictus ('unconquered sun') A name for MITHRA. From the time of the Emperor Aurelian (AD 270–275), until displaced by CHRISTIANITY, this was the official imperial cult of Rome.

Son of Man Title used by JESUS CHRIST to refer to himself, traditionally used to describe Christ's humanity. Its meaning in the NEW TESTAMENT is much debated.

Soteriology Teaching about SALVATION.

Soul (1) The immortal element of an individual man or woman that survives the death of the body. (2) A human being when regarded as a spiritual being.

Spiritualism A religious system or practice that has the object of establishing communication with the dead. Most modern

spiritualist churches derive from a movement in mid-nineteenth-century America. Spiritualists seek to communicate with the dead through such means as table-turning and automatic writing. All mainstream Christian churches denounce Spiritualism.

Steiner, Rudolf (1861–1925) Founder of ANTHROPOSOPHY. He originally followed THEOSOPHY and ROSICRUCIANISM, but broke with these groups and developed his mystical ideas into an educational, ecological, and medical programme for spiritual progress and founded a number of schools.

Stoicism Philosophical school founded by Zeno of Citium (c. 335–263 BC), named after the porch or *stoa* where he taught in Athens. Stoics believed the world order reflected the divine intelligence – the LOGOS which was present in all CREATION. Human beings could attain virtue – harmony with the universe – by learning self-sufficiency, and behaving with courage and self-control.

Suzuki, Daisetz T. (1870–1966) Japanese Zen scholar who played a major part in introducing Zen Buddhism to the Western world. He was sympathetic to CHRISTIANITY.

Swedenborg, Emmanuel (1688–1772) Swedish scientist who became a MYSTIC and visionary. He taught a kind of pantheistic THEOSOPHY (*see* PANTHEISM) centred on JESUS CHRIST, in whom he found a Trinity of Love, Wisdom, and Energy, and founded the New Church.

Synagogue Jewish meeting place for worship and study. Synagogues grew out of the TORAH schools of the SCRIBES during the EXILE. After the destruction of the TEMPLE OF JERUSALEM (AD 70), synagogues became the centres of Jewish life.

Syncretism The growing together of two or more religions making a new development in religion that contains some of the beliefs and practices of both.

Synod Church council; PRESBYTERIAN church court.

T

Talmud The written interpretation and development of the HEBREW scriptures. It is based on the MISHNAH of JUDAS HaNASI, with some excluded teachings and commentary from the debates and controversies of the Schools of Babylon and Palestine. There are two versions: the Palestinian and the Babylonian, which is more detailed and complete.

Targum A (usually) Aramaic translation of a HEBREW SCRIPTURE reading. The translator was expected to make a free interpretation, some of which have become famous in their own right and are used by JEWS alongside the appointed text.

Temple of Jerusalem/ Holy Temple The TEMPLE first built by King Solomon was destroyed in 586 BC. The second temple was dedicated in 515 BC. It was desecrated by the Hellenistic Seleucid king Antiochus Epiphanes but rededicated by JUDAS MACCABEUS.

Rebuilding was begun under Herod the Great in 20 BC. The temple was virtually completed in AD 62, but destroyed by Titus in AD 70.

Tetragrammaton see YHWH.

Theism The belief in one supreme GOD who is both TRANSCENDENT and involved in the workings of the universe.

Theocracy ('divine government') Term describing a state which is constituted on the basis of divine law. CALVIN's regime in Geneva was theocratic.

Theodicy The defence of GOD as both good and omnipotent, which accounts for the existence of suffering and evil. The term was coined in 1710 by Gottfried Leibniz.

Theology (1) A systematic formulation of belief made by, or on behalf of, a particular individual, or CHURCH, or other body of believers. (2) The critical study of CHRISTIANITY, with regard to its origins, SCRIPTURES and other texts, DOCTRINES, ethics, history, and practices.

Theophany A divine appearance, revelation, or manifestation, usually inducing awe and terror in those who witness it – e.g. the appearance of GOD to MOSES on Mount SINAI amidst thunder, lightning, smoke, and trumpet blasts.

Theosophy ('divine wisdom') A term applied to various mystical movements, but which refers particularly to the principles of the Theosophical Society founded by Madame BLAVATSKY in 1875. These comprise a blend of Hindu, Buddhist, and

Christian ideas, together with particular stress on REINCARNATION, immortality, and the presence of GOD in all things.

Tongues, Speaking in see GLOSSOLALIA.

Torah (1) The five books of the Law (the PENTATEUCH) revealed to MOSES; the first division of the HEBREW BIBLE. (2) 'The teaching', the correct response of ISRAEL to GOD, outlined in rules for purity and social justice.

Transcendent That which is above or beyond common human experience and knowledge.

Transept Part of church building at right angles to the NAVE.

Transfiguration The occasion of CHRIST's appearance in glory to three of his DISCIPLES during his earthly ministry. It is celebrated as a feast in the Eastern Churches and by many in the West.

Trinity Christian doctrine of GOD as three Persons, equally. God: the Father, the Son, and the HOLY SPIRIT, constituting the divine unity.

U

Unification Church see FAMILY FEDERATION FOR WORLD PEACE AND UNIFICATION.

Unitarianism Dissenting movement which spread in Britain, Poland, and Hungary from the sixteenth century. Unitarians reject the Christian doctrines of the TRINITY and INCARNATION, and defend a reason-based ethical THEISM.

V

Vatican Councils The first was convened by POPE Pius IX in 1869–70, and resulted in the dogma of Papal Infallibility and attacks on 'modern' thought. The second in 1962–65 was called by John XXIII and led to a drastic modernization of ROMAN CATHOLIC worship and improved relations with other churches.

Venus Roman goddess of love, identified with APHRODITE and honoured as the mother of the Roman people.

Vestments Special garments worn by Christian clergy during liturgical services (see LITURGY).

Voodoo Religion of estimated 75 per cent of the people of Haiti, despite the official domination of Christianity – as well as in the West Indies and parts of South America. Voodoo is highly syncretistic. West African divinities are worshipped, often as Christian SAINTS, and their sanctuaries are closed during the Christian season of LENT.

W

Wesley, John (1703–91) Founder of the METHODIST movement. He travelled through Britain preaching the 'new birth'. Although loyal to the Church of England, he was eventually forced to ordain his own ministers.

Western Wall/Wailing Wall Site in JERUSALEM used by JEWS to lament the FALL OF JERUSALEM and the suffering of the Jews, and to pray for restoration. It is believed to be the only part of Herod's Temple left standing after the destruction of AD 70. (*See* TEMPLE OF JERUSALEM.)

Word of God Christian term for the BIBLE, or part of it.

World Council of Churches Body including many PROTESTANT and ORTHODOX churches, first constituted at Amsterdam in 1948 (*see* CONCILIAR PROCESS, ECUMENICAL MOVEMENT).

Worship Reverence or homage to God which may involve PRAYER, RITUAL, singing, dancing, or chanting.

Wrath The righteous anger of God against SIN.

Y

Yahweh *see* YHWH.

YHWH The 'tetragrammaton', the sacred name of the God of Israel as revealed to Moses. The name means 'I am'. It could not be spoken, and the Hebrew '*Adonai*' ('the Lord') was substituted when the SCRIPTURES were read aloud. The MASORETES put the vowel points for *Adonai* into the name YHWH, which gave rise to the malformation 'Jehovah'.

Yom Kippur/Day of Atonement Jewish day of FASTING and repentance, the most solemn day of the Jewish year.

Z

Zealots Jewish nationalistic party in Roman times who believed the Roman presence defiled their land and flouted the TORAH. In AD 66 they revolted. The war which followed led to the destruction of JERUSALEM and its TEMPLE in AD 70.

Zeus Supreme ruler of the Greek gods. Sometimes the name Zeus stood simply for god, as supreme deity.

Zionism The movement to establish a permanent homeland for JEWS. In 1897 the First Zionist Congress was organized in Basle by Theodor HERZL, in the wake of a wave of European anti-Semitism. Gradually the movement determined that Palestine was the only realistic place to establish the Jewish state, and Jews were encouraged to emigrate and acquire property there.

INDEX

Note: Figures in **bold** denote pages with illustrations

4/9/14